Programming in F

Programming in F

T.M.R ELLIS *University of Oxford*

IVOR R. PHILIPS *The Boeing Company*

Addison-Wesley

Harlow, England • Reading, Massachusetts • Menlo Park, California
New York • Don Mills, Ontario • Amsterdam • Bonn • Sydney • Singapore
Tokyo • Madrid • San Juan • Milan • Mexico City • Seoul • Taipei

© Addison Wesley Longman Limited 1998

Addison Wesley Longman Limited
Edinburgh Gate
Harlow
Essex CM20 2JE
England

and Associated Companies throughout the World.

The rights of T.M.R. Ellis and Ivor R. Philips to be identified as authors of this Work have been asserted by them in accordance with the Copyright, Designs and Patents Act 1988.

The programs in this book have been included for their instructional value. They have been tested with care but are not guaranteed for any particular purpose. The publisher does not offer any warranties or representations nor does it accept any liabilities with respect to the programs.

Many of the designations used by manufacturers and sellers to distinguish their products are claimed as trademarks. Addison Wesley Longman Limited has made every attempt to supply trademark information about manufacturers and their products mentioned in this book. A list of the trademark designations and their owners appears on page xvi.

Cover designed by Senate, London
Cover image courtesy of The Capilano Suspension Bridge & Park,
3735 Capilano Road, North Vancouver, B.C. Canada V7R 4JI
Typeset by 43
Produced by Longman Singapore Publishers (Pte) Ltd.
Printed in Singapore

First printed 1998

ISBN 0-201-17991-1

British Library Cataloguing-in-Publication Data
A catalogue record for this book is available from the British Library

Library of Congress Cataloging in Publication Data
Ellis, T.M.R., 1942-
    Programming in F / T.M.R. Ellis, Ivor R. Philips.
        p.   cm.
    Includes bibliographical references and index.
    ISBN 0-201-17991-1 (alk. paper)
    1. F (Computer program language)   I. Philips, Ivor R.   II. Title.
QA76.73.F16E45   1998
005. 13'3--dc21   98-3580
                                                              CIP

Preface

F is a new programming language developed by Imagine1, Inc., and has been carefully designed to provide a powerful, safe and elegant programming language for engineers and scientists. However, F is not really new, for it is derived from Fortran 90 – the most generally available version of the world's oldest and most widely used scientific programming language. Every F program is also a Fortran 90 and a Fortran 95 program, and F is, therefore, an ideal language to learn both in its own right and if you expect to use Fortran in the future. Appendix C gives a summary of the main differences between F and Fortran 90.

Fortran dates from 1954, when the first FORmula TRANslation system was developed at IBM by a team led by John Backus. Since those early days there have been a number of definitive stages in the development of Fortran – FORTRAN II, FORTRAN IV, FORTRAN 66, FORTRAN 77, Fortran 90 and Fortran 95. The development of Fortran 90 was, in many ways, the most important of all, for it marked the full emergence of Fortran as a modern programming language, with many new features based on the experience gained with similar concepts in other languages, and others which provided Fortran's own contribution to the development of new programming concepts.

Because of its history, however, Fortran 90 and Fortran 95 contain many older features which are retained for compatibility with earlier versions, but which can confuse new programmers and, more seriously, which can encourage bad programming practices. F removes these older, obsolescent, features of Fortran, retaining only those features which are generally accepted as being in accord with modern programming practice. The result is a language which is a true subset of Fortran 90 and Fortran 95, but which is a much smaller language and one which encourages and, in many cases, enforces, good programming practice.

This book is primarily intended for college students who are learning how to program in F (or in Fortran 90 or Fortran 95), and is a natural successor to our similar book about Fortran 90 programming, and is written in such a way as to encourage readers to utilize the power and flexibility of F fully from the outset.

Every chapter of the book follows a similar structure, and is introduced by a short overview of the topic covered in that chapter, with an emphasis on the class of problems that it helps to solve and the key techniques that are being introduced. At several points within each chapter there are short *self-test exercises* which should be used to check, and to reinforce, the material covered thus far. Every chapter also includes a number of worked examples which illustrate both the features of the language that have most recently been introduced and, equally importantly, a recommended approach to the design and development of programs. Finally, at the end of the chapter, before the programming exercises for that chapter, there is a brief checklist of the main features of the chapter, together with a summary of all new syntax introduced.

How to use this book

In line with our overall philosophy of learning through experience, the book is structured in two parts. The first of these covers many of the main features of F, and it is possible to write programs to solve a very high proportion of problems by using only these features. Each chapter contains a number of worked examples, as well as self-test exercises and a substantial number of programming exercises; sample solutions to most of the programming exercises are available via the World Wide Web from our publisher's site (see below), although the majority of these are only available to teachers in possession of the appropriate password. The nine chapters which make up Part I, together with the introductory Chapter 1, can easily, therefore, form the basis of an introductory course in F programming.

Part II develops most of the topics covered in Part I to make the student aware of other possibilities which will both help to solve most remaining problems and introduce alternative, or better, ways of dealing with the more straightforward ones. However, unlike Part I, it is not essential that the student covers all the material. Although the order of presentation creates a logical development, and will frequently utilize material that has been introduced in an earlier chapter, it is feasible to omit certain chapters, or combinations of chapters, for certain categories of students. An *Instructor's Guide* is available via the World Wide Web for teachers using this book, and this topic is discussed there in more detail for those involved in planning courses for particular categories of students.

As already mentioned, every chapter contains several groups of self-test exercises, as well as a set of programming exercises. We strongly recommend that you should attempt all the self-test exercises, and check your answers with those included at the back of the book before proceeding. You should also carefully study the worked examples in each chapter, as these illustrate not only how to code a solution to a particular problem but, more importantly, how to design a program to meet the requirements of the problem.

Once you have completed the chapter you should always attempt some of the programming exercises, *and run your solutions on a computer*, before proceeding to the next chapter. Experience is even more important than theoretical knowledge in programming. Those exercises for which a sample solution is publicly available on the World Wide Web are indicated by an asterisk in this book, although your programs will, almost certainly, differ from these sample solutions. If the difference is substantial then it is worth comparing the two in order to establish how your solution might have been improved; small differences, as a result of individual programming styles, are, however, unimportant.

Additional support via the World Wide Web

This book contains a complete description of the F programming language, and can be used either as a self-teaching book, or as part of a taught course, without the need for any other resources apart from an F compiler and a suitable computer. However, a significant amount of supplementary information is available via the World Wide Web from our publisher's site at

```
http://awl-he.com/computing
```

This information includes a more detailed description of the 102 intrinsic procedures which form an integral part of the F language, a more detailed description of the numerical model which underlies the mathematics used in F programs, an *Instructor's Guide* for those using this book for their teaching, and sample solutions to many of the programming exercises.

Much of this information is publicly available, and may be freely downloaded. However, most of the sample solutions to the programming exercises are available on a restricted basis, as is the *Instructor's Guide*. These restricted items are available only to those having a valid password, which will be provided to teachers using the book by their local Addison Wesley Longman representative.

To the teacher

This book is derived from *Fortran 90 Programming* (Ellis *et al.*, 1994) and shares many of the same concepts as that book. Like that book, therefore, this book contains a wealth of worked examples, all of which have been fully tested, together with a large number of programming exercises at the end of each chapter. Sample solutions to many of these exercises are available via the World Wide Web, although only a small number of these solutions are publicly available. The majority of the sample solutions are contained in the accompanying *Instructor's Guide*, which is available only to teachers who have obtained the appropriate password from their local Addison Wesley Longman representative.

In addition to the programming exercises, each chapter also contains several *Self-test exercises* by means of which students can assess their progress and understanding; solutions to all the self-test exercises are provided at the end of the book.

Like its predecessor, this book introduces both procedures and modules at a very early stage, before there is any discussion of control structures or, indeed, of anything other than simple assignment and list-directed input/output. This means that procedures are treated as a natural basic programming block, and that modules are seen as a natural way of grouping similar entities, with the result that students learn to develop programs in a modular fashion from the outset. Our experience indicates that students have far less trouble with procedures and modules if they are introduced at this early stage than if they are left until most of the other features of the language have been met and the students' own programming styles have begun to form.

Programming is nowadays recognized to be an engineering discipline (**information engineering**), and as such it draws on both art and science. As with any other branch of engineering it involves both the learning of the theory and the incorporation of that theory into practical work. In particular, it is impossible to learn to write good programs without plenty of practical experience, and it is also impossible to learn to write *good* programs without the opportunity to see and examine other people's programs.

This book uses the concept of an English language **structure plan** as an aid to program design, and from their first introduction in Chapter 2 structure plans are developed for all the worked examples throughout the remainder of the book. There are 43 such worked examples and a total of 130 complete programs and subprograms in this book, all of which have been fully tested on either a Power Macintosh or a Pentium computer, using the appropriate F compiler from Imagine1, Inc. Since many of these programs, subroutines and functions may be of more general use there is a special index to them at the end of the book, before the general index.

Each chapter contains two types of exercises for the student. The first are **self-test exercises** which do not require the writing of complete programs, and are designed to enable students to verify their understanding of the material covered in the chapter, or in part of it. Every chapter has a set of these exercises at the end, while most also contain a set in the middle of the chapter. Answers, with explanations where appropriate, to all of these exercises are included at the end of the book. The second type of exercises, which only appear at the end of a chapter, are programming exercises for the student to write *and test on a computer*. As already indicated, example solutions to many of these are available (either publicly or on a restricted basis) via the World Wide Web.

Because we anticipate that students from many different disciplines will wish to learn F, great care has been taken to avoid any bias towards particular scientific or engineering concepts in the worked examples. The purpose of these examples is to help the student to understand how to use particular programming concepts and how to develop well-structured programs using these concepts. Many of these worked examples are, therefore, intended to solve quite general and non-scientific problems which will be understood by students of any background. However F, like Fortran 90, is supremely suitable for numerical problems and Chapters 11 and 17 concentrate on this aspect of programming in F; all the worked examples in these chapters, therefore, do have a strong scientific and numerical bias.

Mention has already been made of the accompanying *Instructor's Guide* which is available via the World Wide Web. This contains a short summary of the major points involved in each chapter, with a note of any particular areas where experience shows that students may have problems. The *Instructor's Guide* also contains example solutions to most of the programming exercises provided in this book. The *Instructor's Guide* is not, however, available to the general public, but only to teachers who are using this book for their teaching; such teachers can obtain the information necessary to download it from the Addison Wesley Longman World Wide Web site by contacting their local Addison Wesley Longman office.

Acknowledgements

This book has been developed from the experience which we have gathered over more than 30 years in teaching, using and implementing various dialects of Fortran. During that time we have both benefited from the advice, assistance and encouragement of a great many people who must, of necessity, remain anonymous. We should, nevertheless, wish to record our thanks to all those who have helped us in so many different ways over the years.

There are, however, several people whose help has been directly related to the writing of this book and we should like to acknowledge their assistance in a more personal manner. Foremost among these is Karen Mosman, our editor at Addison Wesley Longman, who has had to bear the brunt of our complaints when things have not gone according to plan at the publishing end, but who has, nevertheless, contrived to remain charming and helpful at all times. We must also thank Sarah Falconer, our Production Editor at Addison Wesley Longman, who ensured that the various stages involved in the production of this book were carried out with commendable efficiency. We are also grateful to David Epstein, Dick Hendrickson and Walt Brainerd at Imagine1, Inc., both for providing us with the necessary compilers (as well as various caps, shirts, and other items carrying the F logo!), and for commenting on the draft of this book from the perspective of the designers of the F language.

Finally, we owe a great debt of gratitude to our wives, Maggie and Marilyn, for yet again putting up with our destruction of evenings and weekends when the pressure on meeting deadlines was at its greatest, and with the general disruption of normal activities which seems to be an inevitable result of the writing process.

The bridge

On a lighter note, we must finish with a few words about the bridge on the cover of this book.

Those familiar with our earlier books on Fortran programming will be familiar with our penchant for bridges. The first edition of TMRE's FORTRAN 77 book showed the famous Iron Bridge in Shropshire, England – the first bridge in the world to be built entirely of cast iron. As the preface records, 'You can read whatever you like into this – building bridges, developing structures, elegance, style, permanence, etc. – but at least it makes a change from abstract patterns and punched cards!'. The second edition showed the two Forth Bridges near Edinburgh, Scotland, and the preface to that edition records that 'the old Forth railway bridge in the foreground symbolizes old "brute force" technology that has stood the test of time, while the more recent Forth road bridge in the distance symbolizes newer, more elegant technology and the fact that this complements but does not supersede its predecessor'. The cover of our Fortran 90 book incorporates the Fatih Sultan Mehmet Bridge, which crosses the Bosphorous just north of Istanbul, and was opened in 1988, the same year that the technical content of Fortran 90 was finally agreed by the two committees involved, X3J3 and WG5. It was the second longest suspension bridge in the world at that time, and we noted that Fortran was the second most widely used programming language in the world, so they made a good match.

We debated whether to move away from bridges for a book on F, but finally decided that as every F program is also a Fortran 90 program, our book should also show a bridge. But F is smaller than Fortran, so we have chosen a smaller bridge than before. It is the Capilano Suspension Bridge in North Vancouver, Canada, and although smaller than any of our previous bridges it is the longest and highest pedestrian suspension bridge in the world, being 450 feet long and 230 feet above the Capilano River. So, just like F, it is the most impressive example of its class around!

Miles Ellis,
Oxford, England

Ivor Philips,
Bellevue, Washington, USA

February 1998

Contents

Preface   v

1   **Introduction**   **1**

   1.1   What is F? Why is it important?   2
   1.2   What do we mean by 'a computer'?   3
   1.3   Where did F and Fortran come from?
       How did they evolve?   7
   1.4   Why learn F?   11

Part I   **Fundamental Principles**   **15**

2   **First steps in F programming**   **17**

   2.1   From problem to program in three basic steps   18
   2.2   Some basic F concepts   21
   2.3   Running F programs on a computer   26
   2.4   Errors in programs   27
   2.5   The design and testing of programs   30

3   **Essential data handling**   **38**

   3.1   The two fundamental types of numbers   39
   3.2   **real** and **integer** variables   42
   3.3   Arithmetic expressions and assignment   43
   3.4   List-directed input and output of numeric data   49
   3.5   Handling **character** data   56
   3.6   Named constants   62

4   **Basic building blocks**   **68**

   4.1   Programs and modules   69
   4.2   Procedures   71

4.3	Functions	77
4.4	Subroutines	80
4.5	Actual arguments and dummy arguments	83
4.6	Local and global objects	89
4.7	Saving the values of local objects on exit from a procedure	93
4.8	Giving procedure variables an initial value	94
4.9	Procedures as an aid to program structure	95

5   Controlling the flow of your program   **103**

5.1	Choice and decision-making	104
5.2	Logical expressions and **logical** variables	106
5.3	The **if** construct	110
5.4	Comparing character strings	117
5.5	The **case** construct	121

6   Repeating parts of your program   **135**

6.1	Program repetition and the **do** construct	136
6.2	Count-controlled **do** loops	138
6.3	More flexible loops	146
6.4	Giving names to **do** constructs	153
6.5	Dealing with exceptional situations	155

7   An introduction to arrays   **162**

7.1	The array concept	163
7.2	Array declarations	164
7.3	Array constants and initial values	166
7.4	Input and output with arrays	168
7.5	Using arrays and array elements in expressions and assignments	169
7.6	Using intrinsic procedures with arrays	171
7.7	Sub-arrays	172
7.8	Arrays and procedures	177
7.9	Array-valued functions	185

8   Improved building blocks   **193**

8.1	Recursive procedures	194
8.2	Passing procedures as arguments	196
8.3	Creating your own data types	200
8.4	Controlling access to entities within a module	217
8.5	Host association within a module	222
8.6	Gaining more control over **use** association	223

9   **More control over input and output**   **230**

   9.1   The interface between the user and the computer   231
   9.2   Formats and edit descriptors   234
   9.3   Input editing   236
   9.4   Output editing   245
   9.5   **read**, **write** and **print** statements   249
   9.6   More powerful formats   252

10   **Using files to preserve data**   **264**

   10.1   Files and records   265
   10.2   Formatted, unformatted and endfile records   267
   10.3   Connecting an external file to your programs –
        and disconnecting it   269
   10.4   File positioning statements   278

   Intermission –
   Designing, coding and debugging programs   **293**

Part II   **Towards Real Programming**   **295**

11   **An introduction to numerical methods in F**
   programs   **297**

   11.1   Numerical calculations, precision and rounding
        errors   298
   11.2   Parameterized **real** variables   301
   11.3   Conditioning and stability   306
   11.4   Data fitting by least squares approximation   313
   11.5   Iterative solution of non-linear equations   319

12   **More about numeric data types**   **335**

   12.1   **complex** variables   336
   12.2   Non-default data types   344
   12.3   Specifying non-default kinds of variables   345
   12.4   Specifying non-default kinds of constants   346
   12.5   Using non-default kinds to improve portability   347
   12.6   Mixed kind expressions   351

13   **Array processing and matrix manipulation**   **359**

   13.1   Matrices and two-dimensional arrays   360
   13.2   Basic array concepts for arrays having more than
        one dimension   362
   13.3   Array constructors for rank-n arrays   365

13.4	Input and output with arrays	367
13.5	The four classes of arrays	368
13.6	Allocatable arrays	379
13.7	Whole-array operations	390
13.8	Masked array assignment	396
13.9	Sub-arrays	398

14   Pointers and dynamic data structures   **407**

14.1	Fundamental pointer concepts	408
14.2	Using pointers in expressions	413
14.3	Pointers and arrays	416
14.4	Pointers as components of derived types	423
14.5	Pointers as arguments to procedures	431
14.6	Pointer-valued functions	433
14.7	Linked lists and other dynamic data structures	434

15   Additional input/output and file handling facilities   **454**

15.1	Additional edit descriptors for formatted input and output	455
15.2	Non-advancing input and output	457
15.3	Direct access files	464
15.4	Internal files	478
15.5	The **inquire** statement	484

16   Still more powerful building blocks   **494**

16.1	More sophisticated procedure arguments	495
16.2	Accessing non-F procedures from your program	497
16.3	Defining your own operators	499
16.4	Creating generic procedures and operators	505
16.5	Data abstraction and language extension	511

17   More about numerical methods   **523**

17.1	Numerical methods and their limitations	524
17.2	Solving quadratic equations	525
17.3	Newton's method for solving non-linear equations	529
17.4	The secant method of solving non-linear equations	536
17.5	Solution of simultaneous linear equations by Gaussian elimination	543
17.6	Solving a tridiagonal system of equations	553
17.7	Fitting a curve through a set of data points using a cubic spline	557
17.8	Integration and numerical quadrature	567

Afterword – Seven golden rules   589

Appendix A   Intrinsic procedures   591

Appendix B   Reserved words and order of
             statements   601

Appendix C   The relationship between F and
             Fortran 90   605

Appendix D   The ASCII character set   611

Bibliography   613

Answers to self-test exercises   615

Index to programs and procedures   645

Index   649

Introduction

1

1.1 What is F? Why is it important?	1.3 Where did F and Fortran 90 come from? How did they evolve?
1.2 What do we mean by 'a computer'?	1.4 Why learn F?

Computers are used today to solve an almost unimaginable range of problems and yet their basic structure has hardly changed in 40 years. They have become faster and more powerful, as well as smaller and cheaper, but a major factor in the rapidly changing role that they play in today's society is the development of the programming languages which control their every action.

Fortran 90 is the most widely-used version of the world's oldest programming language, and is designed to provide better facilities for the solution of scientific and technological problems and to provide a firm base for further developments to meet the needs of the last years of the 20th century and of the early 21st.

F is a carefully constructed subset of Fortran 90 that retains all of the modern and powerful features of the language, while eliminating most of the older, obsolete features of Fortran that were only retained for compatibility with the past.

This chapter explains the background to both Fortran 90 and its predecessor, FORTRAN 77, and the relationship between F and Fortran 90, and emphasizes the importance of both Fortran and F for the future development of scientific, technological and numerical computation. In particular, the advantages of F over Fortran for both teaching and professional programming are stressed.

1.1   What is F? Why is it important?

Computers first moved out of the research laboratory into industry and commerce in the early 1950s. In many ways their basic design has not changed significantly since then – they have got very much faster, very much more powerful, very much smaller, and, paradoxically, very much cheaper. But, when you get down to details, they work in much the same way now as they did then. Where the massive changes *have* come, however, is in the problems to which computers are applied, and the methods that are used in the solution of these problems. The key to making better and more effective use of computers lies in the **programming languages** which are used to define the problems to be solved and to specify the methods of their solution in terms that can be understood by a computer system.

Note the use of the expression *computer system*, for nowadays we should not simply think of a computer – which is a collection of electronic and electromechanical components and devices – but also of the many computer programs without which it remains simply an inanimate collection of bits and pieces. For many years the actual computer has been referred to as the **hardware**, while the programs that control it make up the **software.** There are many different items of software on all computers, but whether a computer is a large multi-million dollar supercomputer or a small hand-held notebook computer, every single item of software has been written in one of a number of programming languages.

A question that is often asked is 'why are there many different programming languages?', and in an ideal world it is possible that one such language might be sufficient. However, just as there are thousands of natural languages which have evolved over many centuries in different parts of the world, so there are hundreds of programming languages which have evolved over a mere 50 years. Many of these are little used, but there are a small number which are very widely used throughout the world and have been standardized (either through formal international processes or as a result of de facto widespread acceptance) to encourage their continuing use. Most of these major languages are particularly suited to a particular class of problems, although this class is often very wide. Fortran is one such language, and is particularly well suited for almost all scientific and technological problems, as well as to a wide range of other problem areas – especially those with a significant numerical or computational content.

Fortran 90 is the most recent version of the Fortran programming language in general use (although the specification of a revised version known as Fortran 95 was finally approved in 1997), and provides a great many more features than its predecessors to assist the programmer in writing programs to solve problems of a scientific, technological or computational nature. Furthermore, because of Fortran's pre-eminent position in these areas, programs written in Fortran 90 or Fortran 95 can readily be transferred to run, and run *correctly*, on many types of computers in a way that is not always possible when they are written in other languages. Unfortunately, because of the longevity of many Fortran programs, which are often in regular use more than 25 years after being first written, Fortran 90 and Fortran 95 also contain a number of older, obsolete, features which are never used in new programs, but are required in case it is necessary for compatibility with older programs which utilize these features.

The **F programming language** is based on Fortran 90, but with these obsolete features removed in order to preserve the best of Fortran 90 without the clutter of older and redundant language concepts. Furthermore, in order both to simplify the language and to encourage good programming style, F imposes a number of additional constraints on the use of some features of the language.

The result is that while *every F program is a valid Fortran 90 and Fortran 95 program*, and can utilize all the power of Fortran for solving numerical and scientific problems, F programs are cleaner and better written than most Fortran programs because of the absence of older and less well-formulated language constructs.

F is therefore particularly well suited for teaching and learning about programming because it combines the power of a well-established and widely used professional programming language with the elegance, structure and functionality of the best computer science languages. Moreover, because it is available on all major workstations and personal computer platforms F is a powerful development tool for professional programmers who can subsequently submit their F programs to a fully optimized Fortran 90 or Fortran 95 compiler in the knowledge that they are also fully standard-conforming Fortran programs.

Nowadays, almost everyone in the developed world, and a great many outside it, have at some time used a computer and believe that they are familiar with the basic concepts. Frequently, however, this knowledge only relates to a small aspect of the whole computer system, and people are either completely unaware of extremely important concepts or, at best, only partially understand them. Before we start to examine the features of F, and the ways in which we can use them to solve problems, we shall therefore step back slightly and establish (or even re-establish) some of the basic concepts to which we shall return from time to time throughout the remainder of this book.

1.2   What do we mean by 'a computer'?

There cannot be any aspect of modern 20th century life that is not touched by computers, and it is sometimes difficult to believe that they have only existed in anything like their present form for about 50 years. It is hard to accept that the $1000 notebook computer that can be purchased today in thousands of retail outlets is more powerful than any computer that existed 40 years ago, and that, furthermore, the most powerful computers in existence then cost well over 1000 times as much, and occupied at least 10 000 times as much space. Nevertheless, in their essential characteristics such disparate machines are essentially the same – as are virtually all computers anywhere in the world today.

However, even though computers have existed in essentially their modern form for over 50 years, it is only since the early 1980s that they have moved from the realm of the specialist into everyday use in schools, offices and homes throughout the developed world, and there can be little doubt that most of the people who use computers every day do not have any real idea of what a computer actually is.

This book is not going to answer that question, other than to emphasize that, essentially, a computer is merely an inanimate collection of electronic circuits and devices with, usually, a certain amount of electromechanical equipment attached to it. What sets a computer apart from other machines which may be built from similar (or even identical) component parts is its ability to *remember* a sequence of instructions and to *obey* these instructions at a predetermined point in time. Such a sequence of instructions is called a **program**, and what we usually refer to as a computer is more correctly called a **stored-program computer**. How we write a program to instruct the computer to perform the task(s) that we require of it is the subject of this book.

Although we do not need to know anything about exactly how a computer works in order to use it, it is useful to create a conceptual model of a computer which will enable us to understand more easily exactly what we are doing when we write a program.

We have already referred to a computer's ability to remember a sequence of instructions and, not unreasonably, that part of a computer in which such information is stored is known as the **memory**. In fact there are two main types of information stored in a computer's memory, namely a **program** – instructions which the computer is to obey – and **data** – values (numbers, words, and so on) which the computer is to process in a way defined by a program.

This processing is carried out by the **central processing unit** (**CPU**) which consists of (at least) two quite separate parts – a **control unit** which fetches instructions, decodes them, and initiates appropriate action, and an **arithmetic unit** which carries out arithmetic and other types of operations on items of data.

These two parts – the CPU and the memory – could be said to constitute the computer, but there are other essential parts of the system still to be discussed. To be of any practical use a computer must be able to communicate its results to the outside world, and this calls for some form of **output device** such as a display or a printer. Similarly, there must be some way of getting both the program and any variable data it requires into the computer, and therefore an **input device** is needed, such as a keyboard or, on some older computers, a card reader or a paper tape reader. Modern computers may have a wide range of input and output devices attached, including those which interface with instruments or other computers, but the essential concepts remain the same.

Finally, there is the question of large and/or long-term data storage. The devices used to form the memory of a computer are normally transient devices – when the power is switched off they lose the information stored in them and are

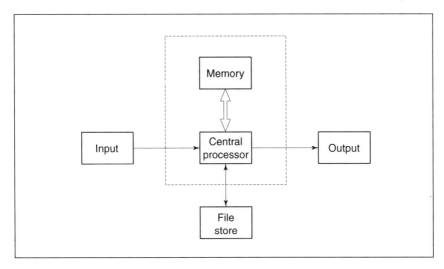

Figure 1.1   An idealized computer.

thus of no use for storage of information other than during the running of a program. In addition, if the computer is to be able to access the information in the memory rapidly it can only be of a relatively small size (typically of the order of a few million characters). A memory of more than this size would place unacceptable burdens on both power requirements and physical space. However, magnetic media, such as disks or tapes coated with a fine magnetic oxide (similar to that used on tapes for domestic cassette or videotape recorders), and optical media, such as a disk whose surface is covered with tiny pits that can be detected by a reflected laser beam, can be used to store very large amounts of information easily and economically, although at the cost of slower access time. Virtually all computers use magnetic media as a **file store** enabling programs and data to be stored in a permanent fashion within the overall computer system, while the use of optical, or magneto-optical, media is becoming increasingly popular due to the enormously greater amounts of data that can be stored in these ways compared to purely magnetic methods. A single unit of program or data stored in such a file store is called a **file**.

Thus a computer can be represented by a simple diagram as shown in Figure 1.1.

The memory and central processor are usually electronic; however, the input, output and file store devices usually also contain mechanical components, with the result that the speed of transfer of information between them and the central processor is many times slower than that between the memory and the central processor. Because of this disparity in speed, most computers arrange for transfers between the central processor and input, output and file store devices to proceed semi-autonomously – and in many cases bypass the central processor and transfer information directly to or from the memory. As a result of this, and because in earlier computers they were usually physically separated

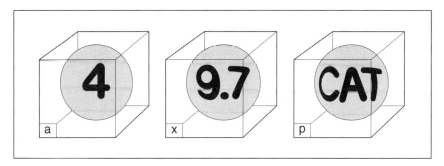

Figure 1.2 A storage model.

from the CPU, these types of device are often referred to as **peripheral devices** – a distinction which has been emphasized in Figure 1.1 by enclosing the memory and central processor in a dashed box.

This idealized structure applies to all computers, although a modern supercomputer may be more elaborate and have thousands of processing units in order to perform many simultaneous calculations; however, the underlying design concepts are still the same. In recent years the development of the **microcomputer** has changed many people's perception of computers, for whereas large computers such as a Cray X-MP supercomputer or a Digital Equipment VAX 11-780 can easily be seen to consist of a number of discrete parts, microcomputers such as a Pentium-based PC or an Apple Macintosh take up only a few square inches of desk space and appear to consist of little more than a television monitor, a keyboard, and a small box, while in a **notebook computer** everything is contained in a single, battery-powered box about the same size as a rather thick pad of paper. Nevertheless, the keyboard is the main input device, the monitor or screen is the main output device, and the small box contains a faster CPU, more memory, and more file store than all but a handful of the most powerful supercomputers of 10 years ago!

Let us now return to the memory and consider its mode of operation. Conceptually, we can use an analogy with a large number of glass boxes, each containing a single ball on which is written a number, or a word, or any other single item that we may wish to store. To distinguish one box from another each has a label attached with an identifying name (see Figure 1.2). Clearly we can find out what is in any of the boxes simply by looking at it, as long as we have the name of the box. Equally clearly, if we wish to put another value in a box we shall first have to remove (or otherwise get rid of) the ball which is already there so as to leave room for the new one. This is exactly the way in which a computer's memory works – if we wish to find out what is stored in a particular location the process does not affect what is stored there, whereas if we store a new value in some location then whatever was already stored there is destroyed and lost.

Now consider the names on the boxes, **a**, **x** and **p**, in Figure 1.2. It is quite clear that these are the names of the *boxes* and not their contents, for if we were

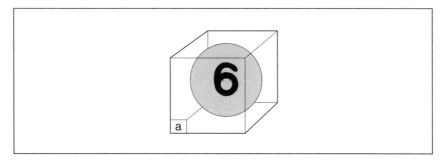

Figure 1.3   An altered storage model.

to store a new ball with the value 6 in box **a** we would not alter its name, and if we now looked at box **a** we would find that it contained the value 6 (Figure 1.3). We shall come back to this when we start to write programs, but it is important to realize from the outset that the names that are used to refer to storage locations in the memory always identify the *location* and not the value that is stored there.

The boxes have, by implication, been open so that the current value may be removed and a new one inserted. To complete the analogy with the computer's memory we must have a rule that says that a box is never left empty; every box must contain a ball, even if it is a blank one or one with the value zero. Because such boxes, or rather the corresponding storage locations in the memory, can have their contents changed at will they are referred to as variable storage locations, or **variables**. Boxes which are identical to these except that they have a sealed lid can have their contents looked at, but it is not possible to replace the contents by a new value. Such storage locations are called constant storage locations, or **constants**.

1.3   Where did F and Fortran come from? How did they evolve?

We have already emphasized that the key feature of a computer is its ability to store a program, or sequence of instructions, and then to obey these instructions in order to solve a particular problem. In the very early days of computing such programs consisted of strings of 0s and 1s known as **machine code** and were unique to a particular type of computer, as well as being almost totally incomprehensible to a human being. It was not long, therefore, before a more compact form was devised in which each group of three **binary digits** (or **bits**) was replaced by a single number in the range 0−7 (the **octal** equivalent of the three-bit binary number). Thus the binary sequence

```
010100011 010 000 010111
```

would be replaced by the octal sequence

```
243 2 0 27
```

This was still a matter for a specialist, although, as there were only a handful of computers in the world at that time, that in itself was of no great importance. Even for a specialist, however, it was difficult to remember which code number represented which operation, and where each data value was kept in the computer's memory. The next development, therefore, was the creation of a mnemonic form for the instructions, and the use of names to identify memory locations. For example

```
LDA 2 X
```

meant *load a special location in the CPU (register 2) with the contents of memory location X*. This is known as **assembly language** programming, and the principles have survived almost unchanged to the present day.

Towards the end of 1953, John Backus proposed to his employers, the International Business Machines Corporation (IBM), that it would be beneficial if a small research group were to be set up to develop a more efficient and economical method of programming their 704 computer than the assembly language used at that time. The proposal was accepted and the group started work almost at once. By mid-1954 an initial specification had been produced for a **programming language** of considerable power and flexibility. This language was to be called the *IBM Mathematical FORmula TRANslation System, FORTRAN*. The project was initially intended purely for use by IBM on a single computer; however, soon after the preliminary report on the language was produced word got out to some of IBM's customers, with the result that the decision was made to make it available to anyone purchasing a 704 computer.

Although, as its name implied, FORTRAN was initially seen as a means of converting mathematical formulae into a machine code or assembly language form that the computer could use, it also embodied several other extremely important concepts. By far the most important of these was that the program was formulated in the *user's* terms, rather than those of the computer, as a result of using an algebraic method of expressing formulae and a 'pidgin English' method of describing the other (non-mathematical) operations. The resulting program was subsequently said to use a **high-level language**, since the method enabled a programmer to write programs without needing to know much about the details of the computer itself.

Since a computer can only understand its own machine code, before a high-level program can be obeyed by a computer it must be **translated** into the appropriate machine code for that computer. A special program (a **compiler**) is used to translate the high-level language program into a machine code program for a specific computer in such a way that the machine code may be kept for use on subsequent occasions. Since the compiler can only translate correct high-level program statements, an important part of its task is to check the syntax (the grammar or the structure) of each statement and to produce **diagnostic** information to help the programmer to correct any errors.

The first *Programmer's Reference Manual* for the FORTRAN language was released in October 1956 and the compiler was finally delivered to customers in April 1957. This was followed 12 months later by FORTRAN II – an improved version of the system with a considerably enhanced diagnostic capability and a number of significant extensions to the language. Despite initial resistance on the grounds that the compiled programs were not as efficient as hand-coded ones, the language soon caught on, and by 1960 IBM had released versions of FORTRAN for their 709, 650, 1620 and 7070 computers. The most important development, however, was that other manufacturers started to write compilers for FORTRAN and by 1963 there were over 40 different FORTRAN compilers in existence! This led to a completely unexpected development of enormous importance, namely program **portability**, since once a program had been written for one computer in a high-level language such as FORTRAN it could be easily moved to another computer with little or no change. This development can, with the benefit of hindsight, be seen to have been the single most important factor in the development of the computer age, for it led to large gains in productivity and, moreover, to the possibility of developing programs which were intended from the outset to be run on a wide range of computers.

One problem that was encountered by these early pioneers, however, was that IBM FORTRAN used specific features of the 704 computer's instruction set and, when they could, the other FORTRAN compilers tended to do likewise. In addition, the advantages to be gained by having a standard language were not fully appreciated, and there were incompatibilities between different compilers, even between those written by the same manufacturer. As a result of pressure from their users as early as 1961, IBM set about developing a still further improved FORTRAN which did away with the machine-dependent features of FORTRAN II. This new system, FORTRAN IV, was released for the IBM 7030 (Stretch) computer in 1962, and later for the IBM 7090/7094 machines. Because programs written in FORTRAN IV were almost totally independent of the computer on which they were to be run, such programs could easily be transferred to a quite different computer, as long as that computer had a FORTRAN IV compiler, thus paving the way for the development of programs which were not directed at any particular type of computer, and which could therefore be used by a much larger community of users than had ever been possible before.

Perhaps the most significant development of all, however, was the decision of the American Standards Association (now the American National Standards Institute, ANSI) to set up a committee in May 1962 to develop an American Standard FORTRAN. This committee, in fact, defined two languages – FORTRAN, based largely on FORTRAN IV, and Basic FORTRAN, which was based on FORTRAN II but without the machine-dependent features. These standards were ratified in March 1966.

The existence of an officially defined standard (ANSI, 1966), which was also effectively an international standard, meant that further development of the language had a firm and well-defined base from which to work. The 1960s and early 1970s saw computers become established in all areas of society, and this dramatic growth led, among other things, to a proliferation of different programming languages. Many of these were oriented towards specific application areas, but a substantial proportion were intended to be **general-purpose languages**. Most noteworthy among these were Algol 60, Algol 68, BASIC, COBOL, Pascal and PL/I.

In the midst of all this language research and development FORTRAN did not remain static. Computer manufacturers wrote compilers which accepted considerable extensions to the standard FORTRAN, while in 1969 ANSI set up a working committee to revise the 1966 standard. Partly because of the many changes in the philosophy and practice of programming during this period, a draft standard did not appear until some seven years had elapsed. During 1977 this draft was the subject of worldwide discussion and comment before a revised version was approved as the new standard in April 1978 (ANSI, 1978); this was subsequently ratified as an international standard in 1980.

The new (1977) standard FORTRAN replaced both the older (1966) FORTRAN and Basic FORTRAN. In order to distinguish the new standard language from the old one, the standard suggested that the new language should be called **FORTRAN 77**.

Although the first FORTRAN 77 compiler was available even before the standard had been approved, it was several years before compilers became widely available, and it was not until the mid-1980s that it could truly be thought of as the 'universal' FORTRAN. In the meantime, however, the computing world had not stood still and many new programming concepts were being developed, as well as many new languages, such as Ada, C and Modula-2. A new ANSI committee, X3J3, was therefore set up in 1980 to develop the *next* FORTRAN standard under delegated authority from the International Organization for Standardization's Fortran Working Group, WG5 (whose current Convenor is one of the authors of this book, TMRE). These committees had originally hoped to produce a new standard by 1986 but underestimated the technical difficulties involved. Nevertheless, the new international standard was finally published in August 1991 (ISO/IEC, 1991), and, as on the previous occasion, the standard suggested an informal name for the new language to distinguish it from its predecessor – **Fortran 90**. This evolutionary process has continued since that time, and the International Standard for a minor revision of Fortran 90 – known as **Fortran 95** – was published towards the end of 1997 (ISO/IEC, 1997).

During the early 1990s, however, it became apparent that although Fortran 90 was a very powerful language, the fact that it contained a great many old-fashioned features for compatibility with earlier versions of Fortran was a serious disadvantage for many purposes – notably teaching, but also for professional use as it made it more difficult to persuade experienced programmers to use the newer features in place of those that they had grown accustomed to. Indeed, most books on Fortran 90 identified a recommended subset of the language and made only passing reference to those features which the authors believed should not be used in new programs. Although these books obviously reflected their authors' personal preferences, there was a remarkable consistency in the choice of 80–90% of the features disapproved of in this way.

In 1995 a group of experienced members of X3J3 took this process one step further and decided to specify a subset of Fortran 90 which would retain all the power of the full language while deleting the obsolete features and exerting more control over the use of some of the other features, notably by eliminating many of the redundant alternative ways of achieving identical results.

This group, who were to become Imagine1, Inc., also negotiated with the authors of a number of existing Fortran 90 compilers for different platforms and by the spring of 1996 were able to announce their new language, called simply **F**, together with arrangements for compilers on all major personal platforms, namely Windows 95/NT-based PCs, Power Macintoshes, and personal computers running Linux.

It is important to recognize that F is a true subset of Fortran 90 and Fortran 95, and that all F programs are therefore also Fortran 90 and Fortran 95 programs. However, F imposes a greater discipline on the programmer by preventing the use of those parts of Fortran which are widely believed to be bad practice in new programs, and by forcing consistency in the way that many aspects of a program are expressed.

The result is that someone who learns to program in F has also learned to program in Fortran, with the added bonus that their Fortran programs will only use the modern parts of Fortran, and that their programs will be written in such a manner as to encourage safety, portability and efficiency.

1.4   Why learn F?

As we have seen, there are, today, a very great many programming languages available throughout the world, some widely available, some not so widely, and some only in one place. However, two languages stand head and shoulders above the others in terms of their total usage. These languages are COBOL (first released in 1960) and Fortran (first released in 1957).

COBOL is used for business data processing and it has been estimated that over 70% of all programming carried out in 1990 used COBOL! Fortran programs probably constitute around 60% of the remainder, with all the other languages trailing far behind.

Fortran was originally designed with scientific and engineering users in mind, and during its first 30 years it has completely dominated this area of programming. For example, most of the analysis of the air flow past a modern aircraft or the path of a NASA Mars-lander is performed by a Fortran program.

The dies which are used in pressing the bodyshells of virtually all mass-produced automobiles are also made by machines controlled by Fortran programs. The control of experiments investigating the sub-atomic particles which constitute the matter of our universe and the analysis of the results of these experiments are mainly carried out by Fortran programs. The structural analysis of bridges or skyscrapers, the calculation of stresses in chemical plant piping systems, the design of electric generators, and the analysis of the flow of molten glass are all usually carried out using computer programs written in Fortran.

Fortran has also been the dominant computer language for engineering and scientific applications in academic circles and has been widely used in other, less obvious, areas, such as musicology, for example. A widely used program in both British and American universities is SPSS (Statistical Package for the Social Sciences) which enables social scientists to analyse survey or other research data (SPSS Inc., 1988); SPSS is written in FORTRAN 77. Indeed, because of the extremely widespread use of Fortran in higher education and industry, many standard **libraries** have been written in Fortran in order to enable programmers to utilize the experience and expertise of others when writing their own Fortran programs. Two notable examples are the IMSL and NAG libraries (Visual Numerics, 1992; NAG Ltd, 1988; Hopkins and Phillips, 1988), both of which are large and extremely comprehensive collection of **subprograms** for numerical analysis applications, to which we shall refer in Chapters 11 and 17 when discussing numerical methods in F programs. Thus, because of the widespread use of Fortran over a period of more than 35 years, a vast body of experience is available in the form of existing Fortran programs. F allows access to all this experience.

Fortran has evolved over 40 years in what has often been a pragmatic fashion, but always with the emphasis on efficiency and ease of use. However, FORTRAN 77 did not have many of the features which programmers using other, newer, languages had come to find invaluable. Fortran 90, therefore, rectified this situation by adding a considerable number of very powerful new features while retaining all of FORTRAN 77. In particular, many of the new features in Fortran 90 enable Fortran programs to be written more easily, more safely and more portably.

Fortran 90, therefore, gave a new lease of life to the oldest of all programming languages, and is also being used as the base from which still more versions of the language are being developed, for example to take advantage of some of the new types of computers, such as **massively parallel computers**, which are being developed as the 20th century draws to a close. The ability to write programs in Fortran will undoubtedly, therefore, be a major requirement for a high proportion of scientific and technological computing in the future, just as the ability to use FORTRAN 77, and before that FORTRAN IV, was in the past.

As we have already explained, F is a subset of Fortran 90 (and of Fortran 95) that includes all the good parts of Fortran and hardly any of the less desirable parts. It is, therefore, an excellent language to learn because it encourages good programming style in the same way as languages such as Pascal, which were designed solely for teaching purposes, while doing so by means of a fully featured language that is totally compatible with current and future scientific and technological programming practice.

This book introduces the F programming language in a way that will encourage embryo programmers to develop a good style of programming and a sound approach to the design of their programs. It must, however, be emphasized that programming is a practical skill, and that to develop this skill it is essential that as many programs as possible are written and tested on a computer. The exercises at the end of each chapter will help here, but it should always be realized that to write fluent, precise and well-structured programs requires both planning and experience − and there are no short-cuts to gaining experience in any walk of life!

PART I

Fundamental Principles

2 First steps in F programming

3 Essential data handling

4 Basic building blocks

5 Controlling the flow of your program

6 Repeating parts of your program

7 An introduction to arrays

8 Improved building blocks

9 More control over input and output

10 Using files to preserve data

First steps in F programming

2.1	From problem to program in three basic steps	2.4	Errors in programs
2.2	Some basic F concepts	2.5	The design and testing of programs
2.3	Running F programs on a computer		

The most important aspect of programming is undoubtedly its design, while the next most important is the thorough testing of the program. The actual coding of the program, important though it is, is relatively straightforward by comparison.

This chapter discusses some of the most important principles of program design and introduces a technique, known as a *structure plan*, for helping to create well-designed programs. This technique is illustrated by reference to a simple problem, an F solution for which is used to introduce some of the fundamental concepts of F programs.

Some of the key aspects of program testing are also briefly discussed, although space does not permit a full coverage of this important aspect of programming. We will return to this topic in the Intermission between Parts I and II of this book.

2.1   From problem to program in three basic steps

It has been claimed that programming is both an art (Knuth, 1969) and a science (Gries, 1991). In fact, it contains elements of both art and science, but in reality it is an **engineering discipline**, and as such it is governed by rules of procedure – albeit rules which contain a large element of pragmatism.

The reason for writing a program, *any program*, is to cause a computer to solve a specified problem. The nature of that problem may vary from manipulating text, which will subsequently be printed on some form of printer attached to the computer (**word-processing**), to landing a spacecraft on a far-off planet; it can vary from controlling the traffic lights in a large city centre to analysing baseball statistics or cricket averages; it can vary from **compiling** an F program to controlling all aspects of the computer system on which the F compiler is running (the **operating system**). It should never be forgotten that *programming is not an end in itself.*

The task of writing a program to solve a particular problem can be broken down into three basic steps.

1. Specify the problem clearly.
2. Analyse the problem and break it down into its fundamental elements.
3. Code the program according to the plan developed at step 2.

There is also a fourth step which, as we shall see, is often the most difficult of all:

4. Test the program exhaustively, and repeat steps 2 and 3 as necessary until the program works correctly in all situations that you can envisage.

We shall discuss the testing of programs briefly later in this chapter, and also in the Intermission between Parts I and II of this book, but will, for reasons of clarity and space, generally omit any reference to testing elsewhere in the book. It is a vitally important part of programming, however, since no one can guarantee to write any program of any sophistication perfectly the first time, and no one would ever claim that a really complex program could be written in such a way that all possible situations have been anticipated and dealt with correctly from the outset.

Equally, it is important that the problem to be solved is specified clearly and unambiguously from the outset. If you are not absolutely clear about what is required it is extremely unlikely that your program will do exactly what was wanted! Specifying exactly the problem that a computer program is to solve is not always easy, but it is not the subject of this book. In all the examples and exercises in this book the problem will be clearly defined at the outset; in real-life programming, however, the problems will frequently not be so clearly defined and you will have to spend a significant amount of effort establishing exactly what is required before starting to develop any programs.

Throughout this book, therefore, we shall concentrate on steps 2 and 3 – especially in the numerous example programs which we shall use to illustrate the concepts being explained. As an example of the approach that we shall use, Example 2.1 illustrates how a simple problem can be converted into an F program.

◻ **EXAMPLE 2.1** ·

1 **Problem**

Write a program which will ask the user for the x and y coordinates of three points and which will calculate the equation of the circle passing through those three points, namely

$$(x - a)^2 + (y - b)^2 = r^2$$

and then display the coordinates (a, b) of the centre of the circle and its radius, r.

2 **Analysis**

There are a number of methods of analysing problems for which programming solutions are required, both formal and informal. The approach that we shall use throughout this book is a refinement of the one that was originally developed by one of us (TMRE) for teaching FORTRAN 77, and which has been used with considerable success to teach many thousands of Fortran programmers for nearly 20 years. It involves creating a **structure plan** of successive levels of refinement until a point is reached where the programmer can readily code the individual steps without the need for further analysis. This **top-down** approach is universally recognized as being the ideal model for developing programs although, as we shall see, there are situations when it is also necessary to look at the problem from the other direction (**bottom-up**).

In this example we shall start by listing the major steps required.

1   Read three sets of coordinates $(x1, y1)$, $(x2, y2)$ and $(x3, y3)$
2   Calculate the equation of the circle $(x - a)^2 + (y - b)^2 = r^2$
3   Display the coordinates (a, b) and the radius r

Now the first and last of these steps are fairly straightforward (once we know something about input and output in F), but the second step is more complicated and might need further analysis. However, we can defer that work until later, or can even delegate it to someone else, by writing this part of the program as a

procedure. We shall not discuss this concept any further at this stage but will simply modify our structure plan to reflect the fact that step 2 will be carried out in a procedure which we shall call *calculate_circle*.

Our structure plan now looks like this:

1 Read three sets of coordinates $(x1, y1)$, $(x2, y2)$ and $(x3, y3)$
2 Calculate the equation of the circle $(x - a)^2 + (y - b)^2 = r^2$ using the procedure *calculate_circle*
3 Display the coordinates (a, b) and the radius r

There is, however, one major potential problem which we have ignored, namely what will happen if there is no solution possible. This might occur if, for example, the points lie on a straight line, or nearly on a straight line, since this will cause the equations which are to be solved to be **ill-conditioned** – a concept that we shall examine further in Chapter 11. For the present we shall ignore this problem in the name of simplicity, but it is an important one, and a proposed solution should always be examined for potential problems before coding is started, and appropriate recovery mechanisms devised. In this case, for example, it would not be too difficult to check for the two situations mentioned before attempting to solve the equations, and to print an appropriate message to the user.

3 Solution

An F program to implement this structure might be as follows.

```
program Circle
   use Geometry

   ! This program calculates the equation of a circle passing
   ! through three points

   ! Variable declarations
   real :: x1,y1,x2,y2,x3,y3,a,b,r

   ! Step 1
   print *,"Please type the coordinates of three points"
   print *,"in the order x1,y1,x2,y2,x3,y3"
   read *,x1,y1,x2,y2,x3,y3        ! Read the three points

   ! Step 2
   call calculate_circle(x1,y1,x2,y2,x3,y3,a,b,r)

   ! Step 3
   print *,"The centre of the circle through these points ", &
           "is (",a,",",b,")"
   print *,"Its radius is ",r

end program Circle
```

```
Please type the coordinates of three points
in the order x1,y1,x2,y2,x3,y3
4.71 4.71
6.39 0.63
0.63 3.06
The centre of the circle through these points is ( 3.502, 1.827)
Its radius is  3.126
```

Figure 2.1   The result of running the solution to Example 2.1.

We shall examine this program in some detail in Section 2.2, but even without any knowledge of F it is relatively easy to see that this program does reflect the structure plan that we had previously developed. Figure 2.1 shows how the screen might appear after running this program.

2.2   Some basic F concepts

The program written in Example 2.1 is a very simple one, but it does contain many of the basic building blocks and concepts which apply to all F programs. We shall therefore examine it carefully line by line to establish these concepts before we move on to look at the language itself in any detail. Before doing so, however, we must emphasize that the code shown in Example 2.1 is not the whole program, since the procedure calculate_circle is also part of the same program. What is shown is simply the **main program** or, more correctly, the **main program unit**. We shall have more to say about the other types of program unit later.

Each line of an F program contains one **statement**, or part of one statement where the statement is continued onto a second or subsequent line, as described below. Each line may have a maximum of 132 characters.

The first line of our program reads

program Circle

Every main program unit must start with a **program** statement which consists of the word **program** followed by the name of the program. This name must follow the rules which apply to all F names and identifiers, namely

- it must begin with a letter – either upper or lower case
- it may only contain the letters A–Z and a–z, the digits 0–9, and the underscore character _ (which must not be the last character of the name)

- it must consist of a maximum of 31 characters.

There are a number of names, known as **reserved words**, which may not be used for any other purpose by the programmer; all such reserved words must be written in lower case only. Reserved words fall into two groups — those such as **program** which have a special meaning in F and another group, known as **intrinsic procedure names**, which we shall meet in Chapter 3. Other names, chosen by the programmer, are referred to as **identifiers**. In this book reserved words are printed in bold typeface to distinguish them from the identifiers chosen by the programmer.

Although the programmer can use both upper and lower case for identifiers, F requires that the same pattern of upper and lower case must be used on every occasion for the same name. Thus, in this example the name of the program has been chosen to be Circle, and all subsequent references to this name must use an upper-case C and lower case for the other letters. Any use of the same letters in different cases, for example circle, CIRCLE or even CiRcLe, will be treated as an invalid representation of Circle and will lead to an error, rather than being treated as a different name; this is because in Fortran programs upper- and lower-case letters are treated as being identical.

The name of the program should be chosen to indicate what the program does and should be different from any other names used for other purposes elsewhere in the program.

Note also that the blank (or space) between the word **program** and the name Circle is included, as in normal English, to make the program easier to read. There may be any number of blanks between successive words in an F statement, as long as there is at least one, but they will be treated as though there was only one by the compiler when it is analysing the program. It is not necessary to include blanks between successive items in a list separated by commas or other punctuation characters, although they may be included if desired to make the program easier to read. It is not permitted to include spaces *within* an F keyword or a user-specified identifier.

```
use Geometry
```

This statement informs the compiler that part of the program is to be found in the module called Geometry. We shall discuss modules in Chapter 4, but for the present will simply note that in this example the procedure calculate_circle will be supplied by means of the module Geometry.

```
! This program calculates the equation of a circle passing
! through three points
```

These two lines are **comments**.

A comment is a line, or part of a line, which is included purely for information for the programmer or anyone else reading the program; it is ignored by the compiler. A comment line is a line whose first non-blank character is an exclamation mark, !; alternatively a comment, preceded by an exclamation mark, may follow any F statement, as can be seen later in this program. We shall normally use comment lines in example programs, but will also use trailing comments where these are more appropriate.

You should always use comments liberally in your programs to explain anything which is not obvious from the code itself. You should always err on the side of caution, since what is clear to you may not be clear to someone else who has to read your program. Indeed, it may not even be clear to you six months after the code was written!

```
! Variable declarations
real :: x1,y1,x2,y2,x3,y3,a,b,r
```

The first of these lines is a comment which indicates that the following line contains one or more **variable declarations**. It is not obligatory, but such comments help a reader to follow the program more easily.

The next line is a **specification statement** and provides important information about the program to the compiler. In this case it specifies that the nine identifiers x1, y1, ..., r are the names of variables which will be used to hold numeric information. As we shall see in Chapter 3, there are several ways in which numeric information may be stored in a computer, but the most common type is known as a **real number**. We shall examine the detailed syntax of variable declarations in Chapter 3.

```
! Step 1
print *,"Please type the coordinates of three points"
print *,"in the order x1,y1,x2,y2,x3,y3"
```

The comment preceding the next block of statements simply indicates that these statements correspond to step 1 of our structure plan.

The following two statements are the first statements to be obeyed during the *execution* of the program, and are called **executable statements**. These particular executable statements are known as **list-directed output statements** and will cause the text contained between the quotation marks (or *quotes*) to be displayed on your computer's default output device, probably the screen. We shall examine the way in which these statements work in Chapter 3.

```
read *,x1,y1,x2,y2,x3,y3       ! Read the three points
```

This statement is clearly closely related to the previous two statements and has a very similar structure. It is called a **list-directed input statement** and will *read* information from the keyboard, or other default input device. It will be discussed in detail in Chapter 3. Note the use of a trailing comment.

```
! Step 2
call calculate_circle(x1,y1,x2,y2,x3,y3,a,b,r)
```

We now move on to step 2 of the structure plan. The **call** statement causes the processing of the main program to be interrupted and processing to continue with the procedure, or **subroutine**, whose name is given in the statement. Thus, as we anticipated in our structure plan, we do not need to know at this stage (or perhaps ever, if someone else writes it!) how the procedure will calculate the coefficients of the equation which defines the required circle. The items enclosed in parentheses following the procedure name are known as **arguments** and are used to transmit information between the main program and the procedure; in this case the relevant information required by the procedure consists of the coordinates supplied by the user, while the information returned by the procedure will be the coordinates of the centre of the circle and its radius. We shall investigate the way in which procedures are used and written in Chapter 4, as soon as we have learned about the various types of data that F can process.

```
! Step 3
print *,"The centre of the circle through these points ", &
        "is (",a,",",b,")"
print *,"Its radius is ",r
```

Step 3 of the structure plan relates to the display of the required results. The first print statement, however, incorporates a new concept — that of a **continuation line**. If the last non-blank character of a line is an ampersand, &, then this is an indication that the statement is continued on the next line. Note that the effect of this continuation is as if the whole of the continuation line follows the previous one (excluding the ampersand). Note, also, that it is not permitted to split a name, or a sequence of characters contained between quotation marks, across two lines. Thus, the example above is permissible because the ampersand comes between two consecutive character strings, "The centre of the circle through these points " and "is (". It would also have been permissible to write

```
print *,"The centre of the circle ", &
        "through these points is (",a,",",b,")"
```

or even

```
print *,"The centre of the circle ", &
        "through these points is ", &
        "(",a,",",b,")"
```

Similarly, the statement discussed earlier, representing step 2 of the structure plan, could also be written

```
call calculate_circle(x1,y1,x2,y2,x3,y3, &
                      a,b,r)
```

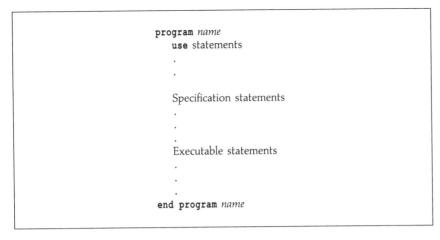

Figure 2.2 The structure of a main program unit.

which would be identical, as far as the compiler was concerned, to the original version since the extra spaces between y3 and a are ignored.

An F statement may have a maximum of 39 continuation lines.

These two **print** statements are different from the earlier ones in that they will print variable information as well as constant character strings. It should be obvious to the reader that they will print, or display, the appropriate text followed by the value of the specified variable or variables, as calculated by the procedure calculate_circle. This extended use will be described in detail in Chapter3.

end program Circle

The final statement of a program must be an **end program** statement, followed by the name of the program, as specified in the initial **program** statement. As might be expected, execution of the **end program** statement brings the execution of the program to an end, and control is returned to the computer's operating system.

The overall structure of an F main program is shown in Figure 2.2.

SELF-TEST EXERCISES 2.1

Attempt all the following tests and then check your answers with the solutions at the end of the book. If you do not get them correct, and you are not sure why your answer is wrong, you should re-read the first two sections of this chapter before proceeding.

1   What are the three steps involved in writing a program?

2   What is usually the most difficult part of the programming process?

3   What are the rules for the names of identifiers in F?

4   What must be the first statement of an F main program? And the last?

5   How is an F statement continued onto a second line?

6   Why are comments important? Give two ways of including comments in your programs.

2.3   Running F programs on a computer

In the preceding sections we have considered an F program in isolation, with little reference to the method by which the program is input to the computer, compiled and executed. This omission is deliberate and is due to the fact that, whereas the F language is uniquely defined, the computer's **operating system** is not. We shall, therefore, digress slightly at this point and look at the broad principles of the overall computer system before returning to discuss the F language in detail.

In the early days of computing, programmers had to do everything themselves. They would load their programs (probably written in an assembly language or even machine code) and press the appropriate buttons on the machine to get them to work. When a program required data they would either type it in or, more probably, load some data cards. When the program wanted to print results programmers would ensure that the printer (or other output device) was ready. Before long, computers developed in two directions – first, magnetic tapes (and later disks) were added to provide backing store, and second, high-level languages such as Fortran became available. Now programmers had to load the compiler first and get it to input their programs as data (of a special kind). The compiled program (possibly on binary punched cards produced by the compiler) would then be input as before. In addition, if any file storage was required, programmers had to load the correct tapes. In some cases a full-time operator was employed to carry out all these tasks, but this of course meant that detailed instructions were required to ensure that the job was processed correctly, and so many programmers still preferred to run their programs themselves.

A major change was heralded by the development at the University of Manchester, in England, of the **multiprogramming** system for the Atlas computer. This took advantage of the high speed of a computer's arithmetic and logical functions compared with its input/output functions to process several programs apparently simultaneously. The effect is similar to that experienced by amateur chess-players when facing a chess master in a simultaneous match, where the master plays against a number of opponents at the same time. In fact, of course, the master moves from one board to another, but, because of his or her much greater ability and speed in assessing the positions of the pieces, the master appears to each opponent to be devoting most of the time to them. The Atlas system took advantage of the (relatively) long delays during input or output of even a single number to leave that program (whose input/output could proceed autonomously) and start to process another.

The next major development took place more or less at the same time at both Dartmouth College and the Massachusetts Institute of Technology in the USA, and led to the concept of **time-sharing**, which placed the user at a terminal through which most input/output took place, with each user having a small **slice** of time in turn. The much slower speed of a terminal allowed more programs to run at once, but, because users were communicating directly with the computer, their work was processed much more quickly in this new **interactive** mode of operation than was possible with **batch** working.

The advent of first multiprogramming and then time-sharing meant that it was no longer possible for a programmer, or even a full-time operator, to carry out all the routine tasks associated with loading and executing a program; too many things were happening in different jobs at the same time. Since the computer was now doing several things at once it was natural that it should be given the additional task of organizing its own work. Special programs were therefore written, called **operating systems**, which enabled a programmer to define what was required in the form of special instructions, and caused the computer to carry out these instructions. What gradually emerged were new languages (**job control languages**) with which programmers instructed the computer how to run their jobs.

With the advent of microcomputers and personal workstations in the 1980s the situation changed again, and although some form of operating system language always exists it is frequently hidden from users who simply type a single command on their keyboards or select an appropriate symbol with a mouse.

Nevertheless, some action is required to run an F program on a particular computer and to identify any specific requirements, and this action will be specific to the particular computer system and compiler being used. Throughout the rest of this book we shall ignore this aspect of running programs, and concentrate on the programs themselves. However, before any programs are actually compiled and executed it will be necessary for the reader to establish exactly how to input the program, and then to compile and execute it, on the particular computer system being used.

2.4 Errors in programs

It is an unfortunate fact that programs often (one might even say usually) contain errors. These fall into two distinct groups – syntactic (or grammatical) errors and semantic (or logical) errors. Before we examine how these two types of errors may occur in F programs, and in order to emphasize the difference between them, we shall consider how they might occur in natural English by considering the well-known saying (among those just starting to read and write) to the effect that

> The cat sat on the mat

If this sentence was being analysed by some automatic device (a robot, perhaps?) which had a good knowledge of English grammar and of the meaning of words, but had no intuition or other means of interpreting what might have been intended by the author, then the mistyped sentence

> The dat sat on the mat

would have no meaning. This is a *syntactic* error, since the word 'dat' does not exist in the English language, and our robot would diagnose it as such. On the other hand, the statement

> The cat sat the on mat

contains only valid English words, but the grammar is incorrect since a preposition ('on') cannot appear between the definite article ('the') and a noun ('mat'). Once again, therefore, our robot would indicate that there was a syntactic error in the sentence.

However, the sentence

> The mat sat on the cat

satisfies all the rules of grammar, and all the words are valid English words. Our robot will, therefore, move to the next stage and try to understand what the sentence means. Here it may have a problem! This is, therefore, an example of a *semantic* error, for there is nothing wrong grammatically (or syntactically) with the sentence; it just doesn't make any sense.

Notice, incidentally, that a typing mistake will not necessarily lead to a syntactic error. For example, the following sentences each have a single typing error, but they are all syntactically correct, and even make sense − though not the sense that was intended:

> The cat spat on the mat
> The cot sat on the mat
> The cat sat on the man

We can see from these examples that a syntactic, or grammatical, error is relatively easy to detect, and an F compiler will always detect any such errors in a program. On the other hand, a semantic, or logical, error may result in a nonsensical meaning, or it may result in a reasonable, but incorrect meaning. In programming terms, a semantic error may result in the program failing during execution, or it may simply result in incorrect answers.

Returning to consideration of F programs, therefore, an example of a syntactic error would be the omission of the comma following the asterisk in the first **print** statement of the program written in Example 2.1:

```
print * "Please type the coordinates of three points"
```

When the compiler is translating this statement it finds that it does not match with either of the valid forms of **print** statement (there is another, as we shall see in Chapter 9), and the appropriate machine code cannot be generated. It will therefore produce an error message such as

```
*** Syntax error
```

or, in F, a more helpful one such as

```
    print * "Please type the coordinates of three points"
#        ^---------------------------------------------^
File Circle.F ; Line 11 # Column 12 ERROR(#74408) ###########
#sample syntax:  print *, EXPR                              ##
#                       ^                                   ##
#                print "format specification", EXPR         ##
#                                            ^              ##
############################################################
```

Since a program may contain more than one error, a compiler will usually continue to check the rest of the program (although in some cases other apparent errors may be caused which will disappear when the first one is corrected). However, no machine code will be produced, and no loading or execution will take place (if these would have been automatically initiated). An **editor** will then normally be used by the programmer to correct the program before it is resubmitted to the compiler.

Errors detected by the compiler (called **compilation errors**) are no great problem. That they are there indicates a degree of carelessness on the part of the programmer, but they can be easily corrected and the program recompiled.

Semantic errors are far more serious, since they indicate that there is an error in the logic of the program. Occasionally this may lead to a compilation error, but usually it will lead either to an error during the execution of the program (an **execution error**) resulting in an abnormal end, or to the program producing incorrect answers. For example, if one number was accidentally divided by zero, leading to a theoretical answer of infinity, this would result in an execution error. On the other hand, if the **read** statement in our program had inadvertently been written as

```
read *,x1,x2,x3,y1,y2,y3
```

then execution of the program would have led to the procedure being asked to determine the circle passing through the points $(x1, x2)$, $(x3, y1)$ and $(y2, y3)$ rather than the one passing through the points $(x1, y1)$, $(x2, y2)$ and $(x3, y3)$ as intended.

This latter example is a type of error with which the computer can give no help, since the program is syntactically correct and runs without causing a failure. It produces an incorrect answer because the logic was incorrect and only a thinking human being can detect and correct it. You should never forget that computers have no intelligence; they will only do what you tell them to do – no matter how silly that may be – rather than what you intended them to do.

Because errors in the logic of a program are often quite difficult to find (the trivial error in a very simple program shown above is hardly typical!), it is very important that programs are planned carefully in advance and that their development is not rushed. This discussion of errors underlines the importance of a planned structure to programs and programming such as that already introduced in Example 2.1, and you should get into the habit of developing structure plans before starting to code even the simplest programs.

2.5   The design and testing of programs

In the subsequent chapters of this book we shall meet the full range of F statements and facilities, and will begin to appreciate the richness of the language, which is the basis of its ability to enable the F programmer to solve an enormously wide range of problems easily and efficiently. The exercises and examples that will be used to illustrate that richness will, however, necessarily be brief, so that their complexity will not get in the way of the points that they are trying to make. Real programs will almost always be substantially larger than those that you will find in this book.

Although all the worked examples will develop the program's design by means of structure plans, it may sometimes seem that this is making the process unnecessarily difficult. *Such an attitude could not be more wrong!*

Computer programming is an activity that is extremely interesting, and one which can often exert a very considerable fascination upon those involved. It is so interesting because it requires a careful blend of knowledge from several different areas, and because the programmer is involved in a creative process which has almost no constraints, beyond the necessity to be logically consistent and obey the syntax and semantics of the language being used. In this, it has similarities with both pure mathematics and with the fine arts. As a consequence of this freedom, the programmer is free to be very creative, but abuse of this freedom will inevitably lead to poor programs.

In mathematics, a correct but ugly proof makes mathematicians uneasy, and they will strive to find an elegant proof to replace it. The same is true for computer programs, and a correct but ugly program will make people want to redesign and rewrite it. It is important to emphasize that this is not just aesthetics coming into play, for there are sound, very practical, reasons for writing elegant programs.

- The first of these is that an ugly program is almost synonymous with poor design, and with coding that was begun before the program was well thought out. This results in programs that can only be made to work correctly with considerable difficulty. Indeed, if a program is badly enough constructed the writer may have an uneasy feeling that it isn't really reliable, even after it has solved several test cases correctly.

  The experience of many people over many years has shown that the time spent in careful initial design, before writing any code, is more than regained during the process of verification (often called debugging). The larger the project the more this principle comes into play. However, this doesn't mean that small projects don't benefit from some initial planning. Careful initial design always pays off, even on the smallest project.

- A second issue, and to many people of even more importance than the initial development of a program, is that of **maintainability** of programs. Programs need maintenance for several reasons. If a programming project goes beyond a relatively small size, it will almost certainly, at some point during its lifetime, be found to have errors in special circumstances that were not thought of, or were incorrectly handled, during the initial design. Programs often have an unexpectedly long life (sometimes to the embarrassment of their authors!). Almost inevitably, most programs will, therefore, be subsequently extended to deal with new problems not in the original requirements. As a result, it is quite normal for more time and effort to be spent in extending and maintaining a program than was spent in originally developing it. The phrase 'write once and read many times' is a truism in programming.

- Finally, if you have written a program of more than parochial interest, you will undoubtedly receive requests from friends and colleagues for copies. The world is full of different types of computers. Imagine your colleagues' distress if they cannot readily compile and execute your program on their machines! You may also find that the computer on which a program was originally developed is being replaced with a new one – a circumstance that seems to be happening with ever-increasing frequency. Therefore, writing **portable programs** is important.

In summary, programs should be well designed before they are begun. This will lead to reliable, efficient, easily maintained, portable programs that are enjoyable to create and to work with.

There are many elements that go into good program design, and many approaches that have been developed to assist programmers to develop well-designed programs. However, regardless of the detailed approach that is used, there are a number of underlying principles that must always be incorporated in the design of any program, of which the following are the most important:

- Completely understand what the program is supposed to accomplish. What are the inputs and outputs supposed to be? This sounds too trivial to be worth mentioning, but it is not. It is all too easy not to have all the facts clearly understood before starting programming. This will lead to much painful and expensive redesign at a later stage.

- Make the input and output clear to understand for the program *user*, even if that user is you. Make the input form as easy as possible and the output form as clear and useful as possible.

- Have a clear design for the method to be used to solve the problem. Write it down. We have already introduced one way to do this and will expand on this in later chapters. However, there are other approaches, and you should choose one that you feel comfortable with. It is surprising how often this stage has to be reworked until a correct solution is found.

- Look to see what functionality you can find in existing procedure libraries. We shall have more to say about this in Chapter 4, but we have already seen in Example 2.1 how a subroutine can be used to avoid the need to write all the program oneself. Reinventing the wheel is not an economical use of your time!

- When writing the program use a modular design. We shall discuss this topic in some detail in Chapter 4 and so will not say more here except to point out that a good rule of thumb is that no single block of code (or *procedure*, see Chapter 4) should be longer than about 50 lines, excluding any comments.

- Use descriptive names for variables and program units and be lavish with comments. Code with few or no comments is usually impossible for even the author to understand once a few weeks have passed since its creation.

- Perform as much error checking on the input as is possible. Moreover, perform checks on the success of the internal stages of a calculation. Include, as part of the output, any problems the program detects and how the accuracy of the answer is being affected. This is actually a somewhat complicated topic and only a few introductory comments can be made here.

  For input error checking, try to catch, and report back to the user, every error that the input data might contain. For example, if one of the data items is the number of items to be processed, this number should be checked to see that it is not negative, and should also be checked to see that it is not so large that the capacity of the program will be exceeded. This is an obvious type of check to make. A less obvious class of checks is on the self-consistency of the data. For example, if a program is supposed to take three points as input and calculate the radius and centre of the circle passing through them, the points should be checked to see that they do not lie on a straight line. If they are exactly collinear the radius is infinite and the coordinates of the centre have become indeterminate. Another check is to test that all the points are distinct. If they are not, then there are an infinite number of solutions.

For errors that can be detected while the program is executing, consider checks on how many iterations are being performed in trying to converge to a solution. If this becomes too large, the user should be informed and given an option to terminate the process.

Returning to the problem of determining the circle through three points, suppose the points are almost collinear or almost coincident. This is more difficult to detect than exact collinearity or coincidence. What does 'almost' mean here? How can a precise numerical value be given for 'almost'? There is a solution. The centre of the circle can be determined as the result of solving a pair of simultaneous linear equations. There are well-established mathematical techniques, which are, however, outside the scope of this book, for estimating the *condition number* of such linear systems of equations. This analysis will detect near linearity or coincidence of points and can be used to report back to the user how many digits, if any, of the answer are accurate.

- Finally, test the program by using cases that execute *every* part of the program, including your input error tests and calculation problem tests. Although it may sound obvious, ensure that you know what the correct answer should be for those tests which are designed to run to completion. Just because your program produces an answer doesn't mean that it is the correct one!

These techniques do not take the interest and challenge out of programming, making it a mechanical process. Instead, they make a program easier to develop and maintain, thereby making the process more interesting and less painful. Both of us have, at some time in our lives, been faced with the problem of trying to find the error in a badly written and badly documented program (written by someone else, of course!) and we do not recommend it to anyone.

We shall return to the question of testing programs in the Intermission between Parts I and II of this book, but we cannot over-emphasize what a vitally important part of the programming process it is. Even with apparently simple programs, such as those which you will write in response to the exercises in the first part of this book, you should always thoroughly test them to ensure that they produce the correct answers from valid data, and react in a predictable and useful manner when presented with invalid data.

SELF-TEST EXERCISES 2.2

1 What is the difference between a syntactic error and a semantic error? Into which category do (a) compilation errors and (b) execution errors fall?

2 Give three reasons for the importance of well-designed programs.

3 Give four issues that should be considered *before* starting on the detailed design of a program.

4 Give four issues that should be considered during the testing of a program.

5 What is the maximum number of characters that may occur in one line of an F program?

6 What is the maximum number of lines that an F statement may be spread over?

SUMMARY

- Programming is an engineering discipline.

- The four basic steps involved in programming are *specification*, *analysis and design*, *coding* and *testing*.

- A structure plan is a method for assisting in the design of a program.

- Top-down design involves refining the problem into successively greater levels of detail.

- The programming of sub-problems identified during top-down design can be deferred by specifying a subprogram for the purpose.

- An F name consists of up to 31 characters, and may be made up from any combination of the 26 upper-case letters A–Z, the 26 lower-case letters a–z, the ten digits 0–9, and the underscore character _; the first character must be a letter and the last character may not be an underscore.

- Upper-case and lower-case letters are treated as being identical for the purpose of distinguishing between identifier names; however, upper-case and lower-case letters must be used in the same arrangement every time the same identifier appears.

- Blank characters are significant and must not appear in names; at least one blank must be used to separate names from each other, and from numbers.

- Keywords are names which have a special meaning in the F language; other names are called identifiers.

- Keywords are reserved words and may not be used for any other purpose; the names of intrinsic procedures are also reserved words.

- Upper-case letters may not be used for reserved words.

- Every main program unit must start with a **program** statement, and end with an **end program** statement containing the same name as the corresponding **program** statement.

- A comment line is a line whose first non-blank character is an exclamation mark, !; a trailing comment is a comment whose initial ! follows a statement. Comments are ignored by the compiler.

- Specification statements provide information about the program to the compiler.

- Execution statements are obeyed by the computer during the execution of the program.

- A list-directed input statement is used to obtain information from the user of a program during execution.

- A list-directed output statement is used to give information to the user of a program during execution.

- A **call** statement is used to transfer processing to a subroutine, using information passed to the subroutine by means of arguments, enclosed in parentheses.

- F syntax introduced in Chapter 2:

Initial statement	**program** *name*
End statement	**end program** *name*
use statement	**use** *name*
Variable declaration statement	**real** :: *list of names*
List-directed input and output statements	**read** *, *list of names* **print** *, *list of names and/or values*
Subroutine call	**call** *subroutine_name* (*argument1, argument2, ...*)

PROGRAMMING EXERCISES

Sample solutions for exercises whose numbers are preceded by an asterisk (for example, 2.2 and 2.3) may be obtained from the World Wide Web at http://awl-he.com/computing.

2.1 Find out how to use the editor on your computer to type and correct an F program. Also find out how to submit your program for compiling and execution.

*2.2 The following simple program contains a number of errors. Identify them and produce a corrected version.

```
program exercise 2.2
 real : number
 ! This program contains a number of errors &
   is not a good example of F at all!
   print *,"This &              ! Trailing
           is a silly           ! comments!
           program
   print *,"Type a number"
   read *,"number"
   print "Thank you. &
          Your number was" number
END exercise
```

Run the corrected program on your computer to check that it does indeed work. If it still does not work, then keep correcting it until it does!

2.3   How many mistakes can you find in the following program?

```
program final test
! This program contains several errors
   real :: Var-1,Var 2,Var_3,Var4

   print "Please type four numbers &
          separated by commas"
   read var-1,var 2,var_3,var4
   ! Now print the numbers to check that they were
   ! input correctly
   print *,"The numbers you typed were:
   print *,var-1,var 2,var_3,var4
   print *,"That's all for now." &
          "How many errors did you find?"
end program final_test
```

*2.4   Write an F program that prints the following message when it is run:

```
Hello World!
```

Now modify your program so that it prints a message similar to the following:

```
Hello World!

My name is Natasha Rudikova, and this is my first program
It won't be my last one, though!

Au revoir!
```

2.5   Write a program that expects three numbers to be entered, but only uses one **read** statement, and then prints them out so that you can check that they have been input correctly.

When typing in the numbers at the keyboard try typing them all on one line

(a)   separated by spaces
(b)   separated by commas
(c)   separated by semi-colons

Then run the program again, but type each of the three numbers on a separate line, followed by ENTER.

This exercise should help you to appreciate how an F program expects input to a list of variables.

2.6   Write a program that asks for the time in the form hh, mm and then prints that time as a message in the following form:

    The time is mm minutes after hh

What do you notice about the result of running this program?

Essential data handling

3

3.1 The two fundamental types of numbers

3.2 real and integer variables

3.3 Arithmetic expressions and assignment

3.4 List-directed input and output of numeric data

3.5 Handling character data

3.6 Named constants

There are two fundamental types of numbers in both mathematics and programming – namely those which are whole numbers, and those which may have a fractional part. In F these are known as integers and real numbers, respectively, and the difference between them is of vital importance. A third fundamental data type allows character information to be stored and manipulated.

This chapter discusses these three basic data types, the ways in which they may be used in calculations or other types of expressions, and the facilities contained within F for the input and output of both numeric and textual information.

Finally, this chapter introduces the concept of a named constant, which can be of great benefit in making programs easier to read and to modify.

3.1 The two fundamental types of numbers

When the first FORTRAN processor was developed in 1954 it introduced two, quite different, ways of storing numbers and of carrying out arithmetic. These have remained essentially unaltered in Fortran since that time, and are therefore the two fundamental types of numbers in F. Before proceeding any further we must establish what they are and how they differ.

An **integer** is a whole number and is stored in the computer's memory without any decimal (or fractional) part. However, because of the way in which it is stored, there are always limits to its size. These limits vary from one computer to another and depend upon the physical design of the computer's memory. We can illustrate this by considering a hypothetical computer which, for ease of comprehension, stores its data in decimal form instead of the binary (base 2) system used by almost all computers. This means that a single digit will be recorded by means of some device which has 10 states (corresponding to the 10 digits) instead of one with two states (for instance, on and off) as required for binary numbers. Each location in the memory used for storing integers will consist of a fixed number of these devices, say eight for the purposes of illustration, which will impose a limit on the size of the number – in this case up to 99 999 999. There remains the question of the sign of the numbers.

Suppose that the device which stored the integer was an electronic equivalent of a milometer or odometer, such as that fitted to a car to record the distance travelled (see Figure 3.1). If the reading is 00 000 000 and the car moves forward two miles (that is, adds 2) the milometer will read 00 000 002. However, if the car now reverses for three miles (that is, subtracts 3) the reading will successively go to 00 000 001, 00 000 000 and finally 99 999 999. Thus the same reading is obtained for a value of −1 as for +99 999 999, and adding 1 to 99 999 999 will give zero. We could therefore adopt a convention which says that readings from 1 to 49 999 999 will be considered to be positive, whereas 50 000 000 to 99 999 999 will be considered to be negative, and equivalent to −50 000 000

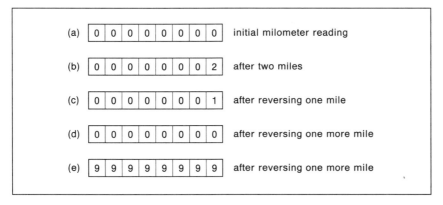

Figure 3.1 Milometer readings during travel.

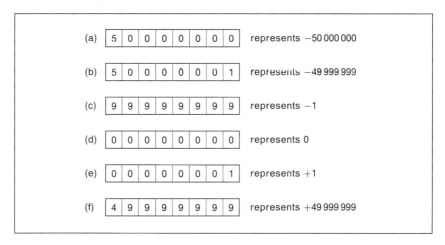

Figure 3.2 Storage of eight-digit integers.

to −1 respectively. Almost all computers work in a similar manner to this, although when using the binary system the effect is that if the first binary digit (or **bit**) is a one then the number is negative, while if it is zero the number is positive.

Using the convention just described, our eight-digit memory location can hold a whole number in the range −50 000 000 to +49 999 999, as shown in Figure 3.2.

The other type of number is called a **real number**. A real number can be regarded as consisting of an integer part and a string of digits representing the fractional part, and clearly one way of storing such a number in an eight-digit memory location would be to assume that, for example, the first four digits come before the decimal point and the second four after it. However, this would mean that the numbers could only lie between −5000.0 and +4999.9999, using the same convention as before regarding the sign, and that all numbers would be stored with exactly four decimal places. Clearly this is too restrictive and another way must be found. One solution might be to allow more digits, but the problem with this approach is that a large number of them will be wasted on many occasions. For example, if 16 digits were allowed, so as to give the same range as for integers, but with eight places of decimals, then on the one hand a number such as 100 000 000.0 cannot be stored because it needs nine digits before the decimal place, even though none of those after it are needed, while on the other a number such as 0.000 000 004 would have to be treated as zero because it needs nine decimal places even though none of the eight before the decimal point are needed.

One solution for our hypothetical computer would be to consider any positive non-zero real number as a fraction lying between 0.1 and 1.0, called the *mantissa*, which is multiplied or divided by 10 a certain number of times, called the *exponent*. Thus 100 000 000.0 would be the same as 0.1×10^9, and 0.000 000 004 would be the same as $0.4 \div 10^8$, or 0.4×10^{-8}.

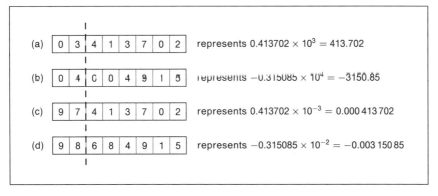

Figure 3.3   Floating-point numbers.

Using this approach, we could define a method of representation which says, for example, that the last six digits represent the mantissa as a fraction to six decimal places (with the first being non-zero), while the first two represent the exponent, that is, the number of times that the fraction is to be multiplied or divided by 10. The same technique as was used for integers to distinguish positive and negative numbers will be used for *both* the mantissa and the exponent. Figure 3.3 illustrates this method, which is known as **floating-point** representation.

This method of representation has two main implications. The first is that all numbers, whatever their size, are held to the same degree of accuracy. In the example being used they will all be stored to an accuracy of six significant digits. Thus the problem of wasted digits does not arise. The second implication is that the limits for the size of the numbers are very much greater than was the case for integers. In our hypothetical computer, for example, real numbers can lie anywhere in the range from -5×10^{48} to $+4.99999 \times 10^{48}$, and at the same time the smallest number that can be differentiated from zero is 0.1×10^{-50} (that is, 10^{-51}).

In our hypothetical computer, therefore, the number 03413702 represents the real value 413.702 or the integer value 3413702, depending upon whether it is interpreted as a floating-point number or as an integer. Note that there is nothing in the number 03413702 itself to indicate which of these two is intended; in this hypothetical example it would be the programmer's responsibility to remember which was intended.

In a real computer exactly the same situation arises, and it is essential that the two methods of number representation are clearly defined; we shall see in the next section how to instruct the computer which method to use. We can already see, however, that it is extremely important that the difference between an integer and a real number is thoroughly appreciated:

- An integer is a whole number, is always held *exactly* in the computer's memory, and has a (relatively) limited range (between about -2×10^9 and $+2 \times 10^9$ on a typical 32-bit computer).

- A real number, on the other hand, is stored as a floating-point number, is held as an *approximation* with a fixed number of significant digits and has a very large range (between about -10^{38} and $+10^{38}$ to 7 or 8 significant digits on the same 32-bit computer).

3.2 `real` and `integer` variables

The whole question of storage of different types of information in a computer can become quite complicated, and we shall return to this topic several times as we develop a fuller understanding of the power and flexibility of the F language. In the last section we saw the importance of informing the computer what type of information is to be processed, and the main way in which we do this is by means of a *variable declaration*. At its simplest this takes the form

   type :: *name*

where *type* specifies the **data type** for which memory space is to be reserved, and *name* is a name chosen by the programmer with which to refer to the **variable** that has been declared.

In Chapter 1 we used an analogy with a series of glass boxes to represent the memory of a computer, and we can extend this analogy so that the box now contains two identifying symbols (see Figure 3.4), one of which is the *name* used in the earlier example, while the other identifies the *type* of information which may be stored in the box.

In general, there will be more than one variable of the same type being declared and so a list of names may be given:

   type :: *name1, name2, ...*

Thus we may declare three integer variables by a statement such as

   integer :: a,b,c

or

   integer :: first_integer,second_integer, &
                third_integer

In a similar way, real variables are declared as

   real :: x,y,z

Note that real values are represented as floating-point numbers.

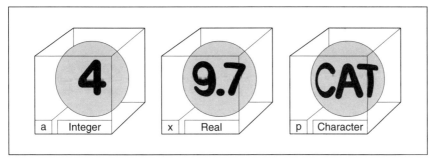

Figure 3.4 A typed storage model.

3.3 Arithmetic expressions and assignment

Once we have declared one or more variables, we can start to use them to solve problems. First, however, we must establish how particular values are stored in the memory locations associated with the specified variables.

In fact, there are only two ways in which a variable can be given a value during the execution of a program – by **assignment** or by a **read** statement. We met the **read** statement in Chapter 2, and will discuss it in some detail in the next section; however, by far the most common means of giving a value to a variable is through an **assignment statement**. This takes the form

name = expression

where *name* is the name of a variable, and *expression* is an arithmetic, or other, expression which will be evaluated by the computer to calculate the value to be assigned to the variable *name*. Thus the statement

```
a = b + c
```

takes the value currently stored in b, adds to it the value currently stored in c, and stores the resulting value in a.

If a, b and c are all real variables, and the values in b and c were 2.8 and 3.72 before the statement was obeyed, then the value assigned to a would be 6.52 – or rather it would be a very close approximation to 6.52, remembering that real arithmetic is always an approximation. Similarly, if a, b and c are all integer variables, and the values in b and c were 17 and 391 before the statement was obeyed, then the value assigned to a would be 408; in this case the answer would, of course, be exact.

Figures 3.5 and 3.6 illustrate what has happened, by reference to the storage model used earlier, but what about the situation shown in Figure 3.7? In this

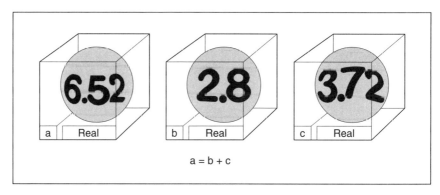

Figure 3.5 Real arithmetic and assignment.

example, the expression uses two real variables, and so the result is clearly real. However, the variable a is integer and so cannot hold a real value.

In this situation, the result of the expression is **truncated** to an integer by, in effect, throwing away the fractional part, or, more formally, by rounding towards zero. Thus, if the values in b and c were 2.8 and 3.72 before the statement was obeyed, as before, then the value of the expression would be 6.52, which would be truncated to 6 before being assigned to a.

In the reverse case, where the value of the expression is integer but the variable to be assigned the value is real, there is less of a problem since the integer result can easily be converted to its real equivalent without any loss of accuracy unless it is so large that it has more precision than a floating-point number can provide. For example, using the hypothetical computer used in Section 3.1 the integer number 12345678 has eight digits of precision and would need to be converted to 0.123457×10^8 (that is, 12345700.0).

A related problem occurs when not all of the entities making up the expression are of the same type, for example if b were real, while c were integer. In this case the rule is quite simple, namely that the integer value is converted to its real equivalent before the calculation is carried out. Note that

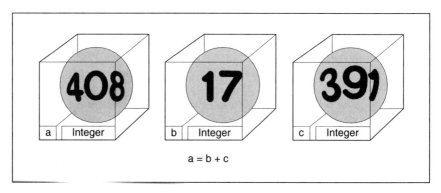

Figure 3.6 Integer arithmetic and assignment.

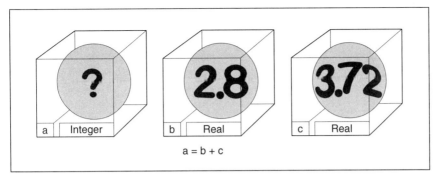

Figure 3.7 Mixed-mode assignment.

this conversion is only for the purpose of evaluating the expression; the integer value stored in c remains unchanged. Moreover, the process described here is something of an oversimplification, to which we shall return shortly, but it is sufficiently accurate for our present discussion.

We must now examine the form of an arithmetic expression in more detail. As in mathematics, an arithmetic expression is created by use of the five primary arithmetic operations – addition, subtraction, multiplication, division and exponentiation (or 'raising one number to the power of another'). Although the addition and subtraction operators use the conventional mathematical operators + and - it is not possible to express the other three operations in quite the same way as in conventional mathematics. Figure 3.8 shows the symbols used to express the five arithmetic operators in F.

We may create expressions of arbitrary complexity, subject to the limit on the length of a statement, by means of these operators, such as

```
a = b+c*d/e-f**g/h+i*j+k
```

However, it is not at all obvious, at first sight, how the above expression will be evaluated!

In this situation, F assigns the same priorities to operators as does mathematics, namely that exponentiation is carried out first, followed by

Operator	Meaning
+	addition
-	subtraction
*	multiplication
/	division
**	exponentiation (or 'raising to the power of')

Figure 3.8 Arithmetic operators in F.

Operator	Priority
**	High
* and /	Medium
+ and –	Low

Figure 3.9 Arithmetic operator priorities.

multiplication and division, followed by addition and subtraction, as shown in Figure 3.9.

Within the same level of priority, addition and subtraction or multiplication and division, evaluation will proceed from left to right, except in the case of exponentiation where evaluation proceeds from right to left. Thus the evaluation of the above expression proceeds as follows, where temp_1 and so on represent variables used by the computer system to store intermediate values, but which are not accessible to the programmer:

1. Calculate f**g and save it in temp_1.
2. Calculate c*d and save it in temp_2.
3. Calculate temp_2/e and save it in temp_3.
4. Calculate temp_1/h and save it in temp_4.
5. Calculate i*j and save it in temp_5.
6. Calculate b+temp_3 and save it in temp_6.
7. Calculate temp_6-temp_4 and save it in temp_7.
8. Calculate temp_7+temp_5 and save it in temp_8.
9. Calculate temp_8+k and store it in a.

In practice many of the temporary variables temp_1, ..., temp_8 will not actually be used as the computer will keep the intermediate results in special high-speed memory locations (called *registers*) to speed up the calculation, but the principle is correct – namely that the calculation proceeds step by step with each step consisting of the evaluation of a sub-expression consisting of one operator having two operands.

This leads us to a refinement of the earlier statement regarding what happens in a **mixed-mode expression**, where not all the operands are of the same type. The evaluation of the expression proceeds as already defined until a sub-expression is to be evaluated which has two operands of different types. At this point, and not before, the integer value is converted to real. The importance of this can be seen by considering the evaluation of the statement

```
a = b*c/d
```

where b is a real variable whose value is 100.0, while c and d are integers having the values 9 and 10, respectively.

Following the rules that have been already described, the value of b*c is first evaluated, with the value of c being first converted to the real value 9.0, to give an intermediate result of 900.0, after which the value of d is converted to its real equivalent before the division is carried out, to give a result to be assigned to a of 90.0, as we would expect.

Now consider what would have happened if the expression had been written in the different, but mathematically equivalent, way

```
a = c/d*b
```

Now when the first operation is carried out both the operands are integer and so the sub-expression c/d is evaluated as an integer operation. Since integers can have no fractional parts the same procedure is carried out as was described for assignment, namely the mathematical result (0.9) is *truncated* to give an intermediate result of zero. This is then converted to its real equivalent (0.0) before being multiplied by the real value of b, but it is already too late, and the result that will be assigned to a is also zero.

This phenomenon, known as **integer division** for obvious reasons, has caught out many a programmer (including both the authors at some time in their careers!). In general, integer division is to be avoided except in situations where programmers know exactly what they are doing and wish to take advantage of the automatic truncation; normally it is preferable to carry out this type of arithmetic using real arithmetic and then to deal with the result as required at the end of the calculation.

The reader should not assume, however, that the order of evaluation does not matter in real (that is, floating-point) arithmetic, for consider the following statement

```
w = x-y+z
```

where x, y and z all have the value 5.678. Clearly the correct value for assignment to w is also 5.678, and with the expression written as above this is, indeed, the result. However, consider what might happen if the statement was written in the mathematically identical form

```
w = x+z-y
```

and the program was executed on a computer which only held real numbers to four significant digits. In this case the first operation (5.678 + 5.678) would result in a 'true' value of 11.356 which would be saved (to four significant digits) as 11.36 before the subtraction took place, leading to a result of 5.682 — an error of 0.004, or 0.07% on a simple addition and subtraction!

In practice, because modern computers carry out their arithmetic in special areas of memory capable of much greater precision than the main memory, this particular example would present no difficulty, but the principle that order of evaluation matters is an important one which will be taken up in more detail in Chapter 11.

We have seen that long expressions can become difficult to read and that the order of evaluation is often important; there are, however, two steps that can be taken to improve matters.

The first of these involves the use of parentheses which, just as in mathematics, alter the order of evaluation. Thus the statement

```
w = x*(z-y)
```

will result in the evaluation of the sub-expression z-y first, with the result being multiplied by x to obtain the value to be assigned to w.

The other thing that can be done is purely cosmetic and involves the use of spaces to make expressions more readable. For example, the expression used earlier in this section could be made easier to read and understand by writing it as

```
a = b + c*d/e - (f**g)/h + i*j + k
```

The spaces are purely for the human reader and are ignored by the F compiler. In this instance, the parentheses are also only for the benefit of the human reader since the exponentiation would, in any case, be carried out first. We shall use spaces around the lowest priority operators in this way in most of the programs in the remainder of this book, but it must be emphasized that this is merely the authors' own style; programmers will develop their own styles as their experience grows.

There are two remaining points to be made at this stage concerning arithmetic expressions.

The first of these concerns the addition and subtraction operators. All five operators have been presented as **binary operators** thus far; that is, they have always had two operands. This is always true of the multiplication, division and exponentiation operators, but the addition and subtraction operators can also be used as **unary operators**, having only one argument:

```
p = -q
x = +y
```

The meaning of these unary operators is obvious and the result is identical to the binary case if a zero were placed before the operator.

The other point to be made concerns **constants**. In Chapter 1, when discussing the concept of a variable by analogy with a glass box containing a ball representing a value, we mentioned that if the box was sealed so that its value could not be changed then it was called a constant. Such constants may have names like variables, as we shall see in Section 3.6, or they may simply appear in an F statement by writing their value. In this latter case they are called **literal constants** because every digit of the numbers is specified *literally*.

All the program examples that have been presented in this section have only used variables, but in most expressions there are also some constant items. Numeric literal constants are usually written in the normal way, and the presence or absence of a decimal point defines the type of the constant.

Thus these are integer constants:

```
123
1000000
-981
0
```

while the following are real constants:

```
1.23
1000.0
-9.81
0.0
```

There is one exception to the rule that real constants must have a decimal point, namely the **exponential form**. This is typically used for very small or very large numbers and takes the form

$$meexp$$

where *m* is called the **mantissa** and *exp* is the **exponent**. The mantissa may be written either with or without a decimal point, whereas the exponent must take the form of an integer. Thus the value 0.000 001, or 10^{-6}, may be written in any of the following ways

```
1e-6
100e-8
0.1e-5
```

and so on.

3.4   List-directed input and output of numeric data

We have already met the **list-directed input/output statements** in Chapter 2, and with our new knowledge about variables and the real and integer data types it is now appropriate to define the format of these statements in more detail. In the form that we shall use them at present they both have an almost identical syntax, as follows:

```
read *,var_1,var_2, ...
print *,item_1,item_2, ...
```

The main syntactic difference between them is that the list of items in a **read** statement may only contain variable names, whereas the list in a **print** statement may also contain constants or expressions. These lists of names and/or other items are referred to as an **input list** and an **output list**, respectively. The asterisk following the **read** or **print** indicates that **list-directed formatting** is to take place. We shall see in Chapter 9 how other forms of input and output formatting may be defined, but the list-directed form is more than adequate for the present.

The list-directed **read** statement will take its input from a processor-defined input unit known as the **default input unit**, while the list-directed **print** statement will send its output to a processor-defined unit known as the **default output unit**. In most systems, such as workstations or personal computers, these default units will be the keyboard and display, respectively; we shall see in Chapter 9 how to specify other input or output units where necessary.

The statement

```
read *,real_var1,real_var2,int_var
```

will, therefore, read three values from the default input unit, normally the keyboard, and store them in the three variables `real_var1`, `real_var2` and `int_var`. A value that is input to a real variable may contain a decimal point, or the decimal point may be omitted, in which case it is treated as though the integer value read was followed by a decimal point. A value that is to be input to an integer variable must not contain a decimal point, and the occurrence of one will cause an error.

We can see, therefore, that the term 'list-directed' is used because the interpretation of the data input, or the representation of the data output, is determined by the list of items in the input or output statement. We shall see in Chapter 9 how to specify our own formatting instead of using the default one supplied by the F processor.

One important point that must be considered with list-directed input concerns the **termination** of each data value being input. The rule is that each number, or other item, must be followed by a **value separator** consisting of a comma, a space, a slash (/) or the end of the line; any of these value separators may be preceded or followed by any number of consecutive blanks (or spaces). If there are two consecutive commas then the effect is to read a **null value**, which results in the value of the corresponding variable in the input list being left unchanged. Note that a common cause of error is to believe that the value will be set to zero!

If the terminating character is a slash then no more data items are read, and processing of the input statement is ended. If there are any remaining items in the input list then the result is as though null values had been input to them; in other words, their values remain unchanged.

We can illustrate how this works by considering the following short program:

```
program list_directed_input_example
    integer :: int_1,int_2,int_3
    real :: real_1,real_2,real_3
!   Initialize all variables
    int_1 = -1
    int_2 = -2
    int_3 = -3
    real_1 = -1.0
    real_2 = -2.0
    real_3 = -3.0
!   Read data
    read *,int_1,real_1,int_2,real_2,int_3,real_3
!   Print new values
    print *,int_1,real_1,int_2,real_2,int_3,real_3
end program list_directed_input_example
```

Figure 3.10 shows the result of reading several different sets of data with this program.

It is also permitted to include special data items of the form $n*c$ or $n*$ where n is an unsigned non-zero integer constant and c is a real or integer data item. The first of these two forms represents n consecutive occurrences of the data item c, while the second represents n consecutive occurrences of a null value. These can be useful where it is required to read a large number of identical values.

	Data input	Result output
(a)	1,2.3,4,5.6,7,8.9	1, 2.300, 4, 5.600, 7, 8.900
(b)	9 8.7 6 5.4 3 2.1	9, 8.700, 6, 5.400, 3, 2.100
(c)	1 2.3	
	4 5.6	
	7 8.9	1, 2.300, 4, 5.600, 7, 8.900
(d)	9,,,5.4,,2.1	9, -1.000, -2, 5.400, -3, 2.100
(e)	1,2.3,4,5.6/	1, 2.300, 4, 5.600, -3, -3.000
(f)	/	-1, -1.000, -2, -2.000, -3, -3.000

Figure 3.10 Examples of list-directed input.

We have already used the list-directed **print** statement, and the statement

```
print *,entity_1,entity_2,entity_3
```

will output the values of *entity_1*, *entity_2* and *entity_3* to the default output unit, normally the display, where each of the three items in the output list may be a variable name, a constant or an expression. The only point to mention here concerns the layout, or **format**, of the results. On output, list-directed formatting causes the processor to use an appropriate format for the values being printed. Exactly what form this takes is processor dependent, but it is usually perfectly adequate for simple programs and for initial testing. In general, however, more control is required over the layout of results, and we shall see in Chapter 9 how this may be achieved. One point that should be mentioned, however, is that every new line of output will be preceded by a single space. This is for historical reasons connected with early versions of Fortran and does not affect the output in any other way; it does, however, mean that output will always start one character in from the left-hand edge of the screen or paper, as appropriate.

We have already discussed the form of integer and real constants in the context of arithmetic expressions and assignment, and they may, of course, be included within an output list if appropriate. Far more useful, however, is the ability to use character constants in output statements to provide textual information. Thus the program that was introduced in Chapter 2 contained a statement of the form

```
print *,"The centre of the circle is (",a,",",b,")"
```

which causes five items to be printed (or displayed), namely

1. The character string: `The centre of the circle is (`
2. The value of the variable `a`
3. The character string: `,`
4. The value of the variable `b`
5. The character string: `)`

It can easily be deduced from this example that a character literal constant consists of a string of characters chosen from those available to the user on the computer system being used, enclosed between quotes.

If the string of characters which is to form a character literal constant contains a quote character then clearly there would be a problem; however, F deals with this by treating two consecutive quotes within a character string as representing a single quote character. Thus the statement

```
print *,"This string includes a ""quotation""!"
```

will result in the following being output to the display, or other output device:

```
This string includes a "quotation"!
```

☐ EXAMPLE 3.1 ·

☐1 Problem

Write a program to read a Celsius temperature and convert it to Fahrenheit, using the formula

$$F = \frac{9C}{5} + 32$$

☐2 Analysis

This is a very simple problem, and can probably be written down without much difficulty. Nevertheless, we shall write a structure plan first.

> **1** Read Celsius temperature (*temp_c*)
>
> **2** Convert to Fahrenheit (*temp_f*)
>
> **3** Print both temperatures

☐3 Solution

```
program celsius_to_fahrenheit

    ! A program to convert a Celsius temperature to Fahrenheit .

    ! Variable declarations
    real :: temp_c,temp_f

    ! Ask for Celsius temperature
    print *,"What is the Celsius temperature? "
    read *,temp_c

    ! Convert it to Fahrenheit
    temp_f = 9.0*temp_c/5.0 + 32.0

    ! Print both temperatures
    print *,temp_c,"C = ",temp_f,"F"

end program celsius_to_fahrenheit
```

Notice that the program name and the names of the two variables have been chosen so as to indicate what their purpose is. We could have chosen any names of up to 31 characters which satisfy the F naming rules, but it is usually sensible to keep variable names somewhat less than this maximum in order to minimize typing and to make the program easier to read. A statement such as

```
temperature_in_fahrenheit - 9.0*temperature_in_celsius/5.0 &
                          + 32.0
```

is perfectly valid, but is much too verbose – to the extent that it would not fit on one line in this book!

The only exception to this is that the name of the main program, which only appears on the **program** and **end program** statements, is often rather longer in order to describe the purpose of the program.

Note also that we have written the calculation in a form that avoids any mixed-mode expression. As we have already seen, it would be perfectly acceptable to write

```
temp_f = 9*temp_c/5 + 32
```

and allow the processor to convert the three integer constants to their real equivalents before carrying out the calculation. However, this is rather lazy programming and can easily lead to mistakes such as writing the mathematically equivalent form

```
temp_f = 9/5*temp_c + 32
```

which causes an integer division to take place, with the result that the statement is effectively reduced to

```
temp_f = temp_c + 32
```

which is clearly wrong!

Arguably, the best way to write this statement is actually

```
temp_f = 1.8*temp_c + 32.0
```

since this eliminates a division operation. However, this is less clearly related to the formula, and it might be preferable, therefore, to include a comment to elaborate:

```
! Use the formula F=9C/5+32 (that is, F=1.8C+32)
temp_f = 1.8*temp_c + 32.0
```

Finally, note that, since we can include expressions in an output list, we could have replaced the last two statements, and their associated comments, by

```
! Use the formula F=9C/5+32 (that is, F=1.8C+32)
! and print both temperatures
print *,temp_c,"C = ",1.8*temp_c+32.0,"F"
```

In this case, of course, we can also remove the declaration of the variable temp_f from the program.

• ◻

SELF-TEST EXERCISES 3.1

1   What is the difference between an integer and a real number?

2   What is the primary advantage of an integer over a real number?

3   What are two advantages of a real number over an integer?

4   What is a declaration statement?

5   Write declaration statements for variables which are to be used for the following purposes:

   (a)   to store the number of men, women and children living in a community, and the ratio of adults to children;
   (b)   to store the dimensions, in feet and inches, of a rectangular box;
   (c)   to store the dimensions, in metres and centimetres, of a rectangular box;
   (d)   to store the number of seconds that an experiment lasts, and the number of photons detected by a piece of experimental apparatus during that time.

6   What is an assignment statement?

7   What are the five arithmetic operators in F? What are their respective priorities?

8   Write a statement to calculate the average of two numbers. Include the declaration of any necessary variables.

9   What will be printed by the following program?

```
program test3_1_9
   real :: a,b,p,q,r
   integer :: x,y,z
   a = 2.5
   b = 4.0
   p = a+b
   x = a+b
   q = a*b
   y = a*b
   r = p/q
   z = x/y
   print *,p,q,r
   print *,x,y,z
end program test3_1_9
```

10   Give four different ways of typing the data so that the statement

```
   read *,a,b,c,d
```

will cause the real variables a, b, c and d to take the values 1.2, 3.456, 7.89 and 42.0.

3.5 Handling character data

Having used **character** constants in some of our **print** statements it is now appropriate to consider how we may declare **character** variables and manipulate **character** data within a program. First, however, we must emphasize that characters and numbers are stored very differently in any computer.

As we have already seen, **real** and **integer** variables can hold a wide range of numbers in a single variable. We must now introduce the concept of a **numeric storage unit**, which is that part of the memory of the computer in which a single **real** or **integer** number can be stored. On most modern computers a numeric storage unit will consist of a contiguous area of memory capable of storing 16, 32, 48 or 64 **bits**, or binary digits. A 32-bit numeric storage unit is capable of storing integers in the range from about -2×10^9 to $+2 \times 10^9$, or real numbers in the range -10^{38} to $+10^{38}$ to an accuracy of about seven significant digits.

Characters, on the other hand, are stored in **character storage units**, typically occupying 8 or 16 bits, each of which can hold exactly one character in a coded form. A **character variable** consists of a sequence of one or more consecutive character storage units. There is no assumption about the relationship, if any, between numeric and character storage units although, in practice, most computers will use the same physical memory devices for both types so that, for example, four 8-bit character storage units may be kept together in what would otherwise be a single 32-bit numeric storage unit.

Programs in F are written using characters taken from the **F character set** which consists of the 26 lower-case letters and the 26 upper-case letters of the Latin alphabet, the 10 decimal digits, the underscore character and 21 additional special characters. These 84 characters are shown in Figure 3.11. Note that keywords and other reserved words in F do not use upper case; in identifiers upper- and lower-case letters are treated as identical although the same usage of upper- and lower-case must be used in all instances of the same identifier; in data or in a character string upper- and lower-case letters are treated as different characters.

In addition to the characters of the F character set all F compilers support a larger set of characters known as the ASCII character set (or, more formally, ISO 646 RV), which is also known as the **default character set**. Any of the

```
A B C D E F G H I J K L M N O P Q R S T U V W X Y Z
a b c d e f g h I j k l m n o p q r s t u v w x y z
0 1 2 3 4 5 6 7 8 9
◊ = + - * / ( ) , . ' : ! " % & ; < > ? $

(where ◊ represents the space, or blank, character)
```

Figure 3.11 The F character set.

graphic characters in this set (but not control characters such as <new line>) may be used as part of a character constant, may be stored in character variables, may be input or output, and may appear in comments.

A character variable is declared in a very similar manner to that used for integer and real numbers, with the important difference that it is necessary to specify how many characters the variable is to be capable of storing. The declaration statement takes the form

```
character(len=length) :: name1,name2, ...
```

This declares one or more **character** variables, each of which has a **length** of *length*. This means that each of the variables declared will hold exactly *length* characters. If a **character** variable is to hold only a single character then it must be declared with a length of 1.

The length specification may be either a positive integer constant or a positive integer constant **expression**. Thus the following three sets of declarations have an identical effect:

1. `character(len=6) :: a,b,c`

2. `character(len=12-6) :: a,b,c`

3. `character(len=4*3 - 12/2) :: a,b,c`

The fact that character variables always hold a specified number of characters leads to a number of potential problems when carrying out assignment or input. Consider, for example, what will be stored in the three variables a, b and c by the following program:

```
program character_example
   character(len=3) :: string_1
   character(len=4) :: string_2,string_3
   string_1 = "End"
   string_2 = string_1
   string_3 = "Final"
end program character_example
```

Here we have three character variables declared, two of length 4, and one (string_1) of length 3. The first assignment statement assigns the character constant End to string_1. We can readily see that the value to be assigned (the constant) has a length of 3 and so it exactly occupies the three storage units which constitute the variable string_1, and all is well.

The next assignment statement is, however, more of a problem. string_1 has a length of 3 and contains the three characters End; string_2, however, has a length of 4, so what will be stored in the four storage units?

The answer is that if a character string has a shorter length than the length of the variable to which it is to be assigned then it is extended to the right with blank (or space) characters until it is the correct length. In this case, therefore, the contents of `string_1` will have a single blank character added after the letter d, thus making a length of 4, before being assigned to `string_2`.

The third assignment statement poses the opposite problem. Here the character constant to be assigned has a length of 5, whereas the variable, `string_3`, only has a length of 4. In this case the string is truncated from the right to the correct length (4) before assignment.

At the end of this program, therefore, the three variables `string_1`, `string_2` and `string_3` contain the character strings End, End◊ and Fina, respectively, where ◊ represents a blank, or space, character.

The importance of this extension and truncation makes it desirable that we restate these rules more formally:

> When assigning a character string to a character variable whose length is not the same as that of the string, the string stored in the variable is extended on the right with blanks, or truncated from the right, so as to exactly fill the character variable to which it is being assigned.

A similar situation can arise during the input of character data by a **read** statement if the number of characters which form the input data is different from the length of the variable into which they are being read. Before discussing this in detail, however, we must examine the way in which character data is input and output by list-directed input/output statements.

The form of any character data to be read by a list-directed **read** statement is normally the same as that of a character constant. In other words it must be delimited by quotation marks. There are some exceptions to this rule, however, in order to cater for common situations where the need for the quotes would be annoying. The delimiting characters are not required if *all* of the following conditions are met:

1. the character data does not contain any blanks, any commas or any slashes (that is, it does not contain any of the value separators discussed earlier);

2. the character data is all contained within a single record or line;

3. the first non-blank character is not a quotation mark, since this would be taken as a delimiting character, or an apostrophe, for compatibility with Fortran in which this is an alternative delimiting character;

4. the leading characters are not numeric followed by an asterisk, since this would be confused with the multiple data item form ($n*c$).

In this case the character constant is terminated by any of the value separators which will terminate a numeric data item (blank, comma, slash or end of record), and it may be repeated by means of a multiple data item of the form $n*c$.

If the character data which is read by a list-directed **read** statement is too long or too short for the variable concerned then it is truncated or extended on the right in exactly the same way as for assignment.

The output situation is rather simpler, and a list-directed **print** statement will output exactly what is stored in a character variable or constant, including any trailing blanks, without any delimiting quotation marks.

Thus we could modify our earlier program to print the values of the three variables as follows:

```
program character_example
   character(len=3) :: string_1
   character(len=4) :: string_2,string_3
   string_1 = "End"
   string_2 = string_1
   string_3 = "Final"
   print *,string_1,string_2,string_3
end program character_example
```

The result of running this program would be the following line of text:

```
EndEnd Fina
```

The ability to assign a character literal constant, or the string stored in a character variable, or to input and output character data, does not in itself take us very far. Just as we can write arithmetic expressions, therefore, so we can also create character expressions. The major difference between character expressions and the other types of expressions, however, is that there are very few things we can actually do with strings of characters!

One thing that we can do, though, is combine two strings to form a third, composite, string. This process is called **concatenation** and is carried out by means of the **concatenation operator**, consisting of two consecutive slashes:

```
char = "Fred"//"die"
```

The composite string will, of course, have a length equal to the sum of the lengths of the two strings which were concatenated to form it, and the variable char will contain the string Freddie, as long as it has a length of at least 7.

This is the only operator provided in F for use with character strings; F does, however, include one important additional capability, namely the identification of **substrings** of character variables. This is achieved by following the character variable name by two integer expressions separated by a colon and enclosed in parentheses. The two integer values represent the positions in the character variable of the first and last characters of the substring. Either may be omitted, but not both, in which case the first or last character position is assumed, as appropriate.

Thus the substring alpha(5:7) represents the three-character substring consisting of the fifth, sixth and seventh characters of the value of the variable alpha, while beta(4:) represents a substring starting at the fourth character of the value of the variable beta and ending at the last character of beta, and gamma(:6) represents a substring consisting of the first six characters of the value of gamma.

It is also permitted to assign a value to a substring without altering the rest of the variable. Thus the following program fragment will result in the variable ch having the value Alpine◊◊, where, as before, ◊ represents a space:

```
program substring
   character(len=8) :: ch
   ch = "Alphabet"
   ch(4:) = "ine"
      .
      .
      .
```

It is instructive to examine this in detail.

The substring ch(4:) is the substring from character 4 to the end of ch – a total of five characters. The character constant "ine" only has a length of 3 so it is extended by adding two blank characters before being assigned to ch(4:). The assignment means that the old substring value ("habet") is replaced by the new value ("ine◊◊"), leaving the rest of ch unchanged. The final result, therefore, is that ch contains "Alpine ".

▢ EXAMPLE 3.2 ·

▢1 Problem

Write a program which asks the user for title, first name and last name, and then prints a welcome message using both the full name and first name.

▢2 Analysis

This program is merely an exercise in simple character manipulation. However, there are some slight difficulties in combining the title, first and last names in a form which will avoid multiple spaces within the composite name. For example, if variables with a length of 12 characters were chosen, then the name Sarah would be followed by seven spaces.

In Chapter 2 we pointed out that many of the detailed aspects of programs can often be carried out in *procedures* which can be written later, or can be written by someone else, or which may already exist somewhere else. The F language contains a number of special procedures, known as **intrinsic procedures**, which provide a great many useful additional features. We shall examine this topic in

some detail in Chapter 4, but for the present we shall merely note that there are
several intrinsic procedures whose purpose is to assist in the manipulation of
character strings. A list of all the intrinsic procedures in F will be found in
Appendix A.

The most useful intrinsic procedure, for our present purpose, is **trim**, which
removes any trailing blanks from the character string provided as its argument.
There would still be a difficulty if the user types one or more blanks before the
name, but we shall assume that this does not happen and ignore the problem for
the present – although there is another intrinsic procedure that could be used to
deal with it.

Armed with this intrinsic procedure we can develop our structure plan:

1   Read title, first name and last name

2   Concatenate the resulting strings together, using **trim** to remove
trailing blanks from the title and first name

3   Print a welcome message using the formal address, and another using
just the first name

3   **Solution**

```
program welcome

   ! This program manipulates character strings to produce a
   ! properly formatted welcome message

   ! Variable declarations
   character(len=20) :: title,first_name,last_name
   character(len=40) :: full_name

   ! Ask for name, etc
   print *,"Please give your full name in the form requested"
   print *,"Title (Mr./Mrs./Ms./Professor/etc: "
   read *,title

   print *,"First name: "
   read *,first_name

   print *,"Last name: "
   read *,last_name

   ! Create full name
   full_name = trim(title)//" "//trim(first_name) &
               //" "//last_name

   ! Print messages
   print *,"Welcome ",full_name
   print *,"May I call you ",trim(first_name),"?"

end program welcome
```

Notice that **trim** has been used in the last **print** statement to ensure that the question mark at the end of the question comes immediately after the name, and not separated from it by several spaces.

3.6 Named constants

Frequently, a program will use certain constant values in many places, and it is not necessarily obvious what a particular constant represents. For example, it might be required to define the maximum number of items that could appear in some dataset, but using the same literal constant in all the places where it must be referred to is prone to error both when typing the program and, even more, when subsequently modifying it, and is less readable than would be the case if a name were used. Furthermore, there are a great many occasions when physical or natural constants, such as the value of π, are required in programs, and there is clearly no intention for these to be altered. F allows us a convenient method of dealing with these situations by defining what are called **named constants** by use of the **parameter attribute** in a declaration statement which takes the form:

> *type*, **parameter** :: *name1=constant_expression1, ...*

where the expression *constant_expression1* may be any expression consisting solely of literal constants, named constants that have already been declared, and operators. We shall see in Chapter 4 that it is also possible for a constant expression to contain certain intrinsic procedures.

Thus, the following statements will declare two real constants and one integer constant:

```
real, parameter :: pi=3.1415926, pi_by_2=pi/2.0
integer, parameter :: max_cases = 100
```

In the first statement `pi` is defined to be a constant, and then `pi_by_2` is defined by means of a constant expression involving `pi`. Since the statement is processed from left to right this is acceptable as `pi` has already been defined before it is used in the definition of `pi_by_2`; if the two constants were listed in the opposite order then there would be an error. There will never be any need to change the values of these two constants, and their definition is purely to make the program easier to read and to avoid errors in typing long constants since, instead of writing, for example

```
area = 3.1415926*r*r
```

we can write

```
area = pi*r*r
```

On the other hand, the integer constant max_cases, which is assumed to represent a limit on the number of cases to be processed by the program, might need to be changed if the size of problem being processed were to change. This is a situation in which there might be many places in the program where the constant value of 100 appears, not all of which refer to the maximum number of cases. Modifying the program to change the maximum would then be highly prone to error. By making the maximum value a named constant the program is easier to read and any change subsequently required need only be made in one place.

Finally, we note that, since the whole reason for giving an entity the parameter attribute is to declare a named constant, it is not permitted to attempt to change its value at a subsequent point in the program. The only way that its value can be changed is by modifying the declaration statement accordingly, and recompiling the program.

SELF-TEST EXERCISES 3.2

1   What is the difference between the *F character set* and the *default character set*?

2   What is the most obvious difference between the declaration of an integer or real variable and the declaration of a character variable?

3   Write declaration statements for six character variables, of which four are to contain character strings of up to 20 characters, one is to contain only a single character, and one is to contain the month of the year.

4   What will be printed by the following program?

```
program Test3_2_4
   character(len=16) :: a,b,c,d
   a = "A kindly giant"
   b = "A small man"
   c = b(:8)//"step"
   d = "for a"//b(8:)
   b = " "//d(:4)//b(9:11)//a(3:6)
   a = a(:2)//a(10:15)//"leap"
   print *,c(:13),d
   print *,trim(a(:12)),b
end program Test3_2_4
```

5   Write a declaration statement for two named constants which can be used to check whether an individual's age renders him or her ineligible for jury service.

SUMMARY

- Variables are locations in the computer's memory in which variable information may be stored; constants are locations in which information is stored which cannot be altered during the execution of the program.

- An integer is a whole number; its representation in a computer is always exact.

- A real number may have a fractional part; it is represented in a computer as a floating-point number which is a close approximation to its true value.

- Integers and real numbers are both stored in numeric storage units.

- All F compilers support the 84 characters which constitute the F character set; most processors also support a number of other characters as part of their default character set.

- Characters in the default character set may be used to form character strings; each character is stored in a separate character storage unit.

- All variables must be declared in a type declaration statement before their first use; a character variable must have its length declared.

- A named constant declaration specifies that the name has the **parameter** attribute; the value of the constant is specified by means of a constant expression consisting of literal constants, named constants that have already been declared, and operators.

- The priority of arithmetic operators in an arithmetic expression is the same as in mathematics; evaluation of the expression proceeds from left to right, within a priority level, except for exponentiation which is carried out from right to left, but may be altered by the use of parentheses.

- If one of the operands of an arithmetic operator is real, then the evaluation of that operation is carried out using real arithmetic, with any integer operand being converted to real.

- If an integer value is assigned to a real variable it is converted to its real equivalent before assignment; if a real value is assigned to an integer variable it is truncated before conversion to integer, and any fractional part is lost.

- Character strings may be concatenated to form a longer character string.

- Character variable substrings may be used wherever the character variables of which they are substrings may be used.

- Character strings are extended with blanks to the right, or truncated from the right, before assignment to make them the same length as the variable they are being assigned to.

- A list-directed **read** statement takes its data from the default input unit, and a list-directed **print** statement sends its results to the default output unit.

- F syntax introduced in Chapter 3:

Variable declarations	**real** :: *list of variable names*
	integer :: *list of variable names*
	character(**len**=*length*) :: *list of variable names*
Named constant declaration	*type* , **parameter** :: *name*=*initial_value* , ...
Assignment statement	*variable_name* = *expression*
Character substring specification	*name*(*first_position* : *last_position*)
	name(*first_position* :)
	name(: *last_position*)
Arithmetic operators	**, *, /, +, -
Character operator	//

PROGRAMMING EXERCISES

*3.1   Write and run a program which will read 10 numbers and find their sum. Test the program with several sets of data, including the following

$$1, 5, 17.3, 9, -23.714, 12.9647, 0.0005, -2974, 3951.44899, -1000$$

Were the answers what you expected?

3.2   The following program is intended to swap the values of var_1 and var_2:

```
program swap
   real :: var_1,var_2

   ! Initialize variables
   var_1=111.111
   var_2=222.222

   ! Exchange values
   var_2 = var_1
   var_1 = var_2

   ! Print swapped values
   print *,var_1,var_2

end program swap
```

The program contains an error, however, and will not print the correct values. Determine the error and correct it so that it works properly.

Now modify the corrected program so that you can enter the two numbers from the keyboard.

3.3   Write a program to input a number x and print the values of $x - 1$, $x + 2$ and $x^2 + x - 2$.

3.4   The reduced mass of a diatomic molecule is given by the expression

$$\mu = \frac{m_a m_b}{m_a + m_b}$$

Write a program that calculates μ, where you enter m_a and m_b from the keyboard.

*3.5   Write a program to print a list of the characters in the F character set, followed by their internal representation on your computer.

3.6   Write a program that reads a six-word sentence, one word at a time, into six variables, and then prints the sentence formed by concatenating the six variables.

3.7   Write a program that reads a sentence consisting of six words separated from each other by a single space into a single variable. The program should then read the number of characters in each of the six words and use this information to store each word in a separate variable. Finally, the program should list these six words, one to a line.

3.8   When visitors come to dinner at his home in Copenhagen, Mr Schmidt always makes them Danish Apple Cake. For four people this requires the following ingredients:

> 675 g of apples
> 75 g of butter
> 150 g of sugar
> 100 g of breadcrumbs
> 150 ml of cream

Write a program which inputs the number of people coming to dinner, and then prints the amount of each ingredient required.

3.9   A woman wishes to build a brick wall 4 ft high along one side of her garden. The bricks are 9 ins long, 4.5 ins wide, and 3 ins high, and there should be 0.5 ins of mortar between bricks. Write a program to calculate how many bricks she will need if the wall is to be 23 ft 6 ins long, and then use this program to calculate the number of bricks needed for walls of different heights and lengths.

3.10   A small business wishes to use a computer program to calculate how to make up the pay packets for its employees. The program should read the total amount to be paid, and print the number of £20, £10 and £5 notes required, and the number of £1, 50p, 20p, 10p, 5p, 2p and 1p coins needed. It is a union requirement that every pay packet should contain at least 40p in coins, and at least one £5 note. Subject to this restriction, the pay packet should contain as few coins and notes as possible. Note that £1 = 100p.

  Write a program to provide the required information, and test it with a wide variety of cases, including those with a total pay of £125.39 and £65.40.

3.11   A body that experiences a uniform acceleration moves a distance s in a time t, where s is given by the formula

$$s = \frac{at^2}{2} + ut$$

where a is the acceleration in metres/sec^2, and u is the initial velocity in metres/sec.

  A body falling freely under gravity is in such a situation, with $a = g = 9.81$ metres/sec^2.

Write a program that asks the user for the body's initial downward velocity (in metres/sec) and time of flight (in seconds). The program should then calculate and print the height from which the body fell.

3.12 Calculate the Coulomb potential at a distance r from a particle with a charge of z. The required formula is

$$\phi(r) = \frac{ze}{4\pi\epsilon r}$$

where $e = 1.6 \times 10^{-19}$ C, $\epsilon = 8.86 \times 10^{-12}$ F/m, and $\pi = 3.1416$. r is specified in metres and z is an integer number.

Basic building blocks

4

4.1   Programs and modules
4.2   Procedures
4.3   Functions
4.4   Subroutines
4.5   Actual arguments and dummy arguments
4.6   Local and global objects
4.7   Saving the values of local objects on exit from a procedure
4.8   Giving procedure variables an initial value
4.9   Procedures as an aid to program structure

In all walks of life, the easiest way to solve most problems is to break them down into smaller sub-problems and deal with each of these in turn, further subdividing these sub-problems as necessary.

This chapter introduces the concept of a procedure to assist in the solution of such sub-problems, and shows how F's two types of procedures, functions and subroutines, are used as the primary building blocks in well-designed programs.

A further encapsulation facility, known as a module, is also introduced as a means of packaging procedures and providing access to global data:

4.1 Programs and modules

Up to this point we have considered our programs to consist of a sequence of statements starting with a **program** statement and finishing with an **end program** statement, as shown in Figure 4.1. Between these two statements there are three main groups of statements, namely **use** statements, which we met in Chapter 2 as a means of accessing modules, specification statements, of which declaration statements are the only ones we have met so far, and executable statements; these three groups of statements must appear in the order shown.

A sequence of statements starting with a **program** statement and ending with an **end program** statement is formally known as a **main program** or main program unit, and there must be exactly one main program unit in an F program.

However, F also has a second type of program unit, called a **module**. This is primarily a means of collecting together a set of related objects – procedures, variables, data types – and making them available to a program in a controlled manner. An F program may contain any number of modules, or it may contain none at all. We shall examine the basic features of modules in this chapter, and will then return to examine them in more detail in Chapters 8 and 16.

The basic structure of a module is not dissimilar from that of a main program unit, see Figure 4.2, but with one very important difference – a module does not contain any executable statements. There can be any number of module program units in a program, and the initial **module** statement of each module specifies the name of that module, which must satisfy the rules laid down for names in F that were listed in Chapter 2, and the **end module** statement must include that name in a similar fashion to the case with the program name on the **program** and **end program** statements.

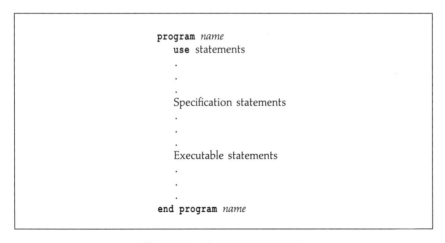

Figure 4.1 A main program unit.

```
                    module name
                       use statements

                          .

                       Specification statements
                          .
                          .
                          .

                    end module name
```

Figure 4.2 A module program unit.

Although a module may not contain any executable statements, it may contain any number of subprograms, each of which defines an F **procedure**. These subprograms are separated from the other statements in the module by a **contains** statement, as indicated in Figure 4.3.

Strictly speaking, these two types of module should be referred to as *private* modules, to distinguish them from a different type of module, called a *public* module, that we shall meet in Section 4.6. However, in accordance with normal practice, we shall simply refer to them as 'modules', and will assume that this term refers to private modules unless otherwise specified.

Before examining the module concept any further, however, it is appropriate to examine the purpose and structure of a procedure as a fundamental building block in F.

```
                    module name
                       use statements
                          .
                          .
                          .
                       Specification statements
                          .
                          .
                          .
                    contains
                       Procedure definitions
                          .
                          .
                          .
                    end module name
```

Figure 4.3 A module program unit containing procedure definitions.

4.2   Procedures

The statements that we met in the last chapter enable us to write programs consisting of a number of lines of instructions that will be obeyed in sequence in order to cause the required actions to take place. However, this is not always the way we do things in real life. For example, look at Figure 4.4. This is a note such as might be left to instruct someone how to prepare the evening meal. It is a sequence of instructions but with one important difference – *not all the instructions are there*. The main part of the preparation is covered in a cookery book (*The Silver Palate Cookbook*, by Julee Rosso and Sheila Lukins), so, instead of writing it all down, the writer simply referred to the appropriate page of the book. There was no point in either copying it out or describing what to do in different words; it was much easier to make use of what had already been written by the authors of the book.

Figure 4.5 shows part of the actual recipe for Raspberry Chicken referred to in the note in Figure 4.4, and we can see that even here the whole recipe is not included. In this case the details of how to prepare the chicken stock and the crème fraîche are to be found elsewhere in the book, on pages 342 and 339 respectively, and it would be wasteful to keep repeating them in the many recipes that use either or both. A cross-reference to the other recipes, therefore, saves space and, incidentally, also keeps the main recipe less cluttered and thus easier to follow.

Both of these situations (use of standard procedures and avoidance of duplication with consequent structural improvements) occur in programming as well. A special section of program which is, in some way, referred to whenever required is known as a **procedure**. Moreover, just as recipes are normally collected together in cookery books, so procedures are collected together in **modules**.

Procedures fall into two broad categories, namely those which are written by the programmer (or by some other person who then allows the programmer to use them) and those which are part of the F language itself. This latter group are known as **intrinsic procedures**, and their names are reserved words and must always be written in lower case. Procedures which are not part of the F language

Miles,
    I thought we might have Raspberry Chicken tonight (see page 87 of the Silver Palate cookbook). I'll be a bit late home, so could you make a start please ?
    Love
        Maggie

Figure 4.4   An example of the use of a standard cooking procedure.

RASPBERRY CHICKEN

Boneless chicken breasts are quick and economical to serve but often dull to eat. In this recipe, ready in minutes, raspberry vinegar lends a bit of welcome tartness, mellowed by chicken stock and heavy cream. A handful of fresh raspberries, poached briefly in the sauce just before serving, adds an elegant note. Wild rice and a simple sautéed green vegetable would be good accompaniments.

2 whole boneless, skinless chicken breasts, about 2 pounds
2 tablespoons sweet butter
¼ cup finely chopped yellow onion
*4 tablespoons raspberry vinegar**
¼ cup Chicken Stock (see page 342), or canned chicken broth
¼ cup heavy cream, or Crème Fraîche (see page 339)
1 tablespoon canned crushed tomatoes
16 fresh raspberries (optional)

    1. Cut each chicken breast into halves along the breastbone line. Remove the filet mignon, the finger-size muscle on the back of each half, and reserve for another use. Flatten each breast half or *suprême* by pressing it gently with the palm of your hand.
    2. Melt the butter in a large skillet. ~~Bring the heat~~, add the ~~suprêmes~~, and cook for ab~~ou~~

Figure 4.5 Using cross-referencing to avoid duplication (reproduced with permission from *The Silver Palate Cookbook*, by Julee Rosso and Sheila Lukin, © Workman Publishing Co., Inc., New York).

may be written in F or, in certain circumstances, in other programming languages; in the latter case they are referred to as **external procedures**. All procedures in an F program (or their interfaces, see 8.2, in the case of external procedures) must be defined within modules.

There is also a further categorization, based upon their mode of use, into what are called **subroutines** and **functions**. Almost all of the intrinsic procedures which are part of the F language are functions and are referred to as **intrinsic functions**. There are also five **intrinsic subroutines**.

The purpose of a function is to take one or more values (or **arguments**) and create a single result, and F contains a number of intrinsic functions for elementary mathematical functions, such as

sin (x) which calculates the value of sin x (where x is in radians)
log (x) which calculates the value of $\log_e x$
sqrt (x) which calculates the value of $\sqrt{x}$.

As can be seen from these examples a function reference takes the general form

name (argument)

or, where there are two or more arguments

name (arg1, arg2, ...)

A function is used simply by referring to it in an expression in place of a variable or constant. Thus

a+b***log**(c)

will first calculate $\log_e c$, then b × $\log_e c$, and finally add this to a. Similarly

-b+**sqrt**(b*b - 4.0*a*c)

will first calculate (b*b - 4.0*a*c), then use the function **sqrt** to find its square root, and finally add this to -b.

There are 97 intrinsic functions available in F; some of these are concerned with standard mathematical functions such as those illustrated above, but many deal with other matters. We shall introduce the intrinsic functions, or families of related intrinsic functions, at appropriate stages as we increase our knowledge and understanding of the F language. A full list can be found in Appendix A for reference.

Many of these functions can have arguments of more than one type, in which case the type of the result will usually (though not always) be of the same type as the arguments. Thus

real :: x,y
y = **abs**(x)

will produce the absolute value of the real variable x (that is, the value ignoring the sign) as a real value and assign it to the real variable y, whereas

integer :: x,y
y = **abs**(x)

will produce the absolute value of the integer variable x as an integer value and assign it to the integer variable y.

Those functions which exhibit this quality are referred to as **generic functions**, since their name really refers to a group of functions, the appropriate one of which will be selected by the compiler depending upon the type of the arguments.

☐ **EXAMPLE 4.1** . . . .

1 **Problem**

A farmer has a triangular field which he wishes to sow with wheat. Write a program that reads the lengths of the three sides of the field (in metres), and the sowing density (in grams per square metre). Print the number of 10-kilo bags of wheat he must purchase in order to sow the whole field.

2 **Analysis**

The key to the solution of this problem is the equation

$$area = \sqrt{s(s-a)(s-b)(s-c)}$$

for the area of a triangle whose sides have lengths a, b and c, where $2s = a + b + c$.

Our structure plan is then quite simple:

1   Read lengths of the sides of the field (a, b and c)
2   Calculate the area of the field
3   Read the sowing density
4   Calculate the quantity of wheat seed required
5   Calculate the number of 10 kilo bags this represents

Step 5 is the only one of these which may cause some slight difficulty. The solution can, however, be easily obtained by considering what will happen if we simply divide the quantity of wheat (in grams) by 10 000 to obtain the number of 10 kilo bags. Unless the result of step 4 was an exact multiple of 10 000 (and remember that real arithmetic is, anyway, only an approximation), then there will be some fractional part in the answer. We may decide that if this is less than 0.1 (that is, one kilo) then we will ignore it, but that if it is more than that then we shall need an extra bag – even though we shall not use all of that bag. If we add 0.9 to the result of this division, therefore, the resulting figure will be the number of bags required, probably plus a fractional part. This fractional part will be lost through truncation when the result is assigned to an integer – which is, of course, what the number of bags should be represented as since it has to be a whole number. We can therefore modify step 5 as follows:

> **5** Calculate the number of 10 kilo bags as 0.0001 * quantity | 0.9 (to allow for a partly used bag)

3 Solution

```
program wheat_sowing

! A program to calculate the quantity of wheat required to
! sow a triangular field

! Variable declarations
   real :: a,b,c,s,area,density,quantity
   integer :: num_bags

! Read the lengths of the sides of the field
   print *,"Type the lengths of the three sides of the field", &
           " in metres: "
   read *,a,b,c

! Calculate the area of the field
   s = 0.5*(a+b+c)
   area = sqrt(s*(s-a)*(s-b)*(s-c))

! Read sowing density
   print *,"What is the sowing density (gms/sq.m.)? "
   read *,density

! Calculate quantity of wheat and the number of 10 kg bags
   quantity = density*area
   num_bags = 0.0001*quantity + 0.9  ! Round up more than 1 kg

! Print results
   print *,"The area of the field is ",area," sq. metres"
   print *,"and ",num_bags," 10 kilo bags will be required"

end program wheat_sowing
```

As we have seen, a function is used to calculate a single value from one or more values supplied as arguments. However, in some situations a procedure is required to return more than one value, and in these situations a subroutine is used instead of a function. In addition to the 97 intrinsic functions, F contains five intrinsic subroutines and we shall use one of these, **date_and_time**, to demonstrate how a subroutine is used.

The result of a function is returned by means of the name of the function, which is why the function reference can be used in place of a variable in an expression. The results of a subroutine, on the other hand, are returned by means of some of its arguments, and the subroutine is invoked by means of a **call** statement, which takes the form

```
call name (arg1, arg2, ...)
```

The intrinsic subroutine **date_and_time** is provided in order that a program can obtain the date and the time from the computer's system clock. There are several ways in which this subroutine may be used, but the one that we shall use here corresponds to a call of the form

```
call date_and_time (date,time,zone)
```

where date, time and zone are character variables of length at least 8, 10 and 5, respectively. On return from the subroutine date will contain a character string of the form *ccyymmdd*, corresponding to the century, year, month and day, time will contain a string of the form *hhmmss.sss*, corresponding to hours, minutes, seconds and milliseconds, while zone indicates the difference between the local time zone and Coordinated Universal Time (also known as Greenwich Mean Time, or GMT) and will contain a string of the form ±*hhmm*, corresponding to a sign (+ or −), hours and minutes.

The following program illustrates how this subroutine might be used to print the date and time (to the nearest minute):

```
program Date_and_time_example

   character(len=10) :: date, time, time_zone

   call date_and_time(date,time,time_zone)
   print *,"The date is ",date(7:8),"/",date(5:6),"/", &
         date(1:4)
   print *,"The time is ",time(1:2),"h ",time(3:4),      &
         "m ",time_zone(:5)

end program Date_and_time_example
```

If this program was executed on a computer in Cape Town, South Africa, at eleven in the morning (local time) on Christmas Day, 1996, then the results produced would be as follows:

```
The date is 25/12/1996
The time is 11h 00m +0200
```

If it was also executed at exactly the same instant on a computer in London, England, then the results produced there would be:

```
The date is 25/12/1996
The time is 09h 00m +0000
```

Both functions and subroutines may, of course, be provided by the user, and both are normally implemented by means of an F **subprogram** which is physically placed within a module, as already indicated in Figure 4.3.

One very important principle which applies to all procedures in F is that *the main program and any subprograms need never be aware of the internal details of any other program unit or subprogram*. The only link between the main program or a subprogram and another subprogram is through the **interface** of the sub-program, which consists of the name of the subprogram and certain other **public** entities of the subprogram. This very important principle means that it is possible to write subprograms totally independently of the main program, and of each other. This feature opens up the way for **libraries** of subprograms, that is, collections of subprograms that can be used by more than one program. It also permits large projects to use more than one programmer; all the programmers need to communicate to each other is the information about the interfaces of their procedures.

4.3   Functions

The intrinsic functions available as part of the F language cover many of the major mathematical functions, as well as meeting other common requirements. However, when developing a program it is often necessary to write our own **function subprograms**.

A function takes a very similar form to the programs we have written so far, except that the first statement of the function is not a **program** statement but is a special **function** statement which takes the form

```
function name(d1,d2, ...) result(result_name)
```

where *d1*, *d2*, ... are **dummy arguments** which represent the **actual arguments** which will be used when the function is used (or **referenced**), and *result_name* is the name of a variable which will be used to store the result of the function. As we might expect by now, the final statement of the function is an **end function** statement, taking the form

```
end function name
```

We could, therefore, write a function to calculate the cube root of a positive real number as follows:

```
function cube_root(x) result(root)
! A function to calculate the cube root of a positive
! real number
```

```
! Dummy argument declaration
real, intent(in) :: x
! Result variable declaration
real :: root
! Local variable declaration
real :: log_x
! Calculate cube root by using logs
log_x = log(x)
root = exp(log_x/3.0)

end function cube_root
```

This function will only work for positive values of x because the method involves taking the log of x. In Chapter 5 we shall see how we can extend this function to handle negative or zero values of x successfully.

There are three very important points to notice about this function.

The first is that the variables log_x and root are not accessible from outside the function. They are called **internal variables** (of the function in which they are declared), or **local variables**, and have no existence outside the function. Thus the main program, or another procedure, could use the names log_x or root for any purpose it wished with no fear of the two uses of the same name being confused with each other. It is this isolation of the inside of a procedure from the outside that makes procedures such powerful tools in the writing of large or complicated programs.

The second point to note is that one of the two local variables, root, also appears in the second part of the initial **function** statement. Every function must have exactly one such **result variable** whose name must appear in the **result** clause of the **function** statement, and which must be declared in the body of the function in the same way as any other variable. When execution of the function is completed the value of the result variable will be used as the value of the function in the expression in which it was referenced.

The final point is that the declaration of the dummy argument x takes a slightly different form from the declarations that we have used up to now, namely the inclusion of the phrase **intent(in)** after the type, **real**. This is the second *attribute* that we have met so far (**parameter** was the other), and like all attributes appears in a declaration statement in order to provide additional information about the object being declared. In this case, it informs the compiler that the dummy argument x may not be changed by the function cube_root. We shall discuss this attribute in detail in Section 4.5 when we discuss the relationship between actual arguments and dummy arguments; for the present we shall simply note that dummy arguments to functions *must* be declared with **intent(in)**.

When the **end function** statement is obeyed it causes execution of the program to return to the point in the calling program at which the function was referenced. The effect is as though a variable had been inserted in the code at that point whose value is the same as that calculated by the function for its result variable. Thus the statement

```
a = b*cube_root(c)+d
```

will cause the cube root of c to be calculated by the function, multiplied by b, have d added, and the result to be stored in a.

In Section 4.1 we stated that procedures in F must always be defined in a module. The purpose of a module is to group together various entities and to make them available in a controlled fashion to programs and procedures that require access to them. Every procedure that is to be made accessible in this way must appear in a **public** statement, which takes the form

public :: *list of names*

This is a specification statement, and must appear with any other specification statements in the module. A suitable module for the function cube_root might, therefore, be as follows:

```
module maths
   public :: cube_root
contains
   function cube_root(x) result(root)
      .
      .
      .
   end function cube_root
end module maths
```

Any program or procedure that wishes to use the cube_root function must contain a **use** statement referencing the maths module. This takes the form

use *module_name*

and must appear immediately after the initial statement, before any specification statements. This will make not only the name of the function available, but also the function's **interface**, that is, the details of its arguments and result. A suitable program to test this function and module is as follows:

```
program test_cube_root
   use maths
   real :: x
   print *,"Type a positive real number"
   read *,x
   print *,"The cube root of ",x," is ",cube_root(x)
end program test_cube_root
```

It is possible, although not usually very useful, to write a function which has no arguments, in which case the initial statement takes the form

function *name*() **result**(*result_name*)

Such a function is referenced in the obvious way:

```
a = b*name() + c
```

Although it is possible to carry out a wide range of operations within a function, it must always be remembered that a function's purpose is to calculate a single value based in some manner on the values supplied as its arguments. Moreover, the operation of a function should be predictable, in the sense that it will always return the same value for the same values of its arguments. This places certain restrictions on the statements that can appear within a function in order to ensure that the function cannot have any **side effects** which might cause a subsequent reference to produce a different result. We have already met one of these restrictions, the requirement that dummy arguments must be specified as having **intent(in)**, which prevents them from being altered, and we shall introduce others when appropriate.

One other such restriction is that a function is not normally allowed to carry out any input or output. The main exception to this prohibition is that **print** * and **read** * statements are permitted; however, these are only really allowed for diagnostic purposes, and should be used with care.

A further restriction is that since subroutines are not restricted in any way, a function is not permitted to call a subroutine either directly or indirectly.

Finally, we must emphasize that, although the function cube_root was referenced in the main program, it could equally well have been referenced in another function or, as we shall see in the next section, in a subroutine. However, a very important point is that a function defined in this way must not refer to itself, either directly or indirectly (for example, through referencing another function which, in turn, references the original function). This is known as **recursion** and is only allowed under special conditions which we shall meet in Chapter 8.

4.4   Subroutines

We have already seen that there are two types of procedures in F – functions and subroutines, and have used both an intrinsic function and an intrinsic subroutine in simple examples. It is now time to examine in rather more detail how a subroutine differs from a function.

A function, as we have seen, is referenced in the same way as a variable simply by writing its name, followed by any arguments it may have enclosed in parentheses; such a function reference causes a **transfer of control** so that, instead of continuing to process the current statement, the computer obeys the statements contained within the function. The execution of the function utilizes the values provided as arguments to calculate a single value (the **result value**) which is available as the value of the function reference, just as writing the name of a variable in an expression provides a value – the value stored in a particular memory location. A **function reference**, therefore, is not a complete statement but is part of an expression, and may appear anywhere that an expression may appear (for example, on the right-hand side of an assignment statement, in an output list, as an argument in another function reference, and so on). We have already used a number of intrinsic functions, which are defined within the F language, and functions which we wrote ourselves, but both types are referenced in the same way:

```
var = fun(arg1, arg2, ...)
print *,fun1(arg1, arg2, ...)
var = fun2(a1, fun3(arg1, arg2, ...), a2, a3, ...)
```

and so on.

A subroutine, on the other hand, is accessed by means of a **call** statement which gives the name of the subroutine and a list of arguments which will be used to transmit information between the calling program unit and the subroutine:

```
call name(arg1,arg2, ...)
```

The **call** statement causes a transfer of control so that, instead of obeying the next statement in the program, the computer obeys the statements contained within the subroutine *name*. When the subroutine has completed its task it returns to the calling program ready to obey the next statement.

Unlike a function, which always returns the result of its execution as the value of the function, a subroutine need not return anything to the calling program unit; however, if it does return any values then these are returned by means of one or more of its arguments.

We can see how this works by writing a subroutine, roots, which calculates the square root, the cube root, the fourth root and the fifth root of a positive real number. This is, clearly, somewhat similar to the function cube_root developed in the last section, but will return four results instead of one; it must, therefore, be written as a subroutine:

```
subroutine roots(x,square_root,cube_root,fourth_root, &
                 fifth_root)
! Subroutine to calculate various roots of a positive real
! number supplied as the first argument, and return them in
! the second to fifth arguments

   ! Dummy argument declarations
   real, intent(in) :: x
   real, intent(out) :: square_root,cube_root, &
                        fourth_root, fifth_root
```

```
    ! Local variable declaration
    real :: log_x

    ! Calculate square root using intrinsic sqrt
    square_root = sqrt(x)

    ! Calculate other roots by using logs
    log_x = log(x)
    cube_root = exp(log_x/3.0)
    fourth_root = exp(log_x/4.0)
    fifth_root = exp(log_x/5.0)

end subroutine roots
```

Note that, although the code is very similar to that written for the corresponding function, in this case the results of executing the subroutine are assigned to variables which are themselves dummy arguments. Notice, also, that these dummy arguments have been given an **intent**(**out**) attribute, to indicate that they are to be used to transfer information from the subroutine back to the calling program. We shall discuss the use of the **intent** attribute with subroutines in the next section (4.5), when we discuss the relationship between dummy arguments and actual arguments in rather more detail. In the calling program unit the corresponding actual arguments will contain the results on return from the subroutine:

```
program subroutine_demo
    use example_module    ! contains the subroutine roots

! A program to demonstrate the use of the subroutine roots

! Variable declarations
    real :: pos_num, root_2, root_3, root_4, root_5

! Get positive number from user
    print *,"Please type a positive real number: "
    read *,pos_num

! Obtain roots
    call roots(pos_num, root_2, root_3, root_4, root_5)

! Display number and its roots
    print *,"The square root of ",pos_num," is ",root_2
    print *,"The cube root of ",pos_num," is ",root_3
    print *,"The fourth root of ",pos_num," is ",root_4
    print *,"The fifth root of ",pos_num," is ",root_5

end program subroutine_demo
```

Since the name of a subroutine is simply a means of identification and does not have any type, the interface for a subroutine is the name of the subroutine, together with the number and type of any dummy arguments.

If a subroutine has no arguments then its initial statement takes the form

subroutine *sub*()

Such a subroutine is called by a **call** statement of the form

    call *sub*()

Finally, as was the case for functions, a subroutine may call other subroutines or reference functions, but it must not call itself, either directly or indirectly (for example, through referencing another procedure which, in turn, references the original subroutine). As with functions, such recursive calls are only allowed under the special conditions which we shall meet in Chapter 8.

4.5   Actual arguments and dummy arguments

We have seen that when a function or subroutine is referenced information is passed to it through its arguments; in the case of a subroutine information may also be returned to the calling program unit through its arguments. The relationship between the **actual arguments** in the calling program unit and the **dummy arguments** in the subroutine or function is of vital importance in this process. The actual mechanism used is unimportant, and may vary from one computer system to another; the important thing to realize is that the dummy arguments do not exist as independent entities – they are a simply a means by which the procedure can identify the actual arguments in the calling program unit.

One very important point to stress is that *the order and types of the actual arguments must correspond exactly with the order and types of the corresponding dummy arguments.*

In Chapter 3 we refined a model that had first been introduced in Chapter 1 so that variables were represented by glass boxes, their values by balls stored in the boxes, and their names and types by labels on the boxes (Figure 4.6).

We may extend this model by the addition of a notice-board for each procedure, with a section for each dummy argument. When the procedure

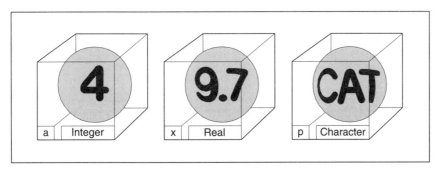

Figure 4.6   A storage model.

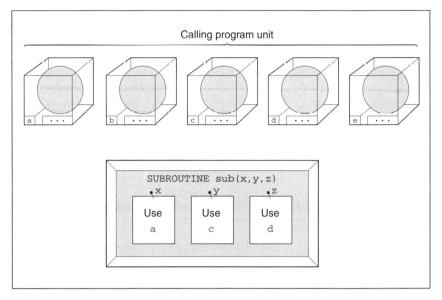

Figure 4.7 A representation of **call** sub(a,c,d).

(function or subroutine) is called from some other program unit we may imagine that a message is pinned up for each dummy argument identifying the corresponding actual argument, as shown in Figures 4.7 and 4.8.

Whenever a reference is made to one of these dummy arguments in the procedure the notice-board will be used to show to which *actual* location in the memory (one of the actual arguments) reference is being made. For example, if the only executable statement in the subroutine was

```
x = y + z
```

then the effect of the call in Figure 4.7 would be as if it was replaced in the calling program unit by the statement

```
a = c + d
```

whereas the effect of the call in Figure 4.8 would be as if it was replaced by the statement

```
b = e + a
```

It follows from this model that, whereas an actual argument may be a variable (an open box) or a constant (a closed and sealed box), a dummy argument is a pseudo-variable, in the sense that the corresponding area of the notice-board may have different notices pinned on it; in the procedure that defines it, it can be used just like any other variable in the procedure. However, it has no existence

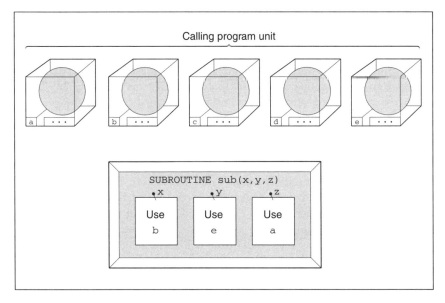

Figure 4.8 A representation of `call` sub(b,e,a).

outside the procedure; whenever it is used it is always in the context of the actual argument being substituted for it.

Because the arguments of a subroutine can be used to transmit information from the calling program to the subroutine, or from the subroutine to the calling program, or for both purposes, it is important that the distinction between dummy arguments which are being used for these different purposes is recognized. This is achieved, as has already been mentioned in the context of a function, by use of the **intent** attribute, and it is now appropriate to examine this in more detail.

Although the **intent** attribute is one of a number of attributes that may follow the type in a declaration statement, it differs from the others in that it may only be used in the declaration of a dummy argument. It can take one of the following three forms:

- **intent(in)** which informs the processor that this dummy argument is used only to provide information to the procedure, and the procedure will not be allowed to alter its value in any way;

- **intent(out)** which informs the processor that this dummy argument will only be used to return information from the procedure to the calling program. Its value will be undefined on entry to the procedure and it must be given a value by some means before being used in an expression, or being otherwise referred to in a context which will require its value to be evaluated;

- `intent(inout)` which informs the processor that this dummy argument may be used for transmission of information in both directions.

As we have already indicated, a subroutine's arguments may have any of the three forms of **intent** attribute, but must be specified to have one of them. In the case of a function, however, the arguments can only be used for giving information to the function, with the result of the function always being returned through its result variable; the dummy arguments in a function must *always*, therefore, be declared with **intent(in)**.

Returning to the notice-board model that we used to illustrate the way in which actual and dummy arguments are related, we find that even this simple model highlights a further difficulty. All the examples that we have used so far have involved either real or integer arguments, but not characters, and we must now briefly examine how these differ from numeric arguments.

The potential difficulty with character arguments relates to the issue of the length to be used in the declaration of the dummy arguments, and can most easily be demonstrated by an example.

Before developing this example, however, we should mention that F imposes certain restrictions on the order of specification statements in a procedure or a main program. In all cases any **use** statements must immediately follow the initial **program**, **function** or **subroutine** statement, and these must be followed in a procedure by the declarations of dummy arguments; in a function the declaration of the result variable must come after the declarations of any dummy arguments. Finally any remaining (local variable) declarations must precede any executable statements in the procedure or main program unit.

EXAMPLE 4.2

1 Problem

Write a procedure which will take two character arguments as input arguments, containing two names (a 'first name' and a 'family name', respectively) and which will return a string containing the two names with exactly one space separating them.

2 Analysis

This problem is similar to that presented in Example 3.2, but with two refinements.

The first, and major, difficulty is that the procedure, regardless of whether it is a function or a subroutine, cannot know the length that will be declared for each of the two names, so how can the corresponding dummy arguments be declared?

As might be expected, this is such a common problem that F provides a solution – an **assumed-length character declaration**. This can only be used for declaring a dummy argument, and involves replacing the length specifier by an asterisk:

```
character(len=*) :: character_dummy_arg
```

This is called an assumed-length dummy argument because it *assumes* its length from the corresponding actual argument when the procedure is executed. If the correspondence between actual and dummy argument is carried out in a way analogous to the notice-board used above then this is clearly no problem as no extra storage is required. Note that character dummy arguments *must* always be declared in this way.

The second difficulty is concerned with removing any redundant spaces at the beginning or the end of the two names and then inserting exactly one between them. In Example 3.2 we met the **trim** intrinsic function, which removes any trailing blanks from its argument. A second intrinsic function, **adjustl**, which moves its argument enough spaces to the left to remove any leading blanks, will enable us to deal with the (unlikely) case that either of the arguments contains leading blanks.

Although it appears that the solution to this problem could be written as either a subroutine or a function, and that a function might be more appropriate since its purpose is to deliver a single result based on its arguments, in this case a subroutine is, in fact, the only possibility. The reason for this is that the result of the procedure call will be a character string of unknown length, and the necessary assumed-length character declaration is only permitted for a dummy argument. The structure plan for the subroutine is straightforward:

Subroutine get_full_name(*first_name,last_name,full_name*)
first_name, *last_name* and *full_name* are all **character**(**len**=(*))

1 Concatenate names, using **adjustl** to remove leading blanks from both names, and **trim** to remove trailing blanks from *first_name*

3 Solution

```
subroutine get_full_name(first_name,last_name,full_name)

! Subroutine to join two names to form a full name with a
! single space between the first and last names

    ! Dummy argument declarations
    character(len=*), intent(in) :: first_name,last_name
    character(len=*), intent(out) :: full_name

    ! Use adjustl to remove redundant leading blanks, and trim
    ! to remove redundant blanks at the end of first_name
    full_name = trim(adjustl(first_name)) // " " //    &
                adjustl(last_name)

end subroutine get_full_name
```

Note that although the dummy arguments are declared to be of assumed length the corresponding actual arguments will have to be declared with specific lengths in the calling program unit. In particular, the length of the actual argument corresponding to the dummy argument `full_name` will determine the nature of the character string representing the full name in the calling program unit. If this is longer than the result of the concatenation then the resulting full name will be extended on the right with blanks in the usual way. If it is shorter then the result of the concatenation will be truncated to the appropriate length. Because of this, there is little point in causing the subroutine to remove any extra blanks at the end of the second name.

Note also that the result of the **adjustl** function reference has been used as the argument to **trim**. The first function, **adjustl**, therefore moves its argument, `first_name`, to the left to eliminate any leading blanks, and the second, **trim**, takes the result and removes any trailing blanks, including any that were introduced by **adjustl**. Strictly speaking, it is not necessary to remove any leading blanks from `first_name` since they do not affect the main problem, which is ensuring that there is only one space between the two names, but while we are tidying up we may as well do everything properly!

Another approach, which avoids the nested intrinsic function references, is to declare two local variables and assign the two names, without leading blanks, to them. There is an apparent difficulty with determining the length for these variables, but once again an intrinsic function comes to our aid. **len**(*character_string*) returns the length of its argument, and can be used in the declaration of other character variables:

```
subroutine get_full_name(first_name,last_name,full_name)

! Subroutine to join two names to form a full name with a
! single space between the first and last names

    ! Dummy argument declarations
    character(len=*), intent(in) :: first_name,last_name
    character(len=*), intent(out) :: full_name

    ! Local variables
    character(len=len(first_name)) :: new_first_name
    character(len=len(last_name)) :: new_last_name

    ! Use adjustl to remove redundant leading blanks
    new_first_name = adjustl(first_name)
    new_last_name = adjustl(last_name)

    ! Use trim to remove blanks at the end of new_first_name
    full_name = trim(new_first_name) // " " // new_last_name

end subroutine get_full_name
```

SELF-TEST EXERCISES 4.1

1   Why should programs be broken into a main program and a set of procedures?

2   What is the difference between a subroutine and a function?

3   What is an intrinsic procedure?

4   What is a generic function?

5   What is the difference between a dummy argument which is declared with an `intent(inout)` attribute, and one which is declared as `intent(out)`?

6   Write the initial statements and the declarations for any dummy arguments for procedures designed to carry out the following tasks. (Don't worry if you don't know how to write the procedure yet; you can specify its interface with a calling program without knowing how to write it.)

   (a)   Count the number of times a specified character appears in a character string;
   (b)   Find the roots of a quadratic equation of the form

$$ax^2 + bx + c = 0;$$

   (c)   Establish whether a whole number is prime. (A number is prime if it is only divisible by itself and by 1);
   (d)   Reverse the order of the characters in a character string;
   (e)   Print an error message based on an error code which may be -1 or an integer in the range 1 to 10;
   (f)   Read whatever is typed at the standard input unit until a whole number greater than zero is typed, and return that number.

4.6   Local and global objects

In the previous section we stressed the very important principle of the **locality of variables**, whereby each program unit is only aware of any variables declared within the program unit itself, referred to as its **local variables**, together with pseudo-variables known as dummy arguments. It is impossible to over-emphasize the importance of this concept because it means that when we are writing a subprogram, or a main program, we do not need to be concerned with a clash of names with those used in another program unit. This is exactly analogous to names within a family.

The Ellis family in Figure 4.9 have called their children David, Sarah and Richard, and refer to them within the family by those names, even though their full names are David Ellis, Sarah Ellis and Richard Ellis. The Jones family, who live a long way away and have never met the Ellis family, have called their children Sarah, Emma and David. Because the two families are in different places

Figure 4.9   Local variables!

and don't even know each other there is never any confusion within their respective families about who David and Sarah are; David and Sarah Ellis are *local* to the Ellis family, while David and Sarah Jones are not part of the Ellis family but are *local* to the Jones family.

The combination of local variables and arguments is the reason why it is possible to write libraries of useful subroutines and functions which can subsequently be used in other people's programs. Someone whom you will never meet can write a procedure, freely using any names for dummy arguments or local variables, secure in the knowledge that there is no possibility of names 'clashing' with names that you have chosen because the names used in the procedure are local to that procedure only.

Nevertheless, there are a number of situations in which it would be very convenient for a set of procedures all to have access to the same set of variables without the need to pass them among themselves as arguments. Similarly, it is often useful for a set of named constants to be available to a defined set of procedures. Both of these problems can be solved by use of modules.

Up to this point, we have only used modules as a means of packaging procedures, but this is only a very small part of the power of the module concept. We have seen that such a module must contain a **public** statement to specify the names of the procedures that are to be made available to any program unit using the module, and a similar concept, using a **public** attribute in the declaration statement, can also be used to specify variables and named constants, and some other entities that we shall meet later, that are to be made available to users of the module. Note that any **public** statements must appear before any declaration statements.

Suppose, for example, that we wished to use the values of π and e in a number of different procedures. We could place their definitions in a very simple module, such as the following:

```
module Natural_constants
    real, parameter, public :: pi=3.1415926, e=2.7182818
end module Natural_constants
```

In order to obtain access to the constants defined in this module the main program, another module or a procedure subprogram must include a **use** statement immediately after the initial statement, and before any specification or executable statements. In this example, therefore, a procedure which begins

```
subroutine Module_example(arg1,arg2)
    use Natural_constants
    .
    .
    .
end subroutine Module_example
```

will have access to the two constants pi and e in exactly the same way as though they had been declared in the subroutine Module_example. Entities which are made available in this way are said to be made available by **use association**.

There is another way to obtain access to objects declared in a module, called **host association**. We shall discuss this in more detail in Chapter 8, but it is worth pointing out here that host association means that any procedures contained in the same module will automatically have access to any entities declared before the **contains** statement. Thus in the following example, the constants pi and e will be available to both sub1 and sub2 without any formality, as will the two real variables global_var1 and global_var2:

```
module example
    public :: sub1,sub2
    real, parameter, public :: pi=3.1415926, e=2.7182818
    real, public :: global_var1,global_var2
contains
    subroutine sub1(a,b,c)
    .
    .
    .
    c = pi*a*b
    .
    .
    .
    end subroutine sub1
    subroutine sub2(x,y,z)
    .
    .
    .
```

```
        global_var1 = x*global_var2
        .
        .
        .
        end subroutine sub2
end module example
```

A function, as well as not being allowed to change the value of its arguments, may not change the values of any variables accessed by host association. Thus, unlike a subroutine, a function could not change the value of either `global_var1` or `global_var2` in the above example.

Note, incidentally, that if it is not required to access the constants or variables outside the module then the **public** attribute may be replaced by **private**:

```
real, parameter, private :: pi=3.1415926, e=2.7182818
real, private :: global_var1,global_var2
```

In this case the entities concerned will be available within the module but will not be accessible from outside. We shall see in Chapters 8 and 16 how useful this can be in developing large programs or libraries of procedures. For the present we shall simply note that every variable or constant declared in a module must have either the **public** or **private** attribute specified as part of its declaration.

We have already mentioned that it is permissible for one module to use another. However, a module is not allowed to use itself, either directly or indirectly (via a recursive chain of other modules), and neither is a module allowed to be accessed by two different methods in the same program unit. In order to help enforce this latter restriction, a **private** statement must always be included in any module which accesses another module by **use** association, other than in one special situation which is discussed below. This prevents any items made available to a module by **use** association being also made available outside this module when it is itself accessed via a **use** statement. A **private** statement consists of the word **private** on a line by itself, and must appear after any **use** statements, but before any other statements in the module:

```
module another_module
    use Natural_constants
    private
    real, parameter, public :: pi_by_two=0.5*pi
    .
    .
    .
end module another_module
```

It is also permitted to combine several modules into a single module. In this case the module must only contain a sequence of **use** statements specifying the modules required, followed by a **public** statement which indicates that everything accessible from the individual modules is to be accessible from this module:

```
module super_module
   use module_1
   use module_2
   .
   .
   .
   use module_n
   public
end module super_module
```

Such a module, which is called a *public* module to distinguish it from the usual form of module which, it will be recalled, is formally known as a *private* module, does not, of course, define anything new, but is simply a convenient method of grouping together a number of (presumably) related items that are already defined in separate modules. It is important to emphasize, however, that the rule about only accessing modules by one route means that any program unit that accesses the module super_module must not also directly access any of the modules that are referenced within it.

We shall return to the subject of modules in Chapter 8, when we shall examine them in rather more detail. For the present, however, we shall simply continue to use them as a convenient way of making certain variables and constants available throughout a program and, especially, as the means of providing procedures in an F program.

4.7 Saving the values of local objects on exit from a procedure

One aspect of local variables in a procedure that we have not yet considered concerns the question of what happens to them after an exit has been made from the procedure.

We have stated that the local entities within a procedure are not accessible from outside that procedure (unless, of course, they are used as actual arguments in a call to another, subsidiary, procedure). It follows, therefore, that once an exit has been made from the procedure then none of the local entities within that procedure can be accessed in any way from anywhere else in the program; in effect, they cease to exist. But what happens if a further call is made to the procedure? Are its local variables still in the state in which they were left when an exit was last made? Or are they, in effect, a new set of local entities which will 'exist' only for this **instance**, or use, of the procedure? (An instance of a procedure is the formal term for its being executed as a result of a **call** or function reference, as appropriate.)

The answer is that, unless special steps are taken, the latter is the case, and the next time that the procedure is referenced the local variables will be in the same state as they would have been if the procedure had never been referenced on an earlier occasion. If it is required to preserve the value of a local variable for the next call to the procedure then it is necessary to explicitly give it a **save attribute** by including the attribute **save** in its declaration:

```
real, save :: list of real variables
```

Note, however, that only local objects may be given a **save** attribute; it is not possible to give the **save** attribute to a dummy argument or a result variable. Note also, that since it is not possible to exit from, and subsequently re-enter, the main program unit, it is not permissible to specify the **save** attribute for any variables declared in the main program.

We shall meet an important use for saved variables in the next section.

4.8   Giving procedure variables an initial value

Several of the examples that we have written thus far have required that some of the variables are given an initial value, and this has been done by means of an assignment statement, or a series of assignment statements. However, there are many situations when a variable in a procedure may be required to have an initial value on the first reference to the procedure, but to then update that value on subsequent references. Such a local variable must, of course, have the **save** attribute, but if the initialization were to be carried out by means of an assignment statement then it would be re-initialized on every entry to the procedure – which would defeat the object of saving the value of the variable!

In the case of a local variable in a procedure it is permissible, therefore, to provide an initial value as part of the declaration of the variable, as long as the declaration statement also contains a save attribute. In this situation the name of the variable is followed by an equals sign and the initial value in a somewhat similar manner to the declaration of a named constant:

```
real, save :: a, b=1.23, c
integer, save :: count=0
```

The initial value need not be a constant, but can be a restricted type of constant expression, known as an **initialization expression**. The restrictions on initialization expressions are intended to ensure that they can be evaluated during compilation and can be summarized as follows:

- All elements of the expression must be constants or references to intrinsic functions with constant arguments.
- Any exponentiation must be to an integer power.
- Any named constants must have already been defined.

We shall meet some other entities that can appear in initialization expressions in later chapters.

Notice, however, that it is not possible to use this form of initialization in the main program, since the **save** attribute can only be used with local variables in a subroutine or function. However, this does not cause any difficulty as the main program is only ever entered once, at the start of execution, and so the difficulty referred to above with using an assignment statement does not arise.

An obvious example of a procedure which requires a local variable with an initial value is one which prints a heading at the top of the next page of output, including the page number:

```
subroutine new_page()

! This subroutine prints a heading and the page number
! at the top of the next page

   ! Local variable
   integer, save :: page=0

   ! Update page number and print heading
   page = page + 1
   print *,"Example page heading Page        ",page

end subroutine new_page
```

In this example, the page number is initialized to zero at the time of the first entry to the subroutine, but on each entry thereafter it has the same value that it had on exit the previous time. Since its value is increased by one each time the subroutine is entered, this has the desired effect.

4.9   Procedures as an aid to program structure

One of the great advantages of procedures is that they enable us to break the design of a program into several smaller, more manageable sections, and then to write and test each of these sections independently of the rest of the program. This paves the way for an approach known as **modular program development** which is a key concept of software engineering.

This approach breaks a problem down into its major sub-problems, or **components**, each of which can then be dealt with independently of the others. In a large project these components may be developed by different people. If necessary, a component may itself be subdivided into further components, just as in any other piece of engineering design. All that is necessary is that the interface between each component and the rest of the program is well defined.

An example of this approach in mechanical engineering is the manufacture of the Airbus A-300. The wings for this aircraft are manufactured in the United Kingdom, while part of the fuselage is manufactured in Italy and the remaining part in France. In order that the front and rear parts of the fuselage join correctly, and that the wings fasten onto the fuselage properly, it is only necessary to provide a detailed specification of exactly how the relevant parts will be joined – the *interface* between these sub-assemblies. The exact specification of, for example, the wingtips has no direct effect on the design of the fuselage.

The interface for a component of an F program consists of two parts. The first, the interface proper, is the list of arguments supplied to the component (or rather to the procedure which is, in effect, the main program unit of the component). The second is the specification of the action of the component.

A structure plan gives very great assistance in modular development as it identifies, in a natural way, the major components of the program. Rather than expanding these components within a single structure plan, as we have been doing up to now, we can treat each of these major components as a separate sub-problem whose solution is to be developed independently. Once developed they can be integrated to form the complete program according to the top-level structure plan. We shall develop this idea further in later chapters, but for the present we shall simply combine the concept of a structure plan with that of a modular program structure.

☐ EXAMPLE 4.3

1 Problem

Write a program which will read a set of 10 experimental results and calculate their mean and standard deviation.

2 Analysis

We can readily identify the three major components of this problem – the input of the data, the calculation of the mean and standard deviation, and the output of the results. Even if we have no statistical knowledge whatsoever, therefore, we could write a structure plan of the following nature:

1   Read 10 real data items ($x1, \ldots, x10$) using the subroutine *input*
2   Calculate the mean and standard deviation using the subroutine *statistics*
3   Print results using the subroutine *results*

Notice that we have specified that the input and output are carried out in subroutines. As well as enabling us to keep the structure of the program as clear as possible, this provides two major benefits.

The first of these is that it means that we can test each of the subroutines separately, thus both simplifying the testing procedure and making it easier to find any errors. For example, a dummy *input* subroutine can be used when testing the main *statistics* subroutine:

```
subroutine input(x1,x2,x3,x4,x5,x6,x7,x8,x9,x10)
   real, intent(out) :: x1,x2,x3,x4,x5,x6,x7,x8,x9,x10
   x1 = 1.5
   x2 = 3.7
   .
   .
   .
   x10 = -7.1
end subroutine input
```

The second benefit is that by breaking up a program into discrete sections in this way we can keep the size of each procedure down to manageable proportions. Experience shows that the longer the procedure, the more difficult it is to read and to test, and hence the less likely it is to work as well as possible. As a rule of thumb, we would suggest that if a procedure, including any comments, reaches a length of more than about 50 lines, so that it can no longer be printed on a single sheet of paper or viewed easily on a screen, then you should examine it carefully to see whether the problem being solved by the procedure might not be better split into two, or more, sub-problems, each of which could be the subject of a separate, smaller, procedure.

We can, therefore, now write a second level of subsidiary structure plans, such as:

Subroutine statistics($x1, \ldots, x10, mean, st\_dev$)
   real :: $x1, \ldots, x10, mean, st\_dev$

1   Calculate mean of $x1-x10$
2   Calculate standard deviation

This provides sufficient information for the main program unit to be written, since the interface with the subroutine statistics is fully defined. The mathematics of how to calculate the standard deviation can be left to the person who is to write this subroutine, since he or she will know the exact form of the subroutine's interface with the calling program unit.

We will not take this problem any further at this stage, however, as the resulting program will be very limited and the concept of modular development has been sufficiently well demonstrated. We shall return to this problem in Chapter 8 when we shall be able to write a program to solve a similar problem with an arbitrary number of data items.

SELF-TEST EXERCISES 4.2

1   What is **use** association?

2   Write suitable specification statements for use in a module which will

     (a)   provide conversion factors to convert between metric units of length, volume and mass (metres, litres and kilograms) and their imperial equivalents (feet, pints and pounds);

     (b)   provide procedures to calculate the mean and standard deviation of a set of data items;

     (c)   provide procedures to carry out five types of analysis on data which may be supplied in either metric or imperial units of length, volume or mass.

3   What is the purpose of the **save** attribute?

4   What is an initialization expression?

5   When can a variable be given an initial value as part of its declaration?

SUMMARY

- F procedures may be subroutines or functions.

- Intrinsic procedures are a special class of procedures which form part of the F language.

- Many intrinsic functions exist in several versions, each of which operates on arguments of different types; such functions are called generic functions.

- All F procedures, other than intrinsic procedures, must be defined in a module.

- An F program consists of one main program unit, and any number of modules.

- Execution of a function is initiated by the appearance of the function name in an expression; execution of a subroutine is initiated by a **call** statement.

- A function is given information to operate on by means of one or more arguments, and delivers a single result.

- A subroutine's arguments are used both to receive information to operate on and to return results.

- The **intent** attribute must be used to control the direction in which arguments are used to pass information.

- A function's dummy arguments must all have **intent(in)**.

- A character dummy argument must be declared with an assumed length, that is (**len**=*).

- Only the arguments of a procedure are accessible outside the procedure; all other variables and constants declared in the procedure are local to that procedure.

- A module may be used to make variables and constants available to several procedures.

- The values of a procedure's local variables may be retained between references by use of the **save** attribute.

- Local variables in a procedure may be given an initial value as part of their declaration as long as they have the **save** attribute.

- Procedures provide the basic building blocks for modular development and top-down program design.

- F syntax introduced in Chapter 4:

Initial statements	**module** *name*
	function *name* (*dummy argument list*) **result** (*result*)
	function *name* () **result** (*result*)
	subroutine *name* (*dummy argument list*)
	subroutine *name* ()
End statements	**end module** *name*
	end function *name*
	end subroutine *name*
Function reference	*function_name* (*actual argument list*)
	function_name ()
Subroutine call	**call** *subroutine_name* (*actual argument list*)
	call *subroutine_name* ()
Module use	**use** *module_name*
contains statement	**contains**
Accessibility statement	**private**
	public
	public :: *list of procedure names*
Assumed length character declaration	**character** (**len**=*) :: *character_dummy_arg*
Accessibility attribute	**public**
	private
Argument intent attribute	**intent** (*intent*)
	where *intent* is **in**, **out** or **inout**
save attribute	**save**
Initialization of local variables	*type*, **save** :: *variable_name* = *initial_value*, ...

PROGRAMMING EXERCISES

Most larger programs are structured in such a way that each of the major functions (input of data, calculation of each type of analysis, printing of results) is handled by a different procedure, or group of procedures, which can be written and tested independently. In the following exercises you should write your solutions in this way, even though it may not be strictly necessary.

Write a structure plan for the program before you start coding.

*4.1   Write a subroutine which, when supplied with the coordinates of two points (x_1, y_1) and (x_2, y_2), calculates the distance of each point from the origin and the distance between the points.

Note that the distance d_1 of point 1 from the origin is given by the formula

$$d_1 = \sqrt{x_1^2 + y_1^2}$$

while the distance d between the two points is given by

$$d = \sqrt{(x_2 - x_1)^2 + (y_2 - y_1)^2}$$

Test your subroutine in a short program to check that it works correctly with several different sets of data.

4.2   Write a function which, when supplied with the coordinates of two points (x_1, y_1) and (x_2, y_2), calculates the distance between the points.

Test your function to make sure that it works correctly.

Now modify the subroutine that you wrote for Exercise 4.1 so that it uses this function to carry out all the necessary calculations.

4.3   Write a function to give the logarithm of a number to base b. (Use the equation $\log_b x = \log_{10} x / \log_{10} b$.)

*4.4   Write a module that contains four integers. Use this module in a program which contains a main program and three subroutines, one to input three integer values from the keyboard, one to calculate the sum of the three integers, and the third to print the result of adding the three numbers together.

Although a trivial program (to put it mildly!), this approach mirrors that used in larger programs where each of the three activities may be quite complicated, and the use of a module to enable data to be easily shared is extremely useful.

4.5   A credit card company produces monthly statements for its customers. Each statement shows the following information:

    (a)   The amount outstanding from last month
    (b)   The interest due on that amount for the month
    (c)   Any payment received since the last statement
    (d)   The total spent with the card since the last statement
    (e)   The total amount now outstanding

The customer can then pay any amount as long as it is at least 5% of the outstanding amount.

Write a program which reads the amount outstanding, details of payments made and total spending, and the current interest rate, and then produces an appropriate statement.

4.6   A builder wishes to calculate the relative costs of building a wall using different sizes of bricks and different types of mortar. The thickness of the wall will always be one brick's depth. Regardless of the size of brick and the type of mortar, the thickness of the mortar will always be 0.5 in. Write a program to help him.

The program should read the size of the bricks and their cost, the cost of the mortar per cubic inch, and the height and length of the wall. It should calculate how many bricks will be required and their cost, how much mortar is required and its cost, and the total cost (excluding labour!).

4.7   The force F due to gravity between two bodies of masses m_1 and m_2 is given by the formula

$$F = \frac{Gm_1m_2}{r^2}$$

where $G = 6.672 \times 10^{-11}$ newtons/metre^2/kg^2, r is the distance between the bodies (in metres), and the masses m_1 and m_2 are measured in kilograms.

Write a program that uses a function to evaluate the force of gravity between two bodies given their masses and separation. Define G as a parameter (and think about where it should be specified).

4.8   In Einstein's famous equation $E = mc^2$, the energy E is in joules if the mass m is in kilograms and c is the speed of light in metres per second (=2.9979 $\times$ 10^8). Write a function to calculate the energy equivalent of a given mass. Roughly how much energy is equivalent to the mass of a sugar cube (approximately 1 gram)?

4.9   Write a program consisting of a main program and two *subroutines*. The main program should read up to 10 positive numbers. It should then use the first subroutine to calculate the arithmetic mean of these numbers (that is, the sum of the numbers divided by n, the number of numbers) and the second to calculate their geometric mean (that is, the nth root of the product of the n numbers). The main program should then print these two means. (Note that the nth root of a real value can be obtained by taking the natural logarithm of the value, dividing it by n, and then taking the exponential of the result.)

Now modify the program so that the subroutines do not have any arguments, but obtain their data, and return their results, through variables made available from a module by **use** association.

4.10   Write a subroutine that calculates the position, velocity and acceleration of a body undergoing simple harmonic motion using the equations given below:

position $= a\sin(nt + \epsilon)$
velocity $= na\cos(nt + \epsilon)$
acceleration $= -an^2\sin(nt + \epsilon)$

Use as starting values $n = 3.14159265$, $\epsilon = 0$, $a = 2.5$. Test the program by specifying your own set of values for t.

4.11   The escape velocity from the surface of a planet (that is, the minimum velocity a projectile must achieve in order that it will never return to the planet's surface, ignoring such things as air resistance) is given by the expression:

$$V_{esc} = \frac{\sqrt{2GM}}{R}$$

where G is the gravitational constant $(6.67 \times 10^{-11} \text{ N/m}^2/\text{kg}^2)$, M is the mass of the planet (in kg) and R is the planet's radius (in metres).

Write a function that accepts the planetary mass and radius as its input and returns the escape velocity. Use your function to compare the escape velocities from the Earth, Jupiter and the Moon using the following data:

Planet	Mass (kg)	Radius (m)
Earth	6.0×10^{24}	6.4×10^6
Moon	7.4×10^{22}	1.7×10^6
Jupiter	1.9×10^{27}	7.1×10^7

4.12 Write a program to convert the ecliptic latitude β and longitude λ of an astronomical object into right ascension α and declination δ using the formulae

$$\alpha = \tan^{-1} \frac{\sin \lambda \cos \epsilon - \tan \beta \sin \epsilon}{\cos \lambda}$$

$$\delta = \sin^{-1}(\sin \beta \cos \epsilon + \cos \beta \sin \epsilon \sin \lambda)$$

where $\epsilon = 0.4091$. Assume that all quantities are in radians.

(Note: Use the **atan2** intrinsic function for the first expression.)

In fact, the right ascension of an astronomical object is generally given in units of time, where 24 hours equals 360 degrees, while the declination is usually given in degrees. Write a subroutine to convert the two quantities from radians into these units, and incorporate it into your solution. (Note that 2π radians equals 360 degrees.)

Controlling the flow of your program

5

5.1 Choice and decision-making
5.2 Logical expressions and logical variables
5.3 The if construct
5.4 Comparing character strings
5.5 The case construct

Up to now our programs have started at the beginning and proceeded to the end without interruption. However, in practice, most problems require us to choose between alternative courses of action, depending upon circumstances which are not determined until the program is executed. The ability of a program to specify how these decisions are to be made is one of the most important aspects of programming.

This chapter introduces the concept of comparison between two numbers or two character strings, and explains how such comparisons can be used to determine which of two, or more, alternative sections of code are obeyed.

An alternative form of choice uses a list of possible values of some variable or expression to determine which of the several alternative blocks of code is actually executed.

5.1 Choice and decision-making

All the programs that we have written so far have started execution at the beginning of the main program, and have then proceeded to execute each statement in turn, in the same unvarying sequential order, until the last statement of the main program is executed. Even the use of procedures has not altered this sequential processing, for the effect has been to transfer control temporarily to another part of the program, obey that sequentially, and then return to carry on at the statement after the procedure reference. What makes computers so powerful – apparently even mimicking some of the powers of the human brain – is their ability to vary the order of execution of statements according to logical criteria which are not determined until after the program has started execution.

In everyday life we frequently encounter a situation which involves several possible alternative courses of action, requiring us to choose one of them based on some decision-making criteria. For example, Figure 5.1 shows a hypothetical discussion about how to get from Vienna to Budapest.

Clearly there are several answers based upon the preferred method of travel and the time available. If we eliminate the details of the answer we see that it has a definite structure, as shown in Figure 5.2. Each of the various alternative forms of transport (or 'actions') is preceded by a condition or test of the form '*if* some criterion holds *then*...', apart from the last form (travel by road) which is included as a final alternative if none of the others are suitable and is preceded by the word *otherwise*.

F has a very similar construction, shown in Figure 5.3, which uses the words **if** and **then** exactly as they were used in the English language example, the words **else if** where the English used *but if*, and the word **else** instead of *otherwise*. In addition, so that there is no doubt about the end of the final 'action', the words **end if** are placed at the very end. The only other difference is that

---

Q: How do I get to Budapest from Vienna?

A: It depends how you want to travel.
   If you are in a hurry *then*
       you should fly from Schwechat airport in Vienna to Ferihegy airport in Budapest;
   but if you are a romantic or like trains *then*
       you should take the Orient Express from the Sudbahnhof to Budapest's Keleti palyudvar;
   but if you have plenty of time *then*
       you can travel on one of the boats which ply along the Danube;
   otherwise
       you can always go by road.

Figure 5.1 An example of decisions in English.

If criterion 1 *then*
    action 1
but if criterion 2 *then*
    action 2
but if criterion 3 *then*
    action 3
otherwise
    action 4

Figure 5.2 English language alternatives.

the criterion on which the decision will be based is enclosed in parentheses. This structure is known as an **if construct** and the initial **if ... then** is called an **if statement**.

The way an **if** construct works is that each decision criterion is examined in turn. If it is true then the following action or 'block' of F statements is executed. If it is not true then the next criterion (if any) is examined. If none of the criteria are found to be true then the block of statements following the **else** (if there is one) is executed; if there is no **else** statement, as in Figure 5.4, then no action is taken and the computer moves on to the next statement, that is, the one following the **end if** statement. There must always be an **if** statement (with its corresponding block of statements) and an **end if** statement, but the **else if** statements and the **else** statement may be omitted if they are not required.

```
if (criterion_1) then
    action_1
else if (criterion_2) then
    action_2
else if (criterion_3) then
    action_3
else
    action_4
end if
```

Figure 5.3 F alternatives.

```
if (criterion) then
    action
end if
```

Figure 5.4 A minimal if construct.

Before we can start to use this facility for taking one of several alternative courses of action we must define the criteria on which the decisions will be based. These all consist of a new type of expression – a **logical expression**.

5.2   Logical expressions and `logical` variables

In the English-language discussion about how to get from Vienna to Budapest the decision depended upon the truth of certain assertions. Thus, '*if* you are in a hurry *then* travel by plane' could be expressed (rather quaintly) as '*if* it is true that you are in a hurry *then* travel by plane', and similarly for the other decision criteria. We see therefore that each decision depends upon whether some assertion is true or false.

The F decision criterion is also an assertion which is either true or false. This is a new concept, not to be confused with numbers or character strings, in which the values *true* and *false* are called **logical values**, and an assertion (or expression) which can take one of these two values is called a **logical expression**. The simplest forms of logical expressions are those expressing the relationship between two numeric values, thus

```
a > b
```

is true if the value of a is greater than the value of b, and

```
x == y
```

is true if the value of x is equal to the value of y. Notice that the sign for the equality relation is two consecutive equals signs.

The two expressions shown above, which express a relationship between two values, are a special form of logical expression called a **relational expression** and the operators are called **relational operators**. Figure 5.5 shows the six relational operators which exist in F, and a few moments' thought will show that they define all possible relationships between two arithmetic values.

There is a certain amount of redundancy in this range of operators, which leads to the possibility of expressing the same condition in several different

```
a <  b  is true if a is less than b
a <= b is true if a is less than or equal to b
a >  b  is true if a is greater than b
a >= b is true if a is greater than or equal to b
a == b is true if a is equal to b
a /= b is true if a is not equal to b
```

Figure 5.5   Relational operators and expressions.

ways. An example of this is that the following four relational expressions are
identical in their effect and will always give the same results:

```
b**2 >= 4*a*c
b**2    4*a*c >- 0
4*a*c <= b**2
4*a*c - b**2 <= 0
```

The mathematically-oriented reader will recognize these as expressing the
condition for a quadratic equation to have real roots.

This variety means that programmers are free to choose their own way of
expressing such conditions. For example, one of us would always use the first
form shown above, as it is the way in which he thinks of the condition (that is,
$b^2 \geqslant 4ac$), while the other prefers the second form.

Notice that, in these examples, the values being compared are not necessarily
expressed as variables or constants but as arithmetic expressions. *All arithmetic
operators have a higher priority than any relational operator* and the arithmetic
expression, or expressions, are therefore evaluated *before* any comparisons take
place.

As we would expect, a relational operator may also be used to evaluate the
relation between two character expressions:

```
string_1 <= string_2
```

However, this is not quite as straightforward as it appears, for we must first
establish what we mean when we state that one character string is greater than
another. Because this issue has a number of complexities which are unrelated
to the primary question of controlling the flow of control in a program, we
shall therefore defer further discussion of comparison of character strings until
Section 5.4, and will restrict ourselves to numeric comparisons until then.

We can now return to the consideration of relational expressions. We have
already established that the result of evaluating such an expression is a logical
value, taking one of the two values *true* or *false*, and it will come as no surprise
to learn that we can declare **logical variables** in which to store such values.
A logical variable is declared in much the same way as a real or integer variable:

```
logical :: var_1,var_2,var_3
```

Once we can declare logical variables the next question is how we can write
the two possible logical values, *true* and *false*, in an F program. We cannot simply
write true or false, as these would appear to be variable names, and so F
requires that these values are enclosed between periods:

```
.true.
.false.
```

Moreover, since we can have logical variables and logical expressions it is natural that we should also be allowed to write functions which deliver a logical value:

```
function logical_fun(arg1, ...) result l_fun
    logical :: l_fun
    .
    .
    .
```

We now return to examining the nature of logical expressions, but before doing that we shall return to consideration of the discussion about the best means of travelling from Vienna to Budapest which was shown in Figure 5.1. In this discussion, the second decision took the following form

> *but if* you are a romantic *or* like trains *then*

Here we have not one decision criterion but two criteria, only one of which needs to be satisfied for the appropriate action to be taken:

> you should take the Orient Express from the Sudbahnhof to Budapest's Keleti palyudvar.

A similar double criterion could have been used to cater for the fact that some people are afraid of flying:

> *If* you are in a hurry *and* you are not afraid of flying *then*
>   you should fly from Schwechat airport in Vienna to Ferihegy airport in Budapest.

In this case the use of the word *and* indicates that *both* the criteria must be satisfied for the specified action to be carried out.

In F we use the same two words to form composite logical expressions, but written as `.or.` and `.and.` in a similar fashion to the two logical values `.true.` and `.false.`. They are called **logical operators** and are used to combine two logical expressions or values. Thus we could write

```
(a<b) .or. (c<d)
```

or

```
(x<=y) .and. (y<=z)
```

In fact the parentheses shown in these examples are not strictly necessary because the relational operators have a higher priority than logical operators, but to human eyes expressions such as

L1	L2	L1.or.L2	L1.and.L2
true	*true*	*true*	*true*
true	*false*	*true*	*false*
false	*true*	*true*	*false*
false	*false*	*false*	*false*

Figure 5.6   The logical operators .or. and .and..

```
a<b.or.c<d
```

can sometimes be confusing, although the judicious use of blank spaces can make the meaning clear:

```
a<b .or. c<d
```

The inclusion of (redundant) parentheses ensures that there is no room for doubt over the true meaning of the expression, and hence of its value:

```
(a<b) .or. (c<d)
```

The effect of the .or. and .and. operators is as one would expect, with .or. giving a true result if *either* of its operands is true, while .and. gives a true result only if *both* are true. Figure 5.6 illustrates this.

Two other logical operators exist which do not have an exact equivalent in normal English usage, namely .eqv. and .neqv.. The first of these (.eqv.) gives a true result if its operands are *equivalent* (that is, if they both have the same logical value), while the other (.neqv.) is the opposite (*not equivalent*) and gives a true result if they have opposite logical values. Figure 5.7 illustrates this.

Essentially, these operators are used in logical expressions to simplify their structure. Thus, the following two expressions are identical in their effect:

```
(a<b .and. x<y) .or. (a>=b .and. x>=y)
a<b .eqv. x<y
```

L1	L2	L1.eqv.L2	L1.neqv.L2
true	*true*	*true*	*false*
true	*false*	*false*	*true*
false	*true*	*false*	*true*
false	*false*	*true*	*false*

Figure 5.7   The logical operators .eqv. and .neqv..

Operator	Priority
.not.	highest
.and.	
.or.	
.eqv. and .neqv.	lowest

Figure 5.8   Logical operator priorities.

There is one further logical operator, **.not.**, which, unlike all the other relational and logical operators, is a unary operator, that is, it has a single operand. The **.not.** operator inverts the value of the following logical expression, so that if the logical expression logical_exp is *true* then **.not.**logical_exp is *false*, and vice versa. As is the case with the relational operators, the effect of the **.not.** operator on an expression can always be obtained in some other way; for example, the following expressions are equivalent in their effect:

```
.not.(a<b .and. b<c)
a>=b .or. b>=c
```

and, of course

```
.not.(a<b .eqv. x<y)
a<b .neqv. x<y
```

In some circumstances the **.not.** operator can make a logical expression much clearer to the human reader.

Just as with arithmetic operators, it is important that the relative priorities of the various logical operators are understood. Figure 5.8 shows their priority order, although it should be noted that, as with arithmetic operators, parentheses can be used to change this order. It should also be noted that any arithmetic operators or relational operators (*in that order*) have a higher priority than any logical operators.

5.3   The **if** construct

We can now return to the basic **if** construct which was informally introduced in Section 5.1, and examine its structure in more detail. The initial statement of the construct is an **if** statement which consists of the word **if** followed by a logical expression enclosed in parentheses, followed by the word **then**:

```
if (logical_expression) then
```

This is followed by a sequence, or *block*, of statements which will be executed only if the logical expression is true. The block of statements is terminated by an **else if** statement, an **else** statement, or an **end if** statement.

The **else if** statement has a very similar syntax to that of an **if** statement:

else if (*logical_expression*) **then**

It is followed by a block of statements which will be executed if the logical expression is true, and if the logical expression in the initial **if** statement, and those of any preceding **else if** statements, are false. The block of statements is terminated by another **else if** statement, an **else** statement, or an **end if** statement.

The **else** statement simply consists of the single word **else** and introduces a final block of statements which will be executed only if the logical expressions in all preceding **if** and **else if** statements are false.

The construct is always ended by an **end if** statement.

There are no restrictions upon what types of statements may appear within a block of statements other than that any multi-statement constructs, such as further **if** constructs, or the **case** and **do** constructs that we shall meet later, must be wholly contained within a single block. It is obvious that no other situation would make any sense!

An **if** construct is, therefore, always introduced by an **if** statement and terminated by an **end if** statement. There may be any number of **else if** statements, each followed by a block of statements, or there may be none. There may be one **else** statement followed by a block of statements, or there may be none; if there is an **else** statement then it, and its succeeding block of statements, must follow all **else if** blocks. This structure is shown in Figure 5.9.

```
if (logical expression) then
    block of F statements
else if (logical expression) then
    block of F statements
else if (logical expression) then

    .
    .
    .

else
    block of F statements
end if
```

Figure 5.9 The structure of an **if** construct.

☐ **EXAMPLE 5.1** •

1 Problem

Example 4.1 calculated the number of bags of wheat that were required to sow a triangular field. Modify this program to deal with the situation in which an exact number of full bags is required in a more aesthetically pleasing manner (and one which is easier to follow).

2 Analysis

In Example 4.1 we added 0.9 to the result of dividing the quantity of seed required by 10 000 (to calculate the number of multiples of 10 kilos required). This used the truncation mechanism to specify an extra bag (which will only be partially used) if the true quantity is not an exact multiple of 10 kilos. A better way would be to use an **if** construct. Since we have already fully analysed this problem in Chapter 4 we shall not repeat this analysis, but will merely show a revised structure plan:

1	Read lengths of sides of field (*a*, *b* and *c*)
2	Calculate the area of the field
3	Read the sowing density
4	Calculate the quantity of seed required
5	Calculate number of full bags needed
6	If any more seed is needed then
	6.1 Add one to number of bags
7	Print size of field and number of bags

We can find out if any more is needed by testing if the amount required is greater than the amount in the bags.

3 Solution

```
program wheat_sowing

! A program to calculate the quantity of wheat required to
! sow a triangular field

    ! Variable declarations
    real :: a,b,c,s,area,density,quantity
    integer :: num_bags

    ! Read the lengths of the sides of the field
    print *,"Type the lengths of the three sides of the field ", &
            "in metres: "
    read *,a,b,c
```

```
! Calculate the area of the field
s = 0.5*(a+b+c)
area = sqrt(s*(s-a)*(s-b)*(s-c))

! Read sowing density
print *,"What is the sowing density (gms/sq.m.)? "
read *,density

! Calculate quantity of wheat in grams and the number of
! full 10 kg bags
quantity = density*area
num_bags = 0.0001*quantity    ! Any part-full bag is excluded

! Check to see if another bag is required
if (quantity > 10000*num_bags) then
   num_bags = num_bags+1
end if

! Print results
print *,"The area of the field is ",area," sq. metres"
print *,"and ",num_bags," 10 kilo bags will be required"

end program wheat_sowing
```

There are two important points to note here. The first is that the relational expression is comparing a real value (quantity) with an integer one (10000*num_bags). In this case the expression is evaluated as if comparing the difference between the two operands with zero; thus the expression

```
quantity > 10000*num_bags
```

is evaluated as if it were

```
(quantity-10000*num_bags) > 0.0
```

To do this 10000*num_bags is converted to its real equivalent and then the real subtraction is performed.

The second point concerns the accuracy of real arithmetic. Real numbers are stored in a computer as an approximation to a defined degree of accuracy and, therefore, when such numbers are used in arithmetic expressions the least significant digits may get lost as a result of round-off. Figure 5.10 illustrates this in the context of hand calculation to six digits of accuracy, where the product of two four-digit numbers requires seven digits to be accurate; the answer is therefore expressed as a six-digit number after rounding the sixth digit. The normal rule is that if the first digit to be omitted (the seventh in this case) is in the range 0−4 then it (and any subsequent ones) are simply dropped, but if it is in the range 5−9 (as in this example) then the last significant digit is increased by one (from 7 to 8 in this case) before the remainder are dropped.

A computer operates in exactly the same way and, therefore, any real arithmetic operation is liable to introduce such a rounding error. Frequently this

Multiply 25.39 by 17.25 to six significant figures:

$$25.39 \times$$
$$\underline{17.25}$$
$$2539$$
$$17773$$
$$5078$$
$$\underline{12695}$$
$$4379775$$

Answer is 437.978

Figure 5.10 Rounding errors in hand calculations.

is of no consequence as the computer is working to a greater accuracy than required for the problem. However, there are four cases where it *does* matter a great deal. One of these is where a large amount of numerical calculation is being carried out and in this case a higher level of accuracy (or *precision*) can be specified, as we shall see in Chapter 11. The second case was mentioned in Section 3.3 and relates to the situation when a large integer value is converted to its real equivalent, with a consequent loss of precision. The third case is the related conversion problem in which a real number is to be truncated before being stored as an integer. The final case is more interesting, and concerns the situation in which we wish to compare or subtract two real numbers which are almost exactly the same. We can illustrate the last two situations by reference to the program we have just written.

Let us suppose that the sides of the field are 130 m, 100 m and 130 m, and that the sowing density is 25 g/m^2. A few moments' calculation shows that the area of the field is 6000 m^2, and hence that 150 kg of seed are required. num_bags should therefore be 15 and the test should find that these contain exactly enough seed. In practice, though, it probably won't be as straightforward as that. For example, the calculation of the area could lead to a value such as 5999.999 999 (to 10 significant figures) or to 6000.000 001. The subsequent calculation of the quantity of seed will give further possible rounding errors leading to a (real) value for 0.0001*quantity of perhaps 14.999 999 99 or 15.000 000 01.

Although for all practical purposes these two values are the same as the true value of 15, when they are truncated to calculate num_bags they will lead to integer values of 14 and 15 respectively. In the first case quantity will clearly be less than 10000*num_bags and so the situation will be compensated for. In the second case, however, it is possible that quantity is fractionally more than 150.0 (for instance 150.000 000 1) and that the relational expression will be true, leading to a calculation of 16 bags!

We can deal with this by *never* testing whether two real values are equal (which is essentially what we are doing here in the borderline case) but rather by testing whether their difference is acceptably small. In this case, therefore, we could say that since the numbers being compared are of the order of 100 000 (actually 150 000 in this example) and since any errors in calculation will, hopefully, be much less than 1%, we should alter the test to read

```
if (quantity > 10000*num_bags+1000) then
   num_bags = num_bags + 1
end if
```

A better way might be to avoid any reference to num_bags and to express the test as follows:

```
if (0.0001*quantity - int(0.0001*quantity) > 0.1) then
   num_bags = num_bags + 1
end if
```

thereby eliminating multiplying quantity by 0.0001, and then multiplying the result by 1000. In this form, the intrinsic function **int** calculates the integer equivalent of 0.0001*quantity, which is the value of num_bags, and subtracts it from the original, real, value. The result of this will be the amount that was lost through truncation which, in this case, represents the amount of seed required in the last, partially filled, bag as a fraction of one bag. We decided in Example 4.1 that if such a bag was less than 10% full then the amount of seed could be ignored. It would probably be advisable, however, to add a comment to explain the test, whichever one is used!

`if` tests are so common in scientific computing that we shall immediately present another example of their use.

EXAMPLE 5.2

1 Problem

Write a function which will return the cube root of its argument.

2 Analysis

In Section 4.3 we wrote a function to meet this requirement which was only valid for positive arguments. We can use an **if** construct to deal with the negative and zero argument cases which were not included in the earlier version.

If the argument is negative then we can use the fact that $\sqrt[3]{(-x)} = -\sqrt[3]{x}$.

The zero argument situation is, however, slightly more complicated, since it is not possible to calculate the logarithm of zero. Our data design and structure plan are therefore as follows:

Data design

Purpose	Type	Name
A Dummy argument: Value whose cube root is required	**real**	x
B Result variable: Cube root of x	**real**	cube_root

Structure plan

> Real function cube_root(x)
>
> **1**   If x = 0
>   **1.1**   Return zero
>   else if x < 0
>   **1.2**   Return −exp(log(−x)/3)
>   else
>   **1.3**   Return exp(log(x)/3)

☐3☐ **Solution**

```
function cube_root(x) result(root)

! Function to calculate the cube root of a real number

    ! Dummy argument and result declaration
    real, intent(in) :: x
    real :: root

    ! Eliminate the zero case
    if (x == 0.0) then
        root = 0.0

    ! Calculate cube root by using logs
    else if (x<0) then
        ! First deal with negative argument
        root = -exp(log(-x)/3.0)
    else
        ! Positive argument
        root = exp(log(x)/3.0)
    end if

end function cube_root
```

One final point that should be made about this function is that calculating the logarithm and then dividing by three is *not* a particularly good way of calculating a cube root. We use it here to demonstrate the use of the **if** construct rather than introducing the more complicated mathematics that a better solution would involve!

5.4 Comparing character strings

In Section 5.2 we mentioned that the six relational operators could be used to compare character expressions and constants (or character *strings* as they are usually referred to), but that the question of determining when one string was greater than another would be left until later. The key to this determination is the **collating sequence** of letters, digits and other characters, which is based on the order of these characters in the American National Standard Code for Information Interchange (ANSI X3.4 1977), which is usually referred to as ASCII. This code, which is used as the internal processor code of many computer systems, is also defined in the International Reference Version (IRV) of the International Standard ISO 646 : 1983; it is included for reference in Appendix D of this book. F lays down six rules for this, covering letters, digits and the space or blank character.

1. The 26 upper-case letters are collated in the following order:
   A B C D E F G H I J K L M N O P Q R S T U V W X Y Z
2. The 26 lower-case letters are collated in the following order:
   a b c d e f g h i j k l m n o p q r s t u v w x y z
3. The 10 digits are collated in the following order:
   0 1 2 3 4 5 6 7 8 9
4. A space (or blank) is collated before both letters and digits.
5. Digits are all collated before the letter A.
6. Upper-case letters are all collated before any lower-case letters.

The position in the collating sequence of the other 22 characters in the F character set is determined by their position in the ASCII collating sequence.

When two character operands are being compared there are three distinct stages in the process:

1. If the two operands are not the same length, the shorter one is treated as though it were extended on the right with blanks until it is the same length as the longer one.

2. The two operands are compared character by character, starting with the left-most character, until either a difference is found or the end of the operands is reached.

3. If a difference is found, then the relationship between these two different characters defines the relationship between the two operands, with the character which comes earlier in the collating sequence being deemed to be the lesser of the two. If no difference is found, then the strings are considered to be equal.

The result of this process is that the relational expression always has the value we would instinctively expect it to have. Thus

    `"Adam" > "Eve"` is *false*

because A comes before E, and is thus *less than* E.

    `"Adam" < "Adamant"` is *true*

because after Adam has been extended the relationship reduces to `" " < "a"` after the first four characters have been found to be the same. Since a blank comes before a letter, this is *true*.

    `"120" < "1201"` is *true*

because the first difference in the strings leads to an evaluation of `" " < "1"`, which is *true* since a blank also comes before a digit.

Finally

    `"ADAM" < "Adam"` is *true*

because the first difference in the strings leads to an evaluation of `"D" < "d"`, which is *true* since upper-case letters come before lower-case letters.

☐ **EXAMPLE 5.3**   ∙

☐1 Problem

Write a function which takes a single character as its argument and returns a single character according to the following rules:

- If the input character is a lower-case letter then return its upper-case equivalent.
- If the input character is an upper-case letter then return its lower-case equivalent.
- If the input character is not a letter then return it unchanged.

2 Analysis

The major problem here is establishing the relationship between upper- and lower-case letters, so that conversions may be easily made. Here we can use the ASCII code (see Appendix D) to good effect due to the existence of the two intrinsic functions **ichar** and **char**. The first of these provides the position of its character argument in the ASCII collating sequence, while the second returns the character at a specified position in that sequence. Thus **ichar**("A") is 65, while **char**(97) is the character a. An examination of the ASCII character set (see Figure D.1 in Appendix D) quickly shows that every lower-case character is exactly 32 positions after its upper-case equivalent. We now have both the information and the means to carry out the conversion and so are ready to design our function.

Although we could simply add or subtract 32 from the ASCII code for the character, as appropriate, it is not then obvious what is happening. We shall therefore define a constant which has the value of this offset, calculated by subtracting the code for an upper-case letter from its lower-case equivalent.

Data design

Purpose	Type	Name
A Dummy argument: Character to be converted	**character**	ch
B Result variable: Converted character	**character**	newch
C Local constant: Offset between upper and lower case in the ASCII character set	**integer**	upper_to_lower

Structure plan

Character function change_case(ch)

1   If $A \leqslant$ ch $\leqslant Z$
     1.1   Return character upper_to_lower places after ch in ASCII
     else if $a \leqslant$ ch $\leqslant z$
     1.2   Return character upper_to_lower places before ch in ASCII
     else
     1.3   Return ch unaltered

3 **Solution**

```
function change_case(ch) result(new_ch)

! This function changes the case of its argument (if it
! is alphabetic)

    ! Dummy argument and result
    character(len=*), intent(in) :: ch
    character(len=1) :: new_ch

    ! Local constant
    integer, parameter :: upper_to_lower = ichar("a")-ichar("A")

    ! Check if argument is lower case alphabetic, upper case
    ! alphabetic, or non-alphabetic
    if ("A"<=ch .and. ch<="Z") then
       ! Upper case - convert to lower case
       new_ch = char(ichar(ch)+upper_to_lower)

    else if ("a"<=ch .and. ch<="z") then
       ! Lower case - convert to upper case
       new_ch = char(ichar(ch)-upper_to_lower)

    else
       ! not alphabetic
       new_ch = ch

    end if

end function change_case
```

SELF-TEST EXERCISES 5.1

1   What is the difference between a logical operator and a relational operator?

2   What are the values of the following expressions?

(a) 1>2
(b) (1+3)>=4
(c) (0.1+0.3)<=0.4
(d) 2>1 .and. 3<4
(e) 3>2 .and. (1+2)<3 .or. 4<=3
(f) 3>2 .or. (1+2)<3 .and. 4<=3
(g) 3>2 .and. (1+2)<3 .eqv. 4<=3

3   What is the purpose of the **if** construct?

4   What are the rules for collating characters?

5   What are the values of the following expressions?

   (a)   `"Me"<"You"`
   (b)   `"Me"<"ME"`
   (c)   `"Me"<"Men"`
   (d)   `"Me"<"Me?"`

5.5   The case construct

In some situations it is necessary to have an ordering built into the decision as to which choice to take because there is an overlap between some of the possible decision criteria. For example, if you are a baseball addict, but especially a Cubs fan, then the decision as to what to do on a Saturday afternoon might look like this:

> *If* it is the baseball season *and* the Cubs are at home *then*
>   Go to Wrigley Field
> *Else if* it is the baseball season *and* the Cubs game is on TV *then*
>   Get a six-pack and watch the game on TV
> *Else if* it is the baseball season *then*
>   Go to any nearby baseball game
> *Else*
>   Rent a baseball video and watch it at home.

It is very clear that the order in which the choices are considered is of vital importance!

Frequently, however, the decision criteria are mutually exclusive, and there is no overlap between them. For example, if you are a Liverpool soccer fan, and are only interested in watching football matches in which they are playing (whether at home or away), then your Saturday afternoon decision plan might be rather different:

> *If* it is the football season *and* Liverpool are playing at home *then*
>   Go to Anfield and support the Reds
> *Else if* it is the football season *and* Liverpool are playing away *then*
>   Go to wherever they are playing and support the Reds
> *Else*
>   Get a six-pack and watch some of your old Liverpool videos at home.

Although this has been written in the same way as the previous example, there is clearly no ordering involved in this decision process and the use of the *if ... else* style is rather misleading. An alternative approach would be to write

Select the appropriate case from the following alternatives:
Case 1: It is the football season and Liverpool are playing at home
Go to Anfield and support the Reds
Case 2: It is the football season and Liverpool are playing away
Go to wherever they are playing and support the Reds
Case 3: Any other situation
Get a six-pack and watch some of your old Liverpool videos at
home

As well as the **if** construct, which caters for the ordered choice situation, F provides another form of selection, known as the **case** construct, to deal with the situation in which the various alternatives are mutually exclusive, and the order in which they are expressed is unimportant. Its overall structure is shown in Figure 5.11.

The initial statement of a **case** construct takes the form

select case (*case_expression*)

where *case_expression* is either an **integer** or a **character** expression. When the **select case** statement is encountered the value of *case_expression* is evaluated, and its value used to determine which, if any, of the alternative blocks of statements in the **case** construct is to be executed.

Each **case** statement takes the form

case (*case_selector*)

or

case default

although there may only be one **case default** statement in a **case** construct.

The *case_selector* determines which, if any, of the blocks of statements will be obeyed, while the **case default** statement, if any, must follow all other **case**

```
         select case (case expression)
         case (case selector)
            block of statements
         case (case selector)
            block of statements

             .
             .
             .
         end select
```

Figure 5.11 The structure of a case construct.

statements, and precedes the block of statements to be obeyed if none of the other **case** statements produces a match.

The *case_selector* can take one of four forms:

case_value
low_value:
: *high_value*
low_value:*high_value*

or it may be a list of any combination of these, where *case_value, low_value* and *high_value* are either literal constants or initialization expressions (see 4.8) of the same type as the corresponding *case_expression*.

The meaning of these four alternatives is almost self-evident, but we shall elaborate them for the avoidance of any doubt:

1. If the *case_selector* takes the form *case_value* then the following block of code is executed if and only if *case_expression* == *case_value*.

2. If the *case_selector* takes the form *low_value*: then the following block of code is executed if and only if *low_value* <= *case_expression*.

3. If the *case_selector* takes the form :*high_value* then the following block of code is executed if and only if *case_expression* <= *high_value*.

4. If the *case_selector* takes the form *low_value*:*high_value* then the following block of code is executed if and only if *low_value* <= *case_expression* .**and**. *case_expression* <= *high_value*.

If none of the specified values or value ranges matches the value of the *case_expression* then the block of code following the **case default** statement, if any, is executed; if there is no **case default** statement then an exit is made from the **case** construct without any code being executed.

Notice that the order in which the various **case** statements, and their following blocks of statements, are written does not matter since the rules governing **case** statements require that there is no overlap; the only exception to this is that the **case default** block, if there is one, must come after all the other case blocks.

Both the **if** and the **case** constructs, therefore, provide a means of selecting one from a set of blocks of statements and executing that block, or of executing none of them if none of the decision criteria is satisfied. As we have already mentioned, one difference between the two constructs is that in the **case** construct the decision criteria must not overlap. The other major difference is that the expression which determines the selection must be a logical expression in an **if** construct, but must be an integer expression or a character expression, but not a real or logical expression, in a **case** construct. This means that, in many situations, a **case** construct provides a more natural way of defining the different cases than is possible with an **if** construct.

☐ **EXAMPLE 5.4** •

☐1 Problem

Read a date in the International Standard form (yyyy-mm-dd) and print a message to indicate whether on this date in Sydney, Australia, it will be winter, spring, summer or autumn. For the purpose of this exercise we shall assume that winter consists of June and July, that spring is August, September and October, that summer is from November until March, and that autumn is April and May.

☐2 Analysis

There are clearly four mutually exclusive cases, depending upon the value of the character string mm, and so the problem is ideally suited for a **case** statement. Although it might be reasonable to assume that the date will be a valid one this is, in general, a dangerous assumption and in any program we should always check that any data is valid before starting to process it. In this example a **case default** statement can easily be used to identify any invalid data. Our data design and structure plan will be as follows:

Data design

Purpose	Type	Name
Date (yyyy-mm-dd)	**character**(**len**=10)	date
Month (for **case**)	**character**(**len**=2)	month

Structure plan

   1   Read date

   2   Extract month from date

   3   Select case on month

       3.1   month is 8, 9 or 10
              Print "spring"

       3.2   month is 11, 12, 1, 2 or 3
              Print "summer"

       3.3   month is 4 or 5
              Print "autumn"

       3.4   month is 6 or 7
              Print "winter"

       3.5   month is anything else
              Print an error message

[3] **Solution**

```
program seasons
! A program to calculate in which season a specified date lies

    ! Variable declarations
    character(len=10) :: date
    character(len=2) :: month

    ! Read date
    print *,"Please type a date in the form yyyy-mm-dd"
    read *,date

    ! Extract month number
    month = date(6:7)

    ! Print season
    select case (month)
    case ("08":"10")
        print *,date," is in the spring"
    case ("11","12","01":"03")
        print *,date," is in the summer"
    case ("04","05")
        print *,date," is in the autumn"
    case ("06","07")
        print *,date," is in the winter"
    case default
        print *,date," is not a valid date"
    end select

end program seasons
```

Note that, because the case selector is a character expression, the case values must be expressed as character constants. An alternative would be to write the selectors for the spring and summer as

```
case ("08","09","10")
```

and

```
case ("11","12","01","02","03")
```

respectively.

Another alternative would be to convert the month to integer form, but since this is slightly awkward it would be difficult to justify in such a simple program, and we shall leave it as an exercise for the adventurous reader.

Finally, it is not necessary to use the variable month at all. The **select case** statement could equally well have been written as

```
select case (date(6:7))
```

although it is then marginally less clear what is going on.

Ideally, the program should also check the validity of the values provided for day and year. We shall leave the addition of these checks for the meticulous reader.

The choice between using a **case** construct and an **if** construct is not always straightforward, and Example 5.5 illustrates how important it is to analyse properly the nature of any decisions before committing yourself to a particular course of action.

EXAMPLE 5.5

1 Problem

Write a program to read the coefficients of a quadratic equation and print its roots.

2 Analysis

This program will use the formula

$$x = \frac{-b \pm \sqrt{b^2 - 4ac}}{2a}$$

where

$$ax^2 + bx + c = 0 \text{ and } a \neq 0$$

It is immediately apparent that there are three possible cases:

1. $b^2 > 4ac$
   in which case the equation will have two real roots;
2. $b^2 = 4ac$
   in which case the equation will have one root (or two coincident roots);
3. $b^2 < 4ac$
   in which case the equation will have no roots (or at least no real roots, and we are not concerned with imaginary roots in this example).

At first sight, since there are three mutually exclusive cases, this seems a natural problem in which to use a **case** statement. However, there are two major difficulties.

The first of these is that the values of the coefficients in this sort of problem will normally be real, and therefore the expression $b^2 < 4ac$ will also be real. The *case_expression* in a **case** statement must, however, be integer or character.

The other problem concerns case 2, where the value of the expression is zero. We have stressed on many occasions that real arithmetic is only an *approximation*. In particular we should *never* compare two real numbers for equality, as two numbers which are mathematically equal will often differ very slightly if they have been calculated in a different way. We avoid this difficulty by comparing the difference between two real numbers with a very small number. Thus we could rewrite the second case as follows:

   2. $|b^2 - 4ac| < small$
   where *small* is a very small number, in which case the equation will have one root;

If we wish to use a **case** statement then we could deal with both of these problems at the same time by dividing the value of $b^2 - 4ac$ by *small* and then assigning the result to an integer for use in the **case** statement. This will mean that if $|b^2 - 4ac| < small$ the result of the division will be between -1 and $+1$, and the integer stored will, as a result of truncation, be zero. If $b^2 - 4ac > small$ then the result stored will be a positive integer, while if $b^2 - 4ac < small$ the result stored will be a negative integer. Notice, however, that there is a further problem in choosing the value of *small* arising from the fact that we shall be dividing $b^2 - 4ac$ by this very small number; it is always possible that dividing by a very small number might lead to a result which is larger than the largest number that can be stored on the computer! This indicates that the approach that we have chosen is not a particularly good one and should *not* be used in a real programming situation; it will, however, suffice for this example of how to use **case** statements.

Note that this analysis has also ignored two other theoretical difficulties. The first of these is the situation if $a = 0$. In this situation the equation is not a quadratic equation and so for this example, in which the coefficients are being typed at the keyboard, we shall simply assume that a non-zero value will be typed for a; it would not be difficult to test for this case and return an appropriate value for x. It does not, of course, matter if b or c is zero, since the equation will still be a quadratic.

The second problem is that the calculation of b^2 and that of $4ac$ could lead to problems if a, b or c is so large that the resulting calculation leads to a value greater than the maximum capable of being stored on the computer system being used (a condition known as **overflow**). Again, since the coefficients are being typed at the keyboard we shall assume that they are 'reasonable' numbers, and will ignore this problem here. Both of these situations should be considered in a comprehensive solution to this, apparently simple, problem. They are discussed in more detail in Chapter 17.

We can now design our program:

Data design

Purpose	Type	Name
A Local constant:		
A small value	**real**	small
B Local variables:		
Coefficients	**real**	a, b, c
Intermediate value	**real**	d
case selection value	**integer**	selector

Structure plan

1 Read the three coefficients a, b and c

2 Calculate $b^2 - 4ac$ $(=d)$

3 Calculate selector (**int**(d/small))

4 Select case on selector:

   4.1 selector > 0
      Calculate and print two roots

   4.2 selector $= 0$
      Calculate and print a single root

   4.3 selector < 0
      Print a message to the effect that there are no roots

We may note here that, since all possible cases have been covered, any one of these cases could be treated as the default case. However, for clarity it is preferable, in this example, to specify all three conditions explicitly, with the result that no default case need be specified.

Before writing the actual program we shall note that, despite the fact that the problem appears to be suitable for a **case** statement, the awkwardness in calculating a suitable value for use as a case selector might make the use of an **if** construct more appropriate. In this case a suitable design would be:

Data design

Purpose	Type	Name
A Local constant:		
A small value	**real**	small
B Local variables:		
Coefficients	**real**	a, b, c
Intermediate values	**real**	d, sqrt_d

Structure plan

---

1 Read coefficients

2 Calculate b^2-4ac, and store it in d

3 If d > small then
   3.1 Calculate and print two roots
   but if d > -small then
   3.2 Calculate and print two equal roots
   otherwise
   3.3 Print message "no roots"

In this situation, the order in which the tests are carried out *does* matter. First we test whether b^2-4ac is greater than small, since this is anticipated to be the most usual case. If it is not then it is zero (for our purpose) or negative. We now test whether it is greater than a very small negative value (-small). If it is, then, since it is also less than or equal to a very small positive value, it can be considered to be zero. If neither of these cases holds then there can be no roots.

We shall write programs in both the ways planned above.

3 Solution

(a) Using a **case** construct

```
program quadratic_by_case
! A program to solve a quadratic equation using a case
! statement to distinguish between the three cases

   ! Constant declaration
   real, parameter :: small=1e-6

   ! Variable declarations
   real :: a,b,c,d,sqrt_d,x1,x2
   integer :: selector

   ! Read coefficients
   print *,"Please type the three coefficients a, b and c"
   read *,a,b,c

   ! Calculate b**2-4*a*c and the resulting case selector
   d = b**2 - 4.0*a*c
   selector = d/small

   ! Calculate and print roots, if any
   select case (selector)
   case (1:)
      ! Two roots
      sqrt_d = sqrt(d)
      x1 = (-b+sqrt_d)/(a+a)
      x2 = (-b-sqrt_d)/(a+a)
      print *,"The equation has two roots: ",x1," and ",x2
```

```
   case (0)
      ! One root
      x1 = -b/(a+a)
      print *,"The equation has one root: ",x1

   case (:-1)
      ! no roots
      print *,"The equation has no real roots"

end select

end program quadratic_by_case
```

(b) Using an **if** construct

```
program quadratic_by_block_if
! A program to solve a quadratic equation using an if
! construct to distinguish between the three cases

   ! Constant declarations
   real, parameter :: small=1e-6

   ! Variable declarations
   real :: a,b,c,d,sqrt_d,x1,x2

   ! Read coefficients
   print *,"Please type the three coefficients a, b and c"
   read *,a,b,c

   ! Calculate b**2-4*a*c
   d = b**2 - 4.0*a*c

   ! Calculate and print roots, if any
   if (d>small) then
      ! Two roots
      sqrt_d = sqrt(d)
      x1 = (-b+sqrt_d)/(a+a)
      x2 = (-b-sqrt_d)/(a+a)
      print *,"The equation has two roots: ",x1," and ",x2

   else if (d>-small) then
      ! One root
      x1 = -b/(a+a)
      print *,"The equation has one root: ",x1

   else
      ! No roots
      print *,"The equation has no real roots"

   end if

end program quadratic_by_block_if
```

SELF-TEST EXERCISES 5.2

1   What is the main difference between a **case** construct and an **if** construct (apart from their syntax)?

2   What restrictions, if any, are there on the case expression in a **select case** statement?

3   What forms may a case selector take? Are there any restrictions on any of these forms?

4   What is meant by overflow on a computer?

5   In a multiple choice situation, when should you use a **case** construct, and when should you use an **if** construct?

SUMMARY

- The ability of a computer program to choose which one of two or more alternative sequences of statements to obey is a major factor in making computers such powerful tools.

- The **if** construct and the **case** construct provide the means for a program to select one of several alternative courses of action.

- An **if** construct uses a logical expression to determine the required course of action.

- A **case** construct uses an integer expression or a character expression to determine the required course of action.

- Relational operators are used to derive logical values from a comparison of two numeric expressions or two character expressions.

- Character expressions are compared by the relation operators using the F collating sequence.

- Logical operators are used to combine two logical values, and thus to allow more complex comparisons.

- Logical variables take one of two values: .**true**. or .**false**..

- F syntax introduced in Chapter 5:

  if construct

  ```
  if (logical_expression) then
      block_of_code
  else if (logical_expression) then
      block_of_code
      .
      .
      .
  ```

```
                              else
                                block_of_code
                              end if
```

case construct

```
                              select case (case_expression)
                              case (case_selector)
                                block_of_code

                                  .

                                  .

                                  .

                              case default
                                block_of_code
                              end select
```

Relational operators   `>, >=, <=, <, ==, /=`

Logical operators   `.and., .or., .eqv., .neqv., .not.`

PROGRAMMING EXERCISES

*5.1 Write a program which will request a number to be typed at the keyboard and will then inform the user whether the number is positive, negative or zero.

Now modify your program so that if it used an **if** construct it now uses a **case** construct, and vice versa.

5.2 Write a program to print out the truth tables for `.or.`, `.eqv.` and `.neqv.` in the same form as the following table for `.and.`

A	B	A.**and**.B
T	T	T
T	F	F
F	T	F
F	F	F

where the value for the third column is printed as the result of executing a logical expression (and *not* by working out the result and simply printing the table!).

5.3 The logical *NAND* operation is the equivalent of performing the `.and.` operation on two operands, followed by a `.not.` operation on the result. Thus

        a NAND b is the same as `.not.` (*a* `.and.` *b*)

Write a logical function to perform the *NAND* operation on its two logical arguments.

5.4 Write a program which reads a number between 1 and 6 from the keyboard and prints out the corresponding word: 'one', 'two', and so on. If a number outside this range is typed the program should print an appropriate message.

Now modify your program so that if it used an **if** construct it now uses a **case** construct, and vice versa.

5.5   Write a program that accepts a positive integer as its input and informs the user of all the following:

(a)   whether the number is odd or even
(b)   whether it is divisible by seven
(c)   whether it is a perfect square (that is, its square root is a whole number).

5.6   Write a program that will determine how much income tax a person pays, given the following basis for taxation:

Income	Tax rate
first £5000	0%
next £15 000	25%
everything over £20 000	32%

5.7   It is often difficult to compare the value of items priced in different currencies. Write a function to convert an amount in any one of the eight currencies shown below to an equivalent amount in one particular currency, which we shall call the *standard currency*. Use this function in a program which reads two amounts in any two of these currencies and calculates which is the lower.
    Use the following table to specify the currencies and their relationships:

$$1 \text{ UK pound} = 1.52 \text{ US dollars}$$
$$= 2.45 \text{ Deutschmarks}$$
$$= 8.60 \text{ French francs}$$
$$= 52.65 \text{ Belgian francs}$$
$$1 \text{ US dollar} = 103.95 \text{ Japanese yen}$$
$$= 1.40 \text{ Swiss francs}$$
$$= 1.31 \text{ Canadian dollars}$$

5.8   The current I drawn by an electrical appliance of power P watts from a supply voltage V volts is given by the formula:

$$I = \frac{P}{V} \text{ amps}$$

An electrical supplier stocks three types of cable, suitable for currents of up to 5 amps, 13 amps and 30 amps, respectively. Write a program that asks the user for the power rating and supply voltage of an appliance, and displays the most suitable cable, or a warning if the appliance cannot be safely used with any of the cables in stock.

*5.9   A firm produces digital watches and sells them for £15 each. However, it gives a discount for multiple orders as follows:

Number ordered	Discount
2−4	5%
5−9	10%
10−29	15%
30−99	20%
100−299	25%
300+	30%

Write a program to input the number of watches required and to print the gross cost, the discount (if any), and the net cost.

5.10   The brightness of a binary star varies as follows. At time $t = 0$ days Its magnitude is 2.5, and it stays at this level until $t = 0.9$ days. Its magnitude is then determined by the formula

$$3.355 - \log_e(1.352 + \cos(\pi(t - 0.9)/0.7))$$

until $t = 2.3$ days. Its magnitude is then 2.5 until $t = 4.4$ days, and it is then determined by the formula

$$3.598 - \log_e(1.998 + \cos(\pi(t - 4.4)/0.4))$$

until $t = 5.2$ days. It then remains at 2.5 until $t = 6.4$ days, after which the cycle repeats with a period of 6.4 days.

   Write a program which will input the value of the time t and print the brightness of the star at that time.

5.11   Write a program which reads three real numbers representing three distances. The program should use these as the arguments to a subroutine which will set three further arguments as follows:

triangle   is set *true* if the three distances could represent the sides of a triangle; that is, no number is greater than the sum of the other two numbers

isosceles   is set *true* if triangle is *true* and exactly two of the sides are of equal length; that is, an isosceles triangle

equilat   is set *true* if triangle is *true* and all three sides are of equal length; that is, an equilateral triangle

The program should then display an appropriate message.

5.12   Write a logical function which has two character arguments, and which returns the value *true* if the first argument contains the second, and *false* otherwise. Thus, if the function is called within, then

        within("Just testing","test")

is *true*, while

        within("Just testing","Test")

is *false*. (Hint: one of the intrinsic functions will help here.)
   Test your function with a driver program which inputs pairs of character strings from the keyboard, and uses the result of a function reference to cause one of the following forms of message to be displayed:

(a)   The phrase 'test' is contained within 'Just testing'
(b)   The phrase 'Test' is not contained within 'Just testing'

Repeating parts of your program

6.1	Program repetition and the do construct	6.3	More flexible loops
6.2	Count-controlled do loops	6.4	Giving names to do constructs
		6.5	Dealing with exceptional situations

A very large proportion of mathematical techniques rely on some form of iterative process, while the processing of most types of data requires the same, or similar, actions to be carried out repeatedly for each set of data. One of the most important of all programming concepts, therefore, is the ability to repeat sequences of statements either a predetermined number of times or until some condition is satisfied.

F has a very powerful, yet simple to use, facility for controlling the repetition of blocks of code, and this chapter explains how this facility can be used to control iterative processes as well as more simple repetitive tasks.

The use of repetitive techniques, however, often leads to situations in which it is required to end the repetition earlier than had been anticipated, and F contains a number of statements to assist in these exceptional cases. By their nature, however, such statements interrupt the normal flow of control through the program and must be used with care if they are not to lead to other problems.

6.1 Program repetition and the do construct

So far, most of our programs have taken rather longer to write than it would have taken to solve the problem by hand! This is because they have consisted of a series of instructions which are executed in sequence *once only*. In many cases the programs would be much more useful if they could be repeated with different sets of data. For instance, Example 3.1 converted a single Celsius temperature to Fahrenheit; it would be much more useful if it could convert a series of temperatures or create a table of equivalent temperatures.

Before we see how we can do this in F let us re-examine the structure plan for Example 3.1:

1	Read Celsius temperature
2	Calculate Fahrenheit equivalent
3	Print both temperatures

There are three main ways in which we could modify this plan to enable the program to convert more than one temperature. The first of these simply states that the process is to be repeated a predetermined number of times, say 10:

1	Repeat the following 10 times
1.1	Read Celsius temperature
1.2	Calculate Fahrenheit equivalent
1.3	Print both temperatures

A more flexible approach would be to ask the user how many temperatures are to be converted:

1	Read number of temperatures to be converted (*num*)
2	Repeat the following *num* times
2.1	Read Celsius temperature
2.2	Calculate Fahrenheit equivalent
2.3	Print both temperatures

A variation on this would be to ask after each conversion if any more conversions were required:

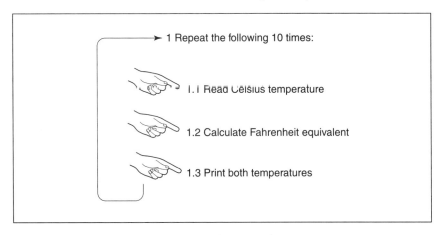

Figure 6.1   A program loop.

1   Repeat the following
   1.1   Read Celsius temperature
   1.2   Calculate Fahrenheit equivalent
   1.3   Print both temperatures
   1.4   Ask if any more conversions required
   1.5   If not then stop repeating this block of code

Yet another variation would be to produce a table of equivalent temperatures in the following way:

1   Repeat the following for each Celsius temperature from 0 to 100 in steps of 5
   1.1   Calculate Fahrenheit equivalent
   1.2   Print both temperatures

Clearly this will produce a table of equivalent temperatures at 5 °C intervals from 0 °C to 100 °C without the need for any data to be read at all.

The repetition of a block of statements a number of times is called a **loop** (see Figure 6.1) and is so important that F contains a special construct with exactly the features that are required. It is called a **do construct** and takes one of the following forms:

do *count=initial, final, inc*
   block of statements
end do

or

> **do** *count=initial, final*
>   *block of statements*
> **end do**

or simply

> **do**
>   *block of statements*
> **end do**

A loop created by use of a **do** construct is called a **do loop**.

6.2   Count-controlled do loops

The first statement of a **do** loop is called a **do statement** and, as we have already seen, takes one of the forms:

> **do** *count=initial, final, inc*
> **do** *count=initial, final*
> **do**

The first two alternatives define a **count-controlled do loop** in which an integer variable, known as the **do variable**, is used to determine how many times the block of statements which appears between the **do** statement and the **end do** statement is to be executed. We shall discuss the third alternative in Section 6.3.

Informally, we can consider the second, slightly simpler, form, in which *inc* is absent, as meaning that the loop is executed for *count* taking the value *initial* the first time that the loop is executed, *initial+1* the next time, and so on until it takes the value *final* on the last pass through the loop.

In a similar manner, we can informally consider the first form to mean that the loop is executed for *count* taking the value *initial* the first time that the loop is executed, *initial+inc* the next time, and so on, with the value of *count* being incremented by *inc* for each subsequent pass; in this case the final pass through the loop will be the one which would result in the *next* pass having a value of *count* greater than *final*.

The formal definition of this process is that when the **do** statement is executed an **iteration count** is first calculated using the formula

$$\mathbf{max}\,(\,(final-initial+inc)\,/inc,\,0)$$

do *statement*	*Iteration count*	do *variable values*
do i=1,10	10	1,2,3,4,5,6,7,8,9,10
do j=20,50,5	7	20,25,30,35,40,45,50
do p=7,19,4	4	7,11,15,19
do q=4,5,6	1	4
do r=6,5,4	0	(6)
do x=-20,20,6	7	-20,-14,-8,-2,4,10,16
do n=25,0,-5	6	25,20,15,10,5,0
do m=20,-20,-6	7	20,14,8,2,-4,-10,-16

Figure 6.2 Some examples of do statements and their effect.

and the loop executed that many times. On the first pass the value of *count* is *initial*, and on each subsequent pass its value is increased by *inc*. If *inc* is absent then its value is taken as 1. The effect of the **max** function is that if *final<initial* then the iteration count will be zero, and the statements in the loop will not be executed at all. Notice, however, that *count* will be set to the value *initial* since this assignment takes place before the iteration count is tested.

The do variable, *count*, must be a scalar integer variable, while *initial*, *final* and *inc* must be integer expressions. Moreover, the do variable may not be accessed by host or use association, nor may it be a dummy argument, the result variable of a function, or a pointer; pointers will be discussed in Chapter 14. Because of its special role, it is not permitted to alter the value of the do variable between the initial do statement and the corresponding **end do** statement by any means other than the automatic incrementation which is part of the do loop processing.

Figure 6.2 shows some examples of the iteration counts for a number of different do statements, and the values that will be taken by the do variable on each pass through the corresponding loops, and it can be seen that our informal description is perfectly adequate as long as care is taken over the last value.

It must always be remembered, however, that the way that a loop works is *not* by looking at the value of the do variable on each pass, but by calculating the iteration count and then decrementing this count by one after each pass is completed. One effect of this is that once the loop has been completed (that is, it has been executed the number of times defined by the iteration count) the do variable will have the value that it would have had on the *next* pass through the loop, if there had been one. Another effect is that if the values of *initial*, *final* and, if it is present, *inc* are such as to result in a zero or negative value for the iteration count then the loop is not obeyed at all, because the value of the iteration count is examined immediately before commencing execution of each pass.

▢ EXAMPLE 6.1 •

1 Problem

Write a program which first reads the number of people taking an exam. It should then read their marks (or scores) and print the highest and lowest marks, followed by the average mark for the class.

2 Analysis

This is a straightforward problem which will use a **do** loop to repeatedly read a mark and use it to update the sum of all the marks, the maximum mark so far, and the minimum mark so far.

Data design

Purpose	Type	Name
Number of people (data)	**integer**	number
Mark (data)	**integer**	mark
Max and min marks	**integer**	maximum, minimum
Sum of all marks	**integer**	total
Average of all marks	**real**	average
do variable	**integer**	i

Since the **do** variable is only used to control the loop we will follow normal programming (and mathematical) conventions and use the name i for this purpose.

Note also that **sum** cannot be used for the name of the variable in which the sum of the marks is stored because **sum** is a reserved word, see Appendix B (B.1); it is the name of an intrinsic procedure, see Appendix A (A.7). We shall, therefore, use the name total instead.

Structure plan

1 Initialize total to zero, maximum to a large negative value, minimum to a large positive value

2 Read number of examinees (number)

3 Repeat number times
    3.1 Read a mark
    3.2 Add it to cumulative sum
    3.3 If it is larger than maximum mark so far set maximum to this mark
    3.4 If it is less than minimum mark so far set minimum to this mark

4 Calculate average

5 Print maximum, minimum and average marks

One aspect that must be very carefully considered is the initialization of the three variables which will be used to save the accumulated sum of the marks, and the maximum and minimum marks. In this example the cumulative sum must obviously start at zero, but what about the maximum and minimum marks? What we shall do (at steps 3.3 and 3.4) is to compare each mark that is read with the highest (or lowest) read previously and store the higher (or lower) as the new maximum (or minimum). It follows, therefore, that initially the maximum must be set to a lower value than any actual marks can take, and the minimum must be set to a higher value than is possible as a mark. If marks are to lie, for example, in the range 0–100 then any values less than zero or greater than 100 could be used for the initial maximum and minimum, respectively. However, as the intrinsic function **huge** is a generic function we can use it to provide the largest possible integer value, which will be more than large enough!

3 Solution

```
program Examination_marks
! This program prints statistics about a set of exam results

    ! Variable declarations
    integer :: i,number,mark,maximum,minimum,total
    real :: average

    ! Initialize variables
    total=0
    maximum=-huge(1)
    minimum=huge(1)

    ! Read number of marks, and then the marks
    print *,"How many marks are there? "
    read *,number
    print *,"Please type ",number," marks, one per line: "

    ! Loop to read and process marks
    do i=1,number
       read *,mark
       ! On each pass, update sum, maximum and minimum
       total = total+mark
       if (mark>maximum) then
          maximum=mark
       else if (mark<minimum) then
          minimum=mark
       end if
    end do

    ! Calculate average mark and output results
    average = real(total)/number
    print *,"Highest mark is ",maximum
    print *,"Lowest mark is ",minimum
    print *,"Average mark is ",average

end program Examination_marks
```

Notice, incidentally, the line after the end of the loop in which the average is calculated. Since both `total` and `number` are integer the expression `total/number` would cause integer division to take place, which would not be appropriate when calculating an average. The intrinsic function **real** converts an integer to its real equivalent, thus forcing a real division to take place. Notice also that the marks must be typed one per line, since each is being read by a separate execution of the **read** statement, during a separate pass through the loop.

It must be emphasized that there are no restrictions on the types of statements that may appear in the block of statements which constitute the **range** of a **do** loop. In particular, other **do** loops may be **nested** within a **do** loop, although the whole of the nested loop must, of course, lie within the outer loop. Example 6.2 shows an example of a nested **do** loop.

EXAMPLE 6.2

1 Problem

Write a program to print a set of multiplication tables from 2 times up to 12 times, where each table should take the form:

x times 1 is x
x times 2 is $2x$
.
.
.
x times 12 is $12x$

2 Analysis

This is an extremely simple program to visualize:

Data design

Purpose	Type	Name
Two values in table	**integer**	i, j

Structure plan

```
1   Repeat for i from 2 to 12
    1.1  Print heading
    1.2  Repeat for j from 1 to 12
             1.2.1  Print "i times j is i*j"
```

```
                    .
                    .
                    .
        3 times      8 is      24
        3 times      9 is      27
        3 times     10 is      30
        3 times     11 is      33
        3 times     12 is      36

        4 times table
        4 times      1 is       4
        4 times      2 is       8
        4 times      3 is      12
        4 times      4 is      16
                    .
                    .
                    .
```

Figure 6.3 Part of the results produced by Multiplication_tables.

3 Solution

```
program Multiplication_tables
! A program to print multiplication tables from 2 to 12 times

    ! Variable declarations
    integer :: i,j

    ! Outer loop defines which 'times table'
    do i=2,12
        print *," "
        print *,i," times table"
        do j=1,12
            print *,i," times",j," is ",i*j
        end do

    end do

end program Multiplication_tables
```

Figure 6.3 shows part of the results produced by running this program.

The next example shows an extension of Example 6.2.

EXAMPLE 6.3

1 Problem

Write a program to print a set of multiplication tables from 2 times up to 12 times, where each table only goes up to 'x times x is x^2'.

2 Analysis

This is a very similar problem to that in Example 6.2, except that the final value of the **do** variable in the inner loop will be different each time it is entered to print a new table. This is more like the situations in which counting loops are normally used, in which some or all of the controlling values are variables, rather than constants:

Data design

Purpose	Type	Name
Two values in table	**integer**	i, j

Structure plan

1 Repeat for i from 2 to 12
   1.1 Print heading
   1.2 Repeat for j from 1 to i
      1.2.1 Print "i times j is i*j"

```
                    .
                    .
                    .
          3 times table
          3 times      1 is      3
          3 times      2 is      6
          3 times      3 is      9

          4 times table
          4 times      1 is      4
          4 times      2 is      8
          4 times      3 is     12
          4 times      4 is     16

          5 times table
          5 times      1 is      5
          5 times      2 is     10
                    .
                    .
                    .
```

Figure 6.4 Part of the results produced by the revised `Multiplication_tables`.

3 Solution

```
program Multiplication_tables
! A program to print multiplication tables from 2 to 12 times

   ! Variable declarations
   integer :: i,j

   ! Outer loop defines which 'times table'
   do i=2,12
      print *," "
      print *,i," times table"
      do j=1,i
         print *,i," times",j," is ",i*j
      end do
   end do
end program Multiplication_tables
```

Figure 6.4 shows part of the results produced by running this program.

SELF-TEST EXERCISES 6.1

1   What is a do loop?

2   What restrictions (if any) are there on the statements which can appear in a do loop?

3   What is a do variable? What restrictions (if any) are there on the ways in which it is used?

4   What is the iteration count? How is it calculated?

5   How many times will each of the loops controlled by the following do statements be executed?

   (a)   do i=-5,5
   (b)   do j=1,12,2
   (c)   do k=17,15,-1
   (d)   do l=17,15
   (e)   do m=100,350,15
   (f)   do n=10,10,10

6   What is the value of the do variable after normal termination of a do loop?

7   What will be printed by the following programs?

   (a)   ```
program loop_test_1
   integer :: i,j,k,l,m,n
   i=1
   j=2
```
```

```
        k=4
        1=8
        m=0
        n=0
        do i=j,k,l
           k=i
           do j=1,m,k
              n=j
              do k=1,n
                 do l=i,k
                    m=k*l
                 end do
              end do
           end do
        end do
        print *,i,j,k,l,m,n
     end program loop_test_1

(b)  program loop_test_2
        integer :: i,j,k,l,m,n
        i=1
        j=2
        k=4
        1=8
        m=0
        n=0
        do i=j,k,l
           k=-i
           do j=1,m,k
              n=j
              do k=1,n
                 do l=i,k
                    m=k*l
                 end do
              end do
           end do
        end do
        print *,i,j,k,l,m,n
     end program loop_test_2
```

6.3   More flexible loops

The examples that have been discussed up to now have all used the **do** variable to control the number of times that the loop is executed. However, there are a great many situations in which it is not possible to determine this number in advance, for example in a mathematical calculation which is to be terminated when some value becomes less than a predetermined value. In this situation we can use the third form of the **do** statement mentioned in Section 6.1, together with a new statement, **exit**, which causes a **transfer of control** to the statement immediately following the **end do** statement. Since this statement will, when executed, cause all the remaining statements in the loop to be omitted, it follows that it is *always* used in association with one of the control statements discussed in Chapter 5.

Thus, for example, the following loop will continue to be executed until the value of term becomes less than the value of small:

```
do
   .
   .
   .
   if (term < small) then
      exit
   end if
   .
   .
   .
end do
! After obeying the exit statement execution continues
! from the next statement (that is, after this comment)
   .
   .
   .
```

Using this form of the **do** statement does incur the risk that the condition for obeying the **exit** statement may never occur. In that situation the loop will become what is known as an **infinite loop**, and will continue executing until the program is terminated by some external means such as exceeding a time limit or switching off the computer! In order to avoid this possibility, we strongly recommend that this non-counting form of the **do** statement is only used when the programmer can be absolutely certain that there is no possible situation in which the terminating condition will not occur. Since such a 100% certainty is rare, we recommend that such loops should normally contain a **fail-safe mechanism** in which a **do** variable is used to limit the number of repetitions to a predefined maximum. Thus, the simple example above should be extended as follows:

```
do count=1,max_iterations
   .
   .
   .
   if (term < epsilon) then
      exit
   end if
   .
   .
   .
end do
! After obeying the exit statement, or after obeying
! the loop max_iterations times, execution continues
! from the next statement (that is, after this comment)
   .
   .
   .
```

One additional advantage of this approach is that the number of times that the loop was executed is always available after an exit has been made from the loop. If this exit was made because the maximum number of iterations had been carried out then the rules given in Section 6.2 tell us that the count will have the value that it would have had on the *next* iteration, max_iterations+1 in the example above. It is therefore trivially easy to determine whether the loop ended because the terminating condition was met, or whether it had carried out the maximum number of allowable iterations without achieving the terminating condition which, in some cases, may indicate that there is an error in the logic of the program. Example 6.4 illustrates this situation, and also shows how using a **do** variable can bring other benefits to loops that do not apparently require one.

☐ EXAMPLE 6.4

1 Problem

A set of examination marks, or scores, for a class is provided, consisting of three items for each examinee: a number which will be used to identify the student, the mark, and a code (F=female, M=male) to indicate the sex of the examinee. The data is terminated by a record containing anything other than F or M for the sex code. It is required to calculate the average mark for the class, and also the average mark for the boys and girls separately.

2 Analysis

The program for this problem needs to produce a sum of all the marks and to count the examinees in order to calculate the class average, and also needs to do the same for the boys and the girls separately. We can use the **do** variable to count the total number of examinees. Our design is therefore as follows:

Data design

Purpose	Type	Name
A Constants:		
Codes for male/female	`character`	`male, female`
Max no. of marks	`integer`	`max_pupils`
B Variables:		
Student number (data)	`integer`	`student_num`
Exam mark (data)	`integer`	`mark`
Sex code (data)	`character`	`code`
Number of each sex	`integer`	`num_boys, num_girls`
Total marks and by sex	`integer`	`total_marks, marks_boys, marks_girls`
do variable	`integer`	`num_pupils`

Structure plan

1. Initialize counts and sums of marks for boys and girls
2. Repeat the following for num_pupils up to max_pupils
   - 2.1 Read next set of data
   - 2.2 Select case on code
     - code is female (=F)
       - 2.2.1 Update sum of girls' marks
       - 2.2.2 Add 1 to count of girls
     - code is male (=M)
       - 2.2.3 Update sum of boys' marks
       - 2.2.4 Add 1 to count of boys
     - code is anything else
       - 2.2.5 Exit from loop
3. Calculate sum of all marks
4. Calculate and print required averages

Notice that we have defined two constants (male and female) to represent the relevant codes (M and F). This is not strictly necessary, especially in such a simple program as this, but it makes the program easier to follow and is good programming practice. Notice also that, since the three averages are not required except at the very end for printing, it is not necessary to declare any variables in which to store them. The only remaining difficulty is deciding on the maximum number of times we shall allow the loop to be repeated. Since the problem refers to a school class a maximum of 100 should be more than sufficient.

3 Solution

```
program Examination_statistics
! This program calculates some simple examination statistics

    ! Constant and variable declarations
    character(len=1), parameter :: male="M",female="F"
    integer, parameter :: max_pupils=100
    character(len=1) :: code
    integer :: student_num,mark,num_boys,num_girls,num_pupils, &
               marks_boys,marks_girls,total_marks

    ! Initialize variables
    num_boys=0
    num_girls=0
    total_marks=0
    marks_boys=0
    marks_girls=0
    ! Read at most max_pupils sets of data
    print *,"Type up to ",max_pupils," exam results."
```

```fortran
      print *,"Each result must consist of the student number," , &
              " the mark, and a code"
      print *,"The code is F for a female student and M for a male"
      print *,"Data should be ended by a zero student number "
      print *,"and mark, followed by any code other than M or F"

do num_pupils=1,max_pupils
   ! Read next mark and code
   read *,student_num,mark,code

   ! Select appropriate action
   select case (code)

   ! Female pupil
   case (female)
      num_girls = num_girls+1
      marks_girls = marks_girls+mark

   ! Male pupil
   case (male)
      num_boys = num_boys+1
      marks_boys = marks_boys+mark

   ! End of data
   case default
      exit
   end select
end do

! Adjust num_pupils to correct number
num_pupils = num_pupils-1

! Calculate total marks
total_marks = marks_boys+marks_girls

! Calculate and print averages
if (num_pupils == 0) then
   print *,"There was no data!"
else
   ! Deal with no terminator case
   if (num_pupils == max_pupils) then
      print *,max_pupils," sets of data read without a", &
              " terminating record"
      print *,"Results are based on these pupils only"
   end if
   print *,"There are ",num_pupils," pupils. Their average", &
           " mark is ",real(total_marks)/num_pupils
   if (num_girls > 0) then
      print *,"There are ",num_girls," girls. Their average", &
              " mark is",real(marks_girls)/num_girls
   else
      print *,"There are no girls in the class"
   end if
   if (num_boys > 0) then
      print *,"There are ",num_boys," boys. Their average", &
              " mark is ",real(marks_boys)/num_boys
```

```
      else
          print *,"There are no boys in the class"
      end if
  end if

end program Examination_statistics
```

Notice that at the exit from the loop we subtracted 1 from num_pupils. We should briefly examine why this was done. There are two cases to consider — either the special terminator data is read, or the maximum number of marks are read with no terminator. Let us look at each of these cases separately.

Assume that the class has 35 pupils. On the first pass through the loop num_pupils is 1 and the first pupil's mark is read. On the next pass num_pupils is 2 and the second pupil's mark is read. On the 35th pass num_pupils is 35 and the 35th, and last, pupil's mark is read. On the next pass num_pupils is therefore 36 and the terminator data is read. On exit from the loop num_pupils is thus one more than the number of pupils.

If no terminator is read, then after max_pupils marks have been read the loop will finish. In Section 6.2 we saw that if a **do** loop completes its specified number of iterations then the **do** variable will have the value it would have had on the next iteration. In our case this will be max_pupils+1 — one more than the number of pupils whose marks were read.

In both cases, therefore, the number of pupils is num_pupils-1. Nevertheless, it is appropriate to print a warning message in the latter case to draw attention to the possible omission of some marks if the fail-safe action of the **do** loop came into effect before data for all the pupils had been processed.

There are two points to note about the calculation and printing of the averages. The first is that a test is made to see if there are any pupils in each category (so as to avoid dividing by zero) and a suitable message printed if there are not. The second concerns the calculation of the average. The program has assumed that the marks are integers, and of course the number of pupils is an integer. An expression such as total_marks/num_pupils would therefore lead to an integer division being carried out and the average given in integer form (truncated, not even rounded!). This is not suitable and so steps must be taken to force a real division.

One approach would be for the sums of marks to be kept in real variables. The ensuing expressions would be mixed-mode and would therefore be evaluated using real arithmetic. Alternatively, the sums can be converted to real form once they have been calculated. The easiest way to do this is to use the intrinsic function **real** which simply produces as its result the real equivalent of its argument, thus once again leading to a mixed-mode expression. It is not necessary also to make the divisor real as the compiler will take care of this anyway when processing the mixed-mode expression.

It is also worth noting that this program breaks the guideline that we gave earlier for the length of a single program unit. An appropriate way of breaking this program into smaller units would be to deal with the input of the data in a subroutine which would return the various totals via its arguments. It is frequently a good idea to deal with data input in a separate procedure as this can simplify testing, by enabling the input procedure to be tested independently of the anaysis of that data, and vice versa. We shall leave the rewriting of this program in this way as an exercise for the student.

The program written for Example 6.4 failed to deal with one important situation, namely what happens if the data supplied is invalid, such as a mark which is outside an acceptable range (for example, 0–100). An error with more serious consequences might be an incorrectly typed (sex) code, leading to premature exit from the loop before all the data had been read. Defining a termination code, say X, and treating anything other than M, F or X would deal with this, if we knew what to do once we had detected the error.

The difficulty, therefore, is not how to detect these situations, but what to do when we have done so. Here we can make use of another new statement, **cycle**. This is very similar to the **exit** statement except that instead of transferring control to the statement *after* the **end do** statement it transfers control back to the start of the loop in exactly the same way as if it, in fact, transferred control *to* the **end do** statement. This means, of course, that the iteration count is decreased by one and the **do** variable, if any, incremented appropriately, before a test is made to determine whether another pass through the loop is required. Although the use of a **cycle** statement will, therefore, avoid incorrectly updating the various counts and sums it will lead to the wrong figure for the total number of pupils. This is easily dealt with, however, by using the sum of the number of boys and the number of girls for this purpose.

An additional case can therefore be added to the **case** construct in the **do** loop to deal with an invalid code:

```
! End of data
case ("X")
   exit
! Invalid code
case default
   print *,"Invalid code - please re-enter data"
   cycle
end select
```

In a similar manner, the two cases which deal with the boys and girls could be modified to deal with invalid marks, using either a nested **case** construct or a block **if** construct:

```
! Female pupil
case (female)
select case (mark)
```

```
case (0:100)
   num_girls = num_girls+1
   marks_girls = marks_girls+mark
case default
   print *,"Invalid mark - please re-enter data"
   cycle
end select
```

or

```
! Male pupil
case (male)
   if (mark>=0 .and. mark<=100) then
      num_boys = num_boys+1
      marks_boys = marks_boys+mark
   else
      print *,"Invalid mark - please re-enter data"
      cycle
   end if
```

A possibly more serious problem is that this approach will reduce the maximum number of iterations of the loop, and hence the maximum number of sets of data that can be read. Since this maximum number is meant to be a fail-safe value, and should never even be closely approached, one solution might be, for example, to use twice the value of max_pupils as the maximum loop count.

6.4 Giving names to do constructs

The examples that we have given above of the use of the **exit** and **cycle** statements should cause no confusion regarding the next statement to be executed. However, the situation with nested loops is less clear. For example, to which statement will the **exit** statement in Figure 6.5 transfer control?

The rule for determining this is that the **exit** statement transfers control to the statement immediately following the **end do** statement belonging to the innermost **do** construct that contains the **exit** statement. Thus, in the code fragment shown in Figure 6.5 the **exit** statement will transfer control to the first executable statement following the second **end do**. This is usually what is wanted, but there will be occasions when it is required to exit from *all* of the enclosing loops, or even from more than the immediately enclosing loop, but not from all of them. A similar rule applies to the **cycle** statement.

For this reason, it is possible to give a name to a **do** construct by preceding the **do** statement by a name, which follows the normal F rules for names and is separated from the **do** by a colon, and by following the corresponding **end do** by the same name:

```
                    do
                     .
                     .
                     .
                    do
                     .
                     .
                     .
                      do
                       .
                       .
                       .
                       exit
                       .
                       .
                       .
                      do
                       .
                       .
                       .
                      end do
                        ! This one (1)?
                       .
                       .
                       .
                     end do
                      ! or this one (2)?
                       .
                       .
                       .
                   end do
                    ! or this one (3)?
                     .
                     .
                     .
                  end do
                   ! or this one (4)?
```

Figure 6.5 Exiting from a nested do loop.

block_name: **do**
                    .
                    .
                    .
                 end do *block_name*

Note that if the initial **do** statement is named in this way then it is mandatory for
the same name to appear on the corresponding **end do** statement, and vice versa.

The **cycle** and **exit** statements may also be followed by the name of an
enclosing **do** construct, in which case control is transferred to, or after,
respectively, the **end do** statement having the same name:

```
outer:   do
             .
             .
             .
inner:       do
                 .
                 .
                 .
                 select case (n)
                 case (1)
                     exit outer
                 case (2)
                     exit inner
                 case (3)
                     cycle outer
                 case (4)
                       cycle inner
                 end select
                 .
                 .
                 .
             end do inner
             .
             .
             .
         end do outer
```

Note that, in this example, the references to inner in two of the case selections are redundant, since that is where they would transfer control to in any case, if no construct name was specified. However, it helps to ensure that there is no doubt in the (human) reader's mind about what is intended.

6.5 Dealing with exceptional situations

All of the control constructs that we have discussed so far have shared one common feature, namely that the construct is entered at only one place (the **if**, **select case** or **do** statement) and is only left at one place (the corresponding **end if**, **end select** or **end do** statement). This is good programming practice, as it enables the programmer to control the logic of the program much more easily than would otherwise be the case. Nevertheless, there are occasionally situations in which this is either inconvenient, or makes programming very difficult, and two additional statements exist to help us in these exceptional situations.

The first of these statements simply terminates execution without the need to find a way of reaching the **end** statement of the main program unit. It consists of the word

stop

and causes execution of the program to be terminated immediately. Typically, this statement will be used when the program has detected some error from which it is not possible to recover.

A closely related statement causes a return from a procedure without the need to find a way of reaching the **end** statement of the procedure. It consists of the word

```
return
```

and causes execution of the procedure to be terminated immediately and control transferred back to the program unit which called or referenced the procedure.

SELF-TEST EXERCISES 6.2

1   What is the difference between a count-controlled **do** loop and other **do** loops? When should the count-controlled form be used?

2   What is an infinite loop? How can it be avoided?

3   What is an **exit** statement used for? What is the effect of executing one?

4   What is a **cycle** statement used for? What is the effect of executing one?

5   What is the purpose of naming a **do** construct? What form does the name take?

6   What does a **return** statement do? When should it be used?

7   What does a **stop** statement do? When should it be used?

SUMMARY

- A sequence of statements which are repeated is called a loop.

- The **do** construct provides the means for controlling the repetition of statements within a loop.

- In a count-controlled **do** loop the number of times the loop is repeated is determined by the value of the iteration count, which is calculated before the first iteration.

- In a count-controlled **do** loop the **do** variable is incremented on each pass through the loop.

- It is not permitted for a program to alter the value of a **do** variable during the execution of a loop, other than through the automatic incrementation process.

- On normal completion of a count-controlled **do** loop the **do** variable will have the value that it would have had on the next pass through the loop, had there been one.

- **do** constructs may be named.

- Execution of an **exit** statement in a loop causes the next statement to be executed to be the one immediately after the **end do** statement of the innermost loop surrounding the **exit** statement, unless the **exit** statement is named, in which case it will be the statement immediately after the **end do** statement having the same name.

- Execution of a **cycle** statement in a loop causes the next statement to be executed to be as though execution had continued with the **end do** statement of the innermost loop surrounding the **cycle** statement, unless the **cycle** statement is named, in which case it will be as though execution had continued with the **end do** statement having the same name.

- The **stop** statement causes an immediate termination of the execution of a program.

- The **return** statement causes an immediate termination of the execution of a procedure.

- F syntax introduced in Chapter 6

do construct	**do** *do_var=initial, final, inc*
	.
	.
	.
	end do
	do *do_var=initial, final*
	.
	.
	.
	end do
	do
	.
	.
	.
	end do
Loop control statements	**exit**
	cycle
Named **do** construct statements	*do_block_name:* **do** *do_var=initial, final, inc*
	do_block_name: **do** *do_var=initial, final*
	do_block_name: **do**
	end do *do_block_name*
	exit *do_block_name*
	cycle *do_block_name*

stop statement	stop
return statement	return

PROGRAMMING EXERCISES

*6.1   Find out how many characters there are in the character set used by your computer; it will probably be 64, 128 or 256. Then write a program to print a list of all the characters in the order of their internal representation (that is, from 0 to 63, 0 to 127, 0 to 255, and so on, as appropriate).

6.2   The international standard paper sizes, such as A4, are defined by the formula

$$2^{1/4-n/2} \times 2^{-1/4-n/2} \text{ metres}$$

where n is the number following the letter A. Write a program to print the international paper sizes in both centimetres and inches (1 inch $=$ 2.54 cm) from A0 down to A6.

6.3   A lever is the simplest machine known to man, and provides a means of lifting loads that would otherwise be too heavy.
   In Figure 6.6, the relationship between the human *Effort* and the actual *Load* is given by the equation

$$Effort \times d_1 = Load \times d_2$$

Write a program that will produce a table of the effort required to raise a load of 2000 kg when the distance of the load from the fulcrum (d_2) is fixed at 2 metres. The program should print out the effort required for levers of lengths differing in steps of 2 metres between two limits (minimum and maximum), which should be input from the keyboard.
   Use the results produced by the program to determine the shortest lever that could be used to raise the load if the maximum effort is equivalent to 25 kg.

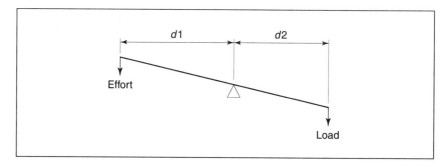

Figure 6.6   Diagram for Exercise 6.3.

6.4   Mrs Smith is moving from Cambridge, Massachusetts, to Cambridge, England, and wants to be able to convert her recipes from American measures to British measures using the following conversions:

US	British
1 cup flour	4 oz flour
1 cup butter	8 oz butter
1 cup sugar	6 oz sugar
1 cup confectioner's sugar	4 oz icing sugar
1 cup milk	8 fl oz milk *or* 0.4 pints milk

Write a program which will read lines of the recipe, each containing the quantity, followed by a space, then the units (which may be ignored), followed by another space and then the name of the ingredient. Your program should convert this data into the number of ounces of the ingredient (or the number of pints in the case of milk), and print the revised list of ingredients. Any lines not containing one of the above ingredients should be left unaltered.

6.5   A sheet metal stamping company buys its metal in rectangular sheets of various sizes − 2, 5 or 10 metres long by 2, 4 or 6 metres wide. It has an order for a number of circular discs of a given diameter (less than one metre) and wishes to waste as little metal as possible.

Write a subroutine which takes the number and diameter of discs required and the size of the sheet, and then calculates the number of sheets of this size required and the percentage of the metal wasted.

Use this subroutine in a program which requests the number and diameter of discs required, and then cycles through all the available sheet sizes automatically and prints the relevant information for each sheet size so that the user can decide which sheet size will produce least wastage.

Finally, modify the program so that the program decides which sheet size to use, based on the least amount of metal wasted.

6.6   The yield of a chemical reaction after time t seconds at a temperature of $T\,°C$ is given by $1 - e^{-kt}$, where $k = e^{-q}$ and $q = 2000/(T + 273.16)$.

Write a program which allows the user to enter the temperature, and which then prints out the yield for each minute until it reaches 95%.

6.7   A simple method of determining whether an integer is a prime number is to try dividing it by all integers less than or equal to its square root, and checking to see whether there is any remainder.

Write a function which will determine whether a number is a prime using this method, and return the value of the first factor found, or one if it is a prime.

Test this function by including it in a simple test program that reads a number from the keyboard and either informs the user that it is a prime or displays one of its factors.

Finally, modify your program to print a list of primes less than 32 768.

6.8   The length, L, of a bar of metal at a temperature T is given by the equation

$$L = L_0 + ETL_0$$

where the temperature is measured in degrees Celsius, L_0 is the length of the bar at $0\,°C$, and E is the coefficient of expansion.

Write a program that will produce a set of tables showing the lengths of various bars of metal at various temperatures, assuming that each bar is exactly one metre long at $20\,°C$. For each type of metal the program should read the coefficient of expansion and the range of temperatures to be covered.

6.9   The Fibonacci Sequence of numbers is one in which each number is the sum of the previous two. It starts

$$1, 1, 2, 3, 5, 8, \ldots \text{ etc.}$$

Write a program to generate the first 36 members of the sequence.

The ratio of consecutive numbers in the series $(1/1, 2/1, 3/2, 5/3, \ldots)$ tends to the so-called Golden Ratio

$$\frac{\sqrt{5}+1}{2}$$

Modify your program so as to determine how far along the sequence you have to go until the difference between the Golden Ratio and that of consecutive numbers is less than 10^{-6}.

6.10   The value of $\sin x$ (where x is in radians) can be expressed by the infinite series

$$\sin x = x - \frac{x^3}{3!} + \frac{x^5}{5!} - \frac{x^7}{7!} + \frac{x^9}{9!} - \cdots$$

where $n! = n \times (n-1) \times (n-2) \times \cdots \times 2 \times 1$

Write a function that uses the above series to calculate $\sin x$ to an accuracy that is provided as an argument to the function. (Hint: $\sin(x + 2\pi) = \sin x$ and we may therefore use a value of x which lies between $-\pi$ and $+\pi$ to reduce the size of the terms of the expression. Once this has been done every term after the second is smaller than its predecessor, and so it is easy to know when to stop the calculation.)

Use this function in a program that calculates the sine of an angle (in degrees) input from the keyboard to an accuracy which is also input from the keyboard.

Finally, modify this program so that it produces a table showing the value of $\sin x$ for x taking values from $0°$ to $90°$ in steps of $1°$, where $360° = 2\pi$ radians. Each line should show the angle (in degrees), the value of $\sin x$ calculated by the program, and the value of $\sin x$ calculated by use of the intrinsic function $\mathtt{sin}$.

*6.11   The pressure inside a can of carbonated drink is given by the expression

$$0.00105 \times T^2 + 0.0042 \times T + 1.352 \text{ atm}$$

where $T\,°C$ is the temperature of the drink. When the pressure exceeds 3.2 atm the can will explode.

Write a program to print the pressure inside the can for the temperature rising in one-degree steps from $15\,°C$ until the can explodes.

6.12   In a simple simulation of a lunar lander, the downward speed V at time $T + 1$
seconds is related to the speed at time T by the expression:

$$V_{T+1} = V_T + 5 - F$$

where the number 5 allows for the acceleration due to gravity, and F is the number of
units of fuel burnt in that second. The height H of the lander above the moon's surface
changes according to the equation

$$H_{T+1} = H_T - V_T$$

Write a program to implement this simple simulation. The lander starts at a height of
200 units, and the user may choose every second how much fuel to burn (between 0 and
10 units). The user should try to achieve a soft landing (which means having a speed of
less than 10 units when H first drops below zero) using the minimum total quantity of fuel.

Your program should print an appropriate message when the lander reaches ground
level!

An introduction to arrays   7

7.1 The array concept
7.2 Array declarations
7.3 Array constants and initial values
7.4 Input and output with arrays
7.5 Using arrays and array elements in expressions and assignments

7.6 Using intrinsic procedures with arrays
7.7 Sub-arrays
7.8 Arrays and procedures
7.9 Array-valued functions

In scientific and engineering computing, it is very common to need to manipulate ordered sets of values, such as vectors and matrices. There is also a common requirement in many applications to repeat the same sequence of operations on successive sets of data.

In order to handle both of these requirements, F provides extensive facilities for grouping a set of items of the same type into an array which can be operated on either as an object in its own right or by reference to each of its individual elements.

This chapter explains the principles of F array processing features. These are considerably more powerful than those of any other programming language, with the exception of Fortran 90 and Fortran 95, and include the construction of array-valued constants, the input and output of arrays, the use of arrays as arguments to procedures, and the returning of an array as the result of a function. For introductory purposes, the description in this chapter is restricted to one-dimensional arrays; multidimensional arrays will be discussed in Chapter 13.

7.1 The array concept

In all that we have said so far, and in all the programs we have written, we have used one name to refer to one location in the computer's memory. However, there are a great many situations when we would like to repeat a sequence of operations on a set of related entities, either by repeating the statements in a loop and having the computer use different variables for each iteration or by simply referring to a complete set and instructing the computer to carry out the same operations on each item in the set.

One way to do this would be to have a group, or **array**, of locations in the memory, all of which are identified by the same name but with an index, or **subscript**, to identify individual locations. Figure 7.1 illustrates this concept, using the same types of boxes as were originally used in Chapter 1 to introduce the concept of named memory locations.

In this example, the whole set of n boxes is called A, but within the set we can identify individual boxes by their position within the complete set. Mathematicians are familiar with this concept and refer to an ordered set like this as the *vector* A and to the individual elements as A_1, A_2, ... A_n.

In F we call such an ordered set of related variables, which have the same name and type, an **array**, and we refer to the individual items within the array as **array elements**. In F, we cannot use the exact mathematical notation for a subscript to identify these elements (although we do borrow the name); instead we follow the name of the array by an identifying *integer* value enclosed in parentheses:

```
A(1), A(2), ..., A(n)
```

More precisely, an array element is defined by writing the name of the array followed by a subscript, where the subscript consists of an integer expression (known as the **subscript expression**) enclosed in parentheses. Thus, if x, y and z

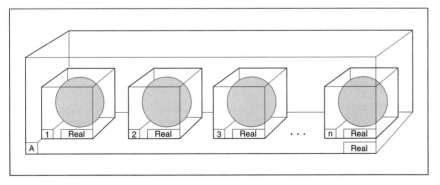

Figure 7.1 An array of memory locations.

are arrays, of any type, and i, j and k are integer variables, then the following are all valid ways of writing an array element:

```
x(10)
y(i+4)
z(3*i+max(i, j, k))
x(int(y(i)*z(j)+x(k)))
```

Notice that function references are allowed as part of the subscript expression, as are array elements (including elements of the same array).

An array element is a scalar object and may be used as such. Thus, if **x** is an array, we may write such statements as

```
print *, x(5)
x(1) = x(2) + x(4) + 1
```

which, respectively, displays the value stored in x(5) and sets the value stored in x(1) to be the sum of the values stored in x(2) and x(4) incremented by 1.

7.2 Array declarations

Up to this point, all the variables that we have used have been **scalar variables**, and the declaration of any such variable has caused the compiler to allocate an appropriate storage unit to contain its values. When we declare an **array variable**, however, the compiler will need to allocate several storage units, and the form of the declaration must be modified to provide information about the size of the array and, hence, the number of storage units that will be required. The way to do this uses a **dimension attribute** applied to the variable name.

Let us consider, for example, a situation in which we require three real arrays, each containing 50 elements. The easiest way to declare these is as follows:

```
real, dimension(50) :: a, b, c
```

This informs the compiler that each of the three variables specified is an array having 50 elements.

As with character variables of differing lengths, you must write a separate declaration for arrays of different sizes:

```
real, dimension(50) :: a, b, c, z
real, dimension(20) :: x, y
```

By default, the subscripts will start at 1; but if we wish the subscripts to have a different range of values then we may, instead, provide the lower bound and the upper bound explicitly, separated by a colon:

```
real, dimension(11:60) :: a, b, c
real, dimension(-20:-1) :: x
real, dimension(-9:10) :: y
real, dimension(0:49) :: z
```

Notice that both negative and zero subscript values are allowed and that the *sizes* of the six arrays declared in this declaration are identical to those declared in the earlier declaration; only their *bounds* are different.

At this point we must mention five technical terms that are of great importance when discussing arrays in F.

- Although all the arrays that have been discussed so far have only had one subscript, F permits up to seven subscripts, each of which relates to one **dimension** of the array. For each dimension there are two bounds which define the range of values that are permitted for the corresponding subscript: the lower bound and the upper bound.
- The number of permissible subscripts for a particular array is called its **rank**.
- The **extent** of a dimension is the number of elements in that dimension and is equal to the difference between the upper and lower bounds for that dimension plus one.
- The **size** of an array is the total number of elements which make up the array; this is, of course, the same as the extent for a rank-one array.
- Finally, the **shape** of an array is determined by its rank and the extent of each dimension; it is possible to store the shape of any array in a rank-one array where the value of each element represents the extent of the corresponding dimension.

In this chapter, we shall only consider rank-one arrays, since this is sufficient for many purposes and will enable us to appreciate many of the particular features of F's array processing facilities without undue complexity. Chapter 13 will then build on this knowledge and experience to discuss the full range of array features.

An array declared in the way shown in the above examples is called an **explicit-shape array** because its bounds are declared explicitly. As we shall see later in this chapter and in Chapter 13, there are other forms of array which do not need explicit declaration of the bounds. For the present, we shall also assume that the bounds are constant, although Section 7.8 will discuss situations in which this restriction may be lifted.

An array element reference and a function reference look the same. An F compiler, just like a human reader, can only tell which is intended by looking at the specification statements and seeing whether or not a dimension attribute has been specified. This can be illustrated by considering the program extract shown in Figure 7.2.

```
program array_or_function
    use functions                      ! module containing
                                       ! function second
    real, dimension(10) :: first    ! first is an array
    integer :: i
    real :: first_i, second_i
      .
      .
      .
    first_i = first(i)                 ! array reference
    second_i = second(i)               ! second must be a function
                                       ! reference since it is not
                                       ! an array
      .
      .
      .
end program array_or_function
```

Figure 7.2 Array and function references.

It can clearly be seen that the two assignment statements have exactly the same form in every way and that the only way of determining what is intended is by noting that the declaration for first includes a dimension attribute, while second, in module functions, is that of a function. The first executable statement therefore assigns the value of the array element first(i) to the variable first_i. The second executable statement refers to a real function second, and the compiler will insert the appropriate instructions to transfer control to the function second with the actual argument being specified by i; the value returned by the function will then be assigned to the variable second_i. It is not unknown, therefore, for missing array declarations to result in misleading compilation error messages about missing functions!

7.3 Array constants and initial values

Before we examine how to use arrays, we must establish how an array constant is defined. Since an array consists of a number of array elements, it is necessary to provide values for each of these elements by means of an **array constructor**. In its simplest form, an array constructor consists of a list of values enclosed between special delimiters, the first of which consists of the two characters (/ and the second of the two characters /):

(/ *value_1*, *value_2*, ... /)

If arr is an integer array of size 10, its elements could therefore be set to the values 1, 2,..., 10 by the following statement:

```
arr = (/ 1, 2, 3, 4, 5, 6, 7, 8, 9, 10 /)
```

This is perfectly satisfactory for a small array, but what if the array had been 500 elements in size? Many tedious lines of code would be required.

To deal with this situation, as well as for the general, and very common, situation in which an array constant is required that has some regular pattern, we can use an **implied do**. This is a special syntax, used with arrays in a number of situations, that uses the **do** loop-counting control mechanism to step through a set of values and/or array elements. It takes the general form

(*value_list*, *implied_do_control*)

where the *implied_do_control* takes exactly the same structure as the **do** variable control specification in a **do** statement. Thus, the assignment statement shown above for the array `arr` could also be written in the more compact and less error-prone form

```
arr = (/ (i, i = 1, 10) /)
```

The index in an implied **do**, in this case `i`, must not be used for any other purpose, except as an implied **do** control in another **array constructor** in the same procedure or main program. Thus, for example, `i` could not also be a dummy argument in the procedure that contained the array constructor.

An implied **do** element does not have to appear on its own and may be freely mixed with single constants, or other implied **do** elements, in the overall list of values which make up an array constructor. For example, the following array constructor defines the sequence of 50 values which are all zero except for the first, which takes the value -1, and the last, which takes the value 1:

```
(/ -1, (0, i = 2, 49), 1 /)
```

Note that the values of `i` in this example are only used for counting and that using the values from 2 to 49 is simply to emphasize to the human reader which array elements will have zero values. We could equally well have written

```
(/ -1, (0, i = 1, 48), 1 /)
```

or even, somewhat confusingly,

```
(/ -1, (0, i = 37, 84), 1 /)
```

Although the above examples only have a single item in the list of values controlled by the implied **do**, there may be as many as necessary, including other (nested) implied **do** elements. Thus, the following array constructor defines a sequence of 100 values which are all zero apart from every tenth value, which takes the value of its position in the list:

```
(/ ((0, i = 1, 9), 10*j, j = 1, 10) /)
```

The list of values in an array constructor must contain exactly the same number of values as the size of the array to which it is being assigned (in either an assignment statement or in an initial value assignment in an array declaration statement):

```
integer, dimension(50), save :: an_array = (/(0, i = 1, 50) /)
integer, dimension(100), save :: another_array = &
        (/ ((0, i = 1, 9), 10*j, j = 1, 10) /)
```

The first of these two initial value declarations can, in fact, be further simplified, as we shall see in Section 7.5 when we examine the way in which arrays are used in expressions and assignment statements.

7.4   Input and output with arrays

An essential feature of using arrays in our programs is the ability to input data to arrays and output results from arrays. There are three possibilities here, depending upon whether we wish to refer to individual array elements, to complete arrays, or to a subset of array elements.

- Array elements are treated in just the same way as scalar variables and so need no further discussion.
- An array name may appear in an input or output list, in which case it refers to the whole array.
- The issue of input and output of sub-arrays is discussed in Section 7.7.

Thus, for example, the following statement would output the five elements of the array p followed by the third and fourth elements of the array q and the whole of the array r:

```
real, dimension(5) :: p, q
integer, dimension(4) :: r
print *, p, q(3), q(4), r
```

In a similar way

```
integer, dimension(5) :: value
read *, value
```

would read five values from the input stream.

7.5 Using arrays and array elements in expressions and assignments

An array element can be used anywhere that a scalar variable can be used. In exactly the same way as a scalar variable, it identifies a unique location in the memory to which a value can be assigned or input and whose value may be used in an expression or output list, and so on. The great advantage is that, by altering the value of the array element's subscript, it can be made to refer to a different location.

The use of array variables within a loop, therefore, greatly increases the power and flexibility of a program. This can be seen in Figure 7.3, where a short loop enables up to 100 sets of survey data to be input and stored for subsequent analysis in a way which is not otherwise possible. Here, we have used the ability to employ individual elements of an array as scalars in a **read** statement and an **if** test.

For most other programming languages, this is the only way that arrays can be used in most types of operations; that is, element by element. However, F enables an array to be treated as a single *object* in its own right, in much the same way as a scalar object. We have already used this fact when, for example,

```
program survey_analysis
    integer, parameter :: max_people = 100
    character(len=12), dimension(max_people) :: first_name, last_name
    character(len=1), dimension(max_people) :: middle_initial
    integer, dimension(max_people) :: age
    character(len=1), dimension(max_people) :: sex        ! m/f
    character(len=11), dimension(max_people) :: social_security
    real, dimension(max_people) :: height, weight
    integer :: i
      .
      .
      .
    do i = 1, max_people
        read *, first_name(i), middle_initial(i), last_name(i) &
                age(i), sex(i), social_security(i), height(i), weight(i)
        if (age(i)) < 0) then
            exit                    ! age < 0 ends data
        end do
    end do
    ! Process data in the eight arrays
      .
      .
      .
end program survey_analysis
```

Figure 7.3 Inputting data to an array.

we assigned an array constant to an array variable in the previous section with a statement of the form

array_name = (/ *list of values* /)

and we should now establish the rules for working with whole arrays.

- Two arrays are **conformable** if they have the same shape.
- A scalar, including a constant, is conformable with any array.
- All intrinsic operations are defined between two conformable objects.

When two conformable arrays are the operands in an intrinsic operation, then the operation is carried out on an element-by-element basis. Thus the following code fragment will result in the arrays a and b having identical values:

```
 .
 .
 .
real, dimension(20) :: a, b, c, d
 .
 .
 .
a = c*d                    ! Whole-array style manipulation

do i = 1, 20               ! Element-by-element style
   b(i) = c(i)*d(i)        ! array manipulation
end do
 .
 .
 .
```

It is immediately obvious that the first style is much easier to read than the second, as well as avoiding the need for the extraneous **do** loop variable, i.

An important point to notice is that the rule is that the *shapes* of two arrays must be the same for them to be conformable. This means that the arrays must have the same rank (that is, the same number of dimensions) and the same extent in each dimension. It does *not* mean that the range of the subscripts need be the same. The importance of this can be seen from Figure 7.4, which shows exactly the same program fragment as that above, except that the bounds of the four arrays are all different, even though their extents are the same. Here the advantage of the F array processing capability becomes really apparent!

The rule that a scalar is conformable with any array means that we can write statements such as

```
array_1 = 10*array_2
```

```
        .
        .
        .
   real :: a(1:20), b(0:19), c(10:29), d(-9, 10)
        .
        .
        .
   a = c*d                        ! Whole-array style manipulation
   do i = 1, 20                   ! Element-by-element style
       b(i-1) = c(i+9)*d(i-10)
   end do
        .
        .
        .
```

Figure 7.4 F array processing.

which will cause every element of the array array_1, whatever its shape, to be assigned a value 10 times the corresponding element of the array array_2, as long as its shape is the same as that of array_1. Furthermore, it means that

```
real, dimension(1000) :: arr
arr = 1.0
```

will set every element of the array arr to one. This would work regardless of the rank or size of arr. It also means that all the elements of an array in a module or a procedure may be initialized in exactly the same way as for scalar variables:

```
real, save :: a = 0.0, b = 0.0
real, dimension(50), save :: c = 0.0, d = 10.0
```

sets all 50 elements of 0 to the value zero and all 50 elements of d to the value 10. Arrays, like scalars, may not be initialized in a main program.

7.6   Using intrinsic procedures with arrays

The F intrinsic procedure library, as we have already seen, contains a considerable number of functions and subroutines which are of great importance in many programming situations. A particularly valuable aspect of the F array processing facilities is that of **elemental intrinsic procedures**, whereby arrays may be used as arguments to many of the intrinsic procedures in just the same way scalars are. If an elemental function has an array as an argument then the result of the function reference will be an array with the same shape as the argument. Thus, if array_1 and array_2 are conformable arrays, the statement

```
array_1 = sin(array_2)
```

assigns the sine of each element of the array array_2 to each corresponding element of the array array_1. Where an intrinsic function has more than one argument then they must all be conformable, as we would expect. Thus the statement

```
arr_max = max(100.0, a, b, c, d, e)
```

will assign to the elements of arr_max the maximum value of the corresponding elements of the arrays a, b, c, d and e, or 100.0 if that is greater, as long as the six arrays arr_max, a, b, c, d and e are all conformable; the scalar value 100.0 is, of course, conformable with any array.

All of the intrinsic functions which it might be reasonable to expect to work with either array-valued or scalar arguments are elemental so that, in particular, the wide range of mathematical functions may be applied equally to array or scalar arguments.

There are also two elemental intrinsic subroutines which can take either scalar or array arguments: **mvbits** and **random_number**. The list of all intrinsic procedures in Appendix A indicates, among other things, which ones are elemental.

There are a number of intrinsic functions especially meant for dealing with arrays. We mention here the functions that are probably the most commonly used. A complete list is given in Appendix A. If arr is a rank-one array:

maxval(arr) The maximum value of the elements of arr

maxloc(arr) The location of the first element of arr having the value **maxval**(arr)

minval(arr) The minimum value of the elements of arr

minloc(arr) The location of the first element of arr having the value **minval**(arr)

size(arr) The number of elements in arr

sum(arr) The sum of the elements of arr.

7.7 Sub-arrays

We have seen how to use whole arrays in expressions. However, it is frequently useful to be able to define a sub-array, consisting of a selection of elements of an array, and to then manipulate this sub-array in the same way that a whole array can be manipulated.

In F, **array sections** can be extracted from a parent array in a rectangular grid (that is, with regular spacing) using **subscript triplet** notation, or in a completely general manner using **vector subscript** notation. In either case, the resulting array section is itself an array and can (with three exceptions that we note later in this section) be used in the same way as an array – for example, in whole-array expressions, passed as an argument to a procedure, or used in an input or output statement.

We have already defined an array element as

array_name (*i*)

where *array_name* is the name of a variable with the dimension attribute (that is, an array) and *i* is an integer expression.

If *i* is replaced by what is called a subscript triplet or by a vector subscript, then, instead of defining an array element, we have defined an array section. In this chapter we will describe only rank-one array sections, deferring higher-rank array sections until Chapter 13.

We will describe subscript triplets first, because they are conceptually simpler than vector subscripts.

A subscript triplet takes the following form:

subscript_1 : *subscript_2* : *stride*

or one of the simpler forms

subscript_1 : *subscript_2*
subscript_1 :
subscript_1 : : *stride*
: *subscript_2*
: *subscript_2* : *stride*
: : *stride*
:

where *subscript_1*, *subscript_2* and *stride* are all scalar integer expressions. A subscript triplet is interpreted as defining an ordered set of subscripts that start at *subscript_1*, that end on or before *subscript_2*, and that have a separation of *stride* between consecutive subscripts. The value of *stride* must not be zero. Note the similarity to a **do** loop.

If *subscript_1* is omitted, it defaults to the lower index bound for the dimension; if *subscript_2* is omitted, it defaults to the upper index bound for the dimension; and if *stride* is omitted, it defaults to the value 1. Note that the first colon must always be included, even if the first subscript is not specified.

Thus, if the array `arr` is declared as

```
real, dimension(10) :: arr
```

then `2:8:3` is a subscript triplet that defines a set of integers that starts at 2 and proceeds in increments of 3 until 8 is reached. Consequently, the set of subscripts is 2, 5 and 8, and `arr(2:8:3)` is an *array* whose elements are `arr(2)`, `arr(5)` and `arr(8)`, in that order.

If the stride is negative, then the subscript order is reversed with the result that `arr(8:2:-3)` is an array whose elements are `arr(8)`, `arr(5)` and `arr(2)`, in that order.

Some other sub-arrays of `arr` are as follows:

`arr(1:10)`   is a rank-one real array containing all the elements of `arr`; it is, in fact, identical to `arr`.

`arr(3:5)`   is a rank-one real array containing the elements `arr(3)`, `arr(4)` and `arr(5)`.

`arr(:9)`   is a rank-one real array containing the elements `arr(1)`, `arr(2)`, ..., `arr(9)`.

`arr(::4)`   is a rank-one real array containing the elements `arr(1)`, `arr(5)` and `arr(9)`.

`arr(:)`   is a rank-one real array containing all the elements of `arr`; it is the same as `arr`.

A simple example of how array sections can simplify code can be seen if we consider how to print the first three elements of an array `work` of size n. Rather than write:

```
print *, work(1), work(2), work(3)
```

we can write the simpler

```
print *, work(1:3)
```

As a more complicated example, suppose we want to print the even-numbered elements of array `work`. Rather than write:

```
integer :: i
do i = 2, n, 2
   print *, work(i)
end do
```

we write the simpler

```
print *, work(2 :: 2)
```

This defines an array section consisting of the even-numbered elements of `work`. As we said earlier, an array section is an array and can, therefore, be printed out as such. This version is both easier to read and less error-prone than the first method. There is one difference between the output produced by the two sets of code. The first piece of code will put out each number on a separate line. The second piece of code will put several numbers on each line of output. Chapter 9 will describe how to gain complete control over the output format.

In a similar manner, array sections can be used for input.

Since they are arrays, array sections may be used in array expressions. For example:

```
integer, dimension(10) :: a
integer, dimension(3)  :: b
  .
  .
  .
b = a(4:6)                  ! Same effect as b(1) = a(4),
                            ! b(2) = a(5), b(3) = a(6)
a(1:3) = 0                  ! Set a(1), a(2), a(3) to 0
a(1 :: 2) = 1               ! Set the odd-numbered elements
                            ! of a to 1
a(1 :: 2) = a(2 :: 2)+1     ! Make each odd-numbered element of
                            ! a equal to one more than the next
                            ! even-numbered element
```

Array sections, since they are arrays, can be used in conjunction with the intrinsic procedures of F. Thus:

```
real, dimension(4) :: a
  .
  .
  .
print *, sum(a(2:4))
print *, sum(a(1:4:2)
```

prints out the value of a(2)+a(3)+a(4) and then the value of a(1)+a(3).

It should be clear that array sections give considerable flexibility in working with regularly shaped sub-arrays.

A good example of the use of array sections defined by subscript triplets will be found in Section 17.5 in the procedure for solving a system of linear equations by Gaussian elimination.

We shall now turn from subscript triplets to vector subscripts. These are used when a non-regular pattern of indices is needed and, hence, a subscript triplet would not work.

A vector subscript is an integer array expression of rank 1, each of whose elements has the value of a subscript in the array section being defined. Thus, if arr1 is an array of size 7 and the rank-one integer array v has a size of 4 and the elements of v have the values 3, 7, 4 and 5, then the array section arr(v) is a rank-one array of size 4 whose elements are, in order, arr(3), arr(7), arr(4) and arr(5). The array v is the vector subscript.

Note that, in the preceding example, the size of `arr(v)` was equal to the size of `v` and the size of `arr` was irrelevant in determining the size of the array section `arr(v)`. Hence, a vector subscript can be used to construct a vector from an array that is longer than that array; for example, if the arrays `p` and `u` are declared as follows:

```
logical, dimension(3) :: p
integer, dimension(5) :: u = (/3, 2, 2, 3, 1/)
```

then `p(u)` is a rank-one logical array of size 5 whose elements are, in order, `p(3)`, `p(2)`, `p(2)`, `p(3)` and `p(1)`. Notice that some of the elements of `p` are repeated.

This is an example of a **many-one array section**. That is, it is an array section with a vector subscript having at least two elements with the same value. A many-one array section must not appear on the left-hand side of an assignment statement, nor may it appear in the input item list of a **read** statement. In both cases, such uses would be ambiguous and are, therefore, forbidden.

We stated earlier that there are three ways in which an array section differs in usage from an array. The second difference is that individual elements of an array section cannot be specified by the index notation. Thus:

```
real, dimension(5) :: a
a(1) = 3.4                    ! Allowed
a(1:3)(1) = 3.4               ! Not allowed
```

The third difference is that an array section with a vector subscript may not be an actual argument if the corresponding dummy argument is modified in any way.

SELF-TEST EXERCISES 7.1

1   What is an array? What is an array element?

2   What is the difference between an array variable and a scalar variable?

3   What is the dimension attribute? How is an array specification written?

4   What (if any) are the constraints on a subscript expression?

5   What are the rank, extent, size and shape of an array?

6   Write declarations for suitable arrays in which to store the following sets of data:

(a) The information collected in an (anonymous) survey of people attending a meeting of Gamblers Anonymous. Each person is asked how much they earn each week, how many times they go gambling each week, how much they lose on average each week gambling, what is their largest single win, what is their largest single loss, and how many weeks they have been a gambling addict.

(b) The data collected in an experiment in which a sample piece of material is fixed in a device which then allows it to be repeatedly hit by a mass of variable weight (but fixed for each experiment) dropped from a specified height until the sample fractures. The mass, height, and number of blows are recorded.

(c) The heights above a base plane at various points on the surface of a three-dimensional model.

(d) The temperature at 6 a.m., noon, 6 p.m., and midnight on each day of a year and the number of days on which the noon temperature was below $-10\,^{\circ}$C, $-9\,^{\circ}$C, $-8\,^{\circ}$C, ... $+30\,^{\circ}$C, and over 30 $^{\circ}$C.

7   What is an array constructor?

8   What is an implied do? How is one used with an array constructor?

9   What are the differences (if any) between input and output to and from arrays and input and output to and from scalars?

10   What is meant by the statement that two arrays are conformable?

11   What is the particular importance of conformable objects?

12   How can arrays be used in expressions?

13   What is an elemental procedure?

14   What are the two kinds of array sections, and how are they specified?

15   How are arrays and array sections similar? How are they different?

7.8   Arrays and procedures

So far, all the array declarations that we have used have been for explicit-shape arrays (that is, they have had constant bounds). However, the requirement for constant bounds would cause a great many difficulties when working with procedures, as can readily be seen by examining the situation that arises if we wish to use an array as an argument to a procedure: how can we declare the dummy argument array in a procedure when we do not know the details about the size or shape of the actual arguments that may be used in references to the procedure?

As we saw in Chapter 4, one of the most important aspects of the argument-passing mechanism is that a procedure does not need to know the details of the calling program unit and that program unit, in turn, does not need to know anything about the procedure except the information about its arguments which form part of the procedure's interface. It would make no sense at all for the bounds of a dummy argument array to be fixed and for all arrays passed as actual arguments to be required to have the same bounds!

The solution to this problem is the **assumed-shape array**. In fact, if an array is a procedure dummy argument, it *must* be declared in the procedure as an assumed-shape array!

An assumed-shape array is a dummy argument array whose shape, as its name implies, is not known but which *assumes* the same shape as that of any actual argument that becomes associated with it. The shape of an array, as we have already seen, is defined by its rank and the extent of each of its dimensions, but since we are only concerned with rank-one arrays at present, we need only consider the extent.

The array specification for an assumed-shape array can take one of two forms:

(*lower_bound*:)

or, simply

(:)

The second form is equivalent to the first with a lower bound equal to 1. In both cases the upper bound will only be established on entry to the procedure and will be whatever value is necessary to ensure that the extent of the dummy array is the same as that of the actual array argument.

How is an actual array argument associated with a dummy array argument? It is as if the actual argument array exactly overlays the dummy argument array. The easiest case to understand is that in which both arrays default to having their subscripts start at 1. In this case, if a is the actual argument and x is the corresponding dummy argument, then x(1) corresponds to a(1), x(2) to a(2), and so on.

Now consider a more complicated case. If, for example, a is declared as

```
real, dimension(b:40) :: a
```

and x is declared as

```
real, dimension(d:) :: x
```

then x(d) will correspond to a(b), x(d+1) to a(b+1), x(d+2) to a(b+2), and so on.

Some examples will make this clearer. Let us consider a subroutine which starts with the following statements:

```
subroutine array_example(dummy_array_1, dummy_array_2)
   real, intent(inout), dimension(:) :: dummy_array_1,   &
                                        dummy_array_2
   .
   .
   .
```

If this subroutine is called from a program unit that contains the declarations

```
real, dimension(10:30) :: a, b
```

by the statement

```
call array_example(a, b)
```

then the two dummy argument arrays will both have lower bounds of 1 and upper bounds of 21. If the subroutine is subsequently called from another program unit (or even from the same one) that contains the declarations

```
real :: p(-5:5), q(100)
```

by the statement

```
call array_example(p, q)
```

then on this occasion both dummy argument arrays will have a lower bound of 1, while the upper bound of dummy_array_1 will be 11 and the upper bound of dummy_array_2 will be 100.

Now suppose we use two array sections defined as

```
integer, dimension(3) :: section = /(5, 1, 2, 5)/
real, dimension(9) :: a
call array_example(a(4:8:2), a(section))
```

In this case, dummy_array_1 will have three elements a(4), a(6) and a(8), while dummy_array_2 will have four elements a(5), a(1), a(2), a(5). These elements will, inside subroutine array_example, be referred to, respectively, as dummy_argument_1(1), dummy_argument_1(2), dummy_argument_1(3), dummy_argument_2(1), dummy_argument_2(2), dummy_argument_2(3), dummy_argument_2(4). Observe that, because the second argument is an array section with a vector subscript, subroutine array_example must not change dummy_argument_2.

For many purposes this may be all that is needed, but there will also be occasions when it will be necessary for a procedure to know the size of the actual arrays associated with its dummy argument arrays. To resolve this problem, the intrinsic function **size** is available to provide the necessary information. Thus, for a rank-one array argument arr, **size**(arr) returns the number of elements in arr.

■ **EXAMPLE 7.1** •

1 Problem

Write a subroutine that will sort a set of names into alphabetic order.

2 Analysis

The need to sort data into numerical or alphabetic order is a very common one in many computer programs and is a need which is easily satisfied with the tools we now have at our disposal. Sorting is a subject on which much research has been carried out over many years; however, for our purposes a simple general-purpose sorting method will suffice. If small amounts of data are to be sorted, it is perfectly adequate; but, if large amounts are to be sorted, one of many specialized sorting methods, such as Quicksort or Pigeon Sort, should be used.

 We shall investigate the method of **straight selection** because it is reasonably efficient and easy to understand. Essentially the method involves searching through all the items to be sorted and finding the one which is to go at the head of the sorted list. This is then *exchanged* with the item currently at the head of the list. The process is then repeated, starting immediately after the item just sorted into its correct place, and so on. Each time, one more item is moved to its correct place. Figure 7.5 shows the progress of such a sort, in which eight numbers are sorted so that the lowest is on the left and the highest is on the right. The two numbers to be exchanged at each stage are circled, although it should be noted that the fourth exchange does not actually take place because the number at the head is already in the correct place.

 This is quite a simple method to code in F; but, before planning the logic, we must first consider how the data to be sorted will be provided and how the sorted list of names will be returned. The major question to be decided is whether the original data is to be sorted or whether a copy is to be made and

Initial order	⑦	①	8	4	6	3	5	2
After first exchange	1	⑦	8	4	6	3	5	②
After second exchange	1	2	⑧	4	6	③	5	7
After third exchange	1	2	3	④	6	8	5	7
After fourth exchange	1	2	3	4	⑥	8	⑤	7
After fifth exchange	1	2	3	4	5	⑧	⑥	7
After sixth exchange	1	2	3	4	5	6	⑧	⑦
After seventh exchange	1	2	3	4	5	6	7	8

Figure 7.5 Sorting by straight selection.

sorted so that the data is also available in its original order. A third possibility, which we shall briefly discuss later, is to leave the original data unchanged but to provide a sorted **index array** which can be used to access the data in alphabetic order. For this example, however, we shall simply reorder the original data.

We can now prepare our data design and structure plan:

Data design

Purpose	Type	Name
A Argument		
Array of names to be sorted	`character(len = *)`	name
	`dimension(:)`	
B Local variables		
Number of items to be sorted	`integer`	number
First name on this pass	`character`	first
	`(len = len(name))`	
Subscript of first name	`integer`	index
Temp for swapping names	`character`	temp
	`(len = len(name))`	
`do` variables	`integer`	i, j

Structure plan

> subroutine alpha_sort(*name*)
>
> **1** Repeat for *i* from 1 to *number*−1
>   **1.1** Save *i* and *name(i)* as current 'earliest' name
>   **1.2** Repeat for *j* from *i*+1 to *number*
>   **1.2.1** If *name(j)* is 'earlier' than current 'earliest' store it and its index
>   **1.3** If step 1.2 found an 'earlier' name swap with *name(i)*

3 **Solution**

```
subroutine alpha_sort(name)

! A subroutine to sort the contents of the array name into
! alphabetic order

    ! Dummy argument
    character(len = *), dimension(:), intent(inout) :: name

    ! Local variables
    character(len = len(name)) :: first, temp
    integer :: number, save_index, i, j

    ! Set number to the number of names to be sorted
    number = size(name)
```

```
                   ! Loop to sort number-1 names into order
                  do i = 1, number-1

                      ! Initialize earliest so far to be the first in this pass
                      first = name(i)
                      save_index = i

                      ! Search remaining (unsorted items) for earliest one
                      do j = i+1, number
                          if (name(j) < first) then    ! An earlier one has been
                              first = name(j)           ! found, so save it
                              save_index = j            ! and its position
                          end if
                      end do

                      if (save_index /= i) then    ! An earlier name was found
                          temp = name(i)           ! so exchange it with the
                          name(i) = name(save_index)  ! "head" of the list
                          name(save_index) = temp
                      end if
                  end do
              end subroutine alpha_sort
```

Notice, in particular, that this subroutine can be written without any knowledge of either the length of the character strings being sorted, because the array name is declared with assumed length, or the number of items being sorted, because it is an assumed-shape array.

The length *is* needed for the declaration of the two temporary character variables first, which is used to store the current earliest name on each iteration, and temp, which is used for temporary storage when two names are being exchanged. It is obtained by use of the intrinsic function **len** applied to the dummy array name.

The number of items to be sorted is required in order to control how many times the two loops are to be obeyed and is obtained by use of the intrinsic function **size**. It should be noted, however, that this will return the number of *elements* in the actual argument associated with the dummy argument array name; if the actual argument array is not full with data to be sorted, then the value returned will not, in fact, be the number of items to be sorted. An easy way around this problem would be to provide the number of items to be sorted as a second argument. However, a more elegant way is to use an **array section** (see Section 7.7) in the calling program unit to pass only that part of the array which is to be sorted.

Finally, note that the array argument name is declared to have **intent(inout)**, since the array must be defined with a set of values before entry to the subroutine (because otherwise there would be nothing to sort!), but it is also used to return the sorted array. If it was required to keep the original order as well having a sorted array, then a slightly modified version of the subroutine might have two array arguments, one with **intent(in)** and the other with **intent(out)**.

One (usually minor) problem with an assumed-shape array is that only the shape of the dummy argument array is known and, hence, the extent in each dimension but not the bounds of the actual argument array. Thus, if we have a subroutine

```
subroutine array_bounds(a, t)
   integer, dimension(:), intent(in) :: a
   integer, intent(out) :: t
   .
   .
   .
end subroutine array_bounds
```

and the calling program unit contains the statements

```
integer, dimension(3:5) :: x
integer :: y
call array_bounds(x, y)
```

then, inside subroutine array_bounds, we will only know that the size of the actual argument x is 3. We will not know that its upper and lower bounds are 3 and 5. As far as subroutine array_bounds is concerned, a will have a (default) lower bound of 1. Thus a(1) will correspond to x(3), a(2) to x(4), and a(3) to x(5).

Frequently this does not matter, but if the bounds are required, then we may supply the bounds through other arguments or by **use** association.

In the simplest case, this might take the form:

```
subroutine explicit(a, b, lower, upper)
   integer, intent(in) :: lower, upper
   real, dimension(lower:), intent(in) :: a, b
   .
   .
   .
```

Alternatively, the relevant values can be provided by means of a module:

```
subroutine explicit_2(a, b)
   use database      ! This module includes the lower
                     ! and upper bounds of a large group
                     ! of arrays, including a and b.
                     ! These bounds are called lower and upper
   real, dimension(lower:), intent(in) :: a, b
   .
   .
   .
```

Whether the array bounds were supplied by a dummy argument or by **use** association from a module, notice that the upper bound cannot be used in the declaration of array dummy arguments since they must be declared as assumed-shape. Knowing the actual lower bound and the size of the array (via the intrinsic function **size**) fixes the upper bound. Hence, it is actually unnecessary to give the upper bound explicitly as a dummy argument.

Whatever the means by which they are made available, or values from which they may be calculated are made available, the bounds are determined using the values that the relevant variables had *on entry to the procedure*, and any subsequent change in the values from which array bounds were initially calculated has no effect on the array bounds. There are two intrinsic functions **lbound** and **ubound** that return, respectively, the lower and upper bounds of an array. Thus, for a rank-one array arr:

- **lbound**(arr, 1) returns the lower bound of arr
- **ubound**(arr, 1) returns the upper bound of arr.

The second argument for **lbound** and **ubound** specifies that the value returned is to be for the first dimension (the only one for a rank-one array) and must be present, even though its value is always 1 for a rank-one array.

In Example 7.1 we created two temporary variables in which to save information during (part of) the execution of the procedure but whose values were not required outside the procedure. Where there is a requirement for scalar variables of this type, there is no problem; but if a local array is required for the duration of the execution of the procedure, how do we know what size to declare it? It cannot be declared as an assumed-shape array, since these must be dummy argument arrays. However, there is a special form of explicit-shape array, known as an **automatic array**, which is provided for this precise purpose.

An automatic array is an explicit-shape array, in a procedure, which is *not* a dummy argument array and whose bounds, or the information necessary to calculate the bounds, are made available through dummy arguments or by **use** association from a module. An automatic array is declared, therefore, in a very similar manner to an explicit-shape array, except that it has non-constant bounds.

We illustrate the concept with the following code fragment. Suppose we want to write a subroutine that takes two input arrays (of size n) and returns an array of size n containing the n largest elements in the two arrays. One way we could choose to accomplish this is to have an automatic array of size $2n$, copy the two arrays into it, sort the $2n$ elements of the automatic array, and then copy the n largest elements of the automatic array into the output array. Thus, we could write:

```
subroutine largest(a, b, c)
    real, dimension(:), intent(in) :: a, b    ! two input arrays
    real, dimension(:), intent(out)::c        ! the output array
    real, dimension(2*size(a))::x             ! double-size
                                              ! automatic array
    x(1:size(a)) = a          ! copy a into the first half of x
    x(size(a)+1:) = b         ! copy b into the second half of x
    call sort(x)              ! sort into ascending order
    c = x(size(a)+1:)         ! copy n largest elements
end subroutine largest
```

Note the use of array sections and array expressions to move the contents of the arrays. Note also that we have postulated the existence of a subroutine called sort that will sort a real array into ascending order.

An automatic object conceptually comes into existence when the procedure defining it is entered and ceases to exist when a **return** or **end** statement is executed. In between, automatic objects can be used in the same way as any other variable. Thus, they can be passed as actual arguments:

```
subroutine auto(x, s)
   real, dimension(:), intent(in) :: x
   real, intent(out) :: s
   real, dimension(3*size(x)) :: a   ! automatic object
                             ! fill a with values
   .
   .
   .
   call next(a, s)         ! use a as an actual argument
end subroutine auto
subroutine next(u, v)
   real, dimension(:), intent(in) :: u
   real, intent(out) :: v
                        ! calculate the value of v
   .
   .
   .
end subroutine next
```

7.9   Array-valued functions

We have met the ways in which arrays can be passed to procedures as arguments and in which a subroutine can return information by means of an array. However, it is often convenient for a function to return its result in the form of an array of values rather than as a single scalar value. Such a function is called an **array-valued function**.

An array-valued function is defined in a similar way to a function whose result is a scalar. The declaration of the type of the result must specify the appropriate dimension attribute, unless it is a pointer – see Section 14.6:

```
function name(.......) result(arr)
   real, dimension(dim) :: arr
   .
   .
   .
end function name
```

The type declaration for *arr* must use an explicit shape for the dimension attribute. The size of the array result is calculated on entry to the function.

Subsequent changes to any of the variables involved in calculating the size of the array will not cause the size of the array to change. Thus, for example, the following function will return an array which is twice the size of its dummy argument `in_arr`:

```
function double(in_arr, ...) result(out_arr)
   real, dimension(:), intent(in) :: in_arr
   real, dimension (2*size(in_arr) :: out_arr
                            ! fill out_arr with values
   .
   .
   .
end function double
```

It is, of course, the responsibility of the program unit which references this function to ensure that the function result is used as a real array that is twice the size of `in_arr`.

Let us now consider a trivial subroutine that simply adds two arrays together, returning the result through a third dummy argument array:

```
subroutine trivial_sub(a, b, c)
   real, dimension(:), intent(in) :: a, b
   real, dimension(:), intent(out) :: c
   a = b+c
end subroutine trivial_sub
```

In this situation, all three dummy argument arrays are assumed-shape arrays and the result will be returned through the dummy argument c, whose shape (that is, whose extent in this rank-one case) is determined by the corresponding actual argument.

It would seem more natural to write this procedure as a function, but although we can still have two assumed-shape dummy arguments, what about the result array variable, which cannot have an assumed shape? The answer in this case is that, since it must be conformable with the two dummy arguments in order for the assignment to take place, we can use their shape in the declaration of the result variable:

```
function trivial_fun(x, y) result(sumxy)
   real, dimension(:), intent(in) :: x, y
   real, dimension(size(x)) :: sumxy
   sumxy = x+y
end function trivial_fun
```

Note that, since all three arrays (x, y and the result array variable sumxy) must be conformable they must all have the same size, and it does not matter which of the two dummy arguments is referred to in the array specification for sumxy. Of course, if this function was being written for other than demonstration purposes, it would be advisable to check that the two arrays were conformable by means of a statement such as

```
if (size(x) /= size(y)) then
    ! Take appropriate error action
    .
    .
    .
end if
```

In most cases, where an array-valued function of varying size or shape is required, there will be at least one dummy argument that can be used to provide the information necessary for the declaration of the result array variable. It is possible, however, that the information needed could come from a module.

An array-valued function can be used in expressions in the same way as an array can. Thus, if `f1` and `f2` are functions, each having a single dummy argument of type real, that return arrays of size 10, it would be legitimate to write code of the form

```
real :: x
real, dimension(10) :: a
    .                       ! set value of x
a = f1(x)*f2(x)
    .
    .
    .
```

Here, `f1(x)` and `f2(x)` are arrays of size 10 that are multiplied together element by element. The result is then stored in a.

■ EXAMPLE 7.2 ●

1 Problem

Write a function that takes two real arrays as its arguments and returns an array in which each element is the maximum of the two corresponding elements in the input arrays.

2 Analysis

This is a very simple exercise that requires only a very simple data design and structure plan. The only complication would be if the two input arrays were (erroneously) of different sizes; however, we shall ignore this and assume that they have identical size:

Data design

Purpose	Type	Name
A Dummy arguments		
Input arrays	**real**(:)	array 1, array 2
B Local variables		
Result variable	**real**(:)	max_array

Structure plan

> **1** Repeat for each element of input array_1
> **1.1** max_array(i) = maximum of array_1(i) and array_2(i).

3 **Solution**

```
function max_array(array_1, array_2) result(maximum_array)

! This function returns the maximum of two arrays on an
! element-by-element basis

   ! Dummy arguments
   real, dimension(:), intent(in) :: array_1, array_2

   ! Result variable
   real, dimension(size(array_1)) :: maximum_array

   ! Use the elemental intrinsic max to compare elements
   maximum_array = max(array_1, array_2)
end function max_array
```

Note that the use of the intrinsic function **max** in an elemental fashion avoids the need to write a loop of the form

```
do i = 1, size(array_1)
   maximum_array(i) = max(array_1(i), array_2(i))
end do
```

SELF-TEST EXERCISES 7.2

1 What is an assumed-shape array? When can one be used?

2 What are the advantages of an assumed-shape array over an explicit-shape array? What are the disadvantages?

3 How can you determine the size of an actual array argument passed to a function or subroutine?

4 What is an automatic array?

5 In what situation can an explict-shape array have non-constant bounds?

6 How is the type of an array-valued function declared? What restrictions (if any) are there on the form of the array that it may return as its value?

SUMMARY

- An array is an ordered set of related variables of the same type which are referred to by a single name.

- The individual items in an array are called array elements.

- Array elements are identified by following the name of the array by an integer subscript expression, enclosed in parentheses. They are scalars.

- An array may have up to seven subscripts, each of which relates to one dimension of the array.

- Each dimension of an array has a lower and an upper bound which, together, define the range of allowable subscript values for that dimension.

- The number of permissible subscripts for an array is called its rank.

- The extent of a dimension is the number of elements in that dimension.

- The size of an array is the total number of elements in the array.

- The shape of an array is determined by its rank and the extent of each dimension.

- The declaration of an array must specify its rank and the bounds for each dimension.

- An explicit-shape array is an array whose bounds are specified explicitly.

- An assumed-shape array is a dummy array argument whose bounds are not specified in the declaration of the array, but which assumes the same shape as the corresponding actual array argument.

- The size of an actual array argument can be determined by use of the intrinsic function **size**.

- An automatic array is an array in a procedure, which is not a dummy argument, which has non-constant bounds, and which obtains the information required to calculate its bounds from outside the procedure at the time of entering the procedure.

- An array-valued constant is specified by an array constructor, which may include one or more implied **do** elements.

- Input and output of arrays may be specified element by element, by whole arrays, or by use of array sections.

- Two arrays are conformable if they have the same shape; a scalar is conformable with any array.

- All intrinsic operators are defined for conformable arrays in addition to scalars.

- Intrinsic operations on arrays take place element by element.

- An array section is a sub-array defined by specifying a subset of the elements of another array.

- Array sections are specified by the use of subscript triplets and vector subscripts.

- An array section is an array.

- Many intrinsic procedures are elemental and may be used with array arguments to deliver array-valued results.

- A function may have an array as its returned value.

- F syntax introduced in Chapter 7

Array declaration	*type*, **dimension** (*extent*) :: *list of names*
	type, **dimension** (*lower_bnd*:*upper_bnd*) :: *list of names*
	type, **dimension** (*lower_bnd*:) :: *list of names*
	type, **dimension** (:) :: *list of names*
Array element	*array_name* (*integer_expression*)
Array constructor	(/ *list of values* /)
	(/ (*value_list*, *int_var* = *initial*, *final*, *inc*) /)
Array section	*array_name* (*b*:*e*:*s*) subscript triplets
	array_name (*b*:*e*)
	array_name (*b*:)
	array_name (:*e*)
	array_name (:)
	array_name (*b*::*s*)
	array_name (:*e*:*s*)
	array_name (::*s*)
	array_name (*v*) vector subscript
	where *v* is a rank-one integer array.
Array input/output	**read** *, *array_element*, *array_name*, *array_section*
	print *, *array_element*, *array_name*, *array_section*
Whole array operations	a = b*c + b + c
	and so on, where a, b and c are conformable arrays

PROGRAMMING EXERCISES

7.1   Write a program which will read up to 20 integer numbers and print them out in the reverse order to that in which they were typed.

7.2   The normal probability function ϕ is defined as:

$$\phi(x) = \frac{1}{\sqrt{2\pi}} e^{-x^2/2}$$

Write a program to evaluate $\psi(x)$ for values of x from -3.0 to $+3.0$ in steps of 0.2, and store these in an array. Display the results in a table with five values to a line.

7.3   In a psychology experiment volunteers are asked to carry out 10 simple tests, and a record is kept of which tests they pass and which they fail. This record consists of a one for a pass and a zero for a fail.
   Write a program which inputs the test results of a set of volunteers and prints the percentage of the volunteers who passed each test.
(Hint: Use an array of size 10 in which to accumulate the passes.)

*7.4   Write a subroutine that has an array as its argument, providing a set of angles (in radians) at which it is required to evaluate the sine of the angle. The subroutine should print a table of all the angles and their sines.
   Write a simple program to enable you to test your subroutine. Use an array constructor to establish the set of angles to be used.

7.5   In a television quiz game, each of six competitors takes part in five rounds and is awarded a score of between 0 and 10 for each round. The winner of each round gains a bonus of five points.
   Write a program which reads the names and scores in each round for each competitor. The program should then calculate any bonuses due for winning a round before calculating the final score for each competitor. Finally, the program should print the names and scores (round by round and total) for the winner and runner-up.

7.6   Write a program that reads and stores two distinct sets of integer numbers and then finds and prints their union and their intersection. (The union is the collection of those items that are in at least one of the sets; the intersection is the collection of those items that are in both sets.)
   Use an array in which to store a set, with unused elements being set to a special value which is not allowed to appear in the set, and write one subroutine to determine the union and another to determine the intersection.
   When you are satisfied that the two subroutines work correctly, alter your program so that the union and intersection are calculated by array-valued functions.

7.7   In an examination, a student is awarded a distinction if he or she has obtained more than 30% above the average obtained by the whole class. To ensure fair marking, the students are identified only by a unique number in the range 1000 to 1999.
   Write a program which will input the marks obtained by the members of the class and which will then print out the average mark and the identifying numbers of any students obtaining distinction, together with their marks.

7.8   The bubble sort is a very simple (and very inefficient) means of sorting an array. It works as follows.
   Compare the first and second elements of the array; if they are in the wrong order then exchange them, otherwise do nothing. Repeat this process for the second and third

elements, then for the third and fourth elements, and so on. At the conclusion of this process, the last value in the sorted sequence will have 'bubbled' along to the last element of the array and will therefore be in the correct place. Now repeat the process, which will result in the next-to-last value being moved to the next-to-last element. Repeat the process until all the values have been moved to their correct places.

(Clearly, improvements can be made by, for example, examining all n elements of the array in the first pass, the first $n - 1$ elements in the second pass, and so on, but you should not feel any obligation to refine your program in this way – the simplest approach will be sufficient for now.)

Write a subroutine to sort the contents of a **character** array using a bubble sort, and test it in a program that reads a set of words from the keyboard.

*7.9   Write two procedures to convert an 8-digit binary number to its decimal equivalent and vice versa. Note that you can store the binary number in an 8-element integer array in which each array element contains either a 1 or 0.

Use these procedures in a program which requests two positive binary numbers in the range 00000000 to 11111111 and calculates their sum by converting them both to integers, adding the integers, and converting the result back to a binary representation. Assume that the result of an addition does not become bigger than $2^8 - 1$.

7.10   The dot product of two three-dimensional vectors a and b is defined as the scalar

$$a \cdot b = a_1 * b_1 + a_2 * b_2 + a_3 * b_3$$

where a is the vector (a_1, a_2, a_3) and b is the vector (b_1, b_2, b_3).

The vector product, c, of the same vectors a and b is defined as the scalar

$$c = a \times b$$

where $c_1 = a_2 * b_3 - a_3 * b_2$, $c_2 = a_3 * b_1 - a_1 * b_3$, and $c_3 = a_1 * b_2 - a_2 * b_1$

Write and test two functions to calculate the dot product and the vector product of two such vectors.

Now use these functions in a third function to evaluate the scalar triple product of three vectors a, b, and c, which is defined as

$$[abc] = a \cdot (b \times c)$$

Write a program to test this function and also to determine the relationship between $[abc]$, $[bca]$ and $[cab]$.

7.11   Write a function that will take the elements of an input array of type **character**(**len** = 1) and return as output the elements of the array in reverse order. (Hint: use array sections.)

Use an actual argument that is a vector subscript to take any three elements of the character array, whose positions are specified by input from a program user, and return them in inverse order.

7.12   Write a subroutine that will take the elements of an integer input array and return the average of all the elements and the first locations and values of the minimum and maximum elements. (Hint: use the array intrinsics listed in Section 7.6.)

Improved building blocks 8

8.1 Recursive procedures
8.2 Passing procedures as arguments
8.3 Creating your own data types
8.4 Controlling access to entities within a module

8.5 Host association within a module
8.6 Gaining more control over use association

Procedures and modules were first introduced in Chapter 4 as the fundamental building blocks in F programming. However, the basic forms used in earlier chapters are somewhat restrictive and this chapter introduces several important extensions.

Recursion is an important mathematical concept, and both functions and subroutines may be delared to be recursive in order to allow their use in appropriate recursive algorithms. Both recursive and non-recursive procedures may also be passed as arguments to other procedures in order to provide still more flexibility to a program.

An important feature of F is its ability to allow programmers to create their own data types, so that they may more readily express problems in their own terms. This derived type concept is fully investigated in this chapter, with several detailed examples.

Derived types and modules are inextricably linked, and the module concept is also further explored and developed in this chapter, especially in connection with host association and data hiding, both of which contribute towards the development of flexible control of both data and procedures.

8.1 Recursive procedures

When first introducing functions and procedures in Chapter 4 we stated that it was not normally permitted for a function or subroutine to reference itself, either directly or indirectly — a concept known as **recursion**. However, there are a number of classes of problem which lend themselves very naturally to a recursive solution, and F does contain facilities for specifying that a function or subroutine may call itself recursively.

We shall examine the situation with functions first, since the concept is easier to understand in this case, and will then extend it to subroutines.

If we wish to allow a function to be called recursively, either directly or indirectly, then we must add the word **recursive** before **function** in the initial statement:

> **recursive function** *recursive_function_name* (...) **result** (*result*)

We can illustrate how this may be used by considering a classic recursive algorithm, namely the calculation of factorials.

■ **EXAMPLE 8.1** ·

1 Problem

Write a function to calculate $n!$

2 Analysis

The factorial of n is written by mathematicians as $n!$ and is defined as follows:

> $0! = 1$, and $n! = n \times (n-1) \times (n-2) \times \ldots \times 2 \times 1$ for $n \geqslant 1$

Another, recursive, way of expressing this is:

> for $n = 0$ $n! = 1$
> for $n \geqslant 1$ $n! = n \times (n-1)!$

We note that n must be not less than zero, and we should therefore take appropriate steps in our function to deal with the situation in which it is called with an illegal value for n. One approach, and the one that we shall adopt, is to return zero in this case, since this is an impossible value for a factorial and can easily be detected, therefore, by the calling program. Note, incidentally, that all recursive algorithms need some condition to end the recursion! In this case the recursion will continue until the function is called with n equal to zero, at which point no more recursive calls will be made, and the recursion will 'unwind'.

We can now easily develop a design for a function to implement this algorithm:

Data design

Purpose	Type	Name
A Dummy argument: The number (*n*) whose factorial is required	**integer**	n
B Result variable: *n*!	**real**	factorial_n

Structure plan

1 Select case on n
 1.1 n=0
   1.1.1 factorial_n = 1
 1.2 n>0
   1.2.1 factorial_n = n * factorial(n − 1)!
 1.3 n<0
   1.3.1 Error − return factorial_n = 0

3 Solution

```
recursive function factorial(n) result(factorial_n)

   ! Dummy argument and result variable
   integer, intent(in) :: n
   real :: factorial_n

   ! Determine whether further recursion is required
   select case(n)
   case (0)
      ! Recursion has reached the end
      factorial_n = 1.0

   case (1:)
      ! More recursive calculation(s) required
      factorial_n = n*factorial(n-1)

   case default
      ! n is negative - return zero as an error indicator
      factorial_n = 0.0

   end select

end function factorial
```

```
recursive subroutine factorial(n,factorial_n)

    ! Dummy arguments
    integer, intent(in) :: n
    real, intent(out) :: factorial_n

    ! Determine whether further recursion is required
    select case(n)
    case (0)
        ! Recursion has reached the end
        factorial_n = 1.0

    case (1:)
        ! Recursive call(s) required to obtain (n-1)!
        call factorial(n-1,factorial_n)

        ! Now calculate n! = n*(n-1)!
        factorial_n = n*factorial_n

    case default
        ! n is negative - return zero as an error indicator
        factorial_n = 0.0

    end select

end subroutine factorial
```

Figure 8.1   A recursive subroutine to calculate $n!$.

A recursive subroutine operates in much the same way, and is specified by including the word **recursive** before **subroutine** in the initial statement of the subroutine:

recursive subroutine *recursive_subroutine_name* (...)

A recursive subroutine to calculate $n!$ is shown in Figure 8.1.

A great many mathematical algorithms lend themselves to a recursive approach, often resulting in a more elegant solution than the non-recursive one. As an example, Section 11.5 discusses the iterative solution of non-linear equations, and Example 11.2 in that section includes both recursive and non-recursive solutions to the problem.

8.2   Passing procedures as arguments

Up to this point, all the dummy arguments in our procedures have been variables – either **real**, **integer**, **character** or **logical**. However, it is also possible to have a procedure as a dummy argument, in which case the dummy argument is called a **dummy procedure**. However, the declaration of a dummy procedure takes a quite different form from that of any other type of dummy argument, for the purpose of the declaration is to provide information about the procedure's **interface** in contrast to a dummy variable where only the type and certain other attributes are required.

The declaration of a dummy procedure takes the form of an **interface block** of the form:

```
interface
   interface_body
end interface
```

where the syntax of the *interface_body* is the same as that of a procedure, but without any declarations of local variables and without any executable statements. For example, the interface block for a function which takes two real arguments and delivers a real result might be

```
interface
   function dummy_fun(a,b) result(r)
      real, intent(in) :: a,b
      real :: r
   end function dummy_fun
end interface
```

If there are several dummy procedures then all the interface bodies may be included in a single interface block:

```
interface
   subroutine one_arg(x)
      real, intent(inout) :: x
   end subroutine one_arg

   recursive subroutine two_args(x,y)
      real, intent(inout) :: x,y
   end subroutine two_args
end interface
```

The interface of the actual procedure argument corresponding to a dummy procedure must agree with that of the dummy procedure except that its name, and the name of any dummy arguments or result variable, may be different. We do strongly recommend, however, that the same names are used in the interface block as in the actual procedure definition at all times; not only does this minimize the chance of accidental errors, but it simplifies the writing of the interface block since the relevant statements can simply be copied directly from the procedure itself.

We have already stated that a function may not call a subroutine, and it is not surprising, therefore, that any dummy procedure arguments in a function must be functions. Moreover, all actual procedure arguments must be module procedures. This latter rule may seem unnecessary, since F requires all procedures to be defined within modules, and thus to be module procedures; however, as we shall see in the next section, it is possible for an F program to reference a procedure written in another language, but since such a procedure will not be a module procedure, such a procedure cannot be used as an actual argument in a call to another F procedure.

Notice, also, that the requirement that an actual procedure argument must be a module procedure means that it is not permissible for an intrinsic procedure to be an actual argument.

□ **EXAMPLE 8.2** ·

1 **Problem**

Chapters 11 and 17 describe three methods for solving a non-linear equation of the form

$$f(x) = 0$$

However, a procedure to solve such an equation must clearly be given access to a function procedure which defines the mathematical function f.

As an example of this concept, write a program which uses a procedure to print the values of a function for a sequence of values between two specified limits, and test the procedure with the following functions and values of x:

1. $x^3 - 3x^2 - 4x + 12$
2. $2e^x - e^{-x}$
3. $\sin 2x - 2 \cos x$

2 **Analysis**

This is a very simple program, as it merely requires a module containing the three functions, a second module (or, if required, the same module) containing the print procedure, and a main program to set things going. We shall, therefore, not bother with the structure plans in this instance and will proceed directly to the solution, using two modules.

3 **Solution**

```
module functions
   public :: f1,f2,f3
contains
   function f1(x) result(fx)
      real, intent(in) :: x
      real :: fx
      fx = x**3 - 3.0*x*x - 4.0*x + 12.0
   end function f1
```

```fortran
    function f2(x) result(fx)
       real, intent(in) :: x
       real :: fx
       fx = 2.0*exp(x) - exp(-x)
    end function f2

    function f3(x) result(fx)
       real, intent(in) :: x
       real :: fx
       fx = sin(2.0*x) - 2.0*cos(x)
    end function f3
end module functions

module use_functions
   public :: list_function
contains
   subroutine list_function(f,x1,x2,xinc)
      ! Dummy arguments
      interface
         function f(x) result(fx)
            real, intent(in) :: x
            real :: fx
         end function f
      end interface
      real, intent(in) :: x1,x2,xinc

      ! Local variable
      real :: x

      ! Loop to print values of f(x) for specified values of x
      x = x1
      do
         print *,"x = ",x," f(x) = ",f(x)
         x = x + xinc
         if (x>x2) then
            exit
         end if
      end do
   end subroutine list_function
end module use_functions

program test_functions
   use functions
   use use_functions

   ! Constants for use with f3
   real, parameter :: pi=3.14159,twopi=2.0*pi,piby4=0.25*pi

   print *,"f(x) = x**3 - 3.0*x*x - 4.0*x + 12.0"
   call list_function(f1,-4.0,4.0,0.5)
   print *,"f(x) = 2.0*exp(x) - exp(-x)"
   call list_function(f2,-10.0,10.0,1.0)
   print *,"f(x) = sin(2.0*x) - 2.0*cos(x)"
   call list_function(f3,-twopi,twopi,piby4)
end program test_functions
```

• ▢

8.3   Creating your own data types

We have now met four types of data that can be processed by F programs – **integer**, **real**, **character** and **logical**, and we shall meet a fifth, **complex**, in Chapter 12. These five data types are called **intrinsic data types**. However, F also includes the capability for programmers to create their own data types to supplement the five intrinsic types. Because these new data types must be derived from the intrinsic data types and/or previously defined new data types they are called **derived types**.

A derived type is defined by a special sequence of statements, which in their simplest form are as follows:

```
type, public :: new_type
   component_definition
   .
   .
   .
end type new_type
```

There may be as many component definitions as required, and each takes the same form as a variable declaration. Unlike the declaration of variables, however, derived type definitions may *only* appear in a module. Note that the definition includes a **public** attribute in order that procedures which use the module may gain access to the new data type; it is also permissible to declare derived types to be **private**, but then the type is only available within the module. We shall come back to this in Chapter 16, but until then all derived types will be given the **public** attribute.

The concept is best illustrated by an example. Let us imagine that a particular program is being used to collect data about individuals, and that each individual is identified by their name (first name, middle initial, last name), their age, their sex, and their social security number. We could define a new data type called person which would contain all this information:

```
type, public :: person
   character(len=12) :: first_name
   character(len=1) :: middle_initial
   character(len=12) :: last_name
   integer :: age
   character(len=1) :: sex        ! M or F
   character(len=11) :: social_security
end type person
```

Once we have defined a new type then we may declare variables of that type in a similar way to that used for intrinsic types:

```
type(person) :: jack, jill
```

Such declarations will, of course, need access to the type definition, which is why such definitions must always be placed in a module.

A constant value of a derived type is written as a sequence of constants corresponding to the components of the derived type, enclosed in parentheses and preceded by the type name:

```
jack = person("Jack","R","Hagenbach",47,"M","123-45-6789")
jill = person("Jill","M","Smith",39,"F","987-65-4321")
```

This form of defining a constant value for a derived type is called a **structure constructor**. Note that it is quite different from the form of a constant for any of the intrinsic types.

In a similar fashion, a **read** statement will expect a sequence of data values which matches the components in both type and order, while a **print** statement will output the value of a derived type variable as a sequence of its component parts.

We may refer directly to a component of a derived type variable by following the name of the variable by a percentage sign and the name of the component. Thus the following statement changes the last name of jill to that of jack, for example, if she had agreed to follow the common practice in many cultures following their marriage!

```
jill%last_name = jack%last_name
```

We may also, of course, use a derived type in the definition of another derived type:

```
type, public :: employee
   type(person) :: employee
   character(len=20) :: department
   real :: salary
end type employee
```

The same notation, using a % character, is then used to obtain a component of a component of a derived type. Thus, if pat is a variable of type employee whose sex had been incorrectly coded, it could be changed by a statement of the form

```
pat%employee%sex = "F"
```

Note that it is permissible for a component name of a derived type to be the same as the name of the derived type itself, although it will usually be clearer if the names are kept distinct.

In the above examples, assignment and operations have only been specified for individual components of objects of derived type. However, much of the power of derived types comes from the ability to work with the complete object without regard to its individual components. Thus we may write

```
staff(1) = pat
```

where `staff` is an array of type `employee` and `pat` is a variable of the same type. In this case the assignment takes place component by component exactly as if we had written a series of separate assignment statements for each component:

```
staff(i)%employee%first_name = pat%employee%first_name
staff(i)%employee%middle_initial = &
                        pat%employee%middle_initial
  .
  .
  .
staff(i)%salary = pat%salary
```

In general this is what is required, but we shall see in Chapter 16 how to alter this behaviour if something else is required.

However, operations between two objects of the same derived type are more difficult because although it would be meaningful to write

```
pat%salary - tom%salary
```

to establish the difference between the salaries of `pat` and `tom`, since both are **real** values, the expression

```
pat%department - tom%department
```

is meaningless because both components are **character** strings. It is not possible, therefore, to write expressions such as

```
pat - tom
```

where `pat` and `tom` are of derived type. We shall see in Chapter 16 how to overcome this apparent restriction, but until then all operations on objects of derived type must be carried out explicitly component by component.

☐ **EXAMPLE 8.3** . . . .

1 Problem

Define two data types, one to represent a point by means of its coordinates (in two-dimensional space only) and the other to represent a line (also in two-dimensional space) by the coefficients of its defining equation. Write a program which reads the coordinates of two points and which then calculates the line joining them, printing the equation of the line.

2 Analysis

We must first establish the format of the two derived types – point and line.

The first of these is easy, as it will consist of two real components, representing the x and y coordinates, respectively.

The representation of a straight line is, however, slightly more difficult. A straight line is defined by an equation of the form

$$ax + by + c = 0$$

and at first sight we could simply use the three coefficients of this equation as the representation of a line. However, these three coefficients are not unique, since, for example, the equations

$$5x - 4y + 7 = 0$$

and

$$10x - 8y + 14 = 0$$

are identical apart from the fact that all the coefficients of the second equation are twice those of the first, and they both, therefore, represent the same line. This will not, however, cause any problems in the use of this data type as long as it is remembered that any non-zero multiple of a, b and c represents the same line. In fact, the only time that it will cause any difficulty is when deciding if two objects of type line are equal (that is, they represent the same straight line). We shall, therefore, use the three coefficients a, b and c in a derived type to define a line.

Returning to the problem being considered, simple algebra (see Figure 8.2) leads us to the conclusion that

$$a = y_2 - y_1$$
$$b = x_1 - x_2$$
$$c = y_1x_2 - y_2x_1$$

Finally, we should note that our program should check that the two points input are not coincident, since in that event it is impossible to define a line joining them. Since this involves two comparisons between pairs of real numbers, representing the x and y coordinates, we shall put the test in a function which will return *true* if the points are distinct, and *false* if they are coincident to within a specified tolerance. In making this test, we shall assume that, for the region of the plane in which we are interested, and for our particular application, two points can be considered as being coincident if both their x and y coordinates differ by less than 10^{-5}.

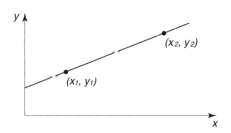

The equation of the line is $ax + by + c = 0$.
The slope of the line is $(y_2 - y_1)/(x_2 - x_1)$ if $x_1 \neq x_2$.
At any point (x, y), other than (x_1, y_1), the slope is $(y - y_1)/(x - x_1)$.
Therefore

$$\frac{y - y_1}{x - x_1} = \frac{y_2 - y_1}{x_2 - x_1} \text{ for } x_1 \neq x_2, \ x \neq x_1, \ y \neq y_1$$

Therefore

$$(x_2 - x_1)(y - y_1) = (y_2 - y_1)(x - x_1) \tag{1}$$

Now, the point (x_1, y_1) also satisfies equation (1) in this form, so we can drop the prohibition that $(x, y) \neq (x_1, y_1)$.
Also, if $x_1 = x_2$ the equation becomes

$$(y_2 - y_1)(x - x_1) = 0 \tag{2}$$

In this case, $y_1 \neq y_2$, since if it did the two points (x_1, y_1) and (x_2, y_2) would coincide and, hence, would not define a straight line. Consequently, we can divide equation (2) by $(y_2 - y_1)$ and obtain

$$x - x_1 = 0$$

In the case where $x_1 = x_2$, this is the equation of the line joining the two points.
Thus, in all cases, equation (1) is the equation of the straight line joining the two (distinct) points. Rearranging (1), we have

$$(y_2 - y_1)x + (x_1 - x_2)y - y_2 x_1 + y_1 x_1 + y_1 x_2 - y_1 x_1 = 0$$

or

$$(y_2 - y_1)x + (x_1 - x_2)y + y_1 x_2 - y_2 x_1 = 0$$

Therefore

$$a = y_2 - y_1$$
$$b = x_1 - x_2$$
$$c = y_1 x_2 - y_2 x_1$$

Figure 8.2 Calculation of the equation of a line joining two points.

We shall place the calculation of the equation of the line in a second function in order to clarify the operation of the main program.

We can now develop our structure plan:

Module geometry
[defines derived types for points and lines]

function distinct_points($p1, p2$) result(*distinct*)
1   Set *distinct true* if x-coordinates or y-coordinates differ

function line_from_points($p1, p2$) result(*join_line*)
1   Calculate and return the coefficients of the line joining the points $p1$
     and $p2$

Program geometry_example
[uses geometry module]

1   Read coordinates of two points
2   If the points are distinct
  2.1   Calculate the coefficients of the line joining the points
  2.2   Print equation of line
     otherwise
  2.3   Print an error message

3 **Solution**

```
module geometry
public :: distinct_points,line_from_points

    ! Type definitions
    type, public :: point
       real :: x,y      ! Cartesian coordinates of the point
    end type point

    type, public :: line
       real :: a,b,c     ! Coefficients of defining equation
    end type line

    ! Constant declaration
    real, parameter, public :: small=1.0e-5

contains

    function distinct_points(p1,p2) result(distinct)
    ! Returns true if the two points supplied as arguments
    ! are not effectively coincident
```

```
! Dummy arguments and result variable declaration
type(point), intent(in) :: p1,p2
logical :: distinct

! Set result true if either pair of corresponding
! coordinates are different
distinct = abs(p1%x - p2%x)>small .or. &
           abs(p1%y - p2%y)>small

end function distinct_points

function line_from_points(p1,p2) result(join_line)
! Returns the line joining the two points
! supplied as arguments

  ! Dummy arguments and result variable declaration
  type(point), intent(in) :: p1,p2
  type(line) :: join_line

  ! Calculate coefficients of line
  join_line%a = p2%y - p1%y
  join_line%b = p1%x - p2%x
  join_line%c = p1%y*p2%x - p2%y*p1%x

end function line_from_points

end module geometry


program geometry_example
! A program to use derived types for two-dimensional
! geometric calculations

use geometry    ! Contains point and line type definitions,
                ! constant small definition, and functions
                ! distinct_points and line_from_points

  ! Variable and constant declarations
  type(point) :: p1,p2
  type(line) :: p1_to_p2

  ! Read data
  print *,"Please type coordinates of first point"
  read *,p1
  print *,"Please type coordinates of second point"
  read *,p2

  ! Test for coincident points
  if (distinct_points(p1,p2)) then
     ! Calculate coefficients of equation representing the line
     p1_to_p2 = line_from_points(p1,p2)

     ! Print result
     print *,"The equation of the line joining these two "
     print *,"points is ax + by + c = 0"
     print *,"where a = ",p1_to_p2%a
     print *,"      b = ",p1_to_p2%b
     print *,"      c = ",p1_to_p2%c
```

```
     else
        print *,"ERROR: The two points supplied are coincident!"
     end if

  end program geometry example
```

Because of the importance of derived types, we shall present a second example of their use – this time in a mathematical context.

☐ EXAMPLE 8.4

① Problem

Define a data type which can be used to represent complex numbers, and then use it in a program which reads two complex numbers and calculates and prints their sum, their difference and their product. Note that the F language does contain an intrinsic data type for representing complex numbers, which we will meet in Chapter 12. However, we shall define our own derived type to represent complex numbers in this example in order to illustrate the power of derived types in extending the F language itself.

② Analysis

Complex numbers are used mainly by electrical engineers and by pure mathematicians, and consist of two parts – a real part and an imaginary part. A complex number is mathematically equivalent to $x + jy$, where x is the real part, y is the imaginary part, and j represents the square root of -1. It is often written in the form (x, y).

The rules for addition and subtraction are very simply derived:

$$(x_1 + jy_1) + (x_2 + jy_2) = ((x_1 + x_2) + j(y_1 + y_2))$$
$$(x_1 + jy_1) - (x_2 + jy_2) = ((x_1 - x_2) + j(y_1 - y_2))$$

while that for multiplication is not much more difficult (as long as we remember that j^2 is equal to -1):

$$(x_1 + jy_1) * (x_2 + jy_2) = ((x_1 * x_2 - y_1 * y_2) + j(x_1 * y_2 + x_2 * y_1))$$

Division is more difficult to work out – which is why we are not bothering with it in this example!

We can express these rules using the parenthesized form of representation as

$$(x_1, y_1) + (x_2, y_2) = (x_1 + x_2, y_1 + y_2)$$
$$(x_1, y_1) - (x_2, y_2) = (x_1 - x_2, y_1 - y_2)$$
$$(x_1, y_1) * (x_2, y_2) = (x_1 * x_2 - y_1 * y_2, x_1 * y_2 + x_2 * y_1)$$

We can now write a structure plan:

> 1   Define a data type for complex numbers
>
> 2   Read two complex numbers
>
> 3   Calculate their sum, difference and product
>
> 4   Print results

③ Solution

```
module complex_arithmetic
! This module contains a derived type definition
! for complex numbers

   type, public :: complex_number
      real :: real_part,imaginary_part
   end type complex_number

end module complex_arithmetic

program complex_example
! A program to illustrate the use of a derived type to perform
! complex arithmetic
use complex_arithmetic

   ! Variable definitions
   type(complex_number) :: c1,c2,csum,cdiff,cprod

   ! Read data
   print *,"Please supply two complex numbers"
   print *,"Each complex number should be typed as two numbers, "
   print *,"representing the real and imaginary parts ", &
          "of the number"
   read *,c1,c2

   ! Calculate sum, difference and product
   csum%real_part = c1%real_part + c2%real_part
   csum%imaginary_part = c1%imaginary_part + c2%imaginary_part

   cdiff%real_part = c1%real_part - c2%real_part
   cdiff%imaginary_part = c1%imaginary_part - c2%imaginary_part

   cprod%real_part = c1%real_part*c2%real_part - &
                     c1%imaginary_part*c2%imaginary_part
   cprod%imaginary_part = c1%real_part*c2%imaginary_part + &
                          c1%imaginary_part*c2%real_part

   ! Print results
   print *,"The sum of the two numbers is ",csum
   print *,"The difference between the two numbers is ", cdiff
   print *,"The product of the two numbers is ",cprod

end program complex_example
```

```
     Please supply two complex numbers
     Each complex number should be typed as two numbers,
     representing the real and imaginary parts of the number
        8 7, 5 3
        11.4, -3.8
     The sum of the two numbers is  20.1,  1.5
     The difference between the two numbers is  -2.7,  9.1
     The product of the two numbers is  119.32,  27.36
```

Figure 8.3 Results produced by the program written for Example 8.4.

Figure 8.3 shows the result of running this program, and it can be seen that a slight improvement would be to print out the three results as parenthesized pairs using statements such as

```
print *,"The sum of the two numbers is (",sum%real_part, &
             ", ",sum%imaginary_part,")"
```

This example illustrates a common dilemma when reading and writing derived data types, namely that in order to control properly the layout of results, or even of data, it is necessary to work at the component level, whereas one of the advantages of using derived types is that the underlying data structure can be ignored. We shall see how to resolve this dilemma in the next section.

* ◻

The derived types that we defined so far have only had scalar components. However, it is also permissible, and often highly desirable, for a derived type to have one or more array-valued components. As in the case of scalar components, these are defined in a similar manner to the declaration of array-valued variables:

```
type, public golfer
   character(len = 15) :: first_name, last_name
   integer :: handicap
   integer, dimension(10) :: last_rounds
end type golfer
```

In this type definition, the fourth component, last_rounds, is an array having bounds of 1 and 10, and will be used to record the golfer's 10 most recent scores.

An important constraint is that the bounds of such array components must be constant expressions. In Chapter 14, however, we shall meet a new concept which will enable us to have the equivalent of variable-size arrays in derived type definitions.

A reference to an element of an array component is written, as we might expect, with the subscript expression in parentheses following the relevant component name. Thus, if a variable of type `golfer` is declared as

```
type(golfer) :: Faldo
```

then the score he achieved in his most recent round is written as

```
Faldo%last_rounds(10)
```

Arrays of derived type are, of course, permitted in F, and are written and used exactly as you would expect. However, matters become slightly more complicated when we have an array of objects which are of a derived type containing an array component, when both the object itself, and a component of the object, will be subscripted. For example, if the details of the members of a golf club are to be held in an array, whose elements are declared as

```
type(golfer), dimension(250) :: member
```

then the last name of an individual golfer will be referred to as

```
member(i)%last_name
```

and the third of the fourth golfer's last 10 rounds will be referred to as

```
member(4)%last_rounds(3)
```

An important restriction is that, in a reference to an object of a derived type having one or more array components, at most one array can have a rank greater than zero. In other words, all array components, except possibly one, must be subscripted. It is therefore permitted to write

```
member%last_rounds(i) = 72
```

in order to set the *i*th round for every member to 72. This works because `member` is an array and `last_rounds(i)` is a scalar, and `member%last_rounds(i)` is, therefore, an array consisting of the *i*th round of every member. Similarly, it is permitted to write

```
member(j)%last_rounds = 72
```

in order to set every round for the *j*th member to 72. However, the statement

```
member%last_rounds = 72            ! ILLEGAL
```

attempting to set every round for every member to 72 is not allowed, because both `member` and `last_rounds` are rank-one arrays.

We can also, of course, include components of another derived type, as long as this has already been defined. Thus we could modify the above definition of a golfer to utilize the previously defined person derived type:

```
type, public golfer
   type(person) :: personal_details
   integer :: handicap
   integer, dimension(10) :: last_rounds
end type golfer
```

In this case, the first name of player declared using this revised type

```
type(golfer) :: Nicklaus
```

could be identified as

```
Nicklaus%personal_details%first_name
```

while the score that he made in his most recent round is

```
Nicklaus%last_rounds(10).
```

◼ EXAMPLE 8.5 ·

1 Problem

Vectors and matrices are two of the most powerful data concepts for many engineering and mathematical applications. Write a module which provides a data type called `vector` and a procedure to multiply two vectors together to obtain their scalar product (or *dot product*). Note that it will also be necessary to provide procedures to create a vector (from a rank-one array) and to provide access to the individual elements of a vector.

2 Analysis

We shall first need to determine how we will define a vector. We shall limit ourselves to vectors having real values, and it is clear that the primary means of storing the elements of the vector will therefore be a real array. However, vectors may be of varying sizes, and so, although we shall store the elements in an array of fixed size, we will also store the number of elements used (the *length* of the vector) as another component of the type. A suitable type definition will, therefore, be

```
type, public vector
   integer :: length
   real, dimension(max_length) :: elements
end type vector
```

where max_length is a **private** named constant which specifies the maximum length of vector permitted. This constant will be declared in the same module so that, if it is required to alter the maximum size of vectors, it will only be necessary to make one change to the module and none to any program that uses the module.

The function to create a vector from an array is quite straightforward but will need to include a check to ensure that the maximum length of a vector is not exceeded:

Function create_vector

Data design

	Purpose	Type	Name
A	Dummy arguments		
	Array containing elements	**real**(:)	array
B	Result variable	vector	v

Structure plan

1   length = **size**(array)

2   If length>max_length
     2.1   Print error message, set length to zero, and exit
     Otherwise
3   Copy first length elements of array to vector

A method for extracting individual elements of a vector will be required, and we shall simply provide a function to copy the vector to an array, thereby returning all the elements in a form in which the calling program can use them. However, it will first be necessary to establish the length of the array in order to ensure that the array is large enough. These two functions are extremely simple:

Function vector_size

Data design

	Purpose	Type	Name
A	Dummy argument		
	Vector whose size is required	vector	v
B	Result variable	**integer**	vec_size

Structure plan

> **1** Set function result to the length component of the dummy argument `vector`

Array-valued function vector_array

Data design

	Purpose	Type	Name
A	Dummy argument Vector to be converted to an array	`vector`	v
B	Result variable	**real**(v%length)	arr

Structure plan

> **1** Set `arr` to elements 1:v%length of the dummy argument `vector`

We can now proceed to consideration of the scalar product function:

Function scalar_product

Data design

	Purpose	Type	Name
A	Dummy argument Vectors to be multiplied	`vector`	v1, v2
B	Result variable	**real**	p
C	Local variable Loop counter	**integer**	i

Structure plan

> **1** If lengths of two vectors are different
>   **1.1** Print error message, set result to zero and exit
>   Otherwise
> **2** Initialize p to zero
> **3** Repeat for i from 1 to `vector%length`
>   **3.1** Add product of corresponding vector elements to p
> **4** Exit with p as function value

⒊ Solution

```
module vectors

    public :: create_vector, vector_size, vector_array, &
              scalar_product

    ! Maximum length for vectors
    integer, parameter, private :: max_length = 10

    ! Derived type definition
    type, public :: vector
       integer :: length
       real, dimension(max_length) :: elements
    end type vector

contains

    function create_vector(array) result(v)
    ! This function creates a vector from elements of an array

       ! Dummy arguments
       real, dimension(:), intent(in) :: array

       ! Result
       type(vector) :: v

       ! Validity check
       if (size(array) > max_length) then
          ! Too long - print warning and set length to zero
          print *, "Error: Vector of length ", size(array), &
                   " requested"
          print *, "Maximum permitted is ", max_length
          v%length = 0
       else
          ! OK - copy array to vector
          v%length = size(array)
          v%elements(1:v%length) = array
       end if
    end function create_vector

    function vector_size(v) result(vec_size)
    ! This function returns the size of a vector

       ! Dummy argument
       type(vector), intent(in) :: v

       ! Result
       integer :: vec_size

       vec_size = v%length
    end function vector_size

    function vector_array(v) result(arr)
    ! This function returns the elements of a vector as an array

       ! Dummy argument
       type(vector), intent(in) :: v
```

```
    ! Result
    real, dimension(v%length) :: arr

    arr = v%elements(1:v%length)
end function vector_array

function scalar_product(v1, v2) result(p)
! This function returns the scalar product of two vectors

    ! Dummy arguments
    type(vector), intent(in) :: v1,v2

    ! Result
    real :: p

    ! Local variables
    integer :: i

    ! Validity check
    if (v1%length /= v2%length) then
        ! Vectors have different lengths
        print *, "Error: Vectors are of different lengths " , &
                    v1%length, " and ", v2%length
        print *, "Zero result returned"
        p = 0.0
    else
        ! OK - calculate dot product
        p = 0.0
        do i = 1, v1%length
            p = p+v1%elements(i)*v2%elements(i)
        end do
    end if
end function scalar_product

end module vectors
```

Of course, the module `vectors` is far from complete. There are many more fundamental capabilities for creating and manipulating vectors that should be added to it, and we shall return to consideration of some of these in Section 16.3. Furthermore, the definition of the type `vector` is wasteful of space, since all entities of type vector are of the same size, regardless of the length of the individual vectors; we shall introduce a technique for dealing with this problem in Chapter 14.

Figure 8.4 shows the results obtained by testing this module with the following program:

```
program test_vectors
use vectors

    integer :: dot
    real, dimension(3) :: a
    real, dimension(20) :: b
    type(vector) :: v, w
    integer :: i
```

```
Length of v is  3
Its elements are ( 1., 2., 3. )
Length of w io  3
Its elements are ( 2., 3., 4. )
Their ocalar product io  20.
Error: Vector of length  20  requested
Maximum permitted is  10
Error: Vectors are of different lengths  3  and  9
Zero result returned
```

Figure 8.4 Results produced by test program for Example 8.4.

```
! Initialize arrays and convert to vectors
a = (/1.0, 2.0, 3.0/)
b = (/2.0, 3.0, 4.0, 5.0, (0.0, i = 1, 16)/)
v = create_vector(a)
w = create_vector(b(1:3))

! Print details of vectors
print *,"Length of v is ", vector_size(v)
print *,"Its elements are (", vector_array(v), ")"
print *,"Length of w is ", vector_size(w)
print *,"Its elements are (", vector_array(w), ")"

! Calculate and print their scalar product
print *, "Their scalar product is ", scalar_product(v, w)

! Test error messages
w = create_vector(b)
w = create_vector(b(1:9))
dot = scalar_product(v, w)

end program test_vectors
```

SELF-TEST EXERCISES 8.1

1   What is the difference between a recursive procedure and a non-recursive procedure? How is each type of procedure specified?

2   How is a dummy procedure declared? What restrictions, if any, are there on the use of a procedure as an argument in a call to another procedure?

3   What is a derived type? From what is it derived?

4   Why are derived types useful?

5   Define a type to store a typical domestic address in your country's standard form.

6   Write a declaration for a variable of the type defined in Question 5, and a single assignment statement to assign your own address to this variable.

7   Define a type to store a person's name and address and the necessary statement
     or statements to read the user's name and address into a variable of this type.

8   What are the restrictions (if any) on the inclusion of an array-valued component in
     a derived type definition?

8.4   Controlling access to entities within a module

The grouping together of related entities into a more complex structure is
common everywhere in engineering and mathematics. For example, a complex
number consists of two real numbers grouped in such a way that they can then be
manipulated as a single entity. This encapsulation is convenient when it is not
necessary to think of the real and imaginary parts separately. Similarly, a set of
$m \times n$ numbers is often combined into a single mathematical structure, an $m \times n$
matrix, which can then be manipulated as a single entity. Much of the power of
mathematics comes from this combination of simpler entities to form new, more
complex, mathematical entities that can then be manipulated as single units at a
higher level.

Derived types provide a similar power in F, and it is good programming
practice to group related variables together in a derived type definition in a
module in order that the type may then be easily used throughout a program.
Furthermore, as we saw in the previous section, procedures that provide
fundamental manipulation capabilities for entities of that type can, and should,
also be put into the same module. This makes program development easier
and maintenance simpler, because all the code relating to the creation and
fundamental manipulation of a particular data type is encapsulated in one place
and not distributed throughout a program.

It is often appropriate to go beyond using derived types and modules in the
ways already described, in order to provide even greater program reliability. The
basic idea is that the component parts of a derived type should *not* be freely
available throughout a program, but should only be available, in a controlled
manner, through procedures provided in the module containing the derived type
definition. This provides greater program safety and control within a program
because if an error in the construction or use of the components of a derived
type entity occurs, then the problem must be located inside the module rather
than potentially being anywhere in the program. This concept is expressed by
saying that the components of a derived type are either **private** (only available
without restriction in the defining module) or **public** (freely available without
restriction throughout a program).

The components of a derived type are made private by preceding the first
component declaration in the derived type definition by the word **private** on a
line by itself:

```
type, public :: complex_number
  private
  real :: a,phi
end type complex_number
```

Note that the privacy only applies *outside* the module in which the type definition appears. Within the module, including all its module procedures, the components are fully accessible.

Finally, note that if the components of a derived type are private then not only is it not permitted to use the % notation with that derived type outside the module, but it is also not permitted to write a structure constructor to define a constant of that type outside the module. Objects of such a type can, therefore, only be manipulated as a whole outside the module, unless procedures are used which have been written to perform detailed manipulation of components of entities of that type, and which are themselves made available through **use** association from the same module, thus providing the security that we require. As a general rule, we recommend that the components of derived types should always be made private, and that all the necessary procedures for accessing their components should, therefore, be incorporated into the same module as the type definition. A good example of where this approach should be used is in the vectors module developed in Example 8.5 where, ideally, the derived type vector should have its components made private so that only the complete object is available to the user, with creation of vectors from arrays, and vice versa, being handled by procedures such as those already incorporated within the module.

☐ **EXAMPLE 8.6** ·

1 Problem

In Example 8.4 we defined a data type to represent complex numbers and used this to carry out addition, subtraction and multiplication. Write a module which contains a similar data type whose components are hidden from the user of the module, and which also contains four procedures to carry out addition, subtraction, multiplication and division between two complex entities.

2 Analysis

We have already carried out most of the work for this new module, other than complex division and the four new procedures to carry out input/output and conversion. Complex division was not discussed in Example 8.4, but is included here for completeness. The formula required is as follows:

$$(x_1, y_1)/(x_2, y_2) = \left(\frac{x_1 * x_2 + y_1 * y_2}{x_2{}^2 + y_2{}^2}, \frac{x_2 * y_1 - x_1 * y_2}{x_2{}^2 + y_2{}^2} \right)$$

Input and output procedures are needed because derived type input and output takes place component by component, and the components will not be accessible outside the module. Two conversion procedures are required in order to allow access to the real and imaginary parts of a complex number, and to create one from the values of the real and imaginary parts. They are all quite straightforward, however, and we can proceed straight to the solution.

3 Solution

```fortran
module complex_procedures
   public :: c_add, c_sub, c_mult, c_div, print_complex, &
             read_complex, create_complex, extract_complex

! Complex data derived type definition
   type, public :: complex_number
      private
      real :: real_part,imag_part
   end type complex_number

contains

   function c_add(z1,z2) result(c_sum)
      type(complex_number), intent(in) :: z1,z2
      type(complex_number) :: c_sum

      c_sum%real_part = z1%real_part + z2%real_part
      c_sum%imag_part = z1%imag_part + z2%imag_part
   end function c_add

   function c_sub(z1,z2) result(c_diff)
      type(complex_number), intent(in) :: z1,z2
      type(complex_number) :: c_diff

      c_diff%real_part = z1%real_part - z2%real_part
      c_diff%imag_part = z1%imag_part - z2%imag_part
   end function c_sub

   function c_mult(z1,z2) result(c_prod)
      type(complex_number), intent(in) :: z1,z2
      type(complex_number) :: c_prod

      c_prod%real_part = z1%real_part*z2%real_part - &
                         z1%imag_part*z2%imag_part
      c_prod%imag_part = z1%real_part*z2%imag_part + &
                         z1%imag_part*z2%real_part
   end function c_mult

   function c_div(z1,z2) result(c_quotient)
      type(complex_number), intent(in) :: z1,z2
      type(complex_number) :: c_quotient
      real :: denom          ! Local variable to avoid calculating
                             ! denominator twice
```

```
            denom = z2%real_part**2 + z2%imag_part**2
            c_quotient %real_part = (z1%real_part*z2%real_part + &
                                     z1%imag_part*z2%imag_part)/denom
            c_quotient %imag_part = (z2%real_part*z1%imag_part - &
                                     z1%real_part*z2%imag_part)/denom
        end function c_div

        subroutine print_complex(z)
            type(complex_number), intent(in) :: z

            print *,z        ! Cannot be done outside module
        end subroutine print_complex

        subroutine read_complex(z)
            type(complex_number), intent(out) :: z

            read *,z         ! Cannot be done outside module
        end subroutine read_complex

        subroutine create_complex(real_part,imag_part,z)
            real, intent(in) :: real_part,imag_part
            type(complex_number), intent(out) :: z

            z%real_part = real_part
            z%imag_part = imag_part
        end subroutine create_complex

        subroutine extract_complex(z,real_part,imag_part)
            type(complex_number), intent(in) :: z
            real, intent(out) :: real_part,imag_part

            real_part = z%real_part
            imag_part = z%imag_part
        end subroutine extract_complex

    end module complex_procedures
```

These procedures can then be tested in a program such as the following:

```
program test_complex
use complex_procedures

    ! Variable declarations
    type(complex_number) :: z1,z2,z3
    real :: re,im

    ! Read a complex number
    print *,"Please type two complex numbers"
    call read_complex(z1)

    ! Read two reals and form a complex number
    read *,re,im
    call create_complex(re,im,z2)

    ! Multiply the two complex numbers and print their product
    z3 = c_mult(z1,z2)
    print *,"The product of these two numbers is"
    call print_complex(z3)
```

```
! Add the two complex numbers and print the real
! and imaginary parts of their sum
z3 = c_add(z1,z2)
call extract_complex(z3,re,im)
print *,"The sum of these two numbers is",re,im

end program test_complex
```

If the module was rewritten to use, for example, the polar method of defining complex numbers then nothing in this latter program would need to be altered, as the program is not aware of the internal form of the complex_number data type and only has access to the real and imaginary parts through module procedures.

This principle of **data hiding** or, more generally, of only allowing access to a restricted set of the entities in a module is extremely important for secure programming, and does not only apply to the components of a derived type. For example, a module which is being used to provide a common database which will be used by a number of procedures in a program might, nevertheless, not wish to allow unlimited access to everything in that database. In a similar manner, a module which contains a collection of procedures to manipulate data in a particular application area might only wish to allow access to the 'top level' of these procedures, and not to those which are used for internal housekeeping, or other purposes which are not the concern of the program unit which is using the module.

As was the case with derived type components, the accessibility of any entity in a module can be either *private* or *public*, and the writer of the module has complete control over such accessibility for every entity. Up to this point we have normally specified that all such entities have been public, but by using a **private** attribute or **private** statement we may restrict the availability of any data objects, types or procedures to the module in which they are defined:

```
private :: internal_procedure

real, private :: internal_value

type, private :: internal_type
   real :: x,y
end type internal_type
```

Note that making a derived type definition private means that no variables of that type can be declared outside the module. This contrasts with the earlier example in which the *components* of a derived type definition were made private, but the derived type itself was not.

8.5   Host association within a module

When we introduced modules in Chapter 4 we identified two uses for them – to enable data entities to be accessed by more than one procedure and to provide an easy way of making the explicit interface of procedures available to any program units that invoke them. In both cases the relevant entities are made available through **use** association. In Section 8.3 we added derived type definitions to the list of entities that can be made available by **use** association.

In Section 4.6 we also introduced the concept of host association, whereby entities declared in the first part of a module, before a **contains** statement, are available for use by any procedures defined in the second part of the module, after the **contains** statement. We used host association in Example 8.5 to make the **vector** derived type definition available to the various procedures in the module, and in Example 8.6 to make the **complex_number** derived type definition similarly available.

Host association, however, does create the potential for complications if a module procedure has a local variable of the same name as one of the entities declared in the first part of the host module. The rules for resolving such conflicts are quite complex, but the essence of them is that the entity in the host is not available if there is a local entity, or one accessible by **use** association, in the procedure with the same name. Consider, for example, the following two modules:

```
module first
   real, public :: z
end module first

module second
   public :: inner
   real, parameter, public :: pi=3.1415926, e=2.7182818
   real, public :: x,y,z
contains
   subroutine inner(x)
      use first
      real, intent(inout) :: x
      real :: y
      .
      .
      .
   end subroutine inner
end module second
```

In this example, the constants pi and e which are declared in the first part of the module second are available in the subroutine inner, but none of the module variables x, y or z are available because of the existence of a dummy argument called x, a local variable called y, and a variable z available by **use** association from the module first.

It is very important, therefore, to check carefully for any name clashes of this type when writing a module containing procedures which expect to obtain access to items from the first part of the module by host association. A compiler will not give any warning of such clashes because the overriding of a potentially host-associated variable by a locally defined variable of the same name is both legal and, in certain circumstances, a useful feature.

Despite these complications, host association is very useful when writing a set of procedures which share certain constant values and/or variables, as it obviates the need for multiple declarations of constants and for lengthy argument lists.

8.6   Gaining more control over use association

We have just seen how a name clash can cause difficulties with host association, and similar problems can also occur when obtaining access to entities in a module by **use** association if the names of one or more of these entities clash with other names, such as local names or the names of entities made accessible by **use** association from another module. In order to deal with this situation an extended form of the **use** statement allows entities in the module to be referred to by a different name in the scoping unit containing that **use** statement:

> **use** *module_name*, *rename list*

where each item in the *rename list* takes the form

> *local_name* => *name_in_module*

Thus, for example, if it was required to use the module `complex_procedures` developed in Example 8.6, but with the four functions called `cplus`, `cminus`, `ctimes` and `cdivide` instead of `c_add`, `c_sub`, `c_mult` and `c_div`, then the use statement would be as follows:

```
use complex_procedures, cplus => c_add, cminus => c_sub, &
                        ctimes => c_mult, cdivide => c_div
```

It is quite often the case that a large module may contain a substantial number of public entities, of which the user of the module only wishes to access a subset. In this case, it is possible to limit the entities made available from the module by another extension of the **use** statement:

> **use** *module_name*, **only**: *only list*

where each item in the *only list* is either the name of an entity in the module, or a renaming of such an entity, as already described. In this case, any public entities in the module whose names do not appear after the **only** keyword will not be accessible to the program using the module; the effect is as if those entities which are omitted had been given the **private** attribute in the module.

Thus, for example, if in the above example it was required that the names of the subroutines create_complex and extract_complex should not be available then the **use** statement would be as follows:

```
use complex_procedures, &
    only: c_add, c_sub, c_mult, c_div, &
        print_complex, read_complex
```

or, if some renaming was also required:

```
use complex_procedures, &
    only: cplus => c_add, cminus => c_sub, c_mult, c_div, &
        print_complex, read_complex
```

SELF-TEST EXERCISES 8.2

1   What is the point of making the components of a derived type **private**?

2   What are the consequences of making the components of a derived type **private**?

3   Under what circumstances can the components of an entity of a derived type with private components be accessed?

4   What is the difference between making the components of a derived type **private** and making the definition of a derived type **private**?

5   What is meant by data hiding?

6   What is the recommended way of controlling the accessibility of entities in a module? Why?

7   How can a program unit restrict the entities in a module that it has access to through **use** association?

8   How can a procedure restrict the entities in the same module that it has access to through host association?

9   What happens if a procedure has a local variable of the same name as a public entity in a module that it is using? How can the procedure have access to both the local variable and the module entity?

SUMMARY

- Procedures may be invoked recursively if the initial statement of the procedure specifies **recursive subroutine** or **recursive function**, as appropriate.

- Dummy procedures must be declared in an interface block which specifies the number and types of the dummy arguments and, in the case of a dummy function, the type of the result.

- Actual procedure arguments must be module procedures; intrinsic procedures may not appear as actual arguments in procedure calls.

- A derived type is a user-defined data type, each of whose components is either an intrinsic type or a previously defined derived type.

- A derived type may only be defined in a module.

- Derived type definitions may have arrays as components, provided that they are explicit-shape arrays having constant bounds.

- Derived type literal constants are specified by means of structure constructors.

- Input and output of derived type objects takes place component by component.

- The components of a derived type may be made private by the inclusion of a **private** statement before any component declarations, in which case the components are inaccessible from outside the module other than by use of module procedures from that module.

- An entity declared in the specification part of a module is available to all procedures contained within that module by host association, unless hidden by a local entity of the same name.

- A **use** statement may specify local names for entities accessible from a module by renaming the module entities.

- A **use** statement may restrict the entities accessible from a module by use of an **only** qualifier.

- F syntax introduced in Chapter 8:

  Initial statements   **recursive function** *name* **(**...**) result (***res_var***)**
                                   recursive subroutine *name* **(**...**)**

  Interface block   **interface**
                                   interface_body_1
                                   interface_body_2

                                   .
                                   .
                                   .

            end interface

Derived type definition	**type, public ::** *type_name* *sequence of component declarations* **end type** *type_name*

	type, public :: *type_name*
	    private
	    sequence of component declarations
	end type *type_name*

Variable declaration	**type** (*derived_type_name*) **::** *list of variable names*
Module entity renaming	**use** *name*, *local_name* => *module_name*, ...
Module entity restriction	**use** *name*, **only:** *list of module public names*

PROGRAMMING EXERCISES

*8.1   Write a program that uses two derived types. The first of these should contain relevant details for an individual, such as first name, middle initial, last name, sex, age, occupation, and anything else you think relevant. The second should contain an address in an appropriate form for your environment.

Use a structure constructor to store your own details, or those of a friend, in variables of these types and then print a message giving these details in a format similar to that below:

```
My name is James D Smith
I am a 23 year-old male student, and I live at
871 rue de la triomphe
Montmartre
Paris
France
```

8.2   Write a function whose only argument is a time interval in seconds, and whose result is the same time interval expressed in hours, minutes and seconds. (Hint: the type of the result of the function will have to be a derived type.)

8.3   The equation of a circle can be written as

$$(x - x_0)^2 + (y - y_0)^2 = r^2$$

where the point (x_0, y_0) is the centre of the circle, and its radius is r.

Define a derived type, along similar lines to those used in Example 8.3, which can be used to represent a circle by its name, the coordinates of its centre, and its radius. Use this derived type in a program which requests the user to provide the coordinates of the centre of the circle, and of a point on its circumference, and calculates the radius of the circle from this information. Finally, the program should print the coefficients of the equation that defines the circle in the form

$$ax^2 + by^2 + cx + dy + e = 0$$

8.4   Using the two derived types that were defined for Exercise 8.1, create a third derived type, called `family`, which contains the names of the father, mother, son and daughter of a 'typical' four-person family, together with their home address. Use this in a program which requests the relevant details for each member of the family, and where they live, and then prints a summary of the family in a form similar to that shown below:

```
The Addison family live in Reading, MA
Wesley is 53
His wife Sheila is 47
Their daughter Lynne is 21 and their son Stephen is 24
```

8.5   Write a function which, when supplied with two arguments of type `point`, as already defined on several occasions, returns the distance between the two points as its result. (Note that this is similar to Exercise 4.1, but using derived type arguments.)

8.6   Define two derived types called `person` and `employee`; `person` should have two components for a personal name and a family name, while `employee` should have three components — one of type `person` to identify the employee by name, and the others to contain the employee's staff number and salary.

   Using the straight selection sorting method described in Example 7.1 write a program which will enable an array of employees to be sorted into any of the following:

   (a) alphabetic order of family name
   (b) increasing order of staff number (that is, lowest staff number first)
   (c) decreasing order of salary (that is, highest salary first)

8.7   In Example 8.3 we wrote a function which calculated the line joining two points. Using the same derived types, write a subroutine for the module `geometry` which calculates the point at the intersection of two lines. Your subroutine should establish whether the lines are parallel and, therefore, have no point of intersection, and return an error flag to indicate whether it was possible to calculate the coordinates of the point of intersection.

8.8   Modify the program that you wrote for Exercise 7.6 so that a set is represented by a derived type consisting of two components: an array to contain the members of the set and an integer count of the number of elements in the set. This avoids the problem of determining which elements of the array are not being used.

8.9   Write a function which has two dummy arguments, `first_person` and `second_person`, both of a derived type which contains, among other things, the first and last names of a person, the age of the person, and the sex of the person. The function should return an integer value indicating the relationship between the two people represented by the arguments, according to the following rules:

   • If the last names are the same then they are related, otherwise they are unrelated, and the function result should be zero.
   • If they are related then a difference in age of over 20 years indicates a parent–child relationship; a difference of less than 20 years, and both ages over 20, implies a marital relationship; a difference of less than 20 years, and at least one aged 20 or less, implies a sibling relationship.

The value of the function should then be as follows:

Husband–wife	1
Father–son	2
Father–daughter	3
Mother–son	4
Mother–daughter	5
Brother–brother	6
Sister–sister	7
Brother–sister	8

If the person represented by the first dummy argument is the older then the result is as shown; if that person is the younger then the value is negated (that is, daughter–father is returned as −3).

Test your function in a program which either reads two sets of personal details from the keyboard or has them as initial values in the main program and uses the function to cause an appropriate message to be printed, along the following lines:

```
Sarah Ellis is the daughter of Miles Ellis
```

8.10   Create two definitions for a derived type called `point` which represents a point in two-dimensional space; the first should use Cartesian coordinates (x, y) and the second polar coordinates (r, ϕ). Place each definition in a different module. Now write a program which uses *both* modules and declares two variables of each type. The program should ask the user for the polar coordinates of two points, and should calculate the equation of the line joining them, in the form

$$ax + by + c = 0$$

Finally the program should print the coordinates of the two points in both polar and Cartesian coordinates, followed by the equation of the line joining them. (Hint: see Example 8.3 for assistance in calculating the coefficients of the equation.)

*8.11   The fact that factoring large integers into prime components is an extremely expensive process forms the basis for many modern encryption algorithms. In 1986 the record was the factoring of an 81-digit number using eight microcomputers, each of which ran for 150 hours. In 1988, a 100-digit number was factorized. Because of such successes, 200-digit numbers are being proposed as the basis for codes used by the United States government. If you wish to work in this area, modern methods for factoring large numbers (the quadratic sieve) are described by Cipra (1988), Gerver (1983) and Richards (1982); Richards also discusses public key codes.

Surprisingly, finding the highest common factor of two integers is a computationally easy problem, solved by the ancient Greeks. The following is Euclid's algorithm for finding the highest common factor of two positive integers a and b.

1.   Let q and r be the quotient and remainder when a is divided by b. It is easy to prove that the highest common factor of a and b is the highest common factor of b and r.
2.   If r is zero, then the highest common factor is b. If r is not zero, replace a and b by b and r, respectively, and repeat step 1.

After, at most, $\min(a, b) + 1$ iterations, the highest common factor will be found.

Write a function to implement Euclid's algorithm. Use this function to find the highest common factor of 26 379 714 and 876 147 and then the highest common factor of 24 019 and 48 611.

8.12   Create a derived type for rational numbers and make its components private. Place this definition in a module, together with a procedure that will create a rational number given two integers (which may be positive or negative). This procedure should reduce the rational number by finding the highest common factor of the numerator and denominator and dividing it into them – you can use the function written in Exercise 8.11 to do this.

Write two more procedures for the module that, given a rational number, will return the numerator and the denominator, respectively.

Test your module by creating rational numbers 5/3, 60/84. Then print out the numerator and denominator of each of the resulting rational numbers.

More control over input and output

9

9.1 The interface between the user and the computer

9.2 Formats and edit descriptors

9.3 Input editing

9.4 Output editing

9.5 read, write and print statements

9.6 More powerful formats

The input and output facilities of any programming language are extremely important, because it is through these features of the language that communication between the user and the program is carried out. However, this frequently leads to a conflict between ease of use and complexity and F, therefore, provides facilities for input and output at two quite different levels.

The list-directed input and output statements that we have been using up to now provide the capability for straightforward input from the keyboard and output to the display or printer. These statements, however, allow the user very little control over the source or the layout of the input data, or over the destination or layout of the printed results.

This chapter introduces the more general input/output features of F, by means of which the programmer may specify exactly how the data will be presented and interpreted, from which of the available input units it is to be read, exactly how the results are to be displayed, and to which of the available output units the results are to be sent. Because of the interaction with the world outside the computer, input and output has the potential for more execution-time errors than most other parts of a program, so F's approach to the detection of such errors is also briefly discussed.

9.1   The interface between the user and the computer

We have now learned how to instruct the computer to manipulate both numeric and character information, to repeat sequences of instructions and to take alternative courses of action depending upon decisions which are only made during the execution of the program. We have seen how we may use procedures to simplify our program structure while simultaneously adding greatly to the flexibility of the options before us, and we have even been able to create new data types to meet our own particular needs. Compared with the sophistication of which we are now capable in these areas, our control over the layout and interpretation of input data and the presentation of results has so far been woefully primitive. The problem arises because it is in this area that the world of the computer (where everything is stored as an electric, magnetic or optical signal in one of only two states) comes face-to-face with the world of the human computer user (where there are an almost infinite number of ways of storing or presenting information). It is the interface between these two worlds that we must now examine.

A graphic example of this problem can be seen in the line of data shown in Figure 9.1, which has the digits 1 to 9 typed in the first nine positions. There are an enormous number of possible interpretations of this, apparently simple, line.

- It could be the number 123456789
- Or it could be the nine numbers 1, 2, 3, 4, 5, 6, 7, 8 and 9
- Or it could be the three numbers 123, 456, 789
- Or it could even be the number 12345.6789
- Or it could represent the four numbers 1.23, 0.45, 67 and 8900
- Or it could be one of hundreds of other valid interpretations of these nine digits

Although these are all real possibilities, we have had little difficulty in dealing with input from the keyboard since the rules that were laid down in Section 3.4 accord with the natural way of presenting data, in most cases, and lead to a quite unambiguous interpretation of what has been typed.

The situation with output, however, has been more problematical since there have been many occasions when we should have liked to have more control over the way in which the results are laid out on the screen. For example, if we wished to print the character string The answers are followed by the values of

123456789

Figure 9.1   A line of input data.

two variables (which are approximately 12.34 and −7.89) we have a potentially vast choice of ways in which to arrange our results. They could all be on one line like this·

```
The answers are 12.34 -7.89
```

or they could be on two lines:

```
The answers are
12.34    -7.89
```

or three lines:

```
The answers are
        12.34
        -7.89
```

or a number of other variations. They could also be printed immediately below the last item, or separated from it by one or more blank lines. The number might be printed with two decimal places, or with five, or in any other way that we might wish. The possibilities are enormous.

As if this was not enough, there is also the question of where the data comes from and where the results are to be sent. The data will often be typed directly at a keyboard, but in larger systems, or for large amounts of data, it will probably be first input to a file in the file store by some quite different means and then read from there. In a similar fashion, results may be displayed on a screen, printed on a printer, or sent to a file. Furthermore, the peripheral device being used for the input or the output may be a local one which is more or less directly attached to the computer, or it may be at some remote site, possibly many miles away.

All of these questions need to be resolved every time any data is input to, or results output from, a program.

Up to this point all our input and output has been carried out using list-directed **read** and **print** statements, and we have not, apparently, considered any of these difficulties at all! In fact, however, the F processor has been taking care of everything on our behalf, and it is now time for us to learn how to specify those aspects over which we wish to exercise control – while leaving the processor to look after the rest.

If we consider the **read** statement first, we find that the source of the data is dealt with by a neat piece of sleight-of-hand. When first introducing the list-directed input and output statements in Chapter 3 we said that the data would be read from the default input unit, which is defined by the particular computer system being used; typically, for personal computers and workstations, it will be the keyboard. In a similar way, the **print** statement sends its results to the default output unit, which is also processor dependent, but which will usually be the computer's display or printer.

The interpretation of the data by a list-directed **read** statement has been dealt with primarily by treating a space or a comma (or a /) as a separator between items of data, and using the 'obvious' interpretation of the data items between the separators.

We should now define more formally how this process actually operates.

The data is considered to be a sequence of alternating values and **value separators**, with the occurrence of a value separator indicating the termination of the previous value. The value separators are of four types:

- a comma, optionally preceded and/or followed by one or more blanks;
- a slash (/), optionally preceded and/or followed by one or more blanks;
- one or more consecutive blanks;
- the end of the record (that is, the line), optionally preceded by one or more blanks.

If there are no values between two consecutive value separators, for example there are two consecutive commas, then the effect is to read a **null value**. The effect of this is to leave the value of the corresponding variable in the input list *unchanged*. This often surprises people!

If a slash value separator is encountered then no more data items are read, and processing of the input statement is ended. If there are any remaining items in the input list then the result is as though null values had been input to them; in other words, their values remain unchanged.

For numeric data, that is all that is to be said, but for character data there is the further rule concerning the requirement for delimiting quotation marks. Because of the above rules concerning terminators, character strings being input by a list-directed **read** statement must be delimited by matching quotation marks unless *all* of the following conditions are met:

- the character data does not contain any blanks, any commas or any slashes (that is, it does not contain any of the value separators discussed earlier);
- the character data is all contained within a single record or line;
- the first non-blank character is not a quotation mark, since this would be taken as a delimiting character, or an apostrophe, for compatibility with Fortran in which this is an alternative delimiting character;
- the leading characters are not numeric followed by an asterisk, since this would be confused with the multiple data item form ($n*c$).

If all of these conditions are met, which essentially means that the character data being input is a single 'word', then it is treated in exactly the same way as numeric data and, in particular, is terminated by any of the value separators which will terminate a numeric data item (blank, comma, slash or end of record); it may also be repeated by means of a multiple data item of the form $n*c$.

For a great many purposes, therefore, list-directed input is perfectly satisfactory. However, the layout of the results by a list-directed **print** statement has been less satisfactory, since each **print** statement causes output to start at the beginning of the next line and prints the various items in a 'reasonable' format. Although the results will always be printed in a readable fashion the programmer has very little control over their layout.

These two list-directed input/output statements are thus restricted in their ability to define both the format of the information and, especially, its source or destination. The remainder of this chapter will examine how we can provide the flexibility needed in many cases for both input and output.

9.2   Formats and edit descriptors

An input statement must contain three distinct types of information – where the data is to be found, where it is to be stored in the computer's memory, and how it is to be interpreted. Similarly an output statement must define where the results are currently stored, where they are to be sent, and in what form they are to be displayed. These processes are illustrated in diagrammatic form in Figure 9.2, and it can be seen that both processes are, in one sense, the same in that they both take information from one place, transform (or edit) it into a different format, and put the edited version in another place.

We have already discussed in some detail how the relevant locations in the computer's memory are identified and, although some minor extensions to the methods already discussed will be presented in later chapters, there is nothing more to add in this regard for the present.

Furthermore, the input/output statements that we have been using so far do not allow us to specify the nature of the external medium, but always use the

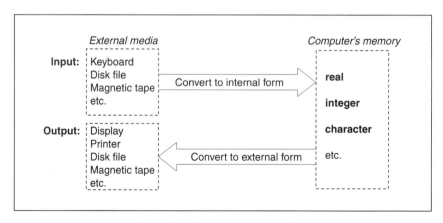

Figure 9.2   Input and output editing.

default input or output unit. We shall see how to change this situation in Section 9.5.

The key element in both the input and output processes, however, is the **editing** of information in one form for presentation in another form, and it is this aspect of input and output which we shall now examine in some detail.

The input and output statements that we have been using thus far have taken the forms

> **read** *, *input_list*
> **print** *, *output_list*

but this has, in fact, been a considerable simplification. Each of these statements also has an alternative form:

> **read** *ch_expr*, *input_list*

and

> **print** *ch_expr*, *output_list*

where *ch_expr* is a character expression.

In both forms the item following the keyword (**read** or **print**) is a **format specifier** which provides a link to the information necessary for the required editing to be carried out as part of the input or output process. This information is called a **format** and consists of a list of **edit descriptors** enclosed in parentheses:

> (*ed_des1*, *ed_des2*, ...)

In the list-directed form which we have been using up to now, the asterisk indicates that the format to be used is a **list-directed format** which will be created by the processor to meet the perceived needs of the particular input or output list — hence its name.

In the new form, the format is called an **embedded format** because it appears as part of the **read** or **print** statement:

> **read** " (*edit_descriptor_list*) ", *input_list*

It is also possible to store such a format in a character variable, and then include the name of the variable, which is, of course, the simplest form of character expression, in the **read** or **print** statement:

> **print** *print_format*, *output_list*

where *print_format* is a character variable containing the format.

In the next two sections we shall present the details of the various edit descriptors, and the ways in which they are used in input and output statements, following which we shall return to the actual statements themselves to examine the question of the source of the data and the destination of the results. For convenience we shall use embedded formats in the examples, but it should be remembered that the form in which the format specifier is stored in a character variable is always an alternative.

9.3 Input editing

We shall start by considering the various edit descriptors that are used for input in conjunction with a **read** statement, since these are the easiest to understand. They fall into two categories — those concerned with the editing of actual data, and those concerned with altering the order in which the characters in the input record are edited, as detailed in Figure 9.3.

The first, and simplest, edit descriptor is used for inputting whole numbers which are to be stored in an *integer* variable, and takes the form

iw

This indicates that the next w characters are to be read and interpreted as an integer. Thus if we wished to read the line shown in Figure 9.1 (which had the digits 1 to 9 typed in positions 1 to 9) as a single integer to be stored in the integer variable n we could write

read "(i9)",n

Descriptor	Meaning
iw	Read the next w characters as an integer
$fw.d$	Read the next w characters as a real number with d digits after the decimal place if no decimal point is present
aw	Read the next w characters as characters
a	Read sufficient characters to fill the input list item, stored as characters
Lw	Read the next w characters as the representation of a logical value
tc	Next character to be read is at position c
tln	Next character to be read is n characters before (tl) or
trn	after (tr) the current position

Figure 9.3 Edit descriptors for input.

If we wished to read the same line as three separate integers (123, 456, 789) then we could write

```
read "(i3,i3,i3)",n1,n2,n3
```

where n1, n2 and n3 are integer variables. This format interacts with the rest of the **read** statement in the following way:

- First the **read** statement recognizes that it requires an integer to store in n1; the format indicates that the first item to be read is an integer occupying the first three character positions (i3). The characters '123' are therefore read and converted to the internal form of the integer 123 before being stored in n1.
- The **read** statement then requires another integer and the format indicates that this is to come from the *next* three character positions (i3). The characters '456' are therefore read and converted to the internal form of the integer 456 before being stored in n2.
- Finally, the process is repeated a third time, causing the characters '789' to be read, converted, and stored in n3 as the integer 789.
- The **read** statement is now satisfied, since data has been read for all of the variables in its input list, and so input of this line of data is complete.

Notice that there is an implied concept of an *index* which is always indicating which is the next character of the input record to be read. Normally this index is moved through the record as characters are read; however, the three tabulation edit descriptors, t, tl and tr, allow the index to be moved without any characters being read.

The first of these, t*c*, causes a tab to character position *c*; in other words the next character to be read will be from position *c*. Thus the statement

```
read "(t4,i2,t8,i2,t2,i4)",x,y,z
```

will, when used with the same line of data, first move the index to position 4 and read the number 45 into x, then move it to position 8 before reading 89 into y, and then move it to position 2 before reading the number 2345 into z. The t edit descriptor thus provides a means not only of skipping over unwanted characters, but also of going back in the record and reading it (or parts of it) again.

The t edit descriptor moves to a character position which is defined *absolutely* by its position in the record, or line of data. The tl and tr edit descriptors, on the other hand, specify a *relative* tab — that is, a move to a character position which is defined relative to the current position. The letters tr followed by a number *n* indicate that the next character is to be *n* positions to the *right* of the current position, while the letters tl followed by a number *n* specify a tab to the *left*, and cause the next character to be *n* positions to the left of (or before) the current position. If `tln` would cause the next position to be before the first character of the record then the pointer is positioned at the start of the record (that is, at the beginning of the line of input data).

The next data edit descriptor is the `f` edit descriptor, which is used for reading real values, and takes a slightly more complicated form than that used for integers:

`fw.d`

This edit descriptor has two different effects, depending upon the layout of the data.

If the data is typed with a decimal point in the appropriate position then the edit descriptor causes the next w characters to be read and converted into a real number. The value of d is irrelevant (although it must be included in the format).

If, on the other hand, the w columns which are to be read as a real number do not contain any decimal point then the value of d indicates where one may be assumed to have been omitted, by specifying that the number has d decimal places. Thus (assuming our usual input record, as shown in Figure 9.1) the statement

`read "(f9.4)",real_num`

will cause the first nine characters to be read as a real number with four decimal places. The variable `real_num` will therefore have the number 12345.6789 stored in it. In a similar way

`read "(f3.1,f2.2,f3.0,tl6,f4.2)",r1,r2,r3,r4`

will cause the value 12.3 to be stored in r1, 0.45 in r2, 678.0 in r3, and 34.56 in r4.

Let us now consider what will happen if the same statement is used to read the line shown in Figure 9.4. The first edit descriptor requires three columns to be read, and since these (.23) contain a decimal point the second part of the edit descriptor is ignored and the value 0.23 stored in r1. In a similar way the `f2.2` descriptor causes the characters '.5' to be read, and r2 is therefore given the value 0.5. The `f3.0` edit descriptor also has its second part overridden by the decimal point in 6.8 and so this is the value stored in r3. Finally, `tl6,f4.0` causes the characters '3.56' to be read, and so this value is stored in r4. Figure 9.5 summarizes the result of reading these two lines of data.

As a general rule, data which is to be stored as real values will be presented to the computer with the decimal points in their correct places. However,

```
.23.56.89
```

Figure 9.4   Another line of data.

```
          read "(f3.1,f2.2,f3.0,tl6,f4.2)", r1,r2,r3,r4

Data:              123456789    .23.56.8

r1 contains        12.3         0.23
r2 contains         0.45        0.5
r3 contains       678.0         6.8
r4 contains        34.56        3.56
```

Figure 9.5 The effect of the f edit descriptor during input.

sometimes, and especially when the data has been collected independently of the programmer, it is presented as whole numbers which need to be processed by the computer as real numbers and on these occasions it can be useful to use a format which, in effect, scales the data appropriately.

There is one further point to be made about the format of real data. In Section 3.3 we saw that a real constant may be written followed by an exponent (for example, 1.5e-6) and a similar format is allowed for numbers being input by a **read** statement. In this case, the exponent may take one of three forms

- a signed integer constant
- e (or E) followed by an optionally signed constant
- d (or D) followed by an optionally signed constant

In the latter two cases the letter (e, E, d or D) may be followed by one or more spaces. The interpretation is identical, regardless of which letter is used.

Thus a real data value may be written in a great many different ways; for example, some of the ways in which the number 361.764 may occur in data are shown in Figure 9.6.

The third major data edit descriptor is the a edit descriptor, which is used to control the editing of character data. It takes one of the forms

a*w*
a

```
            361.764
            3.61764+2
            361764-3
            0.0361764e4
            3617.64d-1
            3.61764E +2
            361.764+0
```

Figure 9.6 Some of the ways in which the real data item 361.764 may be intput.

During input, the edit descriptor a*w* refers to the next *w* characters (just as i*w* and f*w*.*d* refer to *w* characters). However, a character variable has a defined length and any string which is to be stored in it must be made to have the same length. If we assume that the length of the input list item is *len* then the following rules apply:

- If *w* is less than *len* then extra blank characters will be added at the end so as to extend the length of the input character string to *len*. This is similar to the situation with assignment.

- If *w* is greater than *len*, however, the rightmost *len* characters of the input character string will be stored in the input list item. This is the *opposite* of what happens with assignment! The reason for this apparent inconsistency will become apparent when we consider the output of characters in Section 9.4.

An a edit descriptor without any field width *w* is treated as though the field width was identical to the length of the corresponding input list item. Thus, if the three variables ch1, ch2 and ch3 are declared by the following statements:

```
character (len=10) :: ch1
character (len=6) :: ch2
character (len=15) :: ch3
```

then the following two statements will have the identical effect:

```
read "(a10,a6,a15)",ch1,ch2,ch3
read "(a,a,a)",ch1,ch2,ch3
```

Since the form without a field width requires the **read** statement to provide exactly the same number of characters as the length of the variable into which they are to be stored, the question of blank padding or truncation never occurs.

The remaining data edit descriptor is used with logical data, and takes the form

L*w*

where we have used an upper-case L to avoid the potential confusion with the digit 1 that can be caused to human readers by using the lower-case form.

This edit descriptor processes the next *w* characters to derive either a *true* value, a *false* value, or an error. The need to read logical values directly is quite rare and the means of providing the data is somewhat artificial, essentially being based on the first non-blank character in the input field, which must be either an f or a t, or their upper-case equivalents, optionally preceded by a period. Thus any of the following are acceptable as representing *true*:

```
t
true
.T
    .true.
truthful
```

while the following will all be interpreted as *false*:

```
F
False
.f.
    futile
```

Note that if the first non-blank character, other than a period, is not t or f, or their upper-case equivalents, then an error will occur. The input of logical values is not a very common occurrence, but when it is required it is usually in order to read a set of responses to queries, and hence the use of *T, true, False , f,* and so on, as responses for input to the program is often appropriate.

☐ **EXAMPLE 9.1** • • ◦ ◦ ◦ ◦ ■ ■ ■ ■ ■ ■ ■ ■ ■ ◦ ◦ ◦ ◦ ◦ ■ ■ ■ ■ ◦ ◦ ◦ ◦ ◦

1 Problem

A survey, consisting of a maximum of 1000 respondents, has recorded the name, age, sex, marital status, height and weight of a number of people. The information has been recorded as follows:

First name	in columns 1–15
Last name	in columns 21–40
Sex	coded in column 43
	F = female
	M = male
Marital status	coded in column 45
	0 = single
	1 = married
	2 = widowed
	3 = divorced
	4 = cohabiting
	9 = unknown
Age (yrs)	in columns 47, 48
Height (cm)	in columns 51–53
Weight (kg)	in columns 56–62 in the form *kkk.ggg*

The data is terminated by a line which has End of data typed in columns 1 to 11.

Write and test a procedure to read this data and store it in a form suitable for subsequent analysis. Such analysis will require the heights to be stored in metres. You should define a derived type to hold all the data pertaining to one person.

2 Analysis

When developing a large program it is always a good idea first to write and thoroughly test an input procedure. When developing the rest of the program we can then be confident that the data is being correctly input, and can concentrate on the other parts of the program.

The procedure will use a **do** loop to carry out the input, and the only areas to require any particular attention will be the detection of the terminating condition and the conversion of the height in centimetres into metres. This last matter can be dealt with during input by use of an edit descriptor of f3.2, which will cause the data to be interpreted as though it had a decimal point in the required place. Because the format will be quite complicated, and as an example of using non-embedded formats, we shall store the main data format in a character variable. The data will be stored in an array of type person which will be supplied as an argument to the procedure. The maximum number of respondents is not relevant as far as the procedure is concerned since this can be provided as another argument or, preferably, derived by the procedure from the shape of the actual argument array.

Data design

Purpose	Type	Name
A Arguments:		
Array of personal data	person	people
Number of people in survey	integer	number_people
B Local constant:		
Maximum number of data sets	integer	max_people
C Local variables:		
do variable	integer	i
Input data format	character	data_format

Structure plan

1 Set max_people to the size of the dummy argument people
2 Repeat up to max_people times
    2.1 Read next record
    2.2 If terminator found then exit
3 Return number of data sets read

Although the problem, as specified, did not ask for the number of sets of data that were read, this is clearly information that will probably be required during any subsequent processing, and so it seems sensible to provide it.

3 **Solution**

```
module people_survey
   public :: input

   type, public :: person
      private
      character(len=15) :: first_name
      character(len=20) :: last_name
      character(len=1) :: sex    ! M or F
      integer :: marital_status, age
      real :: height, weight
   end type person

contains

   subroutine input(people,number_people)
   ! An input subroutine for a survey

      ! Dummy arguments
      type(person),dimension(:),intent(out) :: people
      integer,intent(out) :: number_people

      ! Local variables
      integer :: i,max_people
      character(len=52) :: data_format
      ! Set max_people to size of input data array
      max_people=size(people)

      ! Display data format
      print *,"Type data as follows: "
      print *,"cols.  1-15 first name"
      print *,"cols. 21-40 last name"
      print *,"col.    43 sex (F=female, M=male)"
      print *,"col.    45 marital status (0=single, 1=married,"
      print *,"             2=widowed, 3=divorced, 4=cohabiting,"
      print *,"             9=unknown)"
      print *,"cols. 47,48 age (in years)"
      print *,"cols. 51-53 height (in cm.)"
      print *,"cols. 56-62 weight (in kg. in the form kkk.ggg)"
      print *," "
      print *,"Data should be terminated by the words ", &
               "'End of data' typed in cols. 1-11"
      print *," "

      ! Define input data format
      data_format = "(a15,t21,a20,t43,a1,t45,i1,t47,i2," &
                  //"t51,f3.2,t56,f7.3)"

      ! Loop to read data
      do i=1,max_people
         read data_format, people(i)
```

```
                        ! Check if this is the terminator record
                        if (people(i)%first_name(1:11) == "End of data") then
                            exit
                        end if
                    end do

                    ! Check to see if a terminator was found
                    if (i>max_people) then
                        print *,"Maximum number of records (",   &
                                max_people,") read"
                        print *,"with no terminator - input halted"
                        ! Save number of data records read
                        number_people = max_people
                    else
                        number_people = i-1
                    end if

                end subroutine input

            end module people_survey
```

A suitable program to test this subroutine might be as follows:

```
    program test_input
    use people_survey

        type(person),dimension(3) :: survey
        integer :: i,number

        ! Get input data
        call input(survey,number)

        ! Print data read
        do i=1,number
            print *,survey(i)
        end do

    end program test_input
```

There are two points to mention about this program. In the module the derived type people has been defined with private components, in accordance with good practice. However, this means that its components are not available outside the module, and that the test program cannot print the data. During testing, therefore, the **private** statement will need to be removed. An alternative would be to put a simple print procedure in the module, but this would be rather extreme for such a simple test. Note also that the data array is very small. A maximum of three data records is sufficient to test that the input procedure will read more than one record successfully, while it is small enough to check what happens if no terminator record is provided. This is the point of testing – to check all possibilities – and an array size of 1000, as specified in the statement of the problem would be absurd for testing!

9.4 Output editing

As we might expect, the edit descriptors used for output are essentially the same as those used for input, although there are some additional ones that are only available for output and the interpretation of the others is slightly different. Figure 9.7 shows the main edit descriptors that are available for output, and we shall briefly examine each in turn.

The i edit descriptor (iw) causes an integer to be output in such a way as to utilize the next w character positions. These w positions will consist of one or more spaces (if necessary), followed by a minus sign if the number is negative, followed by the value of the number. Thus the statements

```
tom = 23
dick = 715
harry = -12
print "(i5,i5,i5)",tom,dick,harry
```

will produce the following line of output (where the symbol ◊ represents a space)

```
◊◊◊23◊◊715◊◊-12
```

If the output is to go to the computer's *printer* then the results which actually appear will be very slightly different, as every line will be preceded by an extra space. The reason for this need not concern us here, other than to mention that it is for compatibility with an additional means for formatting available in Fortran. If the output is sent to a display screen, or most other peripheral devices, the layout will be exactly as defined.

Descriptor	Meaning
iw	Output an integer in the next w character positions
fw.d	Output a real number in the next w character positions with d decimal places
aw	Output a character string in the next w character positions
a	Output a character string, starting at the next character position, with no leading or trailing blanks
Lw	Output $w - 1$ blanks, followed by T or F to represent a logical value
tc	Output the next item starting at character position c
t$l$$n$	Output the next item starting n character positions before (tl) or
t$r$$n$	after (tr) the current position

Figure 9.7 Edit descriptors for output.

The f edit descriptor operates in a similar way, and f*w.d* indicates that a real number is to be output occupying *w* characters, of which the last *d* are to follow the decimal point. Note that the real value to be output is *rounded* (not truncated) to *d* places of decimals before it is sent to the relevant output device. Rounding is carried out in the usual arithmetic way. Thus the statements

```
x = 3.14159
y = -275.3024
z = 12.9999
print "(f10.3,f10.3,f10.3)",x,y,z
```

will produce the following line of output:

```
◊◊◊◊◊3.142◊◊-275.302◊◊◊◊◊13.000
```

Notice that, because the edit descriptors each specify only three places of decimals, the value of x is printed as 3.142 (rounded up), the value of y as −275.302 (rounded down), and the value of z as 13.000 (rounded up).

It is important to realize that, for *all* numeric edit descriptors, if the number does not require the full **field width** *w* it will be preceded by one or more spaces. By allowing more room than is necessary, several numbers may be spaced across the page and the printing of tables becomes relatively easy. An example of this technique is shown in the following program:

```
program tabular_output
   real,parameter :: third=1.0/3.0
   real :: x
   integer :: i
   do i=1,10
      x=i
      print "(f15.4,f15.4,f15.4)",x,sqrt(x),x**third
   end do
end program tabular_output
```

The output format used here specifies that the three items to be printed (x, $\sqrt{x}$, $\sqrt[3]{x}$) are all to use an edit descriptor of f15.4. The three numbers are therefore spread evenly across the page, with the next three directly below them, and so on. The results produced by this program can be seen in Figure 9.8.

As we might expect, the a edit descriptor works in a similar fashion for output as it does for input, and a*w* will, therefore, cause characters to be output to the next *w* character positions of the output record. As was the case for input, therefore, we need to establish exactly what happens if the length of the output list item is not exactly *w*. The rules that apply here are similar to those that we had for input, where *len* is the length of the character variable or constant being output:

```
           1.0000        1.0000        1.0000
           2.0000        1.4142        1.2599
           3.0000        1.7321        1.4422
           4.0000        2.0000        1.5874
           5.0000        2.2361        1.7100
           6.0000        2.4495        1.8171
           7.0000        2.6458        1.9129
           8.0000        2.8284        2.0000
           9.0000        3.0000        2.0801
          10.0000        3.1623        2.1544
```

Figure 9.8 An example of tabular printing.

- If w is greater than *len* then the character string will be right-justified within the output field, and will be preceded by one or more blanks. This is similar to what happens with the i and f edit descriptors.
- If w is less than *len* then the leftmost w characters will be output.

It will be remembered that, during the discussion of the use of the a format for input in Section 9.3, the apparent inconsistency between the truncation on the left during input and truncation on the right during assignment was raised. We can now see that this was necessary to ensure compatibility between input and output. If a character string is output to a field larger than its length then it will have spaces added at the beginning, as with all other types of data. If that same external representation were subsequently to be read back into the computer, using the same format, then it is necessary that the extra blanks at the beginning be removed, and not the important characters at the end! The apparent incompatibility with assignment is, therefore, much less important than the major incompatibility between input and output that would occur if a character string were to be input with truncation at the right.

Note, however, that for *list-directed input* assignment rules apply, and a character string which is too long for the variable it is to be input to will be truncated on the right.

Just as was the case with input, we may omit the field width with an a edit descriptor, in which case the character string being output will occupy exactly the space it requires, with neither leading nor trailing blanks. This form of the a edit descriptor is, therefore, particularly useful on output, since it can enable the same basic format to be used with character variables of different lengths.

Finally, there is the L edit descriptor for use in outputting a representation of logical values. This is perfectly straightforward, and the descriptor Lw will cause $w - 1$ blanks to be output, followed by the letter T or the letter F to indicate *true* or *false*.

There is one further point that should be made at this stage. In the example shown in Figure 9.8, as in several other programs in this section, the same edit descriptor has been repeated several times. A number, called a **repeat count**, may be placed *before* the i, f, a or L edit descriptors to indicate how many times they are to be repeated. Thus the format

```
(i5,i5,i5,f6.2,f6.2,f6.2,f6.2)
```

could be written more succinctly, and more clearly, as

```
(3i5,4f6.2)
```

A repeat count may be used in formats for both input and output to cause repetition of an edit descriptor which is used in conjunction with an input or output list item; it cannot be used to repeat the other edit descriptors, such as t, tl and tr.

The remaining edit descriptors (t, tl and tr) operate in essentially the same way as for input, if we assume that the output record consists initially of spaces, and enable items to be positioned in an exact place in the record (or line).

SELF-TEST EXERCISES 9.1

1   What is a value separator during list-directed input?

2   What are the possible value separators during list-directed input?

3   Under what circumstances may character data be read by a list-directed **read** statement without being enclosed between quotation marks?

4   What is an embedded format?

5   What is an edit descriptor?

6   If the user responds to the following program by typing the nine digits 1 to 9 without any intervening characters, what *exactly* will be printed?

```
program test9_1_6
   integer :: a,b
   real :: c,d
   read "(t6,i4,tl6,i4,tl6,f4.1,tl6,f4.2)",a,b,c,d
   print "(i4,a,i5,a,i5,a,f6.2,a,f6.2,a,f8.3)", &
         a," minus",b," is",a-b,";  ",c," minus",d," is",c-d
end program test9_1_6
```

7   If the user responds to the following program by typing the nine digits 1 to 9 without any intervening characters, what *exactly* will be printed?

```
program test9_1_7
   character(len=6) :: a,b,c
   read "(a8,t1,a4,t1,a)",a,b,c
   print "(t6,a8,tr5,a4,tr5,a)",a,b,c
   print "(t6,a,tr5,a,tr5,a)",a,b,c
end program test9_1_7
```

9.5   read, write and print statements

Now that we have discussed all the major edit descriptors that can be used to assist in the interpretation of data and the presentation of results, it is time to return to the question that we deferred in Section 9.2, namely the source of data and the destination of results.

Both variants of the **read** statement that we have used up to now have taken their input from the default input unit. In order to vary this source of data, and also to allow the possibility of monitoring the success or otherwise of the reading process, we must use a more general form of **read** statement:

   read (*cilist*) *input_list*

where *cilist* is a **control information list** consisting of one or more items, known as **specifiers**, separated by commas. There are a number of specifiers that can be used in conjunction with the **read** statement, but we shall only discuss three of them here; further specifiers will be introduced as they are needed in Chapters 10 and 15. All these specifiers take the same basic form

   keyword = *value*

Such specifiers as are used in a particular case may appear in any order.

There must always be a **unit specifier** in the control information list, which takes the form

   unit = *unit*

where *unit* is the input device (or *unit* in F parlance) from which input is to be taken. *unit* may also be the name of an **internal file**, as we shall see in Chapter 15. It either takes the form of a scalar integer expression whose value is zero or positive, or it may be an asterisk to indicate that the default input unit is to be used. The way in which the unit number is related to a particular peripheral device is, to a large extent, dependent upon the computer system being used. Normally, some units will be **preconnected** and will be automatically available to all programs. The default input unit and the default output unit will always be preconnected in this way, but each F implementation may well have different unit numbers associated with them. Any other peripheral devices or files which the program requires must be given a unit number and connected to the program by an **open** statement (see Section 10.3).

The default input unit will usually be preconnected as unit 1 or unit 5. (This is purely for historical reasons, since IBM, and several other manufacturers, used unit 5 for the card reader and unit 6 for the printer in their early Fortran systems.) We shall assume that it is unit 5, but it must be emphasized that *this is only an assumption*; a particular implementation may use any positive number, or zero, for the default input unit.

With this assumption we may write

```
unit = 5
```

or

```
unit = *
```

to identify the default input unit.

Normally the input will need to be converted from some *external* form such as the characters sent by a keyboard, to an *internal* form suitable for storing in the computer's memory. To carry out this conversion we have already seen that we need a format, and this is identified by a **format specifier** which takes one of the forms

```
fmt = ch_expr
fmt = *
```

in an analogous fashion to the format specifications discussed earlier in this chapter.

Note that the statement

```
read (unit=*,fmt=*) a,b,c
```

is identical in its effect to the earlier list-directed input statement

```
read *,a,b,c
```

The remaining specifier that we shall discuss here is concerned with monitoring the outcome of the reading process, and takes the form

```
iostat = io_status
```

where io_status is an integer variable. At the conclusion of the execution of the **read** statement io_status will be set to a value which the program can use to determine whether any errors occurred during the input process. There are four possibilities:

- The variable is set to zero to indicate that no errors occurred.
- The variable is set to a processor-dependent positive value to indicate that an error has occurred.
- The variable is set to a processor-dependent negative value to indicate that a condition known as an end-of-file condition has occurred; we shall discuss this condition, and the situations in which it can occur, in Chapter 10.

- The variable is set to a processor-dependent negative value to indicate that a condition known as an end-of-record condition has occurred; we shall discuss this condition, and the situations in which it can occur, in Chapter 15

For the present, therefore, we may simply use iostat to determine whether or not the reading of data was carried out successfully by testing the value of the variable in an **if** or **case** construct:

```
read (unit=*,fmt="(5f6.3)",iostat=ioerror) p,q,r,s,t
if (ioerror /= 0) then       ! ioerror is non-zero
    .                        ! Print error/warning message
    .                        ! and take remedial action
    .                        ! before exit from procedure
    return
end if
! Continue with normal processing
    .
    .
    .
```

Output is essentially the reverse of input, so far as the transfer of information is concerned, and as one would expect, the facilities available are essentially the same. The most obvious difference is that for input the word **read** is used in all cases, but for output we have two words. We have used the **print** statement for list-directed output for user-formatted output to the default output unit. To take advantage of the full range of facilities, however, we must use a different word, **write**, in a form of statement which is almost identical to that used for input:

write (*cilist*) *output_list*

Exactly the same specifiers are available as was the case for the **read** statement, although it is impossible to encounter an end-of-file condition or an end-of-record condition during output. The only other difference is the obvious one that an asterisk as a unit identifier refers to the default *output* unit.

As was the case for input, the choice of a unit number for the default output unit is dependent upon the particular implementation. In this book *we shall assume that the default output unit is 6* and that, therefore, the following statements are equivalent:

```
write (unit=6,fmt=*) d,e,f
write (unit=*,fmt=*) d,e,f
print *,d,e,f
```

9.6 More powerful formats

This chapter has described the means whereby a program may define formats for both input and output of considerable complexity. However, a number of other features are available to facilitate still more control of input and output. Probably the most important of these concern multi-record formats, and the repetition of formats.

Let us consider a program that wishes to read 12 real numbers into an array arr, of size 12, typed 4 to a line. With our present knowledge we could write

```
read "(4f12.3)",arr(1:4)
read "(4f12.3)",arr(5:8)
read "(4f12.3)",arr(9:12)
```

However, consider what would happen if we wrote

```
read "(4f12.3)",arr
```

which is the same as writing

```
read "(4f12.3)",arr(1:12)
```

After the **read** statement has used the format to input four real numbers (which are placed in the first four elements of arr) it finds that the input list is not yet exhausted, and that another real number is required. The format *is* completed, however, and it follows that this input record contains no more useful information. There is only one sensible thing to do at this stage – namely to read a new record and interpret its contents using the same format.

Whenever a format is fully used up and there are still items in the input (or output) list awaiting processing, the format will be repeated. The rules governing the point from which it will be repeated are straightforward:

- If there are no nested parentheses then the format is repeated from the beginning.
- If the format contains any nested parentheses then it is repeated from immediately after the left parenthesis corresponding to the rightmost nested parenthesis.
- If the left parenthesis defined above is preceded by a repeat count then the format is repeated including the repeat count.

The following examples should make this clear; an arrow (↑) is shown below the point from which repetition (if any) will take place:

```
(i6,10x,i5,3f10.2)
 ↑
(i6,10x,i5,(3f10.2))
              ↑
(i6,(10x,i5),3f10.2)
     ↑
(f6.2,(2f4.1,2x,i4,4(i7,f7.2)))
      ↑
(f6.2,2(2f4.1,2x,i4),4(i7,f7.2))
                        ↑
(f6.2,(2(2f4.2,2x,i4),4(i7,f7.2)))
      ↑
((f6.2,2(2f4.2,2x,i4),4(i7,f7.2)))
 ↑
```

The repetition of a format can be extremely useful; however, in many cases it is also desirable to be able to define a format which processes two or more separate lines, or (more accurately) **records**. This is achieved by the / edit descriptor, which must be separated from any preceding or succeeding descriptor by a comma, and which indicates the end of the current record.

On input, a / causes the rest of the current record to be ignored and the next input item to be the first item of the *next* record. On output, a / terminates the current record and starts a new one. Thus the statement

read "(3f8.2,/,3i6)",a,b,c,p,q,r

will read three real numbers from the first record and three integers from the second.

Multiple consecutive / descriptors cause input records to be skipped or null (blank) records to be output. Thus the statement

read "(3f8.2,/,/,3i6)",a,b,c,p,q,r

will cause three real numbers to be read from the *first* record and three integers from the *third*. The second record will be skipped and not read. Because a sequence of / edit descriptors separated by commas is rather ugly it is permitted to precede a / edit descriptor by a repeat count, in the same way as with a, f, i and l edit descriptors. Thus an alternative to the previous statement is

read "(3f8.2,2/,3i6)",a,b,c,p,q,r

Multiple / descriptors are particularly useful on output, as we can see in the following program extract, which will produce the output shown in Figure 9.9 if a and b have the values 12.25 and 23.5, respectively:

```
                    Multi-record example


          The sum of 12.25 and 23.50 is 35.75

          Their product is 287.875
```

Figure 9.9 An example of a multi-line output format.

```
write (unit=6,   &
       fmt="(t10,a,3/,a,f6.2,a,f6.2,a," //          &
       " f7.2,2/,a,f10.3)") "Multi-record example", &
       "The sum of",a," and",b," is",a+b,           &
       "Their product is",a*b
```

Finally, it should be pointed out that the combination of a / edit descriptor and a repeated format can provide a very powerful degree of flexibility; thus, the following format

```
(i6,/,(i4,3f12.2))
```

specifies that the first record consists of a single integer, and that the following ones all consist of an integer followed by three real numbers, since the format will be repeated as many times as necessary from the left parenthesis before the i4 descriptor.

◻ **EXAMPLE 9.2** •

1 Problem

A piece of experimental apparatus is monitoring the radioactive decay of a specimen. At approximately regular intervals it records the time since the start of the experiment (in hundredths of a second), the number of α-particles emitted during the interval, the number of β-particles emitted and the amount of γ-radiation in the same period. These are output as an eight-digit number (for the time) and three six-digit numbers. There are five spaces between each number.

Write a program to read this data and to print a table containing the following information: a sequence number for each interval, the length of the interval, the three readings obtained and the average emission of α-particles, β-particles and γ-rays (per second) during the interval. After 1000 time intervals print the time interval which had the highest rate of emission of γ-radiation.

2 **Analysis**

This is a straightforward problem, which is primarily concerned with the use of formats to read the data and lay out the results, apart from one aspect. This type of problem is quite common, and it would obviously be absurd to have to type in all the data every time that the program is run. We shall see in Chapter 10 how to avoid this problem by storing the data in a file. A related issue is that if the data is typed at the keyboard then, in all probability, it will appear on the screen interspersed with the results. We shall ignore this aspect of the problem for now, but will return to it in Example 10.1. We shall use constants (input and output) in which to store the unit numbers, thus making it much easier to change these if it should subsequently be desired to do so. We shall also only test the program with a small number of data items at this stage.

Data design

Purpose	Type	Name
A Constants:		
I/O unit numbers	**integer**	input, output
Maximum number of readings	**integer**	max_readings
B Variables:		
Time since start (data)	**real**	time
Experimental readings (data)	**integer**	alpha, beta, gamma
do variable (and sequence no.)	**integer**	i
Time of last reading and interval	**real**	last_time, period
Average emissions	**real**	av_alpha, av_beta, av_gamma
Maximum average gamma	**real**	max_av_gamma
Interval with max ave. gamma	**integer**	max_interval

Structure plan

1 Initialize maximum gamma radiation and interval
2 Print column headings
3 Repeat max_readings times
    3.1 Read next set of data
    3.2 Calculate length of interval and average emissions
    3.3 Print details
    3.4 If γ-radiation > max γ-radiation then
        3.4.1 Save maximum γ-radiation and interval number
4 Print details of maximum γ-radiation

This is fairly straightforward except for step 2. We shall be printing a table with eight columns and it is sensible to identify these by headings. We can do this by means of a **write** statement which uses a format consisting of a edit descriptors, interspersed with appropriate positioning descriptors to place the column headings in the correct places.

We also need to consider the formats for both input and output. As is often the case, the format of the data is already defined and our format definition must therefore reflect it. In this case it is quite simple:

```
(f8.2,tr5,i6,tr5,i6,tr5,i6)
```

The time is provided in hundredths of a second so the easiest approach is to read it as a real number in seconds with an implied decimal point before the last two digits. The other items are all integers. Notice that we have a repeated sequence (tr5,i6) in the format shown above. We can shorten this format in one of two ways, either by enclosing this sequence in parentheses and preceding it by a repeat count, or by including the leading spaces as part of the numeric field – although this could be dangerous as there is no guarantee that there is not some other data in the input records that we are ignoring (that is, not reading):

```
(f8.2,3(tr5,i6))
```

or

```
(f8.2,3i11)
```

Notice that, although we stated earlier that only data edit descriptors (and the / edit descriptor) were repeatable, the tr edit descriptor in the first alternative has also been repeated. This is allowed when it is part of a repeated sequence which contains at least one repeatable edit descriptor.

Output is always rather different from input in one important respect, namely that we usually have complete control over its format. In this case we wish to produce a table of eight items – a sequence number, a time interval (to one hundredth of a second), three integer values and three averages. Although, at first sight, a suitable format might be

```
(i6,f8.2,3i8,3f8.2)
```

more detailed examination of the layout, and of the expected size of the results, leads to the conclusion that a more aesthetically pleasing layout might be obtained with the format

```
(i6,f8.2,2i6,i7,2f9.2,f10.2)
```

Notice that all the edit descriptors in this format have a field width wider than is necessary in order to space the columns across the page, and also to leave room for column titles.

3 **Solution**

```
program Radioactive_decay
! This program processes experimental data relating
! to radioactive decay

    ! Constant declarations
    ! max_readings is maximum number of sets of data
    ! input and output are the unit numbers for reading
    ! and writing
    integer,parameter :: max_readings=5,input=5,output=6

    ! Variable declarations
    integer :: alpha,beta,gamma,i,max_interval
    real :: time,last_time,period, &
            av_alpha,av_beta,av_gamma,max_av_gamma

    ! Initialize variables
    last_time = 0.0
    max_interval = 0
    max_av_gamma = 0.0

    ! Print headings
    write (unit=output,fmt="(a,t11,a,t17,a,t24,a,t30,a,t37, " // &
        "a,t46,a,t55,a,/,t38,a,t47,a,t56,a)") "Interval",      &
        "Time","Alpha","Beta","Gamma","Average","Average",     &
        "Average","Alpha","Beta","Gamma"

    ! Process max_readings sets of data in a loop
    do i=1,max_readings
        read (unit=input,fmt="(f8.2,3(tr5,i6))") &
            time,alpha,beta,gamma

        ! Calculate interval since last readings
        period = time-last_time
        last_time = time

        ! Calculate average rates of emission
        av_alpha = alpha/period
        av_beta = beta/period
        av_gamma = gamma/period

        ! Print statistics for this interval
        write (unit=output,fmt="(i6,f8.2,2i6,i7,2f9.2,f10.2)") &
            i,period,alpha,beta,gamma,av_alpha,av_beta,av_gamma

        ! Check for maximum gamma radiation in this period
        if (av_gamma > max_av_gamma) then
            max_av_gamma = av_gamma
            max_interval = i
        end if
    end do

    ! Print details of interval with maximum gamma radiation
    write (unit=output,fmt="(t3,a,f7.2,a,i5)")                 &
        "Maximum average gamma radiation was",max_av_gamma, &
        " in interval",max_interval

end program Radioactive_decay
```

```
Interval  Time  Alpha  Beta  Gamma  Average  Average  Average
                                    Alpha    Beta     Gamma
   1      2.56   175    23    401    68.36    8.98    156.64
   2      2.59   168    22    395    64.86    8.49    152.51
   3      2.48   181    27    412    72.98   10.89    166.13
   4      2.51   177    25    410    70.52    9.96    163.35
   5      2.48   166    29    391    66.94   11.69    157.66
Maximum average gamma radiation was 166.13 in interval    3
```

Figure 9.10 Results produced by the Radioactive_decay program.

An example of the results produced by this program can be seen in Figure 9.10.

SELF-TEST EXERCISES 9.2

1   What is the major difference between a **write** and a **print** statement?

2   What is the purpose of an iostat specifier?

3   When is a format, or part of one, repeated?

4   If necessary, where will each of the following formats be repeated from?

    (a) (3i8,2f8.2)
    (b) (3i8,2(tr3,f5.2))
    (c) (3(tr3,i5),2f8.2)
    (d) (3(tr3,i5),2(tr3,f5.2))
    (e) (3i8/2f8.2)
    (f) (3i8,/,2(tr3,f5.2))

5   Write formats and associated input or output statements to read or print the
    dimensions of a box as follows:

    (a) Read the dimensions in metric form, where each side is less than 10 metres
    and the data is typed in the form

        m.cc by *m.cc* by *m.cc*

    (b) Print the dimensions and the volume of the box in the form

        *a * b * c* (=v cubic metres)

    (c) Read the dimensions in feet and inches, where each side is less than 30 feet
    and the data is typed in the form

        ff'ii" by *ff'ii"* by *ff'ii"*

    (d) Print the dimensions and the volume of the box in the form

        *a * b * c* (=v cubic feet)

SUMMARY

- During list-directed input data values are separated by value separators, each of which may be a comma, a slash, a blank, or the end of record, preceded and/or followed by any number of consecutive blanks.

- If there is no value between two consecutive value separators then a null value is read, leaving the corresponding input list item unchanged.

- Character data read by a list-directed **read** statement must be delimited by quotation marks unless it is contained on a single line, does not contain any blanks, commas or slashes, does not begin with a quotation mark, and does not begin with a sequence of digits followed by an asterisk.

- A format specifier is used to provided user-specified data editing on input and output.

- i edit desriptors are used to edit integer data.

- f edit descriptors are used to edit real data.

- a edit descriptors are used to edit character data.

- L edit descriptors are used to edit logical data.

- t, tl and tr edit descriptors are used to control where data is read from in an input record and where it is placed in an output record.

- / edit descriptors are used to identify the end of a record.

- Formats, or parts of formats, are repeated as many times as required until the input or output list has been exhausted.

- **read** and **write** statements with control information lists are used to provide greater flexibility than is possible with the simple **read** and **print** statements which always use the default input and output units.

- The control information list in a **read** or **write** statement consists of a list of specifiers which provide additional information for use during input or output.

- A unit specifier is used to specify the input or output unit to be used for a **read** or **write** statement.

- An fmt specifier is used to specify the format to be used with a **read** or **write** statement.

- An iostat specifier is used to determine whether a **read** or **write** statement was executed without any error, and to provide information about the type of error if one occurred.

- F syntax introduced in Chapter 9

  Input/output statements **read** *format_specifier, input_list*
  read *(cilist) input_list*
  print *format_specifier, output_list*
  write *(cilist) output_list*

Format specifier	(*list of edit descriptors*)
Edit descriptors	i*w*, f*w*.*d*, a*w*, a, L*w* t*c*, t*ln*, t*rn*, /
Control information	unit = *unit*
list specifiers	unit = *
	fmt = *character_variable*
	fmt = "*format_specifier*"
	fmt = *
	iostat = *integer_variable*

PROGRAMMING EXERCISES

9.1   Find out which are the standard input and output units for the computer that you are using. Also find out if any other units are preconnected. If *input* represents the default input unit, and *output* represents the default output unit, find out what happens if you refer to unit * and either *input* or *output* in the same program.

When you have established the answers to these questions run the following programs to see if they behave as you expect.

```
program unit_test_1
! Note that "input_unit" and "output_unit" should be
! replaced in the following declaration by the correct
! unit numbers for the computer you are using

    integer,parameter :: input=input_unit,output=output_unit
    integer :: num1,num2

    write (unit=*,fmt=*) "Type a 4-digit integer"
    read (unit=*,fmt=*) num1
    write (unit=output,fmt=*) "Now type a 3-digit one"
    read (unit=input,fmt=*) num2
    write (unit=output,fmt=*) "The numbers you typed " // &
                              "were as follows:"
    print "(i4,a,i4)",num1," and",num2
end program unit_test_1


program unit_test_2
! Note that "input_unit" and "output_unit" should be
! replaced in the following declaration by the correct
! unit numbers for the computer you are using

    integer,parameter :: input=input_unit,output=output_unit
    integer :: num1,num2

    write (unit=output,fmt=*) "Type a 4-digit integer"
    read (unit=input,fmt=*) num1
    write (unit=*,fmt=*) "Now type a 3-digit one"
    read (unit=*,fmt=*) num2
    print *, "The numbers you typed were as follows:"
    write (unit=output,fmt="(i4,a,i4)") num1," and",num2

end program unit_test_2
```

9.2 Write a program to display a 'multiplication square'. The numbers 1–12 should run across the top of the table and down the side, with the entries holding the relevant product. Thus the first few lines would be:

```
      1  2  3  4  5  6  7  8  9  10  11  12
   X
1     1  2  3  4  5  6  7  8  9  10  11  12
2     2  4  6  8  10 12 14 16 18 20  22  24
3     3  6  9  12 15 18 21 24 27 30  33  36
```

and so on.

9.3 Write a program which will input a date in the form *dd mmm yyyy*, where *dd* and *yyyy* are numeric, and *mmm* is a three-letter representation of the month, and convert it to the number of days since 1 January 1900.

9.4 Write a program that finds the positive difference between two three-digit integer numbers and produces the result of the calculation in the form:

```
The positive difference between n1 and n2 is n3
```

Use formatted **read** and **print** statements in your program.

*9.5 Store 12 five-digit numbers in an array. Purely by changing the output format, print the numbers as

   (a) a single column of numbers;
   (b) four rows of three numbers;
   (c) a single line of numbers.

Now modify the program so that the format is unchanged, but altering the way in which a *single* **read** statement is used can produce the same three formats for the results.

9.6 Write and test a subroutine which prints a real number x, using a field width of 8, according to the following rules:

   1. If $x=\text{int}(x)$ then the number should be displayed as an integer.
   2. Otherwise, if it is possible, x should be printed in fixed point format to at least 3 significant figures.
   3. Otherwise x should be printed in floating point format to as many decimal places as will fit in the space available.

9.7 A railway timetable has to be produced in the following form

Arrival	Departure	Platform	Destination
9.23	9.25	2	Edinburgh
9.28	9.32	1	London
10.41	10.53	3	Sheffield
10.48	10.53	2	Newcastle
11.15	11.18	1	London

Write a program that displays the above timetable on the screen.
Now modify your program so that it asks for up to 10 sets of train details, and then prints them all in the same format as shown above.

9.8   Write a program to print a bank statement. The user should be asked for the opening balance and the amount of each of a number of transactions, which may be debits or credits. Once all transactions have been entered, the program should calculate the final balance and generate a printout of the form:

```
Opening balance:        123.45
Transactions:
Debit     Credit        Total
11.23                   112.22
50.00                    62.22
          25.00          87.22

Closing balance:         87.22
```

Is the **real** data type suitable for such financial calculations?

9.9   The expression

$$\sin\theta\sin\phi - \frac{1}{2}\big(\cos(\theta-\phi) - \cos(\theta+\phi)\big)$$

should be zero for all values of θ and ϕ. Write a program which will produce a square table showing the calculated values of the function for values of θ and ϕ between 0 and 3 radians in steps of 0.25.

9.10   Angles are often expressed in degrees, minutes and seconds, where there are 360 degrees in a full circle, 60 minutes in a degree, and 60 seconds in a minute.

Define a derived type suitable for this form of representation. Then write a program that reads an angle as three integer values, representing the degrees, minutes and seconds, and which then computes its value as a decimal number of degrees, and also its value in radians (where there are 2π radians in a full circle, and π may be taken as 3.141 592 36). The program should display the angle in all three forms, using four decimal places for the value in decimal degrees, and an appropriate number of decimal places for the value in radians.

9.11   A chemist makes five measurements of the rates of three different reactions. The data collected is shown below:

Reaction A	Reaction B	Reaction C
20.6	16.9	90.6
31.2	20.2	100.2
10.9	30.7	98.7
15.4	30.2	117.2
12.1	30.0	88.6

Write a program that calculates the mean rate and standard deviation for each reaction. The standard deviation is given by the formula

$$\sigma = \sqrt{\sum(x_i - \mu)^2}$$

where μ is the mean and x_i is the ith measurement for each reaction. Use formatted output to produce a table consisting of three columns for the experimental data followed by the mean and standard deviation for each reaction.

*9.12 Following an earthquake it is required to print out the seismic measurements recorded at a number of different centres around the world. Write a program which reads several sets of data from the keyboard, each consisting of the longitude and latitude of the recording instrument (as two pairs of integer numbers) and the strength measured on the Richter scale (as a real number). Each set of figures should be stored in a derived type array, each element of which holds the position and strength of the measurement.

Latitudes to the west of the Greenwich meridian are recorded as negative values (thus, $23°48'$ W is recorded as $-23, 48$), and those to the east as positive values. Similarly, longitudes north of the equator are recorded as positive, and those to the south as negative.

Your program should read all the data, and then print the measurements as a table in the following form:

```
Seismic measuremnts recorded after earthquake

    Recording Station          Richter
    Longitude     Latitude     Strength

    nn°nn' N      nnn°nn' W     nn.nn
    nn°nn' S      nnn°nn' E     nn.nn
        .             .             .
        .             .             .
        .             .             .
```

Using files to preserve data

10

10.1	Files and records	10.3	Connecting an external file to your program – and disconnecting it
10.2	Formatted, unformatted and endfile records	10.4	File positioning statements

One of the most important aspects of computing is the ability for a program to save the data that it has been using for subsequent use either by itself or by another program. This involves the output of the data to a file, usually on some form of magnetic or optical media, for input at some later time. Files may be written and read sequentially or, on some types of media, the information in a file may be written and read in a random order. In either case the file may be stored permanently within the computer system, for example on a magnetic or magneto-optical disk which is an integral part of the computer, or it may be stored on some medium, such as a disk or tape, which may be removed from the computer either for safe-keeping or for physical transport to another computer.

This chapter shows how the **read** and **write** statements discussed in the previous chapter can be used to read data from a file and write data to a file, in a sequential manner, and introduces several additional statements which are required when dealing with files. More sophisticated uses of files, including random access to information stored in a file, are discussed later, in Chapter 15.

10.1 Files and records

The input and output facilities that we have met so far allow us to input data and to output results in a wide variety of different ways; however, there has been one major omission which we shall now address. All the programs that we have written have been based on the assumption that when the program is run it reads some data from the keyboard (or other input unit), processes it, produces some results which are displayed on the screen or sent to a printer, and finishes. Once the program has finished nothing remains within the computer system.

This ignores two very important aspects of the normal computing process.

The first is that if there are more than a few lines of data it is usually far more appropriate to type the data into a **file**, possibly using the same editor as is used to type and edit the program, and for the program then to read the data directly from the file. This has the advantage that the data need only be typed once; on all subsequent runs of the program (for example, during testing) there is no need to retype the data. Even if it is not intended to process the data more than once this mode of operation is preferable for larger amounts of data, since it allows for error corrections and/or changes to be made to the data *before* it is read by the program.

For similar reasons, where there are more than a few lines of results to be displayed it is often more convenient to send them to a file which can subsequently be displayed in sections or sent to a printer, or both, as appropriate.

The second aspect that we must consider occurs when the results produced by one program, or some of the results, are required as data for another program, or even another run of the same program. Examples of this type of application range from data processing activities such as payroll calculation or financial accounting, where past records are essential, to analysis of scientific experiments over a period of time, control of airline reservations, scheduling of production, or any other activity which requires knowledge of some past events of the same or similar type.

The **file store** of the computer system is used for this purpose. This consists of special input/output units, usually, though not always, based on either magnetic disks or magnetic tapes, or a combination of the two. Information may be transferred to and from these units by using **read** and **write** statements in a similar manner to that used for data and results transferred via the default input and output units. However, before we examine this in more detail, we must first define two important concepts, namely those of a **record** and of a **file**.

We have already referred to records informally when discussing input and output, and have understood it to refer to a sequence of characters such as a line of typing or a printed line of results. However, a record does not necessarily correspond in this way to some physical entity, but refers to some defined sequence of characters *or of values*. F programs may read and write three types of records – formatted, unformatted and endfile records – and we shall discuss these in some detail in the next section.

A sequence of records forms a file, of which there are two types — external and internal. We shall investigate external files in more detail before we start to examine the records of which they are comprised; internal files will be discussed in Chapter 15.

An **external file** is an identifiable sequence of records which is stored on some external medium. Thus a sheet of printed results is a file. Although this is the formal definition of a file, in general usage a file is normally understood to refer to a file which is part of the computer system's file store. As we have already indicated, there are two main types of storage medium used for this purpose, magnetic tape and magnetic or optical disk, and before discussing files any further it is important to recognize one very important difference between these two types of storage medium, and the effect that this has on the use of files in F programs.

A magnetic tape, which is the older storage medium, is a **sequential** storage medium, in that each record written will normally be written directly after the previous record, so that the normal way of reading magnetic tape records is in the same order as that in which they were written. Magnetic tapes on large computer systems are typically over 2000 ft long (or almost 0.75 km) and may contain as many as 50 million characters or their equivalent, and it would be extremely time-consuming to search for individual records in a random order. On the other hand, magnetic tapes are easy to store and the tape decks that are used to read and write information are relatively economical to manufacture.

A magnetic or optical disk, however, does not record information in a single spiral, like a record, but stores it in the form of a large number of concentric circular **tracks**. This means that information can be retrieved from any part of the surface of the disk in a fraction of a second since, at worst, the read head only needs to travel a few inches to position itself on the required part of the disk. Such a storage unit can therefore be used for **random access** of information as well as sequential access. Moreover, because the technology used in the manufacture of disk drives permits data to be stored very much more densely than is possible on a magnetic tape, a 3.5-inch diameter exchangeable **diskette** (or **floppy disk**) on a personal computer can hold almost 3 million characters, while other types of exchangeable disks may hold as much as a billion characters (a **gigabyte**), while non-exchangeable disks, and those attached to larger computers, may store hundreds of billions of characters.

Because the information anywhere on a magnetic disk (or other similar device) can be accessed so rapidly, and because a disk can hold so much information, a single disk will usually store a large number of separate files of information. Most computers will have some disks permanently (or semi-permanently) mounted, while others will only be loaded when required. On a personal computer, for example, there will normally be a permanently mounted **fixed disk** (or **hard disk**) capable of storing between 100 million and 10 billion characters, while diskettes capable of storing 1–3 million characters will be loaded as and when required to provide more transitory data storage, or to provide a second copy for backup or for transfer of information to another computer.

create the file, and if successful will change its status to `old`, after which any subsequent attempt to open the file as `new` will fail.

If *file_status* is `replace`, and the file already exists, then it is deleted and an attempt made to create a new file with the same name; if this is successful the status is changed to `old`. If the file does not already exist then the action taken will be the same as if `new` had been specified.

Finally, if *file_status* is `scratch` then a special un-named file is created for use by the program; when the program ceases execution (or when the file is closed, see below) the file will be deleted and will cease to exist. Such a file can therefore be used as a temporary file for the duration of execution only.

As well as specifying the initial status of the file, we must also specify what type of input/output operations are allowed with the file. The `action` specifier is used for this purpose, and takes the form

```
action = allowed_actions
```

where *allowed_actions* is a character expression which, after the removal of any trailing blanks, must take one of the three values `read`, `write` or `readwrite`.

If *allowed_actions* is `read` then the file is to be treated as a *read-only* file, and only **read** statements, together with the two file positioning statements **backspace** and **rewind** (see Section 10.4), are allowed on this file; **write** and **endfile** statements are not allowed, thus preventing a program from accidentally overwriting information in the file.

If *allowed_actions* is `write` then the file is to be treated as an output file, and only **write** and **endfile** statements, together with the two file positioning statements **backspace** and **rewind**, are allowed on this file; **read** statements are not allowed.

If *allowed_actions* is `readwrite` then all input/output statements are allowed for this file. Note that if the file status is specified as `scratch` then *allowed_actions* must be `readwrite`; after all, any other value would be meaningless!

The remaining specifiers are all optional, and enable us to specify various requirements regarding the file that is to be opened and to monitor the opening process itself.

The first of these concerns the type of access that is permitted to the file and takes the form

```
access = access_type
```

where *access_type* is a character expression which, after the removal of any trailing blanks, must take one of the two values `sequential` or `direct`; if no access specifier is provided it is assumed to be `sequential`. We shall discuss the meaning of direct access in Section 15.3, but for the present we shall assume that all files are sequential files.

If a file is specified to be a sequential file, a position specifier must be included to instruct the **open** statement where the file is to be initially positioned;

this takes the form

position = *file_position*

where *file_position* is a character expression which, after the removal of any trailing blanks, must take one of the values rewind or append.

If the file did not previously exist then this specifier is ignored and the new file will always be positioned at its initial point. After all, there is nowhere else to position a new file!

If the file does already exist and *file_position* is rewind then the file is positioned at its initial point and a subsequent read or write statement will either read the first record in the file, or write a new first record, as appropriate.

If the file already exists and *file_position* is append then the file is positioned immediately before the endfile record, if there is one, or immediately after the last record of the file (at its terminal point) if there is no endfile record. A subsequent **write** statement will therefore write the next record immediately after the end of the existing information in the file; a **read** statement would, of course, lead to either an error or an end-of-file condition since the file has no records remaining to be read other than an endfile record, if one exists.

If a file is specified to have direct access then a position specifier is not permitted.

Files normally have a name by which they are known to the computer system, and this name is specified by using a **file** specifier, which takes the form

file = *file_name*

where *file_name* is a character expression which, after the removal of any trailing blanks, takes the form of a file name for the particular computer system. If this specifier is not present then status="scratch" must be specified.

Thus if the name of the required file is Imagine1, we could connect the file of that name to a program by means of a statement such as

```
open (unit=9,file="Imagine1",status="old",action="read" , &
      position="rewind")
```

which will connect unit 9 to the specified file. Thereafter any input or file positioning statements using unit 9 will read from that file, starting with the first record; it will not be permitted to write anything to the file.

Alternatively, we could read the name of the required file from the keyboard by a program fragment such as the following:

```
print *,"Please give the name of the output file"
read "(a)",out_file
open (unit=9,file=out_file,status="old",action="write", &
      position="append")
```

where `out_file` is a character variable whose length is great enough to hold the file name. This will allow only output to the specified file, starting immediately after the existing information recorded on the file. Note that, for obvious reasons, it is not permitted to specify that the status of a named file (that is, one with a **file** specifier) is `scratch`.

Because of the different ways in which they are written and read, the records in a file must either all be formatted or all be unformatted, and the specifier

form = *format_mode*

is used to specify which is required. The character expression *format_mode* must take one of the two values `formatted` or `unformatted`, after the removal of any trailing blanks; if it is omitted then the file is assumed to be formatted if it is connected for sequential access, but unformatted if it is connected for direct access (see Section 15.3). Thus the statement

```
open (unit=9,file="datafile",status="old",action="read" , &
      position="rewind")
```

will connect the file `datafile` to unit 9 as a formatted, sequential access file for input only. On the other hand

```
open (unit=7,status="scratch",form="unformatted", &
      action="readwrite",position="rewind")
```

will create a temporary scratch file and connect it to unit 7 as an unformatted, sequential access file.

The next specifier, `recl`, behaves slightly differently depending upon whether the file is connected for sequential or direct access. We shall discuss direct access files in Section 15.3 and, therefore, will only consider its use in a sequential statement for the present. It takes the form

recl = *record_length*

where *record_length* is an integer expression which defines the *maximum* length that the records in the file may have. If the file is a formatted file the length is expressed in characters; if it is an unformatted file then the length is expressed in processor-defined units. In general, this specifier is not required for sequential files, and its main use in this regard is to limit the size of records in a file which will be transferred to some other processor which places a restriction on the size of records in files.

The final specifier that will be discussed here, `iostat`, is concerned with recognizing when an error occurs during the connection process, for example if the named file does not exist or is of the wrong type, and operates in the same way as has already been discussed in connection with the **read**, **write** and

endfile statements. Note that the non-zero values that may be returned in the event of an error during the opening of a file are processor dependent. In the event of any such error during the opening of a file the execution of the program will be terminated unless it is detected by the program:

```
open(unit=13,file="Problem_file",status="old", &
    access="readwrite",position="rewind",iostat=ios)
if (ios /= 0) then
    print *,"Error during opening of 'Problem_file'"
        .
        .
        .
end if
! Continue processing
    .
    .
    .
```

Finally, we should note two important, if self-evident, rules:

- If a file is connected to a unit, then it may not also be connected to another unit.
- If a file is connected to a unit then another file may not be connected to the same unit.

If a file is first disconnected from a unit then it may be connected to another unit, and another file may be connected to the first unit.

Up to this point we have assumed that once a file has been opened it will remain open for the remainder of the execution of the program. This is frequently what is required, but there are occasions when it is required to disconnect a file from the program before the end of execution, or when it is required to specify that some specific action is to take place when such disconnection does take place. A file which has been connected to a program by means of an **open** statement can, therefore, be disconnected by means of a **close** statement, which takes the form

close *(close_specifier_list)*

where the possible specifiers are unit, status and iostat.

The unit and iostat specifiers take the same form as for the **open** statement, while the status specifier is used to determine what is to happen to the file when it has been disconnected from the program. It takes the form

status = *file_status*

where *file_status* is a character expression which, after the removal of any trailing blanks, is either keep or delete. If it is keep then the file will continue to exist after it has been disconnected from the program; if it is `delete` then the file will cease to exist after it has been disconnected. Note that, as was emphasized above, this does not *necessarily* mean that it is physically deleted, merely that it is no longer accessible to the program; for example, if the file is a magnetic tape it may simply be removed from the index of tapes available.

Only the `unit` specifier is required in a **close** statement; if no status specifier is present, then the file is closed as though `status="keep"` had been specified, unless it was opened with `status="scratch"`. If a file has been opened with `status="scratch"` then it will automatically be deleted when it is disconnected from the program, and it is not allowed to specify a close status of `keep`!

☐ EXAMPLE 10.1   ·

☐1 Problem

In Example 9.2 we wrote a program which read up to 1000 sets of experimental data. This is clearly a situation in which it would be absurd to read the data directly from the keyboard; it would be far more sensible to store the data in a file and then to read the data from that file. In this way the data can be created at any convenient time, not necessarily all at once, and checked for accuracy, before being processed by the computer at a later time.

Rewrite the solution to Example 9.2 so that the data is read from a file whose name is provided by the user when running the program, and the results are stored in a second file.

☐2 Analysis

We have already carried out the main analysis for this problem, and the main change is that two additional **character** variables will be required for the names of the file containing the data and of the file to contain the results, and an **integer** variable to record the success, or otherwise, of the attempt to open the required files, together with a small amount of additional 'housekeeping' to open the file at the start of the program.

☐3 Solution

```
program Radioactive_decay
! This program processes experimental data relating to
! radioactive decay which is stored in a file whose name
! is supplied at execution time

   ! Constant declarations
   ! max_readings is maximum number of sets of data
   ! inf and outf are the unit numbers for reading and writing
   integer,parameter :: max_readings=1000,inf=3,outf=4
```

```fortran
! Variable declarations
integer :: alpha,beta,gamma,i,max_interval,ios
real :: time,last_time,period, &
        av_alpha,av_beta,av_gamma,max_av_gamma
character(len=20) :: data_file_name,results_file_name

! Initialize variables
last_time = 0.0
max_interval = 0
max_av_gamma = 0

! Obtain name of data file - allow maximum of 3 attempts
do i=1,3
   print *,"Please give name of data file"
   read "(a)",data_file_name

   ! Open data file on unit number "in"
   open (unit=inf,file=data_file_name,status="old", &
         action="read",position="rewind",iostat=ios)

   ! Repeat request if file not opened satisfactorily
   if (ios==0) then
      exit
   end if
   print *,"Unable to open file - please try again"
end do

! Check to see if file opened successfully
if (i>3) then
   print *,"Three unsuccessful attempts to open file."
   print *,"Program execution terminated."
   stop
end if

! Obtain name of results file
do i=1,3
   print *,"Please give name of results file"
   read "(a)",results_file_name

   ! Open results file on unit number "out"
   open (unit=outf,file=results_file_name,status=" replace", &
         action="write",position="rewind",iostat=ios)

   ! Repeat request if file not opened satisfactorily
   if (ios==0) then
      exit
   end if
   print *,"Unable to open file - please try again"
end do

! Check to see if file opened successfully
if (i>3) then
   print *,"Three unsuccessful attempts to open file."
   print *,"Program execution terminated."
   stop
end if
```

```
! Write headings
write (unit=outf,fmt=" (a,t11,a,t17,a,t24,a,t30,a,t37, " //  &
      "a,t46,a,t55,a,/,t38,a,t47,a,t56,a)") "Interval",      &
      "Time","Alpha","Beta","Gamma","Average","Average",     &
      "Average","Alpha","Beta","Gamma"

! Process max_readings sets of data in a loop
do i=1,max_readings
   read (unit=inf,fmt=" (f8.2,3(tr5,i6))")   &
        time,alpha,beta,gamma

   ! Calculate interval since last readings
   period = time-last_time
   last_time = time

   ! Calculate average rates of emission
   av_alpha = alpha/period
   av_beta = beta/period
   av_gamma = gamma/period

   ! Print statistics for this interval
   write (unit=outf,fmt=" (i6,f8.2,2i6,i7,2f9.2,f10.2)") &
         i,period,alpha,beta,gamma,av_alpha,av_beta,av_gamma

   ! Check for maximum gamma radiation in this period
   if (av_gamma > max_av_gamma) then
      max_av_gamma = av_gamma
      max_interval = i
   end if
end do

! Print details of interval with maximum gamma radiation
write (unit=outf,fmt=" (t3,a,f7.2,a,i5)")                   &
      "Maximum average gamma radiation was",max_av_gamma, &
      " in interval",max_interval

! Also print closing details to standard output device
write (unit=*,fmt=" (t3,a,f7.2,a,i5)")                      &
      "Maximum average gamma radiation was",max_av_gamma, &
      " in interval",max_interval

end program Radioactive_decay
```

Figure 10.2 shows the results sent to the output file by a test using 10 sets of data.

There are three points to comment on in this program. The first of these concerns the procedure adopted to open each file. The **open** statements are each contained in a **do**-loop which allows a maximum of three attempts to open the file; after three unsuccessful attempts the program's execution is terminated by the **stop** statement, which was introduced in Section 6.5, as there is clearly no point in continuing.

The second point concerns the very end of the program, where the final statistics are sent to the standard output device (that is, the display in most cases) as well as to the output file. The main reason for this is so that the user of

```
Interval  Time  Alpha  Beta  Gamma  Average  Average  Average
                                     Alpha    Beta     Gamma
    1     2.56   175    23    401    68.36     8.98    156.64
    2     2.59   168    22    395    64.86     8.49    152.51
    3     2.48   181    27    412    72.98    10.89    166.13
    4     2.51   177    25    410    70.52     9.96    163.35
    5     2.48   166    29    391    66.94    11.69    157.66
    6     2.54   181    25    397    71.26     9.84    156.30
    7     2.51   169    28    407    67.33    11.16    162.15
    8     2.58   159    23    388    61.63     8.91    150.39
    9     2.51   177    26    401    70.52    10.36    159.76
   10     2.47   173    24    398    70.04     9.72    161.13
Maximum average gamma radiation was 166.13 in interval    3
```

Figure 10.2 Results produced by the program written in Example 10.1.

the program can readily see that execution is completed – always a user-friendly action – and if a message is going to be displayed it might as well contain some more useful information than simply a standard closing message such as Execution has now completed.

The final point concerns the number of sets of data. The problem stated that there were exactly 1000 sets of data, and this value is built into the program. However, to provide for more flexibility, it would be better either to read the number of data sets at the start of processing, possibly from the file itself, or to make use of an endfile record to determine the end of the file.

10.4 File positioning statements

There are often situations in which it is required to alter the position in a file without reading or writing any records, and F provides two additional file positioning statements for this purpose. The first of these

backspace (*auxlist*)

causes the file to be positioned just before the *preceding* record (that is, it enables the program to read the immediately previously read record again). As with the **endfile** statement *auxlist* consists of a unit specifier and, optionally, an iostat specifier.

The other file positioning statement is

rewind (*auxlist*)

which causes the file to be positioned just before the *first* record so that a subsequent input statement will start reading or writing the file from the beginning. Once again, *auxlist* consists of a unit specifier and, optionally, an iostat specifier.

These two statements are particularly important when we are dealing with endfile records because, as was mentioned in Section 10.2, if a program has either read or written an endfile record it cannot read or write any more records until either a **backspace** or a **rewind** statement has positioned the file before the endfile record.

One important point about the positioning of a file concerns the writing of information to a file in a sequential manner. The rule in F is that *writing a record to a sequential file destroys all information in the file after that record*. This is, in part, a reminder of the days when all sequential files were on magnetic tape and the physical characteristics of a magnetic tape unit had exactly this effect.

Thus it is not possible to use **backspace** or **rewind** in order to position a file so that only one particular record can be overwritten by a new one, but only so that the rest of the file can be overwritten, or so that a particular record or records can be read. If it is required to overwrite individual records selectively within a file then the file must be opened for direct access, see Section 15.3.

A common use of **backspace** in conjunction with **endfile** is to add information at the end of a previously written file, as in the following example:

```
    .
    .
    .
! Read up to end-of-file
do
    read (unit=8,iostat=ios) dummy
    if (ios<0) then
        exit         ! negative ios means end-of-file
end do
! Backspace to before end-of-file record
backspace (unit=8)
! Now add new information
write (unit=8, ...) ...
! Terminate file with an end-of-file ready for next time
endfile (unit=8)
    .
    .
    .
```

In FORTRAN 77 and earlier versions of Fortran this was the only way of achieving this objective. However, in F (as well as Fortran 90 and Fortran 95) the use of the position specifier in the **open** statement provides a much easier alternative in most such situations:

```
        .
        .
        .
! Open file at the end
open (unit=8,file=datafile,status="old",access="readwrite", &
     position="append",iostat=ios)
if (ios/=0) then
        .         ! Error during opening
        .
        .
end if
! File is now positioned for adding new information
write (unit=8, ...) ...
        .
        .
        .
! Terminate file with an end-of-file ready for next time
endfile (unit=8)
        .
        .
        .
```

EXAMPLE 10.2

1 Problem

A survey has been carried out to obtain statistics concerning the occupation of
people in a certain area. The results of the survey are available in a file for input
to the computer in the following format:

Columns 1–20   Name

Column   23   Sex   = F if female
                        = M if male

Column   25   Job status = 1 if in full-time education
                              = 2 if in full-time employment
                              = 3 if in part-time employment
                              = 4 if temporarily unemployed
                              = 5 if not working or seeking a job

This is followed by one or more items depending upon the job status of the
respondent:

Job status = 1   columns 28, 29   Age
           = 2   columns 28–31   Monthly salary (£)
           = 3   columns 28–31   Monthly salary (£)
                 columns 34–37   Other monthly income (£)
           = 4   columns 28, 29   Age
                 columns 32–34   No. of months unemployed

= 5   columns 28, 29 Age
       column 31   Code
                       = 1 if looking after children
                       = 2 if looking after other relatives
                       = 3 for any other reason

All records in the file may be assumed to be at least 40 characters long.

Since the data is stored in a file there is no need for any special terminating record, as the end of the file can be easily recognized.

Write an input procedure to read the data for processing by another part of the program.

2 Analysis

The major problem here is the variable format of the data, depending on the code which is used to describe the job status (in column 25). In Chapter 15 we shall meet two approaches which can be used to deal with this problem, but we can deal with it here in a cruder, and more time-consuming, way by backspacing and reading the record again using the correct format. Note, however, that all the items in the variable part of the data are numeric, and a careful analysis shows that if we read columns 28 and 29 as the age, 31 as the code for those not working, and 32–34 as the period unemployed, we shall only have to re-read the record for respondents in some form of employment (job status 2 or 3). (Only four columns are allocated for the financial values and they are stated to be in pounds, so no decimal point will be present in the data.)

Although it was not specified in the problem, it will clearly be desirable to define a derived type to represent the data for one person, and to place this definition, together with the various codes, in a module which can be used by both the input procedure and the other parts of the program which will deal with the analysis of the data and the printing of results.

The form of this derived type will clearly allow for all possible variations in the data, even though several of these will not be relevant for any one person. We must therefore set any unused fields to a special value to indicate that they are unused. Since the relevant fields are all numeric, and none of them will be negative, we can set the unused fields to a negative value, which will easily be distinguished from the real data.

The other question which was not specified concerns the opening of the input file. It would be possible for the main program to identify the appropriate file and then open this on a particular unit, communicating this unit number to the input procedure, or the input procedure could deal with this itself. If the file were to be used elsewhere in the program then the former option would probably be preferable, but if the file is only to be accessed to read the data then it would seem better to keep all access to it within the one procedure. We shall adopt this option. Nevertheless, to avoid possible unit number clashes, the unit number to be used will be provided as an argument to the procedure.

Finally, there is always the possibility that an input procedure may detect an error when reading the data and it is important that the calling program unit is aware of this. There are three obvious errors that might occur in a procedure such as this:

1. There is an error during the opening of the file. This will obviously mean that no data has been read! However, it may be possible for the procedure to advise the user of the difficulty if, as here, the filename is being requested interactively, in which case it might be preferable to allow, say, three attempts to open the file before failing.
2. There is an error during the reading of the data.
3. The maximum number of records is read without a terminator.

We shall return the value −1 in the first case, −2 in the second case, and −3 in the last. In the last two cases the actual number of valid records read can also, of course, be returned in the same way as for an error-free case. If there were no errors then the value zero will be returned.

We can now define our data structure and write a structure plan.

Module survey_data

Data design

	Purpose	Type	Name
A	Constants:		
	Sex codes	character(1)	female, male
	Job codes	integer	ft_ed, ft_job, pt_job, no_job, at_home
	At home codes	integer	ch_minder, rel_minder, other
	Code for unused data entries	integer	unused
B	Data type:		
	Individual survey response	[character(20), character(1), integer,integer, integer,integer, real,real]	survey_info

Subroutine input

Data design

	Purpose	Type	Name
A	Arguments:		
	Unit number for data	integer	inf
	Maximum no. of data sets	integer	max_datasets
	Survey data	survey_info	survey_data(:)
	Number of data sets read	integer	num_datasets
	Error code	integer	error_code

Purpose	Type	Name
B Local variables:		
File name for data	**character**(30)	data_file
do variable	**integer**	i
iostat return code	integer	ios
Name (current record)	character(20)	name
Sex	character(1)	sex
Job status	integer	status
Age	integer	age
No. months unemployed	integer	months
At home code	integer	code
Monthly salary	real	salary
Other monthly income	real	income

Structure plan

1 Request name of data file and open it on `inf`
2 Repeat up to `max_datasets` times
    2.1 Read next record up to column 34
    2.2 If end of file then exit from loop
    2.3 If error then set `error_code` to −2 and exit from loop
    2.4 Select case on job status
        status is 1, 4 or 5
        2.4.1 Set unused items to unused
        status is 2 or 3
        2.4.2 Backspace and read record again
        2.4.3 Set unused items to unused
    2.5 Copy local record to array
3 If end of file read set `error_code` to −3
4 Return number of data sets read

Note that a set of local variables are being used for initial input to simplify the programming, and that when the full record has been read in the correct format the final data is then copied to the next element of the main data array.

3 **Solution**

```
module survey
! This module contains a type definition and constants
! for use with the input and processing of survey data,
! together with the input procedure itself

   ! Procedure declaration
   public :: input
```

```
! Type definition for survey response
type, public :: survey_info
   private
   character(len-20) :: name
   character(len=1) :: sex
   integer :: job_status,age,months_jobless,at_home_code
   real :: salary,other_income
end type survey_info

! Various codes
character(len=1),parameter,private ::        &
      female="F",male="M"                      ! sex
integer,parameter,private ::                 &
      ft_ed=1,ft_job=2,pt_job=3,             & ! job status
      no_job=4,at_home=5,                    & ! ----------
      ch_minder=1,rel_minder=2,other=3,      & ! at home code
      unused=-1                                ! unused code
```

contains

```
subroutine input(inf,max_datasets,survey_data,num_datasets, &
                 error_code)
! This subroutine reads up to max_datasets records prepared
! as follows, returning the number read in num_datasets

! Columns 1-20 name
!         23 sex (M or F)
!         25 job status (1-5)
!      28,29 age - for status 1, 4 or 5
!      28-31 monthly salary - for status 2 and 3
!      32-34 other monthly income - for status 3
!      32-34 months unemployed - for status 4
!         31 special code (1-3) - for status 5

   ! Arguments
   integer, intent(in) :: inf,max_datasets
   integer, intent(out) :: num_datasets,error_code
   type(survey_info), dimension(:), intent(out) :: survey_data

   ! Local variables
   character(len=30) :: data_file
   character(len=20) :: name
   character(len=1) :: sex
   integer :: i,ios,status,age,months,code
   real :: salary,income

   ! Ask for name of data file
   ! A maximum of 3 attempts will be allowed to open the file
   do i=1,3
      print *,"Type name of data file"
      read "(a)",data_file
      ! Open file at beginning
      open (unit=inf,file=data_file,position="rewind",   &
            status="old",action="readwrite",iostat=ios)
```

```
   if (ios==0) then
      exit
   end if
   ! Error when opening file - try again
   print *,"Unable to open file - please try again"
end do

! If open was unsuccessful after 3 attempts return error=-1
if (ios/=0) then
   error_code = -1
   return
else
! Successful file opening
   error_code = 0
end if

! Loop to read data
do i=1,max_datasets
   ! Read (part of) next set of data
   read (unit=inf, &
      fmt="(a20,t23,a1,t25,i1,t28,i2,t31,i1,i3)",   &
      iostat=ios) name,sex,status,age,code,months

   ! Check for errors and end of file
   select case (ios)
   case (:-1)              ! end of file - no more data
      exit

   case (1:)               ! error during reading
      error_code = -2
      exit
   end select

   ! Process data read and backspace for more if necessary
   select case (status)
   case (ft_ed,no_job,at_home)
      ! All data for this person already read
      ! so set unused items to unused code
      salary = unused
      income = unused
      select case (status)
      case (ft_ed)
         months = unused
         code = unused
      case (no_job)
         code = unused
      case (at_home)
         months = unused
      end select

   case (ft_job,pt_job)
      ! Backspace and read financial details
      backspace (unit=inf)
      read (unit=inf,fmt="(t28,f4.0,t34,f4.0)")   &
            salary,income
```

```
            ! Set unused items to unused code
            age = unused
            months = unused
            code = unused
            if (status == ft_job) then
               income = unused
            end if
        end select

        ! Record is now fully input, so copy to main data array
        survey_data(i) = survey_info(name,sex,status,age,  &
                                     months,code,salary, income)

    end do

    ! All data input - check if end of file was read
    if (i > max_datasets) then
       error_code = -3
    end if

    ! Save number of records read and return
    num_datasets = i-1

  end subroutine input

end module survey
```

Notice that the checks made that the reading of data from the data file has been error-free have only been carried out the first time that a record is read. This will deal with the problem of detecting the end of file, but there is always a theoretical possibility of some hardware problem causing an error during reading, and this should be checked for in all cases in a 'production' program.

Note also the use of the **return** statement when the procedure is unable to open the data file. This statement was introduced in Section 6.5 and provides a means to return directly to the calling program unit without executing the **end subroutine** statement. This is a good example of when it is particularly useful.

· ▢

SELF-TEST EXERCISES 10.1

1   What is the difference between a formatted record and an unformatted record? When should each type be used?

2   What is the difference between a formatted **read** or **write** statement and an unformatted **read** or **write** statement?

3   What is an endfile record? How is one created?

4   Why must a file be connected to a program before it is used? How is this done?

5 Write appropriate **open** statements to enable a program to use the following files in the manner specified:

(a) A file called `Payroll_Data` which has been prepared by a data preparation operator and is to be read by the program from unit 7;

(b) A file called `Intermediate_results_1` which was produced by another program which carried out the initial analysis of raw data, and which is to be read from unit 11;

(c) A file called `Intermediate_results_2` which is to be produced by this program for further analysis by another program, and which is to be written on unit 8;

(d) A file called `Results` which will be read from and written to on unit 10, and contains experimental results to which additional results will be added as a result of the program's execution;

(e) A file which will be written to and read from on unit 9, and which will be used for storing very large arrays, and other information, during the execution of the program;

(f) A file which will be written to on unit 10, and which will contain the tabulated results produced as a result of the execution of the program.

SUMMARY

- Information that is to be preserved after the execution of a program is ended is stored in a file.

- A file consists of a sequence of records.

- The records in a file may be accessed in a sequential manner, or in a random access manner.

- Writing to a sequential file destroys all records after the one written.

- A file may consist of formatted records and, optionally, one endfile record, or it may consist of unformatted records and, optionally, one endfile record.

- A formatted record is written by a formatted **write** statement, or by some means external to F, and consists of a sequence of characters; it is read by a formatted **read** statement.

- An unformatted record is written by an unformatted **write** statement, and consists of a sequence of values in a processor-dependent form; it is read by an unformatted **read** statement.

- An endfile record is written by an **endfile** statement.

- Reading an endfile record causes an end-of-file condition, which will lead to failure of the program unless detected, for example by use of an `iostat` specifier in a **read** statement.

- A file must be connected to a program by an **open** statement before it is first used.

- An **open** statement must specify the type of file, the type of access allowed to the file, and the position at which reading or writing will start in a sequential file.

- **backspace** and **rewind** statements may be used to position the file prior to a read or write statement.

- F syntax introduced in Chapter 10

File connection statement	**open** (*open_specifier_list*)
File disconnection statement	**close** (*close_specifier_list*)
Unformatted input/ output statements	**read** (*control_information_list*) *input_list* **write** (*control_information_list*) *output_list* where the *control_information_list* does not include a format specifier
Endfile statement	**endfile** (*auxlist*)
File positioning statements	**backspace** (*auxlist*) **rewind** (*auxlist*)
Control information list specifiers	**file** = *file_name* status = *file_status* where *file_status* is one of "old", "new", "replace" or "scratch" action = *allowed_actions* where *allowed_actions* is one of "read", "write" or "readwrite" position = *file_position* where *file_position* is either "rewind" or "append" form = *format_mode* where *format_mode* is either "formatted" or "unformatted" recl = *record_length*

PROGRAMMING EXERCISES

Most of the exercises in this chapter involve the writing of a program to read data from a file. Data can be put in a file either by another program or by typing it into the file using your computer's editor – normally the same one that you use when typing your program.

10.1   Establish how to type data into a file on your computer, and any conventions and/or requirements imposed on you with regard to the names that you may give to your files.

To ensure that you have the details correct, use your editor to create a file containing three lines (or records) each containing four numbers (in any form you wish). Then write a program which reads these 12 numbers into a 12-element array, prints the 12 numbers in any format that you choose, and writes them to a second file as four rows of three. Finally, list the contents of this second file by whatever means is most appropriate on your computer – other than by use of an F program.

*10.2 A file contains a list of 10 integers, stored one per line. Write a program to read this list and write it to another file with the order of the numbers reversed.

10.3 Modify the program you wrote for Exercise 9.12 so that the seismic data is read from a file in which the data from each seismic recording centre is stored as follows:

$ccc \diamond\diamond \pm ll,mm \diamond\diamond \pm LL,MM \diamond\diamond rr.rr$

where *ccc* is the centre's identifying number, *ll,mm* are the degrees and minutes of latitude of the centre (with negative degrees representing west of Greenwich and positive representing east of Greenwich), *LL,MM* are the degrees and minutes of longitude of the centre (with negative degrees representing north of the equator and positive representing south of the equator), *rr.rr* is the strength of the shock on the Richter scale, and $\diamond$ represents a space.

10.4 Write a program that allows a user to type a series of real numbers into a file. Your program should enable the user to check that the data written to the file has been correctly entered (by use of the **backspace** command).

10.5 Modify your solution to Exercise 10.2 so that it can cope with a file with a variable number of integers, up to a maximum of, say, 100. (Hint: you will need to use an iostat specifier in your **read** statement to detect the end of the file.)

Can you think of a way of writing the program so it can deal with an arbitrary, and possibly very large, number of integers (that is, so large that they can't all be held in an array)?

10.6 Write a program to read in the following data from a file:

```
122.25    120.00
135.26    140.00
141.00    100.00
 56.21     50.00
 17.20     17.00
```

The figures in the two columns represent actual and estimated costs of office equipment for a university department. Calculate the error of each estimate as a percentage of the estimate, and write a new file consisting of three columns, the first two being those in the original file and the third column containing the percentage error in the estimate.

Now modify your program so that the output data overwrites the original data in the input file without closing and reopening the file.

10.7 A file contains the text of a business letter – up to 100 lines with no more than 80 characters on a given line. Write a program to count the number of occurrences of the word 'very' in the letter.

Your program should deal correctly with phrases such as:

'Every care has been taken...'
'Very sincerely yours,'
'We are VERY concerned...'

*10.8   Example 10.2 created a module containing an input procedure for a set of survey data. Write an output procedure for the same set of survey data which takes a single argument of type person, as defined in Example 10.2, and prints it in a suitable format, for example

```
Joe Black (M) earns £2432 each month from full-time employment

Susan Jones (F) is aged 15 and is in full-time education

Peter Smith (M) is aged 48 and has been unemployed for 17 months

Ann Knight (F) is aged 53 and does not work
The reason is to look after relatives
```

Write a program to test both the input and output procedures thoroughly.

10.9   Type the following data into a file:

```
12.36    0.004    1.3536E12    2320.326
13.24    0.008    2.4293E15    5111.116
15.01    0.103    9.9879E11    3062.329
11.83    0.051    6.3195E13    8375.145
14.00    0.001    8.0369E14    1283.782
```

By constructing an appropriate formatted input statement, read each line of data from the file into four variables, and determine the number of numbers, n, there are in the file and the absolute value of the largest number, m (that is, the largest number ignoring its sign). Do *not* presume in your program that you know how many lines of data are in the file.

Now read the data again, but this time store each number in an array as its input value divided by the largest value, m. This process is known as *normalizing* the data. Print the values of the normalized array four to a line.

10.10   A file contains a list of names and telephone numbers in the format shown below:

```
Arthur Jones (365) 271-8912
John Smith (011-44-235) 135246
Simon Addison (699) 987-6543
Rachel Jones (444) 361-8990
Jean-Paul Maronne (011-33-1) 34567890
Hideo Takata (011-81-3) 3456-1212
```

and so on.

Write a program to search the file for a particular name (surname, forename or both) and display the line or lines with the phone number.

10.11   Type two or three paragraphs from a book into a file. Then write a program that will count how many times a word typed at the keyboard appears in the file and test it.

Now modify your program to produce a list of all the words in the file and how many times each one occurs.

10.12   A bank wishes to write a simple program to produce statements from a file containing details of the transactions that have taken place during a given period. Each record of the file is laid out as follows:

aaaaaaaa◊◊◊dd◊mm◊yy◊◊◊cccccc◊◊◊nnnnnnn.nn

where *aaaaaaaa*   is the 8-digit account number
       dd◊mm◊◊yy   is the date of the transaction
       cccccc   is the 6-digit cheque number for a debit, and is blank for a credit
       nnnnnn.nn   is the (positive) amount of the credit or debit
(and ◊ represents a space or blank character).

A second file contains details of the balances on the various accounts at the beginning of the period, with each record taking the form

aaaaaaaa◊◊◊±nnnnnnn.nn

where *aaaaaaaa*   is the 8-digit account number
       nnnnnn.nn   is the balance at the end of the last statement period (positive or
                   negative)

The program should read an account number from the keyboard, find the existing balance (if any), and print a statement showing all the transactions which have taken place on that account in the form

```
Statement for Account aaaaaaaa

                    Previous balance     ±nnnnnnn.nn

dd/mm/yy   cccccc   Debit    −nnnnnnn.nn   ±nnnnnnn.nn
dd/mm/yy   cccccc   Debit    −nnnnnnn.nn   ±nnnnnnn.nn
dd/mm/yy            Credit    nnnnnnn.nn   ±nnnnnnn.nn
   .          .        .          .             .
   .          .        .          .             .
   .          .        .          .             .
dd/mm/yy                                    ±nnnnnnn.nn

                    Current balance      ±nnnnnnn.nn
```

The program should also produce an updated file containing the current balances of all account holders. (Note: don't forget about any accounts where there has been neither a credit nor a debit during the period.)

INTERMISSION –
Designing, coding and debugging programs

The first part of this book has presented the fundamental capabilities of the F programming language. With the features that have been discussed, it is possible to write a program to solve almost any problem that you wish. However, as in almost all human activities, providing more powerful capabilities means that more complicated tasks can be more easily and efficiently accomplished. F is no exception to this general principle, and the second part of this book is devoted to describing the advanced features of F that make programming tasks easier to accomplish.

More powerful features can, however, lead to confusion if they are not used properly. Before presenting them, therefore, we shall return once more to a brief discussion of programming techniques in general.

After completing the first part of this book, you should have developed a clear programming style and a thorough understanding of the principles of good programming design. In particular, we have frequently emphasized the importance of developing a program by the method of incrementally refining the design. From bitter experience, the authors are both aware of the temptation to truncate the design stage prematurely and plunge into writing code – and of the disastrous results that succumbing to this temptation usually brings. By repeatedly reminding our readers that effort expended in the design stage invariably saves more effort at later stages, we hope to save the readers of this book from many frustrating experiences.

Unfortunately, in a book such as this, you can only be exposed to small programs, and you are presented with solutions where you have not seen the effort that went into creating them. You will not see any programs in this book where, in terms of the order in which they are referenced, procedures are nested 10 or more deep, and yet such programs are commonplace in the real world of programming.

Real-world problems take from weeks to years to develop and may, in extreme cases, involve hundreds of programmers. In such situations, a disciplined style of programming is essential, and it is important to develop good habits when working with the relatively small problems presented in this book.

It is impossible to be precise, because programming projects are so enormously varied; however, when creating a program, it is reasonable to expend about one-third of the total effort on the design phase. The writing of the code is usually a relatively small part, perhaps less than one-fifth, of the total effort. What consumes the remainder of the time — often more than half of the total effort — is testing the code and modifying it to function correctly (called **debugging**). Good initial design will reduce the often-frustrating debugging effort needed.

We advocate that you should always adopt an incremental approach to both writing and debugging a program. In other words, you should always break your code into small procedures, each one of which has a logically coherent, single, purpose. *Do not write procedures that do too many unrelated tasks.* The motivation is to keep different parts of a program from interacting with each other in subtle and obscure ways. Breaking a program into procedures means that such interactions can occur in a controlled way, only via procedure calling sequences. A good rule of thumb here is to keep procedures to no more than 50 lines of code. In that way, they can be printed on a single sheet of paper and more readily understood. Grouping related sets of procedures into modules will further reduce unwanted interactions.

To debug a program incrementally, each procedure should be thoroughly tested *by itself*. This means that input to the procedure is generated by another part of the program, or by hand, and the output examined for correctness. The set of inputs used to test a procedure should exercise all branches of the code it contains.

It is often very tempting not to test every procedure but, instead, to start trying to make a complete program function. This almost always results in errors being looked for in the wrong place — which is probably the most time-consuming and frustrating part of debugging a program.

Do not build your house without foundations. The incremental debugging approach means that the lowest-level procedures are tested first, then the procedures that use those procedures, and so on until the whole program is verified. The process of developing a set of test problems can often take half of the debugging effort.

Finally, you should keep all the test problems and the results produced during testing. In the course of time almost all non-trivial programs will be modified, and when that day comes it will both save time and provide an added degree of confidence if the modified program can be shown to perform correctly on the same sets of test data as the original version. This does not mean, however, that you should not develop additional tests for any new features added to the program. Thus, over the life of a program, the test suite will incrementally grow with each new modification.

During the second part of this book, many of the exercises at the ends of chapters will involve writing rather more complex programs than has been the case up to now. It will, therefore, be even more important than before that you develop good testing habits as well as good programming habits.

PART II

Towards Real Programming

11 An introduction to numerical methods in F programs

12 More about numeric data types

13 Array processing and matrix manipulation

14 Pointers and dynamic data structures

15 Additional input/output and file handling facilities

16 Still more powerful building blocks

17 More about numerical methods

An introduction to numerical methods in F programs

11.1   Numerical calculations, precision   11.4   Data fitting by least squares
       and rounding errors   approximation
11.2   Parameterized real variables   11.5   Iterative solution of non-linear
11.3   Conditioning and stability   equations

The main area of application for F programs is the solution of scientific
and technological problems – a process which usually involves the
solution of mathematical problems by numerical, as opposed to
analytical, means.

This chapter introduces some of the major limitations that are
imposed on numerical problem solving by the physical characteristics
of computers, as well as by the nature of the problems being solved,
and the means that are provided in F to ensure that the effects of these
constraints are both predictable and controllable. Two of the most
common numerical problems, the fitting of a straight line through a set
of experimental or empirical data and the solution of non-linear
equations, are then discussed, and examples given of how these
problems may be solved in F.

For those particularly interested in this aspect of programming,
Chapter 17 will return to the subject in rather more detail, with
examples of several other commonly required numerical methods.

11.1 Numerical calculations, precision and rounding errors

The F language was primarily designed to help in the solution of numerical problems, although it is certainly not limited to that purpose. Consequently, it is extremely important that the writer *and the user* of such F programs should be aware of the intrinsic limitations of a computer in this area and of the steps that may be taken to improve matters.

We have already met and used the two main types of numbers used in F programs (**real** and **integer**), but it is appropriate at this stage to review their characteristics briefly.

integer numbers are stored exactly, without any fractional part, and all calculations performed upon them, other than division, lead to a result which is mathematically accurate. There could, however, be a problem if, for example, the sum of two integers exceeded the largest integer that a computer could hold. In the case of division, any fractional part in the (mathematical) result is discarded. Typically, **integer** numbers can be in the range -10^9 to $+10^9$. **integer** numbers are normally used for counting and similar operations.

real numbers, on the other hand, are stored as *approximations* to the underlying mathematical values using a **floating-point** representation which allows a wide range of values to be stored with the same degree of precision. Typically, a **real** number will be stored in a computer to about six or seven decimal digits of precision, with an exponent range of around -10^{38} to $+10^{38}$. Some computers, typically those in the supercomputer class, exceed these ranges considerably. Numerical calculations normally use **real** numbers, although in certain circumstances **complex** numbers may also be used (see Section 12.1). Unless otherwise stated, the following discussion of numerical methods will assume that all numbers are **real** numbers.

Having established that **real** numbers used in numerical calculations are approximations, held to a specified degree of precision, we must analyse what effect this may have on the results of such calculations. We discussed this briefly in Chapter 5, when we referred to the manner in which we deal with precision when carrying out manual calculations, but we must now examine the problem in slightly more depth.

In order to illustrate this more easily, we shall assume the existence of a computer which stores its numbers in a **normalized**, decimal, floating-point form; that is, in a decimal equivalent of the way in which (binary) floating-point numbers are stored in a typical computer. We shall further assume that these numbers are stored with four digits of precision. Finally, we shall assume that the exponent must lie in the range -9 to $+9$. Thus, a non-zero normalized decimal number will be of the form $0.d_1 d_2 d_3 d_4 \times 10^p$, where d_1 lies in the range 1 to 9, and d_2, d_3 and d_4 all lie in the range 0 to 9. Normalized means that, except for the number 0, the exponent is adjusted so that $d_1 \neq 0$. The number $0.d_1 d_2 d_3 d_4$ is called the mantissa, while p is called the exponent, which for this

External value	Internal representation
37.5	0.3750×10^2
123.456	0.1235×10^3
123456789.12345	0.1235×10^9
9876543210.1234	cannot be represented – exponent is 10
0.0000012345678	0.1235×10^{-5}
0.9999999999999	0.1×10^1
0.0000000000375	cannot be represented – exponent is -10

Figure 11.1 Number storage on the decimal floating-point computer.

illustration must lie in the range -9 to $+9$. Figure 11.1 shows some examples of the way numbers will be stored in this computer.

Notice that two of the numbers shown in Figure 11.1 cannot be represented on our decimal computer. The first of these, 9876543210.1234, would require an exponent of 10, which is more than the computer will allow. Any attempt to store a number whose exponent is too large, as here, will create a condition known as **overflow** and will normally cause an error at this stage of the processing. Obviously, once a calculation has overflowed, any subsequent calculations using this result will also be incorrect.

A similar situation arises with the final number shown in Figure 11.1, 0.0000000000375; this number requires an exponent of -10, which is less than the computer will allow. This situation, which is known as **underflow**, is less serious than overflow, since the effect is that a number is too close to zero to be distinguished from zero. Many computers will not report this form of error and will store the number as zero; in some numerical calculations, however, it is important to know when underflow has occurred, and so some computer systems do report its occurrence as a non-fatal error. In particular, an unreported underflow can result in an attempt to divide by zero if the divisor is very small or in the wrong result in the case of a test for a number being zero.

We can now look at how our decimal computer will carry out simple arithmetic calculations. Before progressing further, however, we note that most computers carry out arithmetic in a special set of **registers** which allow more digits of precision than does the main memory; we shall, therefore, assume that our computer has arithmetic registers capable of storing numbers to eight decimal digits of precision – that is, twice the memory's precision. When the result of an arithmetic calculation is stored into memory, we will assume that it will be rounded to the computer precision – in our case, four decimal digits.

Consider first the sum of the two fractions 11/9 and 1/3.

The first number, 11/9, will be stored as 0.1222×10^1 on our computer, while the second, 1/3, will be stored as 0.3333×10^0. However, before these two numbers can be added together they must be converted so that they both have the same exponent, where the digits following the space in the following description represent the extra digits available in the arithmetic registers:

$$0.1222 \times 10^1 + 0.0333\ 3 \times 10^1 \rightarrow 0.1555\ 3 \times 10^1 \qquad \text{(in registers)}$$
$$\rightarrow 0.1555 \times 10^1 \qquad \text{(in memory)}$$

Observe that the process is to take the number with the lower exponent, then raise its exponent until it matches the exponent of the other number while correspondingly shifting the mantissa to the right (thus denormalizing it).

The correct internal representation of $(11/9 + 1/3)$, that is, $14/9$, is 0.1556×10^1, and it is worth noting that even this simple calculation, performed in floating-point arithmetic, has therefore introduced an error in the fourth significant figure due to round-off during the calculation.

Consider now the result of a slightly longer calculation in which the five numbers 4, 0.0004, 0.0004, 0.0004 and 0.0004 are added together. Since arithmetic on computers always involves only two operands at each stage, the steps are as follows:

1. $0.4000 \times 10^1 + 0.0000\ 4 \times 10^1 \rightarrow 0.4000\ 4 \times 10^1 \qquad$ (in registers)
$\rightarrow 0.4000 \times 10^1 \qquad$ (in memory)

2. $0.4000 \times 10^1 + 0.0000\ 4 \times 10^1 \rightarrow 0.4000\ 4 \times 10^1 \qquad$ (in registers)
$\rightarrow 0.4000 \times 10^1 \qquad$ (in memory)

and so on.

The result will be 0.4000×10^1, that is, 4.0, when we can easily see that it should be 4.002 when rounded to four significant digits! The denormalization has forced some of the numbers to be effectively zero as far as addition is concerned.

Now consider what would have happened if the addition had been carried out in the reverse order:

1. $0.4000 \times 10^{-3} + 0.4000 \times 10^{-3} \rightarrow 0.8000 \times 10^{-3} \qquad$ (in registers)
$\rightarrow 0.8000 \times 10^{-3} \qquad$ (in memory)

2. $0.8000 \times 10^{-3} + 0.4000 \times 10^{-3} \rightarrow 1.2000 \times 10^{-3} \qquad$ (in registers)
$\rightarrow 0.1200\ 0 \times 10^{-2} \qquad$ (in registers)
$\rightarrow 0.1200 \times 10^{-2} \qquad$ (in memory)

3. $0.1200 \times 10^{-2} + 0.0400\ 0 \times 10^{-2} \rightarrow 0.1600 \times 10^{-2} \qquad$ (in registers)
$\rightarrow 0.1600 \times 10^{-2} \qquad$ (in memory)

4. $0.0001\ 6 \times 10^1 + 0.4000 \times 10^1 \rightarrow 0.4001\ 6 \times 10^1 \qquad$ (in registers)
$\rightarrow 0.4002 \times 10^1 \qquad$ (in memory)

Thus, in this case the result will be 4.002, which is the correct answer to four significant digits.

This example shows that, whenever possible, it is preferable to add positive numbers in order of increasing value in order to minimize errors due to round-off. Similarly, it is preferable to add negative numbers in order of decreasing value in order to minimize errors due to round-off.

A much more serious example of round-off problems comes when we subtract two numbers. Consider, for example, the effect of subtracting 12/41 from 5/17. 5/17 is represented as 0.2941×10^0 and 12/41 as 0.2927×10^0 in our decimal computer, and so the subtraction proceeds as follows:

$$0.2941 \times 10^0 - 0.2927 \times 10^0 \rightarrow 0.0014 \times 10^0 \qquad \text{(in registers)}$$
$$\rightarrow 0.1400 \times 10^{-2} \qquad \text{(in memory)}$$

However, $5/17 - 12/41$ is equal to 1/697, or 0.1435×10^{-2}. The error in the calculation is, therefore, over 2.4%, which is hardly the accuracy we might expect from a computer – even our hypothetical one!

This example illustrates that great care must always be exercised when subtracting numbers that may be almost identical (or summing a series of numbers that may be both positive and negative), because the loss of precision resulting from floating-point calculations can seriously affect the accuracy of the overall calculation.

The reader is cautioned that, even though we used a hypothetical computer with only four significant digits, real machines with six or more significant digits encounter the same round-off problems. We have shown that there can be round-off problems after only four or five additions. Modern computers are capable of speeds in excess of a billion floating-point operations a second. Moreover, some problems can run for days, even on such fast machines. The issue of determining the validity of the answers obtained by performing as many as the 10^{14} floating-point operations such problems may involve is an important one.

We will not continue this discussion here, since the question of arithmetic precision is quite complicated, especially when we turn to multiplication and division. It is enough at this stage to draw attention to the problem. There are several excellent books on this topic, some of which are listed in the bibliography at the end of this book.

To mitigate the effects of round-off, attention must be paid to the numerical algorithms to be employed and to the precision with which the arithmetic operations are to be performed. The first topic is discussed in much detail in books on numerical analysis. In this book we only discuss these topics in an introductory manner. With regard to the second topic, the F language provides different types of numeric variables for those parts of a calculation where loss of precision may be serious. For many problems, although not all, increasing the accuracy of the floating-point calculations is sufficient to obtain satisfactory answers. This is described in the next section.

11.2   Parameterized **real** variables

As we have seen, a **real** value is an *approximation* which represents a numeric value to a specified precision using a **floating-point** representation. The accuracy of this approximation is determined by the form of the floating-point number which is allocated a fixed number of **bits** for the **mantissa** (thus defining the *precision*) and a fixed number for the **exponent** (thus defining the *range* of the numbers). The precision and exponent range are potentially different for every computer. This is a serious hindrance to portability. A program that executes acceptably on one machine may fail on another because of less accuracy or a smaller exponent range.

To permit more precise control over the precision and exponent range of floating-point numbers, **real** variables are, in fact, **parameterized**. That is, they have a parameter associated with them that specifies *minimum precision and exponent range* requirements. This parameter is called the **kind type parameter**. When this parameter is not specified explicitly, the type of the floating-point number is said to be **default real**. The kind type parameter value assigned to a default **real** is processor dependent.

So far, in this book, all **real** variables have been of type default **real**. The rest of this section will explain what the kind type parameter means and how to specify the kind type parameter explicitly.

The following statements illustrate the concept:

```
real :: a, b
real :: c, d
real, dimension(10) :: x, y

integer, parameter :: kind1 = 1, kind2 = 4, kind3 = 2
real(kind = kind2) :: e, f
real(kind = kind1) :: g, h
real(kind = kind3), dimension(10) :: u, v
```

The scalar variables a, b, c and d are of type default **real**, as are the arrays x and y. The second set of variables has been given explicit values for the kind type parameters. Thus, the scalar variables e and f are of kind type 4, the scalars g and h are of kind type 1, and the arrays u and v are of kind type 2. It is important to note that the value to which the kind type parameter is set must be a named **integer** constant. Thus, it would be incorrect to write

```
real(kind = 4) :: e, f  ! Not allowed
```

For any variable or constant that is an intrinsic type, the value of its kind type can be found by using the intrinsic function **kind**. Thus

```
real(kind = kind2) :: x
real :: y
integer :: i,j

i = kind(x)
j = kind(y)
```

will set i to 4 and j to have the value for the kind type of a default **real** number. Note that the kind of y is processor dependent while that of x is not.

The reader will observe that, so far, no specific precision or exponent ranges have been attached to a particular value for a kind type. In fact, each F processor is free to attach any precision and exponent range values it wishes to a particular kind type value. Thus, at first sight, it appears that no portability has been gained, since a variable of kind type 2, for example, may have 14 significant digits of precision and an exponent range of 100 on one machine, while it has six digits of precision and an exponent range of 30 on another.

However, using the kind type in association with the intrinsic function **selected_real_kind** will provide complete portability. This intrinsic function has two optional arguments, p and r. (The subject of optional arguments is discussed in detail in Section 16.1; for the present, references to this and similar functions should be written exactly as shown.)

p is a scalar integer argument specifying the minimum number of decimal digits required, and r is a scalar integer argument specifying the minimum decimal exponent range required. The result of the **selected_real_kind** function is the kind type that meets or minimally exceeds the requirements specified by p and r. If more than one kind type parameter meets the requirements, the value returned is the one with the smallest decimal precision. If there are several such values, the smallest one is returned. If the precision is not available the result is -1, if the range is not available it is -2, and if neither is available it is -3.

The following statements illustrate the concept:

```
real(kind = selected_real_kind(p = 8, r = 30)) :: m
real(kind = selected_real_kind(p = 6, r = 30)) :: n
```

Most computers have provision to store floating-point numbers using one of two precisions, usually referred to as **single-precision** and **double-precision**, with corresponding hardware registers to perform arithmetic operations on them. On a computer that has six significant decimal digits and an exponent range of 40 for its single-precision numbers, m will be stored as a double-precision number, and arithmetic operations on it will be performed using double-precision hardware registers. The variable n, on the other hand, will be stored on the same computer as a single-precision number, and arithmetic operations on it will be performed using single-precision registers.

On a computer that has 15 significant digits and an exponent range of 300 for its single-precision numbers, however, both m and n will be stored as single-precision numbers, and arithmetic operations on them will use single-precision registers.

The important point to notice here is that, regardless of the computer on which the above code is compiled and executed, the code will not have to be changed in any way to meet the specified precision and range requirements. The values returned by the **selected_real_kind** function may change, but that is of no consequence to the program as far as portability is concerned. In fact, because of the lack of portability of the kind type parameter values, we recommend that they *only* be used via the **selected_real_kind** function. The easiest way to do this is to define a named integer constant for use in subsequent variable declarations:

```
integer, parameter :: real_8_30 =   &
                      selected_real_kind(p = 8, r = 30)
   .
   .
   .
real(kind = real_8_30) :: x, y, z
```

Figure 11.2 shows the results of calculating the value of the expression

$$
\left(\sqrt{ \frac{1}{2} \times \frac{3}{4} \times \frac{5}{6} \times \dots \times \frac{2n-1}{2n} } \right)^2 \times \frac{2}{1} \times \frac{4}{3} \times \frac{6}{5} \times \dots \times \frac{2n}{2n-1}
$$

for different values of n. The program was executed on a 32-bit personal computer with the precision required set first at six digits, then at 14 digits. Mathematically, the result of the calculation should be 1, but round-off and truncation effects cause this not to happen exactly. Such effects increase as n increases. Note that the precision 14 answers are better than the precision 6 answers. This additional precision was, however, obtained at the cost of increasing the execution time. On some computers, using double-precision hardware will considerably increase the execution time.

Real literals also, of course, have a kind type parameter and, as with variables, if none is specified then the constant is of type default **real**. The kind type parameter is explicitly specified by following the literal's value by an underscore and the **kind** parameter:

	Six digits of precision		Fourteen digits of precision	
n	Result	Time	Result	Time
100000	0.999971	0.67	1.00000000000004	0.72
200000	1.000095	1.33	1.00000000000003	1.43
300000	1.000227	2.00	1.00000000000004	2.15
400000	1.000415	2.66	1.00000000000003	2.88
500000	1.000048	5.55	1.00000000000006	5.60
1000000	1.000376	12.00	1.00000000000004	13.00
5000000	1.025877	52.00	1.00000000000002	53.00
10000000	1.207035	104.00	1.00000000000104	114.00

Figure 11.2 The effect of different precisions on accuracy and run time.

```
3.14_high      real of kind type high
-4.0E7_low     real of kind type low
2.7            Default real (processor-dependent kind type)
```

where `low` and `high` are named scalar integer constants.

Unfortunately, the kind mechanism can also lead to problems if used without due care, and we must sound some notes of caution.

- In choosing values for the precision, you cannot, unfortunately, do so in total abstraction, freely choosing any precision you might wish. For example, many computers have a precision of between six and seven decimal digits for their single-precision floating-point numbers. Thus, if you choose a precision of 6 for your floating-point variables on such a computer, each **real** variable will be stored in one single-precision unit of memory and the arithmetic will be performed using single-precision registers. If you choose a precision of 7, on the other hand, then the computer will use one double-precision unit of memory in which to store each number and arithmetic will be performed using double-precision registers. Thus, by choosing a precision of 7, you may have inadvertently considerably increased the size of your compiled program and, on many computers, made it run slower than necessary.

- Another effect of the underlying hardware may make you think a process has converged when in fact it has not. Again, taking a computer with between six and seven decimal digits of precision, suppose you ran a program with precision set at 4, then ran it again with precision set at 5, and then finally with precision set at 6. Suppose you notice that your answers are not changing. You *may not*, as a consequence, conclude that your computations have been proved correct. What is in fact happening is that your calculations are all being performed at the *same* actual precision, somewhere between six and seven decimal digits. If you re-read the definition of the **selected_real_kind** function, you will notice that it returns a kind type value that meets or *minimally exceeds* your requirements; it does not have to match them exactly. Thus, in effect, you are executing identical programs, even though you are specifying increasing precision.

- A third class of difficulties can be experienced as a result of the computer providing significantly more precision than requested. Suppose that you specify a precision of 6 for your calculations, and your program executes successfully on a computer where the underlying single-precision hardware has 14 digits of accuracy. This means that your calculations are being executed with considerably more precision than you specified. If this program is subsequently moved to a computer where the underlying single-precision hardware has six digits of accuracy, the program may now fail. This is because, on the second machine, you are now executing with exactly the precision you specified. Thus, when you move your program from a high-precision machine to a lower-precision machine, you should test your program carefully to see if the precision you initially specified should be increased.

Let us sound a final note of caution. The mechanism for specifying higher precision or exponent range should not be used blindly to attempt to get out of numerical difficulties. You may, for example, be using an unstable algorithm or your problem may be ill-conditioned. In such cases you should consider reworking the algorithm or understanding why your problem is ill-conditioned; we shall discuss this topic in Section 11.3.

Furthermore, you cannot specify arbitrarily high precision to get you out of numerical difficulties, as a processor is free to limit the amount of precision it provides. In this context, note that the **selected_real_kind** function will return a negative number when asked for a precision or exponent range that the processor does not support.

Finally, we note that choosing the exponent range is frequently less critical than choosing the precision correctly, and it is permissible not to specify a value for **r** in a reference to **selected_real_kind**, in which case the range provided will be the default range for the precision specified:

```
integer, parameter :: real_8 = selected_real_kind(p = 8)
```

11.3 Conditioning and stability

The previous two sections have shown how important it is for the programmer to be aware of the effect of round-off errors in computer calculations and have indicated some of the approaches that can be used to contain the problem. However, it is also important that the programmer is aware of the likelihood of a particular calculation being seriously affected by such problems. Two factors that are important in assessing this are the **stability** of a numerical process and the **conditioning** of a problem.

A **well-conditioned problem** is one which is relatively insensitive to changes in the values of its parameters, so that small changes in these parameters only produce small changes in the output. An **ill-conditioned problem**, on the other hand, is one which is highly sensitive to changes in its parameters, where small changes in these parameters produce large changes in the output.

If a problem is ill-conditioned, even the best algorithm that can be applied to it will lead to results that are suspect. In such cases the definition of the problem should be examined to see if it can be redefined so that the results can be obtained from different data that is better conditioned. If it is impossible to improve the problem definition, then the answer should be labelled as being sensitive to the values of its input data. It might be appropriate to solve such a problem for sets of slightly different input data to analyse the sensitivity of the answer to the data. The reason for the concern in such situations is that physical data can only be obtained to a certain problem-dependent accuracy. If the data are ill-conditioned, the reliability of any answer obtained is correspondingly suspect.

An example of an ill-conditioned problem is the quadratic equation

$$(x - 1)^2 = 10^{-6}$$

whose roots are 0.999 and 1.001. If the problem is changed slightly to be

$$(x - 1)^2 = 10^{-2}$$

the roots are now 0.9 and 1.1. Thus, a change of 0.009 999 in the constant term of the equation has changed each root by 0.099; a ten times greater change.

This phenomenon does not only occur when the roots are almost equal. Just how unstable the roots of a polynomial can generally be was well illustrated by Wilkinson (1963), who gave a case of a 20th degree polynomial, where the roots were 1, 2, 3, ..., 20, in which changing the coefficient of x^{19} very slightly caused massive changes in about half of the roots.

Another example of an ill-conditioned problem is the pair of simultaneous equations

$$x + y = 10$$
$$1.002x + y = 0$$

whose solution is clearly

$$x = -5000$$
$$y = 5010$$

However, if some round-off, for example on the four decimal-digit machine specified in Section 11.1, had led to the second equation being expressed as

$$1.001x + y = 0$$

then the solution would have been

$$x = -10\,000$$
$$y = 10\,010$$

which is a very great change from the original solution. If the round-off error had led the coefficient of x in the second equation to be 1.000 (to four significant digits) then the problem would have been insoluble!

Clearly, in this case the reason for this extremely ill-conditioned behaviour is that the two equations represent two straight lines which are almost parallel, and therefore a very small change in the gradient of one will cause a very large movement of their point of intersection. Thus, a computer program which generated these equations and then solved them would stand a high probability of being so inaccurate as to be completely useless.

On the other hand, the two equations

$$x + y = 10$$
$$1.002x - y = 0$$

which have (to four significant decimal digits) the solution

$$x = 4.995$$
$$y = 5.005$$

are well conditioned, and a change of the coefficient of x in the second equation to 1.001 or 1.000 would lead to solutions of

$$x = 4.998$$
$$y = 5.002$$

or

$$x = 5.0$$
$$y = 5.0$$

respectively. This well-conditioned behaviour is because, in this case, the two lines are almost perpendicular to each other.

There are techniques which will detect whether, for example, a system of simultaneous linear equations is ill-conditioned, but a discussion of these is beyond the scope of this book. An excellent description of these and other related problems can be found in the book by Atkinson *et al.* (1989).

Related to the conditioning of a numerical process (algorithm) is its stability. A numerical process is said to be **stable** if the answer it gives is the mathematically exact answer to a problem that is only slightly different from the problem given. It is said to be **unstable** if the answer it provides is to a problem substantially different from the one given.

The two principal causes of unstable algorithms are **round-off error**, which we have already discussed, and **truncation error**. Truncation error is the name given to the error caused by terminating a calculation before it is mathematically correct. For example, if a function is being evaluated by a power series, on a computer, it will be necessary to sum only a finite number of terms. In this case the truncation error is the sum of the infinite number of dropped terms. Providing this sum is sufficiently small, and round-off errors are also small, the algorithm will be stable. Other examples of truncation error are estimating the derivative of a function by evaluating it at two close-together points, and estimating the value of a definite integral by evaluating the function at a finite set of well-chosen points.

An example of an unstable algorithm is the following method for calculation of e^{-5}. Suppose we use the power series expansion

$$e^{-x} = 1 - \frac{x}{1!} + \frac{x^2}{2!} - \frac{x^3}{3!} + \cdots$$

with $x = 5$. This series converges for all values of x. Moreover, if the series is truncated after the nth term, it can be shown that the error, E_n, satisfies the relationship

$$|E_n| \leqslant \frac{|x|^n e^{-t}}{n!}$$

for some t such that $0 < t < x$.

Thus, if $x = 5$ and we take the first 25 terms of the series, we are guaranteed that the mathematical error (the truncation error) will be no more than 2×10^{-8}.

The following program to implement this algorithm was executed on a computer with between six and seven decimal digits of precision:

```
program exponential_unstable
    real :: x, ans, term
    integer :: i
    x = 5.0
    ans = 0.0
    term = 1.0

    print "(t5, a, t14, a, t29, a)", "i", "termi", "sumi"
    do i = 1, 25
        ans = ans + term
        print "(i5, tr2, 2e15.6)", i, term, ans
        term = term*(-x)/real(i)
    end do
end program exponential_unstable
```

Figure 11.3 shows the results of running this program, and it can be seen that the answer obtained is $0.673\,748 \times 10^{-2}$. Since the correct answer, to six digits of precision, is $0.673\,795 \times 10^{-2}$ something has gone wrong!

The truncation error was controlled mathematically to be acceptable, and, therefore, the problem must be due to round-off error. Note that each successive term of the calculation is alternating in sign and that, after the sixth term, they are getting smaller in absolute value. This algorithm has, therefore, been designed with bad round-off characteristics.

```
         i       termi        sumi
         1    0.100000E+01  0.100000E+01
         2    0.500000E 01  0.400000E 01
         3    0.125000E+02  0.850000E+01
         4    0.200333E 02  0.123333E 02
         5    0.260417E+02  0.137083E+02
         6   -0.260417E+02 -0.123333E+02
         7    0.217014E+02  0.936806E+01
         8   -0.155010E+02 -0.613294E+01
         9    0.968812E+01  0.355518E+01
        10   -0.538229E+01 -0.182711E+01
        11    0.269114E+01  0.864039E+00
        12   -0.122325E+01 -0.359209E+00
        13    0.509687E+00  0.150478E+00
        14   -0.196033E+00 -0.455557E-01
        15    0.700119E-01  0.244562E-01
        16   -0.233373E-01  0.111889E-02
        17    0.729290E-02  0.841180E-02
        18   -0.214497E-02  0.626683E-02
        19    0.595826E-03  0.686265E-02
        20   -0.156796E-03  0.670586E-02
        21    0.391991E-04  0.674505E-02
        22   -0.933311E-05  0.673572E-02
        23    0.212116E-05  0.673784E-02
        24   -0.461122E-06  0.673738E-02
        25    0.960671E-07  0.673748E-02
```

Figure 11.3 Results produced by using an unstable algorithm to calculate e^{-5}.

To produce a stable algorithm, we can rearrange the calculation as follows. Observe that

$$e^{-x} = \left(e^x\right)^{-1} = \left(1 + \frac{x}{1!} + \frac{x^2}{2!} + \frac{x^3}{3!} + \cdots\right)^{-1}$$

The error, E_n, after truncating n terms of the series satisfies the relationship

$$|E_n| \leqslant \frac{|x|^n e^t}{n!}$$

for some t such that $0 < t < x$.

Thus, if $x = 5$ and we take the first 25 terms of the series, the truncation error is less than 2.9×10^{-6}. Notice that now the terms of the series do not alternate in sign. The error in using the reciprocal of the truncated series as an approximation to e^{-x} is

$$\frac{E_n}{e^x(e^x - E_n)}$$

Therefore, for $x = 5$ the error is less than 1.3×10^{-10}. Proving this is left as an exercise for the interested reader.

A program to implement this algorithm is:

```
program exponential_stable
    real :: x, r_ans, term
    integer :: i
    x = 5.0
    r_ans = 0.0
    term = 1.0

    print "(t5, a, t14, a, t29, a)", "i", "termi", "sumi"
    do i = 1,25
        r_ans = r_ans+term
        print "(i5, tr2, 2e15.7)", i, term, 1.0/r_ans
        term = term*x/real(i)
    end do
end program exponential_stable
```

Figure 11.4 shows the results of running this program. This time the result obtained, $0.673\,795 \times 10^{-2}$, is accurate to six digits of precision. You will

i	termi	sumi
1	0.1000000E+01	0.1000000E+01
2	0.5000000E+01	0.1666667E+00
3	0.1250000E+02	0.5405406E-01
4	0.2083333E+02	0.2542373E-01
5	0.2604167E+02	0.1529637E-01
6	0.2604167E+02	0.1093892E-01
7	0.2170139E+02	0.8840322E-02
8	0.1550099E+02	0.7774898E-02
9	0.9688121E+01	0.7230283E-02
10	0.5382289E+01	0.6959452E-02
11	0.2691145E+01	0.6831506E-02
12	0.1223248E+01	0.6774890E-02
13	0.5096865E+00	0.6751576E-02
14	0.1960333E+00	0.6742653E-02
15	0.7001188E-01	0.6739471E-02
16	0.2333730E-01	0.6738412E-02
17	0.7292905E-02	0.6738081E-02
18	0.2144972E-02	0.6737983E-02
19	0.5958256E-03	0.6737956E-02
20	0.1567962E-03	0.6737949E-02
21	0.3919905E-04	0.6737947E-02
22	0.9333108E-05	0.6737946E-02
23	0.2121161E-05	0.6737946E-02
24	0.4611220E-06	0.6737946E-02
25	0.9606708E-07	0.6737946E-02

Figure 11.4 Results produced by using a stable algorithm to calculate e^{-5}.

observe that the sum does not change after the 22nd addition; this is because, with the modified algorithm, taking the first 23 terms of the series guarantees that the truncation error is less than 3.1×10^{-9}.

Before leaving this example, we must make a comment. This method is almost certainly not the way that the **exp** intrinsic function is implemented by your compiler, which will probably use the techniques of range reduction and a rational approximation. Our purpose in presenting this example is to show that unstable algorithms can usually be replaced by something better. Furthermore, while we have eliminated the problems caused by subtracting numbers, we have not rearranged the calculations to accumulate the sum by adding the various components in order of ascending magnitude. This omission is simply to improve the clarity of the example, and we leave this improvement as an exercise for the interested reader.

SELF-TEST EXERCISES 11.1

1   Define overflow and underflow. Which usually causes the most problems in numerical calculations?

2   In each of the following cases two possible orders of calculation are shown that are mathematically equivalent. Which is the best to use on a computer, and why?

	Order 1	Order 2
(a)	$a * a - b * b$	$(a + b) * (a - b)$
(b)	$(a - b)/c$	$a/c - b/c$
(c)	$(a + b)/c$	$a/c + b/c$
(d)	$a + b + c + d + e$	$e + d + c + b + a$

   where $0 < a < b < c < d < e$ in both cases

(e)	$a/b - c/d$	$((a * d) - (b * c))/(b * d)$

3   How are **real** variables parameterized?

4   What does it mean to be of type default **real**?

5   To achieve numeric portability, how should you use the **kind** capability of **real** variables?

6   Which of the following two programs will give the more accurate results, assuming that you use a machine that has about six digits of precision for single-precision operations? Explain your answer.

```
module prec_def
   integer, parameter, public ::      &
      p3 = selected_real_kind(p = 3)
end module prec_def
```

```
program test_11a
  use prec_def
  real(kind = p3) :: x, y, z
  read "(2f10.4)", x, y
  z = x-y
  print "(t5, a, f14.8, a, f14.8, a, f14.8)",                  &
        "The difference between", x, " and ", y, " is ", z
end program test_11a

module prec_def
  integer, parameter, public ::       &
     p12 = selected_real_kind(p = 12)
end module prec_def

program test_11b
  use prec_def
  real(kind = p12) :: x, y, z
  read "(2f10.4)", x, y
  z = x-y
  print "(t5, a, f14.8, a, f14.8, a, f14.8)",                  &
        "The difference between", x, " and ", y, " is ", z
end program test_11b
```

7   What are the two types of effects that determine the accuracy of a calculation?

8   What are the two effects that contribute to the stability of an algorithm?

9   Define a well-conditioned problem, and an ill-conditioned one.

10 Define what is meant by a stable numerical process and an unstable one. What is the effect of round-off errors on the stability of a numerical process?

11.4   Data fitting by least squares approximation

A frequent situation in experimental sciences is that data have been collected which, it is believed, will satisfy a linear relationship of the form

$$y = ax + b$$

However, due to experimental error, the relationship between the data collected at different times will rarely be identical and can typically be represented graphically as shown in Figure 11.5. Fitting a straight line through the data in such a way as to obtain the fit which most closely reflects the true relationship is, therefore, a widespread need. One well-established method is known as the **method of least squares**.

This method can be applied to any polynomial, or even to more general functions, but for the present we shall only consider the linear case. If we assume that the equation

$$y = ax + b$$

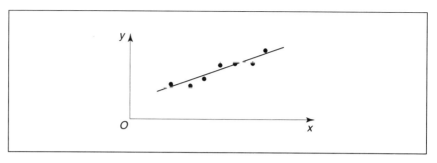

Figure 11.5 Experimental data which exhibits a linear relationship.

is a possible best fit then we can test its accuracy by calculating the predicted values of y for the actual data values of x and comparing them with the corresponding data values. The difference between a calculated value $\hat{y}$ and an experimental value y is called the **residual**, and the method of least squares attempts to minimize the sum of the squares of the residuals for all the data points. Figure 11.6 shows the residuals for the data in Figure 11.5 in graphical form, and it can easily be seen that using the square of the residuals is to give equal emphasis to those predicted values that are too large and those that are too small.

Simple differential calculus leads to the conclusion that the equation that minimizes the square of the residuals is when the two coefficients a and b are defined as follows:

$$a = \frac{\sum x_i \sum y_i - n \sum x_i y_i}{\left(\sum x_i\right)^2 - n \sum x_i^2}$$

$$b = \frac{\sum y_i - a \sum x_i}{n}$$

It is worth noting that it is quite common for one item (or sometimes more) of a set of experimental data to be less accurate than the rest. Clearly this can lead to an erroneous result, and it is, therefore, sometimes appropriate to ignore

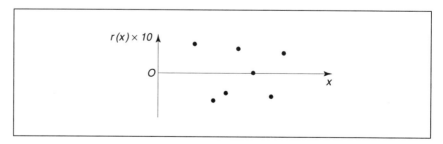

Figure 11.6 Residuals for the data from Figure 11.5.

one item of a data set and then to attempt to fit a straight line through the remaining items.

The value of the sum of the squares of the residuals, often referred to as simply the **residual sum**, can be a good guide as to how closely the equation fits the data. If it is a perfect fit, then all data points will lie on the line and the residual sum will be zero. If it is required to compare the **goodness of fit** of two or more equations, then the one with the lowest residual sum can be taken to be the best fit. It would clearly be possible to use this technique, for example, first to use all data points, and then to repeat the fitting process leaving each data point out of the calculation in turn. Points which contribute excessively to the residual sum would then be candidates for being ignored on the grounds that they contain too much experimental error.

▢ **EXAMPLE 11.1** ·

1 **Problem**

Figure 11.7 shows the results obtained from an experiment to calculate the Young's modulus of the material used to make a piece of wire. Write a program to calculate the value of Young's modulus for this material and the natural (unstretched) length of the wire.

2 **Analysis**

In this experiment the extensions produced in the wire by suspending various weights from it were measured very accurately. Young's modulus is defined by the equation

$$E = \frac{stress}{strain}$$

Weight	Length
10	39.967
12	39.971
15	39.979
17	39.986
20	39.993
22	40.000
25	40.007
28	40.016
30	40.022

The diameter of the wire (in inches) is 0.025

Figure 11.7 Experimental data from Young's modulus experiment.

which can be expressed as

$$E = \frac{f/A}{e/L} \quad \text{or} \quad E = \frac{fL}{Ae}$$

where f is the applied force (that is, the weight), A is the cross-sectional area of the wire (measured at several points and averaged), e is the extension, and L is the unstressed length of the wire.

In this case, in order to eliminate the effect of any curl or kinking in the wire, no measurements were taken in a completely unstressed condition, but the length of the wire was measured instead under an initial load and then under various heavier loads, as indicated in Figure 11.7.

From the above definition of Young's modulus we can derive the equation

$$e = kf$$

where

$$k = L/(AE)$$

However, we do not have the value of e, but rather the value of s (the stretched length), where

$$e = s - L$$

We therefore need to fit the equation

$$s = kf + L$$

to the experimental data. We shall then be able easily to calculate the value of E from k and L.

We are now in a position to design our program and, in accordance with good practice, will place all the constants required for the problem in a module so that they can be easily accessed from the main program as well as any procedures. As both the main program and the subroutine which will carry out the least square fitting follow the method already discussed, we shall omit the detailed data design and structure plan and proceed directly to the program.

3 **Solution**

```
module constants
! This module contains the physical and other constants
! for use with the program youngs_modulus

    ! Define a real kind type q with at least 6 decimal
    ! digits and an exponent range from 10**30 to 10**(-30)
    integer, parameter, public ::                      &
        q = selected_real_kind(p = 6, r = 30)
```

```
    ! Define pi
    real(kind = q), parameter, public :: pi = 3.1415926536_q

    ! Define the mass to weight conversion factor
    real(kind = q), parameter, public :: mtwc = 386.0_q

    ! Define the size of the largest problem set that can be
    ! processed
    integer, parameter, public :: max_dat=100
end module constants

module least_squares
    use constants
    private
    public :: least_squares_line

contains

    subroutine least_squares_line(x, y, a, b)
    ! This subroutine calculates the least squares fit
    ! line ax+b to the x-y data pairs

        ! Dummy arguments
        real(kind = q), dimension(:), intent(in) :: x, y
        real(kind = q), intent(out) :: a, b

        ! Local variables
        real(kind =q ) :: sum_x, sum_y, sum_xy, sum_x_sq
        integer :: n

        ! Calculate sums
        sum_x = sum(x)
        sum_y = sum(y)
        sum_xy = dot_product(x, y)
        sum_x_sq = dot_product(x, x)

        ! Calculate coefficients of least squares fit line
        n = size(x)
        a = (sum_x*sum_y - n*sum_xy)/  &
            (sum_x*sum_x - n*sum_x_sq)
        b = (sum_y - a*sum_x)/n
    end subroutine least_squares_line
end module least_squares

program youngs_modulus
! This program calculates Young's modulus for a piece
! of wire using experimental data, and also calculates
! the unstretched length of the wire

    use constants
    use least_squares

    ! Input variables
    real(kind = q), dimension(max_dat) :: wt, s
    real(kind = q) :: diam
    integer :: n_sets
```

```
      ! Other variables
      real(kind = q) :: k, L, e
      integer :: i

      ! Read data
      print *, "How many sets of data?"
      read *, n_sets

      ! End execution if too much or too little data
      select case (n_sets)
      case (max_dat+1: )
         print *, "Too much data!"
         print *, "Maximum permitted is ", max_dat,        &
                  " data sets"
         stop
      case ( :1)
         print *, "Not enough data!"
         print *, "There must be at least 2 data sets"
         stop
      end select

      print *, "Type data in pairs: weight (in lbs), ", &
               "length (in inches)"
      do i = 1, n_sets
         print "(a, i4, a)", "Data set ", i, ": "
         read *, wt(i), s(i)
      end do

      print *, "What is the diameter of the wire (in ins.)?"
      read *, diam

      ! Convert mass to weight
      wt(1:n_sets) = mtwc*wt(1:n_sets)

      ! Calculate least squares fit
      call least_squares_line(wt(1:n_sets), s(1:n_sets), k, L )

      ! Calculate Young's modulus
      e = (4.0_q*L)/(pi*diam*diam*k)

      ! Print results
      print "(2/,t5, a, f7.3, a)",                             &
            "The unstressed length of the wire is ", L, " ins."
      print "(t5, a, e11.4, a)",    &
            "Its Young's modulus is ", e, " lbs/in/sec/sec"
   end program youngs_modulus
```

Figure 11.8 shows the result of running this program with the data shown in Figure 11.7.

```
How many sets of data?
9
Type data in pairs: weight (in lbs), length (in ins.)
Data set    1:
10 39.967
Data set    2:
12 39.971
Data set    3:
15 39.979
Data set    4:
17 39.986
Data set    5:
20 39.993
Data set    6:
22 40.0
Data set    7:
25 40.007
Data set    8:
28 40.016
Data set    9:
30 40.022
What is the diameter of the wire (in ins.)?
0.025
The unstressed length of the wire is 39.938 ins.
Its Young's modulus is 0.1131E+11 lbs/in/sec/sec
```

Figure 11.8 Results produced by the program youngs_modulus.

11.5   Iterative solution of non-linear equations

Although a straight line fit is often appropriate, many real-life situations will not result in a straight line fit but, rather, in some non-linear relationship of the form

$$y = f(x)$$

If $f(x)$ is a quadratic function, then we can solve the equation

$$ax^2 + bx + c = 0$$

as we showed in Example 5.5, although it should be noted that a deeper analysis of this well-known, but often imperfectly understood, problem will be found in Section 17.2. In general, the function will be more complex than a simple quadratic polynomial and analytic solutions are not possible. In this section, therefore, we shall start to investigate methods to solve the equation $f(x) = 0$ numerically; we shall return to this topic in more detail in Sections 17.3 and 17.4.

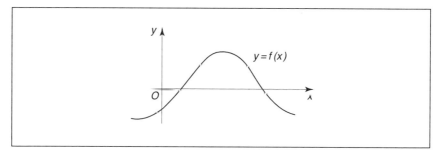

Figure 11.9 $y = f(x)$ and the roots of the equation $f(x) = 0$.

Numerical methods are usually based on calculating an approximation to the true value of a root (or **zero**) of the equation

$$f(x) = 0$$

and then successively refining this approximation until further refining would achieve no useful purpose.

Figure 11.9 shows the graphical representation of a continuous function $y = f(x)$, and it is clear that the roots of the equation

$$f(x) = 0$$

are the values of x at which the curve intersects the x-axis. This leads us to a simple, yet powerful, approach to calculating these roots, based on the observation that if $f(x_i) < 0$ and $f(x_j) > 0$, then there must be at least one root in the open interval $x_i < x < x_j$. Notice, incidentally, that there may be more than one root in the interval; in this discussion, however, we are only interested in finding one of them.

The **bisection method** uses this fact by then evaluating the value of $f(x)$ at the point midway between x_i and x_j and then repeating the process until the value of x is sufficiently close to the true value of the root. As in all **iterative methods**, the problem is in deciding when it is time to stop, or what the **convergence criteria** for the problem are.

Essentially, there are three possible criteria that we might use to terminate an iterative search for a root of the equation, all of which depend upon some value becoming less than some small positive number ϵ. Suppose that the iterative method successively generates the values $x_0, x_1, x_2, \ldots$. Then the convergence criteria are:

1. The magnitude of the function $|f(x_i)|$ should be less than ϵ.
2. The error $|x_i - x_t|$, where x_t is the true value of the root, should be less than ϵ.
3. The difference between successive approximations $|x_i - x_{i-1}|$ should be less than ϵ.

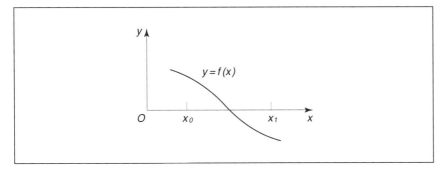

Figure 11.10 Finding an initial interval which contains a root of $f(x) = 0$.

Different methods will use different criteria to terminate the iteration.

In the case of the bisection method, it is clear that, at each step, the interval which surrounds the true value of the root is halved. For example, if the two initial values $f(x_0)$ and $f(x_1)$ have opposite signs, then the root must lie between them, as shown in Figure 11.10, and the value of $f(x_2)$ is calculated, where $x_2 = (x_0 + x_1)/2$.

If the sign of $f(x_2)$ is the same as that of $f(x_0)$, then the root must lie in the interval $x_2 < x < x_1$, while if it is opposite then the root must lie in the interval $x_0 < x < x_2$. In either case the new interval is half the size of the first one (which is, of course, the reason for the name of this method). If $f(x_2) = 0$, then we have found the root exactly and can stop the iteration. Since most functions found in practice do not have roots that are exactly representable as a floating-point number, this is an unlikely (but possible) occurrence.

After n iterations the interval containing the root will, therefore, be of size t, where

$$t = \frac{x_1 - x_0}{2^n}$$

The true root must, therefore, differ from any point within this interval by no more than t and, in particular, must differ from the mid-point of this interval by no more than $t/2$. Rather surprisingly, therefore, even though we do not know the value of the true root, we can use criterion 2 to stop the iteration when we are within a predetermined tolerance of the true value.

The observant reader will have noticed one problem with the procedure outlined above; namely, the assumption that we have two initial values x_0 and x_1 between which the root lies. How do we find these two initial values? And how do we ensure that there is only one root between x_0 and x_1? For the moment, we shall ignore these problems and assume that we have already determined, possibly by graphical means, an initial rough approximation to the root which allows us to choose suitable values for x_0 and x_1; we shall return to this topic again in Chapter 17.

□ **EXAMPLE 11.2** ⦁

1 Problem

Write a program to find the root of the equation $f(x) = 0$ which lies in a specified interval. The program should use a function to define the equation being solved, and the user should input the details of the interval in which the root lies and the accuracy required.

2 Analysis

We have already discussed the mathematics underlying this method, and so can proceed directly to the design of our program.

An initial structure plan might be as follows:

> 1 Read range (`left` and `right`), and `tolerance`
>
> 2 Call subroutine `bisect` to find a root in the interval (`left, right`)
>
> 3 If root found then
>   **3.1** Print root
>   otherwise
>   **3.2** Print error message

> Subroutine `bisect`
> Function dummy argument: `f`
> Real dummy arguments: `xl_start, xr_start, tolerance, zero, delta`
> Integer dummy arguments: `error`
>
> [Note that `zero` is the root found, `delta` is the uncertainty in the root (it will not exceed `tolerance`), and `error` is a status indicator]
>
> 1 If `left < right` then
>
> 2 If `x_left` and `x_right` do not bracket a root then
>   **2.1** Set `error = -1` and return.
>
> 3 Repeat indefinitely (until convergence criteria met)
>   **3.1** Calculate mid-point (`x_mid`) of interval.
>   **3.2** If (`x_mid-x_left`) $\leqslant$ `tolerance` then exit with `zero = x_mid`, `delta = x_mid-x_left`, and `error = 0` to indicate success.
>   **3.3** Otherwise, determine which half interval the root lies in and set `x_left` and `x_right` appropriately.

The only slightly tricky step is step 3.3, in which we determine which of the two half intervals the root lies in. We can expand this step as follows:

3.3.1 If `f(x_mid) = 0` then exit with `zero = x_mid, delta = 0`, and `error = 0`.
Otherwise
3.3.2 If `f(x_left)*f(x_mid)` is less than 0 then
    3.3.2.1 `f(x_left)` and `f(x_mid)` have opposite signs, so set `x_right` to `x_mid`.
Otherwise
    3.3.2.2 `f(x_left)` and `f(x_mid)` have the same sign, so set `x_left` to `x_mid`.

We already know that, since floating-point numbers are approximations, we should never compare two floating-point numbers for equality during this type of process but should rather compare the absolute value of their difference with a very small positive number. Note that a function with a high derivative at a root can have high values in the vicinity of a root, while a function with a small derivative can have small values far from a root. Therefore, the magnitude of the function is generally a poor criterion for terminating the iteration. Thus, we do not use the values of the function to stop the iteration process except to test for the (unlikely) case that we find a point where the function evaluates to zero. Since this unlikely event *might* happen, to create a robust algorithm we include the test in 3.3.1. Instead, the bisection method uses the second (previously mentioned) convergence criterion, in which the size of the bracketing interval is used to stop the process when it becomes less than a specified tolerance.

It will be noticed that once a function value is calculated it is used again, if possible, when the interval is bisected. That is, if the root is in the left half interval, x_left does not change and so f(x_left) need not be recalculated. The same is true for f(x_right) if the root is in the right half interval. This is valuable because most functions encountered in engineering and scientific applications will be expensive to evaluate. The prime measure of a root-finding algorithm's efficiency is how many function evaluations it requires.

Note we have a loop that iterates until the convergence criterion is met. If $\epsilon > 0$ is the tolerance and n is the number of iterations, then we want

$$\frac{x_1 - x_0}{2^n} < 2\epsilon$$

That is,

$$n > \log_2\left(\frac{x_1 - x_0}{\epsilon}\right) - 1$$

This will be satisfied when

$$n = \log_2\left(\frac{x_1 - x_0}{\epsilon}\right)$$

The smaller ϵ, the greater will be the number of iterations. Thus, ϵ should be chosen to be no smaller than is sufficient for our purposes and not so small that it is close to the smallest possible positive computer floating-point number.

Bearing in mind that we will initially evaluate f at r_0 and x_1, then, to satisfy the convergence criteria, we will generally make

$$2 + \log_2 \left(\frac{x_1 - x_0}{\epsilon} \right)$$

function evaluations. There is the (remote) possibility we may encounter a point where f is exactly zero before we perform all these function evaluations. We must, however, assume the worst (and by far the most likely) case in estimating how many function evaluations will be required. This will determine how long we will take to find the root to the desired degree of accuracy.

We shall not continue further with a full data design and structure plan, but will proceed to the solution.

3 **Solution**

```
module constants
! Define a kind type q to have at least 6 decimal
! digits and an exponent range from 10**30 to 10**(-30)
   integer, parameter, public ::                    &
      q = selected_real_kind(p = 6, r = 30)
end module constants

module functions
   use constants
   private
   public :: f

contains

   function f(x) result(fx)
      real(kind = q), intent(in) :: x
      real(kind = q) :: fx
      fx = x+exp(x)
   end function f
end module functions

module interval_bisection
   use constants
   private
   public :: bisect

contains

   subroutine bisect(f, xl_start, xr_start, tolerance, &
                     zero, delta, error)
   ! This subroutine attempts to find a root in the
   ! interval xl_start to xr_start using the bisection
   ! method
```

```
! Function used to define equation whose roots
! are required
interface
   function f(x) result(fx)
      use constants
      real(kind = q), intent(in) :: x
      real(kind = q) :: fx
   end function f
end interface

! Other dummy arguments
real(kind = q), intent(in) :: xl_start, xr_start, &
                              tolerance
real(kind = q), intent(out) :: zero, delta
integer, intent(out) :: error

! Local variables
real(kind = q) :: x_left, x_mid, x_right, v_left, &
                  v_mid, v_right

! Initialize the zero-bounding interval and the
! function values at the end points
if (xl_start < xr_start) then
   x_left = xl_start
   x_right = xr_start
else
   x_left = xr_start
   x_right = xl_start
end if

v_left = f(x_left)
v_right = f(x_right)

! Validity check
if (v_left*v_right >= 0.0 .or. tolerance <= 0.0) then
   error = -1
   return
end if

do
   delta = 0.5*(x_right-x_left)
   x_mid = x_left+delta
   if (delta < tolerance) then
      ! Convergence criteria satisfied
      error = 0
      zero = x_mid
      return
   end if

   v_mid = f(x_mid)

   ! ************************************************
   ! Remove the following print statement when the
   ! program has been thoroughly tested
   print "(2f12.6)",x_left,x_right
   ! ************************************************
```

```
            if (v_mid == 0.0) then
               error = 0
               zero = x_mid
               delta = 0.0
               return
            end if
            if (v_left*v_mid < 0.0) then
               ! A root lies in the left half of the interval
               ! Contract the bounding interval to the left
               ! half
               x_right = x_mid
               v_right = v_mid
            else
               ! A root lies in the right half of the interval
               ! Contract the bounding interval to the right
               ! half
               x_left = x_mid
               v_left = v_mid
            end if
         end do
      end subroutine bisect
   end module interval_bisection

   program zero_find
   ! This program finds a root of the equation f(x) = 0 in a
   ! specified interval to within a specified tolerance of the
   ! true root, by using the bisection method

      use constants
      use functions
      use interval_bisection

      ! Input variables
      real(kind = q) :: left, right, tolerance

      ! Other variables
      real(kind = q) :: zero, delta
      integer :: err

      ! Get range and tolerance information
      print *, "Give the bounding interval (two values)"
      read *, left, right

      print *, "Give the tolerance"
      read *, tolerance

      ! Calculate root by the bisection method
      call bisect(f, left, right, tolerance, zero, delta, err)

      ! Determine type of result
      select case (err)
      case (0)
         print *, "The zero is ", zero,"+- ", delta
      case (-1)
         print *, "The input is bad"
      end select
   end program zero_find
```

```
       -10.000000    0.0000000E+00
        -5.000000    0.0000000E+00
        -2.500000    0.0000000E+00
        -1.250000    0.0000000E+00
        -0.625000    0.0000000E+00
        -0.625000   -0.312500
        -0.625000   -0.468750
        -0.625000   -0.546875
        -0.585938   -0.546875
        -0.585938   -0.566406
        -0.576172   -0.566406
        -0.571289   -0.566406
        -0.568848   -0.566406
        -0.567627   -0.566406
        -0.567627   -0.567017
        -0.567322   -0.567017
        -0.567169   -0.567017
        -0.567169   -0.567093
        -0.567169   -0.567131
        -0.567150   -0.567131
      The zero is    -0.567141 +-     9.5367432E-06
```

Figure 11.11 The solution of $x + e^x = 0$ using **bisect**.

Note that we have included an extra **print** statement in bisect to print the value of the various values being calculated at each iteration. Once the program has been tested this statement would normally be removed.

Figure 11.11 shows the result of running this program to find a root of $x + e^x = 0$ starting at $[-10,0]$ and with a tolerance of 10^{-5}.

For simplicity, we have determined if two function values have opposite signs by multiplying them together and testing whether their product is negative. This can lead to underflow or overflow problems. The reader should consider alternative approaches.

We now present an alternative way of coding module interval_bisection that uses a recursive procedure.

```
module interval_bisection
   use constants
   private

   private :: divide_interval
   public :: bisect

contains

   subroutine bisect(f, xl_start, xr_start, tol,   &
                     zero, delta, error)
   ! Function used to define equation whose roots
   ! are required
```

```
    interface
       function f(x) result(fx)
          use constants
          real(kind = q), intent(in) :: x
          real(kind = q) :: fx
       end function f
    end interface

    ! Other dummy arguments
    real(kind = q), intent(in) :: xl_start, xr_start, tol
    real(kind = q), intent(out) :: zero, delta
    integer, intent(out) :: error

    ! Local variables
    real(kind = q) :: xl, xr

    ! Initialize the zero-bounding interval
    if (xl_start < xr_start) then
       xl = xl_start
       xr = xr_start
    else
       xl = xr_start
       xr = xl_start
    end if

    ! Check if a solution is possible
    if (f(xl)*f(xr) >= 0.0 .or. tol <= 0.0) then
       ! No solution possible
       error = -1
    else
       ! Solution is possible, call divide_interval to
       ! find it
       call divide_interval(f, xl, xr, tol,zero, &
                            delta, error)
    end if

end subroutine bisect

recursive subroutine divide_interval               &
       (f, xl, xr, tol, zero, delta, error)
! Function used to define equation whose roots
! are required
    interface
       function f(x) result(fx)
          use constants
          real(kind = q), intent(in) :: x
          real(kind = q) :: fx
       end function f
    end interface

    ! Other dummy arguments
    real(kind = q), intent(in) :: tol
    real(kind = q), intent(inout) :: xl, xr
    real(kind = q), intent(out) :: zero, delta
    integer, intent(out) :: error
```

```
    ! Local variables
    real(kind = q) :: xm

    ! Remove the following print statement when the
    ! program has been thoroughly tested
    print *, xl, xr

    delta = 0.5*(xr-xl)
    ! Check to see if within the specified tolerance of
    ! the root
    if (delta < tol) then
        ! Yes - return result
        error = 0
        zero = xl + delta
    else
        ! More iterations needed
        xm = xl + delta
        if (f(xl)*f(xm) < 0.0) then
            call divide_interval(f, xl, xm, tol, zero, &
                                 delta, error)
        else
            call divide_interval(f, xm, xr, tol, zero, &
                                 delta, error)
        end if
    end if
  end subroutine divide_interval
end module interval_bisection
```

This code will find an identical root to the previous implementation – looking at the same set of points while finding a solution. However, notice that subroutine divide_interval is not as efficient as the non-recursive code because it does not reuse already-calculated function values. Fixing this is given as one of the exercises at the end of this chapter.

· ▫

SELF-TEST EXERCISES 11.2

1   What are the three main types of convergence criteria for an iterative process?

2   In the method of data fitting by least squares approximation, what is the meaning of the residual and the residual sum?

3   How is the residual sum used as a measure of goodness of fit in a least squares approximation?

4   Name two potential problems with the bisection method for finding the roots of a polynomial.

SUMMARY

- **real** numbers are stored in a computer as floating-point approximations to their true mathematical values.

- All **real** calculations are subject to round-off errors, and the programmer must take care to perform complicated calculations in such a way as to minimize these effects.

- Overflow will occur if a calculation would result in an exponent for a **real** number being larger than the maximum possible exponent allowed. Overflow results in an error condition.

- Underflow will occur if a calculation would result in an exponent for a **real** number being smaller than the minimum possible exponent allowed. The result of underflow is that the result of the calculation is treated as zero; it is not treated as an error by many processors.

- **real** variables may be parameterized in order to provide more than one representation of **real** numbers, with differing degrees of precision or exponent range.

- A processor which supports more than one representation of **real** numbers will specify a different **kind** type parameter for each representation.

- A **real** variable or constant whose **kind** type parameter is not specified is of default **real** type.

- The **selected_real_kind** intrinsic function may be used to determine the **kind** type parameter of the **real** number representation on the current processor which meets, at least, a specified degree of precision and exponent range.

- The use of parameterized **real** variables and constants, in conjunction with the **selected_real_kind** intrinsic function, provides a portable means of specifying the precision and exponent range for numerical algorithms.

- An ill-conditioned problem is one whose results are highly sensitive to changes in its input parameters; a well-conditioned problem is relatively insensitive to such changes.

- A stable numerical algorithm is one which provides a mathematically exact answer to a problem that is only very slightly different from that specified; an unstable process provides an answer to a substantially different problem.

- It is often possible to restate a numerical problem in order to provide a stable algorithm for its solution instead of an unstable one.

- The method of least squares approximation is a simple and effective method of fitting a straight line through a set of data points.

- The residual sum of a least squares approximation can be a good guide as to how closely the line fits the data, and can be used to improve the approximation by omitting data points which contain too much experimental error.

- Iterative methods are normally used to solve non-linear equations.

- The bisection method is a simple iterative method for finding a root of a non-linear equation in a specified interval.

- F syntax introduced in Chapter 11

Variable declarations	**real** (**kind** = *kind-type*) ... :: *list of variable names* where *kind-type* is a named integer constant.
Literal constant definition	*numeric-literal_kind-type* where *kind-type* is a named integer constant.

PROGRAMMING EXERCISES

11.1   Write a program that calculates π using default **real** variables. Print out the answers to as many decimal places as your machine will allow and compare the result with a tabulated value. Repeat this exercise using parameterized **real**s having **kind** types giving 6, 10, 14 and 18 decimal digits of precision. What does this tell you?

11.2   Tabulate the values of $1 - \cos x$ to four decimal places for x between 0 and 10^{-4} in steps of 10^{-5}, using a **real** variable, parameterized to have a precision of 6, for x. Repeat this with a precision of 14 for x.
   Now repeat all of the above using the fact that

$$1 - \cos x = 2 \sin^2 \frac{x}{2}$$

Are you getting better answers? If so, why?

*11.3   Write a program to evaluate the factorial of 200. (Hint: use logarithms.) Compare your result with Stirling's approximation for large n:

$$\log_e(n!) = (n + 0.5)\log_e n - n + \frac{\log_e(2\pi)}{2}$$

11.4   The polynomial

$$63x^3 - 183x^2 + 97x + 55$$

has three real roots between -10 and $+10$. Write a program to find them, using the bisection method.
   (Hint: you must first find intervals in which the roots lie; this can be achieved by tabulating the value of the polynomial for various values of x.)

*11.5   Use the program you wrote for Exercise 11.4 to find those roots of the following equations which lie in the range $-10 \leqslant x \leqslant 10$.

(a) $10x^3 - x^2 - 69x + 72$
(b) $20x^3 - 52x^2 + 17x + 24$
(c) $5x^3 - x^2 - 80x + 16$
(d) $10x^4 + 13x^3 - 163x^2 - 208x + 48$
(e) $x^4 + 2x^3 - 23x^2 - 24x + 144$
(f) $9x^4 - 42x^3 - 1040x^2 + 5082x - 5929$

11.6   Rewrite the recursive subroutine `divide_interval` of Example 11.2 so that it reuses already-calculated function values.

11.7   The Taylor series is a method of calculating an approximation to a particular function. For example, the Taylor series for the function $\sin(x)$ is:

$$\sin(x) = x - \frac{x^3}{3!} + \frac{x^5}{5!} - \frac{x^7}{7!} + \frac{x^9}{9!} - \cdots$$

(where x is an angle in radians, and $n!$ is the factorial function of n; specifically, $n * (n-1) * (n-2) * \ldots * 2 * 1$).

Write a program to evaluate the first five terms of the above series, and compare the accuracy achieved with the intrinsic function **sin**. The algorithm provided by your compiler for the **sin** function is almost certainly more sophisticated than that given here. Now modify your program so that it uses a variable number of terms in the series and keeps adding terms until they become sufficiently small. Note that an efficient program should calculate each term in the series from the previous one. Compare the accuracy obtainable with **real** variables with the precision set to 6 and then set to 14. (Note that if you are using a machine whose single-precision hardware has more than 14 digits of precision, you should set the precision to 14 and then 28 for this exercise.)

11.8   The following set of experimental data is to be fitted by a curve of the form $y = e^{ax}$

x	0.0	0.1	0.2	0.3	0.4	0.5	0.6	0.7	0.8	0.9	1.0
y	1.07	1.40	1.56	2.30	2.92	3.52	4.57	6.00	7.33	9.69	12.04

This can be done as follows. The sum of the squares of the residuals is given by

$$\sum_{i=1}^{10} (y_i - \exp(ax_i))^2$$

and this must be minimized with respect to a. Simple differentiation, therefore, tells us that the following equation needs to be solved for a

$$\sum_{i=1}^{10} x_i(y_i - \exp(ax_i)) \exp(ax_i) = 0, \qquad \text{where } h \text{ is small}$$

Write a program to solve this equation using the bisection method, and hence find the estimated value of a.

11.9 In engineering or scientific problems, it is often required to calculate the derivative of a function; frequently, however, such a derivative is expensive or impossible to compute analytically. One method of calculating the first derivative $f'(x)$ of a function $f(x)$ uses the so-called Newton quotient:

$$f'(x) = \frac{f(x+h) - f(x)}{h}, \qquad \text{where } h \text{ is small}$$

Write a program to compute the Newton quotient for the function

$$f(x) = x^2 - 3x + 2$$

at the point $x = 2$ (where we can readily calculate that the exact answer is 1). Your program should print a table showing the value of h and the calculated value of $f'(x)$, for values of h starting at 1 and decreasing by a factor of 10 on each repetition. You will find that, when h becomes too small, the calculation loses all semblance of accuracy due to rounding errors.

Modify your program to use a new set of values for h in the region which showed the greatest accuracy. What is the best value for h for this function, when $x = 2$?

11.10 Exercise 11.9 showed how rounding errors affected the calculation of the first derivative of a function by means of the Newton quotient. Repeat the exercise, but carrying out all the calculations using **real** numbers in which the precision is set to 14. (Once again, if you are using a machine whose single-precision hardware has more than 14 digits of precision, you should set the precision to 14 and then 28 for this exercise.)

Now repeat the same process, using both default **real**s and the higher-precision **real**s used above, for the following functions at the points specified:

(a) $x^2 - 3x + 2$ at $x = 1.5$ (exact value is 0)
(b) $x^3 - 6x^2 + 12x - 5$ at $x = 1$ (exact value is 3)
(c) $x^3 - 6x^2 + 12x - 5$ at $x = 2$ (exact value is 0)
(d) $x^3 - 6x^2 + 12x - 5$ at $x = 3$ (exact value is 12)

What does this tell you about choosing the value for h?

11.11 This exercise analyses an unstable algorithm. Write a program to calculate the integrals $I_0, I_1, \ldots, I_{10}$, where

$$I_n = \int_0^1 x^n e^{-x} dx, \qquad \text{for } n = 0, 1, 2, \ldots, 10$$

by the recursion formula

$$I_0 = 1 - e^{-1}$$
$$I_n = -e^{-1} + nI_{n-1} \quad \text{for } n \geqslant 1$$

where e is the basis of the natural logarithms. Those who are mathematically inclined can easily verify that this recursion formula is correct by integration by parts.

Use six significant decimal digits of accuracy. Mathematically, the results should all be positive (and should decrease as the subscript increases). Your answers, unless you are using considerably more than the specified accuracy, will show that something is clearly going wrong. What is the problem?

Hint: think about what happens to the small round-off error made in calculating I_0. How does it get magnified in calculating I_1, I_2, I_3, and so on?

A stable algorithm for this problem can be created in a very interesting way. Rewrite the recursion formula as

$$I_{20} = 0 \qquad \text{(We know that } I_n \to 0 \text{ as } n \to \infty).$$

$$I_{n-1} = \frac{e^{-1} + I_n}{n}$$

Write a program based on this algorithm. You will note that the values of I_0, I_1, $\ldots$, I_{10} are all positive and that the values decrease as the subscript increases. In fact, the answers obtained are all correct to six figures of precision. How can this algorithm work when we have arbitrarily set I_{20} to 0 and then worked backwards?

(Hint: think about the error made in I_{19} by setting $I_{20} = 0$. Then the resulting error in I_{18}, $\ldots$.

So, starting with an initial value that was good to six significant digits we obtained wrong answers to the problem. However, starting with a very poor initial value, we were able to obtain six-figure accuracy. This demonstrates some of the power and elegance of numerical analysis.

More about numeric data types

12.1 complex variables
12.2 Non-default data types
12.3 Specifying non-default kinds of variables
12.4 Specifying non-default kinds of constants

12.5 Using non-default kinds to improve portability
12.6 Mixed kind expressions

This chapter introduces the final intrinsic data type in F, to add to the **integer**, **real**, **character** and **logical** data types discussed in earlier chapters. This is the **complex** type, which enables the use of complex mathematics for those application areas, notably electrical and electronic engineering, where its use is essential for all save the simplest problems.

Almost all computers have more than one physical representation for real numbers, providing different degrees of precision and exponent range, and many also provide more than one representation of integers, providing different ranges of integer values. The rest of this chapter shows how F allows the programmer to specify, in a portable fashion, the degree of precision and/or the range of values required, so that the compiler can ensure that the most suitable of the hardware representations is used.

12.1 complex variables

In addition to the real and integer numeric data types, F contains a third intrinsic numeric data type which, although it is not used as much as real or integer variables, does occur from time to time in general applications, and is very important in certain application areas, such as electrical engineering. This type is called **complex** and consists of two parts – a **real part** and an **imaginary part**. In Chapter 8 we defined a derived type for this purpose which enabled us to illustrate several aspects of derived types. In a similar way, the intrinsic **complex** type stores a complex number in two consecutive numeric storage units as two separate **real** numbers – the first representing the real part and the second representing the imaginary part.

A complex variable is declared in a type specification statement of the form

```
complex :: name1, name2, ...
```

while a complex constant is written as a pair of **real** literal constants, separated by a comma and enclosed in parentheses:

```
(1.5,7.3)
(1.59e4,-12e-1)
(-19.0,2.5e-2)
```

The **complex** data type is, thus, a composite type and can be thought of as being an intrinsic version of a derived type, such as the one that we developed in Chapter 8, and, just as it is not possible to access the components of a derived type directly if these are declared as being private, it is not possible to access the real and imaginary parts of a complex number directly. In order to do this, or to create a complex value from two real values representing the real and imaginary parts, we must use one of three intrinsic functions:

real (z)	where z is **complex**, delivers the real part of z
aimag (z)	where z is **complex**, delivers the imaginary part of z
cmplx (a)	if a is **real**, delivers the complex value $(a, 0.0)$ if a is **integer**, delivers the complex value $(\text{real}\,(a), 0.0)$ if a is **complex**, delivers the complex value a
cmplx (x, y)	where x and y must be **integer** or **real**, delivers the complex value $(\text{real}\,(x), \text{real}\,(y))$

All three functions are elemental, and their arguments can, therefore, be either scalar or array-valued.

We can now move to examining how complex numbers are used, and first we note that, in mathematical terms, the complex number (x, y) is written $x + iy$, where $i^2 = -1$, although electrical engineers usually use the letter j rather than i;

If

$$z_1 = (x_1, y_1)$$
$$z_2 = (x_2, y_2)$$

then

$$z_1 + z_2 = (x_1 + x_2, y_1 + y_2)$$
$$z_1 - z_2 = (x_1 - x_2, y_1 - y_2)$$
$$z_1 z_2 = (x_1 x_2 - y_1 y_2, x_1 y_2 + x_2 y_1)$$
$$z_1 / z_2 = \left(\frac{x_1 x_2 + y_1 y_2}{x_2^2 + y_2^2}, \frac{x_2 y_1 - x_1 y_2}{x_2^2 + y_2^2} \right)$$

Figure 12.1 Complex arithmetic.

we shall use j in the following discussion. This definition of a complex number leads to the rules for complex arithmetic which we met in Chapter 8 when defining our own complex derived type; for convenience they are shown again in Figure 12.1.

Both real and integer numbers may be combined with complex numbers in a mixed-mode expression, and the evaluation of such a mixed-mode expression is achieved by first converting the real or integer number to a complex number with a zero imaginary part. Thus, if z1 is the complex number (x1,y1), and r is a real number then

    r*z1

is converted to

    (r,0.0)*(x1,y1)

which will be evaluated as

    (r*x1,r*y1)

Similarly, if i is an integer, then

    i+z1

is evaluated as

    (**real**(i)+x1,y1)

```
program complex_arithmetic
    complex :: a,b,c
    ! Read two complex numbers
    read "(2f8.3)",a,b
    c = a*b
    ! Print data items and their product
    print "(/,t8,a,2f8.3,a)","a = (",a,")"
    print "(/,t8,a,2f8.3,a)","b = (",b,")"
    print "(/,t6,a,2f8.3,a)","a*b = (",c,")"
end program complex_arithmetic
```

Output:
```
12.5    8.4
 6.5    9.6

    a = ( 12.500    8.400)

    b = (  6.500    9.600)

  a*b = (  0.610 174.600)
```

Figure 12.2   An example of complex arithmetic.

In addition to the three intrinsic functions already mentioned, a number of other intrinsic functions are available for use with complex numbers. In particular,

conjg(z)   where z is **complex**, delivers the complex conjugate (x,-y), where x and y are the real and imaginary parts of z, respectively

All of the generic intrinsic numeric functions such as **sin**, **log**, and so on can also be used with complex arguments. A list of these intrinsic functions can be found in Appendix A.

Finally, we should mention that the input and output of complex numbers is achieved by reading or writing two real numbers, corresponding to the real and imaginary parts, using any appropriate edit descriptor. Figure 12.2 shows an example of both complex input and complex output. Note, however, that it is not possible to insert, for example, a comma between the two parts of the complex numbers.

☐ EXAMPLE 12.1   ·

1 **Problem**

When an alternating voltage is applied to an electrical circuit both its phase and its amplitude will be affected by the characteristics of the circuit. In order to simplify calculations relating to such situations, electrical engineers calculate a

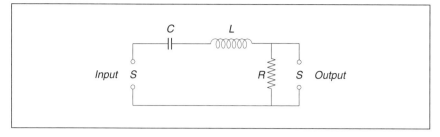

Figure 12.3 A simple electronic filter.

transfer function for the circuit. If the value of the transfer function at a frequency w is $H(w)$, then the amplitude of the output voltage is simply the amplitude of the input voltage multiplied by the magnitude of $H(w)$, while the phase of the output voltage is the phase of the transfer function added to the phase of the input voltage. (The magnitude of the transfer function is its absolute value, while its phase is the arctangent of the imaginary part divided by the real part.)

A very common type of circuit in electronic equipment is a *filter circuit*, such as that shown in Figure 12.3, which consists of a capacitor and an inductor in series, with a resistor in parallel. By varying the sizes of the three components it is possible to produce a *high-pass filter* that passes high frequencies with little attenuation but substantially reduces the amplitude of low-frequency signals, a *low-pass filter* that does the reverse, or a *band-pass filter* that reduces both high- and low-frequency signals allowing only frequencies within an intermediate band to pass without attenuation.

Write a program to produce a table showing the phase and amplitude of the output signal from the circuit shown in Figure 12.3 at different input frequencies, and for different values of the components.

2 Analysis

We can use Kirchhoff's laws to derive the transfer function for this system, which is

$$H(f) = \frac{R}{1/2\pi jfC + 2\pi jfL + R}$$

or

$$H(f) = \frac{2\pi jfRC}{1 - (2\pi f)^2 LC + 2\pi jfRC}$$

where f is the frequency of the signal in Hertz (cycles/sec).

The data design and structure plan for the program is then straightforward:

Data design

Purpose	Type	Name
A Module constants		
π	**real**	pi
2π	**real**	two_pi
B Local variables		
Initial and final frequencies	**integer**	f1, f2
Frequency interval	**integer**	f_inc
Loop variable (frequency)	**integer**	f
Capacitance	**real**	c
Inductance	**real**	L
Resistance	**real**	r
Transfer function	**complex**	h
Output phase	**real**	phase
Output amplitude	**real**	amplitude
Yes/no reply	**character**(1)	answer

Structure plan

> **1** Repeat as long as necessary
> **1.1** Read data values for next case – using subroutine input
> **1.2** Repeat for f from f1 to f2 in steps of f_inc
> **1.2.1** Calculate transfer function
> **1.2.2** Calculate amplitude and phase shift
> **1.2.3** Print frequency, amplitude and phase shift
> **1.3** Ask if another case required
> **1.3.1** If not 'yes' then exit from loop

Since the input procedure simply asks for the relevant information it hardly needs a structure plan.

3 Solution

```
module filter_input

    public :: input
    real,public :: r,c,L
    integer,public :: f1,f2,f_inc

contains

    subroutine input()
    ! This is the input routine for the main program filter

        print *,"What is the value of the capacitance ",  &
                "(microfarads)?"
        read *,c
```

```
      print *,"What is the value of the inductance ",     &
             "(millihenries)?"
      read *,L
      print *,"What is the value of the resistance ",     &
             "(kilo-ohms)?"
      read *,r
      ! Read frequency data
      do
         print *,"Give initial and final frequencies, ", &
                "and increment (hz)"
         read *,f1,f2,f_inc
         ! Check for validity
         if (f1<=f2 .and. f_inc>0.0) then
            exit
         else
            print *,"Data is inconsistent. Please try again"
         end if
      end do
   end subroutine input

end module filter_input

program filter
! This program calculates the transfer function for a simple
! electronic filter, consisting of a capacitor and an
! inductor in series, with a resistor in parallel, and then
! prints the voltage amplification and phase shift that it
! produces on input signals in a specified range of
! frequencies.

   use filter_input

   ! Declarations
   integer :: f
   real :: amplitude,phase
   complex :: h
   character(len=1) :: answer
   real,parameter :: pi = 3.1415926536, twopi = 2.0*pi

   do
      ! Get data for next case
      call input()

      ! Print title for this circuit, and column headers
      print "(a,i5,a,i5,a,/,a,f7.3,a,/,a,f7.3,a,/,a,f7.3,a,) ", &
            "Frequency response between ",f1," hz. and ",        &
            f2," hz.",                                            &
            "for a filter with a series capacitance of ",        &
            c," microfarads",                                    &
            "and a series inductance of ",L," millihenries" ,    &
            "in parallel with a resistance of ",r,               &
            " kilo-ohms is:"
      print "(2/,a,t15,a,t30,a,/,a,t15,a,t30,a,2/)",             &
            "Frequency", "   Voltage", "Phase",                  &
            "  (hz.)", "amplification", "shift"
```

```
! Convert capacitance to farads, inductance to henries,
! and resistance to ohms
c=c*1.0e-6
L=L*1.0e-3
r=r*1.0e3

! Loop for required frequencies
do f=f1,f2,f_inc
    ! Calculate transfer function
    h=cmplx(r,0.0)/cmplx(r,twopi*f*L-1.0/(twopi*f*c))

    ! Amplification factor is absolute value of h
    amplitude=abs(h)

    ! Phase shift is arctangent of imaginary part
    ! divided by real part
    phase=atan2(aimag(h),real(h))
    ! Convert to degrees
    phase=180.0*phase/pi

    ! Print results for this frequency
    print "(i6,t15,f9.3,t30,f5.1)",f,amplitude,phase
end do

! Ask if another case required
print *,"Another case? (Y/N)"
read *,answer
if (answer /= "Y" .and. answer /= "y") then
    exit
end if
end do

end program filter
```

Note that when calculating the transfer function h we used the first form shown in the earlier discussion, namely

$$H(f) = \frac{R}{1/2\pi jfC + 2\pi jfL + R}$$

which was coded in F as

```
h = cmplx(r,0.0)/cmplx(r,twopi*f*L-1.0/(twopi*f*c))
```

where the expression $1/2\pi jfC$ was converted to $-j/2\pi fC$ by multiplying top and bottom by j, remembering that $j^2 = -1$. We could, alternatively, have used the second form of the relationship

$$H(f) = \frac{2\pi jfRC}{1 - (2\pi f)^2 LC + 2\pi jfRC}$$

```
Frequency response between 1000 hz. and 20000 hz.
for a filter with a series capacitance of   0.022 microfarads
and a series inductance of  72.000 millihenries
in parallel with a resistance of    4.700 kilo-ohms is:

Frequency       Voltage      Phase
  (hz.)       amplification  shift

  1000          0.570         55.3
  2000          0.866         30.0
  3000          0.976         12.6
  4000          1.000          0.0
  5000          0.985         -9.8
  6000          0.952        -17.8
  7000          0.911        -24.4
  8000          0.866        -30.0
  9000          0.821        -34.8
 10000          0.778        -39.0
 11000          0.736        -42.6
 12000          0.698        -45.8
 13000          0.662        -48.6
 14000          0.628        -51.1
 15000          0.598        -53.3
 16000          0.569        -55.3
 17000          0.543        -57.1
 18000          0.519        -58.7
 19000          0.497        -60.2
 20000          0.476        -61.6
```

Figure 12.4   An extract from the results obtained from the program filter.

which was derived as a result of multiplying both top and bottom of the first form by $2\pi jfC$. In that case the F expression would have been

```
h = cmplx(0.0,twopi*f*r*c)/ &
    cmplx(1.0-twopi*twopi*f*f*L*c,twopi*f*r*c)
```

Figure 12.4 shows the result of running this program for a particular circuit.

It can clearly be seen that at 4000 Hz there is no attenuation at all, and that there is only a relatively slight attenuation between 2 kHz and 8 kHz. This circuit is, therefore, a simple band-pass filter which substantially attenuates frequencies below 1 kHz and above 15 kHz; it is thus suitable for use in audio equipment, since this is the frequency band which is of most relevance in this type of application. (In practice, since the circuit only contains passive elements, it is unlikely that such a primitive filter would actually be used in high fidelity equipment, but we are not concerned here with the finer points of electronic circuit design!)

12.2 Non-default data types

We first introduced the intrinsic **integer**, **real** and **character** data types in Chapter 3, **logical** in Chapter 5, and **complex** in the previous section of this chapter. However, apart from the discussion of parameterized real data in Chapter 11, we have not yet presented the full potential of any of these data types. For example, the range of values that may be stored in an integer will vary according to how many bits are used to represent it in a computer's memory, while both the range and the precision of real values can vary enormously depending on how they are actually represented by the computer being used. This presents considerable numerical difficulties when attempting to write portable programs.

In order to overcome these problems, F allows all the intrinsic types other than **character** to have more than one form, known as different **kinds**, and provides the means for a program to define which kinds of variables and constants it wishes to use. Each implementation of F will provide at least one kind of each intrinsic data type, known as the **default kind**, and may provide as many other kinds as it wishes. The non-default kinds are identified by means of **kind type parameters**.

For the numeric data types, the kind type parameters allow the specification of the numeric ranges and, for **real** and **complex**, the precisions available. By selecting a kind with a defined range and precision the precision problems resulting from moving programs from one computer to another are greatly reduced.

The kind type parameter for the logical data type, however, is something of an anomaly, because although a logical entity may have a kind type parameter, F attaches no specific meaning to it, and a processor is free to use it in whatever way it wishes for processor-dependent purposes. Typically, it may be used to provide a kind of logical which occupies only a single bit.

There is only one kind of **character** type in F, and it is not permitted to attempt to specify any kind type parameters for **character** objects.

Before discussing how kind type parameters are specified we should briefly examine under what circumstances kind type parameters should be explicitly specified.

Essentially, the numeric data types should have their kind type parameters explicitly specified when the program is expected to be run on more than one type of machine (which is a common situation) and the degree of precision used in calculations is important, or when the default precision or range provided by the machine being used is inadequate for the type of calculations being undertaken.

On the other hand, since non-default logicals are inherently non-portable we recommend that only default logicals should normally be used.

The next two sections will explain how to specify kind type parameters for variables and constants of different types, without going into details of what the values mean. The subsequent sections will then show how to obtain specific effects by varying the values of the kind type parameters for each of the main intrinsic numeric data types.

12.3 Specifying non-default kinds of variables

The kind type parameter associated with a variable is specified by the **kind selector** in the declaration of the variable. If no kind selector is specified then the type is said to be of **default type**. Up to this point (other than during a similar discussion in Chapter 11), all the variables and constants that we have used have been of default type. Thus, in Figure 12.5, the variables x and y are of type default **real**, z is a rank-one default **real** array of size n, i is a default **integer** named constant whose value is 25, and danger is of type default **logical**.

Each data type has its explicit parameterization specified in an identical manner in a modified version of the type declaration statement that we have been using up to now:

type (**kind**=*kind_type*) , ... :: *var_1*, ...

where *type* is one of **integer, real, complex** or **logical**. If the parenthesized **kind**= phrase is omitted then the type is a default type.

kind_type must be a scalar named **integer** constant which has a non-negative value.

Figure 12.6 shows how the same variables and arrays as in Figure 12.5 would be declared with each data type having an explicit value for its kind selector.

```
real :: x,y
complex, dimension(n) :: z
integer, parameter :: i=25
logical :: danger
```

Figure 12.5 Default kind type declarations.

```
integer, parameter :: k2=2, k3=3, k5=5, k10=10
real(kind=k2) :: x,y
complex(kind=k3), dimension(n) :: z
integer(kind=k10), parameter :: i=25
logical(kind=k5) :: danger
```

Figure 12.6 Explicit kind type declarations.

It must be emphasized that only intrinsic data types have kind selectors, and that it is impossible, therefore, to associate a kind selector with a derived type, although kind selectors can, of course, be used with the *components* of a derived type. Thus

```
type,public ::my_point
   real(kind = k3) :: x, y, z
end type my_point
```

defines a derived type each of whose components is real of kind type k3, where k3 is a scalar named **integer** constant having a positive value.

Note, also, that since **complex** numbers are compound entities, consisting of an ordered pair of **real** numbers, the value of the kind selector, whether explicitly or implicitly specified, applies to *both* of the two real components. Thus, the declaration

```
complex (kind=k3), dimension(4) :: v,w
```

defines two rank-one **complex** arrays, v and w, each consisting of eight **real** values of kind type k3 – a real and an imaginary component of each element of each array.

12.4   Specifying non-default kinds of constants

Since variables can be of different kinds, it follows that the same must also apply to constants. Unfortunately, however, the situation here is not quite as straightforward as is the case with variable declarations. In order to specify the kind of a constant the kind type parameter follows the constant, separated from it by an underscore, where the kind type parameter is a scalar named **integer** constant, and takes the value of the required kind type. If the kind type parameter is omitted then the constant is, of course, of the appropriate default type.

The following are examples of **integer** literal constants:

```
628                Default integer
-628_small         integer of kind small
628_large          integer of kind large
```

where small and large are scalar named **integer** constants whose values are non-negative.

real literal constants take a similar form:

```
-1.0               Default real
12.34              Default real
401.2e-5           Default real
-314.2e-3_low      real of kind low
704.2e-3_high      real of kind high
```

where low and high are scalar named **integer** constants whose values are non-negative.

The situation with **complex** literal constants is rather more complicated due to the fact that a **complex** literal constant consists of two **real** constants enclosed in parentheses. The rule in F is that if either of the two components has a kind type specified then the other component must have the same kind type specified. Thus, the following are examples of **complex** literal constants:

```
(1.5,2.7)                   Default complex
(-2.73,17.4e-2)             Default complex
(3.5_low,-12.9_low)         complex of kind low
(1.3e4_high,-1.5e-5_high)   complex of kind high
```

where low and high are scalar named **integer** constants whose values are non-negative.

For **logical** constants, the kind parameter follows the literal value:

```
.true.               Default logical
.false._short    logical of kind short
```

where short is a scalar named **integer** constant whose value is non-negative.

12.5   Using non-default kinds to improve portability

Before discussing how non-default kinds can be used to provide greater control and portability of programs than is possible with default data types there is an important point that must be dealt with, namely that F does *not* require that the values of the kind type parameters have the same meaning on all processors.

At first sight, this would seem to eliminate the possibility of writing portable programs, even though this has been stated to be one of the advantages of using non-default data types. F, however, does provide a number of intrinsic functions that completely eliminate this difficulty for numeric data types.

For *integers*, the value of the kind type parameter specifies what range of integers is required. To provide a convenient way of *portably* specifying the range requirements, the intrinsic function **selected_int_kind** can be used to specify the range required, and cause the F compiler to provide a suitable kind type. Thus a reference to

selected_int_kind (r)

returns a value of the kind type parameter for an integer data type that can represent, *at least*, all integer values n in the range $-10^r < n < 10^r$. If it is not possible to represent all the integer values in this range then the function will return a result of −1. In some cases there may be more than one available kind type which will satisfy the requirement, in which case the one with the smallest range will be returned. If there are several of these then the smallest of these kind type values is returned.

The following example uses this function to define a constant which is, in turn, used in the declaration of a number of variables.

```
program degree
    integer, parameter :: range = selected_int_kind(20)
    integer(kind=range) :: x, y, z

    x = 360_range
    y = 180_range
    z = 90_range
    .
    .
    .
end program degree
```

This extract defines three integer variables x, y and z that can contain values in the range $-10^{20} < n < 10^{20}$. They are initially set to the values 360, 180 and 90, respectively.

Notice that the named constant range is used to set the precision requirements for all integer constants and variables in the program. If the program is moved to a different computer system it will still use variables and constants of a kind which will allow at least the specified range because, even though the relevant kind types returned by the function **selected_int_kind** are processor dependent, it is known that they will be such as to meet the specified range requirement.

Note, however, that the program is not totally portable, because it is possible that the processor cannot support the requested integer range. In this case, the value −1 will be returned by **selected_int_kind**, and the subsequent attempt to declare a variable or constant of this kind will lead to an error. For most programs, though, this should be an extremely rare occurrence.

In the above program fragment we have specified the kind of the constants by writing them in the form 360_range. This is not normally necessary, however, when dealing with integers, since the default integer will almost certainly have a sufficiently large range for any literal constants. We can therefore write statements such as

```
x = 360
```

which are easier to read, and let the compiler take care of the necessary conversions. When we come to consider the situation with non-default reals, however, we shall have to be more careful.

It is important to note that the kind type parameter value returned by the intrinsic function **selected_int_kind** may be for an integer data type that

```
module kind_types
    integer, parameter, public :: &
                      range = selected_int_kind(20)
end module kind_types

program degree
    use kind_types

    integer(kind=range) :: x, y, z

    x = 360_range
    y = 180_range
    z = 90_range

    .
    .
    .

end program degree
```

Figure 12.7   Using a module to specify the kind types of **integer** variables
and constants.

exceeds the requirements specified. Therefore, in subsequent calculations, it would not necessarily be an error to set x, y or z to 10^{25}; whether or not this produced an error, or any type of warning at all, would be completely dependent on the processor on which the program is run.

There is one final point to be made before we leave our discussion of non-default integers. In general, we shall require all the integers in the program, or certainly a substantial proportion of them, to be of the same kind. It will therefore be more satisfactory to place the definition of the kind type in a module so that it can easily be made available to all procedures that require it and, moreover, so that a global change to the range required in the program can be made by simply changing the kind type number in just one statement. Figure 12.7 shows how this program extract would look if written in this way.

For *real numbers*, the value of the kind type parameter specifies the precision as well as the exponent range that is required. Furthermore, in a similar manner to the case with integers, we can use the intrinsic function **selected_real_kind** to assist with portability. Thus the statement

```
integer, parameter :: real_kind = selected_real_kind(p,r)
```

sets the constant real_kind to a kind type parameter for a **real** data type that has at least *p* decimal digits of accuracy and a decimal exponent range of at least *r*. If no such kind type parameter is available on a particular processor for the range requested, the function will return a value of -1 if the precision requested is unavailable, -2 if the exponent range requested is unavailable, and -3 if both are unavailable. If any of these values are used as the kind type in a declaration statement they will, of course, cause a compilation error. If more than one kind

```
module kind_types
   integer, parameter, public :: &
                        real kind = selected real kind(6,30)
end module kind_types

program satellite
   use kind_types

   real(kind=real_kind) :: r, theta, phi

   r = 321.172_real_kind
   theta = 1.47239_real_kind
   phi = 0.172341e-1_real_kind

   .
   .
   .

end program satellite
```

Figure 12.8   Specifying the precision and range of **real** variables and constants.

type parameter value meets the criteria, the one with the smallest decimal precision is returned. If there are several such kind values, then the smallest of the values is returned.

The exponent range argument *r* is optional. This reflects the fact that, for most calculations and processors, selection of the precision is usually (but not always) a more critical issue than selection of the exponent range. If the range argument is omitted, the processor will choose the value of *r*.

Figure 12.8 shows a program fragment which uses **real** numbers having six decimal digits of accuracy and an exponent range of 30.

Just as was the case with integers, it is important to note that the kind type parameter value returned by the intrinsic function **selected_real_kind** may specify a kind type that *exceeds* the specified precision and exponent range requirements. For example, if the program extract in Figure 12.8 was run on a computer which had two real kind types 1 and 2, having precisions and ranges of (5, 30) and (10, 60), respectively, kind type 2 would be selected, with the result that all calculations would use variables and constants which held values to 10 digits of precision. If the program was subsequently run on a computer which also had two kind types 1 and 2, but with precisions and ranges of (6, 40) and (12, 70), respectively, then kind type 1 would be selected, and all calculations would use only six digits of precision. The result might be different from that obtained on the first computer, therefore, but both computer systems would be working to at least six significant decimal digits of precision.

Because its components are **real** values, the value of the kind type parameter for a **complex** entity specifies the decimal precision and exponent range required for its two component **real** numbers. We can therefore use the intrinsic function **selected_real_kind** to specify precision and exponent range requirements for **complex** numbers in a portable manner. Figure 12.9 illustrates the

```
module kind_types
    integer, parameter, public :: &
            complex_kind = selected_real_kind(12,70)
end module kind_types

program accurate
    use kind_types

    complex(kind=complex_kind),dimension(4) :: z

    z(1) = (3.72471778e-45_complex_kind,  &
            723.115798e-56_complex_kind)
    .
    .
    .
end program accurate
```

Figure 12.9 Specifying the precision and range of **complex** variables and constants.

use of non-default **complex** numbers in a program fragment which declares an array of **complex** numbers, each of whose elements has real and imaginary parts having at least 12 digits of precision and an exponent range of at least 70.

Parameterization of **real** (and **complex**) numbers involves more subtle issues (of a numerical nature) than for any other F data type, and has already been discussed in some detail in Section 11.2, for those interested in such matters.

For *logical* data, F assigns no specific meaning to the kind type parameter. Because there is no requirement for an F processor to provide any **logical** data types other than the default kind, and because there is no guarantee, even if they do, that the non-default **logical** types have any particular relationship to each other, the concept is inherently non-portable and not to be recommended.

12.6   Mixed kind expressions

In Chapter 3 we explained how (default) **real** and (default) **integer** values could be used in the same expression, and elaborated the rules relating to the evaluation of such expressions. We also presented the rules governing the assignment of values of one type to a variable of another type.

Clearly, we must now extend these rules to cover the case of expressions involving explicitly parameterized variables and constants. Of course, if all the operands in an expression are of the same type and have the same value for their kind type parameter values, then matters are quite straightforward and, as we would expect, the expression will have a value for its kind type parameter that is the same as that of its operands. It is only when expressions involve operands of different types or different kind type parameter values that the situation may become slightly more complicated.

A number of intrinsic functions are provided to give precise control of kind type parameter values in expressions. The first of these, the intrinsic inquiry function **kind** will return the kind type parameter value of any **integer**, **real**, **complex** or **logical** entity. Thus the statement

```
k1 = kind(0.0)
```

sets k1 to the value of the kind type parameter for default reals, while the statements

```
integer, parameter :: k2=3
integer(kind=k2), dimension(3) :: a
k3 = kind(a)
```

set k3 to 3.

At first sight, this function does not appear to be particularly useful other than for establishing the kind type parameter values of the default intrinsic data types, since it is necessary to know the kind type of a variable before it can be declared, and of a constant before it can be written. However, as we shall see, it does have a role to play in writing portable programs.

A rather more useful feature in this regard, however, is the inclusion of an extra, optional, argument in the type conversion functions **int**, **real** and **cmplx**. We have already met these functions in their simple form, but we shall now briefly re-examine them in their new, more powerful, role.

The intrinsic function **int**(a,kind_type) converts the argument a to an integer. a can be **integer**, **real** or **complex** and can be scalar or array-valued. The value of the result is the integer part of a if it is of type **integer** or **real**, and the integer part of the *real* component of a, if a is **complex**. If the argument kind_type is present then the result of the conversion will be an integer of kind kind_type; if it is not present, as has been the case when we have used it before, then the result will be of type default **integer**. In all cases, if the value of the number being converted lies outside the range of integers which can be represented in the specified kind of integer then the result is undefined – although it will usually result in an error.

Thus the expression

```
j = j + int(x,kind(j))
```

will convert the value of the variable x to an integer of the same kind as the (integer) variable j, before adding it to j and storing the result in j.

In a similar way, the intrinsic function **real**(a,kind_type) converts the argument a to **real**. a can be **integer**, **real** or **complex** and be scalar or array valued. The value of the result is a floating point approximation to a if it is of type **integer** or **real**, and a floating point approximation to the *real* component of a, if a is **complex**. As was the case with **int**, the result will be **real** of kind

kind_type if the argument kind_type is present, and will be default **real** otherwise.

Note, however, that the statement

```
j = int(real(i,kind(x)),kind(i))
```

does not necessarily result in j taking the same value as i, even if they are both of the same **integer** kind. For example, if the three variables in the above statement were declared by means of the following statements

```
integer, parameter :: k = selected_int_kind(10)
integer, parameter :: p = selected_real_kind(6)

integer(kind=k) :: i,j
real(kind=p) :: x
```

then the **integer** variable i potentially has 10 decimal digits of accuracy. When it is converted to a **real** with a requirement for six decimal digits of accuracy, therefore, it must be assumed that some loss of precision may result. When it is subsequently converted back to an integer of the same kind as the original value it is too late to retrieve the lost precision!

For **logical** entities, there is an intrinsic function **logical**(L,kind_type) that converts between different kinds of logicals. The argument L must be of type **logical**. The result has the same value as L and will be of **logical** kind kind_type if the argument kind_type is present, and will be default **logical** otherwise.

There are a number of other intrinsic functions which have an optional argument which defines the kind of the result in the same way as in those described above; a full list can be seen in Figure 12.10. A specification of these, and of all F's intrinsic procedures, can be found in Appendix A.

We now come to the kind type parameter values of expressions, and here we strongly recommend that the intrinsic functions discussed above are always used to ensure that all the elements of an expression are converted to the same kind before any other operations are carried out.

Function name and arguments	Purpose
aint(a,kind)	Truncation
anint(a,kind)	Nearest whole number
cmplx(x,y,kind)	Convert to complex
int(a,kind)	Convert to integer
logical(l,kind)	Convert between kinds of logical
nint(a,kind)	Nearest integer
real(a,kind)	Convert to real

Figure 12.10 Intrinsic functions which have an optional kind argument.

		Operand x_2		
		integer	real	complex
Operand x_1	integer	Kind type parameter value of x_1 if the kind type parameter values of the two operands are equal. Otherwise it is the kind type parameter value of whichever operand has the greatest* decimal exponent range.	Kind type parameter value of the real operand.	Kind type parameter value of the complex operand.
	real	Kind type parameter value of the real operand.	Kind type parameter value of x_1 if the kind type parameter values of both operands are equal. Otherwise, it is the kind type parameter value of whichever operand has the greatest* decimal precision.	
	complex	Kind type parameter value of the complex operand.		

* If they are equal, the kind type parameter value is processor-dependent.

Figure 12.11   Kind type parameter value of x_1 op x_2.

For **logical** entities, the various **logical** operators are only fully defined for operands of the same kind; if they are of different kinds then the kind of the result is processor dependent. It is unlikely that this will cause any difficulties since interpretation of one kind of *true* as another kind is unlikely to be beyond the capability of any F processor! Whatever the kind of the value of a **logical** expression, if it is assigned to a **logical** variable then it will be converted to the kind of that variable.

The rules for determining the kind type parameter value of a numeric expression, however, appear to be quite complicated, although they are quite logical once you sit down and think about it! Figure 12.11 shows how the kind of a simple binary operation is determined, and the kind type parameter value of a more complex expression can then be determined by systematic application of these rules.

It is clear, therefore, that if the kind type parameter values of the operands in an expression are not identical, then the rules for its evaluation are quite complicated, and code written in this way will be difficult to understand, maintain, and convert to a new computer. Whenever possible, therefore, expressions involving operands with differing kind type parameter values should be avoided.

SELF-TEST EXERCISES 12.1

1   How is a complex number represented by an object of **complex** type?

2   What is a kind type parameter? Why are kind type parameters important?

3   What is the relationship between the kind type of a **complex** variable and the kind types of its components?

4   How are explicit kind type parameters specified for variables?

5   How are explicit kind type parameters specified for constants?

6   What intrinsic functions are used to specify values for the kind type parameters of **integer**, **real** and **complex** entities? How are they used?

7   What happens if an impossible **integer** range or **real** precision is requested?

8   If a **real** constant or variable is defined by explicitly stating range or precision requirements, why does it not always meet these requirements exactly?

SUMMARY

- **complex** entities use two consecutive numeric storage units to represent the real and imaginary parts by two real numbers.

- All intrinsic data types, other than **character**, have a parameter called the kind type parameter.

- If the kind type parameter is omitted, the type is said to be of default kind.

- The values of the kind type parameter are system dependent.

- For the numeric data types, the kind type parameter specifies range and precision requirements.

- The kind type parameter of a **complex** variable is the same as the kind type parameter of the two real numbers which represent its two component parts.

- For the **logical** data type, the meaning of the kind type parameter is not defined; it will usually relate to the amount of storage allocated for a logical value.

- The intrinsic functions **selected_int_kind** and **selected_real_kind** enable precision and range requirements to be specified in a portable fashion.

- If all the components of an expression have the same kind type parameter values, the result of the expression also has this kind type parameter value.

- The rules for determining the kind type parameter of an expression in which the components have different kind type parameter values are complicated, and such expressions should be avoided.

- F syntax introduced in Chapter 12

Variable declarations

complex :: *list of variable names*
real (**kind**=*kind-type*) :: *list of variable names*
integer (**kind**=*kind-type*) :: *list of variable names*
complex (**kind**=*kind-type*) :: *list of variable names*
logical(**kind**=*kind-type*) :: *list of variable names*

Literal constant
definitions

(real-part, imaginary-part)
(real-part_kind-type, imaginary-part_kind-type)
numeric-literal_kind-type
logical-literal_kind-type

PROGRAMMING EXERCISES

12.1 The roots of the quadratic equation

$$az^2 + bz + c = 0$$

where a, b and c are **real** values, are given by the formula

$$\frac{-b \pm \sqrt{b^2 - 4ac}}{2a}$$

Allowing for the fact that the expression $b^2 - 4ac$ may be negative (by using **complex** variables), write a program that calculates the roots of such an equation, and use it to find the roots of the following equations:

$$z^2 - 1 = 0$$
$$z^2 + 1 = 0$$
$$z^2 - 3z + 4 = 0$$
$$z^2 - 3z - 4 = 0$$

*12.2 Write a program which reads the values of two **complex** numbers w and z from the keyboard as two pairs of **real** numbers, and calculates the following values:

$$w + z$$
$$\bar{z}$$
$$\bar{w}$$
$$z^2$$
$$z\bar{z}$$

where $\bar{z}$ is the complex conjugate of z. (If $z = x + jy$, then $\bar{z} = x - jy$.)

Test your program with several sets of data, including the following:

(a) $w = 2 + j, z = 4 + 3j$
(b) $w = 8 + 3j, z = 5 + 2j$

12.3 Find out how many kinds of integers your F processor supports. Then write a program which calculates factorials of integers from 1 upwards until the program fails due to integer overflow when the calculation of the next factorial would result in a larger value than the maximum integer value of the kind being used. Repeat this program using each of the available kinds of integers. (Note that Example 8.1 contains two recursive procedures for calculating factorials, one a subroutine and one a function.)

Now modify your program so that it first requests a maximum range for integers and then uses integers of a kind which will allow integers to represent numbers of this size. The program should then request a maximum value of n for which it will calculate $n!$ before starting to produce a list as before.

Use the results of the first program to select several pairs of ranges and maximum factorials, and check that the program now runs without failing.

12.4 Repeat Exercise 12.3 using real variables instead of integers. What does this tell you?

*12.5 Write a program which calculates $1/n!$ for real values of n increasing in steps of 1.0, starting from 1.0 and continuing until the calculated result is not distinguishable from zero. Run this program using the default **real** kind, and then run it again using each available **real** kind in turn.

What does this exercise tell you?

12.6 In Section 12.6 we discussed the importance of the mapping between kind type parameters for **real** variables and the precision used in the hardware of the computer you are using; understanding this relationship will prevent inappropriate precision requests. Write a program to print out a table of the number of decimal digits specified and the actual decimal precision given by your machine. The decimal precision should range from 1 to 30.

12.7 The polar form of the complex number $z(= x + jy)$ is written as (r, θ), where $r = |z|$ (the absolute value of z, which is equal to $\sqrt{x^2 + y^2}$) and $\theta = \tan^{-1}(y/x)$.

Write a function to convert a complex number to its polar form.

If $z = 1 + j$ and $w = 1 + 3j$, write a program which uses your function to print the values of the following expressions in polar form, with θ given in degrees:

z

w

$z * w$

z/w

$z + w$

$z - w$

$2 * z$

z^2

$\sqrt{z}$

12.8 Figure 11.2 shows the result of calculating the expression

$$\left(\sqrt{\frac{1}{2} \times \frac{3}{4} \times \frac{5}{6} \times \cdots \frac{2n-1}{2n}} \right)^2 \times \frac{2}{1} \times \frac{4}{3} \times \frac{6}{5} \times \cdots \times \frac{2n}{2n-1}$$

for various values of n. The result should, of course, be exactly 1.0 but rounding errors will mean that the result, for any reasonably large value of n, will differ slightly from the true value. Write a program to calculate the value of this expression using both six digits of real precision and 14 digits of real precision, and then test it with various values of n in the range 100 000 to 10 000 000.

Now modify your program to measure the time taken to carry out the calculation, and repeat your previous tests.

What does this tell you about real arithmetic on your computer system?

(Note that the intrinsic subroutine **system_clock** may be used to calculate the time between two events, such as the start and finish of a loop. It may be called as follows:

```
call system_clock(count,count_rate)
```

where `count` is a default integer which will be set to a processor-dependent value based on the current value of the processor's internal clock, and `count_rate` is a default integer which will be set to the number of clock counts per second, or zero if there is no clock.)

12.9   Write a program that calculates the roots of $ax^2 + bx + c = 0$, where a, b, c are complex numbers.

Try your program in the case where $a = 1$, $b = -6.000\,01 - 7.999\,99j$, $c = -6.999\,93 + 24.000\,01j$. Run it with the precision first set to 6 and then to 14 decimal digits. The exact answers are $3 + 4j$ and $3.000\,01 + 3.999\,99j$. Unless you have used a sophisticated algorithm, or have a 64-bit machine, you will probably not get very accurate answers when the precision is 6.

Array processing and matrix manipulation

13

13.1 Matrices and two-dimensional arrays
13.2 Basic array concepts for arrays having more than one dimension
13.3 Array constructors for rank-n arrays

13.4 Input and output with arrays
13.5 The four classes of arrays
13.6 Allocatable arrays
13.7 Whole-array operations
13.8 Masked array assignment
13.9 Sub-arrays

In Chapter 7, we discussed the basic principles of F's array facilities in the context of rank-one arrays. In mathematical terms, such arrays are suitable for representing vectors. However, in order to represent matrices or more complex rectangular structures, more than one subscript is required. The same general principles apply to rank-n arrays as were described earlier in the context of rank-one arrays, although the order of the array elements is occasionally important.

As well as extending the basic array concepts to rank-n arrays, however, F contains several other powerful array features which are the subject of much of this chapter. Of particular note are dynamic arrays, whose shape is not determined until execution time.

Finally, the facilities for whole-array processing and sub-array specification are re-examined in the light of multidimensional arrays, and additional concepts are introduced that add still further to the power of F's array processing capability.

13.1 Matrices and two-dimensional arrays

Arrays were first introduced in Chapter 7, and we have already seen how useful they can be in many situations. However, the arrays that we have been using up to now have been restricted to a single subscript, and have been referred to as rank-one or single-dimensional arrays. Although these arrays were perfectly adequate for working with objects such as vectors, they are not appropriate for matrices or objects that are naturally represented by arrays of more than one dimension. F allows us to define arrays with up to seven subscripts, but before dealing with the full generality provided by F for multidimensional arrays, we will, because of their connection with matrices and also for illustrative purposes, briefly discuss two-dimensional arrays in particular.

Mathematically, a matrix is a two-dimensional rectangular array of elements. For example, a 3×4 matrix **A** consists of the elements

$$\begin{bmatrix} A_{1,1} & A_{1,2} & A_{1,3} & A_{1,4} \\ A_{2,1} & A_{2,2} & A_{2,3} & A_{2,4} \\ A_{3,1} & A_{3,2} & A_{3,3} & A_{3,4} \end{bmatrix}$$

F extends the concept of a one-dimensional array, introduced in Chapter 7, in a natural manner, by means of the **dimension** attribute. Thus, to define a two-dimensional array a that could hold the elements of the matrix **A**, we would write

```
real, dimension(3,4) :: a
```

Note that, in the dimension attribute, the number of rows is specified first and the number of columns second. *This order is important.*

As a second example, if we wanted to create three 10×4, two-dimensional arrays, b, c and d, of logical elements, we would write

```
logical, dimension(10,4) :: b, c, d
```

The elements of a two-dimensional array are scalars (that is, they are single entities of the data type involved) and are referenced by a logical extension of the notion used for one-dimensional arrays. For example, a(2,3) is the element of a in the second row and third column. We emphasize that the row position is specified first, followed by the column position. Thus, a(3,2) is a different element from a(2,3), just as $A_{2,3}$ is different from $A_{3,2}$.

The elements of an array, being scalars, can be used anywhere it is legitimate to use a scalar. They can occur in arithmetic expressions, be passed as actual arguments, occur in I/O statements, and so on. For example,

```
a(3,4) = 2.0*a(3,4) + 1.0   ! Doubles a(3,4) and adds 1 to it.
do i = 1,4                  ! Replace row 1 of a by row 3 of a.
   a(1,i) = a(3,i)          ! Row 3 is unaltered.
end do

do i = 1,3                  ! Replace column 2 of a by column
   a(i,2) = a(i,1)          ! 1 of a. Column 1 is unaltered.
end do
```

F provides three intrinsic functions specifically designed for vector and matrix operations, where it is assumed that matrices are stored in two-dimensional arrays and vectors are stored in one-dimensional arrays. Figure 13.1 lists these and their purpose, but it should be noted that F contains a large number of other intrinsic functions which operate on arrays of any dimension. These are described in Section 13.4, but it is relevant to mention here that **maxval**, **maxloc**, **minval**, **minloc**, **product** and **sum** are also useful for work with vectors and matrices and are, therefore, included in Figure 13.1.

The use of some of these intrinsic functions is illustrated by the program shown in Figure 13.2 which establishes a 2 × 3 matrix and its 3 × 2 transpose, and then performs a matrix multiplication to create a 2 × 2 result. A similar multiplication is carried out between the 3 × 2 matrix and a two-element vector to give a three-element vector result.

Note, incidentally, that, although the vector vector_c has been given an initial value by means of a single assignment statement using an array constructor, the matrix matrix_a has been given its value by means of a series of assignment statements, each one setting one element of the array. This is because array constructors are always of rank-one. We shall see in Section 13.3

Name	Result
matmul	Matrix product of two matrices, or a matrix and a vector
dot_product	Scalar (dot) product of two vectors
transpose	Transpose of a matrix
maxval	Maximum value of all the elements of an array, or of all the elements along a specified dimension of an array
maxloc	The location in an array where the maximum value first occurs
minval	Minimum value of all the elements of an array, or of all the elements along a specified dimension of an array
minloc	The location in an array where the minimum value first occurs
product	Product of all the elements of an array, or of all the elements along a specified dimension of an array
sum	Sum of all the elements of an array, or of all the elements along a specified dimension of an array

Figure 13.1   Intrinsic functions for use with vectors and matrices.

```
program vectors_and_matrices
   integer, dimension(2,3) :: matrix_a
   integer, dimension(3,2) :: matrix_b
   integer, dimension(2,2) :: matrix_ab
   integer, dimension(2) :: vector_c
   integer, dimension(3) :: vector_bc

   ! Set intial value for vector_c
   vector_c = (/ 1,2 /)

   ! Set initial value for matrix_a
   matrix_a(1,1) = 1                    ! matrix_a is the matrix:
   matrix_a(1,2) = 2
   matrix_a(1,3) = 3                    ! [ 1 2 3 ]
   matrix_a(2,1) = 2                    ! [ 2 3 4 ]
   matrix_a(2,2) = 3
   matrix_a(2,3) = 4

   ! Set matrix_b as the transpose of matrix_a
   matrix_b = transpose(matrix_a)
   ! matrix_b is now the matrix:   [ 1 2 ]
   !                               [ 2 3 ]
   !                               [ 3 4 ]

   ! Calculate matrix products
   matrix_ab = matmul(matrix_a,matrix_b)
   ! matrix_ab is now the matrix:  [ 14 20 ]
   !                               [ 20 29 ]

   vector_bc = matmul(matrix_b,vector_c)
   ! vector_bc is now the vector:  [ 5 8 11 ]
   .
   .
   .

end program vectors_and_matrices
```

Figure 13.2   An example of matrix and vector multiplication.

how to overcome this problem. Note, also, the use of the intrinsic functions **transpose** and **matmul**. These functions only work with rank-two arrays. Finally, note that we twice assigned a two-dimensional array to another of the same size (when setting matrix_b and matrix_ab). This is similar to the assignment of rank-one arrays, discussed in Chapter 7. We discuss this fully in Section 13.7.

13.2   Basic array concepts for arrays having more than one dimension

In F, an array is formally defined as a compound entity that contains an ordered set of scalar entities, each one of the same type, arranged in a rectangular pattern. An array may have from one to seven dimensions. As we mentioned in

Chapter 7, the **rank** of an array is defined as the number of its dimensions. Incidentally, for those knowledgeable about linear algebra, the rank of an F array has no connection at all with the notion of the rank of a matrix! Although, in the previous section, we followed the widespread, informal, custom of referring to a rank-two array as a two-dimensional array, we shall, in general, use the more correct terminology from now on; thus a vector is stored in a rank-one array, and a matrix in a rank-two array.

The rank of an array is specified by using the dimension attribute in a type declaration statement. Thus the three declarations

```
real, dimension(8) :: a
integer, dimension(3,10,2) :: b
type(point), dimension(4,2,100,8) :: c
```

specify an eight-element rank-one real array a, a $3 \times 10 \times 2$ rank-three integer array b, and a $4 \times 2 \times 100 \times 8$ rank-four array c of the derived type point.

Notice that this form of the dimension attribute is very similar to that used for rank-one arrays, except that the **extent** of each dimension is specified, separated by commas. The rank of the array is the number of items in this list. Once specified, the rank of an array cannot be changed.

For arrays with fixed extents, it is generally good programming practice not to use integers for the extents of arrays but, instead, to use named constants. Thus, for example, we might declare the array c, above, as follows:

```
integer, parameter :: s1 = 4, s2 = 2, s3 = 100, s4 = s1*s2
  .
  .
  .
type(point), dimension(s1, s2, s3, s4) :: c
```

Consistently using the parameter attribute in this way permits the easy change of array sizes in a complex program where several arrays and their extents may have correlated sizes. Such a size change might be required if a program has to be modified to solve larger problems.

On the other hand, if you have arrays dimensioned at three because you are working with three-dimensional vectors, it will not be appropriate to use the parameter attribute in the above way — you are unlikely to decide to change the dimensionality of your space from 3 to 5!

In most of the examples in this book we shall use literal constants for the extents of arrays, for clarity, but when writing real programs you should always consider whether it is more sensible to use a named constant here, just as the same consideration should be applied to *any* use of literal constants in a program.

When we first introduced the various terms used with arrays in Chapter 7, we stated that the **size** of an array is the total number of elements it contains; it is thus equal to the product of the extents of all its dimensions. In the second example above, the array b has extent 3 for its first dimension, extent 10 for its second dimension, and extent 2 for its third dimension; its size is therefore $3 \times 10 \times 2$, or 60. Similarly, the array c has extent 4 for its first dimension, extent 2 for its second dimension, extent 100 for its third dimension, and extent 8 for its fourth dimension; its size is therefore $4 \times 2 \times 100 \times 8$, or 6400. The size of the first array, a, is, of course, the same as its extent, since it is a rank-one array.

One point that we must mention here is that, formally, an array may have any non-negative extent, *including zero*, for any of its dimensions. Although the idea of having an extent of zero in one, or more, dimensions may seem a little strange it is convenient in certain types of problem. However, it has a further implication that, since the size of an array is equal to the product of its extents, if an array has a zero extent for one of its dimensions, its size will be zero, regardless of the extent of any other dimensions.

We also stated, in Chapter 7, that the **shape** of an array is determined by its rank and the extent of each dimension. The shape of any array is therefore representable as a rank-one array whose elements are the extents. For example, if a rank-three array has extents 10, 20 and 30, respectively, for its first, second and third dimensions, its shape is representable as the rank-one array whose elements are, in order, 10, 20 and 30. This concept of the shape of an array will be very important when we come to some of the more advanced uses of arrays later in this chapter.

In Chapter 7, we introduced many of the fundamental features of arrays in the context of rank-one arrays, and all of these features can now be extended to rank-n arrays in a natural fashion. Thus, for example, the array declarations for rank-n arrays may specify lower and upper bounds for one or more of their dimensions:

```
real, dimension(11:18) :: a
integer, dimension(5:7, -10:-1, 2) :: b
type(point), dimension(5:8, 0:1, 100, -3:4) :: c
```

Notice that we have not changed the extents of any of the dimensions of the three arrays a, b and c from the values they were declared to have at the beginning of this section, but only the way that the elements of the arrays are to be referenced. This is an important point that should be clearly understood.

Notice also that, when we specify the lower and upper **index bounds** for a dimension, the extent for that dimension is one plus the difference between the upper and lower index bounds. There is, however, one exception to this, namely that if the lower index bound is greater than the upper index bound then the extent of that dimension is defined to be zero.

It is important to stress that the index bounds of an array are not directly part of its shape. Of course the index bounds determine the array extents, which are part of its shape, but, for example, a rank-one array with index bounds 1 and 10 has the same shape as another rank-one array with index bounds 20 and 29.

Before discussing the ways in which the uses of rank-*n* arrays relate to the similar uses of rank-one arrays with which we are already familiar, we must briefly discuss the order of the elements in an array.

The elements of an array form a sequence known as the **array element order**. It can be visualized as all the elements of an array, of whatever rank, being arranged in a sequence in such a way that the first index of the element specification is varying most rapidly, the next index of the element specification is varying the second most rapidly, and continuing in this manner until the last index of the element specification is varying least rapidly.

To illustrate the concept, let us consider the array `arr` which is declared as follows:

```
real, dimension(4,3) :: arr
```

`arr` is, therefore, a rank-two array of shape (4, 3) with default lower index bounds of 1. The array element order of `arr` is the sequence:

```
arr(1,1), arr(2,1), arr(3,1), arr(4,1),
arr(1,2), arr(2,2), arr(3,2), arr(4,2),
arr(1,3), arr(2,3), arr(3,3), arr(4,3)
```

Notice that this is the same as the order obtained by traversing the first column of `arr`, followed by traversing the second column, and finally the third column. It is for this reason that it is sometimes said that F stores arrays by columns:

The same rule applies regardless of the number of dimensions, although it becomes increasingly difficult to visualize a model, and so it is generally best not to attempt to do so for arrays of rank greater than three!

In general, in F, it is not necessary to be concerned with the array element order. Apart from two situations which we shall discuss in the next two sections, we shall deal with arrays in future without any concern for the order in which the elements are ordered.

13.3   Array constructors for rank-*n* arrays

In Section 7.3 we introduced the concept of an array constructor, as a means of specifying a literal array-valued constant. This takes the form

(/ value_list /)

where each item in *value_list* is either a single value or a list in parentheses controlled by an implied **do**. For example:

```
(/ -1, (i, i = 1, 48), 1 /)
```

defines an array of size 50 whose first element is -1, whose $(i + 1)$th element is i (for $i = 1, \ldots, 48$), and whose 50th element is 1.

An array constructor, however, always creates a rank-one array of values, and, if an array constructor is to be used for arrays with rank higher than one, such as assigning the constructor to a rank-two array, then further steps need to be taken to transform it into an array of the correct shape. This is achieved by using the intrinsic function **reshape**.

This function constructs an array of a specified shape from the elements of a given array. For the current purpose we will use it in the simplest way, in which there are only two arguments. The first argument is the source array (in this application, an array constructor), and the second argument is a rank-one array specifying the required shape. For example

```
reshape ( (/ 1.0, 2.0, 3.0, 4.0, 5.0, 6.0 /), (/2, 3/) )
```

takes the rank-one real array whose elements are 1.0, 2.0, 3.0, 4.0, 5.0, 6.0 and produces, as a result, the 2×3 real array whose elements are

$$\begin{bmatrix} 1.0 & 3.0 & 5.0 \\ 2.0 & 4.0 & 6.0 \end{bmatrix}$$

Notice that the elements of the source array are used *in array element order*; this is one of the few places in F where knowing the array element order is necessary.

The **reshape** function may also be used in a declaration statement to provide an initial value or to define a named constant, and Figure 13.3 shows how the example program used in Figure 13.2 can be improved by declaring the value of the matrix `matrix_a` using an array constructor and the **reshape** function.

Finally, as might be expected, implied **do** elements may be nested, so that an integer array a could be declared and given the value

$$\begin{bmatrix} 11 & 12 \\ 21 & 22 \end{bmatrix}$$

by the following declaration statements:

```
integer :: i,j
real, save, dimension(2,2) :: a = &
            reshape((/ ((10*i+j, i = 1,2), j = 1,2) /), (/ 2,2 /))
```

```
program vectors_and_matrices
    integer, dimension(2,3) :: matrix_a
    integer, dimension(3,2) :: matrix_b
    integer, dimension(2,2) :: matrix_ab

    integer, dimension(2) :: vector_c
    integer, dimension(3) :: vector_bc

    ! Set intial value of vector_c
    vector_c = (/ 1,2 /)

    ! Set initial value of matrix_a
    matrix_a = reshape((/1,2,2,3,3,4/), (/ 2,3 /))
    ! a has the value:   [1, 2, 3]
    !                    [2, 3, 4]

    ! Set matrix_b as the transpose of matrix_a
    matrix_b = transpose(matrix_a)
    ! matrix_b is now the matrix:   [ 1 2 ]
    !                               [ 2 3 ]
    !                               [ 3 4 ]

    ! Calculate matrix products
    matrix_ab = matmul(matrix_a,matrix_b)
    ! matrix_ab is now the matrix:  [ 14 20 ]
    !                               [ 20 29 ]

    vector_bc = matmul(matrix_b,vector_c)
    ! vector_bc is now the vector:  [ 5 8 11 ]
    .

    .

    .
end program vectors_and_matrices
```

Figure 13.3   An improved example of matrix and vector multiplication.

13.4   Input and output with arrays

In Sections 7.4 and 7.7, we showed that, in the context of rank-one arrays, input and output of arrays, or of parts of arrays, could be handled in three ways:

- as a list of individual array elements
- as the complete array, by including the unsubscripted array name in the input or output list
- as an array section.

The first of these cases needs almost no further elaboration, being an obvious generalization of the rank-one case. Thus, using the preceding array a, we could write

```
a(1,1), a(2,2)
```

as the list of an input or output statement. This specifies the diagonal elements of a.

The second case lets us specify the input or output of an entire array by simply putting the array name in the input (or output) list. Use of this capability needs some care, as the array elements will be transferred *in array element order*. This is the second place in F in which knowledge of the array element order is required. Thus, if we write

```
integer, dimension(2,3) :: a
.
.
.
print *, a
```

the elements of a will be printed in the order a(1,1), a(2,1), a(1,2), a(2,2), a(1,3), a(2,3). This might not be the order we wish. Gaining complete control of how the elements are output is discussed in Section 13.9.

The third case is also discussed in Section 13.9.

13.5 The four classes of arrays

When discussing rank-one arrays in Chapter 7, we met three different classes of arrays: namely explicit-shape arrays, assumed-shape arrays and automatic arrays (which are actually a sub-class of explicit-shape arrays). In this section, we shall review these three classes and draw attention to the (minor) differences in their use when their rank is greater than one. There is also a fourth class, deferred-shape arrays, which we have not yet met; this will be discussed in detail in Section 13.6.

Explicit-shape arrays are arrays whose index bounds for each dimension are specified when the array is declared in a type declaration statement. In this context, specified does not necessarily mean fixed. It means that the index bounds can be calculated from information available when the arrays are declared.

The dimension attribute for an explicit-shape array takes the form

dimension (*list of explicit-shape specifiers*)

The rank of the array is the number of *explicit-shape specifiers* given. Each *explicit-shape specifier* specifies the lower and upper index bounds for one dimension of the array and takes the form

lower_bound : upper_bound

or

upper_bound

where *lower_bound* and *upper_bound* are **specification expressions**. A specification statement may be considered, for all practical applications, as being a scalar integer expression; there are some restrictions on the form of this expression but they are unimportant in practice, and will not be given here. If the *lower_bound* is omitted it is taken to be 1.

An example of an explicit-shape array whose bounds are fixed is:

```
type(person), dimension(101:110,20) :: company
```

The variable `company` is a rank-two array of the derived type `person`, where, for example, the first dimension might represent the department within the company, and the second dimension might represent the people in the department; thus `company(i,j)` would be the `j`th person in the `i`th department. The lower and upper index bounds of the array are 101 and 110 for the first dimension, and 1 (default) and 20 for the second dimension. The extents are 10 and 20 for the first and second dimensions, respectively, and the size of the array is 200 (10×20). The shape of the array is specifiable as a rank-one array whose elements have the values 10 and 20.

Explicit-shape arrays with constant index bounds can be specified in type declaration statements in either main programs or procedures.

Only assumed-shape arrays can be procedure dummy arguments. The information about the extents of such arrays is carried implicitly when an actual array is associated with an assumed-shape dummy argument. Notice that it is information about the *extents* of the actual argument that is implicitly available, not information about *index bounds*. The index bounds used inside a procedure are always local to that procedure, constrained only by the need to be consistent with the corresponding extents of the actual arguments.

Assumed-shape arrays may only be dummy arguments of a procedure; they cannot occur in a main program. They take their shape from association with actual arguments when a procedure is referenced, hence the name assumed-shape. The actual argument must be of the same type and have the same rank as the dummy argument.

The dimension attribute for an assumed-shape array takes the form

dimension (*list of assumed-shape specifiers*)

The rank of the array is the number of *assumed-shape specifiers* given. Each *assumed-shape specifier* specifies the lower index bound for one dimension of the array and takes the form

lower bound :

or

$$\vdots$$

If the *lower bound* is omitted, it is taken to be 1. For example, the following function `assumed_shape` has two assumed-shape dummy array arguments, a and b:

```
function assumed_shape(a,b) result(r)
   integer, dimension(:,:), intent(in) :: a
   real, dimension(5:,:,:), intent(inout) :: b
   .
   .
   .
end function assumed_shape
```

The first dummy array argument, a, is of rank 2, with the lower index bounds for both subscripts being 1; the second dummy array argument, b, is of rank 3, with the lower index bound for the first subscript being 5, and the lower index bounds for the other subscripts being 1.

When discussing assumed-shape arrays in Chapter 7, we briefly mentioned the three intrinsic functions **size**, **lbound** and **ubound** in the context of rank-one arrays, and it is now appropriate to re-examine how these functions operate with rank-n arrays.

The function **size** has two arguments, the second of which is optional. The first argument is the name of the array, and the second argument, **dim**, is an integer which, if present, must lie in the range $1 \leqslant$ **dim** $\leqslant rank$, where *rank* is the rank of the array. If **dim** is not present, **size** returns the size of the whole array. If **dim** is present, **size** returns the extent of the array for the specified dimension.

The function **lbound** also has two arguments, of which the second is optional. These arguments follow the same pattern as those for **size**, with the first argument being the name of the array, and the second argument specifying the dimension. If the second argument, **dim**, is present, then **lbound** returns the lower index bound of the specified dimension in the form of an integer. If **dim** is not present, however, the result of the function reference is a rank-one array containing *all* the lower index bounds.

This explains why, in Chapter 7, we stated that this procedure should be used with two arguments, the second being 1, when asking for the bounds of a rank-one array. If, for example, a reference was made to **lbound**(rank_1), where rank_1 is a rank-one array, then the result of the function reference will be a rank-one array, consisting of a single element, and not a scalar value as might have been expected.

The third function, **ubound**, is similar to **lbound**, but returns the upper bound(s) of its first argument.

☐ **EXAMPLE 13.1** ·

1 **Problem**

Write a program to determine whether a polygon is convex.

2 **Analysis**

This type of problem frequently occurs in writing software for computer-aided design (usually abbreviated as CAD) and computer-aided manufacture (usually abbreviated as CAM). Such problems also occur in writing programs for virtual reality applications.

A polygon is an n-sided figure whose boundary consists of straight line segments joining adjacent vertices. Triangles and quadrilaterals, for example, are special cases of polygons (Figure 13.4).

An area is said to be convex if, for any two points in the area, the straight line segment joining them is completely contained in the area. Thus, in Figure 13.5, area A is convex, while area B is not.

It is easy to prove that a triangle is always convex, whereas a quadrilateral may not be.

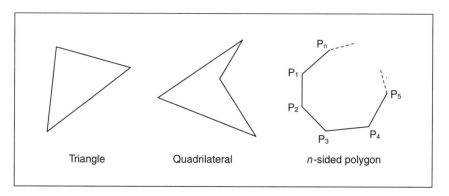

Triangle   Quadrilateral n-sided polygon

Figure 13.4   3-sided, 4-sided, and n-sided polygons.

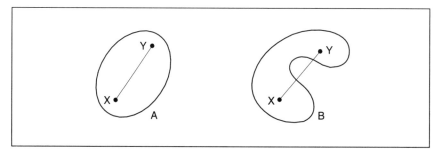

Figure 13.5   Convexity of two-dimensional areas.

The problem of determining convexity will be solved by using a derived type point, consisting of two real numbers, in which to store the coordinates of the vertices. An array of type point will then be used to store the definitions of a polygon.

The mathematical analysis is based on the observation that a polygon is convex if and only if the rotation angles (restricted to be in the range $-180 \leqslant \theta \leqslant 180$) between adjacent sides are either always positive (that is, each side is always rotated in a counterclockwise direction from its predecessor side) or always negative (that is, each side is always rotated in a clockwise direction from its predecessor side). Thus, in the five-sided polygon shown in Figure 13.6, it can be seen visually that the five rotation angles are always in the clockwise direction. Therefore, the five-sided polygon $P_1P_2P_3P_4P_5$ is convex.

By contrast, in the six-sided polygon shown in Figure 13.7, it can be seen visually that the rotation angle between sides P_3P_4 and P_4P_5 is clockwise, whereas all the other angles are counterclockwise. Hence the six-sided polygon $P_1P_2P_3P_4P_5P_6$ is not convex.

It is easily proved by vector analysis that, for convexity, we require, for every three adjacent vertices P_i, P_{i+1}, P_{i+3}, with coordinates (x_i, y_i), (x_{i+1}, y_{i+1}), and (x_{i+2}, y_{2+2}), respectively, that $(x_{i+1} - x_i)(y_{i+2} - y_{i+1}) - (y_{i+1} - y_i)(x_{i+2} - x_{i+1})$ always have the same sign around the polygon. This algorithm will work whether the vertices are given in clockwise or counter-clockwise order. (For those interested in the mathematics, the proof is based on taking the cross product of two adjacent edges. The polygon is convex if the sine of the angle between the edges is always of the same sign — ignoring degenerate cases when three adjacent vertices are co-linear.)

An initial structure plan for the main subroutine is easily developed:

1   Obtain the number of sides of the polygon

2   Set the **logical** variable **convex** to the value **true**

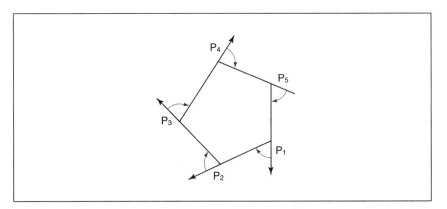

Figure 13.6   A five-sided polygon.

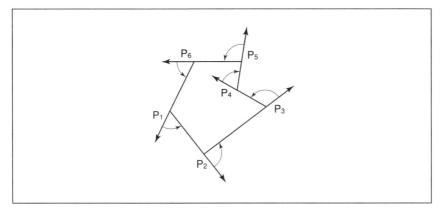

Figure 13.7   A six-sided polygon.

3   Calculate the direction of rotation at the first vertex

4   Repeat for each remaining vertex

   4.1   If direction of rotation has changed

      4.1.1   Set convex to **false**

      4.1.2   Exit from loop

The only difficulty here is the calculation of the direction of rotation at each vertex, and so we shall place this in a function which will return a positive value if the direction is positive (counterclockwise) and a negative value if it is negative (clockwise). We can then easily detect if the direction of rotation has changed by multiplying two successive orientations together and testing to see whether the result is negative. In practice, a few moments' thought shows that we need only use the orientation at the *first* vertex and the current one.

We can now proceed with our data design and structure plan for each procedure; however, we shall not go into the details of the mathematics involved in calculating the direction of rotation at a vertex.

Subroutine `convex_polygon`

Data design

	Purpose	Type	Name
A	Arguments		
	Array of points	`point`	`polygon`
	Convexity of the polygon	**`logical`**	`convex`
B	Local variables		
	Orientation at first vertex	**`real`**	`anti`
	Number of sides	**`integer`**	`n_sides`
	do loop variable	**`integer`**	`i`

Structure plan

> 1   Obtain number of sides of the polygon from **size**(polygon)
>
> 2   Set convex to **true**
>
> 3   Calculate the direction of rotation at the first vertex (anti) using the function orientation
>
> 4   Repeat for each remaining vertex
> > **4.1**   If anti*orientation(current vertex) < 0
> > > **4.1.1**   Set convex to **false**
> > >
> > > **4.1.2**   Exit from loop

Real function orientation

Data design

Purpose	Type	Name
A Arguments		
Array of points	point	p
Number of vertex	**integer**	vertex
B Local variable		
Number of vertices	**integer**	n

Structure plan

> 1   Obtain number of vertices from **size**(p)
>
> 2   Calculate direction of rotation and return as the value of the function

③ Solution

```
module convexity

    public :: convex_polygon
    private :: orientation

    ! Derived type definition
    type, public :: point
        real :: x, y
    end type point

contains

    subroutine convex_polygon(polygon, convex)
    ! This subroutine determines whether a polygon is convex
```

```
! Dummy arguments
type(point), dimension(:), intent(in) :: polygon
logical, intent(out) :: convex

! Local variables
real :: anti
integer :: i, n_sides

anti = 0.0      ! Set initial value of anti

! Set initial value for convex and obtain number of sides
convex = .true.
n_sides = size(polygon,1)    ! n_sides is the number
                             ! of vertices

! Get direction of rotation at first vertex
if (orientation(polygon,1) > 0.0) then
   anti = 1.0
else
   anti = -1.0
end if

! Check direction of rotation at remaining vertices
do i = 2, n_sides
   if (anti*orientation(polygon,i) < 0.0) then
      ! Return immediately a different orientation occurs
      convex = .false.
      exit
   end if
end do
end subroutine convex_polygon

function orientation(p, i) result(orien)
! This function returns the direction of angular
! rotation at a specified vertex i of a polygon.
! Positive if counterclockwise, negative if
! clockwise

   ! Dummy arguments
   type(point), dimension(:), intent(in) :: p
   integer, intent(in) :: i    ! vertex number
   ! Result
   real :: orien

   ! Local variable
   integer :: n

   n = size(p,1)    ! n is the number of vertices

   ! Calculate orientation at this vertex
   if (i == n-1) then
      orien = (p(n)%x-p(n-1)%x)*(p(1)%y-p(n)%y)          &
             - (p(n)%y-p(n-1)%y)*(p(1)%x-p(n)%x)
   else if (i == n) then
      orien = (p(1)%x - p(n)%x)*(p(2)%y - p(1)%y)        &
             - (p(1)%y - p(n)%y)*(p(2)%x - p(1)%x)
```

```
        else
            orien = (p(i+1)%x - p(i)%x)*(p(i+2)%y - p(i+1)%y)   &
                    -(p(i+1)%y - p(i)%y)*(p(i+2)%x - p(i+1)%x)
        end if
    end function orientation
end module convexity
```

The first three points are used to determine the sign of $(x_2 - x_1)(y_3 - y_2) - (y_2 - y_1)(x_3 - x_1)$. We then require that the sign of the corresponding quantity for every three adjacent points has the same sign. This is done in the subroutine convex_polygon.

There is one complication with indexing. When we get to P_{n-1} we must use the points P_{n-1}, P_n, P_1 (not P_{n-1}, P_n, P_{n+1}, because P_{n+1} does not exist, and we want to continue with the first point P_1), and when we get to P_n we must use the points P_n, P_1, P_2. This is taken care of in the function orientation.

We can then easily write a program to test these procedures by asking for, say, six points and then calling convex_polygon to determine the convexity of the resulting polygon:

```
module problem_size
    integer, parameter, public :: number_of_points = 6
end module problem_size

program test_convexity
! This program uses the module convexity to test whether
! a set of points form a convex polygon

    use convexity
    use problem_size

    type(point), dimension(number_of_points) :: polygon
    integer :: i
    logical :: convex

    ! Ask for the point coordinates
    do i = 1, number_of_points
        print "(a, i2)", "Give vertex number ", i
        read *, polygon(i)%x, polygon(i)%y
    end do

    ! Establish polygon's convexity
    call convex_polygon(polygon, convex)
    if (convex) then
        print *, "Polygon is convex"
    else
        print *, "Polygon is not convex"
    end if
end program test_convexity
```

Figure 13.8 shows the result produced by running this program for two polygons, the first with vertices $(0, 0)$, $(1, 0)$, $(2, 1)$, $(2, 2)$, $(1, 3)$, $(-1, 1)$ and the second with vertices $(1, 1)$, $(3, 1)$, $(2, 2)$, $(3, 3)$, $(1, 3)$, $(0, 2)$.

First program run	Second program run
Give vertex number 1	Give vertex number 1
0,0	1,1
Give vertex number 2	Give vertex number 2
1,0	3,1
Give vertex number 3	Give vertex number 3
2,1	2,2
Give vertex number 4	Give vertex number 4
2,2	3,3
Give vertex number 5	Give vertex number 5
1,3	1,3
Give vertex number 6	Give vertex number 6
-1,1	0,2
Polygon is convex	Polygon is not convex

Figure 13.8 Results produced by the program `polygon_test`.

```
Give vertex number 1
1,1
Give vertex number 2
3,1
Give vertex number 3
3,3
Give vertex number 4
1,3
Give vertex number 5
0,2
 Polygon is convex
```

Figure 13.9 Results produced by the modified program `polygon_test`.

Figure 13.9 shows the result of changing the value of `number_of_points` in the module `problem_size` to 5 and running the program again with a different set of points.

The third class of arrays, which was introduced for rank-one arrays in Chapter 7, is *automatic arrays*. An automatic array is a special type of explicit-shape array which can only be declared in a procedure, which is not a dummy argument, and which has at least one index bound that is not constant. The space for the elements of an automatic array is created dynamically when the procedure is entered and is removed upon exit from the procedure. In between entry and exit, an automatic array may be used in the same manner as any other array – including passing it or its elements as actual arguments to other procedures.

We can see the difference between assumed-shape and automatic arrays in the following example:

```
subroutine abc(x)

    ! Dummy arguments
    real, dimension(:), intent(inout) :: x    ! Assumed shape

    ! Local variables
    real, dimension(size(x)) :: e              ! Automatic
    real, dimension(size(x),size(x)) :: f      ! Automatic
    real, dimension(10) :: g                   ! Explicit shape
    .
    .
    .

end subroutine abc
```

In subroutine abc, the arrays e and f are not dummy arguments, but their index bounds are not constant. The upper index bound of e, a rank-one array, is dependent on the shape of the dummy argument x. Both upper index bounds of the rank-two array f depend on the extent of the dummy argument x. Hence, both e and f are automatic arrays. The array g is not a dummy argument, but its index bounds are constant; it is, therefore, not an automatic array.

In this example, the sizes of the automatic arrays e and f both depended on a dummy argument. Another possibility is that their sizes depend on a variable declared in a module.

Automatic arrays are convenient when array space (of variable shape) is needed on a temporary basis inside a procedure, and such arrays are, therefore, often called **work arrays**. The use of automatic arrays for such temporary purposes can enormously simplify calling sequences by eliminating the need for arrays of complicated shape to be passed as arguments.

SELF-TEST EXERCISES 13.1

1   What are the index bounds, extents and size of an array?

2   What is the shape of an array? How can it be denoted?

3   What is the array element order for the array wow, which is declared as follows?

    ```
    real, dimension(2,3,4) :: wow
    ```

4   How is the **reshape** intrinsic function used in connection with array constructors?

5   What are explicit-shape arrays? Can they occur in main programs and procedures?

6   What are assumed-shape arrays? Can they occur in main programs and procedures? Are there any restrictions on the use of assumed-shape arrays?

7   How may the index bounds of a dummy procedure argument be determined?

8   What are automatic arrays and when should they be used?

13.6   Allocatable arrays

In the previous section, we stressed the importance of being able to create temporary arrays whose size could only be determined during the execution of the program. Automatic arrays provide a partial solution to this problem, but a more complete solution is provided by **allocatable arrays**. These provide more flexibility than automatic arrays, because the allocation and deallocation of space for their elements is completely under user control. This is not the case for automatic arrays, since their space is always allocated on entry to a procedure and is always deallocated on exit. We did not previously mention allocatable arrays when we discussed rank-one arrays in Chapter 7. However, an allocatable array can have any rank.

Allocatable arrays are also more flexible than automatic arrays in as much as they can be defined in main programs, procedures or modules.

Using allocatable arrays is slightly more complicated than using any other class of arrays, and consists, essentially, of three steps:

- First, the allocatable array is specified in a type declaration statement.
- Secondly, space is dynamically allocated for its elements in a separate **allocation statement**, after which the array may be used in the normal way.
- Finally, after the array has been used and is no longer required, the space for the elements is deallocated by a **deallocation statement**.

Once space has been allocated for them, allocatable arrays may be used in the same way as any other arrays. Their elements may be defined or referenced, and they may be passed as actual arguments to other procedures although, as might be expected, they may not be used as dummy arguments in a procedure.

An allocatable array is declared in a type declaration statement which includes an **allocatable** attribute. However, since its size is not known when it is declared, it must initially have its shape specifiers set to be undefined by omitting all index bound information for every dimension, and representing the shape of the array in the dimension attribute by a single colon for each dimension:

```
real, allocatable, dimension(:,:,:) :: allocatable_array
```

The rank of the array is, of course, the same as the number of colons, so that the above statement declares a rank-three array.

It will be noted that the type declaration statement for an allocatable array is similar to the type declaration statement for an assumed-shape array. However, an assumed-shape array *must* be a dummy argument to a procedure, and *must not* have an **allocatable** attribute, whereas the opposite is true for allocatable arrays. The two types of declaration statements are, therefore, readily distinguished from each other.

Allocatable arrays are called **deferred-shape** arrays because, when they are initially declared in a type declaration statement, the extent along each dimension is not specified, but is *deferred* until later. We shall meet another form of deferred shape array in Chapter 14.

Unlike all other forms of array that we have met, the declaration of an allocatable array does not, in itself, allocate any space for the array, and it is therefore not usually possible to use the array until further action has been taken. An allocatable array is said to have an **allocation status**, and until space is allocated for its elements, this allocation status is said to be *not currently allocated*, or simply *unallocated*.

An unallocated array has its status changed to *currently allocated*, or simply *allocated*, by means of an **allocate** statement which dynamically allocates space for an allocatable array. It takes the form

allocate (*list of array_specifications*, stat = *status_variable*)

or

allocate (*list of array_specifications*)

Each *array_specification* must consist of the name of an allocatable array, followed by the index bounds for each dimension, enclosed in parentheses:

allocate (arr_1(20), arr_2(10:30,-10:10), arr_3(20,30:50,5))

The stat = *status_variable* element of the **allocate** statement enables the processor to report on the success, or otherwise, of the allocation process in a similar way to that in which an iostat specifier reports on the success of an input/output statement. If the allocation is successful then the integer variable *status_variable* will be set to zero; if there is an error during the allocation, for example if there is insufficient memory for the array or if it is currently allocated, then *status_variable* will be assigned a processor-dependent positive value.

Note that, if an error condition arises during the execution of an **allocate** statement and there is no stat element in the statement, the program will fail. We recommend, therefore, that you should always include a stat element as illustrated in Figure 13.10.

```
        .
        .
        .
    integer :: m, n, error
    real, allocatable, dimension(:,:) :: p
    integer, allocatable, dimension(:,:,:) :: q
    type(vector), allocatable, dimension(:) :: r
        .
        .
        .
    allocate(p(5,1000), q(10,m,n+7), r(-10:10), stat = error)
    if (error /= 0) then
        ! Space for p, q, and r could not be allocated
        print *,"Program could not allocate space for p, q, and r"
        stop
    end if
    ! Space for p, q, and r successfully allocated
        .
        .
        .
```

Figure 13.10 An example of allocation of allocatable arrays, with error checking.

A currently allocated allocatable array is deallocated by the related **deallocate** statement, which has the effect of changing its status to *not currently allocated* and making the memory space that it was using available for other purposes. This statement takes the form

deallocate (*list of currently_allocated_arrays*, stat = *status_variable*)

or

deallocate (*list of currently_allocated_arrays*)

where the meaning and use of the stat element is identical to that for the **allocate** statement. Once an array has been deallocated, the values stored in its elements are no longer available.

It may appear unnecessary to check the deallocation of an array for errors, since it will, presumably, have already been allocated. However, suppose that a program was modified, some time after its initial creation, by inserting some extra statements between the allocation and deallocation of the array. The inserted code might, after performing its calculations, erroneously deallocate the array. It is to guard against such difficult-to-find programming errors that the success or failure of allocation and deallocation statements should always be checked.

The use of **allocate** and **deallocate** statements enables an allocatable array to have its size repeatedly changed, as shown in the following example:

```
real, allocatable, dimension(:) :: varying_array
integer :: i, n, alloc_error, dealloc_error
 .
 .
 .
read *, n                        ! Read maximum size needed
do i=1, n
   allocate(varying_array(-i:i), stat = alloc_error)
   if (alloc_error /= 0) then
      print *,"Insufficient space to allocate array ", &
              "when i = ",i
      stop
   end if
   ! Calculate using varying_array
   .
   .
   .
   deallocate(varying_array, stat = dealloc_error)
   if (dealloc_error /= 0) then
      print *,"Unexpected deallocation error"
      stop
   end if
end do
 .
 .
 .
```

This code fragment first allocates varying_array to be a rank-one array, with index bounds of -1 and $+1$. It performs calculations using the array with this size and shape, and then deallocates it. Next it allocates varying_array again, but this time with index bounds of -2 and $+2$, performs calculations using the array with this new size, and then again deallocates it. This cycle is repeated n times.

If varying_array were not deallocated at the end of every iteration, an error would occur in the second iteration of the loop when the second attempt to allocate a is made.

Note that execution of a **deallocate** statement is not the only way in which an allocated array can lose its allocated status. Exit from a procedure (back to the calling procedure or main program) causes the allocation status of any currently allocated allocatable arrays without the **save** attribute to become **undefined**. Such undefined arrays cannot subsequently be referenced, defined, allocated or deallocated!

As well as causing potential problems, it is bad programming practice to permit the status of an allocatable array to become undefined. An allocatable array which is no longer required should, therefore, always be deallocated before an exit is made from the procedure in which it was allocated. If it will be required

again, and its current values need to be preserved, then it should be declared
with the **save** attribute:

```
character(len=50), allocatable, dimension(:), save :: name
```

If this is done, then the allocatable array will remain allocated when an exit is
made from the procedure and the elements of the array will maintain their values.
If it is not currently allocated on exit from the procedure then it remains in that
state.

This ability for an allocatable array to be saved between references to a
procedure is a major advantage over automatic arrays, which always cease to
exist on exit from the procedure in which they are declared.

The greater control provided by allocatable arrays can also be used to write
programs with more capacity than is possible with automatic arrays, as can be
seen from the following example:

```
subroutine space(n)
   integer, intent(in) :: n
   real, allocatable, dimension(:,:) :: a, b

   allocate(a(2*n,6*n))        ! Allocate space for a
   ! Calculate using a
   .
   .
   .
   deallocate(a)               ! Free space used by a
   allocate(b(3*n,4*n))        ! Allocate space for b
   ! Calculate using b
   .
   .
   .
   deallocate(b)               ! Free space used by b
end subroutine space
```

The subroutine space, therefore, uses $12n^2$ elements for a during execution of
the first part, and then releases this space, and then uses $12n^2$ elements for b
during execution of the second part. Thus, the maximum space required for the
two arrays is that required for $12n^2$ real numbers.

Now suppose the subroutine space was rewritten to use automatic arrays
instead of allocatable arrays:

```
subroutine space(n)
   integer, intent(in) :: n
   real, dimension(2*n,6*n) :: a
   real, dimension(3*n,4*n) :: b
   ! Calculate using a
   .
   .
   .
```

```
        ! Calculate using b
        .
        .
        .
end subroutine space
```

In this case, when the subroutine space begins execution $12n^2$ elements are allocated for a and $12n^2$ elements are allocated for b. A total of $24n^2$ elements are therefore created, and are not released until exit from the subroutine.

Consequently, the version of space using automatic arrays requires twice as many real numbers as does the version using allocatable arrays. If n is large, this extra space requirement could be the difference between success and failure of a program, since a computer only has finite resources available!

Note that we do not even need the allocatable array b, since we could just reallocate the array a appropriately. However, it may make the code clearer to have both a and b – it depends on the nature of the code.

The decision as to whether to use automatic arrays or allocatable arrays will depend upon individual circumstances. If very large arrays are required, or if they need to be saved between procedure calls, then allocatable arrays should be used; on the other hand, if only small arrays are involved, and there is no need to save array values between procedure references, the greater simplicity of automatic arrays may tip the balance in their favour.

There are three main restrictions on allocatable arrays:

- Allocatable arrays cannot be dummy arguments of a procedure.
- The result of a function cannot be an allocatable array.
- Allocatable arrays cannot be used in a derived type definition.

If it is necessary to have a derived type with a variable-size array as a component, pointers must be used; see Chapter 14.

Because of the first of these restrictions, allocatable arrays that are defined in a main program or procedure must be allocated and deallocated in the main program or procedure in which they were initially defined. However, if the type declaration for an allocatable array is placed in a module then the array can be allocated and deallocated by any procedure in the module or by any main program or procedure using the module. We shall see an illustration of this in Example 13.2.

One other point that should be made is that, although an unallocated allocatable array cannot be used in most of the ways in which arrays are normally used, it can be used as an actual argument in a reference to some of the intrinsic inquiry functions, namely **allocated** (which returns the allocation status of an allocatable array), the intrinsic inquiry functions that give information about a type (for example, **digits**), and the intrinsic inquiry functions that give information about type parameters (**kind** and **len**). More information about these functions will be found in Appendix A, but it is worth pointing out here that the **allocated** function can be used to guard against trying to deallocate an unallocated array, or to allocate an array which has already been allocated:

```
    .
    .
    .
real, allocatable, dimension(:) :: work_array
    .
    .
    .
if allocated(work_array) then
   deallocate(work_array)
end if
allocate(work_array(n:m), stat = alloc_stat)
    .
    .
    .
```

The **allocated** function can, of course, only be used on arrays with the allocatable attribute.

▉ EXAMPLE 13.2

1 Problem

Write a program which will determine the minimum and maximum numbers in a file of real numbers, where they occur, and how many of the numbers are less than the mean of all the numbers in the file.

2 Analysis

This is a fairly straightforward problem, apart from the fact that there will need to be an array in which to store the values read from the file, and yet the size of the array clearly cannot be known until execution time. It is thus an ideal situation for an allocatable array.

An initial structure plan might be

> 1 Allocate a suitable work array
>
> 2 Carry out analysis of file

Further thought leads to a refined plan:

> 1 Request maximum size of work array required
>
> 2 Allocate a suitable work array

> 3 Carry out analysis of file
> **3.1** Get name of file
> **3.2** Find maximum and minimum values, and their positions in the file (or array)
> **3.3** Calculate the mean, and count the number of values less than the mean

Steps 1 and 2 can be readily placed in one procedure, while steps 3.2 and 3.3 lend themselves to be placed in separate procedures. If the work array is declared in a module, `work_space`, then the final program structure can easily be developed. Because the data requirements are so simple, as is most of the logic, we shall not give a full data design, nor shall we give detailed structure plans for each procedure, but will simply show the overall structure:

> **1** Call `allocate_space` to do the following:
> **1.1** Request maximum size of the file
> **1.2** Allocate a suitable work array
> **2** Call `calculate` to do the following:
> **2.1** Get the name of the file and open it
> **2.2** Read all the numbers in the file into the work array
> **2.3** Find and print minimum and maximum values, and their positions
> **2.4** Call `num_less_than_mean` to find and print the number less than the mean

3 Solution

```
module work_space
  integer, public :: work_size
  real, allocatable, dimension(:), save, public :: work
end module work_space

module min_max
  use work_space
  private

  public :: allocate_space, calculate
  private :: num_less_than_mean

contains

  subroutine allocate_space()
  ! This subroutine allocates the array work at a size
  ! determined by the user during execution

    ! Local variable
    integer :: error
```

```
      ! Ask for required size for array
      print *,"Please give maximum size of file"
      read *,work_size

      ! Allocate array
      allocate(work(work_size+1), stat = error)
      if (error /= 0) then
         ! Error during allocation - terminate processing
         print *,"Space requested not possible"
         stop
      end if

   ! Work array successfully allocated
end subroutine allocate_space

subroutine calculate()
   ! Local variables
   integer :: i, n, min_p, max_p, open_error, io_stat
   real :: min_v, max_v
   character(len = 20) :: file_name

   ! Get name of data file
   print *,"Please give name of data file"
   read "(a)",file_name

   ! Open data file
   open(unit = 7, file = file_name, status = "old",   &
        action = "read", iostat = open_error)
   if (open_error /= 0) then
      print *,"Error during file opening"
      stop
   end if

   ! Read data until end of file
   do i = 1, work_size
      read (unit = 7, fmt = *, iostat = io_stat)     &
           work(i)
      ! Check for end of file
      if (io_stat < 0) then
         exit
      end if
   end do

   ! Save number of numbers read
   n = i-1

   ! Print details of minimum and maximum numbers
   write(unit = *, fmt = "(a,f15.4)")                &
        "Minimum value is ", minval(work(1:n))
   write(unit = *, fmt = "(a,i10)")                  &
        "Minimum value occurs at position ", minloc(work(1:n))
   write(unit = *, fmt = "(a, f15.4)")               &
        "Maximum value is ", maxval(work(1:n))
   write(unit = *, fmt = "(a,i10)")                  &
        "Maximum value occurs at position ", maxloc(work(1:n))
   ! Calculate number that are less than the mean
   call num_less_than_mean(n)
```

```
      ! Deallocate work array
      deallocate(work)
   end subroutine calculate

   subroutine num_less_than_mean(n)
   ! This subroutine calculates and prints the number of
   ! elements of work(1) to work(n) that are less than
   ! the mean of all the numbers

      ! Dummy argument
      integer, intent(in) :: n

      ! Local variables
      integer :: i, less
      real :: mean

      ! Calculate mean
      mean = sum(work(1:n))/real(n)

      ! Count number less than mean
      less = 0
      do i = 1, n
         if (work(i) < mean) then
            less = less + 1
         end if
      end do

      ! Print number below mean
      write(unit = *, fmt = "(a,i10,a)")                        &
      "There are ", less,                                       &
      " numbers less than the mean of all numbers in the file"
   end subroutine num_less_than_mean

end module min_max

program flexible
   use min_max

   ! Allocate space for the array work
   call allocate_space()

   ! Carry out calculations using the array work
   call calculate()

end program flexible
```

Notice that the module work_space contains only type declaration statements. One is for an allocatable array work, used to hold the array of real
numbers, and the other is for work_size, an integer that is the size of work when
it has been allocated.

Finally, an important point, note that the array work must be given the **save**
attribute. If this were not done the allocation status of work would become
undefined when an exit was made from the subroutine allocate_space — which
would defeat the object of the whole process! A second effect of having the
save attribute is that the values put into work by the subroutine calculate are

```
subroutine allocate_space()

    ! This subroutine allocates the array work at a size
    ! determined by the user during execution

    ! Local variables
    integer :: i, error

    ! Ask for required size for array
    do i = 1, 3
        print *, "Please give maximum size of file"
        read *, work_size

        ! Allocate array
        allocate(work(work_size), stat = error)
        if (error == 0) then
            exit
        end if

        ! Error during allocation - try again (max of 2 times)
        print *, "Space requested not possible - try again"
    end do

    ! Check to see if array was (finally) allocated
    if (.not. allocated(work)) then
    ! No allocation - even after three tries
        print *,"Three attempts to allocate without success!"
        stop
    end if

    ! Work array successfully allocated
end subroutine allocate_space
```

Figure 13.11   An alternative version of the subroutine `allocate_space`.

not lost when an exit is made from the subroutine, and they remain available to other procedures using the module `work_space`.

The general rule is that, if an allocatable array in a module is not given the **save** attribute, when exit is made from a procedure that was referencing the module and the next procedure (or main program) to resume execution is not referencing the module, then the status of the array becomes undefined – a bad situation. To avoid such complications, we recommend that all allocatable arrays be given the **save** attribute and that such arrays be specifically deallocated when they and the values they contain are no longer needed.

As is usually the case in our example programs, we have not taken all the error-checking steps which are desirable (in the cause of clarity and of shortening the length of the program). Figure 13.11, however, shows an alternative version of the subroutine `allocate_space` which checks that the allocation process has been successful, and allows the user to try twice more if it is not successful.

Exactly how far to go in this type of checking will depend upon the environment in which the program is to be used, and, for example, if it will be used only by the programmer or will be part of a widely distributed piece of general-purpose software.

13.7 Whole-array operations

In Chapter 7, in the context of rank-one arrays, we introduced the concept of whole-array processing, whereby two conformable arrays (that is, two arrays which have the same shape) could appear as operands in an expression or an assignment, and the operation or assignment would be carried out on an element-by-element basis. These whole-array operations can be used with conformable arrays of any rank. Thus, if two arrays are declared as

```
real, dimension(10) :: p, q
real, dimension(10:19) :: r
```

then the statement

```
p = q + r
```

has exactly the same effect as the **do** loop

```
do i = 1, 10
    p(i) = q(i)+r(i+9)
end do
```

As we might expect, the same rule applies to arrays of any rank so that if, for example, three rank-four arrays are declared as follows:

```
real, dimension(10,10,21,21) :: x
real, dimension(0:9,0:9,-10:10,-10:10) :: y
real, dimension(11:20,-9:0,0:20,-20:0) :: z
```

then the statement

```
x = y + z
```

has exactly the same effect as the following nest of **do** loops:

```
do i = 1, 10
    do j = 1, 10
        do k = 1, 21
            do l = 1, 21
                x(i, j, k, l) = y(i-1, j-1, k-11, l-11) +    &
                                z(i+10, j-10, k-1, l-21)
```

```
        end do
      end do
    end do
  end do
```

This example makes it very clear that using whole-array expressions is simpler, and hence less error-prone, than using **do** loops! For machines with multiple processing units, whole-array expressions can also make it easier for the compiler to parallelize the code. Thus, whole-array expressions should be used, wherever possible, to simplify code and (possibly) improve performance.

We should now remind ourselves of the rules for working with whole arrays which were stated in Chapter 7:

- Two arrays are conformable if they have the same shape.
- A scalar, including a constant, is conformable with any array.
- All intrinsic operations are defined between conformable arrays.

So far, we have discussed whole-array assignment and expressions in the context of numeric arrays, but the capability to write whole-array expressions is also available for character arrays and logical arrays. Thus, the following code fragment will concatenate each element of string_1 with the corresponding element of string_2, storing the resulting string in the corresponding element of long_string:

```
character(len =7), dimension(3,4) :: string_1, string_2
character(len = 14), dimension(3,4) :: long_string
    .
    .
    .
long_string = string_1//string_2
    .
    .
    .
```

The fact that scalars are conformable with any array means that the following code fragment has the effect of placing a pair of single quotation marks around the strings in every element of the array unquoted and storing the resulting strings in the array quoted:

```
character(len = 20), dimension(4,50) :: unquoted
character(len = 22), dimension(4,50) :: quoted
    .
    .
    .
quoted = """"//unquoted//""""
    .
    .
    .
```

Relational operators also follow the same rules, with the result that the expression

```
A > B
```

where A and B are conformable arrays of some numeric type, results in a logical array of the same shape as A and B and whose element values are obtained by applying the > operator element by element to corresponding elements of A and B. A similar definition will apply to the other relational operators.

For example, if A and B are two-dimensional integer arrays with, respectively, the values

$$\begin{bmatrix} 1 & 2 \\ 3 & 4 \end{bmatrix} \quad \text{and} \quad \begin{bmatrix} -1 & -4 \\ 5 & 2 \end{bmatrix} \quad \text{respectively,}$$

then A > B is the logical array

$$\begin{bmatrix} .\textbf{true.} & .\textbf{true.} \\ .\textbf{false.} & .\textbf{true.} \end{bmatrix}$$

As expected, a scalar is considered to be conformable with any shape array. Thus, A > 2 is the logical array

$$\begin{bmatrix} .\textbf{false.} & .\textbf{false.} \\ .\textbf{true.} & .\textbf{true.} \end{bmatrix}$$

The logical expression in an **if** statement must be scalar. Thus, a logical array must be reduced (somehow) to a scalar value before an **if** test is applied. The intrinsic array-reduction functions **any** and **all** are useful in this context. The function **all**, applied to a logical array, has the scalar value .**true.** if all the array elements are .**true.**; otherwise, the result is .**false.**. By contrast, the function **any**, applied to a logical array, has the scalar value .**true.** if any of the array elements are .**true.**; otherwise the result is .**false.**.

Thus, if we wanted to take some action only if all the elements of a numeric array A are greater than the corresponding elements of a numeric array B, we would write

```
if ( all (A>B) ) then
    .                    ! actions
    .
    .
end if
```

As another example, the logical expression

```
any (A == B)
```

```
function outer_product(x, y) result(outer)
    real, dimension(:), intent(in) :: x, y
    real, dimension(size(x, 1), size(y, 1)) :: outer
    integer :: i, j
    do i = 1, size(x, 1)
        do j = 1, size(y, 1)
            outer(i, j) = x(i)*y(j)
        end do
    end do
end function outer_product
```

Figure 13.12 An array-valued function to calculate the outer product of two vectors.

will evaluate as .**true**. if, and only if, some element of A is equal to the corresponding element of B.

The **any** and **all** intrinsic functions are described in more detail in Appendix A.

The final aspect of whole-array processing that we introduced in Chapter 7 is the concept of an array-valued function. As with all the other concepts that we met originally in the context of rank-one arrays, there is no significant difference in applying the concept to arrays of any rank.

The rule to remember when writing an array-valued function is: the array that is the function result must be an explicit-shape array, although it may have variable extents in any of its dimensions.

An example of an array-valued function outer_product, which calculates the outer product of two vectors, is given in Figure 13.12.

The mathematical definition of the outer product of two vectors x and y is the matrix whose (i, j)th element is $x_i y_j$. In this function we assume that the two vectors are provided as rank-one arrays; the result of the function will be a rank-two array. Note how the extents of the (vector) arrays x and y are obtained by means of the intrinsic function **size**, and then used to define the shape of the function result, outer, and also to control the two **do** loops.

As described in Section 7.6, many of F's intrinsic procedures may be used in an **elemental** manner in whole-array expressions; in other words, they will accept arrays as actual arguments, and will return as their result an array of the same shape as the actual argument in which the procedure has been applied to every element of the array. Thus, if a is a rank-three real array with shape (l, m, n), **sin**(a) is a rank-three real array of shape (l, m, n) in which the (i, j, k)th element is **sin**(a(i,j,k)), for $i = 1, \ldots, l; j = 1, \ldots, m$; and $k = 1, \ldots, n$. The term 'elemental' is used to describe this behaviour, because the intrinsic function is applied element by element to its array arguments. If an intrinsic function is used elementally, then all its array arguments must be of the same shape; if not, the situation would be meaningless.

As a slightly more complicated example, if **a** and **b** are rank-one integer arrays of size n, then **max**(0,a,b) is a rank-one array whose ith element is

max $(0, a(i), b(i))$, for $i = 1, \ldots, n$. Note that the scalar 0 is conformable with a and b.

In addition to the intrinsic procedures that can be used elementally, F also provides many intrinsic procedures specifically designed for array operations. A list of these procedures can be seen in Figure 13.13.

A number of these procedures have an optional argument mask. This is an array of type **logical** that masks the elements of the array being operated on so that array elements are used in the calculation only if the corresponding element in the mask array has the value .**true**.. For example:

```
logical, dimension(3) :: m = (/.true.,.false.,.true./)
integer, dimension(3) :: q = (/1,7,4/)
integer :: s
s = sum(q,1,m)
```

sets s to the sum of the first and third elements of q (that is, 5). If the optional argument m is omitted in the call to **sum**, then s would be set to the sum of all the elements in q (that is, 12).

Many of the procedures in Figure 13.13 contain an optional **dim** argument. For a rank-one array, this argument has no effect. However, for higher-rank arrays, this argument, when present, specifies along which dimension of the input array the procedure is to be applied. The result is an array of rank one less than the rank of the original array. For example, if A is a 3 × 2, rank-two array with value

$$\begin{bmatrix} 1 & 6 \\ 4 & 3 \\ 5 & 2 \end{bmatrix}$$

then **maxval** (A, **dim** = 1) is the rank-one array (**max** $(1, 4, 5)$, **max** $(6, 3, 2)$). That is, the array $(5, 6)$.

Similarly, **maxval** (A, **dim** = 2) is the rank-one array (**max** $(1, 6)$, **max** $(4, 3)$, **max** $(5, 2)$). That is, the array $(6, 4, 5)$.

The use of these array intrinsics is strongly recommended when writing code that manipulates arrays:

- The resulting code will almost always be cleaner and more compact than code written without them.
- The intrinsic procedures are usually provided in assembly language, by the compiler writers, and are consequently very efficient.
- It will require less effort.

In addition to the extension of scalar operations to arrays, and the intrinsics provided to simplify the manipulation of arrays, F also contains two further

Vector and matrix multiply functions

dot_product(vector_a, vector_b)　　　Dot product of two rank-one arrays

matmul(matrix_a, matrix_b)　　　Matrix multiplication

Array reduction functions

all(mask[,**dim**])　　　True if all values are true

any(mask[,**dim**])　　　True if any value is true

count(mask[,**dim**])　　　Number of true elements in an array

maxval(array[,**dim**][,mask])　　　Maximum value in an array

minval(array[,**dim**][,mask])　　　Minimum value in an array

product(array[,**dim**][,mask])　　　Product of array elements

sum(array[,**dim**][,mask])　　　Sum of array elements

Array inquiry functions

allocated(array)　　　Array allocation status

lbound (array[,**dim**])　　　Lower dimension bounds of an array

shape(source)　　　Shape of an array or scalar

size(array[,**dim**])　　　Total number of elements in an array

ubound(array[,**dim**])　　　Upper dimension bounds of an array

Array construction functions

merge(tsource, psource, mask)　　　Merge under mask

pack(array, mask[,vector])　　　Pack an array into an array of rank one under a mask

spread(source, **dim**, ncopies)　　　Replicate an array by adding a dimension

unpack(vector, mask, field)　　　Unpack an array of rank one into an array under a mask

Array reshape function

reshape(source, **shape**[,pad] & [,order])　　　Reshape an array

Array manipulation functions

cshift(array, shift[,**dim**])　　　Circular shift

eoshift(array, shift & [,boundary][,**dim**])　　　End-off shift

transpose(matrix)　　　Transpose of an array of rank two

Array location functions

maxloc(array[,mask])　　　Location of a maximum value in an array

minloc(array[,mask])　　　Location of a minimum value in an array

Note that in the above table [,xyz] indicates that the argument xyz is optional

Figure 13.13　Intrinsic procedures designed for use in array processing.

powerful array handling features which complete the facilities required for powerful and flexible array processing, and these will be described in the final two sections of this chapter.

13.8   Masked array assignment

The **where** construct allows a finer degree of control over the assignment of one array to another, by use of a **mask** which determines whether the assignment of a particular element should take place or, alternatively, which of two alternative values should be assigned to each element. This concept is called **masked array assignment**.

The first, simpler, form of the **where** construct is

```
where (mask_expression)
   array_assignment_statements
end where
```

where *mask_expression* is a logical expression of the same shape as the array variable being defined in the *array_assignment_statements*. The effect is that the assignment statements are only executed for those elements where the elements in the corresponding positions of the *mask_expression* are true. Note, however, that the assignment statement must not be a defined assignment, as described in Section 16.3.

For example, if `arr` is a real array, then the effect of the statement

```
where (arr<0.0)
   arr = -arr
end where
```

is to change the sign of all the elements of `arr` having negative values, and to leave those having positive values unchanged. This is because the expression `a < 0.0` is an array logical expression, of the same shape as `arr`, in which an element is *true* if the corresponding element of `arr` is less than 0, and is *false* otherwise. Consequently, the assignment statement `arr = -arr` is only performed for those elements whose value is less than zero.

Only array assignment statements can appear in a **where** construct.

The simple form of the **where** construct is sufficient for many situations, but there are often cases in which it is desirable to carry out one of two alternative assignments, depending on the value of the corresponding element of the mask array. In these cases, we can use the second form of the **where** construct, which takes the form

```
where (mask_expression)
   array_assignment_statements
elsewhere
   array_assignment_statements
end where
```

The effect of this form of the **where** construct is that the set of array assignment statements immediately following the **where** are only executed for those elements where the elements in the corresponding positions in the mask expression are *true*. Conversely, the set of array assignment statements immediately following the **elsewhere** are only executed for those elements where the elements in the corresponding positions in the mask expression are *false*. Note that all the arrays being assigned values must be conformable with each other, and with the mask array.

The following example illustrates how a **where** construct can be used to replace every non-zero element of the array array by its reciprocal, and every zero element by 1.0:

```
where (array /= 0.0)
    array = 1.0/array
elsewhere
    array = 1.0
end where
```

One very important point to emphasize is that, despite its syntactic similarity to the **if** construct, the **where** construct is *not* a sequential construct. The mask is always an array which is conformable with the array, or arrays, which appear on the left-hand side of the assignment statement, or statements, in the construct, and the effect is as if all the array elements were assigned simultaneously, with the mask either preventing some of the assignments taking place, or causing different ones to take place.

In a **where** construct, masking applies to elemental function references that are *not* within an argument of a non-elemental function. Thus, if z_arr is a real array of the same shape as arr,

```
where (arr > 0)
   z_arr = sqrt(arr)
end where
```

will put the square roots of the elements of arr into the corresponding elements of z_arr only for those elements of arr that are positive. However, in the case of:

```
where (arr /= 0.)
   z_arr = arr/minval(sqrt(arr))
end where
```

because **minval** is not an elemental function, the mask will have no effect on **sqrt**(arr) and the **where** construct is the equivalent of

```
z_arr = arr/minval(sqrt(arr))
```

This will, therefore, fail (with an execution error) if any element of arr is negative.

13.9   Sub-arrays

In Chapter 7, for rank-one arrays, we saw how it was frequently useful, especially in scientific programming, to be able to define a sub-array, consisting of a selection of elements of an array, and to then manipulate this sub-array in the same way that a whole array can be manipulated.

Array sections can be extracted from a parent array, of any rank, in a rectangular grid (that is, with regular spacing) using subscript triplet notation, or in a completely general manner using vector subscript notation. In either case the resulting array section is itself an array and can be used in the same way as an array – for example, in whole-array expressions or passed as an argument to a procedure – except for the three restrictions noted at the end of Section 7.7.

We have already defined an array element as

array_name $(i_1, \ldots, i_k)$

where *array_name* is the name of a variable with the dimension attribute (that is, an array), k is the rank of *array_name*, and the i_j are subscripts.

If any or all of the i_j are replaced by subscript triplets or vector subscripts, then, instead of defining an array element, we have defined an array section. The rank of the array section so defined is the number of subscript triplets and vector subscripts it contains. This definition fits well with the convention that an array element has rank zero, since its definition contains no subscript triplets or vector subscripts.

To illustrate, if the array arr_2 is declared as

integer, dimension(2:9,-2:1) :: arr_2

then arr_2(4:5,-1:0) is a rank-two integer array containing the elements

$$\begin{bmatrix} arr\_2(4,-1) & arr\_2(4,0) \\ arr\_2(5,-1) & arr\_2(5,0) \end{bmatrix}$$

The rank of this array section is the same as that of its parent array; however, this is not necessary. For example, if arr_3 is declared as

```
real, dimension(3,4) :: arr_3
```

then

arr_3(2,:)   is a rank-one real array (because there is only one subscript triplet) whose elements are arr_3(2,1), arr_3(2,2), arr_3(2,3) and arr_3(2,4). In other words, it is the second row of arr_3.

arr_3(:,3)   is a rank-one real array whose elements are arr_3(1,3), arr_3(2,3) and arr_3(3,3). It is, therefore, the third column of arr_3.

arr_3(2,3:4)   is a rank-one array whose elements are arr_3(2,3) and arr_3(2,4).

A good example of the use of array sections defined by subscript triplets will be found in Section 17.5, in the procedure for solving a system of linear equations by Gaussian elimination.

As you would expect, array sections of multidimensional arrays may be used in input or output statements in an obvious way as a generalization of what was described in Section 7.7. Thus, if an array a is defined as

```
real, dimension(5,6,7) :: a
```

the list of elements

```
a(3:4, 1:3, 1)
```

as the list of an input or output statement specifies the elements:

```
a(3,1,1), a(4,1,1),
a(3,2,1), a(4,2,1),
a(3,3,1), a(4,3,1)
```

in the order given.

As in the rank-one case, non-unit strides can be used. Thus, in an input or output statement,

```
a(1:4:3, 2:6:4, 1:3:2)
```

specifies the elements:

```
a(1,2,1), a(4,2,1),
a(1,6,1), a(4,6,1),
a(1,2,3), a(4,2,3),
a(1,6,3), a(4,6,3)
```

in the order given.

In many situations, the obvious way of providing data is not the same as the array element order. For example, consider the situation in which an array x is being used to store a 50 × 8 array of data values.

Since the data may be considered as 50 rows of eight columns, we would normally wish to input or output the array row by row. However, a statement such as

```
print "(8f8.2)", x
```

will print out the data in the following way:

```
x(1,1)   x(2,1)   x(3,1)   x(4,1)   x(5,1)   x(6,1)   x(7,1)   x(8,1)
x(9,1)   x(10,1)  x(11,1)  x(12,1)  x(13,1)  x(14,1)  x(15,1)  x(16,1)
  .        .        .        .        .        .        .        .
  .        .        .        .        .        .        .        .
  .        .        .        .        .        .        .        .
x(49,1) x(50,1)  x(1,2)   x(2,2)   x(3,2)   x(4,2)   x(5,2)   x(6,2)
x(7,2)   x(8,2)   x(9,2)   x(10,2)  x(11,2)  x(12,2)  x(13,2)  x(14,2)
  .        .        .        .        .        .        .        .
  .        .        .        .        .        .        .        .
  .        .        .        .        .        .        .        .
```

which is not at all what was wanted!

On the other hand, using array sections, the statement

```
do i = 1, 50
   print "(8F8.2)", (x(i,:))
end do
```

will cause the results to be printed in the correct arrangement:

```
x(1,1)   x(1,2)   x(1,3)   x(1,4)   x(1,5)   x(1,6)   x(1,7)   x(1,8)
x(2,1)   x(2,2)   x(2,3)   x(2,4)   x(2,5)   x(2,6)   x(2,7)   x(2,8)
  .        .        .        .        .        .        .        .
  .        .        .        .        .        .        .        .
  .        .        .        .        .        .        .        .
```

Note the use of a : in the output list to specify an entire row of the rank-two array x.

We shall now turn from subscript triplets to vector subscripts. These are used when a non-regular pattern of indices is needed and, hence, a subscript triplet would not work.

A vector subscript is an integer array expression of rank 1, each of whose elements has the value of a subscript in the array section being defined. Their use in multidimensional arrays is an obvious extension of that for rank-one arrays.

To illustrate, consider the code:

```
integer, dimension(3) :: u = (/2,1,4/)
integer, dimension(2) :: v = (/7,9/)
real, dimension(5,10) :: a
```

Then a(u,v) is the rank-two array (because it contains two vector subscripts) whose elements are

$$\begin{bmatrix} a(2,7) & a(2,9) \\ a(1,7) & a(1,9) \\ a(4,7) & a(4,9) \end{bmatrix}$$

The size of this array is the product of the sizes of u and v, and the shape of this array is a rank-one integer array whose elements are the size of u and the size of v.

As a more complicated example, if we replace the values of u by (/2,2,4/), then a(u,v) has the elements

$$\begin{bmatrix} a(2,7) & a(2,9) \\ a(2,7) & a(2,9) \\ a(4,7) & a(4,9) \end{bmatrix}$$

Finally, we note that subscripts, subscript triplets and vector subscripts can be used together to define an array section. Thus, if the arrays string and vec are declared as follows:

```
character(len = 10), dimension(3,4,9) :: string
integer, dimension(5) :: vec = (/7,1,3,1,4/)
```

then string(vec,3,5:9:4) is a rank-two character array whose elements are

$$\begin{bmatrix} string(7,3,5) & string(7,3,9) \\ string(1,3,5) & string(1,3,9) \\ string(3,3,5) & string(3,3,9) \\ string(1,3,5) & string(1,3,9) \\ string(4,3,5) & string(4,3,9) \end{bmatrix}$$

As in the case of rank-one arrays, described in Section 7.7, a many–one array section must not appear on the left-hand side of an assignment statement, nor may it be an input item in a read statement.

SELF-TEST EXERCISES 13.2

1 How would you specify two rank-two allocatable arrays called A and B?

2 How would you allocate space so that the array A of the previous exercise has dimension 3 × 4 and B has shape (m, n), where m and n are integer variables?

3 Under what circumstances can an allocatable array, or one of its elements, be passed as an argument to a procedure or be used in an arithmetic expression?

4 What is the allocation status of an array? What are the possible states? How do they occur?

5 How can the allocation status of an allocatable array be prevented from becoming undefined?

6 How can the allocation status of an array be determined while a program is executing?

7 What are the differences between automatic arrays and allocatable arrays? What are the criteria for choosing which to use?

8 How are operators applied in a whole-array expression?

9 How can some intrinsic F functions be used in a whole-array expression?

10 What are the advantages of using whole-array expressions?

11 What is the purpose of a masked array assignment?

12 What is an array section? How is it used?

13 What is the difference between a subscript triplet and a vector subscript? When should each be used?

14 What is the rank of an array section?

SUMMARY

- An array may have up to seven dimensions; its rank is the number of dimensions it has.

- The extent of a dimension is the number of permissible index values for that dimension.

- The size of an array is the number of elements it contains and is equal to the product of its extents.

- The shape of an array is determined by the number of its dimensions and the extent along each dimension. It is representable as a rank-one array.

- The elements of an array are stored in a sequence known as the array element order, in which the first subscript varies most rapidly, then the second, and so on.

- Array constructors define array-valued constants in the form of rank-one arrays. The **reshape** intrinsic function can be used to change this into any specified shape for assignment to an array whose rank is greater than one.

- An allocatable array is an array whose rank is declared initially, but none of its extents, and which is subsequently allocated with bounds specified dynamically during execution.

- The space required for an allocatable array may be released at any time during execution by deallocating the array.

- Allocatable arrays cannot be dummy arguments, function results or components of a derived type.

- To prevent the status of an allocated allocatable array from becoming undefined when a procedure that allocated it is exited, the array can be given the **save** attribute.

- The whole-array processing capability is complemented by a number of intrinsic functions designed for manipulating arrays.

- Masked array assignment is a generalization of whole-array assignment. It is used to control the assignment at the individual element level by employing a conformable logical array expression.

- An array section is a sub-array defined by specifying a subset of the elements of another array.

- Array sections are defined by the use of subscript triplets and vector subscripts.

- F syntax introduced in Chapter 13

Array declaration	*type*, **dimension** (*dim_spec*, ...) :: *list of names*
	where each *dim_spec* (up to a maximum of 7) takes one of the forms:
	  extent
	  lower_bound:*upper_bound*
	  lower_bound:
	  :*upper_bound*
	  :

Allocatable attribute	**allocatable**
Allocate and deallocate statements	**allocate** (*list of array_specifications*, **stat** = *stat_var*) **allocate** (*list of array_specifications*) **deallocate** (*list of allocated arrays*, **stat** = *stat_var*) **deallocate** (*list of allocated arrays*)

Where construct	```where``` *(conformable_logical_expr)*
	   array assignment statements
	```end where```

	```where``` *(conformable_logical_expr)*
	   array assignment statements
	```elsewhere```
	   array assignment statements
	```end where```

Array section	*array_name* $(i_1, i_2, \ldots, i_k)$ where at least one of $i_1, \ldots, i_k$ is a subscript triplet or vector subscript. The rank of the array section is the number of vector subscripts and array triplets it contains.

PROGRAMMING EXERCISES

∗13.1 Write a program that has an explicit-shape rank-two integer array of shape $(4, 5)$ with default index bounds. Fill the array so that the (i, j)th element has the value $10 * i + j$. Print out all the array element values in a rectangular pattern that reflects the array structure.

Now modify your program so that the printed pattern is rotated through $90°$; that is, if the original version treated the first subscript as the row number and the second subscript as the column, then this version should treat the first subscript as the column number and the second as the row number, and vice versa.

13.2 A bus leaves the terminus on the hour and every half-hour between 7.30 a.m. and midnight on Saturdays and Sundays. On all other days it runs on the hour and every 20 minutes between 7.00 a.m. and 6.00 p.m., and on the hour and half-hour between 6.00 p.m. and 11.00 p.m.

Write a program that generates the timetable for the whole week, using a 24-hour clock, and stores it in a rank-two array in which each column contains the times of buses on one day of the week. The program should then print the complete timetable using a single **print** statement.

When you have tested your program, modify it so that for each day of the week it reads up to three triplets which specify the start time of a particular frequency, the end time and the frequency; in the above example the data for Tuesday would therefore be the two triplets (0700, 1800, 20) and (1800, 2300, 30). Test your program with several different patterns. Remember to ensure that buses at the change between frequency patterns (for example, at 6.00 p.m. in the above example) are not scheduled twice!

13.3 The infinity-norm of a vector is defined as the largest of the absolute values of the elements of the vector. Write a function that returns the infinity-norm of a vector whose elements are stored in a rank-one assumed-shape real array which is the only argument to the function. The function should use elemental references to the intrinsic functions to do as much of the work as possible. Test your function on several vectors that have mixtures of positive and negative elements.

The two-norm of a matrix whose elements are a_{ij}, $i = 1, \ldots, m, j = 1, \ldots, n$ is defined to be

$$\sqrt{\sum_{i=1}^{m} \sum_{j=1}^{n} a_{ij}^2}$$

Modify the function just written so that it calculates the two-norm of a matrix, and test it with several matrices of different sizes.

13.4   The intersection of two sets is the set of all elements that occur in both sets. Write a subroutine that has two rank-one, integer, assumed-shape dummy arguments as input and one rank-one, integer, assumed-shape dummy argument as output. The output array should contain the intersection of the two input arrays. The fourth argument of the subroutine should be the number of elements in the intersection.

Test your subroutine with different size sets. For each array, the elements inside the array should be distinct from each other. Be careful that the array used for output is of sufficient size to hold the answer. The subprogram should perform a validity check to test for too small an output array.

13.5   Write a function that has two assumed-shape rank-one real dummy arguments. Internally, form a rank-two real array whose (i, j)th element is the product of the ith element of the first array and the jth element of the second array. The function should scan the product array systematically, to find a 2×2 sub-array that has the largest value for the sum of its elements. Return this sum. Test your function with several sets of inputs.

13.6   The ancient Greeks developed a method of finding all prime numbers up to a specified maximum which is called the Sieve of Eratosthenes. The method is, given the maximum integer n:

1.   Create an integer array A of size n.
2.   Fill A with integers such that A(I) = I, I = 1, ..., n.
3.   Set P = 2.
4.   Go through the array A, setting all integers exactly divisible by P to 0.
5.   Advance P, until either a non-zero A(P) is found, in which case go to step 4, or P > $\sqrt{n}$, in which case go to step 6.
6.   All the numbers in the array that are non-zero must be prime (nothing divided them exactly). Print them out.

Implement this algorithm using an allocatable array for A. The integer n is to be read as input. Try your program for different sizes of n starting at 100. Be careful that you do not set n too large and thereby use an inordinate amount of computer time!

*13.7   Write a function that takes a rank-one integer array as input and whose result is the input array with its elements reversed. Use a vector subscript to accomplish this.

Do it again using a subscript triplet.

Use this function to reverse the elements of the ith row of a rank-two integer array and then reverse the elements of the jth column.

13.8   Write a function that takes a rank-one real array as input, and an integer that lies between 1 and the size of the input array, and whose result is the input array with elements shifted to the left the number of places specified by the integer input. Those element values from the beginning of the array that are replaced by new values should be appended at the other end of the array. This is commonly called a left circular shift. There is an intrinsic function to do this, but the point of this exercise is to write your own.

13.9   Write a subroutine that has a rank-two square integer array as input and as output. The array will contain positive integer values between 0 and 10. The subroutine should modify the input array so that, when an element has a value 10 it is set to 0, when it has a value between 6 and 8 it is increased by 1, when it has a value between 1 and 5 it is decreased by 1, and when it has a value of 0 it is left unchanged.

Test the subroutine by running an array through it repetitively.

13.10   A conservation group is investigating the relative populations of various woodland animals, such as badgers, foxes and squirrels, in a wooded area on the basis of identifying their 'homes'.

The area under observation has been divided into a small 'regions', each $100\,m^2$, forming an $n\,km \times m\,km$ rectangular area. These regions are identified by a coordinate system in which they are numbered from 0 to $10n - 1$ west–east, and from 0 to $10m - 1$ south–north; thus region $(12, 7)$ is the region whose south-west corner is $1200\,m$ east of the 'origin' and $700\,m$ north of it (where the 'origin' of the coordinate system is the south-west corner of the larger area being surveyed).

Within each region the number of fox-holes, badger-setts, squirrel-nests and so on has been recorded in the form of the coordinates of the region, followed by several counts of the form

   k animals

where `animals` is `Badgers`, `Foxes`, or whatever animal's home has been identified.

Thus a particular record, for region $(12, 17)$, might read

   12 17 2 Foxes 1 Badger 5 Squirrels

Write a program to read this data (from a file) and to produce the following initial analyses:

   (a)   The total population of each type of animal, assuming one animal per hole, sett, nest or other type of home;
   (b)   The region or regions with the highest population of each type of animal;
   (c)   The region or regions with the lowest population of each type of animal.

The program should read the dimensions of the area being surveyed (n and m) at the beginning, but it will not be possible to determine the number of different types of animal until all the data has been input.

Test your program with several different sets of data.

Pointers and dynamic data structures

14

14.1 Fundamental pointer concepts
14.2 Using pointers in expressions
14.3 Pointers and arrays
14.4 Pointers as components of derived types

14.5 Pointers as arguments to procedures
14.6 Pointer-valued functions
14.7 Linked lists and other dynamic data structures

It is often convenient to have a pointer to a variable, which can be used to access the variable indirectly. F provides this capability by giving a pointer attribute to a variable, which allows it to point at variables of a specified type.

The use of pointers provides several benefits, of which the two most important are the ability to provide a more flexible alternative to allocatable arrays, and the ability to create and manipulate linked lists. This latter form of dynamic data structure opens the door to powerful recursive algorithms as well as providing the means to tailor the storage requirements exactly to the needs of the problem and the data.

This chapter shows how to use F pointers, and illustrates their potential by several examples which are both powerful and yet elegant.

14.1 Fundamental pointer concepts

All of the variables that we have met so far in F, whether scalar or array, have
shared one common feature, namely that they contain some form of data.
However, there is one further class of variable which does not contain any
data; instead it *points* to a scalar or array variable where the data is actually stored
(see Figure 14.1).

Because their function is to point at where data is stored, rather than to
contain data themselves, variables in this class are called **pointers**.

Pointers are commonly used in situations where data entities are being
created and destroyed dynamically (that is, while a program is executing) and it
is not known beforehand how many such events are going to occur, or in what
order. Simulating the flight control system at an airport is such a case, or
handling a list of requests for cash withdrawals on a national network of cash
machines. It is not feasible to use dynamically allocated arrays efficiently in such
situations, because, when such an array became full, it would be necessary to
allocate another, larger, array and then to copy all the data from the first array
to the second. This would involve significant computer time and enough
memory to contain both arrays simultaneously.

Pointers are also used to manipulate connections between data objects
efficiently. Consider, for example, the situation in which it is required to sort a
large set of data into order, where each item is of a derived type containing
many fields. As we have already seen, sorting an array can involve a

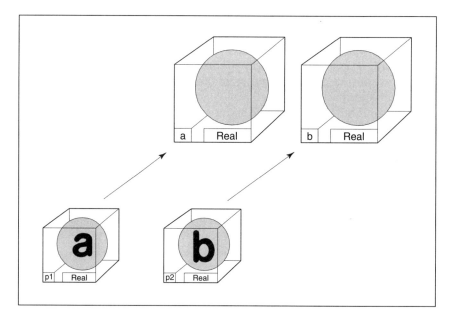

Figure 14.1 Pointers.

considerable number of data movements, and if this is done by moving the objects themselves into the required order there will be a considerable overhead. If, however, there is an array of pointers to the data objects then, instead of interchanging large-sized data objects, it is only necessary to interchange the pointers that are pointing to them. Since pointers are generally small objects, occupying typically only one word of memory, this is much more efficient.

Finally, it should be noted that arrays generally force a rectangular structure on data. This is acceptable if the data is of that nature. However, much data does not fit well into a rectangular pattern; for example, sparse matrices, the structure of neural nets, a road or railroad system, and almost all biological systems. Pointers provide a natural way to emulate the structure of such entities.

A variable in F is declared to be a pointer by specifying that it has the **pointer** attribute in a type declaration statement. For example, the statement

```
real, pointer :: p
```

specifies that the variable p is a pointer that can point to objects of type **real**. It does *not* specify a **real** entity that p is pointing to, only that it *can* point to one. An extremely important feature of this statement is that p can *only* be set to point to entities of type **real**. Any attempt to make it point to data of some other type (intrinsic or derived) will cause a compilation error.

Pointers can, of course, be defined that can point to derived type objects. For example

```
type(employee), pointer :: q
```

defines q to be a pointer variable that can point to objects of the derived type employee.

The general pattern for a pointer type declaration statement is

type specifier, *attribute list*, **pointer** :: *list of pointer variables*

The *type specifier* specifies what type of object can be pointed to, the *attribute list* gives the other attributes (if any) of the data type, and the *list of pointer variables* is a list of all the pointers being defined.

An important aspect of pointers is that every pointer has an **association status** which indicates whether or not it is currently pointing at anything. A pointer's association status when it is initially specified in a type declaration statement is said to be *undefined*.

Before discussing pointer type declaration statements in more detail, it is appropriate to examine how to make a pointer variable point to an object and, in particular, to introduce a concept that makes F's pointers different from those of most other languages.

One potential problem with pointers is that, for reasons that we do not need to elaborate here, they can very easily have a severely detrimental effect upon the execution efficiency of programs. Since execution efficiency has always been of great importance for the class of problems that F is primarily used for, certain steps have been taken to ensure that F compilers can produce as efficient code as is possible, even though a program uses pointers. This is achieved by restricting the variables to which a pointer may point, by requiring that all objects to which a pointer may point have an additional attribute, called the **target attribute**, which, as its name implies, specifies that the object may be pointed to – in other words, that it may be the target of a pointer. Thus, in the following statements

```
real :: a
real, target :: b
real, pointer :: p
integer, pointer :: q
```

the variable p can point to the variable b, because the types match and b has the target attribute; it cannot point to a (even though a is a real variable), because a does not have the target attribute. The variable q cannot point to b because, although b possesses the target attribute, it is of the wrong type, since q can only point to an integer entity.

A pointer can be associated with a target by a **pointer assignment statement**. This is an executable statement which takes the form

pointer => target

where *pointer* is a variable with the pointer attribute and *target* is a variable which has either the target attribute or the pointer attribute, and which has the same type, type parameters and rank as the *pointer* variable. Note that the pointer assignment operator is a composite symbol consisting of an equals sign followed by a greater than sign, without any intervening spaces.

When a pointer points to a target, its association status is said to be *associated*.

Figure 14.2 illustrates some pointer assignment statements and their effect.

In this example, the pointer association status of p, q and r is initially *undefined*. The status of p changes to *associated* after the third statement is executed, that of q after the fourth statement, and that of r after the fifth. Notice that it is legitimate for two or more pointers to be associated with the same target.

In Figure 14.2 the targets all had the target attribute. However, it is also permitted for pointer assignment to take place between two pointers, as illustrated in Figure 14.3.

```
        .
        .
        .
    integer, pointer :: p, q, r
    integer, target :: a, b
    p => a                        ! p points to a
    q => a                        ! q also points to a
    r => b                        ! r points to b
    p => b                        ! Now q points to a
        .                         ! and p and r point to b
        .
        .
```

Figure 14.2 Examples of pointer assignment.

In this example, the pointer association status of u, v and w is initially *undefined*. The pointer u then becomes associated with x and its association status becomes *defined*. The next statement

```
v => u
```

does not, however, set v to point to the pointer u. Instead, the effect is to make v point to *the same target* that u is pointing to. Thus v now points to x, since the pointer u points to x, and the association status of v becomes *associated*. In F, you cannot point to a pointer; however, if you do need pointers to pointers, they can be created indirectly through the use of derived types.

If the *target* is a pointer whose association status is *undefined*, then the status of *pointer* becomes *undefined*, as can be seen in the final statement in Figure 14.3, which sets the association status of u to that of w, that is, *undefined*.

```
        .
        .
        .
    real, pointer :: u, v, w
    real, target :: x
    u => x                        ! u points to x
    v => u                        ! v points to x
    u => w                        ! u now has an undefined
        .                         ! association status
        .
        .
```

Figure 14.3 Examples of pointer assignment where the target is a pointer.

Sometimes it is required to break a pointer's association with a target without setting it to point to another target with a pointer assignment statement, and the **nullify** statement exists for this purpose. This takes the form

nullify (*list of pointers*)

and breaks the association between the specified pointers and their targets, setting the pointer association status of each pointer to *disassociated*:

```
.
.
.
real, target :: a, b
real, pointer :: p, q
p => a                          ! p points to a
q => a                          ! q also points to a
nullify(p)                      ! p is disassociated
.                               ! q still points to a
.
.
p => b                          ! p now points to b
.
.
.
nullify(p,q)                    ! p and q are disassociated
.
.
.
```

There are several things to observe in this example. In the sixth line, the disassociation of p did not affect q even though they were both pointing at the same object. After being disassociated, p can be associated again later in the program, either with the same or with a different object. Finally, the last line illustrates that a **nullify** statement can disassociate several pointers simultaneously.

Because of the importance, in many applications using pointers, of knowing the current pointer association status of pointers, F includes an intrinsic function, **associated**, that will return the association status of a pointer. This function can be used in two ways – with one argument or with two.

In the first case, the function reference **associated**(p), where p is a variable with the pointer attribute, has the logical value *true* if the pointer is currently associated with a target and *false* if it is not.

If a reference to this function contains a second argument, then that argument must have the target attribute, and the result of the function reference will be *true* if and only if the pointer is associated with the specified target.

There is one important restriction concerning the use of the **associated** function, namely that the (first) argument must not have an undefined pointer association status. As a matter of good program design, a pointer should generally only have this status from the time that it is declared until it is first associated with some target. Thereafter it should always be either associated or disassociated. It is strongly recommended, therefore, that pointers should always be either associated with a target variable immediately after their declaration, or nullified, thereby ensuring that their status is disassociated:

```
.
.
.
real, pointer :: a, b, c
integer, pointer :: p, q, r
nullify(a, b, c, p, q, r)
.
.
.
```

There are two restrictions on the use of the pointer and target attributes, both of which are to be expected. The first of these is that a variable with the parameter attribute cannot have either the pointer or the target attribute, while the second is that a variable must not be given both the target attribute and the pointer attribute.

14.2 Using pointers in expressions

We can now begin to investigate how pointers are used in programs to provide additional capabilities that would not otherwise be available. When using pointers, the first, and the most important, rule is that when a pointer appears in a situation where a value is expected (for example, as one of the operands of an operator) it is treated as if it were the associated target, that is, the object being pointed to. This is sometimes called **dereferencing**. Consider, for example, the program fragment shown in Figure 14.4.

In this example, the two pointer assignment statements first associate p with i and q with j. The next statement is a conventional assignment statement, and expects a variable name on the left of the assignment operator and an expression on the right. The expression is analysed first and, since in the arithmetic expression q + 1 the plus operator expects q to have a value, the pointer q is dereferenced and the expression becomes equivalent to j + 1; it will therefore have the value 3. The pointer p on the left-hand side of the assignment operator is also dereferenced, in this case to the variable i. Thus, the effect of the statement

```
p = q + 1
```

is to set the value of i to 3; p is unchanged and continues to point to i.

```
        .
        .
        .
    integer, pointer :: p, q
    integer, target :: i = 1, j = 2
    p => i                          ! Pointer assignment;
                                    ! p points to i
    q => j                          ! Pointer assignment
                                    ! q points to j
    p = q + 1                       ! Assignment (to i)
    if (p-1 == q) then              ! Equality test and
       p => j                       ! pointer assignment
    end if                          ! Assignment (to j)
    p = q + 1
        .
        .
        .
```

Figure 14.4 An example of an arithmetic expression involving a pointer.

In the following statement, the expression p-1 == q results in both p and q being dereferenced to the integers i and j, respectively. The statement is, therefore, testing to see if i-1 is equal to j. Since this is true, the pointer assignment statement p => j is executed, with the result that both p and q point to the same integer variable, j.

In the final line of Figure 14.4, first q and then p is dereferenced to j, with the result that the statement is equivalent to j = j + 1, with the result that j is set to the value 4. The pointer p is unchanged.

Thus the fifth and ninth lines of the example, although they look identical, have different effects – the first modifying the value of i and the second modifying the value of j.

The value of an expression containing pointers, or the effect of an assignment to a pointer, can therefore be seen to depend on the current targets the pointers are associated with. The pointers themselves are unchanged, and continue pointing to their initial targets. In some languages, such as C and C++, pointers can be changed by arithmetic expressions; this is definitely not the case for F.

As another example, if a pointer occurs as an actual argument in a procedure reference, then the target with which it is associated is passed as the actual argument. Of course, the type and type parameters of the pointer must match those of the dummy argument.

The point which these examples are making, and which must be clearly understood, is that there is a significant difference between the behaviour of pointers on the left-hand side of a pointer assignment statement and the behaviour of pointers in a value-demanding situation. To illustrate this difference in a slightly different way from the previous example, consider the statements

```
real, pointer :: p, q
real, save, target :: x=2.0, y=3.0
p => x                          ! p points to x
q => y                          ! q points to y
p = q                           ! Same as x = y; p is unchanged
p => q                          ! p points to y
```

In this example, the assignment statement p = q sets x to have the value 3.0 and leaves the value of p unaltered. On the other hand, the pointer assignment statement p => q sets p to point to y and leaves the value of x unaltered.

We are now able to illustrate how pointers can be used to improve the efficiency of programs involving large objects. Suppose, for example, that we have a derived type large that has many different components, some of them being large arrays. Furthermore, let us suppose that we wish to interchange two objects large_1 and large_2 of type large. This would, previously to this chapter, be accomplished by statements such as

```
        .
        .
        .
type(large) :: large_1, large_2, temp
        .
        .
        .
temp = large_1
large_1 = large_2
large_2 = temp
```

However, this involves three copies of large amounts of data, and also involves the extra storage space for the variable temp. Using pointers will enable the same goal to be achieved considerably more efficiently:

```
        .
        .
        .
type(large), target :: large_1, large_2
type(large), pointer :: p1, p2
p1 => large_1                   ! p1 points to large_1
p2 => large_2                   ! p2 points to large_2
! Now work with p1 and p2 instead of large_1 and large_2
        .
        .
        .
! Interchange pointers so that p1 points to large_2
! and p2 points to large_1
p1 => large_2                   ! p1 points to large_2
p2 => large_1                   ! p2 points to large_1
        .
        .
        .
```

In this version, no large objects are copied; instead only two pointers are reset. However, life is never perfect, and there is a small cost to be paid. In this case, every time that large_1 is required we must write p1, before the exchange has taken place, or p2, after the exchange. This means that, when the program is being executed, an extra step is needed to go from p1 to the object to which it is pointing. Generally, however, this cost is small compared to the saving made through not moving large objects.

Once a pointer has been associated with an object of intrinsic type, the pointer may be used in place of the target object in any context where an object of the type of the target is expected. The dereferencing of pointers to objects of derived type works in an identical manner to the dereferencing of pointers to intrinsic types, as can be seen from the following example:

```
    .
    .
    .
type, public :: point
   real :: x, y
end type point
type(point), target :: pt1
type(point), pointer :: pt
pt => pt1
pt%x = 1.0                    ! Equivalent to pt1%x = 1.0
pt%y = 2.0                    ! Equivalent to pt1%y = 2.0
    .
    .
    .
```

The other situation in which a pointer may occur, and in which it will be dereferenced before being used, is in an input or output statement. Pointers which are associated with a target may occur in the list of items specified in a read or write statement. The pointer is dereferenced, and it is the associated target that data is written from or read into. Thus, if the program extract shown above has a subsequent statement of the form

```
read *,pt
```

the pointer variable pt will be dereferenced to the variable pt1 of type point (as long as pt still points to pt1) and the **read** statement will expect to read two real numbers, which will be read into the two components pt1%x and pt1%y.

14.3 Pointers and arrays

So far, we have only shown pointers that point to scalars. However, as we would expect, the target of a pointer can also be an array. As with scalars, the type declaration statement for an array pointer does not associate the variable with an array; its purpose is to define what sort of arrays the pointer can point to.

The type declaration statement for an array pointer specifies the type of arrays that it can point to, and also the rank of the arrays that it can point to. Note that only the rank is required, not the extents or array bounds.

The dimension attribute of a pointer array cannot specify an explicit-shape or an assumed-shape array, but must take the form of a deferred-shape array, in a similar manner to that used for an allocatable array (see Section 13.6). This does not mean that an array pointer cannot point to an explicit-shape or an assumed-shape array; it is merely a question of how the dimension attribute of an array pointer must be specified.

Although array pointers are similar to allocatable arrays, we will see that they have more capabilities. The deferred-shape dimension attribute for an array pointer is, however, specified in the same way as that for allocatable arrays. The extent of each attribute must, therefore, be specified by a colon, and the total number of colons is the rank of the array.

Thus, the statement

```
real, dimension(:), pointer :: p_array
```

declares a pointer, p_array, which can point only to rank-one, real arrays. Similarly, the statement

```
character(len = 5), dimension(:,:,:), pointer :: p_array2
```

declares a pointer, p_array2, which can only point to rank-three, character arrays whose length attribute is 5.

The array pointers p_array and p_array2 may be associated with any arrays having matching type, type parameters and rank, and which have the target attribute. The extents and index bounds of the arrays can be of any magnitude.

Figure 14.5 shows an example of the use of pointer arrays, and there are several important points to observe. First, p is associated at different times with arrays having different extents, as is q. This is allowed because it is only the rank that matters; the pointer p can point to *any* rank-one, default-real array; the extent of the array does not matter. Similarly, q is made to point to two differently shaped arrays, but their ranks are the same. Finally, note that q would not be allowed to point to the array f because, even though their type and rank are the same, the type parameters, specifically the length attribute, do not match.

Note that, whereas it is legitimate to associate an array pointer with an array section defined by a subscript triplet, it is not permitted to associate one with an array section defined by a vector subscript (see Section 13.9). Thus, in the program fragment shown in Figure 14.6, the first pointer assignment statement associates p1 with a, and p1(i) is interpreted as a(i). The second pointer assignment statement associates p2 with the odd-numbered elements of a. Thus,

```
        .
        .
        .
    integer :: n, u, v, w
        .
        . ! Assign values to n, u, v and w
        .
    real, dimension(10), target :: a
    real, dimension(n), target :: b
    character(len = 5), dimension(u, v, w), target :: d
    character(len = 5), dimension(v, 10, 20), target :: e
    character(len = 4), dimension(v, 10, 20), target :: f
    real, dimension(:), pointer :: p
    character(len = 5), dimension(:, :, :), pointer :: q
    p => a                          ! Associate p with array a
    p => b                          ! Associate p with array b
    q => d                          ! Associate q with array d
    q => e                          ! Associate q with array e
        .
        .
        .
```

Figure 14.5 An example of the use of array pointers.

p2(1) is a(1), p2(2) is a(3), and so on. The third pointer assignment statement is invalid because it attempts to associate p3 with an array section having a vector subscript.

Whatever form of array is being used, once a pointer association has been made the pointer can be used in place of the target array in an expression in exactly the same way as for scalars.

The arrays being pointed to in the previous examples have already been declared in other declaration statements; however, one of the most powerful

```
        .
        .
        .
    real, pointer :: p1, p2, p3
    real, target, dimension(10) :: a
    integer, dimension(3) :: u = (/3, 7, 1/)
    p1 => a                     ! Valid
    p2 => a(1:10:2)             ! Valid
    p3 => a(u)                  ! INVALID!!
        .
        .
        .
```

Figure 14.6 Valid and invalid pointer assignments to array sections.

aspects of array pointers is their use as a means of dynamically creating space for an array when required, and releasing it when it is no longer required. This is carried out by use of the **allocate** statement in a similar fashion to the use of the **allocate** statement to create space for an allocatable array, as discussed in Section 13.6.

The statement takes the form

allocate (*pointer* (*dimension specification*))

or

allocate (*pointer* (*dimension specification*) , stat = *status*)

where *pointer* is a pointer array (that is, it has both the dimension and pointer attributes), *dimension specification* is the specification of the extents for each dimension, and *status* is an integer variable which will be assigned the value zero if the allocation is successful, and a processor-dependent positive value if there is an error, for example if there is not enough memory available. The statement will create an un-named array of the specified size, having the correct type, type parameters and rank, and with an implied target attribute. Because this array does not have a name it can only be referred to by means of a pointer.

After successful execution of the **allocate** statement, the allocation status of *pointer* will become *allocated*, and its association status will become *associated*. Note that, although the stat= portion of the **allocate** statement can be omitted, an undetected allocation error will cause the program to terminate execution. Testing *status* produces more portable and informative code.

Note also that, unlike the situation with allocatable arrays, it is not an error to allocate an array pointer that is currently associated with a target. The effect is to set the pointer to point to the new object just allocated, and to break the connection with the previous target. However, care must be exercised if the first target was also created by an **allocate** statement. This is because, unless another pointer has been set to point to the first target array, the space for the first array will become inaccessible to the program. Not only is this bad programming practice, but it results in the memory becoming cluttered up with unusable space:

```
      .
      .
      .
integer :: error, m, n
real, dimension(:,:), pointer :: p, q
! Calculate values of m and n
      .
      .
      .
```

```
allocate(p(m + n, m*n), stat = error)        ! Allocate p
if (error /= 0) then
   print *, "Allocation Error"
   stop
end if
q => p                                         ! q points to the
                                               ! elements of p
allocate(p(10,n), stat - error)               ! Allocate p again
if (error /= 0) then
   print *, "Allocation Error"
   stop
end if
```

In this code fragment, the pointer p is first set to point to a dynamically created real array of size m + n by m*n. The pointer q is then set to point to the same array. Finally p is allocated again to dynamically create a new array of size 10 by n, and p now points to this new array, and the association of p with the first array is broken. The pointer q, however, is unaffected by the second allocation of p and continues to point at the first m + n by m*n array.

If the pointer assignment statement q => p were removed, however, the space for the first array would become completely inaccessible to the program. A second execution of the original allocate statement would not associate p with the first array, but would, instead, create another array of the same shape.

There is one other point to notice in this example. When p was allocated, the size expressions were not constants, as in the examples previously given for array pointer allocation, but were integer expressions using the variables m and n, which might, for example, have been procedure dummy arguments. The size expressions in an array pointer allocation statement can, in fact, be any scalar, integer expressions.

Note that, if the space for an array pointer is created by an **allocate** statement, and the pointer association status is subsequently set to disassociated by a **nullify** statement, then the space for the elements of the array pointer is *not* deallocated. The space will, however, be inaccessible unless a second pointer has been set to point to it before the **nullify** statement is executed.

To avoid the problems caused through such inaccessible space, the space for an array which was created by a pointer allocate statement can be released by means of a **deallocate** statement, which takes a similar form to that used to deallocate an allocatable array:

deallocate (*pointer*)

or

deallocate (*pointer*, stat = *status*)

The following program uses both allocatable and pointer arrays to illustrate the similarities and the differences between these two forms of dynamic arrays:

```
program space_pointer

   integer, dimension(:), allocatable :: a
   real, dimension(:,:), pointer :: p
   integer :: alloc_error, dealloc_error
   integer :: i                 ! Loop control variable
   integer :: n                 ! Size of diagonal

   ! Read input data
   open (unit = 7, file = "diagonal", status = "old",   &
         action = "read")
   read (unit = 7, fmt = *) n      ! Size of diagonal

   allocate(a(n), stat = alloc_error)
   if (alloc_error /= 0) then
      print *, "Couldn't allocate space for a"
      stop
   end if
   read (unit = 7, fmt = *) a

   ! Allocate space for p
   allocate(p(size(a,1), size(a,1)), stat = alloc_error)
   if (alloc_error /= 0) then
      print *, "Couldn't allocate space for p"
      stop
   end if

   ! Space for p allocated
   p = 0.0                      ! Set elements of p to zero
   do i = 1, size(a,1)          ! Set diagonal of p to the
      p(i,i) = a(i)             ! elements of a
   end do

   ! Calculate using p
   .
   .
   .
   ! Deallocate a and p.
   deallocate(a, p, stat = dealloc_error)
   if (dealloc_error /= 0 ) then
      print *, "Couldn't deallocate space for a and p"
      stop
   end if
   ! Other calculations
   .
   .
   .
end program space_pointer
```

The program uses an allocatable array a to hold the elements of a rank-one **real** array. A **real**, square, rank-two array p is then created whose diagonal elements are the elements of a and whose other elements are zero; the array p is defined by a pointer variable whose element space is created by execution of an **allocate** statement. Once p is allocated, all of its elements are set to zero by a whole-array expression, and its diagonal elements are then set to the elements of a in a **do** loop.

When the calculations are completed, the space for a and p is deallocated. Notice that it is permitted to deallocate allocatable arrays and pointers in the same statement; it is also permitted to allocate arrays of both types in the same statement where this is appropriate. When the space for p is deallocated, the pointer association status of p becomes *disassociated*.

Care must be taken when deallocating pointer arrays to ensure that they are not associated with an object that was not created by a pointer allocation statement. Thus, for example, if a program contains the following statements

```
real, allocatable, dimension(:, :), target :: a
real, pointer, dimension(:, :) :: p
allocate (a(10, 20))
p => a
```

and then the program subsequently attempts to execute the statement

```
deallocate(p)
```

an error will occur because the pointer deallocation statement will attempt to deallocate the space allocated to the allocatable array a. This can be corrected by first nullifying the pointer p

```
nullify(p)
```

which breaks the association between p and a. Alternatively, p could be set to a different target before deallocating a. In either case, it is now reasonable to deallocate a.

The general rule is that a pointer **deallocate** statement must not be used to deallocate any object, scalar or array, that was not allocated by a pointer **allocate** statement. Only objects dynamically created by a pointer **allocate** statement can be destroyed by a pointer **deallocate** statement.

Although we have shown how the space for the elements of an array pointer can be dynamically created and destroyed by use of the **allocate** and **deallocate** statements, these statements can, in fact, also be used to dynamically create and destroy scalar objects of any intrinsic or derived type. For example, in the following code fragment, any_type could be of any derived type that is available to the program at this point, and the **allocate** statement dynamically creates an object of this type with p pointing to it. The pointer p will be dereferenced in any context expecting an object of type any_type, so that, for example, p%c will be interpreted as the c component of the object that p is pointing to.

```
   .
   .
   .
integer :: error
type(any_type), pointer :: p, q
allocate(p, stat = error)
if (error /= 0) then
   print *,"Allocation Error"
   stop
end if
q => p
! Use p and q
   .
   .
   .
nullify(q)
deallocate(p, stat = error)
if (error /= 0) then
   print *,"Deallocation Error"
   stop
end if
   .
   .
   .
```

The **nullify** statement breaks the association between q and p and changes the pointer association status of q to *disassociated*. The status of p is unchanged. Note that if the pointer association status of q had not been set to *disassociated* before p was deallocated, q would have been left pointing to space which was no longer accessible to the program – a situation which, as we have already pointed out, is likely to lead to subsequent program errors.

The **deallocate** statement releases the space created for holding the object of type any_type and sets the pointer association status of p to *disassociated*.

14.4   Pointers as components of derived types

Before we start to use pointers in real programs, there is one other very important concept to be introduced. We have seen that pointers can point to objects of derived type in just the same way as they can point to objects of intrinsic type. However, a pointer can also be a component of a derived type. Such a pointer component of a derived type can point to an object of any intrinsic type or to any accessible derived type, *including the type being defined*. This has several very important implications.

We shall first, however, consider a derived type which contains a pointer component that does not refer to any objects of the same type, for example:

```
type, public :: mine
   integer :: i
   real, dimension(:), pointer :: p
end type mine
```

This is quite straightforward, although it should be noted that objects of this type will need to have space allocated for their pointer component before they can be employed in a useful fashion:

```
type(mine) :: a, b
allocate (a%p(10), b%p(20))
a%i = 1
a%p = 0.0                       ! Fill all elements of a%p with 0
b%i = 2
b%p(1:19:2) = 0.0               ! Fill odd-numbered elements of
                                ! b%p with 0
b%p(2:20:2) = 1.0               ! Fill even-numbered elements of
                                ! b%p with 1
```

To simplify the example, no error check was made in the **allocate** statement.

The ability to have array pointers as components permits us to improve the definition of the vector type that was defined in Example 8.5. In that example, the derived type was defined as:

```
type, public :: vector
   integer :: length
   real, dimension(max_length) :: elements
end type vector
```

where max_length was a named constant which specified the maximum length of vector permitted. This meant that there was considerable wasted space due to the need for every vector to have an array component big enough to cater for the largest vector anticipated.

We can now, instead, define the derived type vector as:

```
type, public :: vector
   real, dimension(:), pointer :: elements
end type vector
```

Observe that we no longer need the length component, because now we can apply the **size** intrinsic function to the elements array to find out the length of a vector.

Using this new type, we could define vectors of length 1, 10, and 20 by code such as the following:

```
        .
        .
        .
integer :: error
type(vector) :: u, v, w
```

```
allocate (u%elements(1), v%elements(10),   &
          w%elements(20) stat = error)
if (error /= 0) then
   print *, "Vector allocation error"
   stop
end if
.                           ! Further processing
.
.
```

Now, unlike the situation when using the earlier vector definition, there is no space wasted when creating space for the elements of a vector. Moreover, we can create vectors of any size we wish, subject only to the size of the computer's memory.

Now we shall consider the situation in which a derived type contains a pointer component which points to an object of the same type. Consider, for example, the following type definition:

```
type, public :: node
   integer :: i
   character(len = 3) :: id
   type(node), pointer :: p        ! p points to objects
                                   ! of type node
end type node
```

With this style of derived type definition, objects can be made to point at each other, as can be seen in the following example:

```
type(node), target :: n1, n2, n3

! Make n1 point at n2
n1%i = 1
n1%id = "E31"
n1%p => n2

! Make n2 point at n1
n2%i = 2
n2%id = "AX4"
n2%p => n1

! Make n3 point at n2
n3%i = 3
n3%id = "CC5"
n3%p => n2
```

Notice that, in order to permit the pointers to be set correctly, n1, n2 and n3 had to be given the target attribute.

This ability to have pointer components that can point to variables of the same type allows the creation of structures in which the relationships between the data elements (usually called nodes) can be arbitrarily complex, as opposed to the entities in an array which always have a rectangular structure (except for the case of an array section with a vector subscript). One of the simplest examples of such a relationship structure is a **linked list**. These are lists in which each node points to a successor (or predecessor) node. Linked lists occur very commonly in applications such as artificial intelligence, compiler writing, simulation, modelling and neural networks. We shall examine this important area in more detail in Section 14.7.

■ **EXAMPLE 14.1** ·

1 Problem

In order to build up a database of professional contacts, a derived type is defined to contain the name, sex, telephone number and address of each contact. It is required to design and maintain this database in such a way that the contact details are always stored in alphabetic order of last names.

2 Analysis

This is, in principle, a simple sorting problem, but with records that may each involve a large number of fields. Sorting the file by any method which involves exchanging data items will, therefore, be inefficient and we should look to using a method that sorts pointers to the data, and not the data itself.

This implies a requirement for an array of pointers. Although this is a relatively common requirement, we have already stated that, because a pointer is an attribute and not a data type, it is impossible to create such an array. We must, therefore, proceed indirectly.

Objects that simulate arrays of pointers can easily be created by using a derived type containing a pointer of the desired type, and then creating an array of that derived type. For example, suppose an array of pointers to integers is required. The following statements will define a derived type `int_pointer` whose only component is a pointer to integers:

```
type, public :: int_pointer
   integer, pointer :: p
end type int_pointer
```

We can then define an array of variables of this type:

```
type(int_pointer), dimension(10) :: a
```

It is now possible to refer to the ith pointer by writing `a(i)%p`.

We can now return to our problem and define a suitable derived type for the contact data, for example:

```fortran
type, public :: contact
   character(len = 15) :: first_name, last_name
   character(len = 20) :: title
   character(len = 1) :: sex
   character(len = 20) :: telephone
   character(len = 40) :: street
   character(len = 20) :: city
   character(len = 20) :: state
   character(len = 10) :: zip
end type contact
```

We shall use a naive sort algorithm called an injection sort. It is not one of the best sort algorithms known, but is an appropriate one for this problem, and also has the advantage that it does not obscure, by its complexity, the way in which we shall use pointers.

An injection sort starts with an empty list and adds items sequentially. When an item is added to the list, it is added so that it is in the correct position as defined by the ordering criteria. This is done by scanning sequentially down the list and, when the correct position is found, moving all the items already in the list (except for the first item, which is simply put in position one), starting at that position, down one position. The new item is then inserted in the position just vacated. In an injection sort, therefore, the list of items processed so far is always in the correct order which will avoid the need for any subsequent sorting; this is a major advantage, for this problem, over many other methods which are more efficient at sorting an existing list.

For reasons of clarity (and brevity!) we shall assume that there is already a set of contact data stored in a file, and will develop a program to sort this into order and then print the ordered list. The provision of an input procedure to, for example, create the initial file from data typed at the keyboard, and further development of the program to preserve the sorted list and to allow it to be subsequently updated, are left as exercises for the reader.

The data design for this problem is quite straightforward, but lengthy, and will be omitted in this example; it can easily be deduced by studying the solution given below. We shall give a structure plan for the sort procedure, but will omit those for the main program and display procedure, as these are relatively trivial.

Subroutine sort

Structure plan

1	Set p_contacts(1) to point at contacts(1)
2	Repeat for i from 2 to n
2.1	Repeat for j from 1 to i-1
2.1.1	If last_name of contacts(i) < last_name of p_contacts(j)

> **2.1.1.1** Move p_contacts(j:) down one place
> **2.1.1.2** Insert contacts(i) at position j
> **2.1.1.3** Cycle for next contact (at step 2)
>   **2.2** Insert contacts(i) at end of list

3 Solution

```
module storage

    ! Field lengths for contact data
    integer, parameter, private :: name_len = 15
    integer, parameter, private :: title_len = 20
    integer, parameter, private :: sex_len = 1
    integer, parameter, private :: phone_len = 20
    integer, parameter, private :: street_len = 40
    integer, parameter, private :: city_len = 20
    integer, parameter, private :: state_len = 20
    integer, parameter, private :: zip_len = 10

    ! Derived type for contact data
    type, public :: contact
        character(len = name_len) :: first_name, last_name
        character(len = title_len) :: title
        character(len = sex_len) :: sex
        character(len = phone_len) :: telephone
        character(len = street_len) :: street
        character(len = city_len) :: city
        character(len = state_len) :: state
        character(len = zip_len) :: zip
    end type contact

    ! Derived type to create an array of pointers to objects
    ! of type contact
    type, public :: contact_pointer
        type(contact), pointer :: pointer_to_contact
    end type contact_pointer

    ! Global data
    integer, public :: n                 ! Number of data records

    ! Array of contacts
    type(contact), allocatable, dimension(:),          &
                   target, save, public:: contacts

    ! Array of pointers to array of contacts
    type(contact_pointer), allocatable, dimension(:), &
                   save, public :: p_contacts
end module storage

module sort_and_display
    use storage
    private
```

```fortran
   public :: sort, display
contains

   subroutine sort()
   ! This subroutine sorts the array p_contacts based on
   ! the alphabetic order of the last_name field of the
   ! array contacts using an injection sort

      ! Local variables
      integer :: i, j            ! Loop control variables

      ! Initialize pointer list
      p_contacts(1)%pointer_to_contact => contacts(1)

      ! Main sorting loop
      main_loop: do i = 2, n

         ! Check current contact against contacts in list
         ! so far
         do j = 1, i-1
            if (contacts(i)%last_name < &
               p_contacts(j)%pointer_to_contact%last_name) &
               then
               ! Shift last part of p_contacts array down
               p_contacts(j + 1:i) = p_contacts(j:i-1)
               ! Insert current contact in list
               p_contacts(j)%pointer_to_contact => contacts(i)

               ! Return to find position for next contact
               cycle main_loop
            end if
         end do

         ! Current contact comes after all items already in
         ! list
         ! Insert it at the end
         p_contacts(i)%pointer_to_contact => contacts(i)
      end do main_loop

   end subroutine sort

   subroutine display()
   ! This subroutine prints the names of people in the
   ! contact list sorted by their last names

      ! Local variable
      integer :: i                ! Loop control variable

      ! Print alphabetical list of names
      do i = 1, n
         print "(t5, a, tr1, a)",                              &
               p_contacts(i)%pointer_to_contact%first_name,  &
               p_contacts(i)%pointer_to_contact%last_name
      end do

   end subroutine display
end module sort_and_display
```

```
program sort_contacts
! This program sorts a list of contacts into alphabetic
! order and then prints the contacts in that order
   use storage
   use sort_and_display

   ! Declaration
   integer :: error

   ! Open data file
   open(unit = 7, file = "contacts", status = "old", &
        action = "read")

   ! Read number of data records
   read (unit = 7, fmt = *) n

   ! Allocate space for all records
   allocate (contacts(n), p_contacts(n), stat = error)
   if (error /= 0) then
      print *,"Allocation error"
      stop
   end if

   ! Read all contact data
   read (unit = 7, fmt = *) contacts
   close (unit = 1)

   ! Sort data into order
   call sort()

   ! Print sorted list
   call display()

   ! Deallocate arrays before ending
   deallocate(contacts, p_contacts, stat = error)
   if (error /= 0) then
      print *,"Error deallocating contacts and p_contacts"
   end if
end program sort_contacts
```

Note that, at the end of the main program, the allocatable array contacts and the array of pointers p_contacts were deallocated. It may be felt that this was unnecessary, since the program is going to end immediately after this anyway. The main reason is that it is good programming style to acquire a habit of always explicitly deallocating allocated arrays and pointers for the reasons discussed earlier; a secondary reason is that it will often detect programming errors such as might occur if a procedure had inadvertently deallocated an array prematurely.

· ◻

There is one final point that should be made regarding the use of pointers as components in derived types, which relates to their occurrence in an input or output statement.

If a derived type ultimately contains a pointer, then an object of that type must not appear in the list of items specified in a **read** or **write** statement, since it is not possible to read or write the value of a pointer. Thus if, during the course of a program's execution, you have built up an elaborate structure of relationships by using derived types containing pointers (a linked list – see Section 14.7 – would be a simple example) and you wish to save the structure in a file before the program terminates, you *must* create a secondary storage scheme for the output that does not involve pointers, and copy the information to that secondary storage before executing the **write** statement.

SELF-TEST EXERCISES 14.1

1   What is a pointer? What is a target?

2   What can a pointer point to?

3   What are the possible association states of a pointer?

4   What is a pointer assignment statement and what forms can it take?

5   How can the pointer association status of a pointer variable be set to disassociated?

6   How can the pointer association status of a pointer variable be determined?

7   What is dereferencing? Give several examples.

8   How do pointers and the input/output features of F interact?

9   How can pointer variables be defined that can point to arrays?

10   How can the space for the elements of an array pointer be created dynamically? How can it be deallocated dynamically?

14.5   Pointers as arguments to procedures

It will be remembered that allocatable arrays cannot be used as dummy arguments of procedures (see Section 13.6). Pointers (and targets), on the other hand, are allowed to be procedure dummy arguments, but only as long as the following conditions are adhered to:

- If a dummy argument is a pointer, then the actual argument must be a pointer with the same type, type parameters and rank.
- A pointer dummy argument cannot have the **intent** attribute.

A particularly important aspect of pointer arguments concerns their allocation and deallocation. In the examples of pointer allocation and deallocation shown so far, the allocation and deallocation have always occurred in the same program unit; however, this is not a necessity, as can be seen from the following program extract:

```
module create_destroy
     .
     .
     .
contains
   subroutine create()
      real, dimension(:), pointer :: p
      allocate (p(100))              ! Error checking omitted
                                     ! for clarity
          .
          .
          .
      call calculate(p)
   end subroutine create

   subroutine calculate(x)
      real, pointer, dimension(:) :: x
      ! Calculate using x
          .
          .
          .
      deallocate(x)                  ! Error checking omitted
                                     ! for clarity
          .
          .
          .
   end subroutine calculate
     .
     .
     .
end module create_destroy
```

The space for the elements of p is allocated in the subroutine create, which then calls the subroutine calculate. This associates the dummy pointer argument x with the actual pointer argument p. After using the array x, the subroutine calculate deallocates it. This also deallocates the actual argument p in subroutine create and sets the pointer association status of p to *disassociated*.

This flexibility is in strong contrast to the situation with allocatable arrays which cannot be used as actual or dummy arguments, and must, therefore, be allocated and deallocated in the same program unit (unless they are in a module – see Section 13.6). However, this flexibility can bring its own problems if care is not taken. We strongly recommend, therefore, that the error checking provided by the stat specifier should always be used, and that in complex programs full use be made of the **associated** and **allocated** intrinsic procedures to establish the status of pointers.

On exit from a procedure, the actual argument takes its association status from that of the dummy argument. Therefore, it is generally inappropriate to set the dummy argument to point to an object local to the procedure that does not have the **save** attribute. Otherwise, the pointer actual argument will have an association status of *undefined*. Moreover, if a pointer is set to point to a dummy argument (which will, therefore, be required to have the **target** attribute), on exit the pointer actual argument will have an association status of *undefined*.

14.6   Pointer-valued functions

To complement the possibility of using a pointer as an argument to a procedure, it is also permitted for a function result to be a pointer. For example

```
module small
   public :: even_pointer

contains

   function even_pointer(a) result(p)
   ! The result of even_pointer is an array
   ! pointer to the even-numbered elements
   ! of the input array a.
      real, dimension(:), target, intent(in) :: a
      real, dimension(:), pointer :: p
      p => a(2::2)        ! p points to an array section
   end function even_pointer

end module small
```

In Section 14.1, where we first discussed pointer assignment statements, we stated that the form of a pointer assignment statement was

pointer => target

We can now generalize this to

pointer => expr

where *expr* is an expression delivering a pointer result. Figure 14.7 shows an example of this extended form of pointer assignment, using the pointer-valued function `even_pointer` shown above.

The program first uses the function to set p to point to the even-numbered elements of the array a. Then q is set to point to the even-numbered elements of the array pointed to by p because, in this statement, p will be dereferenced as the

```
program pointer_function
   use small
   real, dimension(15), target :: a
   real, dimension(:), pointer :: pa, p, q, r

   .
   .
   .

   pa => a
   p => even_pointer(pa)          ! p points to even elements of a
   q => even_pointer(p)           ! q points to even elements of p
   r => even_pointer(q)           ! r points to even elements of q

   .
   .
   .

end program pointer_function
```

Figure 14.7   Pointer assignment of the result of a pointer-valued function.

array it is pointing to. As a result, q therefore points to the array consisting of
a(4), a(8) and a(12). Finally, r is set to point to the even-numbered elements of
q and therefore points to the array consisting of the single element a(8).

14.7   Linked lists and other dynamic data structures

One of the most common uses of pointers is to create what are called linked lists.
These are lists of objects in which every object has a pointer to the next object in
the list, which may not be stored in memory adjacently to its predecessor. In an
array, by contrast, the items are stored sequentially, and the array, at some point
in a program, must have a specific size defined for it. In a linked list, items that are
logically adjacent (that is, *connected*) are not necessarily stored contiguously.
Moreover, items for the list can be created dynamically (that is, at execution time)
and may be inserted at any position in the list. Likewise, they may be removed
dynamically. Thus, the size of a list may grow to an arbitrary size as a program is
executing, constrained only by the memory resources of the computer being
used.

When analysing a problem which is to use linked lists it is frequently
convenient to represent the list in diagrammatic form, as shown in Figure 14.8.
Conventionally, the first item in the list is referred to as the **head** of the list,
while the last item is called the **tail**.

A linked list in F typically consists of a derived type containing fields for the
data plus a field that is a pointer to the next item in the list. The head and the tail
will usually be represented by pointers to the appropriate list items. Example
14.2 illustrates how such a linked list can be used in the simulation of a real-time
system, in which the underlying database is constantly changing.

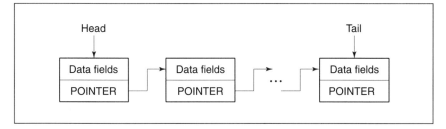

Figure 14.8 A linked list.

☐ **EXAMPLE 14.2** ●

1 **Problem**

We wish to model a national network of cash machines. In this example, however, we shall examine only that part of the program that handles the set of pending requests. We shall assume that requests are processed in the order in which they are received and that, therefore, the set of pending requests will be kept in order in such a way that a new request coming in is added at the end of the set and the next item to be processed comes from the front of the set.

2 **Analysis**

It would be inconvenient to keep such an ordered set, where elements are being added and deleted in an unpredictable order, in an array, and we shall therefore use a linked list. This will consist of a set of objects of a derived type that contains the request information. For this example, we shall assume that these are the cash machine number, the customer's account number, the date and time of the request, and the amount of cash requested.

The derived type will also have one more field which will contain a pointer that can point to entities of the same derived type. During execution, this pointer will be set to point to the next request, in order of arrival. A new request arriving will be linked onto the end of the list; an order for the top-priority request will be satisfied by delivering the request at the front of the list and removing it from the list.

We can, therefore, represent the list of unsatisfied requests as shown in Figure 14.9.

The space for each request will be allocated dynamically when the request arrives. Initially, the list will be empty, and the head and tail pointers will be set to be disassociated.

There are two cases to consider when a new request is being added to the list. The first possibility is that the list is empty. In this case, the head and tail pointers will both be set to point to a new item when it arrives (see Figure 14.10).

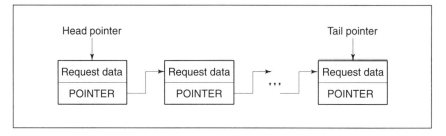

Figure 14.9   The list representing unsatisfied transaction requests.

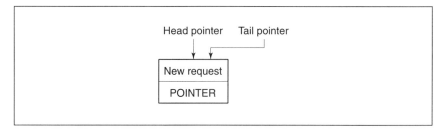

Figure 14.10   The list with only one entry.

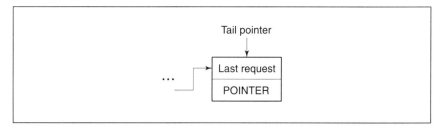

Figure 14.11   The end of the list before adding a new item.

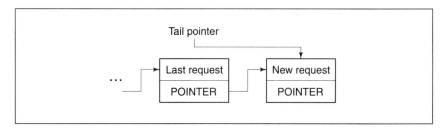

Figure 14.12   The end of the list after adding a new item.

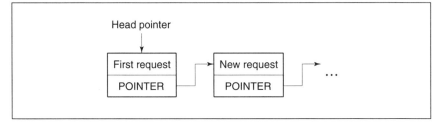

Figure 14.13 The start of the list before removing an item.

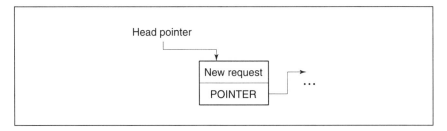

Figure 14.14 The start of the list after removing an item.

If the list is not empty, then the new request can be added at the end of the list by adjusting two pointers. Before the new request is added, the end of the list will be as shown in Figure 14.11, while Figure 14.12 shows the situation after the new request has been added at the end.

When asked to provide the front item in the list, there are three possibilities. The first possibility is that the list is empty, in which case an indication that the list is empty must be returned. The second possibility is that there is only one item in the list, in which case that item should be delivered and the head and tail pointers set to disassociated. The third possibility is that the list contains at least two items, in which case that item should be delivered and the head pointer adjusted so that the second item is now the head of the list. Figure 14.13 shows the start of the list before the first item is delivered in this case, while Figure 14.14 shows how it has changed after the item has been delivered and the head pointer reset.

In this example, and in the next, we shall diverge from our normal practice and proceed directly to a sample solution without showing the data design and structure plan. This is because the code required to implement this model is essentially very straightforward, apart from the statements involved in manipulating the list. In this case, it will be more useful for the reader to examine the code carefully, with the aid of the comments provided, in order to see exactly how the various pointer statements work, than it would be to proceed with the more abstract analysis involved in a structure plan. Such an initial planning stage is, however, vital in writing such a program, as it is with all programming.

3 Solution

```
module data_types
    ! Derived type to record transaction data
    type, public :: request
        integer :: machine
        integer :: customer
        character(len = 8) :: date
        character(len = 4) :: time
        real :: amount
        type(request), pointer :: next
    end type request
end module data_types

module linked_list
! This module contains the procedures to manipulate the
! linked list representing the outstanding transaction
! requests

    use data_types
    private

    public :: init, add, delete, list

contains

    subroutine init(head, tail)
    ! Initialize the empty list

        ! Dummy arguments
        type(request), pointer :: head, tail

        nullify (head, tail)         ! No successor
    end subroutine init

    subroutine add(new, head, tail)
    ! Add a new item to the end of the list

        ! Dummy arguments
        type(request), pointer :: new, head, tail

        ! Check to see if list is empty
        if (associated(head)) then
            ! List is not empty
            tail%next => new          ! Attach new request
            nullify (new%next)        ! at end of list
            tail => new               ! Reset tail pointer
        else
            ! List is empty
            head => new               ! Start up list with new
            tail => new
            nullify (tail%next)       ! No successor
        end if
    end subroutine add

    subroutine delete(head, tail, first)
    ! Return a pointer to the first item in the linked
    ! list, and remove it from the list
```

```
   ! Dummy arguments
   type(request), pointer :: head, tail, first

   ! Check to see if list is empty
   if (associated(head)) then
      ! List is not empty
      ! Check if more than one item in the list
      if (associated(head%next)) then
         ! More than 1 item in the list
         first => head          ! Return pointer to first item
         head => head%next      ! Remove item from list
      else
         ! Only 1 item in the list
         first => head          ! Return pointer to first item
         nullify (head, tail)   ! List is now empty
      end if

   else
      ! List is empty
      nullify (first)           ! Return no element
   end if
end subroutine delete

subroutine list(head)
! List the contents of the list

   ! Dummy argument
   type(request), pointer :: head

   ! Local variable
   type(request), pointer :: ptr

   print *," "
   print *,"Pending Request List"

   ! Check whether list is empty
   if (.not. associated(head)) then
      ! List is empty - print message
      print *,"The list is empty!"
   else
      ! List contains at least one item
      ! Set local pointer to head of list
      ptr => head

      ! Loop to print all items in the list
      do
         ! Print details of this request item
         print *,ptr%machine, ptr%customer, ptr%date,  &
                 ptr%time, ptr%amount

         ! Set pointer to next item
         ptr => ptr%next
         ! Exit loop if there are no more items in the list
         if (.not. associated(ptr)) then
            exit
         end if
      end do
```

```fortran
        end if
      end subroutine list
  end module linked_list

  module make_data
    use data types
    private
    public :: make

  contains

    subroutine make(i, j, x, item)
    ! Subroutine for simulating input requests

      ! Dummy variables
      integer, intent(inout) :: i, j
      real, intent(inout) :: x
      type(request), pointer :: item

      ! Local variable
      integer :: err

      ! Create a new transaction record
      allocate(item, stat = err)
      ! Check that it was created successfully
      if (err /= 0) then
         ! Print error message and terminate processing
         print *,"Machine out of memory"
         stop
      end if

      ! Assign a value to each field of the new record
      item%machine = i
      item%customer = j
      item%date = "06091997"
      item%time = "1215"
      item%amount = x
      i = i + 1
      j = j + 2
      x = x + 10
    end subroutine make

  end module make_data

  program bank
  ! This program simulates the operation of the cash machines
    use data_types
    use linked_list
    use make_data

    ! Declarations
    integer :: i, j, m
    real :: x
    type(request), pointer :: head, tail
    type(request), pointer :: item, first
```

```
i = 1
j = 1
x = 100.0
! Initialize empty list
call init(head, tail)

! Loop to add four items to the list
do m = 1, 4
    ! Create a transaction request
    call make(i, j, x, item)

    ! Add it to the list
    call add(item, head, tail)

    ! Print the current state of the list
    call list(head)
end do

! Loop to remove six items from the list
do m = 1, 6
    ! Remove item from head of list
    call delete(head,tail,first)

    ! Check to see if any item was removed
    if (associated(first)) then
        ! An item was removed - print it
        print *," "
        print *,"Request to be processed is:"
        print *,first%machine,first%customer,first%date,   &
                first%time,first%amount
    end if

    ! Print items remaining in list
    call list(head)
end do

end program bank
```

Note that we have not made the components of type request private. This is left as an exercise for the reader.

Figure 14.15 shows the results produced by executing this program.

```
            Pending Request List
            1 1 060919971215   1.0000000E+02

            Pending Request List
            1 1 060919971215   1.0000000E+02
            2 3 060919971215   1.1000000E+02

            Pending Request List
            1 1 060919971215   1.0000000E+02
            2 3 060919971215   1.1000000E+02
            3 5 060919971215   1.2000000E+02
```

Figure 14.15 The result of testing the banking simulation program.

```
                    Pending Request List
                    1 1 060919971215    1.0000000E+02
                    2 3 060919971215    1.1000000E+02
                    3 5 060919971215    1.2000000E+02
                    4 7 060919971215    1.3000000E+02

                    Request to be processed is:
                    1 1 060919971215    1.0000000E+02

                    Pending Request List
                    2 3 060919971215    1.1000000E+02
                    3 5 060919971215    1.2000000E+02
                    4 7 060919971215    1.3000000E+02

                    Request to be processed is:
                    2 3 060919971215    1.1000000E+02

                    Pending Request List
                    3 5 060919971215    1.2000000E+02
                    4 7 060919971215    1.3000000E+02

                    Request to be processed is:
                    3 5 060919971215    1.2000000E+02

                    Pending Request List
                    4 7 060919971215    1.3000000E+02

                    Request to be processed is:
                    4 7 060919971215    1.3000000E+02

                    Pending Request List
                    The list is empty!

                    Pending Request List
                    The list is empty!

                    Pending Request List
                    The list is empty!
```

Figure 14.15 (*cont.*)   The result of testing the banking simulation program.

Another dynamic data structure that can be created by using pointers is a
tree. This is similar in concept to a linked list, except that each node of the tree
has two or more pointer components. Figure 14.16 shows, diagrammatically,
how a tree with two such components can be represented, and it can be seen
that the tree is always represented as being upside-down! The single node from
which the tree 'grows' is, nevertheless, conventionally referred to as the **root** of
the tree, while each of the linked lists which make up the complete tree is
referred to as a **branch**.

A tree which splits into two branches at each node is called a **binary tree**,
one which splits into three at each node is called a **ternary tree**, and so on.

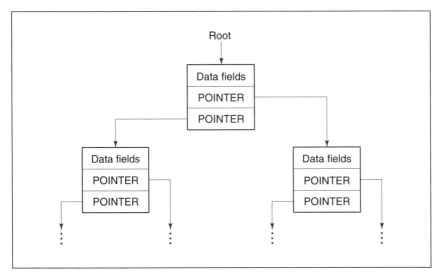

Figure 14.16 A binary tree.

Trees are very useful ways of representing many natural and artificial structures, and lend themselves, in particular, to recursive methods of traversing the branches of the tree in order to carry out various tasks upon the elements at its nodes. Example 14.3 shows how a binary tree can be used in this way to provide a much more efficient form of injection sort than that presented in Example 14.1.

☐ EXAMPLE 14.3 ●

1 Problem

Example 14.1 used an injection sort to order and list a file of contact names and addresses. A much improved version can be developed by storing the contact data in a binary tree instead of in an array.

2 Analysis

We shall use the same derived type for the details of each contact as before, but will define a second derived type from which to create a binary tree, as shown in Figure 14.17.

We can see how the sorting algorithm will work most easily, as is usually the case when working with lists and trees, by expressing the sequence of operations diagrammatically. We shall illustrate how a sequence of names (and associated other data) would be placed in the tree so that a subsequent process can 'walk through' the tree in the correct order. Initially the tree will be empty, and so the first contact, Michael Eaton, will be placed at the root, as shown in Figure 14.18, where we have used a form of representation which, in order to simplify the diagram, only shows the name of the contact.

When the next contact is to be added the last name is compared with the last name of the contact at the root, and the contact placed on the right or left, as appropriate, as shown in Figure 14.19.

Each time a new contact is to be added in the tree a decision is first made whether to go to the left or right of the root, and then to the left or right of the next node on that branch, and so on until the end of a branch is reached. Figures 14.20 to 14.23 show how several more names would be inserted using this approach.

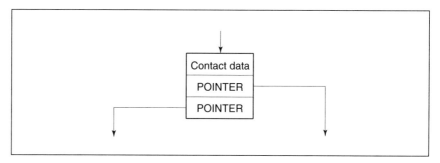

Figure 14.17   A node of a binary tree for a contact database.

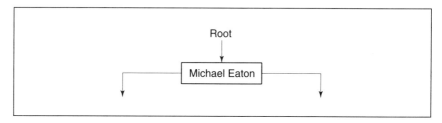

Figure 14.18   The tree after Michael Eaton has been added.

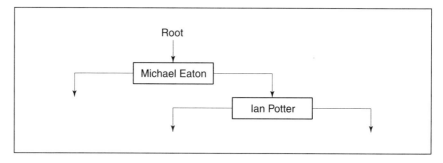

Figure 14.19   The tree after Ian Potter has been added.

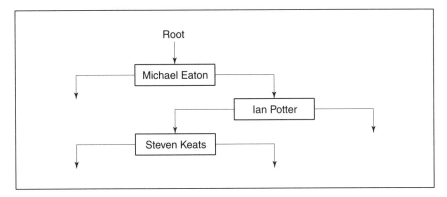

Figure 14.20   The tree after Steven Keats has been added.

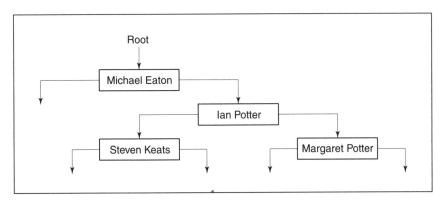

Figure 14.21   The tree after Margaret Potter has been added.

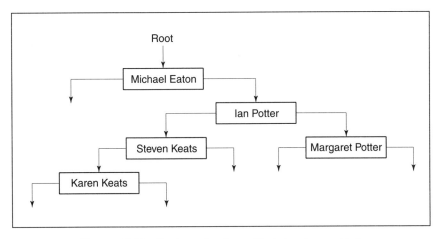

Figure 14.22   The tree after Karen Keats has been added.

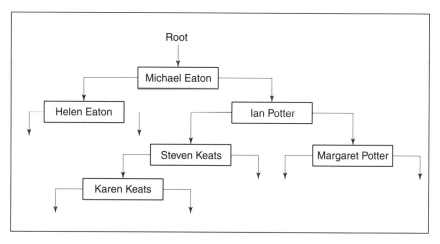

Figure 14.23 The tree after Helen Eaton has been added.

When the data is drawn in this fashion it is clear that, since at each node the item on the left precedes the node alphabetically, and the one on the right succeeds it, the process of printing the names in alphabetic order is simply a question of traversing the tree in a logical fashion. The process is first to move down the leftmost branches of the tree until there are no more nodes; this will be the first item. After printing this name the printing procedure must move up one level and print that name. This is followed by moving to the right node and down any left branches from there, before repeating the same process.

Notice, incidentally, that the order in which the contacts are entered will significantly affect the structure of the tree. Figure 14.24 shows how the tree

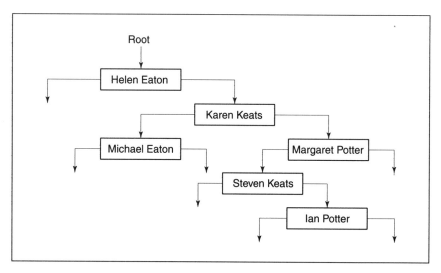

Figure 14.24 The tree if the names are entered in the reverse order.

would look if the same six names were entered as before, but in the reverse order. However, despite the fact that it looks quite different it retains the same properties, and the process described above for 'walking through' the tree will result in exactly the same order.

It is clear from the above discussion, moreover, that both insertion and printing are recursive processes, as, indeed, are most processes carried out on tree-structured data. We shall place two recursive subroutines to carry out these actions in a module, together with the two derived type definitions. As in the previous example we shall omit the data design and structure plan since the algorithm is almost trivially simple and it is the implementation of it using pointers that is of interest.

3 **Solution**

```
module contact_database

    public :: insert_contact, print_names
    ! Field lengths for contact data

    integer, parameter, private :: name_len = 15
    integer, parameter, private :: title_len = 20
    integer, parameter, private :: sex_len = 1
    integer, parameter, private :: phone_len = 20
    integer, parameter, private :: street_len = 40
    integer, parameter, private :: city_len = 20
    integer, parameter, private :: state_len = 20
    integer, parameter, private :: zip_len = 10

    ! Derived type for contact_data
    type, public :: contact_data
        character(len = name_len) :: first_name, last_name
        character(len = title_len) :: title
        character(len = sex_len) :: sex
        character(len = phone_len) :: telephone
        character(len = street_len) :: street
        character(len = city_len) :: city
        character(len = state_len) :: state
        character(len = zip_len) :: zip
    end type contact_data

    ! Derived type for binary tree containing contacts
    type, public :: contact_tree
        type (contact_data) :: data
        type (contact_tree), pointer :: left, right
    end type contact_tree

contains

    recursive subroutine insert_contact(contact, database)
    ! This subroutine inserts a contact in the binary tree

        ! Dummy arguments
        type (contact_data), intent(in) :: contact
        type (contact_tree), pointer :: database
```

```
      ! Check if (sub)tree is empty
      if (.not. associated(database)) then
          ! (sub)tree is empty, so insert contact at root
          allocate (database)
          database%data = contact
          nullify (database%left)
          nullify (database%right)

      ! Compare contact and the root of the (sub)tree
      else if ((contact%last_name < database%data%last_name)    &
          .or. ((contact%last_name == database%data%last_name)    &
          .and. (contact%first_name < database%data%first_name))) &
          then
          ! Contact comes first, so insert it in the left branch
          call insert_contact(contact, database%left)

      else
          ! Insert contact in the right branch
          call insert_contact(contact, database%right)
      end if

   end subroutine insert_contact

   recursive subroutine print_names(database)
   ! This subroutine prints the (sub)tree elements in order

      ! Dummy argument
      type (contact_tree), pointer :: database

      if (associated(database)) then
          call print_names(database%left)
          print "(t6, a, tr1, a)", database%data%first_name,  &
                                   database%data%last_name
          call print_names(database%right)
      end if
   end subroutine print_names

end module contact_database

program sort_contacts
! This program sorts a list of contacts into alphabetic
! order and then prints the contacts in that order

   use contact_database

   ! Declarations
   type (contact_data) :: contact_details
   type (contact_tree), pointer :: contacts    ! Database
   integer :: ios

   ! Ensure that contact database tree is empty
   nullify (contacts)

   ! Open data file
   open(unit = 7, file = "contacts",   &
            status = "old", action = "read")
```

```
! Loop to read contact details and insert them in the tree
do
    read (unit = 7, fmt = *, iostat = ios) contact_details
    ! Test for end of file
    if (ios < 0) then
        ! All data read and inserted
        close (unit = 7)
        exit
    else
        ! Insert this contact in the tree
        call insert_contact(contact_details, contacts)
    end if
end do

! All contacts now in database, so print names in order
call print_names(contacts)

end program sort_contacts
```

As can be seen, the use of recursive data structures and recursive procedures provides an extremely elegant method of processing data. It is also worth pointing out that the sorting of contacts into alphabetic order, first by last name and then by first name, is almost trivially easy.

It must also be emphasized that this method is totally dynamic, and, subject to the size of memory available, will cater equally easily for any number of contacts.

As we have often done, to keep the example as simple as possible, we have not made the components of type `contact_data` private. This is left as an exercise for the reader.

· □

In the last two examples, we have demonstrated the use of two of the most common forms of dynamic data structures based on pointers. These are also two of the simplest forms of linked data structures, and more general structures than lists and trees are feasible, in which the connectivity between nodes can be arbitrarily complex. There is a considerable amount of literature in this area; for those wishing to pursue the topic further, Knuth (1969) provides a comprehensive summary of the topic.

SELF-TEST EXERCISES 14.2

1   What are the restrictions on pointers and targets being procedure dummy arguments?

2   How is the result of a function declared to be a pointer, and what is the restriction on the use of such a function?

3   How can pointers be made components of a derived type? What is such a capability useful for?

4   What is a linked list?

5   Give three advantages of linked lists over arrays.

6   What is a tree structure? What is a binary tree?

7   Give one situation when a list is preferable to a tree, and one where a tree is preferable to a list.

8   Why is recursion useful when working with lists and trees?

SUMMARY

- Being a pointer is an attribute of a variable.
- A pointer type declaration statement specifies what type of entity, scalar or array, implicit or derived type, a pointer can point to.
- A variable can only be pointed to if it has the target attribute.
- A pointer has an association status that can be either undefined, associated or disassociated.
- A pointer can be associated with a target by a pointer assignment statement. The type, type parameters and rank of the pointer and target must agree.
- Once associated with a target, in any situation where the pointer occurs in which an entity of the type of the target is expected, the pointer is dereferenced to obtain the current value of the target.
- The association status of a pointer can be set to disassociated by the **nullify** statement.
- The association status of a pointer can be determined by use of the intrinsic function **associated**.
- The space for the element(s) of a scalar or an array pointer can be dynamically created and released by use of **allocate** and **deallocate** statements, respectively.
- Pointers and targets can be procedure dummy arguments.
- The result of a function can be a pointer.
- Pointers can be components of derived types.
- An array of pointers cannot be declared directly, but can be simulated by means of a derived type having a pointer component.
- A pointer component of a derived type can point to an object of the same type; this enables such structures as linked lists to be created.

- Linked lists and binary trees provide powerful data structuring capabilities, especially when used in recursive algorithms.

- A pointer cannot point to an array section that has a vector subscript.

- F syntax introduced in Chapter 14

Pointer assignment	*pointer_variable => pointer_target*
Pointer attribute	`pointer`
Target attribute	`target`
Allocate and dealocate statements	`allocate` (*pointer*(*dimension_specification*), `stat` = *status*)
	`allocate` (*pointer*(*dimension_specification*))
	`deallocate` (*pointer*, `stat` = *status*)
	`deallocate` (*pointer*)
Nullify statement	`nullify` (*pointer*)

PROGRAMMING EXERCISES

14.1   Exercise 13.6 explained how to find prime numbers by using the Sieve of Eratosthenes. In that exercise you used an allocatable array in which to store the integers to be tested. Modify that program (or write a new one) to use a pointer instead of an allocatable array.

Which approach do you prefer?

14.2   Write a program which asks the user for a positive integer (to test the program, keep this between 5 and 20). The program should then read that number of real numbers and store them in real variables that have been created, when the program is executed, by means of a linked list. The program should then print the numbers with the largest and smallest absolute values, and the mean of all the numbers.

When you have thoroughly tested this program, modify it so that the data is stored via a pointer array.

14.3   Make the components of the type `contact` in Example 14.1 private. Rewrite the code correspondingly.

14.4   Make the components of the type `request` in Example 14.2 private. Rewrite the code correspondingly.

14.5   Make the components of the type `contact_data` in Example 14.3 private. Rewrite the code correspondingly.

14.6   Write a function that has a rank-one, assumed-shape, real dummy argument. The function should, internally, create a rank-two, real pointer array whose (i, j)th element is the ith element of the input array divided by the jth element of the input array. Your procedure should calculate the maximum value in the rank-two array, return it as the function result, and deallocate the space for the pointer array.

14.7 Put the definition for a vector given in Section 14.4 into a module and add procedures for allocating and deallocating space for the elements of a vector, associating the element space of a vector with a user-specified real array, returning a pointer to the element space of a vector (use a pointer-valued function), and adding and subtracting two vectors. Write a suitable program to test your module.

14.8 Devise a derived type to store sparse matrices. These are matrices in which the great majority of elements are zero. The structure need only contain the non-zero elements. Write procedures to create and print sparse matrices, by printing only the non-zero elements and their locations. Write a procedure for adding two sparse matrices.

14.9 A doubly linked list is one in which every data item has pointers to the predecessor element (if any) and the successor element (if any). Define a derived type whose single data field is an integer and whose other fields are for the forward and backward pointers.

Maintain the doubly linked list so that the nodes (the derived type objects) are kept in increasing numerical order. Keep a pointer to the head of the list (initially disassociated). Keep the predecessor pointer of the first node in the list and the successor pointer of the last node in the list disassociated.

Write procedures to add and delete nodes from the list and to print, in order, all elements of the list.

For efficiency, keep a pointer that points to the last node added to the list. Use this pointer to efficiently add and delete nodes to and from the list. If items tend to come in grouped clumps, then it will be more efficient to start a search from the last position a node was added, rather than always start from the head of the list.

14.10 Example 14.3 showed how a binary tree could be used to store data in a pre-sorted order. Using a similar technique write a program that reads a list of words (from a file) and stores them in a data structure in such a way that they can easily be listed in (a) the order in which they were read, (b) the reverse of the order in which they were read, or (c) alphabetic order. (Hint: you will need several pointers for each element.)

14.11 A botanist investigating the habitat of various wild flowers divides the area being surveyed into squares of approximately 3 ft × 3 ft. The survey starts at the south-east corner of the survey area and identifies each square by the number of rows west and the number of rows north of the base corner. For each square, the number of flowers of each type is recorded by writing down the number of rows west and north, followed by the number and name of each flower in that square, for example:

> 6W 19N 37 bluebells 16 snowdrops 1 foxglove
> 7W 19N 13 bluebells 7 daffodils 19 snowdrops 4 dandelions
> etc.

Some areas were inaccessible, and for these the words 'not surveyed' are recorded after the two row numbers.

Write a program to read the data and produce a list of the locations of the five most populous flowers in the survey in the form:

```
The five most populous flowers were as follows:
1 Bluebells (735 found)
   Locations were: 6W 19N (37), 7W 19N (13), ...
2 Forget-me-not (692 found)
   Locations were: 12W 4N (81), 13W 3N (65), ...
```

Note that neither the range of west and north coordinates nor the number of different flowers can be known to the program until all the data has been read.

14.12 Modify the program you wrote for Exercise 14.11 so that the data structure created can be preserved in a file. A subsequent execution of the program can then read this file and use new data to extend the coverage of the survey. (Note that Section 14.4 pointed out that it is not possible to read or write pointer information, and that if a pointer-based data structure is to be written to a file it must first, therefore, be copied into another data structure which does not contain pointers.)

Additional input/output and file handling facilities

15

15.1 Additional edit descriptors for formatted input and output	**15.3** Direct access files
	15.4 Internal files
15.2 Non-advancing input and output	**15.5** The inquire statement

Input and output of information is both the most important part of any computing process, because it is the computer's only means of communicating with the outside world, and one of the most awkward, because the mechanical aspects of the interaction involve many compromises and inelegant activities.

In earlier chapters we have met the most useful features of F's input and output facilities, but there is a great deal more which, although less widely used, is of very great importance in particular classes of work. This chapter first discusses the remaining edit descriptors and input/output specifiers which complete the forms of input and output that have already been introduced, before moving on to introduce three additional methods of input and output.

15.1 Additional edit descriptors for formatted input and output

In Chapter 9 we introduced the principles of formats and edit descriptors, and described those edit descriptors which are most generally used for formatted input and output. However, there are a number of further edit descriptors (Figure 15.1) which can be extremely useful in certain situations, and we shall briefly describe these before moving on to the remaining input/output methods in the F language.

The $iw.m$ edit descriptor is an extended form of the i edit descriptor which only affects the output of integers; if used for input it is treated as though it were iw. On output it specifies the minimum number of digits which are to be printed including, if necessary, one or more leading zeros. The value of m must not be greater than w, while if it is zero and the value of the integer is also zero only blanks are output. Figure 15.2 gives an example of its use.

The next edit descriptor provides an alternative to the f edit descriptor for the output of real numbers, and takes either of the forms

$esw.d$
$esw.dee$

If used for input both forms have exactly the same effect as $fw.d$, and e may have any value (which is ignored).

For output, however, they cause the corresponding real value to be printed in a quite different format from that used by the f edit descriptor. As we have already seen, $fw.d$ will output a real number rounded to d decimal places with an external field of width w; $esw.d$, on the other hand, will output such a number in an external field of width w using an exponential format, where the mantissa has d decimal places, and the exponent consists of either an E, followed

Descriptor	Meaning
$iw.m$	Output integer with at least m digits
$esw.d$ $esw.dee$	Output real values in exponent/mantissa form
sp	Print + signs before positive numbers
ss	Do not print + signs before positive numbers
s	Allow processor to decide whether to print + signs before positive numbers
:	Terminate format if there are no more list items

Figure 15.1 More edit descriptors for input and output.

```
program extended_integer_editing
    integer :: i
    do i=-10,10,5
        print "(i5,i5.2,i5.0)",i,i,i
    end do
end program extended_integer_editing
```

Output

```
-10  -10  -10
 -5  -05   -5
  0   00
  5   05    5
 10   10   10
```

Figure 15.2 An example of i*w.m* editing.

by a sign and two digits, or a sign followed by three digits. In this form the mantissa will either be zero, or its absolute value will be greater than or equal to 1 and less than 10. Thus, using an es12.3 edit descriptor, the value 157.364 91 would be output in one of the following two forms:

```
◊◊◊1.574E+02
◊◊◊1.574+002
```

where, as before, ◊ represents a space. Obviously, only the form without the E is possible if the absolute value of the exponent is greater than 99.

In the extended form, es*w.dee*, which *must* be used if the absolute value of the exponent is more than 999, the exponent will consist of the letter E followed by a sign and *e* digits. Using an edit descriptor of es12.3e4 to output the value 157.364 91, for example, will result in the following result being displayed:

```
◊1.574E+0002
```

The remaining additional edit descriptors are not concerned with controlling the format of individual items, but with more general control of the formatting process. The first three of these control the display of plus signs during the output of numbers by any of the numeric edit descriptors. The sp (*sign print*) edit descriptor affects any numbers output by any following edit descriptors in this format, and causes a + sign to be placed before positive numbers (just as a - sign is placed before negative ones). An ss (*sign suppress*) edit descriptor has the opposite effect, and prevents a + sign being placed before positive numbers. Finally, an s edit descriptor restores the normal (default) situation which, for most systems, will be to omit + signs. Figure 15.3 illustrates the effect of these edit descriptors.

The final descriptor is the : edit descriptor, which is used to terminate a format if there are no more list items. This is not usually necessary, as the format will terminate in any case at the next edit descriptor which requires a list item.

```
             program sign_editing
                real,parameter :: a=1.2,b=-3.4,c=0.0
                integer,parameter :: i=1,j=-2,k=0

                print "(3f6.2,3i6)",a,b,c,i,j,k
                print "(sp,3f6.2,3i6)",a,b,c,i,j,k
                print "(ss,3f6.2,3i6)",a,b,c,i,j,k
                print "(s,3f6.2,3i6)",a,b,c,i,j,k
             end program sign_editing

         Output
             1.20 -3.40  0.00     1    -2     0
            +1.20 -3.40  0.00    +1    -2     0
             1.20 -3.40  0.00     1    -2     0
             1.20 -3.40  0.00     1    -2     0
```

Figure 15.3 An example of the effect of using sp, ss and s edit descriptors.

15.2   Non-advancing input and output

One of the fundamental principles of input and output in F is that every **read**, **write** or **print** statement normally begins a new record. However, there are some situations in which it would be convenient to be able to read part of a record, and read the rest later, or to write part of a record, and write some more later. F provides for this requirement by means of **non-advancing input and output**.

Non-advancing input/output can only take place on a formatted file that is connected to an input or output unit for sequential access, and which is not using list-directed formatting. With non-advancing input/output it is possible to:

- read or write a record by a sequence of statements, each statement accessing a portion of the record instead of one statement processing the complete record;

- be informed of the length (that is, the number of characters read) of a formatted sequential input record; and

- be notified when an end-of-record has been encountered during the processing of a **read** statement.

Non-advancing input or output is specified by the inclusion of an advance specifier in a **read** or **write** statement. This takes the form

advance = *advance_mode*

where *advance_mode* is a character expression which, after the removal of any trailing blanks, is either `yes` or `no`.

If it is `yes`, or if the `advance` specifier is omitted, then input or output, as appropriate, is carried out in the normal (advancing) mode and, at the completion of the statement, the file is positioned after the end of the last record read or written. However, if an `advance=no` specifier is present then the input or output is carried out in non-advancing mode.

In the case of a non-advancing **read** statement there are three possibilities:

- If the **read** statement did not attempt to read beyond the end of the record, and there were no errors and no end-of-file condition set, then the file position is unchanged, and the next **read** statement will start to read the same record, starting immediately after the last character read.

- If the **read** statement did attempt to read beyond the end of the record then an end-of-record condition will be set, and can be tested for by use of the `iostat` specifier. The file will be positioned immediately after the end of the record just read.

  Note that an end-of-record condition is not an error, and so if it is not detected by means of an `iostat` specifier then the program will continue without any indication that some of the data items read may have been null.

- If there was an error, or if an end-of-file condition was set, then the file will be positioned immediately after the end of the record just read.

It is frequently useful, when carrying out non-advancing input, to be able to determine how many characters have been read. This is achieved by use of the **size** specifier, which takes the form

size = *character_count*

where *character_count* is an integer variable. At the conclusion of the non-advancing **read** statement the variable *character_count* becomes defined with the number of characters read, excluding any inserted as padding characters.

Thus, the statement

```
read (unit=input,fmt=in_fmt,advance="yes",size=count,   &
      iostat=read_status) var1,var2,var3
```

will carry out non-advancing input from the file connected to unit `input` using the format defined by the character variable `in_fmt`, and will store the number of characters read in the integer variable `count`. The integer variable `read_status` will be set to an appropriate value to indicate the success, or otherwise, of the reading operation.

Non-advancing output is more straightforward than non-advancing input, and there are only two possibilities:

- If there were no errors then the file position is unchanged, and the next **write** statement will write to the same record, starting immediately after the last character written.

- If there was an error then the file will be positioned immediately after the end of the record just written.

◻ **EXAMPLE 15.1** ◦

1 **Problem**

In Example 10.2 a set of data was read from a file, in which each record had the following format:

Columns 1–20   Name

Column   23   Sex   = F if female
                       = M if male

Column   25   Job status = 1 if in full-time education
                            = 2 if in full-time employment
                            = 3 if in part-time employment
                            = 4 if temporarily unemployed
                            = 5 if not working or seeking a job

This was followed by one or more items depending upon the job status of the respondent:

Job status = 1   columns 28, 29   Age
          = 2   columns 28–31   Monthly salary
          = 3   columns 28–31   Monthly salary
                 columns 34–37   Other monthly income
          = 4   columns 28, 29   Age
                 columns 32–34   No. of months unemployed
          = 5   columns 28, 29   Age
                 column 31   Code
                                  = 1 if looking after children
                                  = 2 if looking after other relatives
                                  = 3 for any other reason

In Example 10.2 an input procedure was written to read the data and store the relevant details in a derived type array for subsequent use by other procedures. The problem of not knowing the format of the whole record until the first part had been read was dealt with by the crude method of only reading the first part of each record, and then backspacing the file and re-reading the rest in the correct format.

Rewrite the input procedure written in Example 10.2 to use non-advancing input, so that each record is only read once.

2 Analysis

The only change that needs to be made to the previous version is in the actual reading of the records. In this case the first three items will first be read using non-advancing input, and then the remaining one or two items, depending upon the code read as the third item. The data design will therefore be exactly as in the previous example, except that we shall define constants for the processor-dependent codes for end-of-file and end-of-record and place them in a separate module; the structure plan will, however, be altered slightly:

Structure plan

1   Request name of data file and open it on *unit*
2   Repeat up to *max_datasets* times
   2.1   Read first three items of next record
   2.2   If end of file then exit from loop
   2.3   If error then set *error_code* to −2 and exit from loop
   2.4   Select case on job status
      status is 1
      2.4.1   Read age
      2.4.2   Set salary, other income, months unemployed and code to unused
      status is 2
      2.4.3   Read salary
      2.4.4   Set age, other income, months unemployed and code to unused
      status is 3
      2.4.5   Read salary and other income
      2.4.6   Set age, months unemployed and code to unused
      status is 4
      2.4.7   Read age and months unemployed
      2.4.8   Set salary, other income and code to unused
      status is 5
      2.4.9   Read age and code
      2.4.10 Set salary, other income and months unemployed to unused
   2.5   Copy local record to array
3   If no end-of-file read set *error_code* to −3
4   Return number of data sets read

3 **Solution**

```
module error_codes
! This module contains PROCESSOR-DEPENDENT error codes

   integer,parameter,public :: end_of_record = -1002,  &
                               end_file = -1001

end module error_codes

module survey
! This module contains a type definition and constants
! for use with the input and processing of survey data,
! together with the input procedure itself

use error_codes
private

   ! Procedure declaration
   public :: input

   ! Type definition for survey response
   type, public :: survey_info
      private
      character(len=20) :: name
      character(len=1) :: sex
      integer :: job_status,age,months_jobless,at_home_code
      real :: salary,other_income
   end type survey_info

   ! Various codes
   character(len=1),parameter,private ::         &
           female="F",male="M"                    !sex
   integer,parameter,private ::                   &
           ft_ed=1,ft_job=2,pt_job=3,             & ! job status
           no_job=4,at_home=5,                    & ! ----------
           ch_minder=1,rel_minder=2,other=3,      & ! at home code
           unused=-1                                ! unused code

contains

   subroutine input(inf,max_datasets,survey_data,num_ datasets, &
                    error_code)
   ! This subroutine reads up to max_datasets records prepared
   ! as follows, returning the number read in num_datasets

   ! Columns 1-20 name
   !          23 sex (M or F)
   !          25 job status (1-5)
   !       28,29 age - for status 1, 4 or 5
   !       28-31 monthly salary - for status 2 and 3
   !       32-34 other monthly income - for status 3
   !       32-34 months unemployed - for status 4
   !          31 special code (1-3) - for status 5
```

```fortran
! Arguments
integer, intent(in) :: inf,max_datasets
integer, intent(out) :: num_datasets,error_code
type(survey_info), dimension(:), intent(out) :: survey_data

! Local variables
character(len=30) :: data_file
character(len=20) :: name
character(len=1) :: sex
integer :: i,ios,status,age,months,code
real :: salary,income

! Ask for name of data file
! A maximum of 3 attempts will be allowed to open the file
do i=1,3
   print *,"Type name of data file"
   read "(a)",data_file
   ! Open file at beginning
   open (unit=inf,file=data_file,position="rewind",   &
         status="old",action="readwrite",iostat=ios)
   if (ios==0) then
      exit
   end if
   ! Error when opening file - try again
   print *,"Unable to open file - please try again"
end do

! If open was unsuccessful after 3 attempts return error=-1
if (ios/=0) then
   error_code = -1
   return
else
! Successful file opening
   error_code = 0
end if

! Loop to read data
do i=1,max_datasets
   ! Read first part of next set of data
   read (unit=inf,fmt="(a20,t23,a1,t25,i1)",   &
         advance="no",iostat=ios) name,sex,status

   ! Check for errors and end of file
   select case (ios)
   case (end_file)              ! End of file - no more data
      exit

   case (end_of_record,1:)    ! Error during reading
      error_code = -2
      exit
   end select

   ! Read more data according to status code
   ! Note that position 1 in the remainder of the record is
   ! position 26 in the original record
   select case (status)
```

```
      case (ft_ed)
         ! Read age and set other items to unused code
         read (unit=inf,fmt="(t3,i2)") age
         months = unused
         salary = unused
         income = unused
         code = unused

      case (ft_job)
         ! Read salary details and set other items to unused
         read (unit=inf,fmt="(t3,f4.0)") salary
         age = unused
         income = unused
         months = unused
         code = unused

      case (pt_job)
         ! Read income details and set other items to unused
         read (unit=inf,fmt="(t3,f4.0,t9,f4.0)") salary,income
         age = unused
         months = unused
         code = unused

      case (no_job)
         ! Read age and months unemployed and set other
         ! items to unused
         read (unit=inf,fmt="(t3,i2,t7,i3)") age,months
         salary = unused
         income = unused
         code = unused

      case (at_home)
         ! Read age and code and set other items to unused
         read (unit=inf,fmt="(t3,i2,t6,i1)") age,code
         salary = unused
         income = unused
         months = unused
      end select

      ! Record is now fully input, so copy to main data array
      survey_data(i) = survey_info(name,sex,status,age, &
                                   months,code,salary,income)

   end do

   ! All data input - check if end of file was read
   if (i > max_datasets) then
      error_code = -3
   end if

   ! Save number of records read and return
   num_datasets = i-1

end subroutine input

end module survey
```

Note that non-advancing input is not specified when reading the record for the second time, as this will always be the last time that a record is read, and it is important that the file is positioned after the end of the record so that the next record will be read properly.

Notice also that, as in the previous version, the checks made that the reading of data from the data file has been error-free have only been carried out the first time that a record is read. This will deal with the problem of detecting the end-of-file which indicates that there is no more data, but there is always a theoretical possibility of some hardware problem causing an error during reading, and this should be checked for in all cases in a 'production' program.

SELF-TEST EXERCISES 15.1

1   What are the advantages of using an es edit descriptor for the output of real numbers over an f edit descriptor?

2   What will be printed by the following program?

```
program test_15_1_2
   integer, dimension(0:6) :: powers_of_two
   real, dimension(0:6) :: inverse_powers_of_two
   integer :: i,j
   powers_of_two = (/ (2**j,j=0,6) /)
   inverse_powers_of_two = (/ (1.0/2**j,j=0,6) /)
   do i=0,6
      print "(i8,i8.4,f8.4,es15.4,es15.4e4)",   &
            powers_of_two(i),powers_of_two(i),   &
            inverse_powers_of_two(i),            &
            inverse_powers_of_two(i),            &
            inverse_powers_of_two(i)
   end do
end program test_15_1_2
```

3   What is the difference between advancing and non-advancing input? When should you use each type?

4   What is the difference between advancing and non-advancing output? When should you use each type?

15.3   Direct access files

In Chapter 10 we defined an external file as a sequence of records, either formatted or unformatted, which exists outside the program on some external medium. We also indicated that such a file could be stored either in a sequential manner, in which records are written and read in sequence, or in a random manner, in which records are written and read in any specified order. Sequential files are perfectly satisfactory for most purposes, but there are a number of situations in which it is more convenient to write and/or read records in a non-sequential fashion – for example, when interrogating a database. F, therefore, allows a file to be written and read in a **direct access** manner as well as in a sequential manner.

To do this, however, the file must first be connected to the program for direct access, rather than the (default) sequential access mode that we have used up to now. This is achieved by using the `access` specifier in the **open** statement for the file:

```
access = "direct"
```

If an **open** statement specifies direct access it must contain a **recl** specifier, which, as we saw in Section 10.3, takes the form

```
recl = record_length
```

When used with a direct access file this specifies that *all* the records in the file will have the same length, *record_length*, which is measured in characters if the file is formatted and in processor-defined units if it is an unformatted file. Since direct access files cannot normally be transferred to another type of computer there is normally no reason for converting the values being written to the file into their character representation, with the result that direct access files are, almost invariably, also unformatted files.

In order to write to, or read from, a direct access file it is necessary to define which record is to be written or read by use of a `rec` specifier in the **read** or **write** statement. This takes the form

```
rec = record_number
```

where *record_number* is an integer expression *with a positive value*, which specifies the **record number** of the record to be read or written. Thus the statement

```
write (unit=7,rec=20) a,b,c,d
```

will write the values of a, b, c and d as an unformatted record to record 20 of the direct access file connected to unit 7, and

```
read (unit=7,rec=next_rec) w,x,y,z
```

will read the record from the same file whose record number is the value of the integer variable next_rec.

Note, also, that if a format used to write (or read) a formatted direct access file specifies more than one record, then each successive record will be given a number one greater than the previous one. Thus the statement

```
write (unit=8,fmt="(10f12.2)",rec=75) array(1:100)
```

will cause 10 records to be written, since the format specifies that each record contains 10 real numbers; these records will be numbered from 75 to 84, inclusive.

If an input or output statement includes a rec specifier then it is a direct access input or output statement; if it does not include a rec specifier then it is a sequential input or output statement. *Note, however, that direct access input or output may not use list-directed formatting, nor may it use non-advancing input or output.*

It is important to understand that, although the records in a file are numbered consecutively, starting at record 1, they may be written in any order. Once a record has been written it may never be deleted, but it may be overwritten. The effect of this can be visualized by imagining a file to consist of a very large number of potential, fixed-size, records available in the file, all of which are 'hidden' by a movable cover in a newly created file, as shown in Figure 15.4. Once record *n* has been written then it becomes available by sliding the cover,

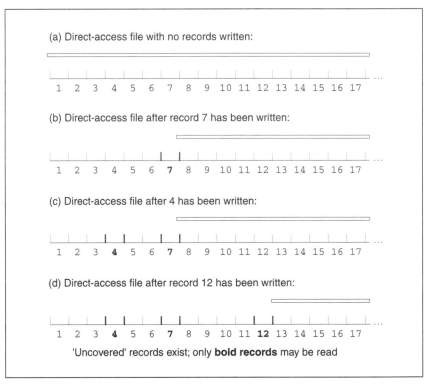

Figure 15.4   A representation of a direct access file.

thus also making visible all those records that 'precede it' (that is, records 1 to $n - 1$) – although such records cannot be read until some value has been written to them.

It may appear, at first sight, that the rule that requires every record in a direct access file to have the same length, namely that defined by the recl specifier in the **open** statement, may be somewhat restrictive. This is not the case, however, since the record will always be extended to the specified length if it would otherwise be too short; the specified record length can, therefore, be considered as a *maximum* record length, and as long as there is no attempt to exceed this maximum there will be no problem.

Note that if an unformatted record would be too short then it will be extended with undefined values in order to make it the correct length. If a formatted record would be too short then it will be extended with trailing blanks.

☐ EXAMPLE 15.2   ·

1 Problem

The superintendent of a college chemistry department wishes to keep a record of all the chemicals in the department's store on a computer, so that each day the record of all material moved from the store to the laboratories can be used to update the quantities held in the store, and identify which items need to be reordered from the suppliers. In other words, the department wishes to develop a simple stock control system.

Define the structure of the master file used to store details of stocks held, and write a program which can be used to update this file with the daily stock movements. Ignore the problems associated with adding new chemicals to the master file, and of deleting unused chemicals, and assume that only the quantities will change.

2 Analysis

The major difficulty with any problem of this nature is that the updating information (that is, the stores documents recording the issue of chemicals, in this case) will be in an arbitrary order, whereas the information in the master file which is to be updated will be stored in a predefined order – which will, by definition, be different from the 'random' order of the data. There are three, well-established, approaches to overcoming this incompatibility:

1 (a) The master data is stored in a sequential file and read into memory at the start of processing.
   (b) All updating of the master file is then carried out in memory.
   (c) At the completion of processing, the updated information is written to a new sequential file, ready for next time.

2. (a) The master data is stored in a sequential file.
    (b) Before starting to update the master file, all the updating details are sorted into the same order as the records in the master file.
    (c) The master file is then updated sequentially.

3. (a) The data is stored in a direct access file.
    (b) The master file is updated in the order of the input data.

Each of these approaches has its advantages and disadvantages. For example, if the master file is small then the much faster updating possible through carrying out the whole process in memory is the dominant factor; however, this approach is not suitable for large master files because of the large memory requirements.

The second approach was the only approach in the days before the widespread availability of disk drives, with their inherent random access capability. For many years almost all business and commercial data-processing programs spent a significant amount of their time sorting files into the correct order for the next operation, with the result that significant efforts were devoted to developing faster and more effective sorting algorithms for different types of sorting needs.

However, with the advent of large and economical random access storage, in the form of magnetic and magneto-optical disks, the third approach is the preferred one, other than for small master files, when the first method may still be preferred. We shall, therefore, use a direct access file to store the details of the stocks held of the various chemicals.

Each record in the file will contain the following fields, for which we shall define a derived type stock_record:

Name of chemical (in its symbolic form, e.g. H2SO4 for sulphuric acid, H_2SO_4)
Units (e.g. grams, litres, etc.)
Current stock level
Reorder level
Unit order quantity
Maximum stock

The program will update the current stock levels and then, when all input data has been processed, will compare the current stocks of every chemical with the reorder level and issue a request to order additional supplies of those below that level. These orders will be for multiples of the unit order quantity to bring the total stock to as close as possible *below* the maximum stock. A refinement would be to include the name and address of the supplier in the file and to print the orders, but that is not necessary for this example.

The only remaining problem is identifying which record in the master file contains the information relating to a particular chemical. Since records in a direct access file are identified by their record number, running upwards from 1, it is clearly necessary to relate the name of the chemical to a record number. We shall adopt a simple, albeit inefficient, method of storing all the chemical symbols in an array and using the index of the name in the array as the record number. We shall, however, return to this in a subsequent refinement to the program.

In order to emphasize the structure of the overall program, and in accordance with good practice, we shall divide the bulk of the code into two subroutines, one to update the master file and the other to produce any necessary reorder requests. In addition we shall require a function to return the record number for a specified chemical, and a subroutine to initialize the **look-up table** of chemicals.

We can now proceed to the final design of the program.

Module `stock_control`

Data design

Purpose	Type	Name
A Module constants		
Size of look-up table	`integer`	`max_names`
Length of names	`integer`	`max_len`
Name of master file	`character(len=20)`	`master_file_name`
Master file unit	`integer`	`master_file`
Record length	`integer`	`rec_len`
B Type definition		
Stock record	`[character(len=max_len),`	`stock_record`
	`character(len=8),`	
	`real, real, real, real]`	
C Module variable		
Look-up table of names	`character(len=max_len)`	`chemical`

Subroutine `get_chemicals`

Data design

Purpose	Type	Name
Dummy argument	`logical`	`error`
Stock record	`stock_record`	`stock`
do loop variable	`integer`	`i`

Structure plan

1 Set `error` to *false*

2 Repeat for `i` from 1 to `max_names`

    2.1 Read data record `i`

    2.2 Store name of chemical in `chemical(i)`

    2.3 If error during reading

        2.3.1 Print warning

        2.3.2 Return with `error` set to *true*

Function record_number

Data design

Purpose	Type	Name
Dummy argument	**character**(**len**=max_len)	item
Function result	**integer**	index_num
do loop variable	**integer**	i

Structure plan

> **1** Repeat for i from 1 to max_names
>   **1.1** If item=chemical(i) exit from loop
>
> **2** If a match was made
>   **2.1** Return value of i
>   otherwise
>   **2.2** Return zero

Subroutine update

Data design

Purpose	Type	Name
Dummy argument	**logical**	error
Amount issued	**real**	amount
Stock record	stock_record	stock
Chemical name	**character**	name
do loop variable	**integer**	i
iostat variable	**integer**	ios
Record number	**integer**	rec_num

Structure plan

> **1** Set error to *false*
> **2** Repeat the following
>   **2.1** Read next update record (name, amount)
>   **2.2** Find index for this chemical using function record_number
>   **2.3** If rec_num > 0 then
>   **2.3.1** Read record index
>   **2.3.2** Update current stock level
>   **2.3.3** Write updated record back to master file
>   **2.3.4** If error during reading or writing then
>   **2.3.4.1** Print warning
>   **2.3.4.2** Return with error set to *true*

otherwise
2.3.5 If name is END then
     2.3.5.1 Exit from loop
    otherwise
     2.3.5.2 Print warning
     2.3.5.3 Return with error set to *true*

Note that an alternative method would have been to carry out the test for the
END input record immediately after the **read** statement. However, this will mean
that the test will be carried out for every update record, whereas the approach
shown above will only check for end of data if the record is not a valid update
record.

Subroutine reorder

Data design

Purpose	Type	Name
Stock record	stock_record	stock
Order quantity	**real**	quantity
do loop variable	**integer**	i

Structure plan

1   Repeat for each record in the file
    1.1   Read the record
    1.2   If error during reading then
        1.2.1   Print warning
       otherwise
        1.2.2   If current stock level < reorder level then
            1.2.2.1   Calculate number of order units required
            1.2.2.2   Print order details

Program stock_update

Data design

Purpose	Type	Name
iostat variable	**integer**	ios
Error flag	**logical**	error

Structure plan

1 Open master file

2 If error during opening

    2.1 Print error message

    otherwise

    2.2 Get list of chemicals on database using subroutine `get_chemicals`

    2.3 If no errors then

        2.3.1 Update stock records using subroutine `update`

        2.3.2 If no errors then

            2.3.2.1 Print list of required orders using subroutine `reorder`

            otherwise

            2.3.2.2 Print error message

        otherwise

        2.3.3 Print error message

3 Solution

```
module stock_control
! This module contains the data and procedures required to
! operate a simple stock control system

    public :: get_chemicals,record_number,update,reorder

    ! Global constant declarations
    integer,parameter,public :: max_names=100,max_len=20
    character(len=20),parameter,public :: &
       file_name="chemical_supplies"
    integer,parameter,public :: file_unit=7

    ! Note that the calculation of the record length is processor
    ! dependent; the following assumes one unit per character
    ! and four units per real value
    integer,parameter,private :: char_store=1,real_store=4
    integer,parameter,public :: &
       rec_len = char_store*(max_len+8) + real_store*4

    ! Derived type for stock records
    type,public :: stock_record
       character(len=max_len) :: name
       character(len=8) :: units
       real :: current,re_order,unit_order,max
    end type stock_record

    ! Look-up table of chemicals in the database
    character(len=max_len),dimension(max_names),private :: &
       chemical

contains
```

```
subroutine get_chemicals(error)
! This subroutine reads the names of the chemicals
! from the database

   ! Dummy argument
   logical, intent(out) :: error

   ! Local variables
   integer :: i,ios
   type(stock_record) :: stock

   ! Initialize error flag
   error = .false.

   ! Read first item from each record and place it in the
   ! look-up array chemical
   do i=1,max_names
      read (unit=file_unit,rec=i,iostat=ios) stock
      if (ios==0) then
         ! Store name in look-up table
         chemical(i) = stock%name
      else
         ! Error in reading master file - abort set-up process
         print *,"Error in reading master file."
         print *,"Processing terminated."
         error = .true.
         exit
      end if
   end do
end subroutine get_chemicals

function record_number(item) result(index_num)
! This function returns the index of item in the look-up
! table chemical

   ! Dummy argument and result variable
   character(len=*), intent(in) :: item
   integer :: index_num

   ! Local variable
   integer :: i

   ! Search for item name in look-up table
   do i=1,max_names
      if (item==chemical(i)) then
         exit
      end if
   end do

   ! Check to see if a match was found
   if (i>max_names) then
      ! No match made - return zero
      index_num = 0
   else
      ! Match made - return index
      index_num = i
   end if
end function record_number
```

```
subroutine update(error)
! This subroutine updates the master file

   ! Dummy variable
   logical, intent(out) :: error

   ! Local variables
   real :: amount
   integer :: i,ios,rec_num
   type(stock_record) :: stock
   character(len=max_len) :: name

   ! Inform user of requirements
   print *,"Type stock issues as chemical followed by        &
         quantity"
   print *,"issued (negative) or received (positive)"
   print *,"To end data type the word END and a zero"

   ! Initialize error flag to false
   error = .false.

   ! Loop to read details and update master file
   do
      read *,name,amount
      ! Get record number for this chemical
      rec_num = record_number(name)

      ! Check if this was a valid name
      if (rec_num>0) then

         ! OK - so update master file
         read (unit=file_unit,rec=rec_num,iostat=ios) stock
         if (ios==0) then
            ! Update current stock and rewrite record
            stock%current = stock%current + amount
            write (unit=file_unit,rec=rec_num,iostat=ios) stock
            if (ios/=0) then
               ! Error during writing
               print *,"Error during updating this ",         &
                     "chemical's record in the master file."
               print *,"The record may now be incorrect!"
               error = .true.
            end if

         else
            ! Error during reading - ignore this data
            print *,"Error during updating this",              &
                  "chemical's record in the master file."
            print *,"The record is unchanged"
            error = .true.
         end if
```

```
      else
         ! Invalid chemical name - check if end of data
         if (name=="END") then
            exit
         else
            ! Unknown chemical - print error message
            print *,name," is not in the master file."
            print *,"This line of data has been ignored!"
            error = .true.
         end if
      end if
   end do
end subroutine update

subroutine reorder()
! This subroutine reorders any chemicals whose stock level
! has fallen below the specified reorder level

   ! Local variables
   integer :: i,ios,num_units
   real :: quantity
   type(stock_record) :: stock

   ! Print header
   print "(a,2/,a,t30,a,2/)",                        &
         "The following items need reordering:",     &
         "Chemical","Quantity"

   ! Loop to check stock levels
   do i=1,max_names
      read (unit=file_unit,rec=i,iostat=ios) stock
      if (ios==0) then
         ! Check if stocks are below reorder level
         if (stock%current < stock%re_order) then
            ! More stock required - calculate order quantity
            quantity = stock%max - stock%current
            num_units = ceiling(quantity/stock%unit_order)
            quantity = num_units*stock%unit_order

            ! Reduce order quantity if it would exceed
            ! maximum stock
            if (stock%current+quantity > stock%max) then
               quantity = quantity - stock%unit_order
            end if
            print "(a,t30,f10.2,tr1,2a,f10.2,tr1,2a)",   &
                  stock%name,quantity,stock%units,        &
                  " (in units of ", stock%unit_order,     &
                  stock%units,")"
         end if
      else
         ! Error during reading - ignore this data
         print *,"Error during checking this ",          &
                 "chemical's record in the master file."
         print *,"No check for reordering made!"
      end if
   end do
```

```
      end subroutine reorder

  end module stock_control

  program stock_update
      use stock_control

  ! This program updates a stock control file of chemicals
  ! and produces a list of order requests

  ! Local variable
      integer :: ios
      logical :: error

  ! Open master file
      open (unit=file_unit, file=file_name, access="direct",   &
            status="old", action="readwrite", recl=rec_len,    &
            iostat=ios)
      if (ios/=0) then
  ! Error during opening master file
          print *,"Error during opening of master file"
          print *,"Please check file and try again"
      else
  ! Get list of chemicals in the data base
          call get_chemicals(error)

  ! Check that list of chemicals read successfully
          if (.not. error) then
  ! No errors, so update master file
              call update(error)

  ! All updating now carried out - check if any errors
              if (.not. error) then
  ! No errors, so search for chemicals in need of reordering
                  call reorder()
              end if
          end if
      end if
  end program stock_update
```

Note that the program has checked, at each stage, that the master file has been read or written without error. *This is extremely important when updating a master file in this way.* However, there is always a danger that an execution error might leave the file in a damaged state, and so it is normally not recommended to update such a file directly in the way that we have done here. One approach is to make a **backup** copy before updating commences, so that if an error should occur the original version of the file can still be used. An alternative is to have a cycle of, typically, three files and to update from one to the next in the cycle; this approach, which is conventionally referred to as the **grandfather–father–son** method, ensures that the previous *two* versions of the file are always available in case an error is detected during, or after, processing. We shall return to this topic in Section 15.5.

The other point that should be mentioned concerns the method of identifying the record number of the master file record associated with a specified chemical. Obviously a sequential search is not very efficient, particularly if there are a large number of records, and so we shall briefly examine an alternative approach.

This establishes the record number corresponding to a particular chemical by using a different form of table, which must be kept in a file because of the method used for inserting new names. This uses what is known as a **hashing technique** to create a special form of table, known as a **hash table**, in which the names are not stored sequentially but, instead, are used to derive an integer in a given range (the same as the extent of the table) which identifies the place in the table at which the name will be stored. If that place is already in use then a new index is calculated, possibly by as simple an algorithm as adding one, and that new index is tried.

The advantage of this approach is that it is only necessary to search a small number of elements of the table to find a name instead of carrying out a sequential search through the whole table until a match is found. A further advantage is that the identical method can be used for inserting new entries, since if an empty cell in the table is encountered before a match is made then that is the correct place to insert the new name; deletion is more difficult as it requires a reorganization of the whole table, but deletion of items from the simpler look-up tables will also require the restructuring of the master file if the 'empty' spaces are to be used for other purposes.

We shall not provide a complete solution to the problem using a hash table, but will present an alternative version of the function record_number which assumes that some other procedure has read the hash table from a file into the array chemical, which is now organized as a hash table and not as a simple look-up table:

```
function record_number(item) result(index_num)
! This function returns the index of item in the hash
! table chemical (in the module)

    ! Dummy argument and result variable
    character (len=*), intent(in) :: item
    integer :: index_num

    ! Local variables
    integer :: i,start

    ! Calculate start point for table search
    start = modulo(ichar(item(1:1))*ichar(item(2:2)), &
                   max_names)+1

    ! Search from here to end of table
    do i=start,max_names
        if (chemical(i)==item) then
            ! Match made - return index
            index_num = i
            return
```

```
          else if (chemical(i)=="") then
             ! Empty cell means item is not in table - return 0
             index_num = 0
             return
          end if
       end do

       ! No match yet made, and all cells full
       ! Search remainder of table
       do i=1,start-1
          if (chemical(i)==item) then
             ! Match made - return index
             index_num = i
             return
          else if (chemical(i)=="") then
             ! Empty cell means item is not in table - return 0
             index_num = 0
             return
          end if
       end do

       ! Complete table has been searched without either finding
       ! a match or finding an empty cell
       ! Return -1 to indicate that table is full
       index_num = -1

    end function record_number
```

Note that the initial point to start searching the table has been determined by multiplying the numeric value of the first two characters in the chemical's name together and then taking the remainder after dividing by the size of the hash table; finally, one is added to obtain a value which lies between 1 and max_names. The method used to calculate the initial value, start, is not particularly important as long as it gives a fairly wide spread of values for any group of names, and it can be determined quickly.

The final point to make about this version is that if the table is full then a negative value has been returned. This can be treated in the same way as zero in this program, but would be of importance in a further procedure which used this function to establish where to insert a new name. If the function returned the value zero, then the name could be inserted at that point, but if it returned a negative value then it would indicate that it was not possible to add any more entries to the table.

15.4 Internal files

An **internal file** is not really a file at all but behaves like one, and can be used to great advantage in particular situations. It is actually a means whereby the power and flexibility of F's formatting process can be used to convert information from one format to another without the use of any external media. Such a file may be a character scalar variable, a character array element, a character substring, or a character array.

In the first three cases the internal file consists of a single record, while if it is an array it consists of a sequence of records, each of which corresponds to one element of the array. In the latter case the whole file must be input or output by means of a single statement, since a **read** or **write** statement on an internal file *always* starts at the beginning of the file.

An internal file can only be read by a sequential formatted **read** statement. It can only be written by a sequential formatted **write** statement, or it can be created by any other appropriate means — for example by an assignment statement or by input from some other source.

An internal file is identified by using the name of a character entity in an input or output statement in place of the unit identifier. Thus we may write

```
character(len=30) :: line
write (unit=line,fmt="(3f10.4)") x,y,z
read (unit=line,fmt="(3(f6.0,tr4))") x,y,z
```

which would first create a character string in the variable `line` consisting of the representations of the values of x, y and z with four decimal places, and would then read these back into the same variables in such a way as to ignore the digits following the decimal point. The effect would, therefore, be to truncate the values of the three variables by eliminating any fractional parts. (Note that the same effect could be achieved by use of the intrinsic function **int**.)

The following example illustrates another use of an internal file, namely to allow a record of an external file to be read more than once without the need to backspace the external file.

■ **EXAMPLE 15.3** •

1 **Problem**

Example 15.1 used non-advancing input to read data in which the format of the second part of each record varied, depending upon the value of a code in the earlier part of the record. An alternative approach would be to use an internal file.

2 **Analysis**

The program will be very similar to that written for Example 15.1 except that after the first three items in each record have been read, the rest of the record will be read into a **character** variable, and then the relevant parts read from that variable, acting as an internal file.

Data design

This will be the same as before, except for the addition of a **character** variable, *input_record*, of length 10 (which is sufficient for the longest case).

Structure plan

> **1**   Request name of data file and open it on *unit*
>
> **2**   Repeat up to *max_datasets* times
>
> **2.1**   Read first three items of next record, and the rest of the record into *input_record*
>
> **2.2**   If end of file then exit from loop
>
> **2.3**   If error then set *error_code* to −2 and exit from loop
>
> **2.4**   Select case on job status
>
> status is 1
>
> **2.4.1**   Read age from *input_record*
>
> **2.4.2**   Set salary, other income, months unemployed and code to unused
>
> status is 2
>
> **2.4.3**   Read salary from *input_record*
>
> **2.4.4**   Set age, other income, months unemployed and code to unused
>
> status is 3
>
> **2.4.5**   Read salary and other income from *input_record*
>
> **2.4.6**   Set age, months unemployed and code to unused
>
> status is 4
>
> **2.4.7**   Read age and months unemployed from *input_record*
>
> **2.4.8**   Set salary, other income and code to unused
>
> status is 5
>
> **2.4.9**   Read age and code from *input_record*
>
> **2.4.10** Set salary, other income and months unemployed to unused
>
> **2.5**   Copy local record to array
>
> **3**   If no end-of-file read set *error_code* to −3
>
> **4**   Return number of data sets read

③ Solution

```
module error_codes
! This module contains PROCESSOR-DEPENDENT error codes

   integer,parameter,public :: end_of_record = -1002, &
                               end_file = -1001

end module error_codes
```

```
module survey
! This module contains a type definition and constants
! for use with the input and processing of survey data,
! together with the input procedure itself

use error_codes
private

   ! Procedure declaration
   public :: input

   ! Type definition for survey response
   type, public :: survey_info
      private
      character(len=20) :: name
      character(len=1) :: sex
      integer :: job_status,age,months_jobless,at_home_code
      real :: salary,other_income
   end type survey_info

   ! Various codes
   character(len=1),parameter,private ::          &
           female="F",male="M"                       ! sex
   integer,parameter,private ::                   &
           ft_ed=1,ft_job=2,pt_job=3,             & ! job status
           no_job=4,at_home=5,                    & ! ----------
           ch_minder=1,rel_minder=2,other=3,      & ! at home code
           unused=-1 ! unused code

contains

   subroutine input(inf,max_datasets,survey_data,num_datasets, &
                    error_code)
   ! This subroutine reads up to max_datasets records prepared
   ! as follows, returning the number read in num_datasets
   ! Columns 1-20 name
   !          23 sex (M or F)
   !          25 job status (1-5)
   !       28,29 age - for status 1, 4 or 5
   !       28-31 monthly salary - for status 2 and 3
   !       32-34 other monthly income - for status 3
   !       32-34 months unemployed - for status 4
   !          31 special code (1-3) - for status 5

      ! Arguments
      integer, intent(in) :: inf,max_datasets
      integer, intent(out) :: num_datasets,error_code
      type(survey_info), dimension(:), intent(out) :: survey_data

      ! Local variables
      character(len=30) :: data_file
      character(len=10) :: input_record
      character(len=20) :: name
      character(len=1) :: sex
      integer :: i,ios,status,age,months,code
      real :: salary,income
```

```
! Ask for name of data file
! A maximum of 3 attempts will be allowed to open the file
do i=1,3
   print *,"Type name of data file"
   read "(a)",data_file
   ! Open file at beginning
   open (unit=inf,file=data_file,position="rewind", &
         status="old",action="readwrite",iostat=ios)
   if (ios==0) then
      exit
   end if
   ! Error when opening file - try again
   print *,"Unable to open file - please try again"
end do

! If open was unsuccessful after 3 attempts return error=-1
if (ios/=0) then
   error_code = -1
   return
else
! Successful file opening
   error_code = 0
end if

! Loop to read data
do i=1,max_datasets
   ! Read next set of data
   read (unit=inf,fmt="(a20,t23,a1,t25,i1,t28,a10)", &
         iostat=ios) name,sex,status,input_record

   ! Check for errors and end of file
   select case (ios)
   case (end_file)              ! End of file - no more data
      exit

   case (end_of_record,1:)    ! Error during reading
      error_code = -2
      exit
   end select

   ! Read remaining data from internal file according to
   ! status code
   select case (status)

   case (ft_ed)
      ! Read age and set other items to unused code
      read (unit=input_record,fmt="(i2)") age
      months = unused
      salary = unused
      income = unused
      code = unused

   case (ft_job)
      ! Read salary details and set other items to unused
      read (unit=input_record,fmt="(f4.0)") salary
      age = unused
```

```
            income = unused
            months = unused
            code = unused

      case (pt_job)
            ! Read income details and set other items to unused
            read (unit=input_record,fmt="(f4.0,tr2,f4.0)")  &
                  salary,income
            age = unused
            months = unused
            code = unused

      case (no_job)
            ! Read age and months unemployed and set other
            ! items to unused
            read (unit=input_record,fmt="(i2,tr2,i3)")       &
                  age, months
            salary = unused
            income = unused
            code = unused

      case (at_home)
            ! Read age and code, and set other items to unused
            read (unit=input_record,fmt="(i2,tr1,i1)") age, code
            salary = unused
            income = unused
            months = unused
      end select

      ! Record is now fully input, so copy to main data array
      survey_data(i) = survey_info(name,sex,status,age,       &
                                   months,code,salary,income)

  end do

  ! All data input - check if end of file was read
  if (i > max_datasets) then
      error_code = -3
  end if

  ! Save number of records read and return
  num_datasets = i-1

end subroutine input

end module survey
```

Note that it would also have been possible for the **read** statement which actually reads the data from the input file to have read the whole record into input_record, and then read everything, including the three common items, from the internal file. This would have had the advantage that the whole input record was always available, at the cost of slightly more complicated formats.

15.5   The inquire statement

For most purposes the statements already described will enable a program to carry out any file operations it requires. There are, however, occasions, especially when writing a general-purpose subroutine, when it would be useful to find out, or check up on, the various details which are applicable to files, such as whether they are formatted, connected for direct access, and so on. This can be achieved by using the **inquire** statement, which takes one of the forms

> **inquire** (unit=*unit_number*, *list of specifiers*)
> **inquire** (**file**=*file_name*, *list of specifiers*)
> **inquire** (iolength=*integer_variable*) *output list*

where the specifiers which may appear in first two forms are shown in Figures 15.5−15.8.

The first form is known as an **inquire-by-unit** statement, and must include a `unit` specifier in the same form as in an **open** statement. Its purpose is to obtain information about the specified unit and/or about the file, if any, that is currently connected to the unit specified. The second form is known as an **inquire-by-file** statement, and must include a `file` specifier in the same form as in an **open** statement. Its purpose is to obtain information about the specified file and/or about the unit, if any, to which the file is currently connected. Both of these forms of the inquire statement may also include an `iostat` specifier in the usual way.

The specifiers used with inquire-by-unit and inquire-by-file fall into four groups.

The specifiers in first group, shown in Figure 15.5, are used in an inquire-by-unit statement, and enable the program to establish whether a specified unit exists, whether a file is connected to a specified unit, and if so, what its name is.

Specifier	Target values and meaning
exist=*unit_existence*	`.true.` or `.false.` Existence of the named unit
opened=*open_status*	`.true.` or `.false.` Whether a file is connected to this unit
named=*name_status*	`.true.` or `.false.` Whether the file connected to this unit has a name.
name=*file_name*	The name of the file connected to this unit, or undefined

Figure 15.5   Unit status specifiers for use with the **inquire** statement.

Specifier	Target values and meaning
exist=*file_existence*	.**true**. or .**false**. Existence of the named file
opened=*open_status*	.**true**. or .**false**. Whether this file is connected to an input/output unit
number=*unit_number*	The unit number of the unit connected to this file, or undefined
name=*file_name*	The name of this file in a processor-defined form

Figure 15.6   File status specifiers for use with the **inquire** statement.

Thus, the statement

```
inquire (unit=unit_number, opened=connected,  &
         named=named_file, name=file_name)
```

will set the logical variable connected *true* if there is a file connected to unit number unit_number and will set the logical variable named_file *true* if the file connected to unit unit_number has a name (that is, it is not a scratch file). If the file has a name then the character variable file_name will be assigned the name of the file, otherwise it will become undefined.

The specifiers in second group, shown in Figure 15.6, are used in an inquire-by-file statement, and enable the program to establish whether a specified file exists, whether the specified file is connected to a unit, and if so, what its number is.

Thus, the statement

```
inquire (file=file_name, opened=connected,  &
         number=unit_number)
```

will set the logical variable connected *true* if the file file_name is connected to an input/output unit, and will set the integer variable unit_number to the unit number of the relevant input/output unit if the file is so connected. This enables a procedure, for example, to test whether a specified file is already connected, and then either to initiate input or output on the appropriate unit or to open the file on a specified unit.

The third group of specifiers is shown in Figure 15.7, and may be used in either an inquire-by-unit or an inquire-by-file to determine the record length of a file, or the next record in a direct access file, respectively. In the latter case, the value returned is $n + 1$ if the last record read or written was record number n, and 1 if the file is connected but no records have yet been read or written.

Thus the two statements

```
write (unit=7,rec=20) a,b,c,d
inquire (unit=7,nextrec=next)
```

will result in the integer variable next being given the value 21.

Specifier	Target values and meaning
recl=*record_length*	The record length of a file connected for direct access, or the maximum record length for a file connected for sequential access, or undefined
nextrec=*record_number*	The number of the next record of a file connected for direct access, or undefined

Figure 15.7 Record-related specifiers for use with the **inquire** statement.

The fourth and largest group of specifiers is shown in Figure 15.8, and enables the program to determine the values of the various attributes which could have been set in an **open** statement for a file.

These specifiers all require a character target and some of them assign it the value that was used for the corresponding specifier in the **open** statement, or the default value if appropriate, or UNDEFINED if the file is not yet connected or it is not possible to determine the correct value. The remaining specifiers ask whether a particular action is allowable and set the target to the characters YES or NO (or UNKNOWN), as appropriate.

Specifier	Target values and meaning
access=*access_type*	SEQUENTIAL, DIRECT or UNDEFINED
sequential=*yes_or_no*	YES, NO or UNKNOWN
direct=*yes_or_no*	YES, NO or UNKNOWN The type of access for which the file is connected
form=*format_type*	FORMATTED, UNFORMATTED or UNDEFINED
formatted=*yes_or_no*	YES, NO or UNKNOWN
unformatted=*yes_or_no*	YES, NO or UNKNOWN The type of formatting for which the file is connected
action=*io_type*	READ, WRITE, READWRITE or UNDEFINED
read=*yes_or_no*	YES, NO or UNKNOWN
write=*yes_or_no*	YES, NO or UNKNOWN
readwrite=*yes_or_no*	YES, NO or UNKNOWN The type of input/ouput for which the file is connected
position=*file_position*	REWIND, APPEND, ASIS or UNDEFINED The initial file position specifed when the file was connected

Figure 15.8 Attribute specifiers for use with the **inquire** statement.

Thus, if the file My_file has been opened for direct access, the statement

```
inquire (unit="My_file",access=access_type)
```

will set the character variable access_type to the value DIRECT. The statement

```
inquire (unit="My_file",sequential=seq,direct=dir)
```

will set the character variable dir to the value YES. It is not possible in this case, however, to state what value will be assigned to the character variable seq since if sequential access is also allowed on the file it may be YES, if sequential access is never allowed on the file it may be NO, but if the processor cannot determine which of these possibilities is true then the value UNKNOWN will be assigned to seq.

Note that any character values which are assigned as a result of executing an **inquire** statement will always be in upper case, except in the case of the name specifier, which will be in whatever form the actual filename is specified.

Note also that if an error condition occurs during execution of an **inquire** statement then all inquiry specifier variables become undefined, other than the iostat variable, if one is specified.

Finally, it should be noted that the value assigned to the target variable of the position specifier assumes that the file has not been repositioned since it was opened. If it has been repositioned then a processor-dependent value will be assigned to the target variable.

The final type of **inquire** statement is known as an inquire-by-output-list, and takes a different form from the other types of **inquire** statement:

```
inquire (iolength=length) output_list
```

where *length* is an integer variable and *output_list* is a list of entities in the same form as an output list for a **write** statement. The effect of this statement is to assign the target variable *length* with the length of the record that would result from using the specified output list in an unformatted **write** statement.

It will be remembered that this is measured in processor-defined units, and that, moreover, it is required when opening a file for direct access. Thus, for example, in Example 15.2, the module stock_control included the following lines:

```
integer,parameter,private :: char_store=1,real_store=4
integer,parameter,public :: &
   rec_len = char_store*(max_len+8) + real_store*4
```

A better approach, using the **inquire** statement, would be to replace these lines in the module by the following declaration:

```
integer,public :: rec_len
```

and to add the following statements before the **open** statement in the main program:

```
type(stock_record) :: record
inquire (iolength=rec_len) record
```

which will set `rec_len` to the correct value for the records which constitute the master file.

Another way in which the **inquire** statement can be useful is in connection with establishing, and maintaining, a grandfather–father–son cycle of tapes in a program which updates a master file. Example 15.2, for example, could be modified so that a cycle of three tapes was used, say `Master_1`, `Master_2` and `Master_3`, in the following manner:

*n*th run	Update from `Master_1` to `Master_2`; delete `Master_3` at end of run.
(*n* + 1th run)	Update from `Master_2` to `Master_3`; delete `Master_1` at end of run.
(*n* + 2th run)	Update from `Master_3` to `Master_1`; delete `Master_2` at end of run.

It is a relatively trivial task to write a procedure which will use **inquire** to determine which two of the three possible files exist, and then to open the one that does not exist as the new master tape (for writing), the one that was created on the last run for reading only, and the third tape so that it can be closed *and deleted* at the successful conclusion of the program's execution. The program will then automatically look after this aspect of its data security.

SELF-TEST EXERCISES 15.2

1   What is the difference in the meaning of the `recl` specifier in an **open** statement for a sequential file and its meaning in an **open** statement for a direct access file?

2   Can a file which has been written with direct access **write** statements subsequently be read as a serial file?

3   Can a file which has been written with sequential **write** statements subsequently be read as a direct access file?

4   What restrictions are there on the form of input and output on direct access files?

5   What is a hash table? How is it used, and what are its advantages over a conventional look-up table? What is its major disadvantage?

6 What will be printed by the following program?

```
program test_15_2_6
    character(len=5), dimension(10) :: line1,line2
    integer :: i
    line1 = (/"one ","two ","three","four ","five ",  &
            "six ","seven","eight","nine ","ten "/)
    do i=1,10
        read (unit=line1,fmt="(a5)") line2(i)
    end do
    write (unit=*,fmt="(10a6)") line2
    read (unit=line1,fmt="(a5)") line2
    write (unit=*,fmt="(10a6)") line2
end program test_15_2_6
```

7 How would you find out the length of the record produced on your computer by the **write** statement in the following program extract? What is it?

```
        .
        .
        .
real :: p,q
real, dimension(7) :: x
real (kind=selected_real_kind(12,30)) :: y,z
        .
        .
        .
write(unit=8,rec=next) p,q,x,y,z
        .
        .
        .
```

SUMMARY

- Various edit descriptors may be used to provide greater control over input and output editing.

- Non-advancing input and output does not start a new record each time the statement is executed.

- Non-advancing input and output may only occur on a sequential file that uses explicit formatting.

- Files may be sequential, direct access or internal.

- The records in a direct access file can be written or read in any order.

- An internal file is a character variable or array, and enables the edit descriptors used in formatting to be used to convert an item in memory into another format.

- A hash table is a convenient method of storing a random set of identifying names for subsequent retrieval.

- The **inquire** statement enables a program to establish details about files at execution time; it can also be used to establish the length of an input/output list.

- F syntax introduced in Chapter 15

inquire statement	inquire (unit=*unit_number*, *list of specifiers*)
	inquire (**file**=*file_name*, *list of specifiers*)
	inquire (iolength=*integer_variable*) *output_list*
Edit descriptors	i*w*.*m*, es*w*.*d*, es*w*.*dee*, :, sp, ss, s
Input/output specifiers	recl = *record_length*
	advance = *advance_mode*
	size = *character_count*
	rec = *record_number*
inquire specifiers	See Figures 15.5, 15.6, 15.7 and 15.8

PROGRAMMING EXERCISES

15.1   Write a program to calculate the values of y, where $y = e^x \sin x$, for x varying from 0 to 20 in steps of 0.5. The sets of values for x and y should be written to an unformatted file, and should also be printed using list-directed formatting.

Now write a second program which reads the results produced by the first program and prints them in the form of a table containing the values of x and y. The program should print this table five times using different formats for both x and y as follows:

1.   Both in f format
2.   Both in f format with any plus signs before the y values printed, but not those before the x values
3. x in f format and y in es format
4.   Both in es format
5.   Both in es format with any plus signs before either being printed

15.2   Write a program which carries out the following input and output actions:

1.   Prints an opening (welcome) message
2.   Prints a request for two integers to be typed
3.   Reads one integer from the keyboard
4.   Reads the second integer from the keyboard
5.   Prints the two numbers
6.   Prints the sum of the two numbers
7.   Prints a farewell message

The program should use list-directed input and output statements.

Note that each printed message will begin on a new line and that the two integers must also be typed on separate lines; if two numbers are typed on the same line in response to the request for two integers then the second will not be read, but the computer will wait for the second number to be typed on a new line.

Now modify the program so that it uses formatted **read** and **write** statements, specifying the default input and output units. Other than, probably, using different field widths when printing the numbers and their sum, the format of the input and output should be identical.

Now modify the program again by changing the first **read** statement (step 3, above) to use non-advancing input and run the program again. Was the result what you expected?

Now change each of the **read** and **write** statements in turn to use non-advancing input or output until all statements are non-advancing. Were the effects what you had expected?

Finally, *without changing anything apart from the specification of advancing or non-advancing input/output*, modify the program so that the initial welcome is on the first line, followed by the request for two integers and the input of both integers on the next line, followed by the listing of the two numbers, their sum, and the farewell message on a third line.

You should now understand how advancing and non-advancing input and output work!

15.3   A simple integer calculator can be simulated by reading a numerical expression from the keyboard involving the operators +, -, * and / and ending with =, and then displaying the result. Write a program to simulate a calculator using each of the following methods:

1.   Read an integer using non-advancing input. Then read characters until a non-space character is read – this must be an operator or an equals sign. If it is an operator then read the next integer and calculate a partial result before looking for the next operator as before; if it is an equals sign then the result can be printed.

2.   Read the complete line into a character variable or array and then use this as an internal file in a similar manner to that described above.

3.   Read the complete line into a character variable or array and then examine each character in turn in order to either create an integer value or identify it as an operator; this is, essentially, what a compiler does when reading a source program – although the number of possibilities in an F program are rather greater than is the case for the very simple syntax of this exercise.

Which did you find the best method? Why?

15.4   Write a program that asks the user for the name of a file and then writes the alphabet, as 26 elements of a character array, to the file. The program should check to see if the file already exists, and if it does it should inform the user and request a new name (which should also be checked in the same way).

Test the program by running it twice with exactly the same filename supplied as input.

*15.5   Type the following data (which is the same as was used for Exercise 10.9) into a file:

```
12.36    0.004    1.3536E12    2320.326
13.24    0.008    2.4293E15    5111.116
15.01    0.103    9.9879E11    3062.329
11.83    0.051    6.3195E13    8375.145
14.00    0.001    8.0369E14    1283.782
```

Write a program that reads each line of the file as one long character string. The program should then use an internal file to extract the four numbers from each line and store them in one row of a matrix as real numbers. Finally, the program should calculate the mean of each column of the matrix.

15.6 A census has been carried out on the population of Smalltown, during which the following data was collected:

Name	Age	Address	Economic status
Sandy T Shaw	26	10, High Street	A
Alan M Jones	56	2, Largeville Road	B
Chris D Jones	54	2, Largeville Road	B
Simon B Taylor	32	7, High Street	D
Paul K Smith	72	5, Largeville Road	C
Tristan T Bloggs	44	8, High Street	E

Enter this information into a file. Write and test a program that reads the file and provides the user of the program with the following options:

(a) Obtain the address of a named person.
(b) Obtain the age of a named person.
(c) Obtain the names of people with a given economic status.

Now modify the program to allow you to add new census data to the file.

15.7 Use the file described in Exercise 15.6 as a direct access file. Write a program that reorders the records in the datafile according to age, with the youngest first, and write the reordered data back to the same file.

15.8 Section 15.5 described a method of using the **inquire** statement to automatically use a 'grandfather–father–son' system of rotating three files.

Write a short program to implement such a system. The program will require access to three named files, only two of which will exist. The program should open the most recently created file and the one that does not exist and copy the contents of the old file to the new one. The program should then read a record from the keyboard and write it to the end of the new file. Finally the unused file should be deleted.

Run the program at least four times and check the contents of the latest version after each run.

15.9 An employer of a company employing around 400 people wishes to create a simple database containing the following items of information about each member of his staff:

Staff number (in the range 1001–4999 for males, 5001–9999 for females)
Name (title, first name and family name)
Job title
Date of joining company (*dd-mm-yyyy*)
Date of last salary change (*dd-mm-yyyy*)
Current salary (annual)
Home address
Home telephone number
Doctor's name
Doctor's telephone number

Write a program which allows the following actions:

    (a)   Add a new member of staff
    (b)   Remove a member of staff
    (c)   Print details for a specified member of staff
    (d)   Update details for a specified member of staff
    (e)   Print a complete staff listing

15.10 Where a large database is being processed it is often neither possible nor appropriate to read all the data from a file into the computer's memory. In these cases the data should be stored in a direct access file in such a way that the required record can easily be identified and read whenever it is required. The solution for Example 15.2 illustrated how a hash table could be used to quickly identify the correct record.

However, that example did not provide the means for inserting and/or deleting entries in the hash table.

Either modify the program written in Example 15.2 or write a separate program which will do this. The program should

    (a)   *for insertion* read the name of the chemical, and then find the first vacant position in the hash table (using the hashing method used in the example program). If there is a vacant position, and the chemical name is not already in the table (human errors can occur!), then the appropriate entry should be made in the table, and the relevant stock control details should be read and written to the master file;

    (b)   *for deletion* read the name of the chemical and find its entry in the hash table. The corresponding record in the master file can easily be deleted, but deleting the entry from the hash table is not necessarily straightforward. Remember that simply deleting it might mean that another entry which originally selected this position, and then used another because it was already in use, would then fail to be found by the hashing routine. There are several possibilities − see if you can find a satisfactory one.

Still more powerful building blocks

16

16.1 More sophisticated procedure arguments

16.2 Accessing non-F procedures from your program

16.3 Defining your own operators

16.4 Creating generic procedures and operators

16.5 Data abstraction and language extension

This chapter completes the examination of the F language by returning to the basic building blocks of the language for the final time. The power of procedures is still further increased by the ability to omit some of the actual arguments or to provide them in a different order from that specified in the procedure heading.

A further extension of procedures, utilizing an interface block, allows the creation of user-defined operators and extended meanings for intrinsic operators in order that the operator notation may be used with objects of derived type. Interface blocks can also be used to enable procedures written in a language other than F to be made available to an F program, and to allow the programmer to define a generic procedure – a concept used extensively by intrinsic procedures, whereby several different versions of the same procedure may co-exist, with the correct one to use on each occasion being determined by the type of the actual arguments.

Finally, all these concepts are drawn together to illustrate how the F language possesses powerful capabilities for data abstraction and language extension.

16.1 More sophisticated procedure arguments

Up to this point, we have stated that the actual argument list and the dummy argument list must match exactly, and that the first dummy argument will correspond to the first actual argument, and so on. However, an alternative approach allows us to omit actual arguments, or to present them in a different order.

These enhanced facilities are provided by **keyword arguments** in which one or more of the actual arguments take the form

keyword = actual_argument

where *keyword* is the name of the dummy argument which is to be associated with the actual argument specified.

This is most easily explained by means of an example. We shall assume that a subroutine exists with the following initial statements:

```
subroutine keywords(first,second,third,fourth)
   integer, intent(inout) :: first,second,third,fourth
```

If we wish to call this subroutine with the corresponding actual integer arguments one, two, three and four then any of the following forms of the **call** statement would have an identical effect:

```
call keywords(one,two,three,four)         ! Positional

call keywords(first=one,second=two,   &   ! Keyword in
     third=three,fourth=four)              ! same order

call keywords(third=three,first=one, &    ! Keyword in
     fourth=four,second=two)               ! different order

call keywords(one,fourth=four,        &   ! Mixed positional
     third=three,second=two)               ! and keyword
```

Note, especially, the last example. It is permitted to mix positional arguments and keyword arguments, but once a keyword argument has appeared then *all* remaining actual arguments must also be keyword arguments.

In itself, the ability to provide the actual arguments in a different order, at the cost of rather more writing, does not seem to be any great advantage. However, when combined with the ability to define **optional arguments** it can become extremely useful. An optional argument is specified by the inclusion of the **optional** attribute in the declaration of the dummy argument:

```
real,intent(...),optional :: dummy_argument_name
```

Note that, in the dummy argument list of a procedure, any optional arguments must follow all non-optional arguments.

Obviously, it will normally be necessary for the procedure to know if an actual argument corresponding to an optional dummy argument has been specified or not – for example in order to allow the use of a default value for the dummy argument – and a logical intrinsic function, `present`, is available for this purpose. This function takes the name of an optional dummy argument as its argument and returns the value *true* if there is a corresponding actual argument, and *false* if there is no corresponding actual argument.

Thus if the subroutine `keywords` was modified so that its last three arguments were all optional:

```
subroutine keywords(first,second,third,fourth)
   integer, intent(inout) :: first
   integer, intent(inout), optional :: second,third,fourth
```

then it could be called with statements such as

```
call keywords(one,two)

call keywords(one,third=three)

call keywords(one,two,fourth=four)
```

and the procedure `keywords` would be able to detect which of the three optional arguments had been supplied and take appropriate action. Note that without using keyword arguments it is only possible to omit arguments from the end of the list of arguments; by using keyword arguments it is possible to omit any argument.

☐ EXAMPLE 16.1   ·

1 Problem

Write a subroutine which takes as its arguments a title (Dr, Mr, Ms, and so on), a family name, and up to three personal names, and returns a single character string containing the title, personal names and family name, with one space between each element.

2 Analysis

This is similar to Example 4.2, apart from the complication of a variable number of personal names, and we can proceed directly to a solution using optional arguments for the personal names.

⌐3⌐ Solution

```
subroutine get_full_name(full_name,title,family_name,p_name1, &
                         p_name2,p_name3)
! Subroutine to join names to form a full name with a single
! space between the title and the first name, and between each
! pair of names

! Dummy argument declarations
   character(len=*), intent(in) :: family_name, title
   character(len=*), intent(in), optional :: p_name1,      &
                                             p_name2, p_name3
   character(len=*), intent(out) :: full_name

! Build up composite name in stages
   full_name = adjustl(title)
   if (present(p_name1)) then
      full_name = trim(full_name) // " " // adjustl(p_name1)
   end if
   if (present(p_name2)) then
      full_name = trim(full_name) // " " // adjustl(p_name2)
   end if
   if (present(p_name3)) then
      full_name = trim(full_name) // " " // adjustl(p_name3)
   end if
   full_name = trim(full_name) // " " // adjustl(family_name)

end subroutine get_full_name
```

16.2   Accessing non-F procedures from your program

In an F program a procedure can only be called from another procedure in the same module, a procedure in another module which has access to the procedure by **use** association, or from the main program if it has access to the procedure by **use** association. In all of these cases the compiler has access to the interface of the called procedure when compiling the calling program unit, and is thus able to check that the calling sequence is correct with regard to whether the procedure is a subroutine or a function, the type and number of arguments, and the type of the result in the case of a function.

It is sometimes possible to call procedures written in languages other than F, but in such a case the compiler clearly does not have access to the procedure's interface at the time that it is compiling the calling program unit. In this situation the programmer must provide this information in the form of an **interface block**.

Such an interface block takes exactly the same form as that introduced in Chapter 8 in the context of a dummy procedure, except that it must be placed with the specification statements in a module (that is, *before* the **contains** statement).

Obviously, the ability of an F compiler to incorporate procedures written in other languages will depend upon the language, the operating system, the version of the compiler, and possibly other factors. However, most F compilers can incorporate compiled versions of Fortran 90 procedures and, although it will generally be preferable to make any minor changes that are necessary for full F language conformance and then compile the resulting code as an F procedure, there are situations when, for copyright or other reasons, this is not possible. Such a situation may typically arise, for example, if it is required to utilize a procedure from an existing Fortran 90 library.

Thus, if the program `curve_fitting_example` requires the use of the Fortran 90 library subroutine `cubic_spline`, which has two real array input arguments, and four real array output arguments together with an integer output argument, then the start of the program might be as follows:

```
module example
   public :: cubic_spline, ...

   ! Interface block for Fortran 90 subroutine cubic_spline
   interface
      subroutine cubic_spline(x,y,a,b,c,d,error)
         real, dimension(0:), intent(in) :: x,y
         real, dimension(0:), intent(out) :: a,b,c,d
         integer, intent(out) :: error
      end subroutine cubic_spline
   end interface
   Other specification statements
   .
   .
   .

contains
   Module procedure definitions
   .
   .
   .

end module example

program curve_fitting_example
use example
   .
   .
   .
   call cubic_spline(...)      ! Fortran 90 procedure
   .
   .
   .
end program curve_fitting_example
```

16.3   Defining your own operators

We have seen how a module can be written to provide the programmer who uses it with new data types and with procedures that will carry out commonly required operations on objects of these types as well as manipulating their component parts. This goes a long way towards enabling the programmer to create a special environment for use in a particular application area, but there is still one major gap in this environment – namely the provision of *operators* for use with objects of these types.

For example, in Example 8.5 we wrote a function `scalar_product` which calculated the scalar product of two objects of type `vector`. This allows a programmer using the vector type to write a statement such as

```
v1_dot_v2 = scalar_product(v1, v2)
```

where v1 and v2 are of type `vector`, and v1_dot_v2 is **real**. However, it would be more natural to write

```
v1_dot_v2 = v1 operator v2
```

where *operator* is some representation chosen by the programmer to represent the scalar product operator, or even

```
v1_dot_v2 = v1 op v2
```

where *op* is one of the intrinsic operators already used in F, but whose meaning has been **extended** for use with two operands of type `vector`.

F provides the necessary facilities for us to define our own operators in either of these ways by use of yet another variant of the interface block.

If we wish to specify our own representation for an operator then it must consist of a name of up to 31 letters enclosed between periods. Note that, as with other user-defined names in F, any combination of upper- and lower-case letters is permitted, but the same pattern of upper and lower case must be used on every occasion. Thus, we could decide to represent the scalar product operator as `.dot.` or `.scalarproduct.`, but *not* as `.scalar_product.` because of the rule that operator names must consist only of letters.

The operator chosen must be declared in an interface block in a module, before any **contains** statement, in the form

```
interface operator (operator_symbol)
   module procedure function_name
end interface
```

where *operator_symbol* may consists of a sequence of up to 31 letters enclosed between periods and *function_name* is the name of a function in the second part of the same module, or available by **use** or host association, that defines the required operation. Notice the use of the reserved word **operator** to denote that we are defining an operator interface for the function that will perform the operation and the reserved words **module procedure** to identify the specific function that will perform the operation. The operator defined in such an interface block is known as a **defined operation**.

The module procedure specified in the defining interface block must be a function having either one or two arguments; if it has one argument then the operator will be a unary operator, while if it has two then the operator will be a binary operator. In either case, the dummy arguments must be non-optional and must be specified as having **intent(in)**.

Returning to the example of the function for calculating the scalar product of two vectors, the inclusion of the following interface block in the module would, therefore, allow the operator .dot. to be used in the way previously shown:

```
interface operator(.dot.)
   module procedure scalar_product
end interface
```

A defined operation specified by such an interface block will be treated as a reference to the function with the operand(s) as the actual argument(s); in the case of a defined binary operation the first, or left-hand, operand will be the first actual argument and the second, or right-hand, operand will be the second actual argument. In the above example we have therefore defined an alternative, and often more convenient, way of using the scalar_product function.

Sometimes, however, it may be more desirable to use one of the existing intrinsic operators to represent the required operation, and this is permissible subject to two additional constraints:

- It is not permitted to *change* the meaning of an intrinsic operator, only to extend it. It must be possible, therefore, to distinguish the extended meaning of the operator from its already defined intrinsic meaning(s) solely by reference to the types of its operands.

- The number of function arguments must be consistent with the intrinsic uses of the operator. Thus, for example, a unary / operator is forbidden.

We could, therefore, extend the meaning of the intrinsic multiplication operator, *, to calculate the scalar product of two vectors by means of the following interface block:

```
interface operator(*)
   module procedure scalar_product
end interface
```

so that a user of the module can simply write statements such as

```
v1_dot_v2 = v1*v2
```

where `v1` and `v2` are of type `vector`.

Whether one defines a completely new operator name or extends an existing intrinsic operator depends on the nature of the problem being solved. Where relevant, we strongly recommend that you consider the analogous mathematical notation.

One final point relates to the visibility of the function used to define the operator. The intention of defining such an operator is that it is used in preference to the equivalent function reference, and we strongly recommend, therefore, that the names of any functions used to define operators should be private to the module, and *not* be available outside the module. This is very easily achieved by listing the names of any functions used for this purpose in a **private** statement in the module. The operators *must* appear in a **public** statement, however, if they are to be available to any procedure or main program that uses the module; they appear in such a statement in the same form as they appear in the **interface** statement:

public :: operator(*operator_symbol*)

Note also that the function used to implement the defined operator must appear in a **public** or **private** statement; since the intention is that the operator form be used outside the module, the function will normally be specified as **private**. Thus the extended * operator described above might appear in an extended version of the module `vectors` as follows:

```
module vectors
    public :: create_vector, vector_size, vector_array, &
              operator(*)
    private :: scalar_product

    interface operator(*)
        module procedure scalar_product
    end interface
    .
    .
    .
contains
    .
    .
    .
end module vectors
```

where the module procedures `create_vector`, `vector_size`, `vector_array` and `scalar_product` appear after the **contains** statement.

This almost completes the set of programming tools necessary for fully utilizing the capabilities inherent in the combination of derived types and modules, but there is one remaining requirement which the reader may not immediately think of.

Although we tend to think of the assignment operator, =, as simply copying the result of the expression on its right to the variable whose name appears on its left, a moment's thought shows us that there is more to assignment than this, for we have already met many cases in which some change is made to the value on the right-hand side of the assignment before it is stored in the location in memory identified by the name on the left-hand side. For example, a **real** value may be converted to an **integer**, including truncation, or a **character** string may be extended with spaces. Assignment is fully defined for all intrinsic data types, but what about derived types?

If an object of a derived type is assigned to an entity of the same type then, as we saw in Chapter 8, by default every component of the derived type value on the right is copied to the corresponding component of the entity on the left. Since this is normally what is required, there is no problem here. But what about assignments where the types are different? In such cases, and even when both operands are of the same type, we can define the meaning we wish for assignment in much the same way as we have just learned to define other operators:

```
interface assignment(=)
   module procedure sub
end interface
```

Note the use of the reserved word **assignment** to indicate we are defining an interface for the assignment operator. Note also that the assignment symbol must be included in the interface statement, even though it cannot be changed from =; this is because the syntax would otherwise be confused with the final use of an interface block that we shall meet in Section 16.4.

The procedure specified in the defining interface block must be a subroutine having exactly two non-optional dummy arguments; the first dummy argument must be specified as having **intent(out)** or **intent(inout)**, while the second must be specified as **intent(in)**. Such a **defined assignment** will be treated as a reference to the subroutine with the left-hand side as the first actual argument and the value of the right-hand side expression as the second actual argument.

It is frequently the case that more than one defined assignment is required, in order to deal with different combinations of operands, and in this case all the relevant subroutines must be defined in a single interface block in either of two ways:

```
interface assignment(=)
   module procedure sub1, sub2, ...
end interface
```

or

```
interface assignment (=)
    module procedure sub1
    module procedure sub2
    .
    .
    .
end interface
```

Note that it is not permissible to have two separate interface blocks, both of which define the assignment operator.

A good example of the use of such a defined assignment can be seen by reference to the module written in Example 8.5, modified to use the improved definition of the derived type vector given in Section 14.4, where two functions create_vector and vector_array created a vector from a rank-one array and copied the elements of a vector to a rank-one array, respectively. A better way might be to rewrite these as subroutines and use them to define assignment between rank-one arrays and vectors by means of the following interface block:

```
interface assignment (=)
    module procedure create_vector, vector_array
end interface
```

With these defined assignments added to the module vectors, it will be possible to write statements such as

```
v1 = a1
```

and

```
a2 = v2
```

where v1 and v2 are of type vector, and a1 and a2 are **real** arrays, instead of the much more clumsy

```
v1 = create(a1)
```

and

```
a2 = vector_array(v2)
```

As was suggested for defined operators, it is usually preferable to hide the name of a subroutine used to provide a defined assignment. To achieve this, in a similar way to that used with operators, the assignment symbol must appear in a **public** statement, and the defining subroutine must appear in a **private** one. For example, with these two subroutines, together with a third subroutine for assigning one vector to another, the module `vectors` would now begin as follows:

```
module vectors

   public :: vector size, operator(*), assignment(=)
   private :: scalar_product, create_vector, vector_array,   &
              vector_assign

   interface operator(*)
      module procedure scalar_product
   end interface

   interface assignment(=)
      module procedure create_vector, vector_array,          &
                       vector_assign
   end interface
   .
   .
   .
contains
   .
   .
   .
end module vectors
```

Note that the third assignment subroutine, `vector_assign`, to assign one vector to another, is necessary because the default assignment operator for the derived type `vector` would result in the pointers in the two vectors pointing at the same element array (that belonging to the vector on the right-hand side of the assignment statement). This is certainly not what we would expect as the result of the assignment of one vector to another.

SELF-TEST EXERCISES 16.1

1   What is the difference between a keyword argument and a positional argument?

2   What are the rules which govern the association of dummy arguments and their corresponding actual arguments?

3   How is an optional argument specified? How does a procedure establish whether an optional dummy argument has a corresponding actual argument?

4   What is an interface block? Name three situations in which one is required.

5   What is meant by a defined operation? How is it defined?

6   What are the constraints on extending the meaning of an intrinsic operator?

7   What is meant by defined assignment? How is it defined?

16.4   Creating generic procedures and operators

We have already encountered examples of what are called *generic* procedures. These are procedures that can accept arguments of more than one type. For example, the intrinsic procedure **sin** can accept arguments that are of type **real** or **complex** and returns a result that is of type **real** or **complex**, correspondingly. This is in apparent violation of the rule that the types of actual arguments and procedure dummy arguments must match.

However, the rule is not really being broken. What is happening is that effectively there are, hidden from the user, two different **sin** functions; one taking a **real** argument and one taking a **complex** argument. An F compiler can tell which one is desired by the type of the actual argument. A generic interface called **sin** exists for user convenience – we do not want to use a different function name based on the type of the actual argument. This is precisely analogous to common practice in mathematics. A similar situation occurs for many of the intrinsic procedures of F – as can be seen from the complete list of F's intrinsic procedures in Appendix A.

There are often cases when it would be convenient if we could write our own generic procedures, and F gives us this ability via yet another variant of interface blocks.

To illustrate the concept, suppose that we want to write a generic procedure that will interchange two values given to it. The values can be either both of type **integer** or both of type **real**. To accomplish this, suppose we have written two subroutines, integer_swap and real_swap, that, respectively, interchange the values stored in two variables of type **integer** and the values of two variables of type **real**. We can write an interface that will define a generic interface named swap to these two subroutines as follows:

```
interface swap
   module procedure integer_swap, real_swap
end interface
```

or

```
interface swap
   module procedure integer_swap
   module procedure real_swap
end interface
```

Note that, unlike an operator or an assignment interface, these module procedures can be either subroutines or functions. However, the set of module procedures in a particular generic interface block must be either all functions or all subroutines – you cannot have a mix of functions and subroutines.

With this interface, we could write code of the form

```
.
.
.
integer :: i, j
real :: x, y
i = 1
j = 2
x = 1.0
y = 2.0
call swap(i, j)
call swap(x, y)
print *, i, j, x, y
.
.
.
```

The first call to swap results in integer_swap being called with the two actual arguments i and j, while the second call to swap results in real_swap being called with the two actual arguments x and y. The result of the **print** statement will therefore be

```
2  1  2.0  1.0
```

The general form of a generic interface is

```
interface generic_name
    module procedure list of module procedures
    .
    .
    .
end interface
```

where *generic_name* is the generic name to be used for the set of procedures specified in the block and *list of module procedures* is a comma-separated list of procedure names. There may be more than one such procedure list; however, all the procedures specified in a generic interface block must be subroutines, or they must all be functions. None of the procedure names, which are called **specific names**, may be the same as the generic name.

It is obviously vital that all the procedures specified by module procedures in such a **generic interface block** can be unambiguously differentiated, and the following rule applies for this purpose:

Any two procedures in a generic interface block must be distinguishable by reference to their non-optional dummy arguments, at least one of which must be different when considered both as positional and as keyword arguments.

The distinction between any two procedures in the interface block can therefore be made because one procedure has a dummy argument for which the other procedure has no equivalent dummy argument, or for which the equivalent dummy argument is of a different type, kind-type parameter or rank. An F compiler can then ensure that the correct procedure is used on each occasion that the generic name is referenced.

☐ EXAMPLE 16.2   • • • • • • • • • • • • • • • • ■ • • • • • • ■

① Problem

In Example 8.3 we developed a function to calculate the equation of a line between two points. It is now required to provide a generic subroutine which will, as its result, give a line which either (a) passes through two specified points, (b) passes through a point perpendicular to a specified line, or (c) passes through a point and is tangent to a specified circle. In the last case, an additional argument specifies which of the two alternatives is to be chosen.

② Analysis

We have already developed a function for the first case, together with a second function which will check to see if a solution is possible, that is, that the two points are not coincident. We could easily combine these into a single subroutine as follows:

```
subroutine line_from_points(join_line,p1,p2,distinct)
! Returns the line joining the two points supplied
! as arguments; distinct is set true if the points
! are distinct and a unique line exists, otherwise
! it is set false and the value of join_line is
! undetermined

    ! Dummy argument declarations
    type(point), intent(in) :: p1,p2
    logical, intent(out) :: distinct
    type(line), intent(out) :: join_line

    ! Set distinct true if either pair of corresponding
    ! coordinates are different
    distinct = abs(p1%x - p2%x)>small .or. &
               abs(p1%y - p2%y)>small

    ! Calculate coefficients of line if points are distinct
    if (distinct) then
        join_line %a = p2%y - p1%y
        join_line %b = p1%x - p2%x
        join_line %c = p1%y*p2%x - p2%y*p1%x

    end if
end subroutine line_from_points
```

Note that the value of small will be obtained by host association from the module containing line_from_points.

It is clear that, although the other two subroutines would have a line and a point as their first two arguments, the third arguments would be a line and a circle, respectively, and so the rules for disambiguating procedures in a generic interface block are satisfied. All that remains is to write a generic interface block.

We must choose a generic name to be used to refer to the three definitions. An obvious name might seem to be line, but this is not allowed because the name of one of the derived types is line, and F, as we know, will not permit, for example, the names line and Line to be used in the same scope. We shall, therefore, use gen_line for the generic name.

We shall not write the other two subroutines in detail (although our readers may wish to complete this example), but will merely indicate the overall structure of the resulting module, and the way in which it can be used.

3 Solution

```
module geometry
public :: gen_line
private :: line_from_points,line_perpto_line,line_tanto_circle

   ! Type definitions
   type, public :: point
      real :: x,y   ! Cartesian coordinates of the point
   end type point

   type, public :: line
      real :: a,b,c   ! Coefficients of defining equation
   end type line

   type, public :: circle
      real :: a,b,r   ! Coefficients of defining equation
   end type circle

   ! Generic procedure definition
   interface gen_line
      module procedure line_from_points
      module procedure line_perpto_line
      module procedure line_tanto_circle
   end interface

   ! Constant declaration (for use only in the module)
   real, parameter, private :: small=1.0e-5

contains

   subroutine line_from_points(join_line,p1,p2,distinct)
   ! Returns the line joining the two points supplied
   ! as arguments; distinct is set true if the points
   ! are distinct and a unique line exists, otherwise
   ! it is set false and the value of join_line is
   ! undetermined
```

```fortran
! Dummy argument declarations
type(point), intent(in) :: p1,p2
logical, intent(out) :: distinct
type(line), intent(out) :: join_line
      .
      .
      .
end subroutine line_from_points

subroutine line_perpto_line(new_line,p1,lin1,distinct)
! Returns the line through the point p1 perpendicular to
! the line lin1; distinct is set true if p1 does not
! lie on the line lin1 and a unique line exists, otherwise
! it is set false and the value of new_line is
! undetermined

    ! Dummy argument declarations
    type(point), intent(in) :: p1
    type(line), intent(in) :: lin1
    logical, intent(out) :: distinct
    type(line), intent(out) :: new_line
      .
      .
      .
end subroutine line_perpto_line

subroutine line_tanto_circle(tangent_line,p1,c1,left,outside)
! Returns the line through the point p1 tangent to the
! circle c1; outside is set true if p1 lies outside
! c1t and a tangent line exists, otherwise
! it is set false and the value of tangent_line is
! undetermined. If left is true the line on the left
! looking from p1 is chosen, otherwise the line on the right

    ! Dummy argument declarations
    type(point), intent(in) :: p1
    type(circle), intent(in) :: c1
    logical, intent(in) :: left
    logical, intent(out) :: outside
    type(line), intent(out) :: tangent_line
      .
      .
      .
end subroutine line_tanto_circle

end module geometry
```

We can now write a main program to test this module:

```fortran
program geometry_examples

use geometry
    type(point) :: p1, p2, p3
    type(line) :: line_1, line_2, line_3
    type(circle) :: c
```

```
            real :: r
            logical :: OK,left
            .
            .
            .
            call gen_line(line_1,p1,p2,OK)        ! line through p1, p2
            .
            .
            .
            call gen_line(line_2,p3,line_1,OK)    ! line through p3
                                                  ! perpendicular to line_1
            .
            .
            .
            left = .false.
            call gen_line(line_3,p1,c,left,OK)    ! line through p1 tangent
                                                  ! to the circle c on the
                                                  ! "right"
            .
            .
            .
        end program geometry_examples
```

Although in many cases it will only be required to define or extend an operator to deal with one combination of operands, there will also be situations in which it would be convenient to use the same operator in several situations, with different combinations of operands. In this case, we may define a generic defined operator in exactly the same way as we defined a *generic procedure*:

```
    interface operator (operator_symbol)
        module procedure list of function names
        .
        .
        .
    end interface
```

Note that all the defining functions for a particular operator *must* appear in the same interface block; it is not permitted to have two different interface blocks defining the same operator.

An example of the need for multiple definitions might be the requirement to define the result of multiplying an object of type vector by a **real** value, in either order, as well as defining the scalar product of two vectors. An appropriate interface block might then be

```
    interface operator(*)
        module procedure scalar_product,real_times_vector, &
                          vector_times_real
    end interface
```

where the two functions `real_times_vector` and `vector_times_real` define the result of the two operations of multiplying a **real** value by a `vector` and a `vector` by a **real** value, respectively.

```
module vectors

    public :: vector_size, operator(*), assignment(=)
    private :: scalar_product, real_times_vector,        &
               vector_times_real, create_vector,         &
               vector_array, vector_assign

    interface operator(*)
       module procedure scalar_product,real_times_vector, &
                        vector_times_real
    end interface

    interface assignment(=)
       module procedure create_vector, vector_array,     &
                        vector_assign
    end interface
    .
    .
    .
contains
    .
    .
    .
end module vectors
```

Finally, it must be noted that automatic transformation of **integer** to **real** will not take place for defined operations, and that if it is required to permit an **integer** to be multiplied by a `vector` using the same syntax then two further functions must be provided and their names included in the interface block.

16.5 Data abstraction and language extension

The ability to define new data types, to be able to encapsulate them in a module together with any relevant operators (including defined assignment) and procedures, coupled with the ability to make any of these operators and procedures generic, and the use of the **private** and **public** attributes to hide the internal details from the user of the module, is collectively known as **data abstraction**. Such abstraction is a key functionality in modern programming practice. In particular, it means that F modules can provide many of the features required for **object-oriented programming** (although not all of them) and for **language extension**. Language extension allows a programmer to extend the language to make it more appropriate for a particular application area. The time spent in developing such a language extension will be more than repaid by the easier and more reliable programs that can then be developed in this application domain.

We conclude the description of the F language, therefore, by showing how to write a module for performing arithmetic with rational numbers. It will use almost all of the features of F while demonstrating data abstraction and language extension.

☐ EXAMPLE 16.3 •

① Problem

A rational number is a number consisting of two parts, an integer numerator and a non-zero integer denominator, whose decimal value is the result of dividing the numerator by the denominator; in other words, it is a fraction. It is required to write a module to create a type for rational numbers and to provide the necessary facilities for rational numbers to be used in arithmetic expressions in the same ways as integer and real numbers. Write that part of the module that contains the specifications for all public entities, together with the procedures necessary to add an integer to a rational number, and a procedure to store the result in a rational-number variable.

We caution that the design presented here is suitable only for working with small problems. If many operations are performed on rational numbers, the numerator and denominator of the result will typically be too large to store in single variables of type **integer**. In fact, this is one of the reasons that floating-point numbers were invented. Such problems can, of course, be solved, but the solutions are too complex for expository material, obscuring the main point of the example (the design of modules) with their complexity.

② Analysis

The specification of a derived type to implement rational numbers is very straightforward:

```
type, public :: rational
   private
   integer :: num, denom
end type rational
```

We must first provide a subroutine for setting the value of a rational number from a pair of integers, incorporating a validity check to test for a zero denominator. We shall also need a function to display a rational number. Two functions should also be provided to extract, respectively, the numerator and denominator of a rational number.

We need to think carefully about the various arithmetic operations that we shall need to provide, and we shall consider the + operator first. There are four

Type of result	Type of left operand	Type of right operand
rational	integer	rational
rational	rational	integer
rational	rational	rational
rational		rational (unary +)

Figure 16.1 Extended cases for operators for rational arithmetic.

possibilities, as shown in Figure 16.1, and an interface block to extend the + operator accordingly might be as follows:

```
interface operator(+)
   module procedure int_plus_rat
   module procedure rat_plus_int
   module procedure rat_plus_rat
   module procedure rat_plus
end interface
```

Similar interface blocks will be required to extend the subtraction, multiplication, division and exponentiation operators.

It will also be necessary to provide extensions to the assignment operator to cover the three cases shown in Figure 16.2.

Notice that we have first analysed the capability that should be provided. This is good style. We next analyse the issues in providing that capability.

The implementation will be such that, after every creation of a new rational value, the numerator and denominator of the result have all common factors removed – see Exercise 8.12.

We must now write the four procedures to implement the + operator. In the case of adding an integer to a rational number, we know that we shall not require any simplification of the result, since the rational number involved in the expression is already in its simplest form. We need only write functions to deal with two cases (integer plus rational and rational plus integer), although, since these will be the same for all practical purposes, we shall only develop a structure plan for the first, int_plus_rat.

Left-hand side	Right-hand side
integer	rational
rational	integer
rational	rational

Figure 16.2 Extended assignment for rational arithmetic.

Data design

Purpose	Type	Name
A Dummy arguments		
Integer value to be added	**integer**	int_num
Rational value to be added	**type**(rational)	rat_num
B Result variable		
Sum of two arguments	**type**(rational)	rat_int_rat

Structure plan

1   Numerator of result is int_num × rat_num%denom

2   Denominator of result is rat_num%denom

3 Solution

```
module rational_numbers
! This module implements rational numbers as an additional
! numeric type

   public :: set_value, operator(+), operator(-),     &
             operator(*), operator(/), operator(**),  &
             assignment(=), numerator, denominator
   private :: int_plus_rat, rat_plus_int, rat_plus_rat, rat_plus
   ! and four similar private statements for the procedures to
   ! implement -, *, / and **
   private :: int_equals_rat, rat_equals_int, rat_equals_rat, &
              reduce_rat

   ! Type definition
   type, public :: rational
      private
      integer :: num, denom
   end type rational

   ! Extended intrinsic operator specifications
   interface operator(+)
      module procedure int_plus_rat
      module procedure rat_plus_int
      module procedure rat_plus_rat
      module procedure rat_plus
   end interface

   ! and four similar interface blocks for -, *, / and **

   ! Extended assignment
   interface assignment(=)
      module procedure int_equals_rat
      module procedure rat_equals_int
      module procedure rat_equals_rat
   end interface
```

```
contains
   ! Initialization
   subroutine set_value(p, q, r)
      integer, intent(in) :: p, q
      type(rational), intent(out) :: r
      if (q == 0) then
         print *, "Cannot have a zero value for a denominator"
         stop
      end if
      r%num = p
      r%denom = q
      call reduce_rat(r)          ! Remove the highest common
                                  ! factor from the two
                                  ! components of r
   end subroutine set_value

   ! Inquiry functions
   function numerator(r) result(n)
      type(rational), intent(in) :: r
      integer :: n
      n = r%num
   end function numerator

   function denominator(r) result(d)
      type(rational), intent(in) :: r
      integer :: d
      d = r%denom
   end function denominator

   ! + functions
   function rat_plus_int(rat_num, int_num) result(r)
   ! Adds an integer to a rational number to give a rational
   ! result

      ! Dummy arguments and result
      type(rational), intent(in) :: rat_num
      integer, intent(in) :: int_num
      type(rational) :: r

      ! Calculate result
      r%num = int_num*rat_num%denom + rat_num%num
      r%denom = rat_num%denom
   end function rat_plus_int

   function int_plus_rat(int_num, rat_num) result(r)
   ! Adds a rational number to an integer to give a rational
   ! result

      ! Dummy arguments and result
      integer, intent(in) :: int_num
      type(rational), intent(in) :: rat_num
      type(rational) :: r
```

```
            ! Calculate result
            r%num = rat_num%num + int_num*rat_num%denom
            r%denom = rat_num%denom
        end function int_plus_rat
            .
            .
            .
    end module rational_numbers
```

Note that, in the subroutine set_value, we have chosen to stop if we encounter a zero denominator; in a working module it would be preferable to take some more constructive action. Also note that, in the same subroutine, a call is made to the subroutine reduce_rat, whose purpose is to establish the highest common factor of the numerator and denominator of its argument, and then to divide both by that factor.

Notice, incidentally, that the second of the two functions detailed above for the + operator could have been written in a slightly shorter way by using the defined operator +, as specified by the first procedure:

```
function int_plus_rat(int_num, rat_num) result(r)
! Adds a rational number to an integer to give a rational
! result

    ! Dummy arguments and result
    integer, intent(in) :: int_num
    type(rational), intent(in) :: rat_num
    type(rational) :: r

    ! Calculate result with defined operator for reverse order
    r = rat_num + int_num
end function int_plus_rat
```

In this instance, a saving of one line of code is achieved at the cost of an extra procedure call and so could hardly be justified. However, if each procedure had been substantially longer, then such a simplification might be justified. Similarly, it might be worth using the extended meaning of one intrinsic operator in the procedure(s) to define another extended operator.

SELF-TEST EXERCISES 16.2

1   What is a generic procedure?

2   How are generic procedures defined? What constraints are there on generic procedures?

3   What are the rules for determining which specific procedure is used to implement a call to a generic procedure?

4   What is a generic operator? How is one defined?

5   What meant by data abstraction? What are the benefits of data abstraction?

SUMMARY

- Actual arguments may be related to dummy arguments either by position or by keyword.

- Dummy arguments declared with the **optional** attribute may be omitted from the list of actual arguments; the intrinsic function **present** determines whether an optional dummy argument has a corresponding actual argument.

- A procedure written in a language other than F must have its complete interface specified in an interface block which must be placed with the specification statements in the main program or a module.

- An interface block may be used to define a new operator, or to extend the meaning of an intrinsic operator; the procedures specified in such an interface block must all be functions.

- An interface block may be used to extend the meaning of assignment for non-intrinsic data types; the procedures specified in such an interface block must all be subroutines.

- An interface block may be used to define generic procedures; the procedures specified in such an interface block must either all be functions or all be subroutines.

- Any two module procedures in an interface block which defines a new operator, an extended intrinsic operator, extended assignment or a generic procedure must be distinguishable solely by reference to their non-optional dummy arguments.

- Data hiding and the ability to define and extend operators and assignment provide the facilities for data abstraction.

- Data abstraction is used for language extension and object-oriented programming.

- F syntax introduced in Chapter 16:

Keyword procedure invocation	**call** *name* (*dummy_arg_name=actual_arg, . . .*) *function_name* (*dummy_arg_name=actual_arg, . . .*) & **result** (*result_var_name*)
Optional dummy argument attribute	**optional**

| Defined operator interface block | ```
interface operator (operator_symbol)
    module procedure list of module function names
    .
    .
    .
end interface
``` |
| Defined assignment interface block | ```
interface assignment (=)
    module procedure list of module subroutine names
    .
    .
    .
end interface
``` |
| Generic procedure interface block | ```
interface generic_name
    module procedure list of module procedures
    .
    .
    .
end interface
``` |

PROGRAMMING EXERCISES

*16.1 Write a procedure which can calculate a revised bank balance after the addition of interest if the account is in credit, or the deduction of interest if it is overdrawn. The interest to be credited or debited is calculated by multiplying the current balance by the appropriate interest rate. Your procedure should be capable of being called from the main program in any of the following ways, where new_balance, old_balance, loan_rate and savings_rate are all integer variables:

(a) `new_balance = update(old_balance,12.5,4.5)`
where the savings rate is 4.5% and the overdraft rate is 12.5%.

(b) `new_balance = update(savings=4.5,balance=old_balance)`
where a default rate of interest is used for any overdraft (loan) interest and the rate for any savings is 4.5%.

(c) `new_balance = update(old_balance)`
where default rates of interest are used for both savings and overdraft

(d) `loan_rate = 12.5      ! that is, 12.5% overdraft interest`
`new_balance = update(old_balance)`
where the specified rate of 12.5% is used for any overdraft interest and the default interest rate is used for any credit balance.

(e) `savings_rate = 4.5      ! that is, 4.5% savings interest`
`new_balance = update(overdraft=12.5,old_balance)`
where the specified rate of 4.5% is used for any savings interest and any overdraft interest is charged at 12.5%.

Test your procedure in a program that uses (at least) all of these methods.
```

16.2   In Section 16.4, we defined a generic subroutine `swap`. Complete and test this definition. Then extend `swap` to also interchange entities of type `complex_number` (as defined in Examples 8.4 and 8.6).

16.3   Complete and test the module `vectors` that was partially developed in Section 16.4. Pay particular attention to the subroutine `vector_assign`.

16.4   In Example 16.2 we wrote part of a module to calculate the coordinates of a point in various ways. Write the necessary code to add to the module `geometry` so that the statement

        point_1 = .centre.circle_1

in a program that uses the module, will cause the variable `point_1` of type `point` to be assigned the value of the coordinates of the centre of the circle `circle_1`, which is itself of type `circle`, and the statement

        point_2 = line_1 .intersects. line_2

will cause the variable `point_2`, also of type `point`, to be assigned the value of the coordinates of the point of intersection of the two lines `line_1` and `line_2`, both of type `line`. Remember to take appropriate action if the lines are parallel.

16.5   Write a module which defines a monadic operator `.qsort.` which sorts an integer array a with n elements using the following algorithm for the QuickSort method.

1.   Set the integer variables i and j to 1 and n, respectively
2.   Decrease j until $a(i) > a(j)$, then swap $a(i)$ and $a(j)$
3.   Increase i until $a(i) > a(j)$, then swap $a(i)$ and $a(j)$
4.   Repeat the last two actions until i and j are equal, and call this value of i (and j) *pivot*

$a(pivot)$ is now in the correct place, and the array has been divided into two sections around pivot, each of which can be sorted separately.

   If both sections have more than one element then save the start and end positions of the smaller section on a stack, and return to sort the larger section. If only one section has more than one element then return to sort that section. If neither section has more than one element then remove the start and end of a section off the stack and return to sort it. If there is nothing left on the stack then the array is fully sorted.

   Note that a stack is a means of storing items in which items can only be removed in the reverse order to that in which they were added to the stack ('last in – first out'), and is a very useful concept in many algorithms. It can be implemented in F as an array and an integer pointer to the top of the stack. In this case an array of dimension $2 \log_2 n$ will be large enough.

   Test the module in which the operator `.qsort.` is defined in a program which includes a statement of the form

        sorted_integers = .qsort.random_integers

where `sorted_integers` and `random_integers` are integer arrays (of the same size).

16.6   Modify your solution to Exercise 16.5 to use a recursive algorithm instead of a stack. (Hint: you will need to use sub-arrays.)

*16.7 Write a program which can be used to encrypt or decrypt a message in the following manner.

A keyword is used to encrypt the message by allocating each letter in the keyword its numeric position in the alphabet, and then replacing each letter of the message by the letter n later in the alphabet, where n is the value of the next letter of the keyword. The keyword is repeated as often as necessary, and the alphabet is considered to be circular (that is, A follows Z). The message must consist only of letters and spaces, with any numbers being spelled out, digit by digit. All letters are encrypted to lower case. Spaces can be simply replaced by the next letter in the keyword, although this can cause slight confusion during decrypting as the letter z and a space will be encrypted to the same character (think about it!); a neater way is to treat the alphabet as having 27 letters, for example a–z plus I, and to replace spaces by I during encrypting, and vice versa during decrypting.

The coded message is written in groups of the same length as the keyword, which forms the first group, with extra random letters being added to the end of the last group if necessary. Thus, if the keyword is *pxadtai* (16, 24, 1, 4, 20, 1, 9) the message *This exercise is crazy* will be encrypted as follows, using a 27-letter alphabet with I as the extra character:

$$
\begin{aligned}
T &\to T + 16 = i \\
h &\to h + 24 = e \\
i &\to i + 1 \quad = j \\
s &\to s + 4 \quad = w \\
\diamond &\to 20 \quad\quad = t \\
e &\to e + 1 \quad = f \\
x &\to x + 9 \quad = f \\
e &\to e + 16 = u \\
r &\to r + 24 = o
\end{aligned}
$$

and so on, leading to the encrypted message

pxadtai iejwtff uodmlfi ypagkbh ngnsoio

Note that, as can be seen from this example, the same letter does not normally encrypt to the same encrypted letter, thus eliminating the well-known method of code-breaking based on frequency counts.

The decryption part of the program will, of course, use the same procedure in reverse.

Your program should use two procedures to carry out the encryption and decryption, respectively. The encryption procedure should have either one or two input arguments. The required argument will be the message to be encrypted. The optional argument will be the keyword to be used for encryption; if this argument is not supplied your procedure must obtain a suitable keyword in some other way. If both arguments are provided the procedure must accept them in either order. The decryption procedure will have only one input argument, namely the message to be decrypted. (Hint: first write and test the encryption procedure; this can then be used to test the decryption one.)

16.8 Modify the program that you wrote for Exercise 16.7 so that encryption and decryption are carried out by two operators, `.encrypt.` and `.decrypt.`. The first of these operators should have two character operands and should deliver the encrypted version of the second operand, using the first operand as the key; the other operator should be a monadic operator. Thus

```
    "pxadtai" .encrypt. "This exercise is crazy"
```

will deliver the result 'pxadtai iejwtff uodmlfi ypagkbh ngnsoio', while

```
    .decrypt. "pxadtai iejwtff uodmlfi ypagkbh ngnsoio"
```

will deliver the result 'this exercise is crazyjmovhf' (where the extra letters at the end are because of the addition by the encrypting operator of extra letters to complete the last block).

16.9 In Example 8.6 we developed a module containing a derived type `complex_number` and four procedures to implement addition, subtraction, multiplication and division with complex numbers. Write a module that allows a user to employ the intrinsic operators +, -, *, and / to carry out these operations on complex numbers instead of using the procedures.

Now extend this module so that any combination of **real**, **integer** and `complex_number` entities (variables or constants) may be the operands for the four operators +, -, *, and /. The module should also extend the assignment operator so that assignment of **real** or **integer** values to complex_number variables works correctly.

16.10 Some programming languages contain a data type known as an *enumeration type*, in which a finite set of discrete values are specified, and variables or constants of that type may only take one of these values. For example, a character enumeration type called `seasons` might only allow the values `"spring"`, `"summer"`, `"autumn"` and `"winter"`, and an integer enumeration type called month might only allow the integers between 1 and 12, inclusive.

Write a module which defines two enumeration types, int_enum and char_enum, for integers and characters respectively, and appropriate operators and so on to allow variables of these types to be used in expressions and in **case** statements. Test your module with a suitable test program.

Note that you will need to determine what to do if the program attempts to assign an illegal value to a variable of one of these types. One possibility might be to print an error message and/or to terminate the program. Another possibility might be to treat such an action in a similar way to overflow during an arithmetic operation and to store a logical variable as part of the type which specifies whether the last attempt to change the variable's value was successful.

Such illegal values could be tested for by the module procedures that access an enumerated variable, or by a special validity-check procedure, and appropriate action taken if a variable is found to have been corrupted.

16.11 Example 7.1 introduced the straight selection sort, Exercise 7.8 introduced the bubble sort and Exercise 16.5 explained the QuickSort algorithm, but all of the procedures written to implement these sorts can only sort items of a specific type. Thus a procedure for sorting integers cannot be used to sort characters. However, it can readily be seen that in all methods there are only two situations when the array is referred to: (a) when elements *i* and *j* of the array are to be compared, and (b) when elements *i* and *j* of the array are to be exchanged.

Write a sorting procedure, using whichever method you prefer, which uses optional arguments to allow it to sort an array which is either integer, real or character type. Also include an additional argument to indicate whether the sorted array is to be in ascending or descending order. Test the procedure in a program which calls it three times — first to sort a set of integers into ascending order, second to sort a set of words into alphabetic order, and third to sort a set of real values into descending order.

16.12 qfpuzkx cutceix jnuuobl tktoqpx jnqnzil kfllndb qldlzpu vxscrpx wovndpk qvdcmdx ikkzmkl hfvcedb vtpjntk jfucfsq qydussy jfyhrdb rjpiekr iocazde vflzxgl hjplnbx vtsictk xfuvbsx srdxjkf jfymzep vjpimwv qldlzde vfvcqcq qhaibvx ikbcbzi etpngpo vgvndbx jnuuobb lodorkl ejuyzmi eiluhcx kyuyzdl qkcxnob qugucpl ejuussb qturskl dkpmszm qkcygns

zhjaq hnjze bnrll gndan huien aiiis dxmns xevfs jjnyt qonnk edsew cdlma qdjav hdzsj ovlej cxvny xpgly tdywq twrkf tzfym klzsy lthgl dtnyl qtlgl vlllx gusly uysut ipsja raazt rtuni ryhrg

(Hint: see Exercise 16.7.)

More about numerical methods

17

17.1 Numerical methods and their limitations

17.2 Solving quadratic equations

17.3 Newton's method for solving non-linear equations

17.4 The secant method of solving non-linear equations

17.5 Solution of simultaneous linear equations by Gaussian elimination

17.6 Solving a tridiagonal system of equations

17.7 Fitting a curve through a set of data points using a cubic spline

17.8 Integration and numerical quadrature

The preceding chapters have described all of F. In this final chapter, we return to the subject of numerical methods, which was first discussed in Chapter 11, showing how they can be programmed in F.

After a brief review of some of the limitations of numerical methods, the bulk of this chapter is taken up with a discussion of some of the most widely used numerical techniques relating to the solution of various types of equations, the fitting of curves through sets of data points, and the integration of functions by numerical quadrature. The exercises at the end of this chapter also briefly describe certain other techniques.

Although the descriptions given in this chapter give a sound basis for the understanding of these and other numerical methods, we cannot emphasize too strongly that this is a highly specialized area. If your programs are likely to involve much numerical work then you should refer to some of the many books devoted to numerical methods, several of which are cited in this chapter.

17.1   Numerical methods and their limitations

In Chapter 11, we introduced some of the basic concepts involved in numerical computation and emphasized that, because of such effects as round-off, conditioning and stability, the choice of the numerical method to be used could substantially affect the result obtained in a particular case. It is not our intention to discuss these concepts any further in this book, but it is important that the programmer should be aware of the strengths and weaknesses of different methods before deciding which one to use in a particular situation.

When writing a program, we are generally trying to solve a problem to which there is an exact mathematical answer. Mathematics abounds with existence theorems which typically state that, given certain conditions, a solution to a specified problem exists. However, the proofs are often non-constructive — in the sense that they can imply an infinity of operations to obtain the desired solution or, even worse, do not even specify what set of operations are required to construct the solution. A second type of difficulty arises from the fact that many existence proofs show that some set of real (or complex) numbers is a solution to a specified problem. The set of real (or complex) numbers forms a continuum. However, on a computer, real or complex numbers can only be specified with a finite precision. For example, neither π nor $\sqrt{2}$ can be exactly represented numerically on a digital computer.

The field of numerical analysis is the design of algorithms (deterministic processes with a finite number of steps) that will approximate, to a specified precision, the mathematical solutions of problems. Moreover, it is a requirement that these algorithms execute efficiently; in other words, that they use as few operations as possible. Finally, it is required that they be robust; that is, that they perform reliably for a large range of inputs and detect and report when they are unable to solve a problem. This is the ideal. In practice, there are still many problems for which we have to settle for less.

In Chapter 11, we also discussed the use of parameterized **real** variables as a means of writing procedures whose precision was both portable and readily changeable. However, we pointed out that relying on increasing the precision of calculations would not always eliminate numerical difficulties. Understanding the underlying reasons for numerical difficulties is important for their correct resolution.

Chapter 11 also introduced two simple, but widely used, techniques in numerical programming, namely the method of least squares for fitting a straight line as an approximation to a set of data points and the bisection method for the solution of a non-linear equation.

In this chapter, we shall examine other, superior, methods of solution of non-linear equations, and will also consider the solution of a system of simultaneous linear equations. We shall also look at more sophisticated methods of interpolation and curve-fitting in which the data does not necessarily lie near a straight line. Finally we shall briefly discuss methods of numerical integration in order, for example, to find the area under a curve.

It is important to emphasize, however, that most of the subprograms developed in this chapter are only examples to illustrate the basic techniques. Some introductory textbooks on numerical analysis are by Dahlquist and Björck (1974), Scheid (1968) and Forsythe *et al.* (1977). A great deal of effort has been expended by many people over many years in refining algorithms for numerical computation, especially to deal with difficult cases. The majority of these have been written in Fortran. With a certain amount of effort, translation into F is possible.

17.2 Solving quadratic equations

We start with what, on the surface, appears to be a simple problem, namely finding the roots of a quadratic equation. We shall, however, see that even such a simple problem involves subtle numerical issues if we are trying to produce robust software. The intent here is to instil a healthy caution in the reader when more complicated problems are being solved.

Everyone who studied algebra in high school learned that the quadratic equation

$$ax^2 + bx + c = 0 \tag{1}$$

where $a \neq 0$, has two roots, given by the formula

$$\frac{-b \pm \sqrt{b^2 - 4ac}}{2a}$$

We shall now examine some of the difficulties which can occur when using this formula on a computer with six decimal digits of precision and an exponent range of 10^{40} (many workstations and personal computers have single-precision hardware close to this situation).

Let us consider the equation

$$x^2 - 6x + 5 = 0$$

If we solve this on a computer by using the above formula, we will obtain answers very close to 1 and 5 (which are the exact roots).

If we multiply the above equation by 10^{30}, we obtain the new equation

$$10^{30}x^2 - 6 \times 10^{30}x + 5 \times 10^{30} = 0$$

The roots of this equation are, of course, still 1 and 5.

Now, using the standard formula, we would calculate

$$\frac{6 \times 10^{30} \pm \sqrt{(6 \times 10^{30})^2 - 4 \times 10^{30} \times 5 \times 10^{30}}}{2 \times 10^{30}}$$

However, on our hypothetical computer, 10^{60} is not a representable number. Consequently, the program would abort with an overflow. Similarly, if the original equation was multiplied by 10^{-30}, we would either abort with a numeric underflow or, if the computer being used simply represents underflow as 0, would obtain the roots

$$\frac{6 \times 10^{-30} \pm \sqrt{(6 \times 10^{-30})^2 - 4 \times 10^{-30} \times 5 \times 10^{-30}}}{2 \times 10^{-30}}$$

$$= \frac{6 \times 10^{-30} \pm \sqrt{0}}{2 \times 10^{-30}}$$

$$= 3 \text{ and } 3$$

which are two very poor answers!

This type of difficulty can sometimes be reduced by scaling the equations before attempting to solve them. For example, we could divide the equation by $\max(|a|, |b|, |c|)$, so that all the coefficients lie in the range $[-1, 1]$. This, unfortunately, is not a complete solution to the scaling problem. Consider, for example, the equation

$$10^{-20}x^2 + 10^{20}x + 10^{20} = 0$$

This has one root near -1 and one root near -10^{40}. If we simply scale the equation by dividing by 10^{20}, we will either get an underflow error, or the coefficient of x^2 will become 0. In the latter case, the equation becomes the linear equation

$$x + 1 = 0$$

This has only one root, $x = -1$, and we have lost the second, large negative, root of the original quadratic.

In situations like this, where one root is in the range of the floating-point numbers, we would like to obtain the representable root and indicate that the other root is too large in absolute value to be represented. In this case, we might resort to transforming the equation by scaling the roots.

Next, let us consider the case where one root is much bigger, in absolute value, than the other. For example, the equation

$$x^2 - 10^6 x + 1 = 0$$

has, to six significant places, the roots 10^{-6} and 10^6. The application of the standard formula gives

$$\frac{10^6 \pm \sqrt{(10^6)^2 - 4}}{2}$$

Because of the round-off errors, since 4 will not significantly add to 10^{12}, this becomes

$$\frac{10^6 \pm \sqrt{10^{12}}}{2} = \frac{10^6 \pm 10^6}{2}$$

So the standard formula gives the roots 10^6 (which is good) and 0 (which is bad).

The usual way employed to solve this case is first to calculate the root in which the sign of $\sqrt{b^2 - 4ac}$ is the same as that of $-b$. This eliminates any round-off problems caused by subtracting two nearly equal numbers. In the above example, since $-(-10^6)$ is positive, we take the positive value of the square root. This will give one root as $(10^6 + 10^6)/2$, or 10^6, which is a good answer. To obtain the other root, we note that the product of the roots of the quadratic equation (1) is c/a. Therefore, once one root has been found accurately, we can obtain the other root by dividing c/a by the first root. In the above example, this would give a second root of $(1/1)/10^6$, or 10^{-6}, another good answer. Note that this technique eliminates the possibility of catastrophic cancellation when two nearly equal numbers are subtracted.

We now proceed to writing a program. In order to reduce overflow problems during computation, we rewrite the standard formula in a different, but mathematically equivalent, way. Thus, the roots of the equation

$$ax^2 + bx + c = 0, \quad a \neq 0$$

are the same as the roots of

$$rx^2 + sx + t = 0, \quad r \neq 0$$

where

$$r = \frac{a}{\max(|a|, |b|, |c|)}$$

$$s = \frac{b}{\max(|a|, |b|, |c|)}$$

$$t = \frac{c}{\max(|a|, |b|, |c|)}$$

```fortran
module library_constants

  ! Define precision
  integer, parameter, public :: lib_prec = &
                                selected_real_kind(p = 6)
    .
    .
    .

end module library_constants


    .
    .
    .


subroutine quad_roots(a, b, c, root1, root2, error)
use library_constants
  ! Dummy arguments
  real(kind = lib_prec), intent(in) :: a, b, c
  real(kind = lib_prec), intent(out) :: root1, root2
  logical, intent(out):: error

  ! Local variables
  real(kind = lib_prec) :: f, r, s, t, d

  ! Check for a = 0
  if (a == 0.0_lib_prec) then
     error = .true.
     return
  end if
  error = .false.

  ! Calculate scaled coefficients
  f = max(abs(a), abs(b), abs(c))
  r = a/f
  s = b/f
  t = c/f

  ! Solve modified equation for first root
  d = sqrt(s*s-4.0_lib_prec*r*t)
  if (s>0.0_lib_prec) then
     root1 = (-s-d)/(r+r)
  else
     root1 = (-s+d)/(r+r)
  end if

  ! Calculate other root
  root2 = (t/r)/root1

end subroutine quad_roots
```

Figure 17.1 An improved procedure for finding the roots of a quadratic equation.

The roots of this equation are

$$\frac{-s \pm \sqrt{s^2 - 4rt}}{2r}$$

What we have accomplished by these manipulations is that the coefficients we are now working with (r, s and t) are all in the interval $[-1, 1]$. Thus overflow problems are diminished.

We will then use the preceding formula to obtain one root only by, as already discussed, taking the sign of the square root so as to match that of the first part of the numerator (that is, match the sign of $-s$). This is to minimize cancellation effects.

Finally, the second root is obtained by dividing c/a by the first root.

A subroutine to implement this algorithm is shown in Figure 17.1. Note that the module `library_constants` is assumed, among other things, to define the constant `lib_prec` as the **kind** type parameter for **real** values.

Using this subroutine to find the roots of the equation

$$x^2 - 10^6 x + 1 = 0$$

we obtain the roots 10^6 and 10^{-6}.

17.3 Newton's method for solving non-linear equations

The bisection method introduced in Section 11.5 has one major strength and one major weakness. The strength is that, because the interval is halved at each iteration, it is guaranteed to converge to a root after a finite, and predictable, number of iterations. The weakness of the method, however, is that it is slow to converge. One of the reasons for this is that the method does not use all the available information. It uses the sign of $f(x)$ at the end-points of the interval, but not the value of $f(x)$ at those points. Another weakness is that, for the method to work at all, the initial two points must bracket a root. In this section and the next, we will show some other commonly used techniques that usually converge considerably faster but have the defect that they sometimes fail to converge at all. Fast convergence is important, because each function evaluation can be expensive.

It is possible to combine interval bisection with such faster methods and retain much of the best of both worlds, namely fast convergence and guaranteed convergence. This combination, however, goes beyond the scope of this book. It is described in Forsythe *et al.* (1977).

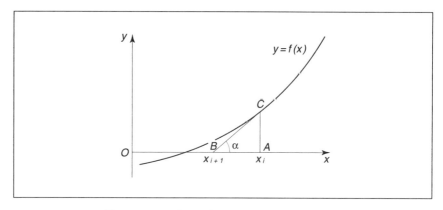

Figure 17.2 Newton's method of approximation.

First we shall discuss **Newton's method**, sometimes known as the **Newton–Raphson method**. This method uses not only function values but also uses the first derivative, or **gradient**, of the curve to help find the next approximation. Figure 17.2 shows how, given the gradient at a point x_i, it is easy to obtain a new estimate x_{i+1} for the root. In this method, we do not bracket a root by an interval but, instead, generate a sequence of approximations that (if successful) tend to the root.

From Figure 17.2 we can readily see that

$$x_{i+1} = OB$$
$$= OA - AB$$
$$= x_i - AB$$
$$= x_i - \frac{AC}{\tan \alpha}$$
$$= x_i - \frac{f(x_i)}{f'(x_i)}$$

where $f'(x_i)$ is the gradient of the curve at the point C, $(x_i, f(x_i))$, which is equal to $\tan \alpha$.

This formula

$$x_{i+1} = x_i - \frac{f(x_i)}{f'(x_i)}$$

is known as **Newton's iteration**, and is the basis for Newton's method of approximation to a root. It is used repeatedly to get a series of values of x (often) converging to a root.

The mathematical conditions under which convergence is guaranteed go beyond the scope of this book and, in practice, are often of limited use.

There will be situations in which the first derivative is not available, or would be very time-consuming to calculate, and in these situations Newton's method is not an appropriate one to choose (but see the description of the secant method in the next section). However, in many cases the derivative is readily available, and in these situations Newton's method will usually converge very rapidly.

It should be noted that Newton's method will converge slowly, sometimes more slowly than interval bisection, if the slope of the function is zero (or almost zero) in a region containing the zero of the function we are trying to find.

The only remaining problem is the determination of the form of convergence criterion to be used. In the bisection method, we used the size of the interval, which we showed to be related to the difference between the approximation to the root and the true value of that root. However, the Newton method does not bracket the root by an interval whose size tends to zero. An appropriate criterion for the Newton method is, therefore, to stop the iteration when a point x_k is found such that

$$|f(x_k)| \leqslant \epsilon$$

where ϵ is a user-specified tolerance. We are, by using this convergence criterion, not insisting that the Newton method find a root exactly. This is because the exact root may not be (indeed, for most functions, is not) a rational number and, therefore, cannot be expressed exactly as a floating-point number. Moreover, when a function is evaluated using floating-point arithmetic, it will not be evaluated exactly. Thus, even if there is a rational number X such that $f(X) = 0$, on a computer it is unlikely that $f(X)$ will be calculated to be exactly zero.

In choosing ϵ, the user must exercise some discretion. If f has a large derivative near a root, we should tolerate a relatively large value of $|f(x)|$ for x being accepted as a good approximation to a zero of f. On the other hand, if f has a small slope near the root, we should adopt a small value for ϵ. Otherwise, $|f(x)|$ may be small, but x could be a long way from the true zero. When working with a new function, some experimentation with the value of ϵ may be necessary.

◼ EXAMPLE 17.1   ●

1 **Problem**

Write a program to find a root of the equation $f(x) = 0$ using Newton's method. The program should use two functions to define the function f and its first derivative, respectively. The user should input the accuracy required together with the x-coordinate of a point which can be used as the starting point for the iteration.

2 Analysis

We have already discussed the mathematics involved in this method and so can proceed to the design of the program. We must, however, note that, generally, the closer the starting value is to the root, the better the convergence will be. Because the Newton method does not guarantee convergence, we shall specify an upper limit for the number of iterations permitted before terminating the process. The data design and structure plan are then quite straightforward:

Data design

Purpose	Type	Name
A Dummy arguments		
Function whose root is required	function	f
First derivative of f	function	f_prime
Start point for interpolation	real	start
Accuracy of result	real	eps
Upper limit for iteration	integer	max_iter
Value of root	real	root
Error/success condition	integer	error
B Local variables		
Current value of $f(x)$	real	f_val
Current value of $f'(x)$	real	f_der
do-loop control	integer	i

Structure plan

1   If eps ≤ 0 then return with error = −3

2   If max_iter ≤ 0, then return with error = −4

3   Set root to initial approximation (start)

4   Repeat up to max_iter times
    4.1   Set f_val to f(root)
    4.2   If | f_val |≤ eps then
        4.2.1   Process has converged, so return with error = 0
    4.3   Set f_der to f'(root)
    4.4   If f_der = 0 then
        4.4.1   Iteration cannot proceed further, so return with error = −2
    4.5   Set root to root-f_val/f_der

5   Process has not converged after max_iter steps, so set error to −1

3 **Solution**

The main program is sufficiently similar to that given in Example 11.2 that we
have not included it here. The subroutine which calculates the root is as follows:

```
module newton
   public :: newton_raphson

contains

   subroutine newton_raphson(f, f_prime, start, eps, &
                             max_iter, root, error)
   ! This subroutine finds a root of the equation f(x)=0
   ! using Newton-Raphson iteration.
   ! The function f-prime returns the value of the derivative of
   ! the function f(x).

      ! Dummy arguments
      interface
         function f(x) result(fx)
            real, intent(in) :: x
            real :: fx
         end function f
         function f_prime(x) result(fpx)
            real, intent(in) :: x
            real :: fpx
         end function f_prime
      end interface
      real, intent(in) :: start, eps
      integer, intent(in) :: max_iter
      real, intent(out) :: root
      integer, intent(out) :: error
      ! error indicates the result of the processing as follows:
      ! =  0 a root was found
      ! = -1 no root found after max_iter iterations
      ! = -2 the first derivative became zero, and so no
      !      further iterations were possible
      ! = -3 the value of eps supplied was negative or zero
      ! = -4 the value of max_iter supplied was negative or zero

      ! Local variables
      integer :: i
      real :: f_val, f_der

      ! Check validity of epsilon
      if(eps <= 0.0) then
         error = -3
         root = huge(root)
         return
      end if

      ! Check validity of max_iter
      if(max_iter <= 0) then
         error = -4
         root = huge(root)
         return
      end if
```

```
        ! Begin the iteration at the specified value of x
        root = start

        ! Repeat the iteration up to the maximum number specified
        do i = 1, max_iter
            f_val = f(root)
            ! Output latest estimate while testing
            print "(2(a, es15.6))", "root = ", root,          &
                    " f(root) = ", f_val
            if(abs(f_val) <= eps) then
                ! A root has been found
                error = 0
                return
            end if

            f_der = f_prime(root)
            if(f_der == 0.0) then
                ! f'(x)=0, so no more iterations are possible
                error = -2
                return
            end if

            ! Use Newton's iteration to obtain next approximation
            root = root - f_val/f_der
        end do

        ! Process has not converged after max_iter iterations
        error = -1

    end subroutine newton_raphson
end module newton
```

Notice that if $\epsilon \leqslant 0$, we have set error to -3 *and* returned an answer of **huge**(root). This is an example of double safety when an error in usage is detected. If a user is so foolish as not to check error returns for problems, the answer returned will be so absurd that a problem should be detected anyway. We have done similarly if the maximum number of interations is not strictly positive. We have also included a **print** statement to show the progress of the iteration; this would normally be removed when the subroutine has been verified to be working correctly.

Figure 17.3 shows the result of running the program with three different starting points using the same function f as was used in Example 11.2, namely $f(x) = x + e^x$. A value of 10^{-6} was used for epsilon in each program execution. The functions f and f_prime are extremely simple to write in this case:

```
module function_definition
    public :: f, f_prime
contains
    function f(x) result(fx)
        real, intent(in) :: x
        real :: fx
        fx = x+exp(x)
    end function f
```

```
          Starting at -10
          root =   -1.000000E+01 f(root) =   -9.999954E+00
          root =   -4.999411E-04 f(root) =    9.990003E-01
          root =   -5.001249E-01 f(root) =    1.063300E-01
          root =   -5.663141E-01 f(root) =    1.299653E-03
          root =   -5.671431E-01 f(root) =    2.322294E-07
          A root was found at x = -0.567143  f(x) = 0.232E-06
          Starting at 0
          root =    0.000000E+00 f(root) =    1.000000E+00
          root =   -5.000000E-01 f(root) =    1.065307E-01
          root =   -5.663110E-01 f(root) =    1.304512E-03
          root =   -5.671431E-01 f(root) =    2.322294E-07
          A root was found at x = -0.567143  f(x) = 0.232E-06
          Starting at 10
          root =    1.000000E+01 f(root) =    2.203646E+04
          root =    8.999592E+00 f(root) =    8.108777E+03
          root =    7.998604E+00 f(root) =    2.984799E+03
          root =    6.996254E+00 f(root) =    1.099529E+03
          root =    5.990771E+00 f(root) =    4.057134E+02
          root =    4.978316E+00 f(root) =    1.502080E+02
          root =    3.951110E+00 f(root) =    5.594418E+01
          root =    2.895422E+00 f(root) =    2.098655E+01
          root =    1.796139E+00 f(root) =    7.822473E+00
          root =    6.828310E-01 f(root) =    2.662305E+00
          root =   -2.107176E-01 f(root) =    5.992851E-01
          root =   -5.418139E-01 f(root) =    3.987834E-02
          root =   -5.670263E-01 f(root) =    1.833178E-04
          root =   -5.671433E-01 f(root) =    4.541133E-08
          A root was found at x = -0.567143  f(x) = 0.454E-07
```

Figure 17.3 Three solutions for $x + e^x = 0$ using the subroutine `newton_raphson`.

```
   function f_prime(x) result (fpx)
      real, intent(in) :: x
      real :: fpx
      fpx = 1.0+exp(x)
   end function f_prime
end module function_definition
```

It will be noticed that, although using a value of -10.0 or 0.0 as the initial value produced extremely fast convergence (4 and 3 iterations, respectively), using $+10.0$ produced a relatively slow convergence which required 13 iterations. A moment's thought about the shape of the function will make the reason for this difference quite clear — namely that for values of x greater than two or three the curve is almost parallel to the y-axis, with the result that Newton's iteration does not work very well. Once again, this emphasizes the importance of thinking about the method to be used *and* the range of values in which it should be used. In the next section we shall meet a third approach to solving this type of problem, and Figure 17.7 shows a comparison of the three methods.

Newton–Raphson iteration can be shown, under certain circumstances, to have superior convergence properties to interval bisection. Whereas the error in the bisection method is only halved at each iteration, the error in Newton's method is approximately proportional to the square of the error of the previous iterate. The mathematical analysis required to show under what circumstances this is true is beyond the scope of this book, but is discussed by Dahlquist and Björck (1974). However, the faster convergence comes at a cost, for Newton–Raphson iteration, unlike interval bisection, does not always converge to a zero. Consider, for example, the case in which $f(x) = x^{1/3}$. The Newton–Raphson iteration in this case is

$$x_{n+1} = x_n - \frac{x_n^{1/3}}{x_n^{-2/3}/3}$$

$$= x_n - 3x_n$$

$$= -2x_n$$

So, if we start at a point x_0, we generate a sequence of iterates x_0, $-2x_0$, $4x_0$, $-8x_0$, $16x_0$, ... Thus, if $x_0 \neq 0$, the sequence will oscillate with ever-increasing amplitude and will definitely not converge to 0 (the answer we are hoping to get) no matter how close to 0 we start the iteration. It will only converge to 0 if we start the iteration at 0 – which is not a very practical algorithm!

17.4   The secant method of solving non-linear equations

As we have seen, Newton's method for the solution of non-linear equations requires the values of the first derivative of the function as well as the values of the function itself. For many functions coming from scientific or engineering problems, calculating the derivative is expensive or (analytically) impossible, and in these situations the **secant method** can be used. This method can be regarded as being derived from Newton's method by replacing the derivative by an estimate of the derivative obtained from the slope of the line joining the last two iterates, as shown in Figure 17.4.

The point where this line (called a secant – hence the name of the method) cuts the x-axis is taken to be the next iterate. Notice that, unlike Newton's method, we now require two values of x to start the iteration. However, unlike the interval bisection method, the two values do not have to have opposite signs for the corresponding function values. It is thus easier to find two values to start the secant method than the interval bisection method.

The equation of the straight line joining the two end-points of the interval can easily be derived by noting that

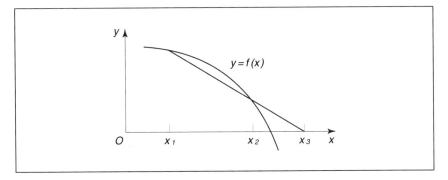

Figure 17.4 The secant method of approximation.

$$\frac{y - f_2}{x - x_2} = \frac{f_2 - f_1}{x_2 - x_1}, \quad \text{for } x_2 \neq x_1$$

where f_1 is the value of $f(x_1)$ and f_2 is the value of $f(x_2)$. The equation of the line is, therefore

$$y = \frac{f_2 - f_1}{x_2 - x_1}(x - x_2) + f_2, \quad x_2 \neq x_1$$

This line cuts the x-axis where $y = 0$. Thus x_3, the x-coordinate of the intersection, satisfies the equation

$$0 = \frac{f_2 - f_1}{x_2 - x_1}(x_3 - x_2) + f_2$$

and, therefore,

$$x_3 = x_2 - \frac{f_2(x_2 - x_1)}{f_2 - f_1}, \quad f_2 \neq f_1$$

The next iterate x_3 is thus calculated as a correction to the point x_2. This is a good form from a computational viewpoint as it tends to minimize round-off errors. For the next iteration we therefore replace x_1 by x_2 and x_2 by x_3. We repeat the iteration until a root is found.

One potential problem is immediately apparent, namely the situation where f_1 and f_2 are the same, or very close to each other. This corresponds to the position shown in Figure 17.5, and clearly will cause the method to fail since the line joining the two end-points is either parallel to the x-axis, or almost parallel to it.

Although less intuitively obvious than the situation shown in Figure 17.5, there are other situations in which the secant method may not converge, and for which another method may be better. It is thus imperative that the **do** loop used

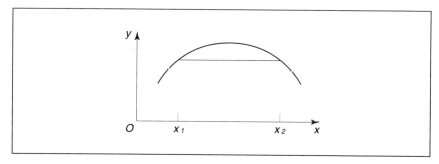

Figure 17.5 A failure position for the secant method.

to control the iteration should have a sensible maximum iteration count, so that another method can be tried in the event that the secant method does not converge to a solution.

As with Newton's method, an appropriate convergence criterion is that the iteration be stopped when a point x is found such that

$$|f(x)| \leqslant \epsilon$$

where ϵ is a user-specified tolerance. The considerations that go into choosing ϵ are the same as those already discussed for Newton's method.

☐ EXAMPLE 17.2 •

1 Problem

Write a program to find a root of the equation $f(x) = 0$ using the secant method. The user should input the accuracy required and the x-coordinates of two points to be used as starting points for the iteration.

2 Analysis

As with Newton's method, the closer the two starting values are to the root, the better the convergence will generally be. We shall ensure that x_2 is the most recent approximation, and will rearrange the initial values, if necessary, so as to ensure that x_2 is the one apparently closest to a root; that is, $|f_2| \leqslant |f_1|$. Furthermore, as already discussed, because the secant method does not guarantee convergence, we will specify an upper limit for the number of iterations permitted before terminating the process.

As with the very similar Example 17.1, the data design and structure plan are quite straightforward:

Data design

Purpose	Type	Name
A Dummy arguments		
Function whose root is required	function	f
Start points for interpolation	real	start1, start2
Accuracy of result	real	eps
Upper limit for iteration	integer	max_iter
Value of root	real	root
Error/success condition	integer	error
B Local variables		
Current values of end-points	real	x1, x2
New end-point	real	x3
Values of $f(x)$ at x1, x2 and x3	real	f1, f2, f3
do-loop control	integer	i

Structure plan

1   If x1 = x2 then return with error = -1

2   If eps ⩽ 0 then return with error = -2

3   If max_iter ⩽ 0, then return with error = -3

4   Set f1 and f2 to f(x1) and f(x2), respectively

5   Repeat up to max_iter times
    5.1   If f1 = f2 then
            5.1.1   Iteration cannot proceed further, so return with error = -5
    5.2   Calculate x3 and f3
    5.3   If |f3| ⩽ eps then
            5.3.1   Process has converged, return with root = x3, error = 0
    5.4   Set x1 = x2, f1 = f2 and x2 = x3, f2 = f3

6   Process has not converged after max_iter steps, so set error to -4

3   Solution

Once again, we shall not include the main program, since it is very similar to the one used in Example 11.2 (and to the one used in Example 17.1). The subroutine which calculates the root is as follows:

```
subroutine secant(f, start1, start2, eps, max_iter,    &
                  root, error)

! This subroutine calculates a root of the equation f(x) = 0
! by use of the secant method
```

```
! Dummy arguments
interface
   function f(x) result(fx)
      real, intent(in) :: x
      real :: fx
   end function f
end interface
real, intent(in) :: start1, start2, eps
integer, intent(in) :: max_iter
real, intent(out) :: root
integer, intent(out) :: error

! Local variables
real :: x1, x2, x3, f1, f2, f3, tempx, tempf
integer :: i

! Check validity of initial points
if(start1 == start2) then
   error = -1
   root = huge(root)              ! Largest number
   return
end if

! Check validity of epsilon
if(eps <= 0.0) then
   error = -2
   root = huge(root)              ! Largest number
   return
end if

! Check validity of max_iter
if(max_iter <= 0) then
   error = -3
   root = huge(root)
   return
end if

! Set up initial pair of points
x1 = start1
x2 = start2
f1 = f(x1)
f2 = f(x2)

! Repeat the iteration up to the maximum number specified
do i = 1, max_iter
   if(f1 == f2) then
      ! No further iterations possible
      error = -5
      root = x2
      return
   end if

   ! Calculate next approximation
   x3 = x1 - f1*(x2 - x1)/(f2 - f1)
   f3 = f(x3)
```

```
      ! Output latest approximation while testing
      print "(2(a, es15.6))", "x3 = ", x3, " f(x3) = ", f3
      if(abs(f3) <= eps) then
         ! A root has been found
         error = 0
         root = x3
         return
      end if

      ! Update bounding points for next iteration
      x1 = x2
      f1 = f2
      x2 = x3
      f2 = f3
   end do

   ! Process has not converged after max_iter steps
   error = -4
   root = x2

end subroutine secant
```

```
      Initial bounds of -10 and 0
      x3 =   -9.090947E-01 f(x3) =    -5.062059E-01
      x3 =   -6.035660E-01 f(x3) =    -5.670793E-02
      x3 =   -5.650210E-01 f(x3) =     3.327245E-03
      x3 =   -5.671572E-01 f(x3) =    -2.181224E-05
      x3 =   -5.671433E-01 f(x3) =    -4.799769E-08
      A root was found at x = -0.567143   f(x) = -.480E-07
      Initial bounds of 10 and 11
      x3 =    9.417774E+00 f(x3) =     1.231458E+04
      x3 =    9.008183E+00 f(x3) =     8.178676E+03
      x3 =    8.198225E+00 f(x3) =     3.642692E+03
      x3 =    7.547775E+00 f(x3) =     1.904067E+03
      x3 =    6.835431E+00 f(x3) =     9.370647E+02
      x3 =    6.145140E+00 f(x3) =     4.725902E+02
      x3 =    5.442788E+00 f(x3) =     2.365284E+02
      x3 =    4.739048E+00 f(x3) =     1.190644E+02
      x3 =    4.025720E+00 f(x3) =     6.004636E+01
      x3 =    3.299963E+00 f(x3) =     3.041160E+01
      x3 =    2.555181E+00 f(x3) =     1.542881E+01
      x3 =    1.788228E+00 f(x3) =     7.767074E+00
      x3 =    1.010730E+00 f(x3) =     3.758335E+00
      x3 =    2.817979E-01 f(x3) =     1.607309E+00
      x3 =   -2.628809E-01 f(x3) =     5.059525E-01
      x3 =   -5.131012E-01 f(x3) =     8.553507E-02
      x3 =   -5.640091E-01 f(x3) =     4.914467E-03
      x3 =   -5.671124E-01 f(x3) =     4.843155E-05
      x3 =   -5.671433E-01 f(x3) =     4.541133E-08
      A root was found at x = -0.567143   f(x) = 0.454E-07
```

Figure 17.6 Two solutions for $x + e^x = 0$ using the subroutine secant.

Note that once the function has been evaluated at a point, that value is saved so it never needs to be recalculated. Also note that we have included a statement so that we can see each new estimate of the value of the root. This **print** statement will normally be removed when we are sure that subroutine secant is working correctly. Observe that, in the case where the iteration reaches a situation where it cannot continue or where the maximum number of iterations have been performed, the value of root is set to one of the last iteration points. This may have some informational value to the user of secant.

Figure 17.6 shows the result of running this program twice, using different initial intervals, with the same function subprogram to define the equation to be solved as was used in Example 17.1 (and in Example 11.2). In both cases a value of 10^{-6} was specified for epsilon, and a maximum iteration count of 20. The first example used the initial interval of -10 to 0, while the second used an initial interval of 10 to 11, which is similar to the case which caused some difficulty for Newton's method in Example 17.1.

It is interesting to examine the actual iterations carried out in these two cases.

Figure 17.7 shows the successive iterates produced by the subroutines bisect (Example 11.2), secant (Example 17.2) and newton_raphson (Example 17.1) using similar starting situations. It can be very clearly seen how the

Bisect	Secant	Newton−Raphson
-5.000000	-10.000000	-0.100000E+02
-2.500000	-9.000000	-0.499941E-03
-1.250000	-0.818189E-03	-0.500125E+00
-0.625000	-0.899422E+00	-0.566314E+00
-0.312500	-0.602525E+00	-0.567143E+00
-0.468750	-0.565136E+00	
-0.546875	-0.567156E+00	
-0.585938	-0.567143E+00	
-0.566406		
-0.576172		
-0.571289		
-0.568848		
-0.567627		
-0.567017		
-0.567322		
-0.567169		
-0.567093		
-0.567131		
-0.567150		
-0.567141		
-0.567145		
-0.567143		
-0.567144		

Figure 17.7 A comparison of the bisection, secant and Newton−Raphson methods.

Newton–Raphson and secant methods are much more efficient in this case than the bisection method, which frequently moves away from the root in the latter stages because of its inability to recognize that one of its end-points is very close to the root.

• ◻

As with Newton's method, it can be shown that, under certain circumstances, the secant method has convergence properties that are superior to the interval bisection method. The error in the secant method is approximately proportional to the 1.6th power of the error of the preceding iterate; see Dahlquist and Björck (1974) for the mathematical analysis. However, as with Newton's method, the cost of the improved performance is that the secant method does not always converge to a root. Note the rate of convergence is not as good as the Newton method, but we have avoided the cost of the derivative evaluation required by the Newton method. The choice between using the secant method or Newton's method, therefore, depends on the cost of evaluating the derivative.

17.5 Solution of simultaneous linear equations by Gaussian elimination

The solution of a system of linear equations is, perhaps, the most common need in engineering and scientific problems, not only because the solution of a physical problem directly often results in the need to solve a system of linear equations, but also because many numerical techniques for solving problems, that apparently have nothing to do with systems of linear equations, work by making appropriate linear approximations internally that then result in the need to solve systems of linear equations.

The method that we shall demonstrate is appropriate for general dense systems of linear equations, where by *general* we mean that the matrix of coefficients of the system of equations has no particular structure. Many physical problems, however, result in matrices of coefficients that do have a special structure, and special numerical techniques have been devised for their solution; see, for example, Dahlquist and Björck (1974) and Golub and Van Loan (1991). By *dense* we mean that most of the elements of the matrix of coefficients of the system of equations are non-zero. In this context, we note that many times a system of equations is sparse (non-dense), and special techniques have been devised for their solution; see, for example, George and Liu (1981) and Duff *et al.* (1986). The numerical solution of sparse systems of linear equations, or those with a special structure, is completely beyond the scope of this book, except for the very special case of tridiagonal systems, which we shall discuss in Section 17.6.

The method that we shall use is known as **Gaussian elimination**, and we shall first illustrate the process by reference to a small 3×3 system of simultaneous linear equations:

$$x_1 + 2x_2 + x_3 = 9 \tag{1}$$
$$2x_1 + 3x_2 - 2x_3 = 7 \tag{2}$$
$$4x_1 + 4x_2 + x_3 = 18 \tag{3}$$

Subtracting 2 times equation (1) from equation (2), and then 4 times equation (1) from equation (3), we obtain the equivalent set of equations:

$$x_1 + 2x_2 + x_3 = 9 \tag{4}$$
$$- x_2 - 4x_3 = -11 \tag{5}$$
$$- 4x_2 - 3x_3 = -18 \tag{6}$$

Subtracting 4 times equation (5) from equation (6), we obtain a further equivalent set of equations:

$$x_1 + 2x_2 + x_3 = 9 \tag{7}$$
$$- x_2 - 4x_3 = -11 \tag{8}$$
$$13x_3 = 26 \tag{9}$$

This completes the Gaussian elimination step. We now perform the **backward substitution** step.

Using equation (9), we obtain

$$x_3 = 26/13 = 2$$

Substituting this value for x_3 in equation (8), we obtain

$$-x_2 - 4 \times 2 = -11$$

and hence

$$x_2 = 11 - 8 = 3$$

Substituting these values for x_2 and x_3 in equation (1), we obtain

$$x_1 + 2 \times 3 + 2 = 9$$

Therefore

$$x_1 = 9 - 6 - 2 = 1$$

The solution of the original system of equations is therefore $x_1 = 1$, $x_2 = 3$, $x_3 = 2$.

Having seen how Gaussian elimination operates in the context of a simple example, we shall now discuss the general case. Suppose we have a system of n linear equations in n unknowns:

$$a_{1,1}x_1 + a_{1,2}x_2 + \ldots + a_{1,n}x_n = b_1$$
$$a_{2,1}x_1 + a_{2,2}x_2 + \ldots + a_{2,n}x_n = b_2$$
$$\vdots$$
$$a_{n,1}x_1 + a_{n,2}x_2 + \ldots + a_{n,n}x_n = b_n$$

Gaussian elimination will turn this system of equations into an equivalent system of equations of the form

$$c_{1,1}x_1 + c_{1,2}x_2 + \ldots + c_{1,n}x_n = d_1$$
$$c_{2,2}x_2 + \ldots + c_{2,n}x_n = d_2$$
$$\vdots$$
$$c_{n,n}x_n = d_n$$

In this form all the coefficients below the diagonal are zero, and the matrix of coefficients, for obvious reasons, is said to be **upper triangular**. As we shall see, in this form, the system of equations can be solved with no further manipulation.

Gaussian elimination works by subtracting multiples of the first equations from all the other equations below it in such a way that the resulting equations each have a coefficient of 0 for x_1. Thus, the initial system of equations becomes

$$a_{1,1}x_1 + a_{1,2}x_2 + \ldots + a_{1,n}x_n = b_1$$
$$a_{2,2}^{(1)}x_2 + \ldots + a_{2,n}^{(1)}x_n = b_2^{(1)}$$
$$a_{2,2}^{(1)}x_2 + \ldots + a_{2,n}^{(1)}x_n = b_2^{(1)}$$
$$\vdots$$
$$a_{n,2}^{(1)}x_2 + \ldots + a_{n,n}^{(1)}x_n = b_n^{(1)}$$

Specifically, for $j \geqslant 2$, the jth equation is obtained by subtracting the first equation, multiplied by $a_{j,1}/a_{1,1}$, from the original jth equation. The superscripts on the coefficients are used to denote that this is step 1 of the process. The solution of the second set of equations is the same as that of the original system of equations.

We now repeat the process again on the $(n-1) \times (n-1)$ system of equations consisting of the second to the nth equations. Subtracting appropriate multiples of the second equation from the equations below it, we obtain a system of equations in which all the equations after the second have zero for the coefficient of x_2.

Proceeding iteratively, after $n - 1$ steps, we obtain a system of equations of the form

$$a_{1,1}x_1 + a_{1,2}x_2 + a_{1,3}x_3 + a_{1,4}x_4 + \ldots + a_{1,n-1}x_{n-1} + a_{1,n}x_n = b_1$$
$$a_{2,2}^{(1)}x_2 + a_{2,3}^{(1)}x_3 + a_{2,4}^{(1)}x_4 + \ldots + a_{2,n-1}^{(1)}x_{n-1} + a_{2,n}^{(1)}x_n = b_2^{(1)}$$
$$a_{3,3}^{(2)}x_3 + a_{3,4}^{(2)}x_4 + \ldots + a_{3,n-1}^{(2)}x_{n-1} + a_{3,n}^{(2)}x_n = b_3^{(2)}$$
$$a_{4,4}^{(3)}x_4 + \ldots + a_{4,n-1}^{(3)}x_{n-1} + a_{4,n}^{(3)}x_n = b_4^{(3)}$$
$$\vdots$$
$$a_{n-1,n-1}^{(n-2)}x_{n-1} + a_{n-1,n}^{(n-2)}x_n = b_{n-1}^{(n-2)}$$
$$a_{n,n}^{(n-1)}x_n = b_n^{(n-1)}$$

This process, as we have already seen, is called Gaussian elimination, and the $a_{i,i}^{(i-1)}$ (the elements along the diagonal) are called **pivots**.

Now the nth equation is solved for x_n by dividing by $a_{n,n}^{(n-1)}$. This value is then substituted into the $(n - 1)$th equation, which can then be solved for x_{n-1}. The values for x_n and x_{n-1} are substituted in the $(n - 2)$th equation, which is then solved for x_{n-2}. We proceed backwards through the set of equations in this way until we finally put the values determined for $x_n, x_{n-1}, \ldots, x_3, x_2$ into the first equation and solve it for x_1. This process, for obvious reasons, is called **back substitution**.

We can see that the Gaussian elimination process will fail if, at the ith step, the coefficient $a_{i,i}^{(i-1)}$ is 0. We would in this case be unable to make all the coefficients of x_i in the equations below it 0, since subtracting any multiple of 0 leaves a number unchanged. If this situation occurs, however, we could interchange the ith equation with one below it that does not have a 0 for the coefficient of x_i, and then proceed. If there is no such equation, then it can be proved that the original system either has no solution or an infinite set of solutions. Observe that changing the order of occurrence of the equations does not change their solution.

In fact, we can go somewhat beyond this interchange procedure. If a pivot element is small, then large multiples of the equation containing it must be used during the elimination process. This will multiply any errors (due to round-off effects) in the other coefficients of this equation. Intuitively, we can see that this is undesirable. So, for reasons of numerical stability, at the beginning of the ith step, we will reorder the equations from the ith one down, so that the one that has the largest absolute value for the coefficient of x_i becomes the ith equation. In books on numerical analysis, you will see this equation reordering process referred to as **partial pivoting**. Proving mathematically that this is a good choice for a stable algorithm would, however, go beyond the scope of this book.

☐ **EXAMPLE 17.3**

1 **Problem**

Write a program to read the coefficients of a set of simultaneous linear equations, and to solve the equations using Gaussian elimination.

2 **Analysis**

We have already discussed the Gaussian elimination method in some detail, and so we can proceed to the design of the program. We shall write one procedure to carry out the Gaussian elimination, and a second to perform the back substitution. Both of these procedures will be used by a third procedure to actually solve a set of equations. Because we shall not want the two subsidiary procedures to be available on their own, we shall encapsulate all three procedures in a module, which will make only the solving procedure public.

An initial structure plan for the Gaussian elimination algorithm is as follows:

1 Repeat for i taking values from 1 to $n-1$
  1.1 Rearrange the order of the ith, $(i+1)$th, ... , nth equations so that the one with the largest absolute value for the coefficient of x_i becomes the ith equation
  1.2 If $a_{i,i} = 0$ then
    1.2.1 Return an error message to indicate that no solution is calculated
    Otherwise
    1.2.2 Subtract multiples of the ith equation from all subsequent equations so that the coefficients of x_i in the subsequent equations become 0

Now we can amplify the steps of this loop. The coefficient of x_i in equation i is $a_{i,i}$, and the coefficient of x_i in equation j is $a_{j,i}$. To make the coefficient of x_i in the jth equation zero, we must therefore subtract $a_{j,i}/a_{i,i}$ times the ith equation from the jth equation.

We will store the coefficients of the system of equations (the $a_{i,j}$) in a **real** rank-two array a and the right-hand sides of the equations (the b_i) in a **real** rank-one array b. The revised structure plan for the Gaussian elimination algorithm then becomes:

1 Repeat for i from 1 to $n-1$
    1.1 Find the row k of array a that has the largest value for $|a(j,i)|$, for $j = 1, \ldots, n$
    1.2 If this largest absolute value is 0 then
        1.2.1 Return an error message
    Otherwise
        1.2.2 Interchange row i and row k of the array a, and also interchange element i and element k of the array b
    1.3 Repeat for j from $i+1$ to n
        1.3.1 Subtract $a(j,i)/a(i,i)$ times row i from row j and similarly for the b array.

We can now turn to implementing the algorithm for back substitution. When the Gaussian elimination step has been completed, the ith equation is of the form

$$\sum_{j=i}^{n} a_{i,j} x_j = b_i, \quad i = 1, 2, \ldots, n$$

where the as and bs are the values resulting from all the manipulations of the Gaussian elimination process. That is, the coefficients of $x_1, x_2, \ldots, x_{i-1}$ are zero in the ith equation. Consequently, we can easily solve the ith equation for x_i, expressing it in terms of $x_{i+1}, x_{i+2}, \ldots, x_n$. Specifically,

$$a_{i,i} x_i + \sum_{j=i+1}^{n} a_{i,j} x_j = b_i, \quad i = 1, 2, \ldots, n$$

Thus,

$$x_i = a_{ii}^{-1} \left(b_i - \sum_{j=i+1}^{n} a_{i,j} x_j \right), \quad i = 1, 2, \ldots, n$$

This formula is used first with $i = n$, then with $i = n - 1, \ldots$, then with $i = 2$, and finally with $i = 1$. Note that, because of the row interchanges in the Gaussian elimination step, $a_{ii} \neq 0$, $i = 1, 2, \ldots, n$. Thus, it will always be possible to divide by a_{ii}.

We also note that after b_i has been used to calculate x_i it does not appear in any subsequent formulae; the solution x_i can therefore be stored in b_i, once b_i has been used to calculate x_i.

An outline structure plan for the back substitution procedure is now very straightforward:

1   Repeat for i from n down to 1
  1.1   Initialize s to $b(i)$
  1.2   Repeat for j from $i+1$ to n
    1.2.1   Subtract $a(i,j) \times b(j)$ from s
  1.3   Set $b(i)$ to $s/a(i,i)$

We shall not, in order to save space, proceed further with the design phase, which is quite straightforward, but will simply present the final solution.

③ Solution

We have already indicated that the two subroutines gaussian_elimination and back_substitution will be called by a third subroutine, which we shall call gaussian_solve. Because we do not want a user to be able to call gaussian_elimination or back_substitution directly, all three subroutines will be put in a module called linear_equations, with only gaussian_solve being public.

```
module linear_equations
    private :: gaussian_elimination, back_substitution
    public :: gaussian_solve

contains

    subroutine gaussian_solve(a, b, error)
    ! This subroutine solves the linear system Ax = b
    ! where the coefficients of A are stored in the array a
    ! The solution is put in the array b
    ! error indicates if errors are found

        ! Dummy arguments
        real, dimension(:,:), intent(inout) :: a
        real, dimension(:), intent(inout) :: b
        integer, intent(out) :: error

        ! Reduce the equations by Gaussian elimination
        call gaussian_elimination(a, b, error)

        ! If reduction was successful, calculate solution by
        ! back substitution
        if (error == 0) then
            call back_substitution(a, b)
        end if
    end subroutine gaussian_solve

    subroutine gaussian_elimination(a, b, error)
    ! This subroutine performs Gaussian elimination on a
    ! system of linear equations
```

```fortran
! Dummy arguments
! a contains the coefficients
! b contains the right-hand side
real, dimension(:, :), intent(inout) :: a
real, dimension(:), intent(inout) :: b
integer, intent(out) :: error

! Local variables
real, dimension(size(a, 1)) :: temp_array ! Automatic array
integer, dimension(1) :: ksave
integer :: i, j, k, n
real :: temp, m

! Validity checks
n = size(a, 1)
if(n == 0) then
   error = -1            ! There is no problem to solve
   return
end if
if(n /= size(a, 2)) then
   error = -2            ! a is not square
   return
end if
if(n /= size(b)) then
   error = -3            ! Size of b does not match a
   return
end if

! Dimensions of arrays are OK, so go ahead with Gaussian
! elimination
error = 0
do i = 1, n-1
   ! Find row with largest value of |a(j,i)|, j = i, ..., n
   ksave = maxloc(abs(a(i:n, i)))

   ! Check whether largest |a(j,i)| is zero
   k = ksave(1)+i - 1
   if(a(k,i) == 0.0) then
      error = -4         ! No solution calculated
      return
   end if

   ! Interchange row i and row k, if necessary
   if(k /= i) then
      temp_array = a(i, :)
      a(i, :) = a(k, :)
      a(k, :) = temp_array
      ! Interchange corresponding elements of b
      temp = b(i)
      b(i) = b(k)
      b(k) = temp
   end if
```

```
      ! Subtract multiples of row i from subsequent rows to
      ! zero all subsequent coefficients of x sub i
      do j = i+1, n
         m = a(j, i)/a(i, i)
         a(j, :) = a(j, :) - m*a(i, :)
         b(j) = b(j) - m*b(i)
      end do
   end do
end subroutine gaussian_elimination

subroutine back_substitution(a, b)
! This subroutine performs back substitution once a system
! of equations has been reduced by Gaussian elimination

   ! Dummy arguments
   ! The array a contains the coefficients
   ! The array b contains the right-hand side coefficients
   ! and will contain the solution on exit
   real, dimension(:, :), intent(in) :: a
   real, dimension(:), intent(inout) :: b

   ! Local variables
   real :: s
   integer :: i, j, n
   n = size(b)

   ! Solve for each variable in turn
   do i = n, 1, -1
      s = b(i)
      do j = i+1, n
         s = s - a(i, j)*b(j)
      end do
      b(i) = s/a(i, i)
   end do
end subroutine back_substitution

end module linear_equations
```

A main program which will use the subroutine `gaussian_solve` to solve a system of linear equations is as follows:

```
program test_gauss
! This program defines the coefficients of a set of
! simultaneous linear equations, and solves them using the
! module procedure gaussian_solve

   use linear_equations

   ! Allocatable arrays for coefficients
   real, allocatable, dimension(:, :) :: a
   real, allocatable, dimension(:) :: b
```

```
           ! Size of arrays
           integer :: n

           ! Loop variables and error flag
           integer :: i, j, error

           ! Get size of problem
           print *, "How many equations are there?"
           read *, n

           ! Allocate arrays
           allocate (a(n, n), b(n))

           ! Get coefficients
           print *,"Type coefficients for each equation in turn"
           do i = 1, n
              read *, a(i, :), b(i)
           end do

           ! Attempt to solve system of equations
           call gaussian_solve(a, b, error)

           ! Check to see if there were any errors
           if(error <= -1 .and. error >= -3 ) then
              print *, "Error in call to gaussian_solve"
           else if(error == -4) then
              print *, "System is degenerate"
           else
              print *, " "
              print *, "Solution is"
              do i = 1, n
                 print "(a, i2, a, f6.2)", " x(", i, ") = ", b(i)
              end do
           end if

        end program test_gauss
```

Note that, for large problems, this code can be made more efficient by use of pointers, in order to avoid exchanging large numbers of arrays and array sections; Exercise 17.8 at the end of this chapter gives you the chance to make such an improvement.

Figure 17.8 shows the results produced when this program was used to solve the following set of equations:

$$2x_1 + 3x_2 - x_3 + x_4 = 11$$
$$x_1 - x_2 + 2x_3 - x_4 = -4$$
$$-x_1 - x_2 + 5x_3 + 2x_4 = -2$$
$$3x_1 + x_2 - 3x_3 + 3x_4 = 19$$

```
How many equations are there?
4
Type coefficients for each equation in turn
2 3 -1 1 11
1 -1 2 -1 -4
-1 -1 5 2 -2
3 1 -3 3 19

Solution is
x( 1) =   2.00
x( 2) =   1.00
x( 3) =  -1.00
x( 4) =   3.00
```

Figure 17.8 Solving a set of simultaneous linear equations using test_gauss.

17.6   Solving a tridiagonal system of equations

One form of sparse system which is particularly important is known as a **tridiagonal system** for reasons which become obvious when we examine such a system:

$$a_{1,1}x_1 + a_{1,2}x_2 = b_1$$
$$a_{2,1}x_1 + a_{2,2}x_2 + a_{2,3}x_3 = b_2$$
$$a_{3,2}x_2 + a_{3,3}x_3 + a_{3,4}x_4 = b_3$$
$$\ddots \qquad \vdots$$
$$a_{n-1,n-2}x_{n-2} + a_{n-1,n-1}x_{n-1} + a_{n-1,n}x_n = b_{n-1}$$
$$a_{n,n-1}x_{n-1} \quad + a_{n,n}x_n = b_n$$

Systems of equations of this type occur frequently in the solution of partial differential equations, and are also found in cubic and bicubic curve fitting, as we shall see in Section 17.7. In order to emphasize the form of such a system, it is common practice to use a different terminology for the coefficients, namely

$$d_1x_1 + c_1x_2 = b_1$$
$$a_2x_1 + d_2x_2 + c_2x_3 = b_2$$
$$a_3x_2 + d_3x_3 + c_3x_4 = b_3$$
$$\ddots \qquad \vdots$$
$$a_{n-1}x_{n-2} + d_{n-1}x_{n-1} + c_{n-1}x_n = b_{n-1}$$
$$a_nx_{n-1} + d_nx_n = b_n$$

Clearly the computation involved in solving a system of this nature should be much simpler than in the general case, since in each column there is only one element to be eliminated. Furthermore, and this is another reason why we have used a different terminology, considerable savings can be made in storage requirements by storing only these tridiagonal coefficients (as three one-dimensional arrays) and ignoring the zero elements which occupy the remainder of the matrix of coefficients.

We shall not give an exhaustive account of the mathematics involved in deriving a solution method, as it is similar to that used in the previous section when discussing Gaussian elimination, except that, providing no pivoting is performed, we only need to subtract a multiple of an equation from the equation immediately below it in order to transform the original set of equations into a new, upper triangular set

$$
\begin{aligned}
D_1 x_1 + c_1 x_2 &= B_1 \\
D_2 x_2 + c_2 x_3 &= B_2 \\
D_3 x_3 + c_3 x_4 &= B_3 \\
&\ \ \vdots \\
D_{n-1} x_{n-1} + c_{n-1} x_n &= B_{n-1} \\
D_n x_n &= B_n
\end{aligned}
$$

We can readily see that the c_i coefficients are unaltered by the transformations, and that

$$D_1 = d_1$$

and

$$B_i = b_1$$

Furthermore, when processing the $(i + 1)$th equation in order to eliminate x_i, we shall use a multiplier m_i which is equal to a_{i+1}/D_i to give a new equation

$$D_{i+1} x_{i+1} + c_{i+1} x_{i+2} = B_{i+1}$$

where

$$D_{i+1} = d_{i+1} - m_i c_i$$

and

$$B_{i+1} = b_{i+1} - m_i B_i$$

It can be shown that in some situations pivoting can be eliminated. One example of such a situation is where the system of equations is diagonally dominant; that is, for each row, the absolute value of the diagonal term is greater than or equal to the sum of the absolute values of the other terms. Using our original notation for tridiagonal systems, this requires that $|a_{i,i}| \geq |a_{i,i-1}| + |a_{i,i+1}|, i = 1, 2, \ldots, n$. Here, we interpret $a_{1,0}$ and $a_{n,n+1}$ as

```fortran
subroutine tri_gauss(a, d, c, b, error)

! This subroutine performs Gaussian elimination with no
! pivoting on a tridiagonal, diagonally dominant, system
! of linear equations

    ! Dummy arguments
    ! Array a holds the subdiagonal coefficients
    ! Array d holds the diagonal coefficients
    ! Array c holds the above-diagonal coefficients
    ! Array b holds the right-hand-side coefficients
    ! error is a variable that indicates success or failure
    real, dimension(:), intent(in) :: a, c
    real, dimension(:), intent(inout) :: d, b
    integer, intent(out) :: error

    ! Local variables
    real :: m
    integer :: n, i

    ! Validity checks
    n = size(a, 1)
    if (n == 0) then
        ! There is no problem to solve
        error = -1
        return
    end if
    if ( n /= size(d,1) .or.                 &
         n /= size(c,1) .or.                 &
         n /= size(b,1) ) then
        ! The arrays of coefficients do not have the same size
        error = -2
        return
    end if

    ! Calculate new coefficients of upper diagonal system
    do i = 1, n-1
        m = a(i+1)/d(i)
        d(i+1) = d(i+1) - m*c(i)
        b(i+1) = b(i+1) - m*b(i)
    end do
    error = 0
end subroutine tri_gauss
```

Figure 17.9 A subroutine for Gaussian elimination on a tridiagonal system.

```
subroutine back_tri_substitution(d, c, b)

! This subroutine performs back substitution to a
! tridiagonal system of linear equations that has been
! reduced to upper triangular form

   ! Dummy arguments
   ! d is the array of diagonal coefficients
   ! c is the array of above-diagonal coefficients
   ! b is the array of right-hand-side coefficients
   ! and will contain the solution on exit
   real, dimension(:), intent(in) :: d, c
   real, dimension(:), intent(out) :: b

   ! Local variables
   integer :: i, n

   n = size(d)
   b(n) = b(n)/d(n)
   do i = n-1, 1, -1
      b(i) = (b(i)-c(i)*b(i+1))/d(i)
   end do
end subroutine back_tri_substitution
```

Figure 17.10 A subroutine for back substitution on an upper triangular system.

being zero. The proof that diagonal dominance eliminates the need for pivoting goes beyond the scope of this book.

An F implementation of this method, in which no pivoting is performed, is shown in Figure 17.9, while Figure 17.10 shows a suitable back-substitution procedure.

We shall use these subroutines as part of a method for curve fitting in the next section. The development of a procedure for solving tridiagonal systems with pivoting is given as an exercise at the end of this chapter.

We will put tri_solve, a subroutine that solves a tridiagonal system by calling tri_gauss and then back_tri_solve, in the same module called tridiagonal_systems. Since only tri_solve is supposed to be directly called by a user, all entities in the module will be private except tri_solve. This module could be written as follows:

```
module tridiagonal_systems
   private :: tri_gauss, back_tri_substitution
   public :: tri_solve

contains

   subroutine tri_solve(a, d, c, b, error)
   ! This subroutine solves a diagonally dominant tridiagonal
   ! system by Gaussian elimination and back substitution
```

```
      ! Dummy arguments
      ! Array a holds the subdiagonal coefficients
      ! Array b holds the diagonal coefficients
      ! Array c holds the above-diagonal coefficients
      ! Array d holds the right-hand-side coefficients
      ! Array b will contain the solution on exit
      real, dimension(:), intent(in) :: a, c
      real, dimension(:), intent(out) :: d, b
      integer, intent(out) :: error

      call tri_gauss(a, d, c, b, error)
      if(error == 0) then
         call back_tri_substitution(d, c, b)
      end if
   end subroutine tri_solve

   subroutine tri_gauss (...)
      .
      .
      .
   subroutine back_tri_substitution (...)
      .
      .
      .
end module tridiagonal_systems
```

17.7   Fitting a curve through a set of data points using a cubic spline

We have considered the solution of equations of various types at some length, because this is a very common requirement in scientific programming. However, another important application is the fitting of an equation to a set of (usually) experimental data with a view to using this equation to predict further results. In Chapter 11 we considered the simple case in which it was believed that the data satisfied a linear relationship. We shall now briefly examine a more general case.

As usual in numerical analysis, there are a number of different methods for fitting a curve to a set of discrete data points; however, by far the best known, and the most widely used, are those methods which are based on **splines**. A spline was an instrument once used by draughtsmen to enable them to draw a smooth curve through a set of points. It consisted of a flexible wooden (or sometimes metal) strip which was constrained (by pins) to pass through the data points. Because the spline would take up the shape which minimized its potential energy the resulting curve was a smooth one.

Mathematically, splines are curves consisting of n polynomial pieces, each one of the same degree k, joined together such that the curve has $k - 1$ continuous derivatives at the join points, as shown in Figure 17.11.

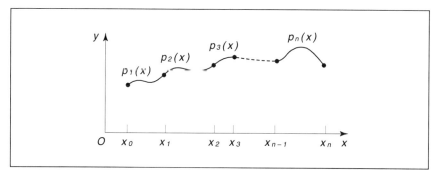

Figure 17.11 A spline curve.

Let us suppose we are given some finite interval $[a, b]$ and a set of points $x_0, x_1, \ldots, x_n$ in $[a, b]$ such that $a = x_0 \leqslant x_1 \leqslant x_2 \leqslant \ldots \leqslant x_n = b$. The points $x_0, x_1, \ldots, x_n$ are called **knots**.

Now, let $k \geqslant 0$ be a fixed integer, and P_i be a polynomial of degree k, $i = 1, 2, \ldots n$. Then a spline s of degree k on $[a, b]$ is defined as

$$
s(x) = \left\{
\begin{array}{ll}
P_1(x) & \text{on} \quad [x_0, x_1] \\
P_2(x) & \text{on} \quad [x_1, x_2] \\
\vdots & \\
P_n(x) & \text{on} \quad [x_{n-1}, x_n]
\end{array}
\right\}
$$

The polynomials must be such that, at $x_1, x_2, \ldots, x_{n-1}$, $s(x)$ has $k - 1$ continuous derivatives.

Such a spline is said to be C^{k-1}, referring to the $k - 1$ continuous derivatives at the knots.

It might be asked why objects as complicated as splines are used when we could simply, given n points, fit a polynomial of degree $n - 1$ through them. The reason is that polynomials of degree more than three tend to oscillate considerably between the given data points, with the amount of oscillation tending to increase as the degree of the polynomial increases. Thus the intrinsic shape represented by a set of data points is usually badly represented by higher-degree polynomials. Splines, on the other hand, conform much better to the shape implied by the data, even though, in practice, they are rarely of degree higher than three.

Here, to illustrate the concept, we shall concentrate on **cubic splines**.

The cubic spline is the mathematical equivalent of the draughtsman's physical instrument and enables the construction of a smooth curve which passes through all the data points. Furthermore, as a measure of its smoothness, its first and second derivatives are continuous everywhere within the range of the data points. Thus, we shall analyse a C^2 cubic spline, and will show the simplest method for constructing such a spline. There are many other, more sophisticated methods based on what are known as basis functions. Dierckx (1993) gives an introduction to such methods for those who are interested in this subject.

A cubic spline actually consists of a set of cubic polynomials, one for each pair of data points. These polynomials are chosen so that they obey the following criteria:

1. In each interval $[x_i, x_{i+1}]$, $i = 0, \ldots, n-1$, the spline consists of a cubic polynomial $s_i(x)$.

2. The spline passes through each data point, and so

$$s_i(x_i) = y_i \text{ and } s_i(x_{i+1}) = y_{i+1}, \quad \text{for } i = 0, \ldots, n-1$$

3. At each of the points where two sub-intervals join the first and second derivatives must be continuous, and so, for $i = 1, \ldots, n-1$

$$s'_{i-1}(x_i) = s'_i(x_i)$$
$$s''_{i-1}(x_i) = s''_i(x_i)$$

For fairly obvious reasons, round-off errors will be less if we express the cubic polynomials as functions of $(x - x_i)$ rather than as functions of x, with the result that we shall require to find the coefficients of the equations

$$s_i(x) = a_i(x - x_i)^3 + b_i(x - x_i)^2 + c_i(x - x_i) + d_i \tag{1}$$

for $i = 0, \ldots, n-1$

We now consider, for $i = 0, 1, \ldots, n-1$, how to find a_i, b_i, c_i and d_i. For a particular i, we have two conditions

$$s_i(x_i) = y_i$$
$$s_i(x_{i+1}) = y_{i+1}$$

We need two more conditions to fix a_i, b_i, c_i and d_i.

For the moment, suppose that we know the second derivatives at $x_0, x_1, \ldots, x_n$. We shall call these derivatives $\sigma_0, \sigma_1, \sigma_2, \ldots, \sigma_n$. Now, for $i = 0, 1, \ldots, n-1$, we have the two extra conditions needed to determine a_i, b_i, c_i and d_i. At this stage, of course, we do not know what values to assign to the σ_i. We shall see later that the continuity conditions on the first and second derivatives we require at $x_1, \ldots, x_{n-1}$ will (with two extra conditions) determine the values of σ_i, and hence the values of a_i, b_i, c_i and d_i.

We now proceed with the analysis to determine a_i, b_i, c_i and d_i in terms of y_i, y_{i+1}, σ_i and σ_{i+1}. First, we let

$$h_i = x_{i+1} - x_i \quad \text{for} \quad i = 0, 1, \ldots, n-1$$

The h_i are, therefore, the distances between successive pairs of data points.

For $i = 0, 1, \ldots, n - 1$, substituting x_i for x, and y_i for $s_i(x_i)$ in equation (1) and rearranging, we obtain

$$d_i = y_i \tag{2}$$

Substituting $x = x_{i+1}$ in equation (1), we obtain

$$y_{i+1} = a_i h_i^3 + b_i h_i^2 + c_i h_i + d_i$$

Using equation (2) and rearranging, we now obtain

$$c_i = \frac{y_{i+1} - y_i}{h_i} - a_i h_i^2 - b_i h_i \tag{3}$$

Now, differentiating equation (1) twice, we have

$$s_i''(x_i) = 6a_i(x - x_i) + 2b_i$$

Substituting $x = x_i$ and $x = x_{i+1}$ in this equation leads to

$$\sigma_i = 2b_i$$
$$\sigma_{i+1} = 6a_i h_i + 2b_i$$

Thus, from these two equations, we have

$$b_i = \frac{\sigma_i}{2} \tag{4}$$

$$a_i = \frac{\sigma_{i+1} - \sigma_i}{6h_i} \tag{5}$$

Substituting equations (4) and (5) in equation (3), we obtain

$$c_i = \frac{y_{i+1} - y_i}{h_i} - \frac{\sigma_{i+1} - \sigma_i}{6h_i} h_i^2 - \frac{\sigma_i}{2} h_i$$

$$= \frac{y_{i+1} - y_i}{h_i} - \frac{\sigma_{i+1} + 2\sigma_i}{6} h_i \tag{6}$$

Equations (2), (4), (5) and (6) thus determine a_i, b_i, c_i and d_i, for $i = 0$, $1, \ldots, n - 1$, once we know the values of the σ_is. Our next step, therefore, will be to determine the values of the σ_i.

Recall that we required the spline to have a continuous first derivative at each x_i, for $i = 1, 2, \ldots, n - 1$. This requirement, which we have not yet used, will determine the σ_i.

Differentiating equation (1), we obtain

$$s_i'(x) = 3a_i(x - x_i)^2 + 2b_i(x - x_i) + c_i$$

Substituting $x = x_i$ and $x = x_{i+1}$ in this equation, we obtain

$$s_i'(x_i) = c_i \tag{7}$$

and

$$s_i'(x_{i+1}) = 3a_i h_i^2 + 2b_i h_i + c_i \tag{8}$$

For continuity of the first derivative at x_i, $i = 1, 2, \ldots, n-1$, we require

$$s_{i-1}'(x_i) = s_i'(x_i)$$

Substituting equations (7) and (8) into this equation, we obtain

$$3a_{i-1} h_{i-1}^2 + 2b_{i-1} h_{i-1} + c_{i-1} = c_i$$

Substituting equations (4), (5) and (6) into this equation, we have

$$\frac{3(\sigma_i - \sigma_{i-1})h_{i-1}^2}{6h_{i-1}} + \sigma_{i-1} h_{i-1} + \frac{y_i - y_{i-1}}{h_{i-1}} - \frac{(\sigma_i + 2\sigma_{i-1})h_{i-1}}{6}$$

$$= \frac{y_{i+1} - y_i}{h_i} - \frac{(\sigma_{i+1} + 2\sigma_i)h_i}{6}$$

Grouping terms together, we have

$$\sigma_{i-1}\left(-\frac{h_{i-1}}{2} + h_{i-1} - \frac{h_{i-1}}{3}\right) + \sigma_i\left(\frac{h_{i-1}}{2} - \frac{h_{i-1}}{6} + \frac{h_i}{3}\right) + \frac{\sigma_{i+1} h_i}{6}$$

$$= \frac{y_{i+1} - y_i}{h_i} - \frac{y_i - y_{i-1}}{h_{i-1}}$$

Thus, multiplying by 6, for $i = 1, \ldots, n-1$,

$$h_{i-1}\sigma_{i-1} + 2(h_{i-1} + h_i)\sigma_i + h_i\sigma_{i+1} = 6\left(\frac{y_{i+1} - y_i}{h_i} - \frac{y_i - y_{i-1}}{h_{i-1}}\right) \tag{9}$$

Equation (9) gives us $n-1$ linear equations in the $n+1$ unknowns σ_0, $\sigma_1, \ldots, \sigma_n$.

We therefore need two more equations to be able to calculate a unique solution, and, hence, a unique cubic interpolating function. This is usually achieved by applying some form of constraint to the spline at the end-points x_0 and x_n. This is desirable in any case since extra constraints on a curve fit are frequently required at the end-points of an interval. In design work, for example, the curve may be required to blend into some existing curve. There are a number of possibilities, of which some common ones are:

- Force the second derivative of the spline to be zero at the end-points:

$$\sigma_0 = \sigma_n = 0$$

- Force the third derivative of the spline to be continuous at the points adjacent to the end-points. This means that

$$a_0 = a_1 \qquad \text{and} \qquad a_{n-1} = a_n$$

which leads to the two further equations

$$\sigma_0 h_1 - \sigma_1(h_0 + h_1) + \sigma_2 h_0 = 0$$
$$\sigma_{n-2} h_{n-1} - \sigma_{n-1}(h_{n-2} + h_{n-1}) + \sigma_n h_{n-2} = 0$$

- Force the first derivative (the gradient) at the end-points to be the same as that of the true curve $y = f(x)$; this assumes that further information is available about the gradient of this curve at these points. Thus

$$s_0'(x_0) = f_0' \qquad \text{and} \qquad s_{n-1}'(x_n) = f_n'$$

which leads to two further linear equations in σ_0 and σ_1, and in σ_{n-1} and σ_n, respectively.

Different treatment of the end-points will be appropriate for different situations, but it will be noticed by the observant reader that, in the first and third cases, we have tridiagonal systems of n equations in n unknowns. The second case also has n equations in n unknowns, but is not strictly tridiagonal; however, it is a trivial task to convert it to tridiagonal form.

We discussed the solution of a tridiagonal system in Section 17.6, and since the above system of equations is diagonally dominant (do you see why?), we can use the subroutines developed in that section in the calculation of the coefficients of a cubic spline. A subroutine which will calculate the values of the coefficients for a tridiagonal system of equations using the first of the above criteria for treatment of end-points ($\sigma_0 = \sigma_n = 0$) is shown below; it has been encapsulated in a module, which in turn uses the earlier module tridiagonal_systems.

```
module spline
    use tridiagonal_systems
    private
    public :: cubic_spline

contains

    subroutine cubic_spline(x, y, a, b, c, d, error)
    ! This subroutine calculates the coefficients of a
    ! cubic spline through the set of data points with
    ! x-coordinates in the array x and corresponding
    ! y-coordinates in the array y.
    ! The coefficients of the cubic polynomials will be
    ! put in arrays a, b, c, d
    ! error will indicate the success or failure of the fit
```

```fortran
! Dummy arguments
real, dimension(0:), intent(in) :: x, y
real, dimension(0:), intent(out) :: a, b, c, d
integer, intent(out) :: error

! Local variables
integer :: n, i
real, dimension(0:size(x, 1)-2) :: h      ! Automatic array
! Automatic arrays for tridiagonal equations
real, dimension(0:size(x, 1)-1) :: t, u, v, w

! Validity checks
n = size(x) - 1
if(n < 1) then
    ! There is no problem to solve
    error = -1
    return
end if


if( n+1 /= size(y) .or.   &
     n /= size(a) .or.   &
     n /= size(b) .or.   &
     n /= size(c) .or.   &
     n /= size(d)) then
    ! The array sizes don't correspond.
    error = -2
    return
end if


! Test that the x-coordinates are either strictly
! increasing or strictly decreasing
if( x(0) < x(1) ) then
    ! Test that x-coordinates are ordered increasingly
    do i = 1, n-2
        if(x(i) < x(i+1)) then
            cycle
        end if
        ! x-coordinates aren't monotonically increasing
        error = -3
        return
    end do
else if(x(0) == x(1)) then
    ! x-coordinates aren't distinct
    error = -3
    return
else
    ! Test that x-coordinates are ordered decreasingly
    do i = 1, n-2
        if(x(i) > x(i+1)) then
            cycle
        end if
```

```
                              ! x-coordinates aren't monotonically decreasing
                              error = -3
                              return
                          end do
                      end if

                      ! Data is OK
                      error = 0

                      ! Set h array to interval lengths
                      do i = 0, n-1
                          h(i) = x(i+1) - x(i)
                      end do

                      ! Fill up coefficient arrays for the tridiagonal system
                      do i = 1, n-1
                          t(i) = h(i-1)
                          u(i) = 2.0*(h(i-1)+h(i))
                          v(i) = h(i)
                          w(i) = 6.0*((y(i+1)-y(i))/h(i) - (y(i)-y(i-1))/h(i-1))
                      end do

                      ! Set end-point conditions
                      u(0) = 1.0
                      v(0) = 0.0
                      w(0) = 0.0
                      t(n) = 0.0
                      u(n) = 1.0
                      w(n) = 0.0

                      ! Calculate the sigma values
                      call tri_solve(t, u, v, w, error)
                      if (error /= 0) then
                          print *, "An 'IMPOSSIBLE' error has occurred - call " &
                                   //"consultant."
                          stop
                      end if

                      ! Calculate the spline coefficients from the sigmas
                      do i = 0, n-1
                          a(i) = (w(i+1)-w(i))/(6.0*h(i))
                          b(i) = w(i)/2.0
                          c(i) = (y(i+1)-y(i))/h(i) - (w(i+1)+2.0*w(i))*h(i)/6.0
                          d(i) = y(i)
                      end do

                  end subroutine cubic_spline

              end module spline
```

The subroutine cubic_spline can be used by any program which wishes to obtain a set of spline coefficients to fit a particular set of data, and which can then use these coefficients to create a mathematical model of the curve to use in whatever way is appropriate.

The following program uses this subroutine to fit a spline through 18 unevenly spaced points in the range $-3 \leqslant x \leqslant 3$, which lie on a curve defined by a function f, and then prints out the values of the interpolated and actual functions at a series of intermediate values:

```
module test_function
    function f(x) result(fx)
        real, intent(in) :: x
        real :: fx
        fx = exp(-0.5*x*x)
    end function f
end module test_function

program spline_test
! This program tests the subroutine cubic_spline

    use spline
    use test_function

    ! Maximum coefficient for data points
    integer, parameter :: n = 17

    ! Local variables
    integer :: error,i,j
    real, dimension(0:n) :: x
    real, dimension(0:n) :: y
    real, dimension(0:n-1) :: a, b, c, d
    real :: z, zj, yz

    ! Set x-values
    x = (/ -2.95, -2.6, -2.1, -1.8, -1.4, -1.0, -0.75,  &
            -0.3, -0.05, 0.2, 0.55, 0.9, 1.25, 1.6, 1.7, &
            2.1, 2.4, 3.0 /)

    ! Calculate y-coordinates corresponding to data
    ! values of x
    do i = 0, n
        y(i) = f(x(i))
    end do

    ! Call cubic_spline to fit a set of n polynomials
    call cubic_spline(x, y, a, b, c, d, error)
    if (error /= 0) then
        print *, "Error ", error
        stop
    end if

    ! Now compare interpolated values with true ones, using
    ! an evenly spaced set of values between -2.8 and +2.8
    print "(t9, a)", "x exp(-0.5x**2) Spline value"
    do i = 0, 14
        ! Calculate z (the value to be used)
        z = -2.8 + 0.4*i
```

```
      ! Find in which interval z lies
      do j = 0, n-1
         if( x(j) <= z .and. z <= x(j+1) ) then
            exit
         end if
      end do

      ! Calculate s(z) for x(j) <= z <= x(j+1)
      zj - z-x(j)
      yz = ((a(j)*zj + b(j))*zj + c(j))*zj + d(j)

      ! Print comparative results
      print "(t6, f6.2, 2es15.6)", z, f(z), yz
   end do
end program spline_test
```

The result of running this program is shown in Figure 17.12.

We observe that the fit is of only moderate accuracy. If we wanted to improve it, we could add more data points.

In the preceding discussion, we have presented the spline method of fitting curves through a set of data points as a two-dimensional problem; however, the method can easily be extended to three or more dimensions, for example to calculate the equation of a surface, $z = f(x, y)$, through a set of points whose heights above some base plane have been measured on a rectangular grid. **Bicubic patches**, in three dimensions, exhibit the same continuity with adjacent patches at their common boundaries as do the two-dimensional cubic spline polynomials at their common points. Such **bicubic spline interpolation** is therefore often used to create mathematical models of surfaces using, for example, data obtained by remote sensing devices such as satellites or oceanic depth sounders; these mathematical models of the surface can then be used by a drawing

x	exp(-0.5x**2)	Spline value
-2.80	1.984110E-02	2.041820E-02
-2.40	5.613478E-02	5.589126E-02
-2.00	1.353353E-01	1.353666E-01
-1.60	2.780373E-01	2.781599E-01
-1.20	4.867523E-01	4.868935E-01
-0.80	7.261491E-01	7.261713E-01
-0.40	9.231164E-01	9.229984E-01
0.00	1.000000E+00	9.999883E-01
0.40	9.231163E-01	9.229935E-01
0.80	7.261490E-01	7.261460E-01
1.20	4.867522E-01	4.867610E-01
1.60	2.780373E-01	2.780372E-01
2.00	1.353353E-01	1.354428E-01
2.40	5.613475E-02	5.613475E-02
2.80	1.984108E-02	2.099702E-02

Figure 17.12 Results produced by the test program spline_test.

program which will plot a graphical representation of the surface as viewed from any particular angle, or which will produce a contour map of the surface.

One final point to emphasize is that we have assumed throughout the foregoing discussion that the spline polynomials must pass through *all* the data points. However, just as in the case where a linear fit is expected (see Chapter 11), when the data is the result of experimentation it is likely that there may be small errors in that data. In these situations, therefore, we may require the spline to be a good fit to the data, but not necessarily to pass through all the data points. This involves a somewhat more complex mathematical treatment, and we will not go into the matter here. It is sufficient to emphasize that some form of least squares approximation is normally used so that data points which will produce significant perturbations if an exact fit is used will have less effect when a least squares fit is used.

17.8   Integration and numerical quadrature

A common problem in science and engineering is the need to evaluate the definite integral of a function. That is, if the function is f, we want

$$I = \int_a^b f(x)dx$$

We shall, for simplicity, assume that $a < b$. There is no loss of generality, because

$$\int_a^b f(x)dx = -\int_b^a f(x)dx$$

In many practical problems, the function f cannot be integrated analytically, and we cannot, therefore, find a known function F such that

$$F'(x) = f(x) \quad \text{on } [a, b]$$

If we could, then $I = F(b) - F(a)$.

If we cannot find such an F then we must turn to numerical techniques. The process of numerically calculating the value of a definite integral is known as **numerical quadrature** (the term **integrate** is used for the numerical solution of differential equations). We will present here a simple version of a method that demonstrates the algorithmic basis for more sophisticated methods.

We recall that a definite integral over a finite interval (we will not deal with infinite intervals here) can be interpreted as the area lying between the curve $y = f(x)$ and the x axis on the interval $[a, b]$. This is shown in Figure 17.13.

The integral I is equal to the area shaded in the figure. Consequently, it is clear that the area, and hence I, can be calculated by subdividing the interval

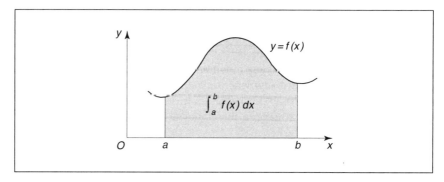

Figure 17.13 $\int_b^a f(x)dx$ interpreted as an area.

$[a, b]$ into n subintervals and summing the areas of these subintervals, as shown in Figure 17.14.

In Figure 17.14 we have subdivided the interval $[a, b]$ by an increasing sequence of x_i, such that $a = x_0 < x_1 < x_2 \ldots x_{n-1} < x_n = b$.

Now let the length of the ith interval be h_i, so that $h_i = x_i - x_{i-1}$, $i = 1, 2, \ldots, n$. Note that we are not assuming that the x_i are uniformly spaced, so that the h_i may be unequal.

We are going to estimate $\int_{x_{i-1}}^{x_i} f(x)dx$ by the area of the trapezium formed by joining the point $(x_{i-1}, f(x_{i-1}))$ to the point $(x_i, f(x_i))$ by a straight line. This is shown shaded in Figure 17.15.

Since the area of the trapezium, T_i, is given by the formula

$$T_i = \frac{h_i(f(x_{i-1}) + f(x_i))}{2}$$

we can deduce that

$$I_i \doteq \frac{1}{2} h_i \{f(x_{i-1}) + f(x_i)\}, \quad i = 1, 2, \ldots, n$$

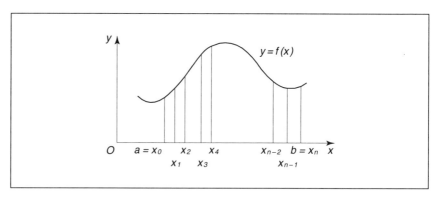

Figure 17.14 Calculating an area by subdividing it into smaller sub-areas.

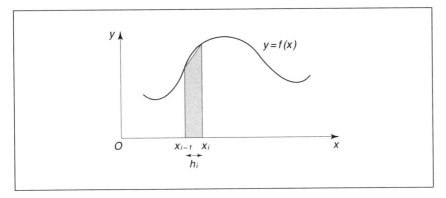

Figure 17.15 Estimating an area by use of a trapezium.

It follows, therefore, that

$$I = \sum_{i=1}^{n} I_i \doteq \sum_{i=1}^{n} \frac{1}{2} h_i \left\{ f(x_i) + f(x_{i+1}) \right\}$$

Before we examine the use of this formula to obtain an approximation to I, however, there are two questions that should be answered. The first concerns the accuracy of the approximation; ideally, we would like to be able to specify an error tolerance and not have it exceeded. The second question concerns how many points are required to meet a specified error tolerance, and how they should be positioned. These two questions, as we shall see, are intimately related.

Before we begin the analysis, we note that, intuitively, the best way to position the x_i is to group them most closely in regions where f' is changing most rapidly and to have them relatively sparse in regions where f' is not changing very fast. Thus, as shown in Figure 17.16, we would group x_i and x_{i+1} close together in regions where the second derivative of f is high. We do not, however, wish to group the x_i closer than necessary, because this would result in

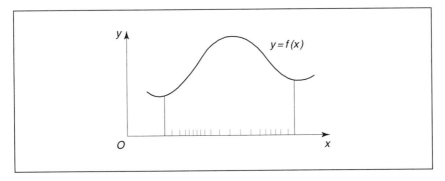

Figure 17.16 Uneven spacing of intervals to improve accuracy.

the need for extra function evaluations, and it is the number of function evaluations required that is the efficiency measure of a numerical quadrature algorithm.

We now start to analyse how many x_i are needed and how to position them, by first estimating the error created by using the approximating trapeziums. Using Taylor's theorem, expanding about x_{i-1}, with three terms, we see that

$$I_i = \int_{x_{i-1}}^{x_i} f(x)dx$$

$$= \int_{x_{i-1}}^{x_i} \left\{ f(x_{i-1}) + (x - x_{i-1})f'(x_{i-1}) + \frac{1}{2}(x - x_{i-1})^2 f''(x_{i-1}) + \ldots \right\} dx$$

$$= f(x_{i-1}) \int_{x_{i-1}}^{x_i} dx + f'(x_{i-1}) \int_{x_{i-1}}^{x_i} (x - x_{i-1}) dx$$

$$+ \frac{1}{2} f''(x_{i-1}) \int_{x_{i-1}}^{x_i} (x - x_{i-1})^2 dx + \ldots$$

$$= f(x_{i-1}) \left[x\right]_{x_{i-1}}^{x_i} + \frac{1}{2} f'(x_{i-1}) \left[x - x_{i-1}^2\right]_{x_{i-1}}^{x_i}$$

$$+ \frac{1}{6} f''(x_{i-1}) \left[x - x_{i-1}^3\right]_{x_{i-1}}^{x_i} + \ldots$$

$$= f(x_{i-1})(x_i - x_{i-1}) + \frac{1}{2} f'(x_{i-1})(x_i - x_{i-1})^2$$

$$+ \frac{1}{6} f''(x_{i-1})(x_i - x_{i-1})^3 + \ldots$$

Since we are going to be dealing with h_is that are relatively small, and if the higher derivatives of f are well behaved (that is, not too large), we can ignore the terms involving $h_i^4, h_i^5, \ldots$ and commit no significant error. Thus, we have, effectively,

$$I_i = h_i f(x_{i-1}) + \frac{1}{2} h_i^2 f'(x_{i-1}) + \frac{1}{6} h_i^3 f''(x_{i-1})$$

Now, examining T_i, we have, using Taylor's theorem expanding about x_{i-1}

$$T_i = \frac{1}{2} h_i \left\{ f(x_{i-1}) + f(x_i) \right\}$$

$$= \frac{1}{2} h_i \left\{ f(x_{i-1}) + f(x_{i-1}) + (x_i - x_{i-1})f'(x_{i-1}) \right.$$

$$+ \frac{1}{2}(x_i - x_{i-1})^2 f''(x_{i-1}) + \ldots \left. \right\}$$

$$= h_i f(x_i) + \frac{1}{2} h_i^2 f'(x_{i-1}) + \frac{1}{4} h_i^3 f''(x_{i-1})$$

Again, we commit no significant error by ignoring the terms in h_i^4, h_i^5, ... and have, effectively,

$$T_i = h_i f(x_i) + \frac{1}{2} h_i^2 f'(x_{i-1}) + \frac{1}{4} h_i^3 f''(x_{i-1})$$

Therefore,

$$I_i - T_i = \left(\frac{1}{6} - \frac{1}{4}\right) h_i^3 f''(x_{i-1}) = -\frac{1}{12} h_i^3 f''(x_{i-1})$$

This, then, is the estimate we shall use for calculating the error caused by approximating the ith integral by the trapezoidal rule. We will call the error E_i. Thus, $E_i = -\frac{1}{12} h_i^3 f''(x_{i-1})$. The total error E committed will thus be given by the equation

$$E = \sum_{i=1}^{n} E_i = -\frac{1}{12} \sum_{i=1}^{n} h_i^3 f''(x_{i-1})$$

It appears from this that we need to be able to evaluate the second derivative of f in order to calculate the error. Furthermore, we have, as yet, no method for determining how to choose the x_i. We shall now proceed to eliminate the need for explicit values of f'' and at the same time create an algorithm for choosing the x_i.

Consider the ith sub-interval $[x_{i-1}, x_i]$. Suppose we split it at the mid-point m_i into two sub-intervals J_1 and J_2 and apply the trapezoidal rule to each sub-interval. Let us assume that the trapezoidal rules give areas of J_i' and J_i'' with errors E_i' and E_i''. We shall denote $\int_{x_{i-1}}^{m_i} f(x)dx$ by I_i' and $\int_{m_i}^{x_i} f(x)dx$ by I_i''. This leads to

$$I_i - T_i = E_i = -\frac{1}{12} h_i^3 f''(x_{i-1}) \tag{1}$$

$$I_i' - J_i' = E_i' = -\frac{1}{12} \left(\frac{h_i}{2}\right)^3 f''(x_{i-1})$$

$$= -\frac{1}{96} h_i^3 f''(x_{i-1})$$

$$I_i'' - J_i'' = E_i'' = -\frac{1}{12} \left(\frac{h_i}{2}\right)^3 f''(x_{m_i})$$

$$= -\frac{1}{96} h_i^3 f''(x_{i-1})$$

Note that, in the previous line, we are assuming the interval is so small that, effectively, $f''(m_i) = f''(x_{i-1})$.

Now, adding the last two equations we get

$$I_i' + I_i'' - (J_i' + J_i'') - L_i' + E_i'' = \frac{1}{48} h_i^3 f''(x_{i-1})$$

Now $I_i = I_i' + I_i''$, so

$$I_i - (J_i' + J_i'') = E_i' + E_i'' = -\frac{1}{48} h_i^3 f''(x_{i-1}) = \frac{1}{4} E_i$$

What this equation tells us is that, if we split the ith interval up into two equal sub-intervals and use the trapezoidal rule on each piece, the error is reduced by a factor of 4.

For convenience, let $C_i = J_i' + J_i''$. Then,

$$I_i - C_i = \frac{1}{4} E_i \qquad\qquad (2)$$

Subtracting equation (2) from equation (1), we obtain

$$C_i - T_i = \frac{3}{4} E_i$$

and, therefore,

$$E_i = \frac{4}{3}(C_i - T_i)$$

This equation tells us that we can obtain the value of the error committed by use of the trapezoidal rule on the ith interval by applying it three times, once to the whole interval and once to each half interval. By making the reasonable assumption that we are dealing with intervals so small that f'' can be regarded as effectively constant on the interval, we have eliminated the need to know values of f'' in calculating the error E_i.

Let us suppose that the integral is wanted with an error no greater than ϵ (specified by the user). We know that the total error E is given by

$$E = \sum_{i=1}^{n} E_i$$

Therefore, if $|E_i| \leq \epsilon h_i / (b - a)$ for each i, then

$$|E| \leqslant \sum_{i=1}^{n} |E_i|$$

$$\leqslant \sum_{i=1}^{n} \frac{\epsilon h_i}{b-a} = \frac{\epsilon}{b-a} \sum_{i=1}^{n} h_i = \frac{\epsilon(b-a)}{b-a} = \epsilon$$

and the requirement is met.

A suitable algorithm will, therefore, start with the whole interval and test to see if the error is less than $\epsilon h_i/(b-a)$.

If not, then the interval is split into two equal sub-intervals and the process is repeated on each sub-interval until the criterion is met. To guard against the process failing to converge, the user should specify a limit on how small a sub-interval may become before the process is terminated as not converging.

We shall define the algorithm in the form of a structure plan, but before doing so we must note an important fact. Quadrature algorithms are judged by how many function evaluations are required to determine the integral. In the method outlined above, when an interval is split into two, the values at the two end-points can be reused as end-points of the two sub-intervals. The only additional function value required is at the mid-point of the original interval. We therefore have an economical algorithm in which no function evaluations are wasted.

We also note that the process we have described is naturally recursive. We shall therefore develop a subroutine `adaptive_quadrature` that will be called by the user. This subroutine will perform some validity checks and then calculate the initial function values to be used by a recursive subroutine `adap_quad`. This recursive subroutine will perform the numerical quadrature by calling itself as many times as are appropriate.

For `adap_quad`, let the left and right end-points be xl and xu, respectively, and let $fl = f(xl)$, where f is the function to be integrated, and let $fu = f(xu)$. A suitable structure plan is then as follows:

1   If the interval length h has become too small then
     1.1   Set an error flag and return
2   Calculate the mid-point `xm` of the interval, and the value `fm` of `f(xm)`
3   Calculate the value `t` of the trapezoidal estimate of the integral over the whole interval
4   Calculate the value `c` of the sum of the trapezoidal rule applied to the two sub-intervals
5   Estimate the error `e = (c-t)/3` (using `c` as the answer)
6   If $|e| \leqslant \epsilon h/(b-a)$ then
     6.1   Return `c` as the value of the integral over `[xl,xu]`

> Otherwise
> **6.2** Split `[xl,xu]` into two equal sub-intervals `[xl,xm]` and `[xm,xu]`
> **6.3** Call `adap_quad` using the sub-interval `[xl,xm]`
> **6.4** Call `adap_quad` using the sub-interval `[xm,xl]`
> **6.5** If no errors occur in either call, return the sum of the two values
> received as the value of the integral over `[xl,xb]`
> [Note that this is the recursive step]

A module containing both subroutines is as follows:

```
module numerical_quadrature
    private :: adap_quad
    public :: adaptive_quadrature

contains

    subroutine adaptive_quadrature(f, a, b, eps, &
            subdivide_limit, answer, error)
    ! This subroutine integrates the function f from a to b
    ! using an adaptive method based on the trapezoidal rule.
    ! eps is the user-specified error tolerance.
    ! subdivide_limit is a user-specified smallest interval
    ! size to use.
    ! answer is the calculated answer.
    ! error is the success/failure indicator.

        ! Dummy arguments
        interface
            function f(x) result(fx)
                real, intent(in) :: x
                real :: fx
            end function f
        end interface
        real, intent(in) :: a, b, eps, subdivide_limit
        real, intent(out) :: answer
        integer, intent(out) :: error

        ! Validity checks
        if(eps <= 0.0) then
            error = -1
            return
        end if
        if(subdivide_limit <= 0.0) then
            error = -2
            return
        end if

        if(a < b) then
            call adap_quad(f, a, b, f(a), f(b), subdivide_limit,  &
                        eps/(b-a), answer, error)
        else if(a > b) then
            call adap_quad(f, b, a, f(b), f(a), subdivide_limit,  &
                        eps/(a-b), answer, error)
```

```
      if(error == 0) then
         answer = -answer
      end if
   else
      error = 0
      answer = 0.0
   end if
end subroutine adaptive_quadrature

recursive subroutine adap_quad(f, xl, xu, fl, fu,           &
                          lower, delta, answer, error)
! This subroutine performs an adaptive numerical
! quadrature using the trapezoidal rule

   ! Dummy arguments
   interface
      function f(x) result(fx)
         real, intent(in) :: x
         real :: fx
      end function f
   end interface
   real, intent(in) :: xl, xu, fl, fu, lower, delta
   real, intent(out) :: answer
   integer, intent(out) :: error

   ! Local variables
   real :: h, t, c, xm, fm, e, ans1, ans2

   h = xu - xl
   if(abs(h) < lower) then
      ! Interval has become too small
      error = -3
      answer = huge(answer)
      return
   end if
   t = h*(fl+fu)/2.0
   xm = xl+h/2.0
   fm = f(xm)
   c = h*(fl+2.0*fm+fu)/4.0
   e = (c - t)/3.0

   if(abs(e) <= delta*h) then
      ! Trapezoidal rule has achieved required accuracy
      ! The print statement is only for during development
      ! It will be removed when code is certified as
      ! functional
      print "(a, es12.4, a, es12.4, a, tr3, a, es12.4)",   &
         "Interval Used (", xl, ", ", xu, ")", "h =", xu - xl
      error = 0
      answer = c
   else
      ! Subdivide the interval
      call adap_quad(f, xl, xm, fl, fm, lower, delta,      &
                  ans1, error)
```

```
                    if(error /= 0) then
                        return
                    end if
                    call adap_quad(f, xm, xu, fm, fu, lower, delta,     &
                                   ans2, error)
                    if(error /= 0) then
                        return
                    end if
                    answer = ans1+ans2
                end if
            end subroutine adap_quad
        end module numerical_quadrature
```

We shall test this module by evaluating $\int_{0.1}^{1}(1/x)dx$ with an accuracy of 0.01 and by evaluating $\int_{0}^{\pi/2} \cos x dx$, also with an accuracy of 0.01, using the following functions:

```
module test_functions
    public :: f, g

contains

    function f(x) result(fx)
        real, intent(in) :: x
        real :: fx
        if( x == 0.0 ) then
            print *, "Cannot calculate the reciprocal of 0"
            stop
        end if
        fx = 1.0/x
        return
    end function f

    function g(x) result(gx)
        real, intent(in) :: x
        real :: gx
        gx = cos(x)
        return
    end function g
end module test_functions
```

Note, incidentally, that

$$\int_{0.1}^{1}(1/x)dx = \left[\ln(x)\right]_{0.1}^{1} = \ln(1) - \ln(0.1)$$

$$= 0 + 2.302\,585 = 2.302\,585$$

and

$$\int_{0}^{\pi/2} \cos x dx = \left[\sin x\right]_{0}^{\pi/2} = \sin(\pi/2) - \sin(0) = 1.0 - 0.0 = 1.0$$

A suitable test program is shown below

```fortran
program test_quadrature
   use test_functions
   use numerical_quadrature

   ! Declarations
   real, parameter :: pi=3.1415926

   real :: a, b, accuracy_tolerance, value
   real :: smallest_subdivision
   integer :: error

   ! Calculate integral of f on [0.1, 1.0]
   a = 1.0e-1
   b = 1.0
   accuracy_tolerance = 1.0e-2
   smallest_subdivision = 1.0e-5
   call adaptive_quadrature(f, a, b, accuracy_tolerance,       &
                           smallest_subdivision, value, error)

   ! Print result or error message, as appropriate
   select case (error)
   case (0)
    print "(2/, 2(a, es9.1),/, a, es14.6,/,2(a, f14.4, /), /)", &
          "Value of integral of x**(-1) from ", a, " to ", b,   &
          "with accuracy tolerance ", accuracy_tolerance,       &
          "is ", value,                                         &
          "Correct answer is ", -log(a)
   case (-3)
      print *,"Failed to converge to a solution for first "      &
           //"problem"
   case (-1)
      print *,"Epsilon was less than or equal to zero"
   case (-2)
      print *,"Subdivide_limit was less than or equal to zero"
   end select

   ! Calculate integral of g on [0, pi/2]
   a = 0.0
   b = pi/2.0
   accuracy_tolerance = 1.0e-2
   call adaptive_quadrature(g, a, b, accuracy_tolerance,       &
                           smallest_subdivision, value, error)

   ! Print result or error message, as appropriate
   select case (error)
   case (0)
    print "(2/, 2(a, es12.6),/, a, es14.6,/,2(a, f14.4, /), /)",&
          "Value of integral cos(x) from ", a," to ", b,        &
          "with accuracy tolerance ", accuracy_tolerance,       &
          "is ", value,                                         &
          "Correct answer is ", 1.0
```

```
        case (-3)
           print *,"Failed to converge to a solution for second "    &
                   //"problem"
        case (-1)
           print *,"Epsilon was less than or equal to zero"
        case (-2)
           print *,"Subdivide_limit was less than or equal to zero"
        end select
     end program test_quadrature
```

The results of running this program are shown in Figure 17.17.

In the first case, we would expect the subdivision points to be clustered more closely as we move towards the origin, since the second derivative of the function x^{-1} becomes increasingly large as we approach the origin. The printed output verifies this is happening. Also, the second derivative of $\cos(x)$ becomes small near $\pi/2$, so we would expect longer steps to be taken in that vicinity. The printed output verifies this expectation also.

In the above example, a relatively low accuracy tolerance of 10^{-2} was used. To illustrate that life is not always straightforward, however, Figure 17.18 shows the result of repeating the same calculations with tolerances set to 10^{-5}, 10^{-6}

```
Interval Used ( 1.0000E-01,  1.1406E-01)   h = 1.4063E-02
Interval Used ( 1.1406E-01,  1.2812E-01)   h = 1.4062E-02
Interval Used ( 1.2812E-01,  1.4219E-01)   h = 1.4063E-02
Interval Used ( 1.4219E-01,  1.5625E-01)   h = 1.4062E-02
Interval Used ( 1.5625E-01,  1.8438E-01)   h = 2.8125E-02
Interval Used ( 1.8438E-01,  2.1250E-01)   h = 2.8125E-02
Interval Used ( 2.1250E-01,  2.6875E-01)   h = 5.6250E-02
Interval Used ( 2.6875E-01,  3.2500E-01)   h = 5.6250E-02
Interval Used ( 3.2500E-01,  4.3750E-01)   h = 1.1250E-01
Interval Used ( 4.3750E-01,  5.5000E-01)   h = 1.1250E-01
Interval Used ( 5.5000E-01,  7.7500E-01)   h = 2.2500E-01
Interval Used ( 7.7500E-01,  1.0000E+00)   h = 2.2500E-01

Value of integral of x**(-1) from   1.0E-01 to 1.0E+00
with accuracy tolerance   1.000000E-02
is          2.3080
Correct answer is       2.3026

Interval Used ( 0.0000E+00,  3.9270E-01)   h = 3.9270E-01
Interval Used ( 3.9270E-01,  7.8540E-01)   h = 3.9270E-01
Interval Used ( 7.8540E-01,  1.5708E+00)   h = 7.8540E-01

Value of integral cos(x) from  0.000000E+10 to 1.570796E+00
with accuracy tolerance   1.000000E-02
is          0.9940
Correct answer is       1.0000
```

Figure 17.17   Results produced by the adaptive quadrature test program.

```
Value of integral of x**(-1) from   1.0E-01 to   1.0E+00
with accuracy tolerance   1.000000E-05
is      2.3025906
Correct answer is       2.3025851

Value of integral cos(x) from 0.000000E+00 to 1.570796E+00
with accuracy tolerance   1.000000E-05
is      0.9999952
Correct answer is       1.0000000

Value of integral of x**(-1) from   1.0E-01 to   1.0E+00
with accuracy tolerance   1.000000E-06
is      2.3025856
Correct answer is       2.3025851

Value of integral cos(x) from 0.000000E+00 to 1.570796E+00
with accuracy tolerance   1.000000E-06
is      0.9999995
Correct answer is       1.0000000

Failed to converge to a solution for first problem

Value of integral cos(x) from 0.000000E+00 to 1.570796E+00
with accuracy tolerance   1.000000E-07
is      0.9999999
Correct answer is       1.0000000
```

Figure 17.18 More accurate results produced by `test_quadrature`.

and 10^{-7}. The **print** statement has been removed from the subroutine **adap_quad** in order not to produce too much output.

Note that the required accuracies were obtained except when we requested an accuracy of 10^{-7} for $\int_{0.1}^{1}(1/x)dx$. What do you think went wrong, and how would you fix it?

We must caution the user that, while the principle of adaptively changing the step size and using the subdivision results to estimate errors is frequently employed, more sophisticated algorithms based on this idea are often used. We have kept the mathematics as simple as possible so that we could concentrate on principles.

We finish our discussion of numerical quadrature on a faint note of gloom. Any numerical quadrature process will usually require the evaluation of the given function f at a finite number of points $x_1, x_2, \ldots, x_p$.

Now consider the function

$$\phi(x) = f(x) - k(x - x_1)^2(x - x_2)^2 \ldots (x - x_p)^2$$

where k is a constant.

For $i = 1, 2, \ldots, p$, $\phi(x_p) = f(x_p)$, because the term we have subtracted from f will be 0 at each x_i. So, to a numerical quadrature procedure

$$\int_a^b \phi(x)dx = \int_a^b f(x)dx$$

while, mathematically

$$k \int_a^b (x - x_1)^2 \ldots (x - x_p)^2 dx = \int_a^b f(x)dx - \int_a^b \phi(x)dx$$

Clearly, by making k large enough, the difference between $\int_a^b f(x)dx$ and $\int_a^b \phi(x)dx$ can be made as large as we please!

This fact puts a note of uncertainty into all numerical quadrature algorithms. However, for most practical problems, it is not significant.

SELF-TEST EXERCISES 17.1

1   What are the advantages and disadvantages of each of the three methods introduced for solving non-linear equations (bisection method, Newton's method, and secant method)?

2   What is partial pivoting? Why is it important in Gaussian elimination?

3   What is the major difference between a cubic spline curve-fitting algorithm and one using a polynomial? What are the advantages of each method?

4   What is adaptive quadrature? Why is caution necessary in accepting the result of any numerical quadrature?

PROGRAMMING EXERCISES

Most of the following examples use the procedures developed in this chapter as a means of experimentation with their accuracy and usefulness. However, the opportunity is also taken to introduce several further techniques in the form of programming exercises. For more details concerning these, and other, numerical methods you should consult an appropriate numerical analysis text.

17.1   In Exercise 11.4 you wrote a program to solve a polynomial equation using the bisection method, and then used it again in Exercise 11.5 to find those roots of the following polynomials which lie in the range $-10 \leqslant x \leqslant 10$. Modify your program, if necessary, to print the number of iterations taken and use it to find the roots again, saving the roots and the number of iterations in a file.

(a) $10x^3 - x^2 - 69x + 72$
(b) $20x^3 - 52x^2 + 17x + 24$
(c) $5x^3 - x^2 - 80x + 16$
(d) $10x^4 + 13x^3 - 163x^2 - 208x + 48$
(e) $x^4 + 2x^3 - 23x^2 - 24x + 144$
(f) $9x^4 - 42x^3 - 1040x^2 + 5082x - 5929$

Now replace the subroutine that uses the bisection method by one that uses Newton's method and run the program again, taking care that you do not overwrite the results saved in a file by the previous program.

Finally, repeat the process, using the secant method.

Now write another program to list the three sets of results in a form suitable for comparing the effectiveness of the three methods.

17.2 Use the programs you wrote for Exercise 17.1 to produce a similar comparison for the following functions:

(a) $\sin(3x + \pi/4)$
(b) $\sin 3x \cos x$
(c) $\sin 5x + 5 \cos x$
(d) $2 - e^{\sin x}$
(e) $\tan(x + \pi/6)$
(f) $\sin(e^{x/3})$

17.3 Use Newton's method to calculate the following values:

(a) the square root of 5;
(b) the cube root of 7;
(c) the seventh root of 2000.

17.4 Use the Gaussian elimination method, described in Section 17.5, to solve the following systems of simultaneous linear equations:

(a) $\quad 2x + 3y + \ z = 4$
$\quad\quad x - 2y - \ z = 3$
$\quad -2x + \ y + 3z = 4$

(b) $\quad 2x + \ y - \ z = 3$
$\quad\quad 4x - \ y - 3z = -3$
$\quad\quad x + 3y + \ z = 4$

(c) $\quad -2x - \ y + 4z = 4$
$\quad\quad x + 2y - 2z = 1$
$\quad\quad 3x + 4y - 6z = -1$

(d) $\quad x - 2y - z + w = 3$
$\qquad 3x + y + z - 2w = 3$
$\qquad -2x - 3y + 2z - w = 4$
$\qquad x + y - z + w = 0$

(e) $\quad x \qquad\qquad + t = 1$
$\qquad 2y - z \qquad\quad = 5$
$\qquad 2x \qquad - w \qquad = 1$
$\qquad\qquad 2z + w \qquad = -3$
$\qquad y \qquad\quad - 2t = 3$

How did your program deal with systems (c) and (e)?

17.5 Use the Gaussian elimination method, described in Section 17.5, to solve the following system of simultaneous linear equations:

$$10x + 7y + 8z + 7w = 32$$
$$7x + 5y + 6z + 5w = 23$$
$$8x + 6y + 10z + 9w = 33$$
$$7x + 5y + 9z + 10w = 31$$

If the coefficients had been obtained by experimental means, or as the result of some earlier calculation, there could be some slight errors in them. In order to test the effect of this, change the coefficients on the right-hand side of the equations by one in the fourth significant figure (about 0.03%) to 32.01, 22.99, 32.99 and 31.01, and run the program again to find a new solution. Did the result surprise you?

Now change the same coefficients by one in the third significant figure to 32.1, 22.9, 32.9 and 31.1, and run it again.

This example (which is due to T.S. Wilson) illustrates the problem of ill-conditioned systems which was first mentioned in Chapter 11.

17.6 Modify the module `tridiagonal_systems` that was developed in Section 17.6 so that partial pivoting is performed when solving tridiagonal systems, and test it with a suitable tridiagonal system.

17.7 The subroutine `gaussian_elimination`, in Example 17.3, subtracts a multiple of the whole of row i from row j. This is unnecessary, because elements 1 to $i - 1$ of row i are zero, and element i of row j will become zero after the subtraction. Modify the subroutine to be more efficient.

Test both your modified subroutine and the original one in a program that uses the computer's clock (or some other means) to measure the time taken for solution by each version of a 10×10 system of equations.

17.8 Modify the subroutine `gaussian_elimination` written in Example 17.3, or the modified one produced for Exercise 17.7, to use pointers to eliminate the actual interchange of rows of the coefficient matrix. Modify subroutine `back_substitution` accordingly. Test this new version on a 10×10 system of equations. What were the run times compared to the original version?

17.9 In order to simplify usage and, generally, make programming simpler and safer for those solving linear systems of equations, create a derived type `square_matrix` and a derived type `vector`. Rewrite the module that was developed in Example 17.3 to use these derived types. Test your module using the various sets of equations that were solved in Exercise 17.4.

17.10 In Section 17.5 it was mentioned that iterative methods were sometimes more suitable than Gaussian elimination for the solution of simultaneous equations, especially when many of the coefficients are zero. One of the best-known iterative methods is the Gauss–Seidel method, which can be summarized as follows.

In the discussion in Section 17.5 we considered the set of simultaneous equations

$$a_{11}x_1 + a_{12}x_2 + \ldots + a_{1n}x_n = b_1$$
$$a_{21}x_1 + a_{22}x_2 + \ldots + a_{2n}x_n = b_2$$
$$\vdots$$
$$a_{n1}x_1 + a_{n2}x_2 + \ldots + a_{nn}x_n = b_n$$

We shall obtain a sequence of vectors which converge to the correct solution vector to the system of equations. We will call these successive approximations $x^{(0)}$, $x^{(1)}$, $x^{(2)}$, ..., and will let

$$x^{(i)} = \begin{bmatrix} x_1^{(i)} \\ x_2^{(i)} \\ \vdots \\ x_n^{(i)} \end{bmatrix}$$

where the superscripts denote which approximate solution is being referred to. The Gauss–Seidel method gives an iteration to obtain $x^{(i+1)}$ from $x^{(i)}$.

We proceed by first rearranging the system of equations, by row interchanges, so that the diagonal elements are all non-zero. If we cannot achieve this, the system of equations is degenerate. After this rearrangement, for $i = 1, 2, \ldots, n$, we divide the ith equation by a_{ii}. This means each diagonal coefficient of the system of equations is 1. We will use primes to denote the coefficients of the resulting system.

In this system, we can rearrange the equations as

$$x_1 = b'_1 - (a'_{12}x_2 + a'_{13}x_3 + \ldots + a'_{1n}x_n)$$
$$x_2 = b'_2 - (a'_{21}x_1 + a'_{23}x_3 + \ldots + a'_{2n}x_n)$$
$$\vdots$$
$$x_n = b'_n - (a'_{n1}x_1 + a'_{n2}x_2 + \ldots + a'_{n,n-1}x_{n-1})$$

We can now use $x_2^{(i)}, x_3^{(i)}, \ldots, x_n^{(i)}$ on the right-hand side of the first equation, to obtain $x_1^{(i+1)}$. We then use $x_1^{(i+1)}, x_3^{(i)}, x_4^{(i)}, \ldots, x_n^{(i)}$, the right-hand side of the second equation, to obtain $x_2^{(i+1)}$. Note that we immediately use $x_1^{(i+1)}$ in obtaining $x_2^{(i+1)}$. We then use $x_1^{(i+1)}, x_2^{(i+1)}, x_4^{(i)}, x_5^{(i)}, \ldots, x_n^{(i)}$, on the right-hand side of the third equation, to obtain $x_3^{(i+1)}$. Again, notice that we immediately use $x_1^{(i+1)}$ and $x_2^{(i+1)}$ in obtaining $x_3^{(i+1)}$. Formally:

$$x_j^{i+1} = b_j' - \sum_{k=1}^{j-1} a_{jk}' x_k^{(i+1)} - \sum_{k=j+1}^{n} a_{jk}' x_k^{(i)}, \qquad \text{for } j = 1, \ldots, n$$

The conditions under which this process is guaranteed to converge to the solution vector go beyond the scope of this book.

A suitable convergence criterion will be the third type described in Section 11.5, namely that the difference between successive approximations should be less than a small value. This can be expressed in this context as

$$|x_j^{(i+1)} - x_j^{(i)}| < \epsilon, \qquad \text{for all } j$$

Write a subroutine to implement the Gauss–Seidel method, and modify your existing program for the solution of simultaneous equations (or the one in Section 17.5) to use this subroutine. Use this new program to solve the five systems of simultaneous equations given in Exercise 17.4.

Which method proved to be most suitable for each system?

17.11   A solid shape is formed by rotating the curve $y = f(x)$ about the x-axis. The volume of such a shape is

$$A = \int_a^b \pi f(x)^2 dx$$

where a and b are the start and end of the curve on the x-axis. Write a subroutine that has a function f and the limits a and b as arguments, and returns the volume of the corresponding solid shape by evaluating the above integral. Use the adaptive quadrature method described in Section 17.8.

Confirm that for $f(x) = x$, $a = 1$, and $b = 3$, the volume contained is $\frac{28\pi}{3}$ units.

17.12   Investigate how the number of function evaluations required by the subroutine adaptive_quadrature to calculate $\int_{-1}^{1}(1/x)dx$ varies as the precision requirements are increased.

17.13   Using the subroutine adaptive_quadrature, calculate π to 4, 5 and 6 decimal places by integrating the equation for a circle of radius 1 with its centre at the origin over the range 0 to 1. How many function evaluations were required? You will encounter numerical difficulties. Why?

17.14   Using the subroutine adaptive_quadrature, calculate π to 4, 5 and 6 decimal places by evaluating $\int_0^1(1 + x^2)dx$. How many function evaluations were required?

17.15   Modify the subroutine adaptive_quadrature so that it additionally returns its estimate of the error. Repeat Exercises 17.13 and 17.14 using your modified algorithm. You will again encounter numerical difficulties in the first case.

17.16   Modify the subroutine adaptive_quadrature to use parameterized **real** numbers so that you can repeat Exercises 17.13 and 17.14 to obtain π to 12 decimal places. How many function evaluations were required?

17.17 Write a program, or programs, to perform the following actions:

1. Calculate a set of values of $f(x)$, for x within a specified range (for instance, from $x = -10$ to $x = +10$ in steps of 0.5), and tabulate these.
2. Use these tabulated values to interpolate a set of splines, or other approximating curves, through these points.
3. Use the subroutine `adaptive_quadrature` to find the definite integral of the original function between two specified values of x, and also of the interpolated curves between the same values.
4. Display the difference between the two integrals as one measure of the goodness of fit.

Test your program(s) on the following functions:

(a) x^2
(b) $x^2 + 3x - 5$
(c) x^3
(d) $2x^3 - 3x^2 - 6x + 4$
(e) x^4
(f) $3x^4 + 5x^3 - 2x^2 + 7x - 9$
(g) $\sin 2x$
(h) $\sin(x/2 + \pi/3) \cos x$
(i) $e^{-x^2/2}$

*17.18 Exercises 11.8 and 11.9 showed how the Newton quotient could be used to calculate the first derivative of a function, but also showed how the choice of h in the formula for the quotient

$$f'(x) = \frac{f(x+h) - f(x)}{h}$$

where h is small, was critical to the accuracy of the calculation. Euler's method for the solution of first order differential equations of the form

$$\frac{dy}{dx} = g(x, y)$$

where $y = y_0$ when $x = x_0$ uses the Newton quotient to replace the derivative on the left-hand side of the equation:

$$\frac{f(x+h) - f(x)}{h} = g(x, y)$$

or

$$f(x + h) = f(x) + hg(x, y)$$

If we know the value of $f(x)$ for some initial value of x (for example, $x = 0$) then we can calculate the value at $x + h$, then at $x + 2h$, and so on. However, our experience in Exercises 11.8 and 11.9 might lead us to suppose that the choice of h will be critical, and this supposition is normally correct.

Euler's method usually requires h to be so small that it is frequently impractical and other methods have to be employed. However, it can be modified, by techniques similar to that used for creating the adaptive quadrature subroutine of Section 17.8, to make it more practical. Such modifications are beyond the scope of this book. Consult Dahlquist and Björck (1974) for an introduction to such techniques.

Use Euler's method in a program to solve the following problem.

It is well-known that in a vacuum a steel ball and a feather will fall at the same speed under the influence of gravity. However, in atmosphere there is always some air resistance which will lead to the steel ball hitting the ground first. This retarding force is normally assumed to be proportional to the square of the velocity, leading to the following equation (from Newton's second law):

$$ma = mg - cv^2$$

where m is the mass of the ball, a is its downward acceleration, g is the acceleration due to gravity, v is the velocity of the ball, and c is some constant. This, in turn, leads us to the first-order differential equation

$$\frac{dv}{dt} = a = g - kv^2$$

where $k = c/m$.

Assuming that for a steel ball of mass 1 kg the value of k is 0.001, write a program to tabulate the downward velocity of a 1 kg steel ball dropped from a stationary hot-air balloon at a great height, and hence calculate the terminal velocity of the ball (that is, the maximum speed that can be attained, which will be achieved when the retarding force due to air resistance equals the accelerating force due to gravity).

Run your program for a range of values for h in order to determine the best value (that is, the time interval between 'samplings' in this case).

17.19 Use the program you wrote for Exercise 17.18 to find the terminal velocity of a man jumping from the balloon. Assume his mass to be 100 kg and k to be 0.004.

When he has reached his terminal velocity he opens a parachute, with the result that k becomes 0.3. Modify your program to find how this affects his speed. (Hint: you may need to alter h again.)

17.20 Radioactive elements decay into other elements at a rate given by the equation

$$\frac{dm}{dt} = -rm$$

where m is the mass of the original material still present at time t, and r is constant property of the element known as the decay rate.

Analytical solution of this equation leads, among other things, to the conclusion that the mass of the original material is reduced by one half in a time T, known as the half-life of the substance, where $T = (\log_e 2)/r \ (\approx 0.693/r)$.

Use Euler's method to calculate the mass remaining, over a period of 500 years, of an initial 10 kg radioactive substance whose half-life is 200 years. Experiment with different values of h, starting with $h = 20$ years.

17.21 In your program for Exercise 17.20 you calculated the change in mass of an element due to radioactive decay. In general, the amount of this mass lost in energy is infinitesimal compared with that converted into another element, and can be ignored. It is simple, therefore, to calculate the mass of the new element, given the initial mass present, after a given time.

However, in many cases, this new element itself decays into a third element. In this situation, clearly, a pair of simultaneous differential equations are required to describe the process.

An example of this process is the decay of strontium 92 (with a half-life of about 162 minutes) into yttrium 92 (with a half-life of about 327 minutes), which in turn decays into zirconium.

Write a program which will use Euler's method to calculate how many atoms there will be of each element at 15-minute intervals over a 10-hour period, assuming that there were 10^{20} atoms of pure strontium 92 at the start of the experiment.

Run your program again using time intervals of 5, 10 and 20 minutes.

AFTERWORD
Seven golden rules

This book is called *Programming in F*, and we hope that we have made it clear that there is much more to programming than simply writing the code. Indeed, we have emphasized that coding will often represent little more than 20–25% of the total effort involved, with some 30–35% being spent on the design, and the remainder being spent in testing and debugging. We will sum up our philosophy, therefore, in what we call the *Seven Golden Rules of Programming*.

1. *Always plan ahead* It is invariably a mistake to start to write a program without having first drawn up a program design plan which shows the structure of the program and the various levels of detail.

2. *Develop in stages* In a program of any size it is essential to tackle each part of the program separately, so that the scale and scope of each new part of the program is of manageable proportions.

3. *Modularize* The use of procedures and modules, which can be written and tested independently, is a major factor in the successful development of large programs, and is closely related to the staged development of the programs.

4. *Keep it simple* A complicated program is usually both inefficient and error-prone. F contains many features which can greatly simplify the design of code and data structures.

5. *Test thoroughly* Always test your programs thoroughly at every stage, and cater for as many situations (both valid and invalid) as possible. Keep your test data for reuse if (when) your program is modified in the future.

6. *Document all programs* There is nothing worse than returning to an undocumented program after an absence of any significant time. Most programs can be adequately documented by the use of meaningful names, and by the inclusion of plenty of comments, but additional documentation should be produced if necessary to explain things that cannot be covered in the code itself. A program has to be written only once – but it will be read many times, so effort expended on self-documenting comments will be more than repaid later.

589

7. *Enjoy your programming* Writing computer programs, and getting them to work correctly, is a challenging and intellectually stimulating activity. It should also be enjoyable. There is an enormous satisfaction to be obtained from getting a well-designed program to perform the activities that it is supposed to perform. It is not always easy, but it should be fun!

Happy programming!

APPENDIX A
Intrinsic procedures

A.1 How to find out about F's intrinsic procedures

The F language includes a rich set of intrinsic procedures, both subroutines and functions, which are intended to facilitate the solution of scientific, statistical, mathematical and other problems. These intrinsic procedures are part of the F language because it is only with a complete set of tools that a solution to a problem is 'easy' and elegant. This appendix lists all the intrinsic procedures contained within the F language with a brief indication of their purpose and calling sequence. In order to save space, and because most programmers will only use a relatively small subset, a full description of these procedures is not included here. In general this information will be found in the manual that accompanies each F compiler, but a more complete description is also available from our publisher's World Wide Web pages at the following URL:

```
http://awl-he.com/computing
```

Several of the intrinsic procedures listed in the following sections have already been discussed earlier in this book and in these cases the section in which they are so discussed is indicated following the description of the procedure.

A.2 Intrinsic procedure classes and their descriptions in this appendix

In addition to the five intrinsic subroutines, one of which is elemental, there are three classes of intrinsic functions: elemental, inquiry and transformational.

An elemental procedure is one that is specified for scalar arguments, but may also be applied to array arguments.

In a reference to an elemental intrinsic function:

- If the arguments are all scalar, the result is scalar. If an argument is an array, the shape of the result agrees with the shape of the argument with the greatest rank; all arguments must be conformable.
- The elements of the result have the same values as would have been obtained if the scalar-valued function had been applied separately, in any order, to corresponding elements of each argument.
- When a **kind** argument is present, it must be a scalar integer initialization expression with a non-negative value that specifies a representation method for the function result that exists on the processor.

An inquiry function is one whose value depends on the properties of its principal argument; in most cases the argument *value* need not be defined.

A transformational function is a function which is neither an elemental function nor an inquiry function; most transformational functions have one or more array-valued arguments or an array-valued result.

In the remaining sections of this appendix each procedure is described in a consistent format in which the name of the procedure and its calling sequence appear first followed by a brief description. Where a procedure has one or more optional arguments these are enclosed in square brackets.

In most cases the description of the procedure will include the type and purpose of all the arguments, but for more comprehensive details you should refer to the World Wide Web pages identified in Section A.1, which contain a very full description of all 102 procedures.

A.3   Numerical and mathematical intrinsic procedures

All of these procedures are elemental functions except for **dot_product** and **matmul**, which are transformational functions, and **random_number** and **random_seed**, which are subroutines.

abs (a) returns the absolute value of a, which must be of a numeric type; if a is complex, **abs** (a) returns the real square root of the sum of the squares of the complex parts.

acos (x) returns the arccosine of the real argument x in the range $0 \leqslant$ **acos** (x) $\leqslant \pi$, where $|x| \leqslant 1.0$.

aimag (z) returns the imaginary part of the complex argument z. (12.1)

aint (a[,kind]) returns the real argument a truncated to a whole number; the result is the value of the largest whole number that does not exceed the magnitude of a and whose sign is the same as the sign of a. If kind is present the result has the kind type kind, otherwise its kind is default real. (12.6)

anint (a[,kind]) returns the nearest whole number to the value of the real argument a. If kind is present the result has the kind type kind, otherwise its kind is default real. (12.6)

asin (x) returns the arcsine of the real argument x in the range $-\pi/2 \leqslant$ **asin** (x) $\leqslant \pi/2$, where $|x| \leqslant 1.0$.

atan (x) returns the arctangent of the real argument x in the range $-\pi/2 \leqslant$ **atan** (x) $\leqslant \pi/2$.

atan2 (y,x) returns the arctangent of y/x in the range $-\pi <$ atan2 (y,x) $\leqslant \pi$. At least one of the arguments must be non-zero. If y is zero the result is 0.0 if x is positive and π otherwise; if y is non-zero then the sign of the result is the same as that of y; if x is zero the absolute value of the result is $\pi/2$.

ceiling (a) returns the least integer greater than or equal to the real argument a.

conjg (z) returns the conjugate of the complex argument z. (12.1)

cos (x) returns the cosine of the real or complex argument x.

cosh(x) returns the hyperbolic cosine of the real argument x.

dot_product(vector_a,vector_b) is a transformational function which returns the dot product of two numeric or two logical vectors; if the arguients are numeric then the result type is the same as the type of the expression vector_a*vector_b; if they are logical the result type is logical. If the vectors have zero size then the result is 0 or *false*, as appropriate. (13.1)

exp(x) returns e raised to the real or complex power x.

floor(a) returns the greatest integer less than or equal to the real argument a.

fraction(x) returns the fractional part of the real argument x.

log(x) returns the natural logarithm of the real or complex argument x; if x is real it must be positive; if x is complex it must be non-zero. (4.2)

log10(x) returns the logarithm of the real argument x to base 10; x must be positive.

matmul(matrix_a,matrix_b) is a transformational function which returns the matrix product of two numeric or two logical matrices. If the arguments are numeric then the result type is the same as the type of the expression matrix_a*matrix_b; if they are logical the result type is logical. (13.1)

max(a1,a2[,a3,...]) returns the maximum value of its arguments, which must all be real or all be integer. (7.6, 7.9)

min(a1,a2[,a3,...]) returns the minimum value of its arguments, which must all be real or all be integer.

modulo(a,p) returns the modulo of a with respect to p; a and p must both be real or both be integer. For integer arguments, the result r is such that a = q*p + r, where q is an integer, the signs of p and r agree, and the inequalities $0 \leqslant$ **abs**(r) $<$ **abs**(p) hold. For real arguments, the result r is such that r = a - floor(a/p)*p. If p is zero, the result is processor dependent.

nearest(x,s) returns the nearest machine-representable real number different from the real argument x in the direction of the real, non-zero, argument s.

nint(a[,kind]) returns the integer nearest to that of the real argument a. If kind is present the result has the kind type kind, otherwise its kind is default integer. (12.6)

random_number(harvest) is a subroutine which returns pseudo-random number(s) from the uniform distribution over the range $0 \leqslant$ harvest < 1.0, where harvest may either be a real scalar or a real array. (7.6)

random_seed([size][,put][,get]) is a subroutine which either restarts the pseudo-random number generator used by **random_number** or returns generator parameters. If there are no arguments then the seed will be set to a processor-dependent value; otherwise there must be exactly one argument present. If the integer variable size is present it will be set to the size n of the seed array; if the rank-one integer array put of size n is present the seed array will be reset to the values supplied; if the rank-one integer array get of size n is present it will be set to the current values of the seed array.

sign (a,b) returns the absolute value of the argument a set to the same sign as b; both arguments must be real, or both must be integer.

sin (x) returns the sine of the real or complex argument x. (4.2, 7.6)

sinh (x) returns the hyperbolic sine of the real argument x.

sqrt (x) returns the square root of the real or complex argument x. If x is real, it must be non-negative; if x is complex, the real part of **sqrt** (x) is non-negative; if the real part of **sqrt** (x) is 0, the imaginary part is non-negative. (4.2)

tan (x) returns the tangent of the real argument x.

tanh (x) returns the hyperbolic tangent of the real argument x.

A.4 Numeric inquiry functions

digits (x) returns the number of significant digits in x, which may be integer or real.

epsilon (x) returns a positive number that is almost negligible compared to 1.0, and of the same type and kind as x.

huge (x) returns the largest number in the processor's numerical model of the same type and kind as x. (6.2)

kind (x) returns the kind value of x, which must be of an intrinsic type. (11.2, 12.6)

maxexponent (x) returns the maximum exponent in the processor's numerical model for a real number of the same kind as the real argument x.

minexponent (x) returns the minimum exponent in the processor's numerical model for a real number of the same kind as the real argument x.

precision (x) returns the decimal precision of real values with the same kind as x, which may be real or complex.

radix (x) returns the base of the processor's numerical model for values of the same type and kind as x, which may be integer or real.

range (x) returns the decimal exponent range in the processor's numerical model for integer or real numbers with the same kind as x, which may be of any numeric type.

tiny (x) returns the smallest positive number in the processor's numerical model of the same type and kind as x.

A.5 Character intrinsic functions

All of these procedures are elemental functions except for **repeat** and **trim**, which are transformational functions, and **len**, which is an inquiry function.

adjustl (string) returns a character value with the leading blanks of the character argument string removed and the same number of trailing blanks added at the end. (4.5)

adjustr(string) returns a character value with the trailing blanks of the character argument string removed and the same number of leading blanks added at the beginning.

char(i) returns the character in a specified position in the ASCII collating sequence; i must lie in the range $0 \leqslant i \leqslant 127$. (5.4)

ichar(c) returns the position of a character in the ASCII collating sequence. (5.4)

index(string,substring[,back]) returns the starting position of the character argument substring within the character argument string. If the logical argument back is absent, or present with the value *false*, the result is the lowest value of i such that string(i:i+len(substring)-1) = substring, or zero if there is no such value; if back is present with the value *true*, the result is the maximum value of i less than or equal to **len**(string)-**len** (substring) such that string(i:i+**len**(substring)-1) = substring, or zero if no such i exists. If **len**(string)<**len**(substring) the result is 0; if **len**(substring)=0 the result is 1.

len(string) is an inquiry function which returns the length of the character argument string. (4.5)

len_trim(string) returns the length of the character argument string without counting any trailing blank characters; if string is all blanks, the result is 0.

repeat(string,ncopies) is a transformational function which returns a character value which is produced by concatenating ncopies copies of the character argument string. If either string is zero length or ncopies is zero, the result is a zero length string.

scan(string,set[,back]) scans a string for any one of the characters in a specified set of characters. The result is an integer which is the first instance of a member of the characters in the character argument set that appears in the character argument string, counting from the left; if the logical argument back is *true*, the search is from the right, but the count is still from the left. If no character of string is in set, or if the length of either string or set is zero, the result is 0.

trim(string) is a transformational function which returns the character argument string with any trailing blanks removed; if string contains no non-blank characters, the result has zero length. (3.5)

verify(string,set[,back]) returns 0 if every character in the character argument string is also in the character argument set or if string has zero length. If a character in string is not in set, the result is its position in string. If the logical argument back is *true*, then the search is from the right.

A.6 Bit intrinsic procedures

Although F does not have an intrinsic bit type, it does contain 12 procedures for manipulating bits held within integers. These procedures are based on those originally specified in the US Military Standard MIL-STD 1753, and are based on a model in which an integer consists of s consecutive bits numbered from 0 to $s - 1$.

All of these procedures are elemental functions except for **bit_size**, which is an inquiry function, and **mvbits**, which is an elemental subroutine.

bit_size(i) is an inquiry function which returns the number of bits in the integer i.

btest(i,pos) returns *true* if bit pos of the integer argument i is 1; otherwise *false*.

iand(i,j) returns the logical AND of the integers i and j.

ibclr(i,pos) returns the integer i with bit pos set to zero.

ibits(i,pos,len) returns a right-adjusted sequence of bits extracted from the integer argument i of length len beginning at bit pos; all other bits are 0.

ibset(i,pos) returns the integer i with the pos bit set to one.

ieor(i,j) returns the exclusive OR of the integers i and j.

ior(i,j) returns the inclusive OR of the integers i and j.

ishft(i,shift) returns the integer i logically shifted shift places to the right (for shift negative) or to the left (for shift positive).

ishftc(i,shift[,size]) returns the value of the integer i with its size rightmost bits circularly shifted shift places to the right (for shift negative) or to the left (for shift positive); if size is absent, then all the bits are shifted circularly.

mvbits(from,frompos,len,to,topos) is an elemental subroutine which copies a sequence of len bits from the integer from, starting at position frompos, to the integer to, starting at popsition topos; the other bits of to are unaltered. (7.6)

not(i) returns the logical complement of the bits of the integer i.

A.7   Array processing intrinsic functions

The availability of a considerable number of the intrinsic procedures for use in array processing was discussed in Chapters 7 and 13, especially the latter, and the most important of them were described in detail there. This section contains a complete summary of all 21 array intrinsics.

In the following descriptions many of the procedures follow similar conventions:

- Array-valued arguments may be of any type, unless otherwise specified.
- The optional logical argument mask is used by some of the functions to select the elements of one or more of the arguments to be operated on by the function.
- When referring to the rank of the (primary) array argument, an italicized *r* is used.
- A scalar is defined as an array of rank 0.
- The term *positive* always means *strictly positive*, that is, greater than 0.

Furthermore, in the functions **all**, **any**, **lbound**, **maxval**, **minval**, **product**, **sum** and **ubound**, but not **cshift**, **eoshift**, **size** and **spread**, the optional argument dim, when present, requires that the corresponding actual argument is not an optional dummy argument of the calling program unit. This is because the functions in the first list all return either a scalar or an array based on the presence or absence of dim, and the function must, therefore, be able to determine the presence or absence of dim from the list of actual arguments.

All of these procedures are transformational functions except for **lbound**, **shape**, **size** and **ubound**, which are inquiry functions, and **merge**, which is an elemental function.

all(mask[,dim]) returns *true* if all elements of the logical array argument mask are *true* along dimension dim or if mask has zero size; otherwise *false*. (13.7)

any(mask[,dim]) returns *true* if any of the elements of the logical array argument mask is *true* along dimension dim; otherwise *false* (including the case in which mask has zero size). (13.7)

count(mask[,dim]) returns the number of *true* elements of the logical array argument mask along dimension dim; it returns zero if mask has zero size.

cshift(array,shift[,dim]) returns an array of the same type as array created by performing a circular shift on an array expression of rank one or circular shifts on all the complete rank-one sections along a given dimension of an array expression of rank two or greater. Elements shifted out at one end of a section are shifted in at the other end. Different sections may be shifted by different amounts and in different directions.

eoshift(array,shift[,boundary][,dim]) returns an array of the same type as array created by performing an end-off shift on an array expression of rank one or end-off shifts on all the complete rank-one sections along a given dimension of an array expression of rank two or greater. Elements are shifted off at one end of a section and copies of a boundary value are shifted in at the other end. Different sections may have different boundary values and may be shifted by different amounts and in different directions.

lbound(array[,dim]) is an inquiry function which returns all the lower bounds or a specified lower bound of array. (7.8, 13.5)

maxloc(array[,mask]) returns a rank-one integer array of size r containing the location of the first element of array having the maximum value of the elements identified by mask. Each element of the result is the subscript corresponding to the element of array having the maximum value in that dimension; if there is more than one such element then the value returned is the first such subscript in array-element order. The ith subscript of the rank-one array returned is positive and less than or equal to the extent of the ith dimension of array. (7.6, 13.1)

maxval(array[,dim][,mask]) returns the maximum value of the elements of the real or integer array argument array along dimension dim (if present) corresponding to the true elements of mask (if present). If array has zero size, or if every element of mask is *false*, the result is the negative number of largest magnitude of the type and kind of array. (7.6, 13.1, 13.7)

merge(tsource,fsource,mask) is an elemental function which returns an array of the same type as tsource and fsource, created by selecting the corresponding element of tsource where mask is *true*, and of fsource where mask is *false*.

minloc(array[,mask]) returns a rank-one integer array of size r containing the location of the first element of array having the minimum value of the elements identified by mask. Each element of the result is the subscript corresponding to the element of array having the minimum value in that dimension; if there is more than one such element then the value returned is the first such subscript in array element order. The ith subscript of the rank-one array returned is positive and less than or equal to the extent of the ith dimension of array. (7.6, 13.1)

minval(array[,dim][,mask]) returns the minimum value of the elements of the real or integer array argument array along dimension dim (if present) corresponding to the true elements of mask (if present). If array has zero size, or if every element of mask is *false*, the result is the positive number of largest magnitude of the type and kind of array. (7.6, 13.1, 13.7)

pack(array,mask,vector) returns a rank-one array of the same type as array created by packing the elements of array under the control of mask. If vector is present, the size of the result is the same as the size of vector; otherwise the result size is the number of *true* elements in mask unless mask is scalar with the value *true*, in which case the result size is the size of array. The result can be unpacked by the intrinsic function **unpack**.

product(array[,dim][,mask]) returns the product of the elements of array along dimension dim (if present) corresponding to the *true* elements of mask (if present); if array has zero size or if mask has no *true* elements the result has the value one. (13.1)

reshape(source,shape[,pad][,order]) returns an array of a specified shape constructed from the elements of the array argument source. The elements of the result, taken in permuted subscript order order(1), ..., order(n) if order is present or in order 1, ..., n if it is absent, are those of source in array-element order followed, if necessary, by the elements of the array argument pad in array-element order, followed, if necessary, by additional copies of pad in array-element order. (13.3)

shape(source) is an inquiry function which returns the shape of source as a rank-one array of size r.

size(array[,dim]) is an inquiry function which returns either the extent of array along a specified dimension (if dim is present) or the total number of elements in the array. (7.6, 7.8, 13.5)

spread(source,dim,ncopies) returns an array of rank $r + 1$ created by copying source along a specified dimension (as in making a book from copies of a single page).

sum(array[,dim][,mask]) returns the sum of the elements of array along dimension dim (if present) corresponding to the *true* elements of mask (if present); if array has zero size or if mask has no *true* elements the result has the value one. (7.6, 13.1, 13.7)

transpose(matrix) transposes an array of rank two; element (ij) of the result has the value matrix (j, i).

ubound(array[,dim]) is an inquiry function which returns all the upper bounds or a specified upper bound of array. (7.8, 13.5)

unpack(vector,mask,field) unpacks a rank-one array into an array under the control of a mask. The element of the result that corresponds to the ith *true* element of mask, in array-element order, has the value vector(i) for $i = 1, 2, \ldots, t$, where t is the number of *true* values in mask. The other result elements have either the corresponding array element of field, if field is array-valued, or the scalar value of field if it is a scalar. The inverse operation of packing an array into a rank-one array is performed by the intrinsic function **pack**.

A.8 Type conversion and manipulation intrinsic functions

All of these procedures are elemental functions except for **selected_int_kind** and **selected_real_kind**, which are transformational functions.

cmplx(x[,y][,kind]) returns a complex value of kind type kind, if present, or of default kind otherwise. If x is non-complex the result has a real part of x and an imaginary part of y if y is present, or an imaginary part of 0.0 if y is not present; if x is complex then y must not be present. x may be of any numeric type, and y of either real or integer type. (12.1, 12.6)

exponent(x) returns the exponent part of x. If x is zero the result is zero; otherwise the result is one plus the integer part of the log to the base 2 of x in the processor's numerical model.

int(a[,kind]) returns an integer value of kind type kind, if present, or of default kind otherwise. If a is real it is truncated and converted to integer; if a is complex its real part is truncated and converted to integer; if a is integer it is converted to kind kind, if necessary. (12.6)

logical(l[,kind]) returns a logical value converted to kind type kind, if present, or to default logical kind otherwise. (12.6)

real(a[,kind]) returns a real value of kind type kind, if present, or of default kind otherwise. If a is integer it is converted to real; if a is complex, the real part is converted to the appropriate kind; if a is real it is converted to the appropriate kind. (6.2, 12.1, 12.6)

rrspacing(x) returns the reciprocal of the relative spacing of numbers near x in the processor's numerical model; x must be real.

scale(x,i) returns xb^i where b is the base in the processor's numerical model representation of x; x must be real and i must be integer.

selected_int_kind(r) is a transformational function which returns a processor-dependent kind value that represents all integers n such that $-10^r < n < 10^r$. If there is more than one such kind, the value returned is the one with the smallest decimal exponent range, unless there are several such kinds, in which case the smallest kind is returned; if no such kind is available the result is -1. (12.5)

selected_real_kind([p][[,]r]) is a transformational function which returns a processor-dependent kind value that represents real values with decimal precision of at least p digits (see **precision**) and a decimal exponent range of at least r (see **range**); either argument may be present, or both may be. If more than one kind meets the criteria, the value returned is the one with the smallest decimal precision, unless there are several such kinds, in which case the smallest kind is returned; if no such kind is available, the result is -1 if the precision requested is not available, -2 if the exponent range is not available, and -3 if neither is available. (11.2, 12.5)

set_exponent(x,i) returns the real number in the processor's numerical model whose fractional part is the fractional part of the model representation of x and whose exponent part is i; if x is zero then the result is 0.

spacing(x) returns the absolute spacing of numbers near x in the processor's numerical model if this is within range, otherwise the result is the same as **tiny**(x).

A.9   Miscellaneous inquiry functions

allocated(array) returns *true* if array is currently allocated; otherwise *false*. array may be any type of array, but must have the allocatable attribute. (13.6)

associated(pointer,target) returns *true* if pointer is associated with a target and target is not present, or if target is the target that pointer is associated with, otherwise *false*; the result is also *false* if either pointer or target is disassociated. pointer may be of any type, and must have the pointer attribute; target may be a pointer or a target, but must have its pointer association status defined if it is a pointer. (14.1)

present(a) returns *true* if the optional argument, a, of the procedure in which the reference to **present** occurs is present; otherwise *false*. (16.1)

A.10   Time and date intrinsic subroutines

date_and_time([date,][time,][zone,][values]) returns current date and time. The first three arguments, if present, are character variables of length 8, 10 and 5 which will be set to the date (*ccyymmdd*), the time (*hhmmss.sss*) and the time difference ($\pm hhmm$) with respect to Coordinated Universal Time (UTC) – also known as Greenwich Mean Time (GMT); if any of these values are not available they are set to blanks. The fourth argument, if present, is an integer array of dimension 8, whose elements will be set to the following values: year, month, day, minutes difference from UTC/GMT, hours, minutes, seconds, milliseconds; if any of these values are not available the corresponding array element is set to -**huge**(0). (4.2)

system_clock([count,][count_rate,][count_max]) returns integer data from a real-time clock. All arguments, if present, are integers; the first is set to a value based on the current value of the system clock, the second is set to the number of processor clock counts per second, and the third to the maximum value that count can take before it is reset to zero. If there is no clock, count and count_rate are set to -**huge**(0) and count_max is set to zero.

APPENDIX B
Reserved words and order of statements

B.1 Reserved words

Programs written in F may not use the names of any F keywords, or the names of any of F's intrinsic procedures, for any other purpose, and these **reserved words** have been printed in bold type throughout this book in order to emphasize that they are reserved. In addition, there are a number of Fortran 90 and Fortran 95 keywords and intrinsic procedures that are not used in F but which are, nevertheless, reserved words in F to avoid any problems if the F program should subsequently be compiled with a Fortran 90 or Fortran 95 compiler. A complete list of all reserved words in alphabetical order is provided in Table B.1, with each reserved word being followed by one of three identifying symbols:

[F] to indicate that the word is an F keyword, and has a specific meaning in the F language.

[I] to indicate that the word is the name of an F intrinsic procedure (function or subroutine).

[X] to indicate that the word is a name that has some significance in Fortran 90 or Fortran 95, although it is not used in F.

If a reserved word falls into two categories, then both symbols appear.

Table B.1 Reserved words in F.

abs [I]	achar [X]	acos [I]
adjustl [I]	adjustr [I]	aimag [I]
aint [I]	all [I]	allocatable [F]
allocate [F]	allocated [I]	and [F]
anint [I]	any [I]	asin [I]
assignment [F]	associated [I]	atan [I]
atan2 [I]	backspace [F]	bit_size [I]
btest [I]	call [F]	case [F]
ceiling [I]	char [I]	character [F]
close [F]	cmplx [I]	complex [F]
conjg [I]	contains [F]	cos [I]
cosh [I]	count [I]	cpu_time [X]
cshift [I]	cycle [F]	date_and_time [I]

601

Table B.1 (*cont.*) Reserved words in F.

dble [X]	deallocate [F]	default [F]
digits [I]	dim [X]	dimension [F]
do [F]	dot_product [I]	dprod [X]
elemental [X]	else [F]	elseif [F]
elsewhere [F]	end [T]	enddo [T]
endfile [F]	endforall [X]	endfunction [F]
endif [F]	endinterface [F]	endmodule [F]
endprogram [F]	endselect [F]	endsubroutine [F]
endtype [F]	endwhere [F]	eoshift [I]
epsilon [I]	eq [X]	eqv [F]
exit [F]	exp [I]	exponent [I]
false [F]	file [F]	floor [I]
forall [X]	fraction [I]	function [F]
ge [X]	go [X]	goto [X]
gt [X]	huge [I]	iachar [X]
iand [I]	ibclr [I]	ibits [I]
ibset [I]	ichar [I]	ieor [I]
if [F]	in [F]	index [I]
inout [F]	inquire [F]	int [I]
integer [F]	intent [F]	interface [F]
intrinsic [F]	ior [I]	ishft [I]
ishftc [I]	kind [I]	lbound [I]
le [X]	len [F,I]	len_trim [I]
lge [X]	lgt [X]	lle [X]
llt [X]	log [I]	log10 [I]
logical [F,I]	lt [X]	matmul [I]
max [I]	maxexponent [I]	maxloc [I]
maxval [I]	merge [I]	min [I]
minexponent [I]	minloc [I]	minval [I]
mod [X]	module [F]	modulo [I]
mvbits [I]	ne [X]	nearest [I]
neqv [F]	nint [I]	not [F,I]
null [F]	nullify [F]	only [F]
open [F]	operator [F]	optional [F]
or [F]	out [F]	pack [I]
parameter [F]	pointer [F]	precision [I]
present [I]	print [F]	private [F]
procedure [X]	product [I]	program [F]
public [F]	pure [F]	radix [I]
random_number [I]	random_seed [I]	range [I]
read [F]	real [F,I]	recursive [F]
repeat [I]	reshape [I]	result [F]
return [F]	rewind [F]	rrspacing [I]
save [F]	scale [I]	scan [I]
select [F]	selectcase [F]	selected_int_kind [I]
selected_real_kind [I]	set_exponent [I]	shape [I]
sign [I]	sin [I]	sinh [I]
size [I]	spacing [I]	spread [I]
sqrt [I]	stop [F]	subroutine [F]
sum [I]	system_clock [I]	tan [I]
tanh [I]	target [F]	then [F]
tiny [I]	to [F]	transfer [X]

Table B.1 (*cont.*)   Reserved words in F.

transpose [I]	trim [I]	true [F]
type [F]	ubound [I]	unpack [I]
use [F]	verify [I]	where [F]
write [F]		

B.2   Order of statements in F programs

F contains a considerable number of non-executable statements whose purpose is to provide information about variables, constants and procedures that the program is using. Although there is considerable freedom as regards the order of these statements, F does impose some constraints on the overall order of statements, and the rest of this appendix summarizes the required order for each type of program unit.

In each of the remaining sections of this appendix those statements or modifiers enclosed in square brackets are optional, but if present must occur in the order shown.

B.3   Main program statement order

The order of statements in the main program must be as follows:

program *program-name*
    [**use** statements]
    [**intrinsic** statements]
    [local entity declarations]
    [executable constructs]
end program *program-name*

B.4   Subroutine statement order

The order of statements in a subroutine must be as follows:

[**recursive**] **subroutine** *subroutine-name* ([dummy-argument-list])
    [**use** statements]
    [**intrinsic** statements]
    [dummy argument declarations]
    [local entity declarations]
    [executable constructs]
end subroutine *subroutine-name*

B.5   Function statement order

The order of statements in a function must be as follows:

[**recursive**] **function** *function-name* ([dummy-argument-list]) &
        result (*result-name*)
    [**use** statements]
    [**intrinsic** statements]
    [dummy argument declarations]

```
        result definition
        [local entity declarations]
        executable construct
        [executable constructs]
    end function function-name
```

B.6   Module statement order

The order of statements in a private module must be as follows:

```
module module-name
    [use statements]
    [private]                    ! Must be present if there are
                                 ! any use statements
    [accessibility statements]
    [intrinsic statements]
    [module entity declarations]
[contains]
    [subprogram definitions]
end module module-name
```

A public module is used for a somewhat different purpose, namely to merge two or more modules into a single module. The order of statements in this form of module is as follows:

```
module module-name
    use statement
    [use statements]
    public
end module module-name
```

APPENDIX C
The relationship between F and Fortran 90

In this appendix, we discuss the differences between F and Fortran 90. Unlike Fortran 90, F is not defined in an international standard. It is formally defined by the syntax rules published by Imagine1, Inc., which can be found in Adams *et al.* (1996), but is, in practice, defined by Metcalf and Reed (1996). Inevitably, we shall use terms from Fortran 90, a significantly more complicated language than F, that do not occur in F. For F programmers who wish to pursue Fortran 90, we refer them to Ellis *et al.* (1994).

As stated in Chapter 1, Fortran has had a long history which, in order to preserve the considerable investment in existing programs, has been carried forward in the last version of Fortran, that is, Fortran 90. F is designed to be a subset of Fortran 90 containing only modern features. Thus, F contains no features categorized as obsolescent in the Fortran 90 standard. No new Fortran 90, Fortran 95 or F programs should use these old features. They are:

- Fixed form for source code.
- The computed go to statement.
- The double precision (real) data type.
- The character* method of expressing the length of a character variable.
- The use of data statements to initialize variable values.
- Statement functions.
- A function result can have an assumed character length.
- A dummy argument that is an array may have assumed size.

Fortran 90 contains more elaborate, but upward compatible, versions of some of the capabilities of F. In general, these provide increased functionality, resulting in a more elegant method of programming than is permitted by F:

- The first of these concerns the accessibility of items encapsulated in modules, where the style we encourage in Fortran 90, in which all entities are declared **private** and a **public** statement lists all those items that are to be accessible from outside the module, is, in our view, clearer and easier to use than the method enforced in F, particularly for large, complex programs.
- The second concerns Fortran 90's **if** statement, which greatly simplifies the writing of exit conditions for loops.
- The third of these is when writing very simple programs, where Fortran 90's ability to define derived types and to initialize variables in a main program can greatly simplify such programs. However, this flexibility can be abused when writing larger programs.

The remainder of this appendix lists these and all the other features of Fortran 90 which are not present in F (other than the obsolescent features detailed above), grouped by topic within the main areas of the F (or any other) programming language.

C.1 General concepts

Source

- Statements may occur on the same source line, separated by semicolons.
- Statements may be labelled.
- Additional source text may be inserted ('included') from files.
- Tokens can be split across lines.
- A continuation line can begin with an &. This permits a character string to be split over more than one line.

Names

- Names can terminate with an _.
- Names are case sensitive.
- Keywords do not have to be lower case.
- There are no reserved words.

End

- The final statement of a main program, procedure or module may be an **end** statement without a matching name, or even without a matching program unit type (that is, **program**, **function**, **subroutine** or **module**).

Statement order

- Fortran 90 has more statements than F and therefore requires more complicated ordering rules.

C.2 Program units

Main programs

- A main program does not have to begin with a program statement.
- Variables can be initialized in a main program.

Functions

- Functions do not have to be placed in modules. They are then said to be external.
- The type of a function does not have to be specified in a result clause.
- Dummy arguments or values accessible by host or use association can be modified.
- Functions, subject to restrictions on their use, can use all the input/output capabilities available in Fortran 90.
- Character dummy arguments do not have to have an assumed length.
- A dummy argument may be a subroutine.
- The **intent** attribute can be omitted.

- Optional dummy arguments can be interleaved with non-optional arguments.
- A **save** statement can be used.
- There are no restrictions on subroutines that may be called.
- There are statement function statements. They consist of a single statement.
- An entry statement permits execution to begin at a point other than the first executable statement.

Subroutines

- Subroutines do not have to be placed in modules. They are then said to be external.
- The **intent** attribute can be omitted.
- Optional dummy arguments can be interleaved with non-optional arguments.
- An entry statement permits execution to begin at a point other than the first executable statement.
- A subroutine with no arguments need not have parentheses and can be called without using parentheses.
- Character dummy arguments do not have to have an assumed length.

Internal procedures

- A procedure may occur inside another procedure or main program, in which case it has access to the variables in its host by host association.

Intrinsic procedures

- There are more intrinsic procedures.
- Actual arguments that are kind values can be scalar integer initialization expressions.

Modules

- Modules default to having public accessibility.
- A module may be accessible by more than one path.
- A module with default public accessibility is not restricted as in F.
- All entities in a module can be declared to be either public or private. These can be overridden by specific lists in other public or private statements.

Use

- An only list can be empty.
- Renaming can cause an accessible entity to have more than one local name

Interfaces

- Because Fortran 90 does not require that procedures be in modules, it is sometimes necessary to specify a procedure interface by use of an interface block.
- Generic names can involve procedures not contained in modules.
- An interface body can be empty.
- A procedure in an interface block can have the same name as the generic name.
- An intrinsic procedure name can occur in an interface body without use of an intrinsic statement.
- A generic interface can redefine the meaning of an intrinsic procedure, within certain limits.

C.3 Data types

Type rules

- There are rules for implicit typing of variables based on the first character of their names.
- An implicit none statement turns off the implicit typing rules.

Attributes

- The attributes of an entity are not necessarily all declared in the same statement.
- Intrinsic functions may be explicitly declared to have the **intrinsic** attribute.
- The :: token in a **type** declaration statement is sometimes optional.

Real numbers

- There is a second floating-point data type – double precision – which corresponds to a **real** data type with a kind type parameter value which selects a hardware representation having greater precision than that used for **real**.
- Literal constants do not have to have a fractional part and may, for a double-precision literal, have a D (instead of E) as an exponent letter.

Complex numbers

- The real and imaginary parts of a complex literal may have different kind type parameters.

Characters

- Variables and literal constants can have a kind type parameter (to specify differing character sets).
- Literal constants may be delimited by apostrophes.
- Constants may be qualified by substrings.

Kind parameters

- Kind parameters can be set to constant scalar integer expressions.

Length selectors

- Length selectors can be set to the values of specification expressions.

Arrays

- An array constructor index can be a dummy argument, a **pointer**, a function **result**, or a variable accessed by **use** or host association.
- The index variable of an array constructor can also be used outside the constructor and may be saved or initialized.
- Dimensions can be specified after the :: token in a type declaration statement.
- Arrays can be specified in a **dimension** statement.
- Parts of an array in an input or output list can be specified with an implied **do**.
- Sequence association is permitted.

Derived types
- Definitions may appear outside modules and do not necessarily contain access specifications.
- A **private** type may have private components.
- A sequence statement in a derived type definition permits objects of this type to be used in an equivalence statement.

C.4   Specification features

Initialization
- A data statement can be used to initialize a variable.
- A block data statement can be used to initialize variables in named common.
- Variables with initial values do not necessarily have the **parameter** or **save** attribute.

Common
- A common statement is a feature that allows different procedures and main programs access to a shared set of variables, possibly using different names to refer to the same entity. Use and host association are less error-prone.

Equivalence
- An equivalence statement is a way of letting different variables share the same space in computer memory.

C.5   Execution features

Continue
- There is a continue statement. It is commonly used in an alternative form of the **do** construct.

Stop
- A **stop** statement can have a stop code.

C.6   Control features

Relational operators
- There are alternative forms for the ==, /=, <, <=, >, >= operators.

Do constructs
- A comma can appear after the **do**.
- A while clause is permitted – permitting termination to be based on a logical condition.
- A continue statement is permitted.
- The index can be a default **real**, a double precision real, a **pointer**, a dummy argument, a function result or accessed via **use** or host association.

Go to

- There is a go to statement that permits an (almost) arbitrary jump of execution within a procedure or a main program.

If

- An **if** construct can be named.
- There is an **if** statement that is not part of an **if** construct.

Case

- A **case** construct can be named.
- Case values and expressions can be of type **logical**.
- The default selector does not have to be the final **case** selector

Where statements

- Where statements can occur by themselves; that is, outside a **where** construct.

C.7   Input/output

Namelist

- A namelist statement is a way of identifying a set of variables by one name.

I/O formats

- A format can be specified in a format statement.
- Some commas in a format list are optional.
- A format specification can contain a character string for an edit descriptor.
- There are more edit descriptors.

Open

- There are more specifiers for the **open** statement.
- There are optional ways of specifying the unit and fmt values.
- Blanks may be used more freely in a format list.
- The status connection specifier can be set to the (system-dependent) value unknown.
- The status connection specifier can be omitted; if so, it defaults to unknown.
- If the status connection specifier has the value scratch, the action connection specifier does not have to have the value readwrite.
- If the status connection specifier has the value new, then the action connection specifier does not have to have the value read.
- The action connection specifier can be omitted. The result is system dependent.
- The position connection specifier can have the value asis.
- Open statements can be applied to a unit that is already connected, thus modifying the existing connection status.

APPENDIX D
The ASCII character set

There are a number of different coding systems for characters on different computer systems. However, F always assumes the system known as ASCII for the purpose of comparing characters by means of the four relational operators <, <=, >= and >. This code was originally an American standard code, but also forms the basis for the widely used seven-bit international standard coding system known as ISO 646.

The following table shows the ASCII coding system, and is laid out in a *hexadecimal* fashion, as is conventional for such tables, corresponding to the actual pattern of bits in the coded character representation. The order of characters in this table thus runs from the top to the bottom of the first column, and then from the top to the bottom of the next column to the right, and so on. To find the decimal value corresponding to a particular character you should multiply the column number by 16 and then add the row number; thus A corresponds to $65(4 \times 16 + 1)$, while } corresponds to $125(7 \times 16 + 13)$. Note that, as elsewhere in this book, the symbol ◊ represents a space; those positions where no character is shown are used for other (non-graphic) purposes.

The ordering of any characters not shown in the figure is not specified in F.

	0	1	2	3	4	5	6	7
0			◊	0	@	P	`	p
1			!	1	A	Q	a	q
2			"	2	B	R	b	r
3			#	3	C	S	c	s
4			$	4	D	T	d	t
5			%	5	E	U	e	u
6			&	6	F	V	f	v
7			'	7	G	W	g	w
8			(	8	H	X	h	x
9			)	9	I	Y	i	y
10			*	:	J	Z	j	z
11			+	;	K	[	k	{
12			,	<	L	\	l		
13			-	=	M	]	m	}
14			.	>	N	^	n	~
15			/	?	O	_	o	

Figure D.1 ASCII coding system.

Bibliography

Adams J.C., Brainerd W.S., Martin J.T. *et al.* (1996). *Key Features of F.* Albuquerque, NM: Unicomp

ANSI (1966). *American National Standard Programming Language FORTRAN. (ANSI X3.9-1966)*. New York: American National Standards Institute

ANSI (1978). *American National Standard Programming Language FORTRAN. (ANSI X3.9-1978)*. New York: American National Standards Institute

Atkinson L.V., Harley P.J. and Hudson J.D. (1988). *Numerical Methods with FORTRAN 77: A Practical Introduction*. Wokingham: Addison-Wesley

Cipra B.A. (1988). PCs factor a 'most wanted' number. *Science*, **242**, 1634–5

Dahlquist G. and Björck A. (1974). *Numerical Methods*. Englewood Cliffs, NJ: Prentice-Hall

Dierckx P. (1993). *Curve and Surface Fitting With Splines*. Oxford: Clarendon Press

Duff I.S., Erisman A.M. and Reid J.K. (1986). *Direct Methods for Sparse Matrices*. Oxford: Clarendon Press

Ellis T.M.R., Philips I.R. and Lahey T.M. (1994). *Fortran 90 Programming*. Wokingham: Addison-Wesley

Forsyth G.E., Malcolm M.A. and Moler C.B. (1977). *Computer Methods for Mathematical Computations*. Englewood Cliffs, NJ: Prentice-Hall

George A. and Liu J.W. (1981). *Computer Solution of Large Sparse Positive Definite Systems*. Englewood Cliffs, NJ: Prentice-Hall

Gerver J.L. (1983). Factoring large numbers with a quadratic sieve. *Mathematics of Computation*, **42/163**, 287–94

Golub G.H. and Van Loan C.F. (1991). *Matrix Computations* 2nd edn. Baltimore, MD: Johns Hopkins University Press

Gries D. (1991). *The Science of Computer Programming*. Berlin: Springer-Verlag

Hopkins T. and Phillips C. (1988). *Numerical Methods in Practice: Using the NAG Library*. Wokingham: Addison-Wesley

ISO/IEC (1991). *Information technology – Programming languages – Fortran. (ISO/IEC 1539 : 1991 (E))*. Geneva: ISO/IEC Copyright Office

ISO/IEC (1997). *Information technology – Programming languages – Fortran – Part 1: Base Language. (ISO/IEC 1539-1 : 1997 (E))*. Geneva: ISO/IEC Copyright Office

Knuth D.E. (1969). *The art of computer programming, Volume 1 – Fundamental Algorithms*. Reading, MA: Addison-Wesley

Metcalf M. and Reid J. (1996). *The F programming language*. Oxford: Oxford University Press

NAG Ltd (1988). *The NAG Fortran Library Manual – Mark 13*. Oxford: NAG Ltd

Richards I. (1982). The invisible prime number. *American Scientist*, **70**, 176–9

Scheid F. (1968). *Theory and Problems of Numerical Analysis*. New York: McGraw-Hill

SPSS Inc. (1988). *SPSS-X User's Guide* 3rd edn. Chicago: SPSS Inc.

Visual Numerics Inc. (1992). *IMSL Fortran Numerical Libraries, Version 2.0.* Houston, TX: Visual Numerics Inc.

Wilkinson J.H. (1963). *Rounding Errors in Algebraic Processes.* Englewood Cliffs, NJ: Prentice-Hall

Answers to self-test exercises

Self-test exercises 2.1 (page 25)

1 • Specifying the problem.
   • Analysing the problem, and breaking it down into its main components.
   • Writing the code to solve the problem.

2   The most difficult part of the whole process is usually the testing, and the elimination of errors (usually referred to as *debugging*). The next most difficult is the analysis of the problem and the design of the program (step 2, above).

3 • They must begin with a letter.
   • They must contain only letters, digits and the underscore character, _.
   • The last character must not be an underscore, _.
   • They must contain between 1 and 31 characters.
   • Upper-case and lower-case letters are treated as being equivalent for the purpose of distinguishing between identifiers; however, the same pattern of upper and lower case must be used whenever an identifier is used.

4   The first statement must be a **program** statement, and the last must be an **end program** statement containing the same name as the **program** statement.

5   If the last non-blank character of a line is an ampersand (&), then the statement is continued on the next line.

6   Programs are usually read many times, often by several different people, over their lifetime. Comments provide explanations of what is happening, and why, where this is not immediately obvious from the code itself, and thus make the program easier to understand by anyone who is reading it.

```
! A comment may be a line whose first non-blank character
! is an exclamation mark
a = 1      ! or it may be a trailing comment following
b = 2      ! any program statement, in which case the
c = 3      ! first non-blank character after the end of
d = 4      ! the statement must be an exclamation mark.
e = &      ! A trailing comment may also follow a
    5      ! continuation marker
```

Self-test exercises 2.2 (page 34)

1 A syntactic error is an error in the syntax, or *grammar*, of a statement. A semantic error is an error in the logic of the program; that is, it does not do what it was intended to do.

Compilation errors (errors detected during the compilation process) are usually the result of syntactic errors, although some semantic errors may also be detected. Execution errors (errors that occur during the execution of the compiled program) are always the result of semantic errors in the program.

2
- A well-designed program is easier to test.
- A well-designed program is easier to maintain.
- A well-designed program is easier to port to other computer systems.

3
- Ensure that the purpose of the program is fully understood.
- Ensure that the data requirements (the inputs) and the reporting requirements (the outputs) are fully understood and specified.
- Divide the overall problem into smaller, more manageable, sub-problems.
- Check to see if some, or all, of the functionality required in your program already exists in procedure libraries.

4
- Use meaningful names.
- Use plenty of comments.
- Ensure that your program carries out as many checks on the validity of the data it reads as is possible (and realistic). A program that attempts to process invalid data will never produce a meaningful answer!
- Test each part of your program thoroughly.

5 A line may contain up to 132 characters.

6 A statement may consist of up to 40 lines.

Self-test exercises 3.1 (page 55)

1 An integer is a whole number, and has no fractional part. A real number does have a fractional (or decimal) part.

2 Integers are stored exactly in the memory of a computer, and all operations using only integers result in exact answers. Real numbers are stored as (very accurate) approximations to their 'true' values, and operations involving real numbers result in approximations to the mathematically correct answer.

3
- Real numbers encompass a very much wider range than integers − typically between -10^{38} and $+10^{38}$ on a 32-bit computer, as compared with between -2×10^9 and $+2 \times 10^9$ on the same computer for integers.
- Most arithmetic calculations involve numbers with fractional parts, and only real numbers can represent such values.

4 A declaration statement is a statement that identifies a name that will be used to represent a variable, and which also specifies the *type* of information (such as real or integer numbers) that will be stored in that variable.

5 **(a)** **integer** :: men,women,children
     real :: adults_to_children

   (b) **integer** :: l_ft,l_ins, & ! Length in ft and ins
          h_ft,h_ins, & ! Height in ft and ins
          d_ft,d_ins   ! Depth in ft and ins

   Note that the above declaration assumes that measurements are to the nearest inch. If fractions of an inch are required then the three variables l_ins, h_ins and d_ins should be **real**.

   (c) **real** :: length,height,depth

   The same approach could be used as for (b), but since the metric system is a decimal one, it is more natural to use real numbers and extract the centimetres when required.

   (d) **real** :: time
     integer :: photons

   It is reasonable to assume that the time will be measured to a greater accuracy than the nearest second. The number of photons must be a whole number, however.

6 An assignment statement causes the result of an expression to be assigned to a variable; that is, the value of the result is stored in the memory location identified by the variable name.

7 In order of decreasing precedence (priority), the five arithmetic operators are the exponentiation operator (**), followed by the multiplication (*) and division (/) operators, and then by the addition (+) and subtraction (-) operators.

8 **real** :: a,b,av
   av = 0.5*(a+b)

Note that the statement

   av = (a+b)/2.0

is also correct, but it is usually preferable to multiply rather than to divide, wherever possible, as multiplication is an intrinsically more accurate (and faster) process than division.

9 6.500, 10.000, 0.650
   6, 10, 0

The exact spacing of the numbers, and the number of decimal places for the real values, may vary from computer to computer, but will follow essentially the same layout as shown above. Note that it is, theoretically, possible that the second number on the second line will be printed as 9 if the result of multiplying 2.5 by 4.0 resulted in a value of, for example, 9.999 999 9 as a result of insignificant round-off errors during the calculation.

10 ● 1.2 3.456 7.89 42.0
   ● 1.2,3.456,7.89,42.0
   ● 1.2
     3.456
     7.89
     42.0
   ● 1.2   3.456   7.89   42

and many other variations on the same theme.

Self-test exercises 3.2 (page 63)

1   The F character set consists of the 52 alphabetic characters of the Latin alphabet (upper- and lower-case letters), the 10 decimal digits, the underscore character, and 21 other specified characters. Only these characters may appear in F statements, other than in comments or character constants which may contain any characters available on the processor.

The default character set is that set of characters which the processor supports.

2   The declaration of a character variable includes a length specification.

3   `character(len=20) :: a,b,c,d`
        `character(len=1) :: x`
        `character(len=9) :: month ! September is the longest`

4   A small step for a man
        A giant leap for mankind

(Neil Armstrong's first words as he became the first man to step onto the surface of the moon in 1969)

5   If we assume that the limits for jury service are 21 and 70, then a suitable declaration might be:

        `integer, parameter :: min_age=21, max_age=70`

Self-test exercises 4.1 (page 89)

1   Breaking a program up into a main program and a set of procedures enables the top-down design approach to be carried through into the structure of the code, so that each procedure carries out a single, well-defined task. This also means that each procedure can be tested independently of the rest of the program.

2   A function returns a single result through the result variable. A function's arguments may only be used to provide information to the function, that is, they are `intent(in)`. A function is referenced by its name appearing as part of an expression.

A subroutine uses its arguments both to provide information to the subroutine and to return results to the calling program unit. A subroutine is referenced by means of a `call` statement.

3   An intrinsic procedure is one which is defined as a part of the F language, and which is provided by the F processor.

4   A generic function is a function which exists in several versions to carry out the same function on arguments of different types. For example, if `int_var` and `real_var` are integer and real variables, respectively, **abs**(`int_var`) will calculate the absolute value of `int_var` and return the result as an **integer** value, while **abs**(`real_var`) will calculate the absolute value of `real_var` and return the result as a **real** value.

5   A dummy argument declared as **intent**(**inout**) may be used both to provide information to the procedure and to return results from the procedure; it may be used freely throughout the procedure. A dummy argument declared as **intent**(**out**), on the other hand, is used only to return results from the procedure, and is undefined on entry to the procedure; it must therefore be given a value in an assignment statement, or by some other means, before being used in an expression.

6   (a) **function** count(char,string) **result**(number)
               character(**len**=*), **intent**(**in**) :: char,string
               integer :: number

Note that the dummy argument char must be declared with **len**=*, even though we know that the corresponding actual argument will be of length 1.

(b) **subroutine** quadratic(a,b,c,root1,root2)
            real, **intent**(**in**) :: a,b,c
            real, **intent**(**out**) :: root1,root2

(c) **function** prime(n) **result**(factor)
            integer, **intent**(**in**) :: n
            integer :: factor
            ! The function will return a factor, or zero if
            ! the number n is a prime

(d) **function** reverse(string) **result**(new_string)
            character(**len**=*), **intent**(**in**) :: string
            character(**len**=*) :: new_string

or, alternatively

      subroutine reverse(string)
            character(**len**=*), **intent**(**inout**) :: string
            ! The reversed string will replace the original one

(e) **subroutine** error(error_num)
            integer, **intent**(**in**) :: error_num

(f) **subroutine** get_number(n)
            integer, **intent**(**out**) :: n

Note that it is not appropriate to use a function for this purpose, as functions are not expected to carry out input operations, other than for diagnostic purposes.

Self-test exercises 4.2 (page 98)

1   **use** association associates a name in a procedure with an entity in a module having the same name, thereby making the entity in the module available in the procedure. (Note that we shall introduce a more complete definition in Chapter 8.)

2   (a) `real, parameter, public :: m_to_ft = 3.282, &`
    `         l_to_pt = 1.762, kg_to_lb = 2.232`

    (b) `public :: mean,st_dev   ! mean and st_dev are the`
    `                        ! names of two procedures`

    (c) `public :: analysis1,analysis2,analysis3,     &`
    `                analysis4,analysis5`
    `     real, parameter, private :: m_to_ft - 3.282, &`
    `         l_to_pt = 1.762, kg_to_lb = 2.232`

    Since all five procedures may need to convert between metric and imperial values it is sensible to make the relevant conversion constants available by host association; they will not, however, be available outside the module in this example.

3   The **save** attribute causes the value of a local variable in a procedure to be preserved between calls to the procedure; if it is not specified then on every entry to the procedure the values of local variables are undefined.

4   An initialization expression is a restricted form of constant expression containing only constants or references to intrinsic functions with integer or character arguments, and in which any exponentiation is to an integer power. A value assigned to a procedure variable in its declaration as an initial value must be a constant or a constant expression.

5   A variable can only be initialized as part of its declaration if it is a local variable in a procedure and has the **save** attribute.

Self-test exercises 5.1 (page 120)

1   A logical operator has two logical operands; a relational operator has two numeric, or two character, operands. Both give a logical result.

2   (a) *false*
    (b) *true*
    (c) Because of possible round-off errors in the evaluation of the expression `(0.1+0.3)` it is not possible to predict with absolute certainty what will be the result
    (d) *true*
    (e) *false*
    (f) *true*
    (g) *true*

3   An **if** construct is used either to select one of several alternative blocks of statements to be executed or to determine whether a single block of statements is executed.

4   • The 26 upper-case letters are collated in alphabetic order.
    • The 26 lower-case letters are collated in alphabetic order.
    • Upper-case letters are collated before lower-case letters.
    • The 10 digits are collated in increasing numerical order.
    • Digits are collated before A.

- Space (blank) is collated before both letters and digits.
- Other characters are collated in the order in which they appear in the ASCII code.

5   **(a)** *true*
       (b) *false*
       (c) *true*
       (d) *true* (blank comes before ? in the ASCII code, see Appendix D)

Self-test exercises 5.2 (page 131)

1   The order of the blocks and their preceding **if**, **else if** or **else** statements matter in an **if** construct because each test is carried out in sequence and the selection criteria may overlap. The order does not matter in a **case** construct, because the case selectors cannot overlap.

2   The **case** expression must be an **integer** or **character** expression. It cannot be a **real** or **logical** expression.

3   The **case** selector may take any of the following forms:

```
value
low_value:high_value
low_value:
:high_value
```

or a combination of these. The values must be **integer** or **character** literal constants or initialization expressions of the same type as the **case** expression.

4   Overflow occurs when a calculation gives rise to a value which is too large to be represented by the numeric type being used.

5   A **case** construct is the more appropriate when there is no overlap between the criteria for making the choice, and the basis for making the choice is, or can easily be, an **integer** or **character** value. An **if** construct is the more appropriate if there is an overlap between the criteria (and hence the order in which the test are made may matter), or if the decision must be made using **real** or **logical** values.

Self-test exercises 6.1 (page 145)

1   A **do** loop is a means of specifying that a sequence of statements (between the **do** statement and the corresponding **end do** statement) is to be repeated a number of times.

2   There are no restrictions on the statements that may appear within a do loop, although any **if**, **case** or **do** constructs must be completely enclosed within the loop.

3   The **do** variable is the **integer** variable specified in a count-controlled **do** statement which is incremented at the end of each pass through the loop. It is not permitted to alter the value of the **do** variable during the execution of the loop.

4   The iteration count is the count of the number of times a count-controlled **do** loop is to be obeyed. It is calculated before the start of execution of the loop as the maximum of (*final* − *initial* + *inc*)/*inc* and zero.

5 (a) 11 times
   (b) 6 times
   (c) 3 times
   (d) 0 times (that is, the loop will not be obeyed at all)
   (e) 17 times
   (f) once

6 What it would have been on the *next* pass through the loop, if there had been one.

7 (a) 10 8 2 8 0 0

Since l is greater than m, and k is positive, the second loop is never obeyed, although its **do** variable, j, is set to the value it would have had on the first pass, had there been one. The two innermost loops are never obeyed either, and their **do** variables are unaltered. The outermost loop has an iteration count of one, and its **do** variable, i, is set to the value it would have had on the second pass, had there been one.

(b) 10 -2 9 9 64 0

The only difference between this program and the previous one is that k is set to $-i$ at the start of the outermost loop, thus causing the second loop to count down from 8 to 0 in steps of -2. On the first pass through this loop the third loop is obeyed once, but on subsequent passes it is not obeyed at all as n is less than l.

Self-test exercises 6.2 (page 156)

1 A count-controlled **do** loop contains the information necessary to determine how many times the loop is to be repeated as part of the **do** statement; other forms of **do** loop decide when to stop repeating the loop on the basis of a condition that occurs during the execution of the loop.

A count-controlled loop is most appropriate if the nature of the problem requires that the loop be repeated a predefined number of times, regardless of the results of the loop repetition. A count-controlled loop is also appropriate in situations where some other means is expected to determine the exit condition, in order to provide a *fail-safe* mechanism in case the exit condition never occurs.

2 An infinite loop is one which never reaches an exit condition. It can be avoided by always using a count-controlled loop to place an upper limit on the number of times a loop is executed.

3 An **exit** statement is used to provide a means of terminating the execution of a loop when some condition occurs; it causes an immediate branch to the statement immediately after the **end do** statement of the innermost loop currently being executed.

4 A **cycle** statement is used to end the processing of the statements in a loop *for this iteration*; it causes an immediate branch to the start of the loop in an identical fashion to that which occurs when the **end do** statement is executed, including the incrementing of the **do** variable, if any. In a count-controlled **do** loop, therefore, the execution of a **cycle** statement on the last pass through the loop has the effect of terminating the execution of the loop.

5 A **do** construct is named so that an **exit** or **cycle** statement in a nested block **do** can exit from more than the innermost loop, or cycle to the start of other than the innermost loop; this is achieved by following the **exit** or **cycle** statement by the name of the loop it is required to **exit** from or **cycle** back to. The name, which follows the normal rules for F names, must precede the **do** statement, separated from the **do** by a colon, *and* follow the corresponding **end do** statement.

6 A **return** statement provides a means of returning from a procedure to the calling program unit in the same way as occurs when execution of the procedure reaches the **end** statement. It is useful in an exceptional situation where there is no requirement to execute the remainder of the procedure, for example if an error has occurred.

7 A **stop** statement terminates processing of the program in the same way as occurs when execution reaches the **end** statement of the main program unit. It is normally only used after a catastrophic error has meant that no further processing is meaningful.

Self-test exercises 7.1 (page 176)

1 An array is equivalent to an ordered set of variables having the same name and type. An array element is one of the individual variables that forms part of the array.

2 An array variable occupies several memory locations, each of which can be independently accessed and contains a separate value. A scalar variable occupies a single memory location and contains a single value.

3 A dimension attribute consists of the word **dimension** followed by the lower and upper bounds for the array subscript(s), separated by a colon, enclosed in parentheses, or simply by the upper bound, in which case the lower bound is one. It appears as an attribute in a declaration statement:

```
real, dimension(10:50) :: arr1,arr3
integer, dimension(25) :: arr2
```

4 A subscript expression must be a scalar integer expression.

5
- The rank of an array is the number of permissible subscripts for the array; each subscript refers to one of the dimensions of the array.
- The extent of a dimension of an array is the number of elements in that dimension.
- The size of an array is the total number of elements in the array.
- The shape of an array consists of the rank of the array and its extent in each dimension; it can be represented by a rank-one array in which the value of each element is the extent of the array in the corresponding dimension.

6 (a)
```
integer, parameter :: max_gamblers=100
real, dimension(max_gamblers) ::      &
                wages,av_loss,max_win,max_loss
integer, dimension(max_gamblers) ::  &
                gambles_per_week,num_weeks_addict
```

(b)
```
integer, parameter :: max_tests=20
real, dimension(max_tests) :: mass,height
integer, dimension(max_tests) :: num_blows
```

```
(c)  integer, parameter :: max_points=50
     real, dimension(max_points) :: x,y,z
```

```
(d)  real, dimension(366) :: temp_6am,temp_noon,  &
                             temp_6pm,temp_midnight
     integer, dimension(-11:31) :: noon_temp
```

The first four arrays have subscripts from 1 to 366, to allow for an entry for every day of the year, including a leap year. The last array uses subscripts from −10 to 30 to accumulate the count of days on which the noon temperature is equal to the subscript value, with `noon_temp(-11)` being used for temperatures less than −10° and `noon_temp(31)` being used for temperatures over 30°.

7   An array constructor is an array-valued constant. It consists of a list of values contained between (/ and /) delimiters.

8   An implied **do** is a means of using the count control part of the **do** loop syntax to control stepping through a list of values. It is used in an array constructor to avoid the need for repeated values or repeated sequences of values.

9   The occurrence of a scalar variable in an input or output list causes the input or output of a single value. The occurrence of an array variable in an input or output list, on the other hand, causes the input or output of the same number of values as the size of the array.

10   Two arrays are conformable if they have the same shape.

11   Whole-array operations are possible between two conformable objects; that is, all intrinsic operations are defined between conformable objects. Note that a scalar is conformable with any array, and is treated as an array of the same shape, every element of which has the value of the scalar.

12   Arrays can be used in expressions in the same way as scalars, as long as all the objects in the expression are conformable.

13   An elemental procedure is a procedure whose arguments may be scalar or array-valued, and will return a scalar result if the actual arguments are scalar and an array-valued result if they are arrays. In the latter case each element of the result is obtained by applying the procedure to the corresponding element(s) of the input argument(s).

14   An array section can be specified by a subscript triplet or a vector subscript. Array sections are themselves arrays. A subscript triplet consists of three scalar integer expressions separated by colons. If a value is omitted it takes a default value. For example, if a is a rank-one array of size 10,

```
a(2:8:3) consists of a(2), a(5), a(8)
a(4::2) consists of a(4), a(6), a(8), a(10)
a(1::2) consists of all the odd elements of a
a(::) consists of all the elements of a
```

A vector subscript is defined by an integer array. It is of the form a(v), where a is a rank-one array and v is a rank-one **integer** array. For example, if a and v are defined as

```
real, dimension(10) :: a
integer, dimension(3), parameter :: v = (/ 4, 2, 9 /)
```

then

   a(v) consists of a(4), a(2), a(9), in that order

If v were initialized by the value (/ 2, 3, 2 /), then

   a(v) consists of a(2), a(3), a(2), in that order.

15   Array sections are similar to arrays in that array sections are (nameless) arrays and, with certain exceptions, can be used in expressions, in input/output lists, or as actual arguments, in the same manner as arrays.
   Array sections differ from arrays in that individual elements cannot be specified: for example, by notation of the form a(1::3)(3). Secondly, an array section with a vector subscript may not be an actual argument if the corresponding dummy argument is not specified as **intent(in)**, nor may it be pointed to. Finally, if an array section is defined by a many−one vector subscript, it may not appear on the left-hand side of an assignment statement or in the input list of a **read** statement.

Self-test exercises 7.2 (page 188)

1   An assumed-shape array is a dummy argument whose rank is specified but whose shape is not known but is assumed from the corresponding actual argument. An assumed-shape array is used in a procedure which is designed to accept actual array arguments of different sizes.

2   An assumed-shape array can be a procedure dummy argument. This permits actual arguments be as large or as small as required each time the procedure is executed.
   The disadvantage of an assumed-shape array is that only the shape of an actual argument is available in the called procedure.

3   Use the intrinsic function **size**.

4   An automatic array is an explicit-shape array, which is not a dummy argument, whose bounds are defined in terms of variables which are either dummy arguments, or whose values are available on entry to the procedure by host association.

5   An explicit-shape array may have non-constant bounds if

- the array is a dummy argument
- the array is an automatic array
- the array is a function result.

6   The type of an array-valued function is declared in a type declaration statement in the body of the function. The result of an array-valued function cannot be an assumed-size array.

Self-test exercises 8.1 (page 216)

1   A recursive procedure may invoke itself, both directly and indirectly. A non-recursive procedure may not invoke itself, either directly or indirectly.

   A recursive procedure's initial statement has the word **recursive** before **function** or **subroutine**, as appropriate. The absence of the **recursive** qualifier means that the procedure is non-recursive.

2   A dummy procedure is declared by means of an interface block which specifies the name of the procedure, the names, types and attributes of all its dummy variables, and, in the case of a function, the name, type and attributes of the result variable.

   Dummy procedures in functions must be functions. All dummy procedures must be module procedures, and must, therefore, be written in F.

3   A derived type is a user-defined data type. It consists of one or more components each of which is either of an intrinsic type or of another derived type. A derived type is, therefore, ultimately derived from entities of intrinsic types.

4   Derived types allow data types to be created which reflect the nature of the problem being solved and the data that it uses.

5   (a) ```
type,public :: UK_address
    character(len=50) :: house_name
    integer :: number
    character(len=30) :: street,village,town,county
    character(len=10) :: post_code
end type UK_address
```

   (b)  ```
type,public :: US_address
    integer :: number
    character(len=30) :: street,city
    character(len=2) :: state
    integer :: zip_code
end type US_address
```

6   (a) ```
type(UK_address) :: my_UK_home
my_UK_home =   &
    UK_address("The Old Manor House",   &
               3,"High Street",   &
               "Little Uffington",   &
               "Wokingham",   &
               "Berks.","RG26 9QZ")
```

   (b)  ```
type(US_address) :: my_US_home
my_US_home =                                   &
    US_address(19725,"Main Street"             &
              "Chicago"                        &
              "IL",60689)
```

7   ```
type,public :: person
    character(len=20) :: first_name,last_name
    type(US_address) :: address
end type person
type(person) :: individual
```
```

```
print *,"Please type name and address in the order"
print *,"first name, last name, number and street,"
print *,"city, state (2 letters), zip code"
read *,individual
```

Note that it would also be possible to read the data by specifying each component, as shown below, but this is not necessary:

```
read *,individual%first_name,individual%last_name,  &
        individual%address%number,                  &
        individual%address%street,                  &
        individual%address%city,                    &
        individual%address%state,                   &
        individual%address%zip_code
```

8   An array-valued component of a derived type must be an explicit-shape array with constant bounds. (It may also be a deferred-shape array, as we shall see in Chapter 13.)

Self-test exercises 8.2 (page 224)

1   Making the components of a derived type **private** means that only the type, and not its internal structure, is accessible elsewhere in the program.

2   If the components of a derived type in a module are made **private**, then only the type itself is available outside the module; inside the module, however, the components are available in the normal way. This means that the author of the module can ensure that the components of the derived type can only be accessed in an approved fashion, for example through procedures which are also defined in the module, thus avoiding the danger of a program inadvertently corrupting the inner form of variables of that type.

3   The private components of a derived type entity can be accessed from within the module in the normal way, as if the components were not specified as being **private**. In other words, the privacy only applies *outside* the module in which the derived type definition appears.

4   Making the components of a derived type **private** means that a program unit which has access to the module in which the derived type definition appears has access to the type, and can declare and use variables of that type, but cannot access the components directly. Making the definition of the derived type **private** means that it is not accessible at all outside the module, and is only, therefore, for use by procedures which are part of that module.

5   Data hiding is the principle of only allowing access to a restricted set of entities within a module, namely those which any program units using the module need to know about. It allows the writer of a module to improve the security of programs by controlling the way in which programs, for example, access the data, or parts of the data, on which their program is operating.

6   Only those entities that are required by a user of the module should be given explicit **public** accessibility. All other entities should be declared to be **private**. Derived type definitions should normally be defined with private components, and public procedures should be provided to access or manipulate these components as required.

7   The **only** qualifier in a **use** statement causes only those entities listed after the **only** qualifier to be accessible by **use** association.

8   The declaration of an entity in a procedure, or the availability of an entity in a procedure through **use** association, causes any entity of the same name in the first part of the host module to be innaccessible via host association.

9   If a local name is the same as a name made available through **use** association an error will result (unlike the situation with host association). The module entity can be renamed in the **use** statement to avoid this problem.

Self-test exercises 9.1 (page 248)

1   A value separator is a character which is used to determine the end of one input item (and the start of the next).

2   Value separators during list-directed input are a comma, a slash, a blank or the end of record, ignoring any blanks before or after the value separator.

3   A character string which
   ● is contained within a single line
   ● does not contain any value separators
   ● does not have a quotation mark or an apostrophe as its first character, and
   ● does not begin with a number followed by an asterisk

may be input without delimiting quotation marks.

4   An embedded format is a list of edit descriptors, enclosed in parentheses, and further enclosed in quotation marks, which is included as part of an input or output statement.

5   An edit descriptor is a specification of how a sequence of characters on the external medium is to be converted to a value in the computer system, or vice versa.

6   `6789 minus 4567 is 2222; 234.50 minus 12.34 is 222.160`

7   `◊◊◊◊◊◊◊345678◊◊◊◊◊123400◊◊◊123456`
        `◊◊◊◊◊345678◊◊◊◊◊◊◊1234◊◊◊◊◊123456`

where ◊ represents a space.

Self-test exercises 9.2 (page 258)

1   A **print** statement always sends its output to the default output unit (normally the computer's display screen or printer). A **write** statement sends its output to the unit specified in the statement.

2   To obtain information about the success, or otherwise, of the input/output operation.

3   A format is repeated when all the edit descriptors have been used and there are still items in the input or output list which have not been processed.

4   The formats will be repeated from the place identified by an arrow below:

(a) `(3i8,2f8.2)`
          ↑

(b) `(3i8,2(tr3,f5.2))`
                ↑

(c) `(3(tr3,i5),2f8.2)`
          ↑

(d) `(3(tr3,i5),2(tr3,f5.2))`
                        ↑

(e) `(3i8/2f8.2)`
          ↑

(f) `(3i8/2(tr3,f5.2))`
                  ↑

5   **(a)** **read** `"(3f4.2,tr4)"`,height,width,depth

The data is assumed to be provided in the order shown; the three variables height, width and depth must be declared as **real** variables.

(b) **print** `"(4(f4.2,a))"`,height," * ",width," * ",   &
            depth," (= ",height*width*depth," cubic metres)"

(c) **read** `"(3(i2,tr1,i2,tr5)"`,h_ft,h_ins,w_ft,w_ins,   &
            d_ft,d_ins

Note that the third use of the tr5 edit descriptor will appear to move beyond the end of the data, but since there is no more data to be read it will not be used in any case.

(d) **print** `"(4(i2,a,i2,a))"`,h_ft,"'",h_ins,""" * ",w_ft,   &
            "'",w_ins,""" * ",h_ft,"'",h_ins,""" (= ",   &
            v_ft3,"'",v_ins3,""" (cubed)"

Note the use of double quotation marks to represent a single quotation mark (representing inches). The volume of the box is assumed to have been calculated elsewhere and the result, in cubic feet and cubic inches, stored in v_ft3 and v_ins3.

Self-test exercises 10.1 (page 286)

1   A formatted record is produced by a formatted output statement, or by some external means, and consists of a sequence of characters. An unformatted record is produced by an unformatted output statement, that is, one with no format specifier, and consists of a sequence of values.

Formatted records should be used if the file is to be transferred to another type of computer, or if it is required to list the file subsequently. Unformatted records should be used if the information written to the file is to be subsequently read by the same program, or by another F program which has been compiled by the same F compiler on the same type of computer.

2   A formatted **read** or **write** statement must include a format specifier, and each statement may process several records, as defined by the format. An unformatted **read** or **write** statement must not include a format specifier, and always processes exactly one record.

3   An endfile record is a special record, of no defined length, which is written by an **endfile** statement. If a **read** statement reads an endfile record it will result in an execution error unless it is detected by means of an **iostat** specifier, and appropriate action taken.

4   A file must be connected to a program so that the program knows on which logical unit the input or output is to take place. The connection is carried out by an **open** statement.

5   (a) **open** (unit=7,**file**="Payroll_Data",status= "old",   &
                  action="read",iostat=open_status)

Note that the file will be formatted by default, so it is not necessary to specify this.

(b) **open** (unit=11,**file**="Intermediate_results_1",   &
            status="old",action="read",   &
            iostat=open_status)

The question does not state whether the file is unformatted, but if produced by another program it will usually be formatted.

(c) **open** (unit=8,**file**="Intermediate_results_2",   &
            status="new",action="write",iostat=open_status)

Since this file is being created for use elsewhere we shall assume that it does not already exist, and that a formatted file is appropriate.

(d) **open** (unit=10,**file**="Results",status="old",   &
            action="readwrite",position="append",   &
            iostat=open_status)

(e) **open** (unit=9,status="scratch",form="unformatted",   &
            action="readwrite",iostat=open_status)

(f) **open** (unit=10,**file**=file_name,action="write",   &
            status="new",iostat=open_status)

As the name of the file is not specified it has been included as a variable, which can either be given a value in the program or input from the keyboard. We shall assume that this file does not already exist.

Self-test exercises 11.1 (page 312)

1   For floating-point numbers, overflow occurs when an attempt is made to create a number whose exponent is larger than possible for the computer being used. This is always fatal. Similarly, underflow occurs when an attempt is made to create a number with an exponent that is too small. On some computers, the result will be zero. On others, it will be fatal.

For integers, overflow occurs if an attempt is made to calculate a number that is larger than possible for the computer being used. Similarly, underflow occurs when an attempt is made to calculate a number that is too small. In either case, the attempt is fatal.

2   **(a)** `(a+b)*(a-b)` is preferable because a^2 and b^2 are more likely to overflow or underflow than a-b or a+b.

      (b) `(a-b)/c` is preferable because it involves one less division and hence is likely to be more accurate in the case when a and b are almost equal.

      (c) This is really the same as (b), since either a or b could be positive or negative. Therefore the form `(a+b)/c` is preferable.

      (d) `a+b+c+d+e` is preferable because adding numbers in increasing order of magnitude minimizes round-off errors.

      (e) `a/b-c/d` is generally preferable because it involves no multiplications and is consequently less prone to round-off errors. There is also the possibility that a*d, b*c, or b*d might overflow or underflow.

3   **real** variables are parameterized by specifying a kind type parameter in their declaration:

     real(kind=n**),** ... :: *list of variable names*

4   Default **real** is the kind of **real** used if no kind type is specified in a **real** declaration statement.

5   The intrinsic procedure **selected_real_kind** may be used to determine the correct kind type parameter for a particular precision and/or exponent range, to improve portability. Thus the statement

     real(kind=selected_real_kind(p=6,r=30))**::** x

defines x to be a floating-point variable with at least six decimal digits of precision and a decimal exponent range of at least 30.

     If a program is to be executed on a variety of machines it is generally preferable to specify explicitly a **kind** having the precision and/or exponent range required to avoid numeric portability problems; this is particularly true when more than normal precision is required.

6   Program `test_11b` will generally give more accurate results. Program `test_11a` is requesting that the variables x, y and z have at least three decimal digits of precision. The compiler will therefore select single-precision computer memory locations to store them and will correspondingly use single-precision registers to perform arithmetic operations on them. Program `test_11b` is requesting at least 12 decimal digits of accuracy. Most computers must use more than one word in memory to store the variables x, y and z and will use double-precision hardware registers to perform arithmetic operations.

     Note that, on a computer where the accuracy given by a single word or register is at least 12 significant decimal digits, there would be no accuracy differences in the answers obtained (since minimum precision requirements are being specified).

7   The accuracy of a calculation is determined by the conditioning of the problem (that is, how sensitive the answer is to small changes in the input) and by the stability of the algorithm employed (that is, whether it gives a mathematically correct answer to a problem that differs only slightly from that specified). If either condition is not satisfied the answer must be regarded with suspicion.

8 The stability of an algorithm is affected by round-off effects (caused by the use of finite-precision floating-point arithmetic) and by truncation errors (the terminating of a process before it is mathematically correct). Since many mathematical processes imply an infinite number of operations, some level of truncation error is often unavoidable.

9 A well-conditioned problem is one in which the answer changes only slightly when the problem changes slightly. An ill-conditioned problem is one in which a small change in the problem causes a large change in the answer. If you have an ill-conditioned problem it is worthwhile seeing if it can be reformulated to be well conditioned.

10 A well-conditioned (or stable) numerical process is one that gives the mathematically correct answer to a problem that is only slightly different from the one specified. An ill-conditioned (or unstable) process is one in which the answer given is the mathematically correct answer to a problem that is substantially different from the one specified. If you have created such a process it is worthwhile redesigning and reprogramming it to be stable. Round-off error, which introduces errors at each stage of a numerical calculation, is the prime cause of unstable algorithms. Stable algorithms are designed so that these errors do not grow substantially as a calculation proceeds.

Self-test exercises 11.2 (page 329)

1 • The magnitude of some quantity related to the process becomes less than some specified value. For example, the value of a function whose root you are trying to find becomes, in absolute value, acceptably small.
   • The magnitude of the difference between two successive approximations becomes less than some specified tolerance. When this occurs we conclude that, since the process isn't changing much between iterations, we have probably converged to an answer. Sometimes, this is not true.
   • The magnitude of the difference between the calculated answer and the mathematically correct answer is acceptably small. It is rare to be able to use this criterion since we usually cannot mathematically bound the answer.

2 The residual, at a point, is the difference between the calculated value (determined from the least squares fit) and the specified value at that point. The residual sum is the square root of the sum (taken over all the data points) of the squares of the residuals.

3 The residual sum provides a measure of how good the fit is to the whole data set. The smaller the residual sum the better the overall fit. Since it involves the squares of the residuals, it is unaffected by whether the fit passes above or below the data points.

4 The bisection method requires that it is provided initially with two points at which the function takes opposite signs. If this cannot be done then the process cannot start. Notice that this is a stronger requirement than just knowing an interval that contains a root.
   A second, possibly harmless, problem is that an interval containing the function sign change may have more than one function root. The interval bisection method will only find one of the roots. It will not even indicate that other roots are present.

Self-test exercises 12.1 (page 354)

1   A **complex** variable or constant is stored as two consecutive **real** numbers, with the real part coming first.

2   All the intrinsic data types in F, other than **character**, may be parameterized. In other words, they have associated with them subsidiary information that further specifies the data type. These parameters are called kind type parameters. In the case of integers, for example, the kind type parameter specifies the range of integers that a variable of that type of integer can store.

   Kind type parameters are important, in the case of numeric variables, because they permit the portable specification of precision and range requirements. In the case of **logical** variables they are less important because their effect is processor dependent, and involves the amount of storage used to store logical values.

3   In a similar manner to **real** variables, a **complex** variable may have its kind type explicitly declared, or may be allowed to default. The kind type parameters for the two **real** components of a **complex** variable are the same as the kind type parameter of the **complex** variable.

4   Explicit kind type parameters for variables are specified by adding kind type specifiers to the type declaration statements. For example:

```
real(kind=selected_real_kind(p=6)) :: x
integer(kind=k3), dimension(9) :: arr
```

5   Explicit kind type parameters for numeric and logical constants are specified by appending an underscore and the value of the kind type parameter to the constant; for example:

```
12.34_short_real_kind
5678_long_int_kind
```

6   For **integer** variables the intrinsic function **selected_int_kind**(r) returns the kind type value, for the current computer, of a kind type that can represent all integers in the range $(-10^r, 10^r)$.

   For **real** variables the intrinsic function **selected_real_kind**(p,r) returns the kind type value, for the current computer, of a real data type that can represent numbers in the ranges $(10^{-r}, 10^r)$ and $(-10^r, -10^{-r})$, with at least p decimal digits of accuracy. Both arguments are optional, although at least one must always be present.

   Kind type values are machine dependent. Therefore, the above functions should be used to specify minimal accuracy and range requirements in a portable manner. Both arguments are optional, although at least one must always be present.

   Since **complex** values are defined by an ordered pair of **real** values, the precision and range of the real and imaginary parts of a **complex** variable can also be specified by use of the intrinsic function **selected_real_kind**. For example, the declaration:

```
complex(kind=selected_real_kind(p=12,r=30)), dimension(5) :: z
```

declares z to be an array of five **complex** numbers whose real and imaginary parts each have a precision of at least twelve significant digits and a decimal exponent range of at least 30.

7   If an impossible **integer** range or **real** precision is requested the functions **selected_int_kind** and **selected_real_kind** will return negative integer results. This will cause a compilation error if they are used to set the **kind** value for an **integer** or **real** variable or constant.

8   The F rules state that a compiler must at least meet the specifications (if it can). A compiler is free, therefore, to satisfy precision and range requirements by exceeding them.

The underlying reality of the hardware for most computers is that only two precisions and exponent ranges are provided, and all precision and range requests are mapped onto those two choices in the best manner possible.

Self-test exercises 13.1 (page 378)

1   The index bounds of an array are, for each dimension, the lower and upper bounds the index for that dimension is permitted to take in specifying an array element. They are integers and may be positive, negative or zero. The extent of an array along a dimension is the number of possible index values along that dimension. The size of an array is the number of elements it contains. The size is, therefore, the product of the extents.

2   The shape of an array is the rank (the number of dimensions) and the extents (size) along each dimension. Since, for an n-dimensional array, the shape is specified by n positive (possibly zero) numbers, the shape may be represented by a rank-one array of size n whose elements are the extents for each dimension.

3   The array element order is:

```
wow(1,1,1), wow(2,1,1), wow(1,2,1), wow(2,2,1), wow(1,3,1),
wow(2,3,1), wow(1,1,2), wow(2,1,2), wow(1,2,2), wow(2,2,2),
wow(1,3,2), wow(2,3,2), wow(1,1,3), wow(2,1,3), wow(1,2,3),
wow(2,2,3), wow(1,3,3), wow(2,3,3), wow(1,1,4), wow(2,1,4),
wow(1,2,4), wow(2,2,4), wow(1,3,4), wow(2,3,4)
```

4   The **reshape** function takes a rank-one array as input and constructs from it an array of any shape, taking the elements of the rank-one array in array element order.

5   An explicit-shape array is one in which the extents for each dimension of the array are explicitly given. The extents may be scalar integer expressions as well as constants, except in a main program, where they must be constant.

6   An assumed-shape array is a dummy argument array that takes its shape from the actual argument array. Its extents are specified using colons.

Assumed-shape arrays can only be dummy arguments. They cannot, for example, occur in a main program or be a function result.

7   The intrinsic functions **lbound** and **ubound** return the lower index bounds of an array and the upper index bounds of an array, respectively.

8   Automatic arrays can only occur in procedures. They are arrays that are not dummy arguments but whose index bounds depend on the procedure's dummy arguments or variables accessed by host association. Automatic arrays are useful when a procedure needs some temporary work space whose size depends on the input arguments.

Self-test exercises 13.2 (page 402)

```
1        integer, allocatable(:,:) :: a, b

2        integer :: error
         allocate(a(3,4), b(m,n), stat=error)
         if (error /= 0) then
            ! Error processing
            .
            .
            .
         end if
         ! Arrays were successfully allocated
         .
         .
         .
```

3   After the array has been successfully allocated it, or its elements, may be used in the normal manner. Before it is allocated, however, the array may still be used as an argument to the intrinsic function **allocated** (which returns the allocation status of an allocatable array).

4   The allocation status of an array defines whether or not it has been allocated. There are three possible states:

- Not currently allocated. All allocatable arrays have this status at the beginning of an executable program. An allocatable array also has this status after the successful execution of a **deallocate** statement.
- Currently allocated. This is the status of an allocatable array after the successful execution of an **allocate** statement.
- Undefined. An allocatable array (without the **save** attribute) has this status if it is not deallocated prior to exit from a procedure. This is bad programming practice because such an array cannot be subsequently employed in any useful way.

5   By executing a **deallocate** statement before executing a **return** or **end** statement in the procedure in which the allocatable array was defined. If such an array is defined in a module, it cannot become undefined.

6   The allocation status of an allocatable array (that doesn't have the undefined status) is determined by use of the intrinsic function **allocated**. This function returns *true* if its argument is allocated and *false* if it is not.

7   An automatic array has index bounds that are functions of the dummy arguments (or variables available by host association). This is not so for an allocatable array. The space for an automatic array is created when a procedure is entered and removed upon exit from the procedure. By contrast, the space for an allocatable array is allocatable and deallocatable anywhere in a procedure or main program. An allocatable array may have the **save** attribute, while an automatic array may not.

8   Operators in a whole-array expression are applied element-wise to each element position in the arrays comprising the expression.

9   All intrinsic functions that are elemental may be used in a whole-array expression. They are applied element-wise to each element position of their array arguments.

10   Whole-array expressions greatly simplify code and therefore make it considerably more readable and maintainable.

11   A masked array assignment permits detailed control over the assignment of one array to another by using a logical mask to control how the assignment is to proceed, on an element-wise basis. For example:

```
real, dimension(m,n) :: x
where (x < 0.0) x = 2.0*x
```

has the effect of replacing every negative element in x by twice its value and leaving the positive elements unaltered.

12   An array section is extracted from an array by a specified pattern. An array section is itself an array. Array sections may be used in a similar manner to any other array.

13 ●   A subscript triplet specifies an array section according to a rectangular pattern. For example, in the following extract the last line specifies an array section that is a rank-one array consisting of the elements x(3,2,1), x(5,2,1) and x(7,2,1):

```
integer, dimension(9,4,10) :: x
        .
        .
        .
x(3:7:2,2,1) = ...
```

  ●   A vector subscript, on the other hand, can be used to define an array section extracted in an irregular manner from its parent array. For example, in the following extract the array hold will contain the values of x(3,4,1), x(2,4,1), x(3,4,1) and x(1,4,1):

```
integer, dimension(5,4,10) :: x
integer, dimension(4) :: extract = (/3,2,3,1/)
integer, dimension(4) :: hold
        .
        .
        .
hold = x(extract,4,1)
```

From the above discussion it is clear that a subscript triplet should be used whenever the extraction pattern can be expressed in a rectangular pattern, whereas a vector subscript should be used when the extraction pattern is irregular.

14   The rank of an array section is the number of subscript triplets and vector subscripts it contains.

Self-test exercises 14.1 (page 431)

1   A **pointer** is a variable that, instead of containing data itself, points to another variable where the data is stored.
    A variable can only be pointed at if it has the **target** attribute. This is to permit the compiler to generate efficient code.

2   A **pointer** can only be made to point to objects of the type specified in its type declaration statement that have the **target** attribute.

3 • Undefined: This is the status when a **pointer** is initially specified in a type
declaration statement.

  • Associated: This is the status when a **pointer** is associated with a specific
target.

  • Disassociated: This is the status when a **pointer** has been associated with a
target and the association has subsequently been broken (by a **nullify**
statement).

4   A **pointer** assignment statement associates a **pointer** with a **target**. There are
two forms:

  • Where the object on the right-hand side of the assignment statement is a
variable with the **target** attribute:

```
real, pointer :: p
real, target :: a
p => a
```

    This associates the **pointer** p with the **target** a.

  • Where the object on the right-hand side of the assignment statement is a
pointer, pointing to variables of the same type and attributes:

```
real, pointer :: p,q
real, target :: a,b
p => a
q => p
```

    The second **pointer** assignment statement makes q point to a (not to p, because
pointers cannot be pointed at).

5   The **pointer** association status of a **pointer** variable can be set to disassociated
by use of the **nullify** statement. For example, using the pointers of the preceding
question, the statement

```
nullify (p,q)
```

breaks the association of p with a and q with a.

6   The **pointer** association status of a **pointer** variable is determined by use of the
intrinsic function **associated** which returns *true* if the **pointer** supplied as its actual
argument is associated with a target, and *false* if it is not. Note that the actual argument
pointer association status must not be undefined.

7   When a **pointer** occurs in an expression where a value is expected, the value of
the **target** the **pointer** is associated with is used. This is called dereferencing. For
example, if the variables p and a are defined as:

```
integer, pointer :: p
integer, target :: a = 1
p => a
```

then the following assignment statements all have the same effect:

```
a = a + 1
a = p + 1
p = a + 1
p = p + 1
```

Note that in the last two examples p is unaltered.

8   It is not possible to read or write a **pointer**. Consequently, a variable of a derived type that contains a **pointer** cannot occur in an input or output statement. Otherwise, a **pointer** in an input or output statement is dereferenced to its associated **target**.

9   The **pointer** p in the following example can point to any rank-three array of integers:

```
integer, dimension(:,:,:), pointer :: p
integer, dimension(4,3,2), target :: a
p => a
```

The **pointer** assignment statement associates p with the rank-three integer array a.

10   The space for the elements of an array **pointer** can be allocated and deallocated dynamically by means of the **allocate** and **deallocate** statements.

Self-test exercises 14.2 (page 449)

1   If a procedure has a **pointer** or **target** dummy arguments, then:

- An actual argument corresponding to a **pointer** dummy argument must be a **pointer** with the same type, type parameters and rank.
- A **pointer** dummy argument cannot have the **intent** attribute.

2   To permit a function to return a **pointer** as its result the **result** variable must be defined to be a **pointer**:

```
function ours(a) result(p)
   integer, intent(in) :: a
   real, dimension(:), pointer :: p
      .
      .
      .
   p => ...
end function ours
```

3   A **pointer** can be a component of a derived type in the same way as any other type of entity:

```
type, public :: other
   integer :: i
   integer, dimension(:), pointer :: point
   type(other), pointer :: node
end type other
```

This derived type contains two pointers – one to a rank-one array of integers and the other to an object of the same derived type.

Pointer components in derived types are useful for creating linked lists, trees, and so on. They are also useful when a component array of variable size is required.

Any derived type that contains (or ultimately contains) a **pointer** cannot be used in an input or output statement.

4   A linked list, in its simplest form, is a data structure in which each element of the structure consists of data and a pointer to the next element of the list.

5   The advantages of linked lists over arrays are:

- A linked list is superior for data structures in which the elements are added to the list in random order. It is easy to add an element to its position in the list by adjusting pointers – the element itself does not have to be moved (a considerable time saving if the element is large). It is also possible for elements to be shared between different linked lists without duplicating the element.
- The size of a linked list does not have to be predefined – elements can be added freely at any time during execution. Thus, space can be used efficiently.
- The elements of a linked list can be freely deleted during execution of a program, thus easily releasing space during program execution for use by other parts of the program.

6   A tree structure is a set of connected data elements (called nodes) in which each node of the list has at most one parent (node pointing to it) and only one node (the root) has no parent.

A more formal definition is that a tree is a finite set of nodes with a distinguished node, called the root, and where the non-root nodes are themselves disjoint (that is, having no elements in common) trees. The non-root nodes are called subtrees.

A binary tree is one in which each node has a maximum of two subtrees (or branches).

7   A list is preferable to a tree when each node has only one predecessor and one successor. For example, the children of one set of parents may be kept as a list in order of their ages.

A tree is preferable to a list when each node can have more than one successor node associated with it. For example, a family tree (note the common terminology) showing the parental structure is best kept as a tree structure.

8   Recursion is useful in dealing with lists and trees because formal definitions of lists and trees are best done recursively. Using recursion to write programs involving lists and trees usually results in simpler programs because the structure of the algorithms now matches naturally the structure of the data.

Self-test exercises 15.1 (page 464)

1   For very large or very small numbers the exponent form used by the es edit descriptor will almost always give a meaningful result, whereas an f edit descriptor may give an error result (for example, a row of asterisks) if the number is too large for the field width specified, or zero if the number of decimal places specified is too small.

2	1	0001	1.0000	1.0000E+00	1.0000E+0000
	2	0002	0.5000	5.0000E-01	5.0000E-0001
	4	0004	0.2500	2.5000E-01	2.5000E-0001
	8	0008	0.1250	1.2500E-01	1.2500E-0001
	16	0016	0.0625	6.2500E 02	6.2500E-0002
	32	0032	0.0313	3.1250E-02	3.1250E-0002
	64	0064	0.0156	1.5625E 02	1.5625E-0002

3   An advancing input statement (the default) always starts reading from the beginning of a new record. A non-advancing input statement will start reading the same record as was read by the last read statement, beginning immediately after the last character read, unless the previous **read** statement attempted to read beyond the end of the record, or the previous **read** statement gave rise to an error or end-of-file condition, or the file position has been changed, in which case it will start at the beginning of the next record.

Non-advancing input should be used if it is necessary to read part of an input record before reading the rest of it – for example, if its contents cannot be determined until the first item, or items, have been read. Otherwise, advancing input should normally be used.

4   An advancing output statement (the default) will always start writing a new record. A non-advancing output statement will write to the same record as the last output statement, beginning immediately after the last character written, unless the previous **write** gave rise to an error, in which case the writing will start at the beginning of a new record.

Non-advancing output should be used if it is required to output a record in two, or more, stages. Otherwise, advancing output should normally be used.

Self-test exercises 15.2 (page 488)

1   A **recl** specifier for a sequential file specifies the maximum length of a record in the file. A **recl** specifier for a direct access file specifies that all the records in the file will have the specified length. In both cases the length is measured in characters if the file is formatted, and in processor-defined units if it is unformatted.

2   Yes. As long as it is first closed and then reopened for sequential access.

3   No. One of the reasons is that every record in a direct access file must have the same length, whereas there is no guarantee that this is the case for a sequential file.

4   Direct access input and output may not use list-directed formatting, nor may it use non-advancing input or output.

5   A hash table is a table in which data is entered in a random order in such a way that it can be quickly found again. In its simplest form, an appropriate algorithm is used to convert the value to be stored into an integer key which lies in exactly the same range as the permissible subscripts of the table. This key is then used to identify the first place to look, and if this place is full (on entry) or contains the wrong value (on retrieval) then a further algorithm defines where to look next – for example in the next element of the array.

A hash table normal consists of several tables, implemented as a single rank-two array or as several related rank-one arrays, with one containing the identifying data (for example, a name), and the others containing additional data that can be extracted from the table once the correct subscript has been found.

6   one one one one one one one one one one
       one two three four five six seven eight nine ten

The result of the first **write** statement is because each time the **read** statement in the loop is obeyed it starts at the beginning of the internal file line1, even though that file contains 10 records. When the internal file is read by a single **read** statement, however, each element of line2 requires a new record from the internal file, and so all 10 words are correctly read.

7   The following program will provide the length of the record:

```
program record_length_inquiry
  real :: p,q
  real, dimension(7) :: x
  integer, parameter :: k=selected_real_kind(12,30)
  real(kind=k) :: y,z
  integer :: record_length
  inquire (iolength=record_length) p,q,x,y,z
  print *,"The record length is ",record_length
end program record_length_inquiry
```

Self-test exercises 16.1 (page 504)

1   A positional actual argument corresponds with a dummy argument through its position in the list of arguments. A keyword actual argument includes the name of the corresponding dummy argument and may appear anywhere in the list of actual arguments; note, however, that once a keyword argument has appeared, then all subsequent actual arguments must be keyword arguments.

2   When using positional actual arguments, each actual argument corresponds to the dummy argument in the same position in the list of arguments. If any optional arguments are omitted from the list of actual arguments then all subsequent arguments must also be omitted.

When using keyword arguments, each actual argument corresponds to the dummy argument whose name precedes the actual argument, separated from it by an equals sign. Such actual arguments may be in any order.

If both positional and keyword arguments appear in a procedure invocation, then all actual arguments after the first keyword argument must be keyword arguments.

3   An optional dummy argument is declared with the **optional** attribute.

The intrinsic procedure **present** can be used to determine whether an actual argument was supplied to correspond with any specified optional dummy argument.

4   An interface block is used to specify the interface of a procedure, to define a defined or extended operator, and to extend the assignment operator.

Some examples of situations in which an interface block is required are:

- the declaration of a dummy procedure
- the declaration of an external procedure (that is, one not written in F)
- the definition of a defined operator
- the definition of an extended meaning for an intrinsic operator
- the definition of an extended meaning for the assignment operator.

5   A defined operation is a unary or binary operator which either extends the meaning of an intrinsic operator, for use with operands of types for which the intrinsic operator is not defined, or defines a new operator for use with any specified types of operands.

A defined operation is defined by means of an interface block, and a function which defines the actions to be taken.

6 ● It is not permitted to change the meaning of an intrinsic operator, but only to extend it. It must, therefore, be possible to distinguish any new meanings from the intrinsic meanings solely by reference to the types of its operands.

● The number of arguments in the defining function must be consistent with the intrinsic uses of the operator.

7   Defined assignment is an extension of the meaning of the assignment operator when used with derived types. It is defined by means of an interface block, together with a subroutine having exactly two non-optional arguments, the first, `intent(out)`, corresponding to the object on the left of the assignment operator and the second, `intent(in)`, corresponding to the expression on the right of the assignment operator.

Self-test exercises 16.2 (page 516)

1   A generic procedure is a procedure which may accept actual arguments of more than one type, returning a result, or results, of a type appropriate to the arguments supplied.

2   A generic procedure is defined by means of an interface block which specifies two, or more, procedures, one of which will be used for each combination of acceptable types of actual arguments.

The only constraints on generic procedures are that it must be possible to distinguish between the different cases solely by reference to their non-optional dummy arguments.

3 ● All the procedures specified in a generic interface block must be functions, or they must all be subroutines.

● Any two procedures in a generic interface block must be distinguishable by reference to their non-optional dummy arguments, at least one of which must be different, whether considered as positional arguments or as keyword arguments.

4   A generic operator is a defined operator, ar an extended intrinsic operator, which is defined in an interface block by two, or more, functions, each of which is to be used to implement a particular combination of operands.

5   Data abstraction encompasses the ability to define new types, procedures and operators, including generic ones, and to encapsulate them in a module in such a manner that only the highest level of detail is available to the user of the module. This allows a user to concentrate on the problem without having to worry about the underlying detail of these application-oriented extensions to the F language.

Self-test exercises 17.1 (page 580)

1   The bisection method has the advantage that it is guaranteed to converge to a root to within a specified tolerance. It has the disadvantages that it can only be started when an interval with a function sign change is known, and it converges relatively slowly because it only uses information about the sign of the function – not its magnitude.

Newton's method has the advantage that, when it converges, it converges rapidly. It has the disadvantages that it must be started close to a root to guarantee convergence (sometimes even this is insufficient) and that the derivative of the function must be calculated.

The secant method also has the advantages that, when it converges, it converges rapidly (but not as fast as Newton's method) and doesn't require derivatives to be evaluated. It has the same disadvantage as Newton's method, namely that convergence is not always guaranteed.

Consequently, the best root-finding algorithms use a blend of methods to achieve a guaranteed convergence that is faster than interval bisection.

2   Partial pivoting is the name giving to the process in Gaussian elimination in which the current pivot row is exchanged with the row having the largest element in absolute value in the column below the current pivot.

It is important to perform partial pivoting in order to have a stable algorithm.

3   The major difference between a cubic spline curve fit and one using a polynomial is that the cubic spline uses a set of cubic polynomial pieces (one for each data sub-interval), whereas a polynomial fit will involve one high-degree polynomial over the entire range of the data set.

The cubic spline will almost always produce a superior fit because high-degree (and we mean degree greater than 5) polynomials tend to oscillate badly between the points at which they interpolate the given data. A polynomial fit will be slightly faster to evaluate than a cubic spline fit. However, this is almost never a good reason to choose a polynomial fit over a spline fit.

4   Adaptive quadrature is a method of calculating the values of definite integrals. It does it by splitting the entire interval of integration up into sub-intervals using more (and smaller) sub-intervals where the function being integrated is varying most rapidly.

Caution is necessary in accepting the result of any numerical quadrature process because two different functions may have the same values at the points employed by the numerical quadrature process to estimate the numerical value of the definite integral.

Index to programs and procedures

This book contains well over 100 complete programs and procedures, all of which have been fully tested. This index details all of these programs and procedures, as well as many of the modules that have been developed in the book.

The first section of the index lists the main program units, while the second lists complete modules, other than those whose sole purpose is to act as a 'container' for one or more procedures. The last two sections list all the individual functions and subroutines.

Many of these programs, procedures and modules are specific to the problem being solved, and should be considered simply as examples of how to write F programs, but a number of them can be used with little or no modification to solve more general problems. Particular examples of this latter category are those concerned with sorting and with the implementation of various numerical methods – but you should remember that it is always preferable to use procedures from a good numerical library.

Main programs

Cash machine simulation   440–1
Celsius to Fahrenheit conversion   53
Character assignment example   57
Character handling example   59
Circle through three points   20

Date and time example   76
Defines and solves a set of simultaneous linear equations by Gaussian elimination   551–2
Demonstration of the use of multiple roots subroutine   82
Determination of a polygon's convexity   376
Driver program for flexible array handling example   388

Electronic filter design   341–2
Exam statistics   141
Examination statistics   149–51
Example of complex arithmetic   338
Example of list-directed input   51

Find a root of a non-linear equation using the bisection method   326

Main program for chemical stock control system   476
Multiplication tables   143
Multiplication tables (compressed)   145

Radioactive decay   257
Radioactive decay – file-based   275–7

Seasons in Australia   125
Simple complex arithmetic using a derived type   208
Solving a quadratic equation (using a case construct)   129–30
Solving a quadratic equation (using an if construct)   130
Sort and print a set of contacts using an injection sort   448–9
Sort contacts using an injection sort and then print them   430
Sowing a triangular field   75
Sowing a triangular field (improved)   112–13

Test for complex number processing module   220–1
Test for vector processing module   215–16

Test program for cube root function 79
Test program for definite integral module 577–8
Test program for dummy procedure example 199
Test program for line/point geometric module 206
Test program for population survey input procedure 244
Tests cubic spline procedure 565–6

Welcome message 61

Young's modulus for a wire under tension 316–17

Modules

Allocatable work space 386

Definition of a complex number type 208
Demonstration of the use of procedures as arguments 199
Derived type complex number processing 219–20
Determination of the convexity of a polygon 374–6

Geometry of lines and points 205–6

Injection sorting of a linked list contact database 428–9
Input procedure and global variables for electronic filter design program 340–1

Least squares approximation for Young's modulus calculation 316
Linked list derived type definition for cash machine simulation 438

Natural constants (global) 91

Physical constants for use with Young's modulus program 316
Population survey 243–4
Population survey using files 283–6
Processor-dependent input/output error codes 461, 480
Program constants for use with bisection method procedures 324

Rational number arithmetic 514–16

Storage for a linked list for a contact database 428

Type definition and input procedure for survey data analysis 461–3, 48–3
Type definition and procedures for chemical stock control system 472–6
Type definitions and procedures for binary tree to store contact details 447–8
Type definitions and procedures for simple geometric calculations 508–9

Vector processing 214–15

Functions

Calculate the scalar product of two vectors 215
Calculate the size of a vector 214
Calculation of $2e^x - e^{-x}$ 199
Calculation of $\sin 2x - 2\cos x$ 199
Calculation of the line joining two points 206
Calculation of $x^3 - 3x^2 - 4x + 12$ 198
Change case of alphabetic characters 120
Convert a vector to an array 214–15
Create a vector from an array 214
Cube root of a positive real number 77–8
Cube root of a real number 116

Defines first derivative of $y = x + e^x$ 535
Defines $y = x + e^x$ 534
Denominator of a rational number 515
Derived type complex number addition 219
Derived type complex number division 219–20
Derived type complex number multiplication 219
Derived type complex number subtraction 219
Determination of whether two points are effectively distinct 205–6
Determine the direction of rotation at a vertex of a polygon 375–6

Function defining the non-linear equation $y = x + e^x$ 324

Maximum values of two arrays 188

Numerator of a rational number 515

Obtain hash table index of a specified chemical 477–8
Obtain look-up table index of a specified chemical 473

Recursive factorial calculation 195

Sum of a rational number and an integer as a rational number 515
Sum of an integer and a rational number as a rational number 515–16
Sum of an integer and a rational number as a rational number using a defined operator 516
Sum of two arrays 186

Subroutines

Add an item at the end of the list for cash machine simulation 438
Alphabetic injection sort 429
Analyse the contents of a file 388

Back substitution on an upper triangular system of equations 556
Bisection method of recursively solving a non-linear equation 327–8
Bisection method of solving a non-linear equation 324–6

Calculate equation of line joining two points 507
Calculate the number of elements of an array less than their mean 388
Calculates coefficients of a cubic spline through a set of points 562–4

Derived type complex number component extraction 220
Derived type complex number creation 220
Derived type complex number input 220
Derived type complex number output 220
Determine the convexity of a polygon 374–5

Example of automatic array manipulation 184

Finds a root of a non-linear equation using Newton–Raphson iteration 533–4
Finds a root of a non-linear equation using secant method 539–42
Forms a correct name from title, family name and up to three personal names 497

Gaussian elimination on a tridiagonal system of equations 555

Improved solution of a quadratic equation 528
Initialize the list for cash machine simulation 438
Initialize a rational number 515
Input procedure for electronic filter design program 340–1
Input procedure for population survey 243–4

Insert a contact into a binary tree (recursively) 447–8
Integrates a function using an adaptive method 574–5

Least squares approximation to a linear fit 316

Multiple roots of a positive real number 81–2

Order chemicals whose stock is too low 475–6

Performs an adaptive numerical quadrature 575–6
Performs back substitution after Gaussian elimination 551
Performs Gaussian elimination on a system of linear equations 549–51
Personal name manipulation 87
Personal name manipulation (alternative version) 88
Population survey input procedure (file-based) 284–6
Print a linked list contact database 429
Print contact details in a binary tree (recursively) 448
Print page numbers 95
Print the contents of the list for cash machine simulation 439–40
Program to tabulate the values of a function 199

Read chemical names from stock control database 472–3
Recursive divide interval subroutine for bisection method 328–9
Recursive factorial calculation 196
Remove an item from the head of the list for cash machine simulation 438–9

Simulate input requests for cash machine simulation 440
Solve simultaneous linear equations by Gaussian elimination 549
Straight selection alphabetic sorting 181–2
Subroutine to analyse contents of a file 387
Sum of two arrays 186
Survey data input subroutine (using an internal file) 48–53
Survey data input subroutine (using non-advancing input) 461–3

Update master chemical stock control file 474–5

Work space allocation 386–7, 389

Index

The F language includes over one hundred intrinsic procedures, all of which are described in Appendix A, pages 591–600. However, only those intrinsic procedures which are discussed in the body of this book, as part of the discussion of other language features, are included in this index.

/ edit descriptor 253–4
: edit descriptor 456
=> operator 410

a edit descriptor 236, 239–40, 245–7, 256
access specifier 271, 465
action specifier 270, 271
actual argument 77, 82–5, 88, 176–8, 185, 197–8, 414, 495
 procedure 197–8
Ada 10
action specifier 457–8
Airbus A-300 95–6
Algol 60 10
Algol 68 10
allocatable array 379, 380–4, 388–9, 419, 421, 432
allocatable attribute 379–80
allocated intrinsic function 384–5, 432
allocate statement 379–82, 419–20, 422
allocation status 380–2, 419
all intrinsic function 392
Anfield 121–2
ANSI 9–10
any intrinsic function 392
argument 24, 72–3, 76, 81, 90
 actual 77, 82–5, 88, 176–8, 185, 197–8, 414, 495
 character 86
 dummy 77–8, 82–6, 88, 176–9, 183, 196–7, 369–70, 380, 414, 431–3, 495, 496
 keyword 495–6

 optional 495–6
 order 83
 shape 172
arithmetic
 complex 337–8
 integer 44
 real 44, 47
arithmetic expression 45, 48
arithmetic operator 45–6
arithmetic unit 4
array 163–7, 174–5, 177–8, 360–1
 allocatable 379–84, 388–9, 419, 421, 432
 assumed-length 182
 assumed-shape 178, 182–3, 186, 368–70, 378, 380, 417
 automatic 184, 368, 377–9, 383–4
 bounds 164–5, 177–8, 183, 364, 368
 conformable 170, 172, 186, 390–2
 constant 166, 170
 constructor 166–8, 170, 365–6
 declaration 164, 168
 deferred-shape 368, 380, 417
 derived type 210
 dimension 165, 170
 element 163–9, 173
 element order 365–6, 368, 400
 explicit-shape 165, 177, 184, 368–9, 377, 417
 expression 175, 185
 extent of a dimension 165, 170, 178, 183, 363–4, 369
 initialization 168, 171
 input 168, 367–8, 400

array (*cont.*)
  object 169
  output 168, 367−8, 400
  pointer 416−17, 419−21
  rank 165, 170, 178, 363, 368−9, 380, 399
  section 173−6, 179, 182, 185, 398−401, 417−18
  shape 165, 170, 172, 178, 183, 364, 369, 379, 391
  size 165, 363−4, 369
  subscript 163, 165, 169, 170
  target 419
  two-dimensional 360−1
  work 378
array processing 170, 390−3
  intrinsic functions 394−5, 596−8
array section
  input/output 399
array variable 164
array-valued function 185, 187, 393
ASCII character code 56, 117, 119, 611
ASCII collating sequence 117, 119
assembly language 8
assignment 60
  defined 502−4, 513
  derived type 202
  integer 44
  masked array 396−8
  mixed-mode 44−5
  operator 502
  pointer 410, 412, 415, 418, 420, 433
  real 44
assignment statement 43, 57−8
associated intrinsic function 412, 432
association
  host 91−2, 222−3, 500
  use 91−2, 183−4, 218, 222−3, 497, 500
assumed-length array 182
assumed-length dummy argument 86−8
assumed-shape array 182−3, 186, 368−70, 378, 380, 417
Atlas computer 26
attribute
  allocatable 379−80
  dimension 164−6, 168, 173, 185, 360, 363, 368−9, 379, 417
  intent 78, 80, 82, 85−6, 182, 500, 502
  optional 495
  parameter 62−3, 78
  pointer 409
  private 92, 200, 221, 224
  public 90, 92, 200, 221
  save 94−5, 383, 388−9, 433
  target 410, 417, 425

automatic array 184, 368, 377−9, 383−4
automatic object 185

back substitution 546
backspace statement 269, 271, 278−9
backup, file 476
Backus, John v, 8
BASIC 10
batch computing 27
bicubic patch 566
bicubic spline interpolation 566−7
binary digit 7
binary operator 48
binary tree 442−7
bisection method for solution of non-linear equations 320−4, 529, 542−3
bit 7
bit intrinsic procedures 595−6
bottom-up 19
bound
  lower 164−5, 178−9, 183−4, 364−5, 368−70
  upper 164−5, 178−9, 183−4, 364, 368−9
branch, tree 442
bridge
  Capilano Suspension x
  Fatih Sultan Mehmet x
  Forth x
  Iron Bridge x
bubble sort 188

C 10
CAD 371
call statement 23−4, 76, 81, 83, 93, 495
CAM 371
Capilano Suspension Bridge x
case construct 111, 122−3, 152, 251
case default statement 122−4
case expression 122−3
case selector 123, 125
case statement 122−3, 126−7
central processing unit 4
central processor 5
character
  argument 86
  concatenation 59
  constant 52, 56, 125
  dummy argument 86−7
  expression 107, 123, 125
  intrinsic functions 594−5
  literal constant 52
  storage unit 56
  substring 59, 60
  variable 56, 57, 235
character declaration 56

character set
  ASCII 56, 611
  default 56
  F 56
character string
  comparison 117−18
  delimiter 233
Chicago Cubs 121
clock, system 76
close statement 270, 274−5
COBOL 10−11
collating sequence 117
  ASCII 117, 119
  F 117
comment 22−3
  trailing 23
comparison
  real number 127
compilation error 29
compiler 8
complex arithmetic 337−8
complex constant 336
complex declaration 336
complex literal constant 347
  default kind 347
  non-default kind 347
complex number 207, 336, 350−1
  imaginary part 336
  input/output 338
  real part 336
complex variable 336
component
  array-valued 209−10
  derived type 200−1, 211, 217−18, 221, 346
  interface 95−6
  private 217−18
  problem 95−6
  public 217
computer
  1620 9
  650 9
  7030 9
  704 8, 9
  7070 9
  709 9
  7090/94 9
  Atlas 26
  notebook 3, 6
  parallel 12
  stored-program 4
computer-aided design 371
computer-aided manufacture 371
computing
  batch 27

interactive 27
concatenation operator 59
conditioning 306−8
conformable arrays 170, 172, 186, 390−2
constant 7, 48
  array 166, 170
  character 52, 56, 125
  default kind 346−7
  derived type 201
  exponential 49
  integer 49, 62
  literal 49
  named 62−3, 90
  non-default kind 346−7
  real 49, 62
constructor
  array 365−6
  structure 201, 218
contains statement 70, 91, 222, 498−9
continuation line 24−5
control information list 249
control unit 4
convergence 305, 543
  criteria 320, 531, 538
convexity 371−2
CPU 4, 6
cubic spline 557−66
curve fitting 557−66
cycle statement 152−3

Dartmouth College 27
data 4
  format of 231−2
data abstraction 511−16
data fitting
  least squares approximation 313−16
data hiding 221
data structure
  recursive 449
data type 42
deallocate statement 379, 381−2, 420, 422−3
debugging 31, 294
  incremental 294
declaration
  character 56
  complex 336
  derived type 200−1
  integer 42
  logical 107
  pointer 409
  real 23, 42
  variable 23, 42
decryption 520−1

default
  character set 56
  input unit 50, 232, 235, 249−50
  kind 302, 344
  output unit 50, 232, 235, 251
  type 345
default **real** 302
deferred-shape array 368, 380, 417
defined assignment 502−4, 513
defined operation 500, 511
defined operator 501, 503−4, 510
  generic 510
delimiting character 58, 233
dereferencing 413, 416
derived type 200
  array 210
  array-valued component 209−10
  assignment 202
  component 200−1, 211, 217−18, 221,
    346
  constant 201
  declaration 200−1
  input 201
  operations 202
  output 201
  pointer component 423−5
  use for language extension 207
derived type definition 200−1, 209, 218, 221
design
  modular 32
  program 30−2
diagnostic 9
dimension 165, 170
dimension attribute 164−6, 168, 173, 185, 360,
    363, 368−9, 379, 417
direct access file 272, 464−7, 487
  record length 467
diskette 266
division
  integer 47, 142
dot_product intrinsic function 361
double-precision 303−5
do
  implied 167, 366
do construct 111, 137−8
  named 153−5
do loop 138−40, 151−2, 173, 277, 391
  count-controlled 138
  fail-safe mechanism 147, 151
  nested 142
  range 142
do statement 138−9, 146−7, 167
do variable 138−40, 147, 151, 167
  incrementation 138−9

dummy argument 77−78, 82−6, 88, 176−9, 183,
    196−7, 369−70, 380, 414, 495−6
  assumed-length 86−8
  character 86−7
  pointer 431−3
  procedure 178, 196−7
dummy procedure 498

edit descriptor 235−6, 245, 455
  / 253−4
  : 456
  a 236, 239−40, 245−7, 256
  es 455−6
  f 236, 238−9, 245−6, 455
  i 236−7, 245, 455
  L 236, 240−1, 245, 247
  s 456
  sp 456
  ss 456
  t 236−7, 245, 248
  tl 236−8, 245, 248
  tr 236−7, 245, 248
editing
  input 234−5
  output 234−5
editor 29
electronic filter 339, 343
elemental function 171−2, 188
elemental intrinsic procedure 171, 393−4, 591
elemental subroutine 172
else if statement 105, 111
else statement 105, 111
embedded format 235
encryption 520−1
end do statement 138−9, 146, 152
end file statement 270, 279
end function statement 77−8
end if statement 105, 111
end module statement 69
end program statement 25, 54, 69
end select statement 122
end type statement 200
end-of-file condition 250−1, 269, 458
end-of-record condition 251, 458
endfile record 268−9
endfile statement 268, 270−1
end statement 185
entity
  public 77
enumeration type 521
Eratosthenes
  Sieve of 405
error 30
  compilation 29

execution 29
    numerical 47
    program 27
    round-off 268, 307–9
    semantic 27–8
    syntactic 27–9
    truncation 308–10, 312
error checking 32–3
es edit descriptor 455–6
Euclid's algorithm for finding the highest common
    factor 228
Euler's method for solution of first order
    differential equations 585–6
evaluation
    order of 48
executable statement 23, 69
execution error 29
exit statement 146–7, 152–3
explicit-shape array 165, 184, 368–9, 377, 417
exponent 49, 302
    real data format 239
exponent range 302–3, 306, 349–51
exponential constant 49
expression
    arithmetic 45, 48
    character 107, 123, 125
    evaluation 45–7
    initialization 94, 123
    integer 123
    logical 106, 108–11, 123
    mixed kind 351–4
    mixed-mode 46, 54
    pointer 413–15, 433
    relational 106–7, 113, 118
    specification 369
    subscript 163–4
    whole-array 391–2
extended operator 499–501, 510, 513
extension
    F language 207
extent 165, 170, 178, 183, 363, 369
    zero 364
external file 266
external procedure 72

F character set 56
f edit descriptor 236, 238–9, 245–6, 455
fail-safe mechanism 147, 151
Fatih Sultan Mehmet Bridge x
file 5, 265–6
    backup 476
    connection 270
    creation 269
    direct access 464–7, 487

existence 269–70
    external 266
    formatted 457
    internal 249, 478–80
    scratch 271
    sequential access 465
file specifier 270, 272, 484
file store 5–6, 265–7
    device 5
filter
    band-pass 339, 343
    electronic 339, 343
first derivative of a function 333
fixed disk 266
floating-point number 41–42
floating-point representation 294, 301
floppy disk 266
format 235, 237, 455
    as a character variable 235
    embedded 235
    list-directed 50, 235, 267
    multi-record 252
    repeated 252–4
    result 52
format specifier 235, 250
formatted file 457
formatted input statement 267
formatted output statement 267
formatted record 267
form specifier 270, 273
Forth Railway Bridge x
Forth Road Bridge x
Fortran v, 2–3, 7, 11–12, 22, 39, 58, 245, 249,
    279
Fortran 90 v, 2–3, 10–12, 279, 605–10
    library 498
    procedure 498
Fortran 90 Programming vii
Fortran 95 v, 2–3, 10–12, 279
FORTRAN 8–10, 12, 39, 77, 279
FORTRAN II 9
FORTRAN IV 9
function 72
    array-valued 185, 187, 393
    elemental 171–2, 188
    generic 73–4
    inquiry 592
    intrinsic 72–3, 75, 81, 172
    logical 108
    pointer-valued 433–4
    reference 73, 75, 77, 80–1, 93, 164–6,
        172
    restrictions on 80, 86, 92
    result 75, 77

function *(cont.)*
  statement order 603
  transformational 592
function interface 79
function statement 77−9, 86
function subprogram 77

Gauss-Seidel iterative solution of simultaneous
    linear equations 583−4
Gaussian elimination solution of simultaneous
    linear equations 543−52, 554−7
generic
  defined operator 510
  function 73−4
  interface 505−8
  procedure 505−7, 510
goodness of fit 315
grandfather-father-son file hierarchy 476, 488

hard disk 266
hardware 2
hash table 477
hashing technique 477
head of a list 434
high-level language 8
highest common factor
  Euclid's algorithm 228
host association 91−2, 222−3, 500
  rules governing 222

i edit descriptor 236−7, 245, 455
IBM 8−9, 249
  1620 computer 9
  650 computer 9
  7030 computer 9
  704 computer 8−9
  7070 computer 9
  709 computer 9
  7090/94 computer 9
identifier 21−2
if construct 105, 110−11, 115, 122−3, 251
if statement 105, 110−11
ill-conditioned problem 20, 306−8
imaginary part of a complex number 336
Imagine1, Inc. v, 11
implied **do** 167, 366
  element 167
IMSL 12
incremental program design 293−4
index array 181
infinite loop 147
initial value 94
  main program 95
initialization expression 94, 123

injection sort 427, 443−7
input
  device 4−5
  editing 234−5
  list-directed 23, 49, 58−9, 247, 250
  non-advancing 458, 464, 479
input list 50
input procedure 152
input statement
  formatted 267
  unformatted 268
input unit
  default 50, 232, 235, 249−50
inquire-by-file 484−5
inquire-by-output-list 487−8
inquire-by-unit 484−5
inquire statement 484−8
inquiry function 592
  miscellaneous 600
  numeric 594
instance of a procedure 93
Instructor's Guide vi−vii, ix
integer
  assignment 44
  constant 49, 62
  expression 123
  variable 42
integer arithmetic 44
integer division 47, 142
integer number 39−41
integer declaration 42
integer literal constant 346
  default kind 346
  non-default kind 346
integer numbers
  storage of 294
integer variable 56
integration 567−80
intent attribute 78, 80, 82, 85−6, 182, 500, 502
interactive computing 27
interface
  component 95−6
  function 79
  generic 505−8
  operator 500
  procedure 72, 197, 497
  subprogram 77
interface block 197, 497−8, 505−8, 510, 513
interface body 197
interface statement 501
internal file 249, 478−80
intrinsic datatype 200
intrinsic function 72−3, 75, 81, 172
  allocated 384−5, 432

all 392
any 392
associated 412, 432
dot_product 361
int 352
kind 352
lbound 184, 370
len 182
logical 353
matmul 361−2
maxloc 172, 361
maxval 172, 361
minloc 172, 361
minval 172, 361
present 496
product 361
real 352−3
reshape 366
selected_int_kind 347−9
selected_real_kind 303−6, 349−51
size 172, 179, 182, 184, 186, 370
sum 172, 361
transpose 361−2
trim 61−2
ubound 184, 370
intrinsic procedure 22, 60−2, 71, 140, 171, 175, 198
  array processing 172, 394−5, 596-8
  bit 595−6
  character 594−5
  elemental 171, 393−4, 591
  mathematical 592−4
  numerical 592−4
  time and date 600
  type conversion and manipulation 599
intrinsic subroutine 72, 75, 172
int intrinsic function 352
iostat specifier 250−1, 268−70, 273−4, 278−79, 458
Iron Bridge x
iteration count 138
iterative solution of non-linear equations 318−24
  convergence criteria 320

job control language 27

keyword argument 495−6
kind intrinsic function 352
kind selector 345
  complex 346
kind type 302−3, 344, 348
  default 344
kind type declaration 345−6

kind type parameter 302−4, 344−6, 348, 350−4
  logical 344
Kirchoff's laws 339

L edit descriptor 236, 240−1, 245, 247
language extension 207, 511−16
lbound intrinsic function 184, 370
least squares approximation 313−16, 567
len intrinsic function 182
length 57
library
  Fortran 90 498
  procedure 12, 90
  subprogram 77
linked list 426, 431, 434−7, 442
list
  head 434
  linked 426, 431, 434−7, 442
  tail 434
list-directed
  format 50, 235, 267
  input 23, 49, 58−9, 247, 250
  output 23, 49, 59
  print statement 232, 234
  read statement 232−3
literal constant 49
  character 52
Liverpool F C 121−2
local variable 78, 89−90
locality of variables 89
logical
  expression 106, 108−11, 123
  function 108
  operator 108−10
  value 106−7
  variable 107
logical data type 351
logical declaration 107
logical intrinsic function 353
logical literal constant 347
  default kind 347
  non-default kind 347
loop 137, 169
  do 138−40, 151−2, 173, 277, 391
  infinite 147
lower bound 164−5, 178−9, 183−4, 364−5, 368−70

machine code 7−8, 29
magnetic disk 266
magnetic tape 266−7
main program 21, 24, 69, 94
  initial values 171
  initialization 95

main program (*cont.*)
  statement order 603
  structure 25
maintainability 31
Manchester, University of 26
mantissa 49, 302
many-to-one array section 176, 401
  restrictions on 176
masked array assignment 396−8
Massachusetts Institute of Technology 27
mathematical intrinsic procedures 592−4
matmul intrinsic function 361−2
matrix 360−1
  multiplication 362
  upper triangular 545
maxloc intrinsic function 172, 361
maxval intrinsic function 172, 361
memory 4−6
microcomputer 6
minloc intrinsic function 172, 361
minval intrinsic function 172, 361
mixed kind expression 351−4
mixed-mode
  assignment 44−5
  expression 46, 54, 337
Modula-2 10
modular design 32
modular program development 95−7, 293
module 71, 77, 79, 90−1, 183, 200
  entity accessibility 221, 223−4
  entity renaming 223−4
  private 70, 93
  public 70, 93
  statement order 604
module procedure 197−8, 505−6
module procedure statement 500
module statement 69
mouse 27
multi-record format 252
multiprogramming 26−7

NAG 12
named constant 62−3, 90
nested **do** loop 142
Newton quotient 333
Newton's iteration 530, 535
Newton's method for solution of non-linear
  equations 529−36, 538, 542−3
Newton−Raphson method for solution of
  non-linear equations 530
non-advancing
  input 458, 464, 479
  input/output 457
  output 459

read statement 458
write statement 459
non-linear equations
  bisection method 320−4, 529, 542−3
  iterative solution 318−24
  Newton's method 529−36, 538, 542−3
  Newton−Raphson method 530
  secant method 536−43
notebook computer 3, 6
null record 253
null value 50, 233
nullify statement 412, 420, 422−3
number
  floating-point 41−2
  integer 39−41
  real 23, 40−2
numeric inquiry functions 594
numeric storage unit 56
numerical intrinsic procedures 592−4
numerical methods 524−9
  limitations of 524−9
numerical quadrature 567−80

object-oriented programming 511
only clause 223−4
open statement 249, 270−4, 277, 279, 465, 486
operating system 18, 26−7, 267
operation
  defined 500, 511
operator
  => 410
  arithmetic 45−6
  assignment 502
  binary 48
  concatenation 59
  defined 501, 503−4, 510
  extended 499−501, 510, 513
  interface 500
  logical 108−10
  pointer assignment 410
  priority 45−6, 107−8, 110
  relational 106, 108, 110
  unary 48
  user-defined 499−500
optical disk 266
optional argument 495−6
optional attribute 495
order of arguments 83
order of statements 603−4
output
  device 4−5
  editing 234−5
  list-directed 23, 49, 59
  non-advancing 459

output list 50
output statement
  formatted 267
  unformatted 268
output unit
  default 50, 232, 235, 251
overflow 127, 299

parallel computer 12
parameterized **real** variable 301−6
parameterized type declaration 345
parameter attribute 62−3, 78
parenthesis 48
partial pivoting 547
Pascal 10, 12
peripheral device 6
PL/I 10
pointer 408−25, 427, 431−7, 442−7
  array 416−17, 419−21
  assignment 410, 412, 415, 418, 420, 433
  assignment operator 410
  association status 409, 411−12, 420, 422−3, 433
  declaration 409
  dereferencing 413, 416
  derived type component 423−5
  expression 433
  input/output of 431
  target 410−14
pointer-valued function 433−4
pointer attribute 409
portability 9, 31, 347−51
position specifier 270−2, 279
precision 114, 294, 299−306, 344, 349−51
preconnected input/output unit 269
present intrinsic function 496
prime numbers
  calculation of 405
printer
  output to 245
print statement 23−5, 29, 50, 52, 56, 62, 80, 235, 251
  list-directed 232, 234
priority
  operator 45−6, 107−8, 110
private module 70, 93
private attribute 92, 200, 221, 224
private statement 92, 218, 244, 501, 503−4
procedure 20, 70−1
  argument 178
  dummy argument 196, 498
  elemental 591
  external 72
  Fortran 90 498

generic 505−7, 510
  input 152
  instance 93
  interface 72, 197, 497
  intrinsic 60−2, 71, 140, 171, 175, 198
  module 505−6
  non-F 198, 497−8
  recursive 449
  size 97
procedure library 12, 90
product intrinsic function 361
program 4
  loop 137
  main 21, 69, 94
  testing 18
program design 30−2
  incremental 293−4
program development
  modular 95−7, 293
program repetition 136
program testing 96, 152, 294
  incremental 294
programming language 8
program statement 21, 25, 54, 69, 77, 86
public entity 77
public module 70, 93
public attribute 90, 92, 200, 221
public statement 79, 90, 92, 501, 503−4

quadratic equations
  solution of 525−9
quadrature
  numerical 567−80
QuickSort 519

random access 266
range 344, 348
rank
  array 165, 170, 178, 363, 368−9, 380, 399
Raspberry Chicken 71−2
rational number 512−16
read statement 23, 29, 43, 50, 58, 80, 235, 237, 249, 265, 271
  list-directed 232−3
  non-advancing 458
real
  assignment 44
  constant 49, 62
  variable 42
real arithmetic 44, 47
  accuracy of 113−14
real number 23, 40−2
  comparison 114−15

real number comparison 127, 203
real part of a complex number 336
real declaration 23, 42
real intrinsic function 142, 151, 352−3
real literal constant 346
　default kind 346
　non-default kind 346
real numbers
　storage of 294
real variable 56
　parameterized 301−6
recl specifier 273, 465−7
record 265−6
　endfile 268−9
　formatted 267
　input/output 253
　null 253
　unformatted 268
record length
　direct access 467
record number 465−6
recursion 80, 83, 92, 194, 196, 447
recursive data structure 449
recursive function statement 194
recursive procedure 327, 449
recursive subroutine statement 196
rec specifier 465−6
relational expression 106−7, 113, 118
relational operator 106, 108, 110
renaming module entities 223−4
repeat count 247−8, 253
reserved words 22, 71, 140, 270, 601−3
　list of 601−3
reshape intrinsic function 366
residual 314
residual sum 315
result
　function 75
　subroutine 75
result value 80
result variable 78, 86, 186
result clause 77−8
return statement 156, 185, 286
rewind statement 269, 271, 278−9
root
　tree 442
round-off 300−1
　error 268, 307−9
rounding 299
　error 113−14

s edit descriptor 456
save attribute 94−5, 383, 388−9, 433
scratch file 271

secant method for solution of non-linear
　　equations 536−43
select case statement 122, 125
selected_int_kind intrinsic function 347−9
selected_real_kind intrinsic function 303−6,
　　349−51
semantic error 27−8
sequential access file 267, 465
　writing to 279
shape
　argument 172
　array 165, 170, 178, 183, 364, 369, 379,
　　391
side effects 80
Sieve of Eratosthenes 405
single-precision 303, 305
size
　array 165, 363, 369
　zero 364
size intrinsic function 172, 179, 182, 184, 186,
　　370
size specifier 458
software 2
software engineering 95
solution of a tridiagonal system of linear
　　equations 553−7
solution of first order differential equations
　Euler's method 585−6
solution of simultaneous linear equations
　Gauss-Seidel iterative method 583−4
　Gaussian elimination 543−52, 554−7
sorting
　bubble sort 188
　injection sort 427, 443−7
　QuickSort 519
　straight selection 180
specification expression 369
specification statement 23, 69, 79, 86, 165
specifier
　access 271, 465
　action 270−1, 457−8
　file 270, 272, 484
　format 235, 250
　form 270, 273
　iostat 250−1, 268−70, 273−4, 278−9, 458
　position 270−2, 279
　recl 273, 465, 467
　rec 465−6
　size 458
　status 270, 274−5
　unit 249, 268, 270, 274−5, 278−9, 484
spline
　cubic 557−66
sp edit descriptor 456

ss edit descriptor 456
stability 306, 308−12
stable algorithm 310−11
stable process 308
statement 21
  allocate 379−82, 419−20, 422
  assignment 43, 57−8
  backspace 269, 271, 278−9
  call 23−4, 76, 81, 83, 93, 495
  case default 122−4
  case 122−3, 126−7
  close 270, 274−5
  contains 70, 91, 222, 498−9
  cycle 152−3
  deallocate 379, 381−2, 420, 422−3
  do 138−9, 146−7, 167
  else if 105, 111
  else 105, 111
  end 185
  end do 138−9, 146, 152
  end file 270, 279
  end function 77−8
  end if 105, 111
  end module 69
  end program 25, 54, 69
  end select 122
  end type 200
  endfile 268, 270−1
  executable 23, 69
  exit 146−7, 152−3
  function 77−9, 86
  if 105, 110−11
  inquire 484−8
  interface 501
  list-directed input 23, 49, 58−9, 250
  list-directed output 23, 49, 59
  module 69
  module procedure 500
  nullify 412, 420, 422−3
  open 249, 270−4, 277, 279, 465, 486
  print 23−5, 29, 50, 52, 56, 62, 80, 235, 251
  private 92, 218, 244, 501, 503−4
  program 21, 25, 54, 69, 77, 86
  public 79, 90, 92, 501, 503−4
  read 23, 29, 43, 50, 58, 80, 235, 237, 249, 265, 271
  recursive function 194
  recursive subroutine 196
  return 156, 185, 286
  rewind 269, 271, 278−9
  select case 122, 125
  specification 23, 69, 79, 86, 165
  stop 155−6, 277
  subroutine 82, 86
  type 200−1, 209, 218
  use 69, 79, 86, 90−2, 224
  write 251, 256, 265, 271
statement order 86, 603−4
  function 603
  main program 603
  module 604
  subroutine 603
status
  allocation 380−2, 419
  pointer association 409, 411−12, 420, 422−3, 433
status specifier 270, 274−5
stop statement 155−6, 277
storage unit
  character 56
  numeric 56
stored-program computer 4
straight selection sorting 180
structure 30
  main program 25
structure constructor 201, 218
structure plan 19−20, 53, 61, 74−75, 87, 96−97, 112, 116, 119, 124, 128−9, 136−7, 140, 142, 144, 149, 181, 188, 195, 205, 208, 212−13, 242, 255, 283, 322−3, 340, 372−4, 385−6, 427, 428, 460, 469−72, 480, 514, 532, 539, 573−4
sub-array 172, 174−5, 398
sub-problem 95−6
subprogram 12, 70, 77
  function 77
  library 77
  name 77
subroutine 24, 72, 80
  elemental 172
  intrinsic 72, 75, 172
  result 75, 82
  statement order 603
subroutine statement 82, 86
subscript 163, 165, 169−70
  triplet 173−5, 398−401, 417
  vector 173, 175−6, 398, 400−1, 417−18
subscript expression 163−4
substring
  character 59−60
sum intrinsic function 172, 361
syntactic error 27−9
system clock 76

t edit descriptor 236−7, 245, 248
tabulation edit descriptor 237
tail of a list 434
target 410−14, 416, 419, 431

target attribute   410, 417, 425
terminator   50–1
ternary tree   442
testing   18, 30–1, 33, 96, 152, 244, 294
time and date intrinsic subroutines   600
time-sharing   27
tl edit descriptor   236–8, 245, 248
top-down   19
transfer of control   80, 146
transformational function   592
transpose intrinsic function   361–2
tree   442–7
   binary   442–7
   branch   442
   root   442
   ternary   442
tridiagonal system of linear equations
   solution of   553–7
trim intrinsic function   61–2
truncation   44, 47
   error   308–10, 312
tr edit descriptor   236–7, 245, 248
type conversion and manipulation intrinsic
   functions   599
type statement   200–1, 209, 218

ubound intrinsic function   184, 370
unary operator   48
underflow   299
unformatted input statement   268
unformatted output statement   268
unformatted record   268
unformatted **write** statement   487
unit
   connection   269
   number   249
   preconnected   249, 269
unit specifier   249, 268, 270, 274–5, 278–9,
   484
unstable algorithm   309–10, 312
unstable process   308

upper bound   164–5, 178–9, 183–4, 364, 368–9
upper triangular matrix   545
user-defined operator   499–500
use association   91–92, 183–4, 218, 222–3, 497,
   500
use statement   22, 69, 79, 86, 91–2, 224
   only clause   223–4

value
   logical   106–7
   null   233
value separator   50, 233
variable   7, 42
   array   164
   character   56–7
   declaration   23, 42
   integer   42, 56
   local   78, 89–90
   locality of   89
   real   42, 56
   result   78, 86
vector   360–1, 424–5
   multiplication   362
vector subscript   173, 175–6, 398, 400–1, 417–18

well-conditioned problem   306, 308
WG5   10
where construct   396–8
whole-array expression   391–3
whole-array processing   390–3
word-processing   18
work array   378
World Wide Web   vi–ix
Wrigley Field   121
write statement   251, 256, 265, 271
   non-advancing   459
   unformatted   487

X3J3   10–11

Young's modulus   315–16

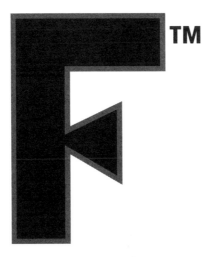

TM

The F language was developed by Imagine1, Inc.

Visit our Web page at

www.imagine1.com/imagine1

or send questions to

info@imagine1.com

Imagine1 has compilers for most Unix systems, Linux, Windows 95/NT, and the Macintosh PowerPC

Free try-and-buy compilers let you experiment with small programs

The educational compilers let you write new code using all modern techniques

The Professional compilers also let you access existing Fortran 77 procedures and procedures written in other languages

The Super-Pro compilers are highly optimized for compute-intensive applications

There are a wide variety of additional books and resources available

There is an e-mail reflector devoted to issues

There are even hats, T-shirts and polo shirts available with an attractive big blue

The web page at

www.imagine1.com/imagine1

has the latest information about compilers, platforms, books, memorabilia, educator resources, and lots of examples of F codes

Contact
Imagine1, Inc
1874 San Bernardino Ave NE
Albuquerque, New Mexico, 87122
USA

1 505 797 8787
1 505 856 1501 fax

info@imagine1.com